# PASSION'S TRIUMPH OVER REASON

# Passion's Triumph over Reason

*A History of the Moral Imagination from Spenser to Rochester*

CHRISTOPHER TILMOUTH

OXFORD
UNIVERSITY PRESS

# OXFORD

UNIVERSITY PRESS

Great Clarendon Street, Oxford OX2 6DP

Oxford University Press is a department of the University of Oxford.
It furthers the University's objective of excellence in research, scholarship,
and education by publishing worldwide in

Oxford  New York

Auckland  Cape Town  Dar es Salaam  Hong Kong  Karachi
Kuala Lumpur  Madrid  Melbourne  Mexico City  Nairobi
New Delhi  Shanghai  Taipei  Toronto

With offices in

Argentina  Austria  Brazil  Chile  Czech Republic  France  Greece
Guatemala  Hungary  Italy  Japan  Poland  Portugal  Singapore
South Korea  Switzerland  Thailand  Turkey  Ukraine  Vietnam

Oxford is a registered trade mark of Oxford University Press
in the UK and in certain other countries

Published in the United States
by Oxford University Press Inc., New York

© Christopher Tilmouth 2007

The moral rights of the author have been asserted
Database right Oxford University Press (maker)

First published 2007

British Library Cataloguing in Publication Data
Data available

Library of Congress Cataloging in Publication Data
Data available

Typeset by Laserwords Private Limited, Chennai, India
Printed in Great Britain
on acid-free paper by
Biddles Ltd., King's Lynn, Norfolk

ISBN 978-0-19-921237-8

1 3 5 7 9 10 8 6 4 2

*To all those who have put their faith in me.*
*With grateful thanks.*

# Acknowledgements

Though doubtless fated to be read first, this page is written last, at the end of a ten-year period during which I have incurred more debts than can be easily recorded. Embedded within this book is a doctoral thesis which I began under the supervision of Fred Parker and ended under that of Colin Burrow. To both I am grateful: to Fred for asking searching, formative questions; to Colin for insisting that even passions require a method. The thesis, principally a study of Hobbes and Rochester, was examined by Paul Hammond and Richard Tuck in 2001. It was at Richard Tuck's instigation that I later incorporated a discussion of France's *libertins érudits* into the present work. My debt to Paul, though, and also to Gordon Campbell, is still greater since it was they who, as subsequent Press readers, redeemed my typescript from its worst errors and indulgences. My other, most enduring debts are to Howard Erskine-Hill and John Kerrigan, both of whom (along with Colin Burrow) offered me the practical support which enabled me to persist with this project under otherwise adverse circumstances. Other people, too, have given their friendship, advice, or both along the way, and to them I am equally grateful. Anne Barton, Susan James, and Quentin Skinner all read and commented generously on early manifestations of parts of this book, and I have profited likewise from the sustained support and interest of Sarah Cain, Phil Connell, Bill Davies, James Lawson, Bart van Es, Daniel Wakelin, and James Warren. The writing of these acknowledgements gives me the chance also to thank my OUP editors, and to say—though words can hardly be enough—how much I owe in everything I do to Kevin Wylie.

# *Contents*

# Introduction

## PASSION'S TRIUMPH OVER REASON

This is a book about governance and the passions, a history of philosophical, theological, and above all literary constructions of the idea of self-control (and indeed self-indulgence) in the period 1580 to 1680. It traces three movements essential to the story of moral psychology during this time: first, the decline (from an initial position of dominance) of an austerely rationalist model of self-governance, one centred on ideas of psychomachia and a hostility to the passions; second, the growth of two alternative traditions, grounded in Augustinianism and a reinterpretation of Aristotle respectively, which revalued the affections as controlled but morally constructive forces, qualities to be harnessed, not eliminated; and third (but very differently), the emergence of a libertine ethic of indulgence, an outlook preoccupied not with restraint but with sexual conquests, the cultivation of power, and a longing for constant motion. The first of these ethics fractured in the early 1600s under the pressure of a growing recognition that reason was weak, human self-delusion impenetrably complex, and the forces of corporeal passion and self-interest more invasive in determining man's actions than had previously been imagined. Burdened by such knowledge, Jacobean writers wavered in their adherence to that earlier humanist ideal which had posited an ascetic, supposedly transcendental faculty of reason as the mind's sovereign power. Seventeenth-century Calvinism, however, and some Counter-Reformation theologies of the same period offered an alternative to this disillusionment in the idea of moral regeneration, a regeneration which created newly 'sanctified' affections—and thus a better kind of passion—within the soul. Equally, alongside this Augustinian response, a revived Caroline interest in Aristotle provided another solution to the falterings of self-governance, one premised on a deliberate marriage between reason and the emotions, the former actively cultivating the latter so as to make them integral to the moral life. Meantime, though, a third, libertine ethic also arose on the back of the collapse of psychomachic thinking, its development fuelled both by those same factors which had first subverted reason's hegemony and by the consequent interest in re-evaluating the value and delights of the passions. This libertinism was at its most potent during Charles II's reign, but was ultimately undermined by its own extravagance, giving way in the 1680s to a more moderate hedonistic ethic, one less inclined to emphasize outright egotism and more inclined to embrace the newly emergent values of magnanimity and generosity.

Such, then, is the broad trajectory of this book, a summary in abstract terms of passion's triumph over reason. The narrative itself begins, in Chapter 1, with a sketch of three rationalist models of self-control—Socratic, Stoic, and 'Aristotelian'—all of them available to an Elizabethan courtier of the 1580s. In the early modern period the domain of ethical reflection was organized (implicitly at least) around precisely such rival definitions of governance, each offering comment on how best the conflicting parts of the psyche might be ordered. The shared aim of these competing ideals was to ensure that man's actions would be determined only by suitable motivations, thus guaranteeing his ability to act virtuously. For many humanist moralists of the sixteenth century, even those who invoked selective Aristotelian principles, the fulfilment of this aim generally entailed using reason to suppress the passions (since, if left unchecked, the latter would drive men to intemperance). The common emphasis on psychomachia, reason's fight to defeat the emotions, followed from this. However, according to early Calvinist opinion (also a concern of Chapter 1), such rationalist self-determination was not possible. For Calvinists reason itself was as ineradicably corrupt as the rest of the soul, and could only be regenerated through a visitation of God's grace. Even then, such regeneration was only partial, empowering the elect to initiate a psychomachic conflict between spirit and flesh but without, in this life, giving them the means to win such a fight.

These different emphases, humanist and Calvinist, are felt again in *The Faerie Queene*, the subject of Chapter 2. There, even Spenser's choice of form (personification allegory) instantiates the psychomachic confrontations which he evidently saw as intrinsic to human nature; and because the eternal recurrence of that psychomachia is a given of this poem, Spenserian man, even at his best, is never capable of achieving anything more than a stumbling Aristotelian continence. He cannot, in other words, realize the permanence and perfection of true Aristotelian virtue. The one thing he can hope for as he strives to fulfil his rationalist moral goals is that he may receive the fleeting assistance of God's grace, and that that grace will give him at least a faltering grasp over his perturbations. That said, the fact that within the fiction of the poem the *Faerie Queene*'s heroes *do* habitually receive this divine help indicates that to Spenser's way of thinking, as for so many other sixteenth-century moralists, rationalist goals clearly were worth fighting for, their difficulty notwithstanding.

Spenser's work provides a subtle illustration of the contours of rationalist, psychomachic moralizing, but the next two chapters of this book chart, through case studies of four late Elizabethan and Jacobean plays, some of the questions which were brought to bear upon that outlook, questions which ultimately undermined it. Chapter 3 focuses on *Hamlet*, and evokes two contrary attitudes at the heart of that play, both of them damaging to prevailing rationalist assumptions. On the one hand, Hamlet longs to be swept up in precisely the kind of passion condemned by Spenser and his contemporaries, since without such affective stimulation he proves incapable of acting emphatically. To that end he even heroizes Senecan fury—just as Seneca's villains themselves appeared strangely charismatic on the Elizabethan stage. On the other hand, though, in other moods the Prince vilifies the flesh and man's passions, embracing the very same austere ethics elsewhere celebrated by sixteenth-century moralists. The problem is that it is in the name of those values that he then subjects Gertrude to a vicious psychological assault, and the effect of *that* association is to cast such ascetic morals in a negative light, exposing their potential unnaturalness and inhumanity.

This is a theme, too, in my fourth chapter, which is again concerned with plays of a similarly challenging effect. *Julius Caesar*, for one, questions the possibility of man's ever satisfying any rational, virtuous ideal given his propensity for self-delusion. That problem is manifested in Brutus, who struggles throughout this tragedy to imagine himself as one motivated by republican and Stoic values, only to witness the shattering of that pretence as his sense of guilt engulfs him in the latter two acts. *Bussy D'Ambois*, meantime, explores the overwhelming power of corporeally engrained affections such as sexual passion, presenting these as ungovernable, explosive forces before which man is helpless, his rationalist pretensions notwithstanding. Chapman appropriates the idioms of Aristotelian meteorology both to express this point and to capture, in figurative terms, the core principle of Stoic monistic psychology, namely, that reason and passion are two extremes on a single mental continuum, the one (reason) proving itself susceptible to a form of drastic inversion which transforms it into the other. *Troilus and Cressida* compounds these disturbing concerns with another—that of the devious, pervasive influence exercised by self-interest in distorting our judgements. Awareness of this human reality is endemic amongst *Troilus*'s characters, and drives them into a neurotic preoccupation with emulation and with the proto-Hobbesian idea that man is engaged in a perpetual race against his fellow beings. These three tragedies, then, pursue a searching examination of the mind's subtlest contours, one analogous to that performed by Montaigne in his *Essays*, and in so doing they expose the limitations of previous constructions of human psychology. The rationalist estimate of the strength of enemy forces within (the passions to be defeated through psychomachia) proves, by their lights, all too naïve.

In Chapter 5 I turn to the Augustinian and newly revived Aristotelian traditions, which offered seventeenth-century writers a way around some of these problems, a way of appropriating the passions to moral purposes. In his *Citie of God* Augustine had identified St Paul's contrasting orders of love, the carnal and the spiritual, as two possible points of orientation for the will. A will regenerated by God's grace (working in co-operation with man's own endeavours) would ground itself, according to Augustine, in spiritual rather than carnal love, and would then express that disposition through a range of sanctified, morally valuable emotions. This idea, developed by both English Calvinists and French Counter-Reformation theologians, shaped the image of human nature which Herbert and Crashaw brought to bear upon their poetry. Thus Herbert's verse takes as its imaginative starting point a focus upon the condition of man's heart and its motions. It explores the unifying, centripetal effect which a feeling for God's love exerts over the self, but it also dwells on the capacity of man and God to share in common emotions, to sympathize with each other. Crashaw's reveries emphasize, rather, the vibrant, sensuous force of the holy affections, their capacity to unfold and amplify the soul, and their role in connecting man to the outside world. Whilst some writers were pursuing this Augustinian perspective, though, others were re-examining Aristotle's and Aquinas's works and finding there an argument which affirmed both the practical usefulness of the passions and their intrinsic place *within* a rationalist conception of virtue. From this trend stemmed several university plays which dwelt upon the political as well as ethical implications of thus incorporating the emotions into rational life; but the influence of such Aristotelianism can also be measured in *Paradise Lost*, not least in Milton's anatomy of the psychology of sin and self-delusion, which clearly draws on Thomist sources. Milton combines elements from Augustine's and Aquinas's ethics in his poem, on the one hand depicting a series of intuitively managed, prelapsarian appetites, on the other hand advocating a model of rational self-consciousness which Adam seems ill-equipped to realize (at least until after the Fall). Likewise, in the last books of his epic, Milton gives us both Pauline love and an Aristotelian conception of 'rational liberty', the latter a source (amongst other things) of an affirming sense of magnanimity.

Having put the theological case for the rehabilitation of the passions, I move on, in the second part of my book, to examine a very different riposte to late Tudor ethics and a very different model of the affections, that of Thomas Hobbes. Hobbes overturned traditional rationalist and psychomachic models of human nature, declaring that the passions, not reason, constituted the proper, primary determinants of human conduct. He posited, too, a new ideal of happiness, equating felicity with a constant motion of the self from the satisfaction of one appetite to the next, and he accorded fear and the lust for power critical roles in that kinetic process. Equally, he recast reason as an instrumental, not a transcendental, faculty, insisting that its true function was to calculate the optimal means of satisfying the passions' interests, not to intuit its own, supposedly eternal values. In line with this, he presented morality, for the most part at least, as a social construction, rather than an absolute. And he maintained that all these points were merely empirical observations, truisms about the nature of human psychology—an argument which implicitly reduces ascetic, psychomachic constructions of the mind to the status of delusions, wished-for but unrealizable ideals which (if man pursues them) can only be a source of torment. In actual fact Hobbes's commitment to his own pragmatic propositions was at best unstable. As I argue in an addendum to Chapter 6, his works are actually suffused with a language of moral absolutism and an adherence to divine law which undermines his relativist discourse. However, the rakish amongst his Restoration readers preferred to ignore this side of his argument, concentrating only on his innovations in which they saw the justification for a new ethic of libertinism.

Chapters 7 and 8 focus on precisely that libertine ideal, first generally and then with specific reference to the works of John Wilmot, Earl of Rochester. Chapter 7 sketches the various intellectual inheritances which contributed to Restoration libertinism: namely, Hobbism (a bastardized, popular misrepresentation of Hobbes's philosophy), cavalier libertine verse, French *libertin* poetry, and the Anglo-French tradition of Epicurean scholarship. All these factors combined with the political and economic climate of the late Interregnum and early Restoration to produce the peculiar phenomenon of English libertinism, an ethic particularly favoured by the circle of wits gathered around the Duke of Buckingham. This ethic established not so much governance as a lack of governance as its rule, making self-interest the principal measure of value and establishing a constant forward momentum in pursuit of appetites as its normative ideal. As is familiar, a taste for riotous self-indulgence and a general hostility towards Christian morals also accompanied this outlook. Such behaviour supposedly reflected the libertine's distinctive honesty, his willingness to confront and accept the visceral realities of his own self, where others preferred to hide from such truths by hugging the delusions of rationalism. Yet Restoration libertinism was also, I suggest, a matter of the *performance* of outrageous opinions. A poet like Oldham deliberately exaggerated the villainy of his libertine persona in his *Satyr against Vertue*. He also invested equal creative energy in penning two recantations of that poem. The effect of these manoeuvres was to obscure from uninitiated readers the true degree of 'sincerity' in such performances, rendering the libertine inscrutable and unpredictable to all but his own coterie. These themes are observable in a host of comedies, lyrics, and satires of the period 1660 to 1680, and in their most refined form in Etherege's *Man of Mode*, in which the Restoration game of manners provides a surreptitious vehicle through which to play out a Hobbist struggle for power.

Some of Rochester's lyrics, too, celebrate the libertine ethos of conquest and motion, and these are the first concern of Chapter 8, but many of his poems expose instead the inadequacies of so kinetic a notion of happiness. Rochester's imagination demonstrates an often anxious preoccupation with images of boundlessness and self-dissolution, threats to which appetitious indulgence gives rise. Furthermore, other works underline desire's propensity to disappoint at its very moment of fulfilment (when fruition proves less pleasurable than was expectation). One masochistic, rather perverse 'solution' to *this* problem, developed in, for example, 'The Mistress', is to introduce pain into one's delights, this as a way of rejuvenating stale pleasures. In his 'Satyre against Reason', though, the Earl offers a more practical alternative, that of simply moderating the appetites, checking the process of self-indulgence before it cloys. To argue for this is inevitably to challenge one of the norms of libertinism, and this same satire pursues that course still further by also attacking the isolation and mistrust which the competitive, egotistical world of Hobbist values fostered. Both here, then, and also in works such as *Lucina's Rape*, in which Rochester attacks Charles for his sexual excesses yet also laments his own complicity in that folly, the Earl can be seen moving away from the libertine ethic towards a more moderately Epicurean hedonism. This shift, commensurate with the growth of Epicureanism traced in the coda to this book, is also in keeping with Rochester's much-voiced admiration for generosity—the very value which was to supersede egotism as the informing ideal of the moral imagination in the next generation of ethical writers, the Whig essayists of King William's England.

Such, then, are the various concerns of this history. It goes without saying that they do not, collectively, amount to a comprehensive survey of moral sensibility across the seventeenth century. There are other stories to be told of that period besides this one of passion's triumph over reason—not least, Beiser's account of seventeenth-century theology which discovers in the latter a narrative of precisely the *sovereignty*, the victory, of reason over its enemies.[1] At a more particular level it should be noted, for example, that the intellectual life of Stoicism in fact persisted in both France and England long after 1600, the point at which I turn away from it.[2] Equally, Chapman's dramatic output does not stop where I do, with *Bussy D'Ambois*: his later

---

[1] See Beiser 1996.      [2] See Barbour 1998; Røstvig 1954; Shifflett 1998.

plays are notoriously different in kind from that early, disillusioned work, precisely because Chapman turned, subsequently, to doctrinaire Stoicism for his material. It is true, too, that the Neoplatonism in *The Faerie Queene* powerfully resists those more ascetic aspects of Spenser's moral vision which I emphasize in Chapter 2. Again, psychomachia did live out a vibrant, if more restricted literary life long after the last death throes of Jacobean tragedy—for example, in Caroline court masques and in *The Pilgrim's Progress*. At the other end of this book's spectrum, it is also self-evident that there was more to first-generation Restoration comedy than merely the Hobbism and libertinism of writers like Etherege and Sedley on which I concentrate;[3] more, too, to Restoration poetry than just Buckingham's court wits' agenda. Having said this, though, the present book nonetheless takes a deliberately bold and expansive view of its subject matter, tracing a field of evolving ethical thinking across a 100-year period and amidst a range of different works, philosophical and theological as well as literary. Until recently, studies of early modern attitudes to the passions tended to concentrate either on expository (rather than literary) texts,[4] or on particular authors and issues—Spenser's treatment of moral psychology, for instance, or Hobbes's analysis of the emotions.[5] The last decade has witnessed a shift towards a more integrated examination of this field, with critics paying especially close attention to the interrelationship between literary works and Renaissance discourses of physiology.[6] However, the price of that same cross-disciplinary integration has been a tendency to present too homogenizing a view of early modern concepts of the passions. Paster's recent work, for example, treats Thomas Wright's *Passions of the Minde in Generall* as if it were normative,[7] when in fact that distinctly Thomist treatment of the affections is only one of several analytical frameworks with reference to which Shakespeare and his contemporaries could have conceptualized the emotions. This study aims to present a more discriminating account of ideas of affectivity in the period. However, my further, greater concern here (following on from the work of Schoenfeldt and others[8]) is to emphasize the interaction between literary

[3] R. D. Hume 1983: 146, 158, 160, 162–3, 166.

[4] See, e.g., Cottingham 1998; Gardiner, Metcalf, and Beebe-Center 1970; Gaukroger 1998; Hirschman 1977; S. James 1997; Levi 1964.

[5] Reid 1982 and Herbert 1989, respectively.

[6] See, e.g., Hillman and Mazzio 1997; Paster 1993 and 2004; Paster, Rowe, and Floyd-Wilson 2004: ch. 6; Sawday 1995. The roots of this approach lie in earlier works such as Babb 1951; Bamborough 1952; Campbell 1930.

[7] See Paster 2004, e.g., where Wright (along with the equally Thomist but much later theologian Edward Reynolds) is frequently invoked to stand for 'early modern English culture', but where figures like Thomas Rogers, William Perkins, and indeed Cicero are glaringly absent.

[8] See Schoenfeldt 1999; Cefalu 2004a; and Paster, Rowe, and Floyd-Wilson 2004: chs. 1, 2.

and theoretical texts which occurred in the *ethical* plane in particular, this by showing how far each of those fields of writing influenced the other in determining attitudes to the governance of the passions.


## A HISTORY OF THE MORAL IMAGINATION

Many of the connections explored in this book do take the form of straight-forward allusions in one work to another, and there are occasions when it is appropriate to think in terms of one author making a deliberate, meditative response to themes and questions posed *by* another (or posed *within* some broader interpretative tradition arising from the work of another). Aquinas, for example, as discussed in Chapter 1, obviously does respond directly to Aristotle, and Hobbes's account of anger is similarly positioned in relation to Aristotelian analyses of the same passion. So too, Milton is shown to allude to Thomist accounts of self-delusion in Chapter 5, Shadwell to Hobbes's definition of the will in Chapter 8. I argue in Chapter 2 that Spenser draws, amongst other things, on a broad tradition of ideas about temperance and virtue stemming from Macrobius and Cicero; in Chapter 7, that the author of 'Upon the Beadle' does the same in invoking a 'Hobbist' nostalgia for man's premoral state; and in Chapter 8, that Rochester does likewise in deploying Augustinian ideas of prelapsarian sexuality in his poem 'The Fall'. As all these examples indicate, the approach to literary/intellectual history exemplified by Skinner especially has a direct application here: these writers do address specific philosophical propositions as if responding to the 'conversations' of their philosophical contemporaries and predecessors.[9]

However, this model of direct forms of address tends (more by accident than design) to make literature the subordinate partner in a one-way relationship, an expressive vehicle which versifies concepts but does little more. By contrast, one of the assumptions of this, my own book is that direct allusion does not in fact constitute the most important mode of interaction linking literary and conceptual materials. The various theories of governance presented in this work are all premissed on *models* of man's moral psychology. Although the respective proponents of these theories purported, in their own day, to be representing observed or otherwise scientific truths, they seem to us, now, to have offered only imaginative constructions of the nature of the mind, different ways of imagining what the self might be like when it is determining to act. Each

---

[9] Cefalu (2004*a*: 14–15, and, more widely, chs. 1, 2) provides a collection of case studies of this kind, demonstrating that early modern 'literary' texts often presented cogent analyses of specific ethical theories.

ethic treated here—Augustinian, Aristotelian, Epicurean, libertine—is, after all, founded on assumptions about the moral possibilities of human nature, man's capacity (or otherwise) for good; and those *pre*rational assumptions are crystallized in the images, and in the ideals captured as images, which characteristically accompany these different moral theories. The dominant image in Erasmus's *Enchiridion*, for example (discussed in Chapter 1), is one of warfare and psychomachic struggle. Preoccupied with an essentially lugubrious idea of what man is like, Erasmus instinctively views the passions as enemies within, and constructs Christian selfhood in terms of an internecine struggle led by a noble but besieged faculty of reason. That image of psychomachia binds together a host of sixteenth-century moral philosophies, connecting them, too, to the wider context of early Calvinist ideas of man. It is *this* kind of connection, I suggest, which is ultimately more significant than localized allusions in uniting otherwise disparate textual materials—more significant, that is, for poetic writers in particular.

Connections built around shared root-images are especially pertinent in tying philosophical texts to *literary* ones, since the latter do not characteristically treat moral themes through overt processes of rational argumentation. Although the exactitude of Spenser's language and allegorical thinking allows us to identify certain specific intellectual influences acting upon his work (Bryskett, for example, or Elyot), he does not really participate in a dialogue with, say, Erasmus's *Enchiridion* in the way that Locke consciously does with Filmer in his *Two Treatises*. The greater part of Spenser's connection with sixteenth-century ethics is one of shared imagery, a predisposition to start out from the same assumptions—the same image of man—as does Erasmus or Thomas Rogers; and it is through that prerational language more than any other that he engages with his predecessors. If we look at this same point from the other side, it is also evident that it is Spenser's psychomachic assumption, his core image of man, which dictates the extent to which he *can*, in *The Faerie Queene*, directly reflect particular conceptual subtleties drawn from Aristotle's ethics. That core image, as I argue in Chapter 2, circumscribes the degree to which Spenser is able to accept Aristotelian notions of habituation. Whilst he can body forth the latter's distinction between mere incontinence and the greater extreme of outright vice—these, gradations of evil traversed through a process of negative habituation, and captured by Spenser in images of liquefaction and somnolence—he cannot represent those same gradations in their positive aspect (as Aristotle does), as a distinction between continence and the permanence of virtue. Spenser cannot do this because the latter—perfectly engrained virtue—is incompatible with his (though not with Aristotle's) prior assumptions about what man is like. In Spenser's imagination such consistency and moral perfection are, on earth at least, unattainable.

Examples of just such moral imagery abound in this study. When Chapman appropriates the idioms of Aristotle's *Meteorologica*, for example, he does so because the various explosive phenomena of the weather and what we now term plate tectonics capture what he sees as the uncontrollable eruptiveness of sexual passion. He does so, also, because the *Meteorologica* is built around a language of fluid transfers and interfusions which matches his own sense, in *Bussy D'Ambois*, of the fluid medium connecting body and soul. It is thus the underlying *image* of human nature which dictates the choice of intellectual associations as Chapman strives to find an analogous language in which to figure his idea of the psyche. Imagery proves integral, too, in helping competing writers—literary as well as philosophical—to discriminate their different shades of hedonism or their different ideals of self-realization. Montaigne and Cotton, for instance, each alike define their Epicureanisms in the figurative terms of savouring and relishing. Meantime, Rochester's images of 'generosity' must compete for appreciation alongside Milton's language of 'magnanimity'. Above all, though, the most important image at work in this book (dominating Part II in fact) is that of continuous, hurtling, forward motion—specifically the perception that man is committed to a constant process of momentum. It is that prerational conceit which informs Hobbes's construction of human nature as he reimagines the self in something other than psychomachic terms. Motion is an informing image, too, in Tacitus, *Troilus and Cressida*, and a host of libertine poems, French as well as English. It captures both the freneticism and the exhilaration of the libertine chase to indulge serial appetites. When Rochester *seems* to echo Hobbes's philosophy, it is largely because he is reproducing precisely such kinetic assumptions about human nature as also underlie *Leviathan* and *The Elements of Law*; and he does *that* not because he is thinking about Hobbes in particular, but because he is reflecting the ethos of his own society, an ethos which itself draws upon the guiding image of man *presupposed* in Hobbes's philosophy. Rochester, then, formulates his criticism of libertine society in imagist terms, and those terms resonate with Hobbes's own. His own poetic imagination, dwelling on the unremitting motions of appetite, is drawn periodically to terrifying ideas of boundlessness: boundless pursuit, unbounded desire, loss of bearings within a boundless space, the dissolution of the sense of self into something boundless, and so on. Hurling movement, precipitation, consumption, and obliteration dog his verse. These are the threatening associations which libertine kinesis provokes in his mind, and it is on such instinctive bases that he gravitates, instead, towards the moderations of traditional Epicureanism. Crucially though, in so *graphically* articulating his disillusionment with libertine motion, Rochester prepares the ground for others, too, to abandon that Hobbist ethic (in that they are encouraged to do so by his and others' arresting language). It is in so far as literary works do this, criticizing the imaginative presuppositions on which philosophical positions such as Hobbes's are based, that they are able to help determine the subsequent fortunes of those theoretical texts. Rochester, not being a contributor to a philosophical 'conversation' (not being the author of an anti-Hobbesian treatise, for example), cannot exert a *direct* influence over the progress of seventeenth-century moral philosophy; but he and others like him can change the imaginative context within which such logical discourses are received, and in that respect they can determine what sort of critical fortune purely philosophical works will meet with. Hobbes's popularity needs must dwindle when, with the decline of Restoration libertinism, the vision of motion at the heart of his philosophy becomes seen as a source less of exhilaration than of frantic anxiety. The relationship between literary and philosophical treatments of governance and the passions is, therefore, more dialectical, more of a two-way or circular exchange, than may at first appear.

It is in this sense that I present here a history of what might best be called the 'moral imagination';[10] and that history is constructed on the premiss that images and assumptions, as much as the declared beliefs and principles which reflect them, evolve over time in collusion with the ideological needs of the different groups which articulate them. This, then, is the larger story behind this history of passion's triumph over reason.

[10] This phrase is deliberately reminiscent of Stachniewski's 1991 book *The Persecutory Imagination*, which examined the influence exerted by Calvinist modes of consciousness over late sixteenth- and seventeenth-century works of literature, most notably Milton's.

# Part I

# Governance and the Passions

# 1

## Positions in Early Modern Moral Thought

On what terms might an Englishman of the 1580s, preoccupied with the task of fashioning himself as a gentleman, have conceived his project? To what ethical traditions might he have looked for insight and inspiration? This book begins by addressing these questions with the intention of thereby framing Spenser's *Faerie Queene* within a larger discourse, the discourse of self-governance. To that end the following chapter offers three brief sketches, one of Socratic and Stoic, one of Aristotelian, and one of early Calvinist attitudes to human nature.[1] It traces these traditions' respective views of reason, the passions, grace, virtue, habituation, and *akrasia* (or weakness of will); this with the aim of demonstrating how far a psychomachic view of the mind, and a dismissive view of the passions and the body, dominated ethical thinking (indeed, the moral imagination) in late sixteenth-century England.

What unites the three classical positions outlined here is their common emphasis on the role of reason in ruling the mind. Reason thus understood intuits transcendental values, grasping a divinely sanctioned, eternally present morality which is the bond of all society. Passions, by contrast, are conceived—by most, if not by Aristotle—as wholly disruptive to this order, and hence as forces to be suppressed or eradicated. This dualistic opposition at the heart of the discourse of governance gives rise to an emphasis on psychomachia, an emphasis instantiated in the very form of Spenser's *Faerie Queene*. The soul is imagined as a battleground upon which reason fights the passions, and those passions become enemies within the gates (enemies the more sinister because they are typically viewed as ineradicable, eternally recurrent). Calvinist outlooks, of course, demonstrate no comparable faith in rational autonomy. Rather, they cast reason as itself the victim of that ineradicable corruption within, which again stems from man's carnal and passionate tendencies but which, on this Protestant argument, can only be

---

[1] For practical reasons I examine the various classical traditions here as discrete intellectual threads. Most contemporary humanists would have been less concerned to observe such boundaries, but they did recognize the existence of conflicting opinions, for example about the nature and worth of the passions.

corrected through the regenerative effect of God's grace. According to this much more negative image of human nature, the mortification of the flesh to which grace gives rise is, furthermore, a rare achievement, one the full realization of which is reserved for the next life. In the meantime, even the elect must face a life of sometimes desperate moral paralysis, dogged by sinful affections against which the spirit (empowered by grace) must struggle. This assumption, too, is a crucial starting point for *The Faerie Queene*, to which work this chapter thus offers a prelude.

## SOCRATES AND THE STOICS

Although first published in 1503, Erasmus's *Enchiridion Militis Christiani* was translated into English thrice and printed a dozen times between 1520 and 1576,[2] so there is good reason to regard its distinctively Socratic[3] moral ideals as indicative even of *late* Tudor opinion on the subject of governance. Erasmus's moral psychology in this work is grounded on a familiar dualism: fallen man has 'two natures', mind and body, the one possessed of reason, the other of passions which constantly 'stryue to go before reason', their rightful ruler.[4] These two, coexistent natures delight in opposites: the mortal body savours 'thynges vysyble ... temporall' and 'erthly', whilst the mind, despising 'thinges that are seen' as 'transytory', seeks what is 'true ... permanent ... celestiall'.[5] Reason counsels man to dismiss the material goods beloved of the body because they are only superficially pleasurable—'the vayne ymages ... of thynges' admired by the crowd in Plato's cave—and because such worldly goods are mutable, being either consumable or subject to the vagaries of Fortune.[6] By contrast, the spiritual goods perceived by and attained through reason offer 'immutable ... pure' pleasure—not least in that they are inalienable, pertaining to a life lived 'inwardly in the spiryte' which fluctuating worldly circumstances cannot touch.[7] Given this superiority of mind over body, Erasmus concludes that man should 'withdrawe ... as moche as [he] can from ... sensyble thynges' and the passionate appetites which they occasion, absenting his mind from the body through 'the despysynge of thynges corporall' and 'contemplacyon ... of thynges spirytuall'.[8] To do this, to identify oneself with the life of reason (what Aristotle calls the best that is within man (*Nicomachean Ethics* (*NE*)

---

[2] Devereux 1983: 104–16.

[3] I follow Vlastos (1991) in characterizing as 'Socratic' Plato's early dialogues, the moral psychology in which is bipartite. The middle dialogues and their tripartite psychology are invoked later in this book.

[4] Erasmus 1981: 60, 61–2.     [5] Ibid. 61.      [6] Ibid. 139.      [7] Ibid. 106.

[8] Ibid. 66, 106.

$1177^b34$) ),[9] is to anticipate dying, since death is precisely the moment at which the mind is finally released from the tainted body. Hence Montaigne: 'the premeditation of death, is a fore-thinking of libertie. He who hath learned to die, hath unlearned to serve. ... To know how to die, doth free vs from all subjection and constraint.'[10] Such premeditation frees man from both his fear of death and the otherwise enslaving demands of the bodily appetites which manifest themselves as passions.

The debt to Plato's *Phaedo*, both here and throughout the *Enchiridion*, is self-evident. Erasmus's combination of ethical and epistemological ideals derives from there. In the *Phaedo* Socrates repeatedly attacks the body, senses, and appetites as sources of deception, impediments which try to falsify reason's judgements: 'For this body ... raiseth wars, seditions, ... by its inordinate lusts ... [To] perceive any thing ... clearly, we must withdraw from the body' (66a–e).[11] The ideal of governance which follows from this is plain. Wise men will 'abstain from all [bodily] pleasures ... not permitting their appetites and passions to carry them away in pursuit of sensual delights ... but abstracting ... their minds from all ... splendid trifles' (82c–83a).[12] Mind and reason, then, exert absolute sovereignty over appetite and passion, even seeking to eradicate such impulses. The sensible pleasures and pains to which these passions and appetites answer are described as nails which 'fastneth the Soul to the Body, and make it corporeal, thinking all things to be true, that the body dictateth' (83d).[13] The soul must be trained to resist such false judgements if it is to maintain its purity and thereby its capacity to fuse with the divine after death.

Reason's obligation to 'constraine [and] master ... all passions', and where they cannot be 'wholly quench[ed]', at least to have 'the vpper hand of them',[14] is thus the principal theme of this and many another Platonically minded moral treatise of the sixteenth century (at least in Northern Europe). The emphasis in such works is markedly dualistic, but also psychomachic and allegorizing. Hence Erasmus, in advocating the subjugation of the passions, dramatizes them not merely as evil, but as intruders within the gates, aliens within who would corrupt man's soul, tearing it from his better self if once indulged. Pleasure becomes, in his language, 'the bayte wherby men are allured ... to ... myschefe'; sorrow 'letteth men and dryueth them from vertue'; fear and recklessness are 'mad counseylours' both; wrath is 'indurate', hope 'flatering'; love 'layeth handes violently on al thynges'.[15] Importantly, the existence of such rebellious impulses makes *akrasia* (the experience of knowing what it is right to do, yet not doing it) possible, this because man

---

[9] References to Aristotle are to Aristotle 1995.    [10] Montaigne 1603: 34.
[11] Plato 1675: 107–8.    [12] Ibid. 153.    [13] Ibid. 156.
[14] La Primaudaye 1618: 13.    [15] Erasmus 1981: 63.

can lose the psychomachic fight against these impostors within. *Akrasia* is therefore entertained as a constant threat by Erasmus (though not by the early Plato[16])—just as it had been by St Paul in his celebrated dictum, 'I see another law in my members, warring against the law of my mind, and bringing me ... to ... sin' (Rom. 7: 23). According to this view of things, there is always, beneath or behind one's apparent self, a potential *alter ego*, a world of passions never to be eradicated, against which the Christian must mount a 'contynual warre'[17]—and this idea will prove especially important in Spenser's *Faerie Queene*. In Erasmus's eyes, Christian moral life amounts to a constant process of crucifying these passions, applying the doctrine of the Cross—the lesson of Christ's example—to one's own self-governance: 'Whan thou art moued with gluttony haue in mynde how he dranke gall with eysell ... When yre prouoketh the lette hym come immedyatly to thy mynde, whiche lyke a lambe before the shearer helde his peace.'[18] It is man's lot perpetually to re-enact the death of Christ, to use reason and faith to master and extinguish his passions, 'burying ... all bodily affections, to the end [he] maie rise againe'.[19]

Here, then, is one familiar psychomachic model of the mind, and clearly it bears comparison with another: namely, that which is articulated in Cicero's *Tusculan Disputations*, perhaps the most celebrated guide to Stoic philosophy in the sixteenth century (Epictetus's much-circulated *Enchiridion* notwithstanding). In Cicero's treatise, as in Plato's *Phaedo*, the body is presented as a prison-house from which the immortal soul must free itself; the philosopher's task is to 'practise' dying, withdrawing from his passions and living by reason; and Cicero (in contrast to most ancient Stoics) also adopts Socrates' bipartite psychology, maintaining that the soul has just two parts: a rational power which must command man's passionate power if he is to cultivate virtue and tranquillity (*Disputations*, 2. 21. 47, 4. 5. 10).[20] But beyond this the *Disputations* also advocate principles more distinctive to Stoicism itself—Stoicism's emphasis upon showing indifference to bodily suffering, for example, and its adoption of a rigorous definition of the true good. Cicero presents the good as encompassing *only* those qualities which pertain to the achievement of virtue, to moderation, courage, prudence, and justice (2. 13. 30–2).[21] He insists that pain is 'ryght small in comparison' to virtuous qualities. Indeed, in Du Vair's later words, virtue positively '*helpeth* her selfe as wel by pouertie as by

---

[16] Vlastos 1991: 48, 86–91.    [17] Erasmus 1981: 61.    [18] Ibid. 179.
[19] Erasmus 1965: 125. This comment is one of many in the latter part of Erasmus's *Praise of Folie* supportive of the position maintained in the *Enchiridion*. *Folie* does, though, take an equivocal stance on the matter of governing the passions (see Paster, Rowe, and Floyd-Wilson 2004: 26–8).
[20] Cicero 1561: sigs. L7$^v$, S6$^v$.    [21] Ibid. sig. K7$^{r-v}$.

riches, by sicknes as by health'.[22] Hence, where moral perfection demands as much, the Stoic must regard with indifference the need to suffer pain. Further, he should be indifferent to all 'goods' of body and fortune. The latter are certainly preferable additions to life, but are not, for the Stoic, essential to true happiness, because such happiness is immune to the vagaries of fortune, pain, poverty, torture, and the like. In Zeno's terms, pain is a thing 'repugnaunt to nature' (*Disputations*, 2. 12. 29)[23] which man may rightfully evade just as he rightfully pursues other 'preferable indifferents' ('wealth, reputation, health, strength'),[24] but since none of these will contribute to true happiness as such, none may be sought or avoided at *virtue*'s expense.

Such, then, are 'right reason's' prescriptions for governance, and it is with those precepts in mind that Cicero develops his theory of the passions. These *perturbationes animi* are agitated movements which disrupt the soul's equable calm, preventing reason from operating judiciously (3. 4. 7).[25] Like the judgements of right reason, all passions have reasoned or cognitive components, but in passions the latter are *misguided* opinions about the good or evil facing an individual, and they characteristically induce violent impulses. Delight, for example, arises when man judges that the prospect before him offers some immediately present good about which he should feel enraptured. The alternative belief, that he is facing a present evil, induces distress. Beliefs about future goods prompt desire, those about future evils, fear. All such passions, Cicero argues—he defines thirty-two others—are grounded on a mistaken measure of good and evil (namely, what profits the 'preferable indifferents' of body and fortune) rather than on virtue. Passions are characteristically premised on 'an earnest opinion ... that [man] ought to flye that, whyche in deede he ought not', a judgement, therefore, contrary to right reason (4. 11. 26).[26] Worse still, these perturbations, a 'smoke' which 'obscure[s] the eye' of true understanding,[27] typically multiply themselves. Every misguided desire provokes an equally intemperate fear of disappointment and an aversion for those things which seem to threaten this. Reason is lost amidst this proliferation: 'For when [affective impulses] are departed once from reason' (*Disputations*, 4. 18. 42), which even a partial indulgence of passion implies, the disordered soul cannot arrest their motions—at least until the passions have lost their 'freshe[nesse]' (3. 23. 55).[28]

Cicero's reference to 'freshe[nesse]' and the observation that pain diminishes with time even though the conditions which first occasioned it remain unchanged is proof for Stoics that there is nothing either good or bad

---

[22] Du Vair 1598: 18.     [23] Cicero 1561: sig. K6$^v$.

[24] Diogenes Laertius, in Long and Sedley 1987: i. 354.     [25] Cicero 1561: sigs. N4$^{r-v}$.

[26] Ibid. sig. T3$^v$.     [27] Du Vair 1598: 34.

[28] Cicero 1561: sigs. U2$^v$, Q3$^r$. See Nussbaum 1994: 381–2.

but thinking makes it so.[29] Once the beliefs on which passions are based
are recognized for what they are—mere opinions, neither necessary nor
true—reason's rule can be restored. Indeed, it is by persistently reminding
the mind of this truism that reason resists the passions. Here again then, as
with Socratic Platonism, psychomachia and a bipartite opposition are essential
features of the soul. Right reason must rule the mind; the passions, in being
associated with 'the filth of the bodie and contagion of the senses',[30] are still to
be imagined as intruders within the gates; and that perception demands that
man should continue to see himself as engaged in a psychomachia, fighting to
expel invaders from his soul and to hold off *akrasia*. But if for Platonism the
passion's insurrections are an eternal recurrence, if Erasmus's Christian soldier
is permanently, miserably at war, the same is not true for Cicero. In his view,
reason's rule can be maintained without passion ever even arising if man both
schools himself in Stoic values and learns to accept the constraints of the human
condition—if he thus fortifies his judgement in advance against the misguided
opinions on which passions thrive. A man who recognizes the inevitability that
humans will err need never grow angry at those who wrong him.[31] Equally, if
he accepts that suffering is part of his lot and expects it, it will not agitate him
(*Disputations*, 3. 17. 36–7).[32] The wise man who appreciates these things and
adapts to them will achieve an impenetrable tranquillity of mind, the end-goal
of Stoic governance. For the majority, though, this Ciceronian dream is a
rarity; periodic returns to psychomachia remain man's everyday reality as he
strives to quell ever-inventive passions determined to corrupt him.[33]

## VARIETIES OF ARISTOTELIANISM

Aristotle's *Nicomachean Ethics* gives rise to a very different tradition of
governance, one which emphasizes the cultivation (rather than suppression)
of the passions. According to Aristotle, man is virtuous only if he shapes
his every action with reference to 'the mean', a situation-specific measure
of proportion and appropriateness. However, virtue is as much a matter of
right feeling as of right acting, and proportionate *action* on its own is thus
insufficient. To achieve true moral excellence, man must also respond to every

---

[29] The opening pages of Montaigne's 'That the taste of goods or evilles doth greatly depend
on the opinion we have of them' offer a celebrated Renaissance elaboration of this Stoic theme
(Montaigne 1603: 127–9). Montaigne concludes with the piquant observation that 'Externall
accessions take both savor and color from the internall constitution: As garments do not
warme-vs by their heate, but by ours' (ibid. 137).
[30] Lipsius 1939: 81.      [31] Cf. Seneca 1620: 535–6.
[32] Cicero 1561: sigs. P2$^r$–3$^r$.      [33] Hence Shifflett 1998: 1–4, 17–18, 29–30.

situation by *feeling* (only) a proportionate degree of passions and desires: 'both fear ... confidence ... appetite ... anger ... pity ... pleasure and pain may be felt both too much and too little ... but to feel them at the right times, with reference to the right objects, towards the right people, with the right aim, and in the right way, is ... characteristic of excellence [virtue]. Similarly with regard to actions also there is excess, defect, and the intermediate' (*NE* 1106$^{b}$19–24).[34] Hence the virtue of courage, for example, is achieved only when man rightly balances his feelings of fear and confidence and then acts according to Aristotle's ideal of military conduct. Temperance depends upon a moderation of the desire for pleasures of taste and touch (namely, food, drink, and intercourse), the temperate man striking a mean between an unnatural insensibility and the cravings of slavish hedonism. But if moderated passion is thus important, so too, to be truly good in Aristotle's sense, man must also be habitually (not merely incidentally) virtuous. His virtues must be permanent states of character, not fleeting impulses. Here again, though, man can only successfully predispose himself to *act* virtuously if he also predisposes himself to *feel* in the right way, to entertain the kinds of passion and desire which support virtue.[35] The cultivation of feeling and the formation of dispositions are both, then, intrinsic to Aristotelian virtue; but why so?

To begin with the cultivation of feeling: Aristotle takes it for granted that man cannot avoid encountering passions on a daily basis. His body makes demands upon him, and his social world stimulates him with endless opportunities, so that desire (and the particular passions through which it manifests itself) needs must be constant facts of life, demanding careful management. More than that, though, these passions and desires are not merely problems to be negotiated; they are also positive forces which the soul, Aristotle argues, needs to harness for its own good. In his *De Anima* Aristotle, having first enumerated the core faculties of man's mind (the understanding which intuits rational truths, the imagination which judges sense-impressions, the desiring power which drives man forward in all his actions), then divides *orexis*—the generic term for desire—into three forms: 'for appetite is the genus of which desire [*epithumia*, or craving for pleasures], passion [*thumos*, or spirited emotion], and wish [*boulēsis*, or rational desire] are the species' (*De Anima* 414$^{b}$2–3).[36] All three of these impulses are conceived as different expressions of the same one, unified desiderative power known as the *orektikon* (432$^{a}$22–$^{b}$7).[37] *Boulēsis* is, admittedly, qualitatively different from the other two forms. Where reason identifies a particular course of action as truly good

---

[34] Cf. Rorty 1980: 104–5, 108–9.      [35] Cf. Cooper 1999: 238.

[36] Plato likewise attributes distinct desires and pleasurable goals to each of the three parts of the soul (*Rep.* 580d).

[37] See Nussbaum 1986: 275–6.

for the self, that same judgement then generates a desiderative impulse which reaches forward longingly in support of reason's plan. This wish is *boulēsis*. It differs from *epithumia* and *thumos* in that *those* desirous impulses, though also shaped by cognitive judgements, support *non-rational* objectives rather than actions selected by reason.[38] Nevertheless, despite this difference, all three are manifestations of a single *orektikon*, and that element of the soul is distinct in nature from both reason and the imagination. Crucially for Aristotle, this appetitive faculty is in fact the most important of man's non-rational capacities, since without *orexis* man simply cannot act. Whether it works in conjunction with the cognitive prescriptions of the practical intellect or of the imagination, the desiring power focuses man's goals at each given moment; and this same desire, transforming itself into particular passions, then provides the physical power to activate the body in pursuit of those same goals. As Aristotle puts it in *De Motu Animalium*, 'the organic parts are suitably prepared [for action] by the affections, these again by desire, and desire by ... thinking or ... sense-perception' (702$^a$17–19).[39] Desire, then, in its three different kinds and its various passionate manifestations, provides the dynamo which initiates all purposive movement. It and the affections are essential to us, and must be managed, because they function as intermediaries between mind and body.

All of this *begins* to demonstrate why the would-be virtuous man must learn to cultivate his passions for his own ends. To be morally virtuous, such a man must, ultimately, perform good deeds, but he can only do that if he first shapes all his mind's motive powers to support his moral purposes; if, that is, he brings under his command all parts of the desiderative power, passions included. The achievement of such control is possible because, as already intimated, desires depend upon the guidance of a cognitive power—whether reason or the imagination—to give them direction. When imagination (the register of superficial judgements, which take the senses' representations at face value) assumes the guiding role over the *orektikon*, it typically identifies some immediate sensuous object as 'good'. It then provokes the lower forms of desire at least—*boulēsis* too if man's reason is corrupted—to yearn for this object. But such goals tend, in the event, to be only 'apparent goods' (433$^a$28), proving themselves sources of evil in reality. Desire thus guided actually finds itself producing 'movement *contrary* to [true rational] calculation' (433$^a$25)—that is, contrary to uncorrupted intellect and *its* judgements about what is good. When, by contrast, precisely that intellect (and not the imagination) guides the *orektikon*, the outcome is much better: true goodness is realized. In this latter case, where *boulēsis* is obviously primary, the desiring power in its

---

[38] Cooper 1999: 240–4, 256.          [39] See Nussbaum 1986: 277–8.

lower forms (*epithumia* and *thumos*) can also be made to 'share in reason' and hanker after the intellect's chosen goal. Through 'advice ... reproof and exhortation', those lower impulses, like *boulēsis*, can be 'persuaded' to align themselves with reason's dictates, this rather than heeding the senses' whims (*NE* 1102$^b$30–5). Aristotelian governance aims to achieve exactly this, making the entire *orektikon* 'participate' in reason.[40]

Desire driven thus by rational goals is, in Aristotle's view, morally valuable, and so too are the passions which are expressions of that desire. Hence, whereas in the Socratic and Stoic traditions passions are intrinsically reprehensible, reflections of misguided judgements about what sorts of goods are valuable, this philosophy offers a different perspective. Here the passions, if commensurate with reason, become the very manifestations of a virtuous soul. Such points are much supported by those Continental moralists who draw on Aristotle. Valerius, for example, observes of the emotions in his *Casket of Iewels* (translated 1571) that 'certayne' such 'inclinations are ingrafted in liuyng creatures' by a benevolent 'nature', for which reason he divides affections into those which are always good, those which are evil, and those 'betwixt bothe' which, if 'Iudged by mediocrity', can be turned to moral purposes.[41] Similarly, both Castiglione in his *Book of the Courtier* (1528, translated 1561) and Thomas Wright in *The Passions of the Minde* (1601, 1603) insist that passions are 'not wholy to be extinguished ... but ... to be ... stirred vp *for the seruice of vertue*'.[42] 'The affections' lend virtue a much-needed impulsive power: 'anger ... helpeth manlinesse: hatred against the wicked helpeth justice, and likewise the other vertues are aided by affections' which, if once removed, 'woulde leave reason very feeble ... like a shipmaister ... without winde'.[43] Du Plessis-Mornay echoes this Plutarchan point, as does Montaigne:

the soules actions ... have neede of this impulsion of passion; valor ... cannot be perfected without ... choller, ... Compassion serveth as a sting vnto clemencie, and wisedome to ... governe our selves, is by our owne feare rouzed vp; and how many noble actions, by ambition ... ? ... no ... *glorious vertue, can be without some immoderate ... irregular agitation*.[44]

The passions and desiring power are to be cultivated, then, for the motive force which they bring to moral actions.

Why, though, does Aristotle also regard the formation of predispositions as so intrinsic a feature of virtue? The explanation for this lies in the distinction

---

[40] The mechanism by which the non-rational parts of the *orektikon* are persuaded to share in reason is discussed in Cooper 1999: 245–6.

[41] Valerius 1571: sigs. B7$^v$–8$^r$.

[42] Wright 1971: 17. Cf. Castiglione 1928: 272.     [43] Castiglione 1928: 272.

[44] 'Du Plessis-Mornay' 1602: 166–7; Montaigne 1603: 329. The common source is Plutarch's *Moralia* 452b.

he makes between virtue and mere continence. In any given situation man certainly *can* act righteously solely because his reason commands that he should so act and because that reason, backed by the impulse of *boulēsis*, has vigour enough to overwhelm opposing tendencies in the soul's non-rational part. The lower passions and desires, although inclining to contrary goals, can, under these circumstances, be forced into obedience—this, the Socratic-Erasmian model of virtue. But a person who does this will not be (on Aristotle's terms) virtuous: he will only be continent (that is, strong-willed). Crucially for Spenser (as we shall see), the continent man always teeters on the edge of vice. If his reason once fails to overrule antagonistic lower desires, the non-rational part (typically championed by *epithumia*) will immediately drag him into sin—initially in the form of *akrasia* as he knowingly does wrong, but latterly in the form of vice proper if he becomes so habituated to misconduct that he loses all rational consciousness of right and wrong. The continent man, then, cannot be said to be truly virtuous, to be *predisposed* to virtue, because he achieves his righteousness only by forcing intractable materials into temporary obedience. In order to be virtuous in the larger sense, he must train his soul such that its lower desiring powers react to every situation, habitually, in a 'virtue-friendly' rather than 'virtue-resistant' way. This is precisely the condition of the man truly predisposed to be virtuous. His perfected *orektikon* anticipates the judgements of reason as a matter of habit. It always already inclines, in all its forms, towards the course of action which reason, judging on its own terms, then endorses as indeed proper. In this man the lower desires (and their attendant passions) want to do, of their own accord, what reason likewise approves of as the good. At most, the intellect in this soul, far from having to cajole these motions of the desiderative power into obedience, need only fine-tune them.

The achievement of this inner self-alignment dispels the threat of *akrasia* and ensures that the agent will, hereafter, be consistently virtuous. But how is so beneficial a disposition to be established in the first place? How can non-rational powers be trained? One answer, given by both Plato and Aristotle, stems from the observation that *thumos* (the medial category of *orexis*) develops in children well before reason and its aspirations do (*Rep.* 441a; *Pol.* 1334$^b$22–4). That *thumos*, Cooper notes, is focused around the human appetite for competitive exertion, and parents and legislators must capitalize on this impulse in educating their young.[45] They must encourage children to associate their spirited *thumos* appetite with the public standard of excellence, nobility of soul, and particularly with the self-discipline which that nobility demands. A boy, when he fixes on this goal of self-discipline in imitation of his

---

45  Cooper 1999: 276–8.

elders, thereby satisfies his *thumos* desires: he gratifies his competitive impulse to assert himself and demonstrate his excellence. However, in his doing this, a part of his soul learns habitually to incline towards (and delight in) actions of a kind which are also compatible with mature, rational virtue. Hence, whilst at this stage the child's motivation is self-regarding rather than the product of a rational calculation about man's true *telos*, nevertheless a foundation is laid here which the faculty of reason (when it develops during later adolescence) will then readily be able to appropriate to its higher purposes.[46] Castiglione captures this broad point for sixteenth-century readers with a description of human development modelled on Aristotle's *Politics* ($1334^b12-27$):

Even as ... in generation the body goeth before the soule, so doth the unreasonable part of the soule goe before the reasonable: ... which is plainely ... discerned in ... babes, who ... immediatly after ... birth utter anger and fervent appetite, but afterwarde in process of time reason appeareth .... [Similarly] ought there to be a ground made first with custome, which may governe the appetites not yet apt to conceive reason: and with that good use leade them to goodnesse: afterwarde settle them with understanding [when she] shew her light.[47]

Whilst the nurturing of these developmental associations is important, though, so too (argues Aristotle) is the more mundane process of imitative behavioural conditioning. If man—at first simply in imitation of others' examples, or in response to others' instruction—repeatedly adopts certain modes of conduct, and if those particular modes of conduct are in fact morally good, he will thereby engender (over time) virtuous habits within himself. Such habitual reiteration will engrain within the soul valuable forms of behaviour which will then *predispose* that soul to feel and act rightly in the future, that is, predispose it to *be* virtuous. Again Castiglione offers a crisp formula for this principle of habituation: 'such ... properties be ingendred in us', he says, 'as our doings are'.[48]

This approach to moral education is forcefully articulated in Bryskett's Aristotelian work *A Discourse of Civill Life* (*c*.1582), which combines Cinthio's *Tre Dialoghi della Vita Civile* with excerpts from Piccolomini and Guazzo. The idea of habituation is a constant refrain here. Bryskett sees it as a legislator's duty to provide the young with 'a true and certaine *forme* of life' according to which they may fashion themselves in 'honest ... vertuous liuing'.[49] Equally, fathers must 'frame the manners and disposition of their children' so as to ensure that the basely appetitious powers within their juvenile bodies do not gain 'ouermuch strength'.[50] Any body thus 'drawne to ... ill habit' will become overly keen on sensual pleasures to the extent that the mind will be unable

---

46 Ibid. 263, 276–9; Rorty 1980: 77, 79.    47 Castiglione 1928: 283.
48 Ibid. 297.    49 Bryskett 1606: 42.    50 Ibid. 52–3.

to govern it. Such tendencies established in infancy will, if tolerated, become still more powerfully ingrained during puberty at which time lusts of the flesh and anger begin to hold sway—the more so because reason, at this age, is scarcely 'tasted'.[51] It is at the moment of adolescence, then, above all, that orderly habits of mind must be established: the unruly, irrational powers, 'two vnbridled colts', should be 'tamed and broken' by reason, 'broken' implying a fracturing of existing habits and a reconfiguring of the psyche so as to make it operate on more rational bases.[52] The 'setled habits' which constitute moral virtue must, Bryskett argues, be established in the appetitious parts of the soul in particular, 'for virtues are grounded in those parts which are without reason, but yet are apt to be ruled by reason': these should be predisposed (made 'supple') so as to be receptive to—indeed, to anticipate themselves—reason's governance.[53] And that in turn is done through 'industry', 'the long practise of many vertuous operations'.[54]

This, then, is the Aristotelian account of governance. Like Plato, Aristotle retains reason as the absolute arbiter of moral value; and, like Plato, he recognizes the importance of *akrasia* and the threat of hedonism which ministering to the body potentially involves. But otherwise his theory departs markedly from the *Phaedo* and *Tusculan Disputations*. Here there is no wholesale dismissal of man's affections; none (or very little) of Socrates' or the Stoics' dualistic emphasis and their other-worldliness; psychomachia is no longer the dominant metaphor; and habituation is accorded a critical role. To this degree, Aristotle's innovations are immense. Those same innovations are also evident, though, in Aquinas's *Summa Theologiæ*, and since that work will be important to my argument later in this book it is worth giving it some initial attention here.

Aquinas's psychology mirrors that of the *De Anima*. He contends that man's imagination (wherein all his perceptions are registered) bluntly identifies objects, goals, or opportunities in the external world, which are either pleasant or repugnant to the senses, as being correspondingly either good or bad. These first judgements then prompt matching impulses of pursuit or flight apropos each such object—these, the instinctive motions of the so-called sensitive appetite (which in fact manifest themselves as one or other of man's passions). Such impulses, though, are in themselves insufficient to initiate bodily action. The ultimate cause of all deeds (to which the sensitive appetite must refer itself) is man's will: actions arise only because they are commanded by the will (or intellectual appetite) which takes the form at any given moment of

---

[51] Bryskett 1606:106.        [52] Ibid. 114–15.        [53] Ibid. 209.
[54] Ibid. 115, 209. For further discussion of theories of habit, including Renaissance comments on this theme, see Murray 1996: 179–98.

an 'affection'—that is, *another* impulsive motion rather like a passion except that it does not (as passions do) induce a commotion within the soul (*Summa Theologiæ* (*ST*) 1a. 82. 5 ad 1).[55] This will, not the sensitive appetite, must consciously, and after consideration, move the soul to pursue a particular course of action; but the will's consent is itself determined by yet other factors. What the senses communicate to the imagination is also reported to the cogitative power, the faculty which bridges the gap between the soul's sensitive and rational parts. The cogitative power (or particular reason) provides a rational judgement as to the *real* merits of the *particular* external object, goal, or opportunity placed before it, sensual preferences aside. It does so under the larger guidance of the understanding, or universal reason, which provides a *general* measure of virtue (1a. 81. 3). The will's ruling is governed, ideally at least, by these two rational forces (*Disputed Questions on Truth* (*QDV*) 25. 1),[56] which concur in determining that it should either consent to or oppose what the sensitive appetite, driven by the imagination and expressed through the passions, desires. That consent or opposition is the act of will which finally determines actual behaviour in any given situation.

If the will does not immediately consent (because the understanding questions the worth of the goal towards which the sensitive appetite leans), that intellectual appetite will, instead, love and desire—these number amongst its 'affections'—whatever alternative goal has been proposed by the rational powers. However, Aquinas insists that, just as the lower relies on the higher appetite's consent to operate, so the higher appetite can only induce bodily action by going through the lower (*ST* 1a. 80. 2 ad 3). This is because only the sensitive appetite, through the medium of its various passions, has the power to make the physiological changes to the body which must occur if man is to become physically capable of exerting himself. Physiologically, sensitive passions take the form of alterations to the shape of the heart, and it is that organ 'from which motion takes its beginning' (*QDV* 26. 3). As the latter dilates or contracts under the influence of different passions, so the distribution of blood and spirits to all parts of the body—a distribution on which muscular exertion depends—is varied. Each individual passion in fact gives the heart a specific 'disposition suitable for carrying out', and making the body carry out, 'that to which the sense appetite' at that moment and in that particular emotional form, 'inclines'. Hence the will's dependence on

[55] References to the *Summa* (*ST*) are to Aquinas 1964–81. Cf. 1a2ae. 31. 4 and S. James 1997: 61–2. Wright is typical of Thomist scholars of the time in noting the existence of these 'affections' of the will (different in kind from the passions of the sensitive appetite) in his *Passions of the Minde* (1971: 31–2). The 'affections' are analogous to Aristotle's *boulēsis*, as Aquinas's so-called concupiscible and irascible passions are to *epithumia* and *thumos* respectively.

[56] References to *The Disputed Questions on Truth* (*QDV*) are to Aquinas 1952–4: vol. iii.

the lower passions. Where the two appetitive powers, rational and sensitive, initially disagree, the will *must* therefore redirect the sensitive appetite to endorse its (the will's) own alternative desires. In effect, the will must induce, in the sensitive appetite, new *passions* conducive to its own aspirations.

This willed modification of the lower appetite can be brought about because the rational powers in fact have the capacity to 'excite and temper' our passions (*ST* 1a. 81. 3 ad 3). Reason need only present what it deems to be good directly to the imagination as pleasant, and what it deems to be evil as painful (*QDV* 25. 4). By thus influencing the 'forms' of the imagination, the very basis of the sensitive appetite, it can redirect the latter to produce passions which favour reason and the will's own, rational courses (*ST* 1a. 81. 3 ad 3).[57] This is Aquinas's account of that process of persuasion by means of which reason, according to Aristotle (*NE* $1102^b30-5$) and indeed Plutarch (*Moralia* 442c), 'ranges and orders' sensitive desire.[58] One especially important manifestation of this mechanism is man's ability to set one *kind* of sensitive passion alongside or against another as the will dictates. According to Aquinas, man has within him 'not only a bent towards what is beneficial and away from what is harmful'—this, the realm of the sensitive appetite's 'concupiscible' passions—but also a power of 'resistance to contrary and destructive forces' which 'block' his aspirations or otherwise 'menace' him—this, the province of his 'irascible' passions (*ST* 1a. 81. 2). The irascibles, especially when driven on by the will, may act as 'champions and defenders' of the concupiscibles, attacking those 'obstacles' and 'threats' which stand between man and his desires; but equally irascible passions may be invoked by the will specifically to counteract the sensitive appetite's initial, concupiscible inclinations, and even to make the soul 'submit to pain' when reason judges this the right thing to do.[59] Irascible impulses, then, like *thumos* in the later Plato's and also Aristotle's psychology, are instrumental in helping reason to reroute man's sensitive desires and in determining the soul to act, instead, in accordance with the good.

If in developing his psychology of the passions Aquinas outdoes Aristotle, he nonetheless stays close to his master in emphasizing the importance of habituation in making man truly virtuous. On the one hand, Aquinas notes that, because in any given situation reason will present man with a whole array of possible goods that he might pursue, the will must be habituated to be decisive both in choosing one such good to pursue and in getting on with it (1a2ae. 50. 5 ad 3).[60] On the other hand, though, this well-conditioned will must also, over time, predispose the sensitive appetite to incline rightly, since man cannot act without the latter's assistance. That lower appetite,

---

[57] Cf. Kretzmann 1993: 145–6.　　[58] Plutarch 1603: 66.
[59] Cf. S. James 1997: 58.　　　[60] Cf. *ST* 1a2ae. 55. 1.

when properly trained, should become predisposed always already to incline towards what the will, in a given particular instance, likewise prefers. As it becomes so disposed, the sensitive appetite will, increasingly, be drawn away from the senses' immediate pleasures (which it would otherwise naturally favour). It will become conditioned, instead, to prefer right from the start the course of action which the will, driven by rational judgement, will then subsequently advocate to it (1a2ae. 56. 4 ad 2, ad 3). Given such habituation, man, argues Aquinas, can be truly virtuous (as opposed to merely continent). Boyle's *Aretology* (1645–7) usefully encapsulates these points in the equestrian imagery so characteristic of the Renaissance language of governance: 'we cannot deny, but by the Influence of the Vertus of the Will, the Sensitiue Appetite may ... acquire good Inclinations and laudable Habitudes: and so may be called Vertuus by Participation: as in the Art of Riding ... the Habitude of Horsmanship is ... principally in the Rider; but yet may be in som sort said to be in the Hors, in Respect of his being Drest.'[61] Again, as with Aristotle, this habituation is achieved in practice through reiteration, as the cumulative effect of repeated instances of right willing, right sense appetition, and right feeling (*ST* 1a2ae. 51. 2, 51. 3). In proportion as it is achieved, the threat of *akrasia* and psychomachia, otherwise so prevalent a feature of Christian experience for Aquinas, as for Paul, recedes. Habituation is thus, for Aquinas, an effective way of defeating sin, making it a fruitful source of hope and success in his account of Christian spiritual life.

As I will show in Chapter 5, this latter, most positive aspect of the Aristotelian tradition was to find favour in Britain from the 1620s onwards, when moralists would increasingly take for granted both the possibility and the moral value of cultivating the passions, and when Aristotelian theologians such as Bishop Reynolds would elaborate on the theory of *akrasia*; but in Spenser's time the dissemination and acceptance of Aristotelian and Thomist thought was more limited. Selected elements of this philosophy *were* to be found in the writings of Castiglione, Valerius, Bryskett, and Wright, and certainly one partly Thomist, partly Hellenistic principle was a commonplace by the end of the Tudor period: by 1600 it was widely accepted (as per *QDV* 26. 3) that passions were, physiologically, alterations in the heart.[62] Hence Melanchthon defines pleasure as a dilation of the heart which boosts the circulation of blood, vital spirits, and natural heat throughout the body, and thereby induces a pleasant feeling conducive to good health.[63] Anger, in which the blood itself boils, is, according to Du Plessis-Mornay, a more intense version of this same movement: 'in anger, the hart ... labours and beates, & then the

---

[61] Boyle 1991: 12.        [62] See, e.g., 'Du Plessis-Mornay' 1602: 131–5; Wright 1971: 33.
[63] Babb 1951: 13–14.

spirits being chased, doe heat the blood, and the actions of the members are troubled, by the suddaine moouing of the spirits and confusion of the blood; but especially ... the spirits ... doe mount [upwards],... fiering the nerues and substaunce of the braine, which causeth a shaking.'[64] Sorrow and grief, by contrast, are contractions of the heart which have the opposite effect to pleasure (and are therefore damaging—even lethal—to the body).[65] In such miseries, Mornay again notes, 'the hart (as being ... close shut) is weakened, by drying & languishing, for not hauing the libertie of the spirits: wherefore, if it continue long ... it prepares the death of the body'.[66] These different passions, Wright argues, by either promoting or restricting bodily vigour, 'inuite [our] Nature to prosecute the good that pleaseth, & ... flie the euill that annoyeth' (be that good and evil as measured by the sensitive appetite *per se*, or by the sensitive appetite acting under the will's guidance). The point in all these cases is, as Paster emphasises,[67] that much of man's body (as well as his mind) is involved in his passions.

This, then, is one principle of the Aristotelian-Thomist synthesis which received some appreciation from the late Tudor period onwards (a theme to which I shall return). For the most part, though, it remains clear that, when Spenser claimed to present in *The Faerie Queene* the 'morall vertues ... as Aristotle hath deuised' them, he had in mind a rather different, more partial understanding of Aristotelian philosophy than that which I have modelled hitherto.[68] *His* Aristotle was generally less indulgent of, less forgiving towards, the passions and the body, and much more concerned with *akrasia* and the negative (but not positive) aspects of habituation. In order to make sense of these facts, I want to conclude this section by focusing on a distinctly sixteenth-century version of Aristotelianism, one which concentrated on the *Socratic* affinities in the *Nicomachean Ethics* and which emphasized not the value, but the rebelliousness, of the passions. There is no better example of this reading of Aristotle than Thomas Rogers's *Anatomie of the Minde* (1576).

Rogers defines his nominal ideal of governance in opposition to both the Stoics and the Peripatetics. Appropriating extracts from Lactantius's *Divine Institutes*, he chastises the Stoics for being too severe, the Peripatetics for being too prodigal, in their attitudes to managing the passions. To suppose that men should have no emotions, as the Stoics do, is to defy human physiology, since the passions are 'grafted ... in [man] by nature[,] ... cherefulnesse ... in the Splene, anger in the Gaule, luste in the Lyuer, ... feare in the harte'.[69] Such enemies within—as Rogers at this point tends to see these passions—are,

---

[64] 'Du Plessis-Mornay' 1602: 122–3.     [65] Babb 1951: 13–14.
[66] 'Du Plessis-Mornay' 1602: 125.     [67] Paster 2004: *passim*.
[68] Spenser 1977: 737. References to *The Faerie Queene* are to this edition.
[69] T. Rogers 1576: f. 1ᵛ. Cf. Lactantius 1964: 435.

anyway, morally *necessary*: it is the 'propertie of vertue, in the mydst of anger to … suppresse that vnruly affection … & … to bridle … desire from coueting', because 'he haue no vertue which hath not that in the suppressing of which the … office of vertue consisteth'.[70] In Rogers's opinion the passions are important to virtue, first, in a purely negative sense, as evils for it to work on. Without them, virtue has no enemy to fight, nor therefore the means to realize itself. Psychomachia is, according to this paradigm, an absolute fact of the moral life, its constant presence the *sine qua non* of virtue.[71] Hence the Stoic project permanently to eliminate man's passions in fact spells the end, not the perfection, of virtue. Rogers, though, swiftly moves on to develop another ideal which pulls against this first, opening position. He argues forcefully that 'to be moued with affections *to a good purpose* is commendable'.[72] To be angry, covetous, or the like may, sometimes, be positively right. He adds, furthermore, that since a man who is 'neuer moued in mind, can neuer be … good to himselfe, or profitable to others[,] … haue [perturbations] we must, and vse them we maye (and that aboundauntly) in honest wyse'.[73] Passions, on this latter, now distinctly Aristotelian argument, are the components of desire which reason must necessarily appropriate to achieve its ends and which ought, consequently, to be regarded in a positive light. They alone *move* man to act (as Aristotle had said in *De Motu*), and must therefore be harnessed by reason if it is to achieve anything.[74]

If, however, these last remarks endorse an Aristotelian perspective, it is Rogers's first, Socratic view, with its assumption that the passions are largely negative, which dominates the bulk of the *Anatomie*. With the exception of chapter 1, Book 1 is solely concerned with the irrational, sinful aspects of feeling. Indeed, such is the negativity with which Rogers regards the *particular* passions, he frequently quotes Stoic strictures against them. Tellingly, he follows the *Tusculan Disputations* in his classification of man's passions. Although he quotes Aristotle's distinction between good and bad pleasures, the remainder of his citations on pleasure—drawn from Cicero, the Stoics, and Plato—are wholly critical, hence his own summary judgement: 'this perturbation belongeth not vnto a reasonable creature … but rather vnto Beasts'.[75] With the exception of delectation, pleasure's different species are all criticized. The comments on 'oblectation' are typical: 'This …, except it be carefully restrayned by the raynes of reason,… so ouercommeth a

---

[70] T. Rogers 1576: ff. 1ᵛ–2ʳ. Cf. Lactantius 1964: 435.
[71] T. Rogers 1576: f. 2ʳ. Cf. Lactantius 1964: 435.
[72] T. Rogers 1576: f. 2ᵛ.　　[73] Ibid. f. 3ʳ.
[74] Lactantius emphasizes this point, here mentioned only briefly by Rogers. See Lactantius 1964: 434, 438–9.
[75] T. Rogers 1576: f. 3ᵛ.

man, that it makes him effeminate, and so spoyleth him of discretion, that
his onely care ... is howe to fyll himselfe with pleasure.'[76] This description
of oblectation begins 'The *Stoikes* saye', that of boasting begins 'according
to ... *Cicero*', and explicitly acknowledged debts of this sort pervade what
follows.[77] Other authorities commonly cited include Diogenes, Chrysippus,
and Zeno, none of them likely to exemplify the seemingly Aristotelian stance
of Rogers's earlier moral theory. Rogers even attacks Stoics like Chrysippus for
indulgently allowing that a wise man might love, preferring Zeno's opinion
that love is 'an vnsatiable desyre,... extreeme enemie to vertue, ... more to be
shunned then any other Perturbation'.[78] The actual content, then, of Book
1 belies the Aristotelian posturing of its first chapter, and the same is true
of Book 2, 'Of ... Vertues'. There, no effort is actually made to connect each
virtue with the control of some specific passion which it characteristically
uses 'in honest wyse'. Although numerous virtues are analysed, passions
only come to the fore in discussions of fortitude and temperance. Rogers
agrees with Aristotle that 'fortitude consists between two extremities, fear,
and folish boldenes',[79] and cites three definitions of temperance, the third
Aristotle's:

(1) a vertuous habite of the minde, whereby we abstaine from all vaine ... pestilent
    pleasures;
(2) to couet nothing whereof [the soul] shoulde afterwarde repent;
(3) a certaine meane about things belonging to the pleasures of the boddie ... which
    desireth nothing but that he ought, when he ought, and as he ought.[80]

However, there is little in the first two definitions here to imply the utilization
of moderate, controlled passions which Rogers endorses at the beginning of
his treatise, and it is striking that the third definition, which does broach that
theory, was later deemed extraneous and excised in the *Paterne of a passionate
minde* (1580), an abridged second edition of Rogers's *Anatomie*.

Rogers, then, does little to substantiate his initial, somewhat Aristotelian-
sounding theory of governance. There is no real exploration of what the
passions can do for man, or any hint of the proposition which lies at the heart
of Aristotle's ethics, that virtue depends upon the rational cultivation of certain
positive *habits* of feeling. Despite Rogers's professed theory, it remains the case
that what really interests him—crucially, what most grips his imagination—is
the darker side of the passions, their depravity and involvement in an eternal
psychomachia, pitted against reason. In the end, he cannot imagine these
affections as anything but negative, or see the mind in other than a defensive,

---

[76] T. Rogers 1576: f. 6ᵛ.        [77] Ibid. ff. 6ᵛ, 8ᵛ.        [78] Ibid. ff. 18ᵛ–19ʳ.
[79] Ibid. f. 139ᵛ.        [80] Ibid. ff. 109ᵛ–10ᵛ.

struggling posture, as a beacon beset on all sides by its own irredeemably corrupt powers. This emphasis is (I suggest) representative of later Tudor moral thought. The author of the *Genealogie of Vertue*, for example, also begins his treatise by trumpeting the affections as 'motions of the soule, wherby the heart is stirred ... to the following after good', yet is elsewhere quick to preoccupy himself, instead, with the mortification of the flesh.[81] Both this writer and Rogers seem positively to delight in a scourging of human nature and its passions, so much so that their work is more readily reminiscent of Calvin than of Aquinas.

## CALVINISM

As is well known, the driving refrain of Calvin's *Institutes*, reflected too in the work of the English Calvinists who shaped theological sensibility in late Elizabethan England, is that there is nothing but depravity within the body and soul of unregenerate man. Self-examination can only prompt a despondent realization that man, unaided, has no real aptitude for goodness (*Institutes*, 2. 3. 9); is equipped with 'nothinge', no capacity, 'towarde the well orderinge of his lyfe' (2. 1. 3); and is polluted by wickedness in his every member (2. 3. 2).[82] According to William Perkins, 'man before he be iustified, is', in the Pauline sense, 'nothing but flesh'.[83] His 'cogitations', 'desires', and 'outward behauiour' are all powered by sinful concupiscence (Richard Rogers).[84] On this account, the humanists' dream of rational self-governance and moral autonomy is therefore doomed to failure. As the humanists correctly imagine, man is indeed beset by a litany of corrupting emotions, the 'Affections, and Lusts' of Galatians 5: 24, which Perkins takes particular care to anatomize and which inspire in Rogers eight lines of vitriolic adjectives capped by the conclusion that the heart is nothing but 'a filthie sinkehole, out of which ... vnsauorie stinkes doe arise'.[85] However, as Calvin emphasizes, these passions are only evil because man's entire nature (of which they are but one expression) is polluted (*Institutes*, 3. 3. 12).[86] By that same token, and contrary to humanist aspirations, Calvinists follow Luther in insisting that the intellectual powers too, the very things which should defeat the wayward passions, are themselves wholly depraved before regeneration. Thus Calvin figures reason as a faculty immersed in error and delusion, one incapable of grasping divine truths (2. 2. 25), and the will, Aquinas's intellectual appetite,

---

[81] Anon. 1603: sig. C6ʳ.     [82] Calvin 1561: ff. 21ᵛ–2ʳ, 3ʳ, 18ʳ.
[83] Perkins 1604: 417.     [84] R. Rogers 1603: 4.
[85] Perkins 1604: 450; R. Rogers 1603: 88.     [86] Calvin 1561: f. 130ᵛ.

is likewise so 'bounde to peruerse desires, that yt can couet no good thynge' (2. 2. 12).[87] The little good there still is in these powers—these faculties on which the rationalist philosophers base all their hopes—remains inaccessible in the absence of God's regenerative process of sanctification. In Richard Rogers's phrase, understanding, conscience, memory, and will are all, for the most part, '*filled*' with the 'filthinesse of sinne'.[88] As such, they cannot function as the autarkic source of self-government of which Erasmus and others dream.

According to Calvin, God's grace is, notoriously, the only power which *can* rejuvenate man's ethical self (*Institutes*, 2. 3. 5, 6, 8), exciting in the hearts of the elect (those predestined for regeneration) a 'loue, desire & endeuour of righteousnesse', and then 'confirmyng' them 'to perseuerance' in that enterprise (2. 3. 6).[89] Hence, when David first began to sense his own depravity and discovered within himself a penitential impulse, he did so, Calvin argues, solely because he had lately received from God what Donne calls 'the grace to begin' (2. 2. 27).[90] The human will, in and of itself, is 'no cause at all' in *initiating* such regeneration, and even once the lifelong journey towards sanctification is under way, the will acts only as God's agent, as the mechanism within man which God appropriates to drive forward his own purposes.[91] As Article 10 of the Thirty-Nine Articles argues, man himself is incapable of repairing his soul: he cannot, 'by his own natural strength and good works, ... turn and prepare himself' for God ('for the heart', Perkins says, 'is vncapable of any good desire, or purpose' until it be regenerated by 'preuenting grace'[92]). When grace *is* imparted, though, its effects are overwhelming (*Institutes*, 2. 3. 10, 13), forcibly crucifying the old Adam within (3. 3. 9) and imposing upon the self a new heart and spirit, a will that is 'created newe' in so far as it is transformed from evil to good (2. 3. 6).[93] Yet, clearly, in all this there is no room for Erasmus's, Cicero's, or Aquinas's vision of moral autonomy: man's moral revolution, if it comes at all, is an essentially passive, not a self-generated, affair.

What grace first imposes upon the elect as they begin to experience regeneration is a sudden, absolute, and thus deeply unpleasant sense of their own spiritual inadequacy; yet that very consciousness is, for Calvin, a sign of spiritual progress (2. 2. 10).[94] Hence when Perkins measures the depths of Christian humiliation (the sinner's terror, his sensitivity to God's anger bruising his heart, his willingness to think 'more vily of himselfe then any other can doe'), paradoxically one can already sense in such prose the approaching promise of salvation.[95] We feel corruption, Perkins later argues,

---

[87] Calvin 1561: ff. 15ᵛ–16ʳ, 11ʳ.    [88] R. Rogers 1603: 3.
[89] Calvin 1561: ff. 19ʳ–21ᵛ, 20ʳ.    [90] Ibid. f. 17ʳ.    [91] Perkins 1604: 11.
[92] Ibid. 51.    [93] Calvin 1561: ff. 22ʳ, 23ᵛ–24ʳ, 129ʳ⁻ᵛ, 20ʳ.
[94] Ibid. f. 9ᵛ. Cf. R. Rogers 1603: 10, 94.    [95] Perkins 1603: 434–5.

'not by corruption, but by grace; and therefore men, the more they feele their inward corruption, the more grace they haue'.[96] This strangely comforting guilt then provokes another urge, again fuelled by grace: namely, an impulse to mortify the flesh, to crucify that part of the soul which continues to harbour sinful appetites.[97] The re-created will, in other words, is stimulated to initiate a psychomachia, one akin to that imagined by Erasmus but always more dependent on divine assistance. Importantly though, this psychomachia also compares with that described by Erasmus, in that it proves to be a lifelong experience. Regenerate man, far from embodying moral perfection, remains (throughout his mortal life) 'oppressed with [the] weight of our fleshe' (*Institutes*, 2. 3. 9).[98] He carries within him a 'spryng' of evil perpetually inciting him to 'lust ... couetousnesse, ... ambition' and such like, in which respect his body, especially, is a continual 'burden' (3. 3. 10, 14).[99] In attempting to eradicate sensual impulses, the spirit thus faces an endless inner warfare of the kind invoked in Galatians 5: 17, a struggle which even Paul discovered could disrupt man's *every* action and which thus attracts Luther's particular attention in his commentary on this same epistle.[100] The sheer desperation of this struggle is graphically captured by Perkins in his *Combat of the Flesh and Spirit*:

the godly man is like a prisoner that is gotten forth of ... gayle, and that he might escape ... striues ... to runne an hundred miles ...; but because he hath ... waightie bolts on his legges, cannot ... creepe past a mile ... and that with chafing his flesh and tormenting himselfe. So the seruants of God doe ... endeauour to obey God in all his commandements: ... yet because they are clogged with the bolts of the flesh, they performe obedience both slowly and weakely, with diuers slippes and falls .... A Christian is not one that is free from all euill cogitations, from rebellious ... motions of will and affections .... But ... he is the sound Christian that feeling himselfe laden with the corruptions of his ... nature, ... fights against them by the grace of Gods spirit.[101]

The clear suggestion here is that sanctified man, in all his slips and falls, will continue to sin in deed as well as thought throughout his mortal life. Perkins's envisaged psychomachia is, as such, a substantial, painful affair—and not least because the conflict between spirit and flesh is not one *between* separate entities, distinct faculties, but *within* each part of man's self. It is a fight 'betweene the heart and the heart'; a fight in which the mind 'is carried against

[96] Ibid. 567.
[97] See *Institutes*, 3. 3. 8 (Calvin 1561: f. 129ʳ); Perkins 1604: 143–5. The latter provides a taxonomy of ways of crucifying the flesh.
[98] Calvin 1561: f. 22ʳ. Cf. Articles 9 and 16 of the Thirty-Nine Articles.
[99] Calvin 1561: ff. 129ᵛ, 131ᵛ.
[100] See Luther 1961: e.g. 148–9; Perkins 1604: 418.   [101] Perkins 1603: 571.

it selfe, the will against it selfe, ... the affections against themselues: by reason they are [all] partly spirituall, and partly carnall'.[102] The soul, then, tears itself apart, oscillating between its Janus faces.

There is some immediate consolation for the elect in face of this life of warfare. With the first impact of his grace, God (argues Perkins) seals a man's fate. That first stroke of justification delivers a 'deadly' wound to man's carnality, after which the flesh 'continually dieth ... by little and little'.[103] From that point onwards, sin's dominion within the soul is destroyed (*Institutes*, 3. 3. 11).[104] It does not thereby cease to 'dwell' amongst man's members, but it does at least cease to 'reigne' (3. 3. 11, 13).[105] Nevertheless, sin remains potent enough to ensure that the psychomachic struggle persists, and the progress which man makes towards abolishing such resistance is painfully slow (3. 3. 9), dependent (at every stage) on further infusions of corroboratory or co-operating grace (2. 2. 25, 2. 3. 14).[106] Over and again grace must intervene to rejuvenate a flagging will otherwise broken by its own carnality. This combat ends only with death, when the flesh is at last 'vtterly abolished' within the elect and their redemption is accomplished (3. 3. 9).[107] Until then, the experience of affliction remains a daily and aching reality, regenerate man even at times losing all sense of the grace buried within him so that he becomes instead 'like a man in a traunce', one who 'by his own sense and by the iudgement of the Physition is taken for dead'.[108]

This, then, is the vision of life and of self-governance (such as it is) which Calvinism bequeathed to Elizabethan England. It constitutes a markedly different story from that of the hopes and aspirations of Erasmus, Cicero, or even Thomas Rogers; but it is a story, nevertheless, which dwells, as theirs do (and with the same lugubrious fascination), upon the negative, degraded aspects of the soul; a story, too, which places psychomachia at the centre of man's consciousness and makes it—here in conjunction with grace—a pivotal image of the moral imagination. I shall return to these commonplace themes and to the traditions which embrace or deny them throughout this book. However, it will already be obvious that the confluence between Calvinism and humanist ethics sketched above is nowhere more apparent than in Spenser's *Faerie Queene*, and it is therefore to that text (and the fractious nature of Elizabethan moral thinking which it exposes) that I turn in my next chapter.

---

[102] Perkins 1603: 447; 1604: 417.        [103] Perkins 1603: 567.
[104] Calvin 1561: f. 130ʳ.
[105] Ibid. ff. 130ʳ–1ʳ. See further on this point Perkins 1604: 414–15.
[106] Calvin 1561: ff. 129ᵛ, 16ʳ, 24ʳ; Perkins 1603: 451. Cf. Perkins 1603: 567; 1604: 51.
[107] Calvin 1561: f. 129ᵛ; Perkins 1603: 569, 567. Cf. Perkins 1604: 417–18.
[108] Perkins 1603: 450–1.

# 2

---

# Spenser, Psychomachia, and the Limits of Governance

Whereas the previous chapter presented a general survey, this one focuses on a single work, *The Faerie Queene* (1590, 1596), and examines the ways in which Spenser's moral imagination, his image of human nature, shapes that epic. Psychomachia, I argue here, dominates *The Faerie Queene*. Man, for all his aspirations to the contrary, is shown to be beset by recurrent, intrusive, bodily lusts, and by passions which are characteristically (if not universally) negative in their moral inflection. These corrupting elements pull against Spenser's knights as they pursue their quest to 'fashion [themselves] in vertuous and gentle discipline', to make reason the governing power of their souls.[1] The poem, then, turns upon the supposition (familiar from Chapter 1) that human nature is essentially flawed, carrying within it the agents of its own destruction. The epic's heroes fight against these retrograde forces, inner impulses that would otherwise draw them into sin; but the progress made in such struggles is typically faltering. Although in times of destitution the knights do receive the emphatic support of God's grace (in which respect Spenser recalls something of the Calvinism previously discussed), their own self-determined victories are, for the most part, precarious affairs, short-lived triumphs wherein reason suppresses, but can never eradicate, rebellious passions. The result is thus a mode of governance which remains ever prone to fracture (during mortal life at least) and which bestows no security on its subject. Yet, for all that, Spenser nowhere abandons his faith in the primacy of right reason, or questions the psychomachic framework within which his understanding of governance is constructed. He may trace the limitations of human moral achievement and man's dependence on grace, but he nevertheless affirms the value of humanist and rationalist ideas of self-mastery. Right reason is always, here, the sovereign power within the mind, whose standards man should aspire to. For that reason, Spenser's epic, like Erasmus's *Enchiridion* or Perkins's *Combat of the*

---

[1] Spenser 1977: 737.

*Flesh*, establishes a benchmark at the outset of this book, against which can be measured developments in the history of the moral imagination over the next hundred years.

In developing these, the broad themes of this chapter, I begin by discussing the portrayal of carnality in the poem, especially that of the body's intrusive lust, which persistently unbalances attempts to delineate an ideal of chaste sexuality. So too, I sketch the ambivalent but often corrupting influence exerted by the passions (pity and anger, above all) in shaping man's conduct and drawing him into immorality. The focus then shifts to Book II of *The Faerie Queene* and the role of temperance therein. Whereas previous critics have at best noted Spenser's *interest* in the Aristotelian distinction between incontinence and intemperance, I argue, more exactly, that he dramatizes the causal relationship between these two conditions. Spenser meticulously tracks the manner in which the one, incontinence, degenerates into the other, intemperance, as man slides deeper into sin. Crucially, though, he does not accord a similar narrative role to Aristotle's parallel distinction between the positives, continence and temperance. Aristotelian temperance involves a form of moral perfection which is, I suggest here, unattainable according to Spenser's way of thinking. Unlike continence, it hinges upon the eradication of psychomachia, the education of the passions so as to make them habitually concordant with the demands of virtue; yet such perfection is incompatible with the fallen and ever-corrupting nature of man as Spenser imagines it. The most *his* knights can hope for is continence, a muscular resistance to the soul's wayward passions. Guyon's moral story, the major concern of this chapter, epitomizes precisely such limitations. Repeatedly battling against the flaws in his own psyche (flaws which periodically overwhelm him), Guyon concludes his quest in the Bower of Bliss with an especially precarious performance of self-mastery. His affiliation, both here and throughout Book II, with shamefastness has met with little comment amongst commentators, but historically this quasi-virtue had in fact long been congruent with continence, just as its superlative counterpart, Arthur's desire for praise, was with temperance proper. This subtlety, too, thus reflects the different scales of moral attainment in play at the heart of Spenser's poem—not least because Arthur *is* seen to achieve moral perfection in Book II, whereas Guyon does not. Guyon's, though, is always the more human example, and I therefore close this chapter by detailing some other instances of fractious virtue elsewhere in *The Faerie Queene* which are comparable to his own.

# THE FLESH, THE PASSIONS, AND THE RECURRENCE OF BACKSLIDING IN *THE FAERIE QUEENE*

Every book of *The Faerie Queene* manifests anxieties about the intrusive force of 'the flesh' as understood both in its narrow sense of sexuality and more broadly as a synecdoche for the passions in general. Time and again Spenser charts processes of degradation as characters backslide from their brief moments of moral triumph into the carnal depravity which for Erasmus, Thomas Rogers, and Perkins alike is the constant refrain of the human condition. Red Crosse, for example, may begin Book i by defeating Errour (i. i. 24), but it is not long before we find him abandoning Una (Truth), and though in doing so he protests disgust at her apparent lasciviousness, the narrator tells us that the actual motive for his flight is 'gealous fire' (i. ii. 5. 6). Sudden sexual jealousy, not moral outrage, in fact prompts this furious departure. The illusory squire who is found embracing an equally illusory Una immediately prior to this moment serves only to externalize Red Crosse's own secret longings, and it is from those dark, desirous 'thoughts'—intimations of his own carnality—more so than from Una herself, that Spenser's hero flees (i. ii. 12. 3–4). In doing so, Red Crosse is 'diuided into double parts' (i. ii. 9. 2), not least in the metaphorical sense that his own psychomachia begins here.[2] His next encounter, which comes immediately, is with Sansfoy, escort to Duessa (manifestly the Whore of Babylon, and therefore an emblem of fleshliness). What is significant in this engagement is not that Red Crosse defeats Sansfoy but, rather, that he takes the latter's place as the Whore's lover and protector. In meeting Sansfoy, he has met an image and anticipation of one part of his fractured self, a figure which he duly becomes. In attempting to deny and escape his carnality, he has driven himself towards it all the more fully. (Indeed, in terms of the logic of allegory, Red Crosse is the cause of this very encounter, having created the Sansfoy—the faithlessness—within himself which he now meets.) This increasing complicity with fleshliness remains the theme in subsequent cantos. Whilst Duessa recounts her 'pitiful' life story, Red Crosse's 'quicke eyes' busy themselves admiring her (i. ii. 26. 5–7). When the couple then encounter Fradubio, the self-evasive tendencies which first initiated this moral descent manifest themselves anew. Since what Fradubio narrates in his autobiography is a mirror of Red Crosse's own recent experiences, and the hero is sufficiently aware of this fact to become 'Full of sad feare and ghastly dreriment', he responds to the talking tree by plugging

---

[2] Hamilton, in Spenser 1977: 45.

the hole through which it has spoken and thrusting its bleeding branch into the ground 'That from the bloud he might be innocent' (I. ii. 44. 4, 6). Having thus silenced a voice which might have saved him, Red Crosse then completes his degrading journey by kissing Duessa for the first time. The step from this to the opening of Canto vii, which finds the couple '[bathing] in pleasaunce' by a fountain's side, is an inevitability (I. vii. 4. 2). When Red Crosse drinks of the waters and is instantly emasculated, we are invited to imagine that he has imbibed that very spirit 'fram'd of liquid ayre' which came to him in his first erotic dream and which even then threatened to '*melt* ... his manly hart' (I. i. 45. 3, 47. 5). He is lost to sensuality, the Orgoglio[3] figure who imprisons him hereafter.

In Red Crosse, then, sexual passion, the body's most characteristic passion, directly intrudes upon virtuous spirituality. Elsewhere, of course, Spenser attempts to enforce a stabilizing distinction between 'filthy lust' and chaste, virtue-inspiring love (III. iii. 1. 6–9).[4] The Garden of Adonis in Book III, Canto vi, for example, offers a vision of controlled sexuality validated by the purposes of reproduction. Adonis, commonly the passive victim of a sexual predator, can instead be found in this garden 'Ioying his godesse, and of her enioyd' (III. vi. 48. 2), the narrator's epanalepsis ('Ioying ... enioyd') emphasizing the healthy mutuality of the sexual pleasure in which Adonis and Venus exult. Such 'Pleasure' is also figured here as the allegorical offspring of a marriage between a now tamed and 'stedfast' Cupid (III. vi. 50. 6) and Psyche (the human soul), this a vision which again endorses sexual delight so long as it is exercised within the controlling structure of marriage.[5] Cantos ix and xii, similarly, advocate a careful circumscription of the body's sexual impulse. This time we are presented with Scudamore who is barred from reaching his beloved Amoret, trapped within the House of Busirane, because the latter is encircled by fire. The fire wall divides before Britomart, the book's symbol of chastity; but when Scudamore attempts 'With greedy will, and enuious desire' to traverse it, it rages all the more (III. xi. 26. 3). To the extent that his passions thus feed the fire, the flames clearly are, in some sense, Scudamore's own unwitting production: it is precisely his own passionate greed and jealousy which keeps him from his lover inside the house.[6] She, meanwhile, is left to suffer violation at the hands of Busirane (the epitome of masculine sexual aggression and appetitiousness) until such time as Britomart can bring the power of absolute, confident chastity to her aid. Importantly, though, when Britomart does that, Amoret insists that her

---

[3] Etymologically, the name suggests a condition of being 'swollen with lust' (Spenser 1977: 97).
[4] Cf. III. v. 1–2.      [5] Lewis 1958: 342. Cf. Hamilton 1961: 138–40, 143–8.
[6] Hamilton, in Spenser 1977: 406.

assailant must not be killed, 'For else her paine / Should be remedilesse, sith none but hee, / Which wrought it, could the same recure' (III. xii. 34. 5–7). This observation immediately invites an identification between Busirane and Scudamore since our assumption—confirmed by III. xi. 11. 8–9—is that it is actually Scudamore who originally wrought the wound in Amoret's heart.[7] In saying, now, that Busirane did it, Amoret implicitly turns the latter (like the fire wall) into a function of Scudamore's own self: both villain and fire represent the aggressive sexual passion within each male which bars him from a temperate and thus lasting union with his beloved. That power must be quelled, but not eliminated, by the constraining principle of chastity—Busirane must be bound but not slain—because reproduction depends, after all, upon *maintaining* precisely such male lust. In the Neoplatonic ending of the 1590 text, Amoret and Scudamore do eventually combine in 'sweet counteruayle' to form their hermaphroditic whole (III. xii. 45–7), but their union is as much bodily as it is spiritual. Here again male sexuality (Scudamore's Busirane) is, in the end, assimilated within a larger, ordered relationship.

However, despite the encouraging example of all these cases, the achievement of chastity—Spenser's enforcement of the boundary which keeps chaste love aloof from Red Crosse's 'filthy lust'—ultimately proves fractious. Britomart, for example, is in fact wounded in the very moment of her triumph here (III. xii. 33. 4–5). Granted, it may be because she takes on that wound (and thereby matches Amoret's experience) that she *can* step into the weaker woman's place; but nevertheless, the bloody tarnishing of Britomart's 'snowie' purity needs must suggest the fragility of the virtuous ideal in play at this point, the ease with which the body might evade chastity's governance. Likewise, that same threat manifests itself again, indeed obscenely, midway through Book IV (here indicating that in issuing the second part of *The Faerie Queene* Spenser felt compelled to register anew the flesh's disruptiveness). In this latter instance, whilst Britomart (that is, chastity) sleeps, Amoret—now her travelling companion—is captured by Lust. In a sense we are told anew here, and in more detail, of how Amoret first came to be captured by Busirane (since Busirane is himself the epitome of 'sinfull *lust*' (IV. i. 4. 2) ). In seeing Lust now actually kidnap Amoret, a kidnap the *consequence* of which had been the theme at the end of Book III, cause seems at this point to postdate effect—as if Spenser were intent on underlining the circularity of his narrative, its repetition-compulsion.[8] This therefore familiar Lust, Amoret's assailant, is figured as a grotesque penis, his 'neather lip'

[7] Hadfield 1996: 139.
[8] Similarly, in Book II we are shown the dead Mordant first and then, much later, the young Verdant seemingly destined to become him.

> ... like a wide deepe poke, downe hanging low,
> In which he wont the relickes of his feast,
> And cruell spoyle, which he had spard, to stow:
> And ouer it his huge great nose did grow,
> Full dreadfully empurpled all with bloud;
> And downe both sides two wide long eares did glow,
> And raught downe to his waste, when vp he stood ...
>
> (iv. vii. 6. 1–8)

In personifying Lust, Spenser presents a man who has become his own member, as if that were the totality of his being, and (true to that idea) this penis has its own gluttonous appetite. The mutation is the greater, though, because either the scrotum is doubled, presented once in the lower lip which forms a poke, and again in the pendulous ears, or we are offered an inverted physiology, the testicular ears hanging *outside* the scrotal sack of the lip. The poem offers some reassurance against this horror in that Lust is subsequently slain, castrated by the virginal Belphœbe's arrow, which leaves 'all his hairy brest with gory bloud ... fild' (iv. vii. 31. 9). (Spenser perhaps betrays a masochistic pleasure here in so violently chastising the rebellious member.) However, the intensely graphic impression generated by this very purple passage is not so easy to dispel; nor is the sting in the tail embedded in a remark which Aemylia now makes to Amoret:

> He [Lust] with his shamefull lust doth first deflowre,
> And afterwards themselues [his female victims] doth cruelly deuoure.
>
> (iv. vii. 12. 8–9)

The primary sense in the second line here construes 'themselues' as the *objects* of Lust's devouring, but there is also a suggestion that women themselves, once first deflowered by an aggressor, may become their own devourers, willing agents who play an active role in their own incorporation into carnality. With such sentiments Spenser again reinforces the backdrop of violent corporeal resistance which intrudes garishly into Book iii's vignettes of chastity and sucks men back into the forms of psychomachia and depravity which I outlined in Chapter 1. However, if the governance of sexual appetite is thus one arena within which the poem's heroes are drawn away from moral ideals towards carnality, the same phenomenon can also be seen in Spenser's treatment of the passions more generally. They too are more often a source of instability than the subject of successful circumscription.

The surface texture of *The Faerie Queene* is thick with passions, both because Spenser is everywhere concerned to identify the emotions which motivate human conduct and because the moral evaluation of these forces is a critical element in his understanding of governance. There are times when his heroes do succeed in keeping such passions in check, or even in turning them to good effect, and such achievements are typically allegorized (perhaps in homage to Plato's *Phaedrus*) as acts of good horsemanship. Hence Arthur and his horse symbolically work as one in treading down the rebellious affections which attack Alma's castle (II. xi. 19. 7–8). Guyon likewise exudes self-mastery in Book v when he alone amongst Florimell's wedding guests can steady Brigadore (v. iii. 34)—just as only Alexander could command Bucephalus.[9] Being long practised in that art of moral dressage applauded in Boyle's *Aretology*, Guyon (sometimes at least) 'well [can] menage' his horse's 'pride' (II. iv. 2. 2). More commonly, though, the passions (like sexual appetite) run amok, dragging Spenser's heroes into sin, and when they do so, equestrian incompetence may be the first sign of such backsliding. Red Crosse's impending degradation, for example, is prefigured in his horse the moment he first appears: 'His angry steede did chide his foming bitt, / As much disdayning to the curbe to yield' (I. i. 1. 6–7). A similar tension bubbles beneath the surface as Artegall courts Britomart in Book IV. Cowed by her grave demeanour, Artegall suppresses the 'looser thoughts' which Britomart's presence stimulates in him; yet the result is that his passion only grows 'more fierce and faine, / Like to a stubborne steede' (IV. vi. 33. 8–9). Bad horsemanship, then, here points the way to the chaos which the passions all too often unleash within the world of the Fairy Queen.

These initial generalizations aside, though, the positive and (more typically) negative effects of the passions portrayed in Spenser's poem are perhaps best illustrated by turning to two particular affections: namely, pity and anger. That the first of these is of ambiguous moral value is a point neatly encapsulated by Bryskett in his *Discourse*: 'Pittie ought alwaies to be before … men, as a thing … without which they are vnworthy the name of humanitie: yet must not this pittie extend so farre for any particular … as thereby to confound the vniuersall order of things.'[10] In keeping with this judgement, Spenser presents pity as a passion which civilizes the savages as they respond to Una's and to Calepine and Serena's torments (I. vi. 12. 5; I. vi. 31. 4; VI. iv. 3; VI. iv. 11). The same passion is also a defining quality of Arthur and Calidore's moral sensibilities (witness, e.g., VI. i. 17–18). At those moments in Canto viii of each book when Arthur in particular dispenses grace, we always find him ruing some hero's 'pitteous plight', be it Guyon's (II. viii. 24. 5), Amoret's (IV. viii. 20. 3), or Red Crosse's:

> … with percing point
> Of pitty deare his hart was thrilled sore,
>
> .   .   .   .   .   .   .   .
>
> For ruth of gentle knight so fowle forlore …
>
> (I. viii. 39. 1–4)

---

[9] Montaigne 1603: 156.     [10] Bryskett 1606: 35.

Spenser himself is acutely conscious of his own pitying response to such events (witness I. iii. 1–2; III. viii. 1; and IV. i. 1), and that we are encouraged to emulate this sentiment is evident in Book I when our mirrors, the royal couple who listen to Red Crosse's story, 'passionate' appropriately (I. xii. 16. 1–6). Pity, then, in all these contexts, is celebrated for its obvious moral worth. Yet equally (if not more often), pity has, as Burrow has argued, the propensity to lead Spenser's heroes into disastrous error, in which regard it is a cause for anxiety.[11] I shall return to this point later in discussing Guyon, but it can be illustrated here by recalling the part which pity plays in propelling Red Crosse into carnality. The false Una, whom Red Crosse initially rebuffs, furthers her seductive purposes by aiming to 'stirre vp gentle ruth' in the knight (I. i. 50. 8). In this she succeeds: he does indeed 'rew' her predicament (I. i. 53. 8). The similarly corrupting 'Fidessa' then has the same effect a few pages later (I. ii. 21. 7–8). Here and in Burrow's examples, pity's pliability, its capacity to promote misguided causes as well as good ones, is thus exposed. Importantly though, the knights themselves—and often also their readers—seem unable to determine, at the moment of first appearance, whether or not a given impulse of compassion will incline man to good or evil. Pity, in short, blindly leads the mind, its ethical value emerging only in retrospect (and therein lies part of its danger).

Much of what is true of pity is equally true of anger. Philosophically, rage's propensity to corrupt is obviously a commonplace of Western ethics, but anger has also long held a special moral status.[12] Plato, for example, in writing his middle and later dialogues, the *Republic*, *Phaedrus* (253d–7b), and *Timaeus* (69e–73a), replaced his earlier bipartite psychology with a tripartite one, retaining reason as one mental force, but now arguing for a new categorical distinction *within* the sphere of the passions—a distinction between *epithumia*, man's irrational appetite for pleasures, and *thumos*, his more vigorous impulse of anger or indignation (*Republic* 439d). According to this new model *thumos*, anger, has a peculiar aptitude for serving as reason's natural auxiliary and fighting against injustice (440d, 441a). Hence, when *epithumia* prompts man to act contrary to reason, it is *thumos* which makes him grow indignant with himself, directing anger against that desire.[13] This, obviously, is the theory underlying Aquinas's distinction between the concupiscible and the irascible passions and his proposition that the latter are especially prone to assist reason; but it also informs Aristotle's treatment of anger in the *Rhetoric* and *Nicomachean Ethics*. In Book 7, chapter 6, of the latter (in a passage later redeployed by Aquinas in the *Summa*, 1a2ae. 46. 4), the arousal of anger is again

---

   [11] Burrow 1993: 111, 120–39.
   [12] Theories of anger are discussed in Braden 1985: 10–13, 22, 75; Burrow 1993: 208–17; Kerrigan 1996: 112–19; Miola 1992: 151–9.
   [13] See further Cooper 1999: 130–5.

said to be determined by a rational component, what Dihle calls 'a preconceived knowledge of what retaliation or just punishment should be like':[14] 'reason or imagination informs us that we have been insulted ... , and anger, reasoning as it were that anything like this must be fought against, boils up straightaway' (*NE* 1149ᵃ31–3).[15] The crucial phrase here is 'anything like this' (*tōi toioutoi*), since it implies that the initial excitement of anger is determined by a general principle, the rational judgement that anger and vengeful retaliation are usually justifiable in cases where one has been unfairly slighted. Where reason identifies an attack on one's own (and therefore on the institutions of) honour, nobility, and virtue, it generally demands a public defence of the same. In this context *thumos*, being the obedient servant of reason as well as the proud guardian of individual self-respect, impulsively asserts itself in the form of an angry desire for revenge. The problem is that such *thumos* makes only incomplete reference to reason and, if it goes unchecked, may therefore initiate action which subsequently proves to have been misguided: 'as do hasty servants who run out before they have heard the whole of what one says, and then muddle the order, ... so anger by reason of the warmth and hastiness of its nature, though it hears, does not hear an order' (1149ᵃ26–31). Aristotle's rationalized anger is not, then, perfect; but it is unique amongst the passions in manifesting a peculiar moral force. This fact was recognized by Spenser's literary forebears, witness Tasso's *Allegory* for *Gerusalemme Liberata*: 'The *Irefull* vertue is that, which ... is [least] estranged from the nobility of the soule ...: so is it the dutie of the irefull ... part ... to be armed with reason against concupiscence, and with that vehemencie ... (which is proper vnto it) to ... driue awaie whatsoeuer impediment to felicitie. But when it doth not obey Reason ... it falleth out, that it fighteth not against concupiscence.'[16] Bryskett likewise identifies as a particular virtue 'Mansuetude', which 'holdeth the reines ... to bridle the vehemency of anger, shewing when, where, with whom, for what cause, ... and how long it is fit ... to be angry; and likewise [when] to let them loose, and ... spurre forward the mind ... slow in apprehending the iust causes of wrath'.[17]

These same distinctions, systematically deployed in Chapman's *Iliads*,[18] play a critical part in *The Faerie Queene*. Spenser may not reflect the full edifice of Platonic and Thomist tripartite psychology,[19] but he does offer numerous

[14] Dihle 1982: 57.

[15] For further such rationalization of anger see Aristotle, *Rhet.* 1370ᵇ13–14 and Seneca, *De Ira* 1. 2. 4–5, 1. 3. 4, 2. 26. 1–4, 3. 21. 1–5.

[16] Tasso 1981: 92. Cf. Braden 1985: 75; Burrow 1993: 208–10; Miola 1992: 158.

[17] Bryskett 1606: 240–1.     [18] Burrow 1993: 207–17; Ide 1980: 24–33, 75–9.

[19] The case that *The Faerie Queene does* reflect the kind of psychological tripartition seen in such Continental sources as Ficino's *Phaedrus* commentary, Gelli's *Circe*, Piccolomini's *Vniuersa*

instances of characters driven to energetic, virtuous action specifically by their wrath, a moral or Aristotelian anger. Sometimes this is in defence of their own reputations, as when Satyrane, irritated by his inability to slay the witch's monster, 'Greatly [grows] enrag'd' and then tackles the beast with his bare hands (III. vii. 33. 5). So too Red Crosse, injured by the dragon, becomes 'yet more mindfull of his honour' and is thereupon sufficiently 'Inflam'd with wrath' to cleave off the creature's tail (I. xi. 39. 1, 6). Guyon is also so disgusted by Cymochles' behaviour that he consciously applies 'wrathfull fire' to his courage (II. vi. 30. 6–9), mapping fury on to a pre-existent virtue to redouble his power. When not fired by self-defence, the rage felt by Spenser's heroes derives, instead, from an indignant sympathy for others' sufferings. Arthur feels as much when he encounters Scudamour and Britomart outnumbered two to one in Book IV: 'His mighty heart with indignation sweld, / And inward grudge fild his heroicke brest' (IV. ix. 32. 3–4). In Book I, when Arthur locates Red Crosse in the prison and is 'thrilled sore' with compassion, that feeling quickly converts to 'furious force, and indignation fell' on the trapped knight's behalf (I. viii. 39. 6). Likewise, Red Crosse in turn burns 'With firie zeale … to auenge' Terwin's 'piteous' death (I. ix. 37. 4–5).

The specific values propelling these instincts of anger vary, inevitably, from moment to moment throughout Spenser's poem. At one instant we find Una urging Red Crosse to add faith to his force, and precisely that reminder of

*Philosophia*, or Tasso's *Allegory* for *Gerusalemme*, has been variously made. Woodhouse (1967: 354) presents the three sisters, Medina, Perissa, and Elissa, as one instance thereof, but in practice each squabbling sibling is just as irascible as the other (II. ii. 28), and whilst Perissa and Sansloy do epitomize excessive concupiscible pleasure, Elissa and Huddibras's *distinctive* trait is their 'melancholy', not any kind of irascibility (II. ii. 17. 8, 35. 4). These couples, far from being separate faculties, are two extremes on a single continuum for which the medial point is Medina. As will become apparent hereafter, a more plausible Thomist triad is that between Guyon, Cymochles, and Pyrochles (Hankins 1971: 29; Morgan 1986: 15), not least because, in so far as Arthur finds Cymochles more threatening than Pyrochles, lustful desire does indeed prove more hostile to virtuous reason than does anger. But although both Guyon and Arthur try (at II. v. 13 and II. viii. 51 respectively) to appropriate Pyrochles to their purposes, thus making anger servant to reason, neither knight succeeds. Nor is the defeat of these two brothers as integral to Spenser's epic as is the turning of Tancred and Rinaldo to Godfrey's purpose in Tasso's *Gerusalemme*, for example (witness Tasso 1981: 88–91; Burrow 1993: 84–99). In fact, this instance of tripartition is more incidental than essential to *The Faerie Queene*, and that last point is equally true of two other alleged examples of the phenomenon cited by Hankins (1971: 30, 123–5), both the lion and Satyrane's decisions to place their irascible qualities at Una's service. Again, neither of these figures is actually more than an occasional presence in the allegory as we have it. A further, quite separate argument of the same kind, Hankins's attempt (1971: 146–7) to identify Book IV's Bruncheval with the dark, concupiscible horse of Plato's *Phaedrus*, also flounders because at the point in the poem where Bruncheval is introduced there is no corresponding white, irascible steed to give point to any Platonic analogy. (Florimell's white horse is, textually speaking, a very distant antithesis.) Finally, if this last instance seems to border on being wilful, Reid's examples of Spenserian tripartition (1982: 370–3) are still more arbitrary. Tripartition is not, therefore, at the heart of Spenser's vision of man.

his Christian duty stimulates his righteous 'gall' (i. i. 19). Some verses later it is rather fear of 'shame'—that is, a worldly shame—which turns him 'Halfe furious ... , / Resolv'd ... to win' (i. i. 24. 1–4). In Canto V Red Crosse and Sansjoy alike are moved to rage by ideas of honour, but Red Crosse is the one who prevails because 'quickning faith', 'shame', and a sense of service for his 'Ladies sake' all drive his anger (i. v. 12. 3–8). In this last case, though, surreptitiously, passion has moved us into different territory. The other instances of anger discussed hitherto are essentially virtuous, examples of an affection turned to good, providing a spirited level of animation to help realize reason's goals. But the last instance—where anger serves to defend Duessa—is not like that. It stands as a timely reminder that anger, like pity, may be corrupted (in this case by an underlying sexual appetite), and that under those conditions anger serves, rather, to precipitate man into a downward spiral of sin.

Further to this last point, it is precisely 'fire and greedy hardiment' which first drive Red Crosse into Error's den (i. i. 14. 1), 'rage' which blinds him to the jealous nature of his feelings as he witnesses Una's apparent infidelity (i. ii. 5. 6–9), and 'the flame of furious despight' which draws him into ignoble bloodlust once he defeats Sansjoy (i. v. 14. 5). (The latter having capitulated, Red Crosse nevertheless longs 'To bath [his blade] in bloud of faithlesse enemy' (i. v. 15. 2–3)—this, the degenerate aspiration of a once pure knight 'Whose manly hands imbrew'd in guiltie blood / Had neuer bene' when Una first knew him (i. vii. 47. 3–4).[20]) Guyon, unhorsed by Britomart at their first encounter, likewise displays an ignobly impetuous wrath (iii. i. 9–11). The most disastrous instances of misguided anger, though, are reserved for Book iv and the violent encounter between Britomart and Artegall, in which each harms the other. Narratorial comment leaves us in no doubt about the depravity to which anger has here led the knight of justice, for 'What yron courage euer could' think

> ... with hands impure
> To spoyle so goodly workmanship of nature,
>
> .    .    .    .    .    .    .    .    .    .
>
> Certes some hellish furie, or some feend
> This mischiefe framd, for their first loues defeature,
> To bath their hands in bloud of dearest freend ...
>
> (iv. vi. 17. 1–8)

The fact that Artegall fights here whilst still blind to his opponent's true identity is, allegorically, precisely the point: anger, at its worst, induces just

---

[20] Hamilton, in Spenser 1977: 77.

such blindness, reminding us that it originates in the soul's irrational, all too corruptible part.

Anger, then, like pity, is a problematic tool of governance. Its potential moral value is clear; but so too is its great (if not greater) propensity to lead the soul astray. Humanist philosophical sources ranging from Aristotle through to Bryskett envisage an ideal soul which (thanks to its careful habituation) would tend always to respond to the world with appropriate feelings. This soul could also, if need be, consciously determine its own passions, controlling their deployment. But Spenserian heroes lack such advantages. For the most part they—and often we, as readers—are blindly led by their passions. This is true even when those affections turn out to serve a virtuous end. Only latterly (if at all) does it become clear to the knights whether or not a particular instance of anger has really been for the good. The motivational passions in this poem—those passions which drive individuals forward in their actions, and thereby give impetus to the narrative—therefore tell an equivocal story. Their moral value varies with the individual circumstances of each moment. However, if we now turn to what one might call the pageant passions, the displays of allegorized and anatomized passions which dominate the work's set pieces, these add a more conclusively negative note to Spenser's image of man's affections. They fuel the overriding impression of the poem that more often than not man's emotions drive him towards sin and carnality.

The threatening, negative power of man's passions is certainly the dominant theme of Spenser's masques, one aspect of his passion-pageantry. The evidence here scarcely requires comment. Book I's masque of the seven deadly sins, for example, bluntly presents each sin as at root a *passionate* disposition associated with a bestial state and responsible for catastrophic physical degradation in the sinner himself. The infernal House of Mammon offers a similar cavalcade of degrading perturbations (II. vii. 22), whilst in the House of Busirane both the tapestries and the masque of Cupid depict the ubiquitous self-enslavement and barracking emotions associated with the Petrarchan love tradition. In all these cases Spenser's graphical energies are turned to one end: the programmatic display of the passions' assault on the soul.

Alongside these masques sit the poem's extended anatomizations of certain particular affections, and here too the passions subject to such attention—despair in Book I, jealousy in Book III, care in Book IV, envy in Book V—are negative ones, powerful threats to rational autonomy with which characters must engage psychomachically to survive. The first such engagement, Red Crosse's encounter with Despair, is the culmination of a process which begins with the defeat of Sansjoy. Just as Red Crosse had previously killed Sansfoy only to become him, so too, having overwhelmed Sansjoy, he himself gradually becomes joyless. That descent begins with sad disillusionment when Red Crosse discovers the true foundations of the House of Pride (I. v. 46–vi. 2), continues with his imprisonment, and ends in the confrontation with Despair. The assault of this passion is, as such, slow and surreptitious. Its first victim, Trevisan, who meets Red Crosse whilst fleeing from Despair, is, primarily, an allegory of one facet of Red Crosse, since it is *he* who is really fleeing from despair here, fleeing from a sense of his own moral and spiritual inadequacy. (Though Arthur has by now freed Spenser's hero from prison, he cannot free him from his own carnality, that which first brought him to his miserable condition and which must remain within him until the House of Holinesse brings justification and regeneration to his soul.) This being so, the meeting with Trevisan is, in practice, yet another self-encounter for the knight, which is why Trevisan, having testified to his own 'byting griefe', can immediately expose Red Crosse's 'like infirmitie' (I. ix. 29. 2, 30. 8). If, though, Trevisan personifies the hero's flight from despair hitherto, their encounter, now, also allegorizes Red Crosse's willingness to confront that self-evasiveness and face his nemesis.

The arguments with which Despair meets Red Crosse, and the subtle diffusion of their two voices, each into the other, in stanzas 41 and 42 (I. ix. 41–2), both confirm the extent to which the one figure is internalized within the other. Despair, making 'a secret breach' in Red Crosse's consciousness (I. ix. 48. 3), meticulously rehearses the knight's former sins. He also articulates the fear of 'like mishaps' yet to come, which makes death, now, seem inviting (I. ix. 45. 5–9). Despair, though, only knows of these things because he speaks from within Red Crosse's guilty 'conscience':

> [Despair] to [Red Crosse's] fresh remembrance did reuerse
> The vgly vew of his deformed crimes …
>
> (I. ix. 48. 3–6)

As the verb 'reverse' implies, the demon acts as an inward mirror, a creature within the soul turning escaping thoughts of past actions back upon the mind. This image also captures the self-absorption of the despairing man. Suicide—Despair proceeds to offer Red Crosse a selection of appropriate instruments—is the logical outward manifestation of this inward tendency, a reversing of action back upon the self. At this point only the intercession of Una, reminding Red Crosse of the 'greater grace' promised to the elect (those 'that chosen art' (I. ix. 53. 5–7) ), can break his reflexive condition.

The Despair Canto provides a telling reminder of what is for Spenser the passions' psychomachic power, their constant propensity to drag the soul into sin—in this case by taking Red Crosse to the brink of suicide. Although the knight's subsequent experiences under Caelia's guidance to some extent overwrite the anxiety induced by this episode, the sense of the passions' destructive potency remains, just as it does in Perkins's account of the regenerate man's mortal life. Perkins's Christian too, though an escaped prisoner, constantly slips, falls, and pitches himself back into self-torment under the burden of his corrupted nature. In Perkins and Spenser alike, the passions are prime agencies responsible for inducing this crisis, which is why for Spenser they are, more often than not—and the potential virtues of pity and anger notwithstanding—a critical impediment to good governance.

## THE LEGEND OF SIR GUYON AND THE PROBLEM OF TEMPERANCE

Thus far I have suggested that *The Faerie Queene*'s heroes find themselves constantly slipping into sin under the twin influences of lust and a predominantly negative array of passions. Book II in particular (that to which I now turn in detail) crystallizes these same issues; but it also presents both a larger conception of virtue, a theory of moral degradation, and a focus upon grace and the human condition which are again illustrative of the limits placed upon moral achievement throughout Spenser's epic.

The theme here is temperance, generally understood, and it is this virtue which most directly seeks to combat and overcome man's many negative passions. Temperance is defined in opposition to precisely the background of carnality already so vividly exemplified in Red Crosse. 'Behold the image of'

> ... feeble nature cloth'd with fleshly tyre,
> When raging passion with fierce tyrannie
> Robs reason of her due regalitie,
> And makes it seruant to her basest part:
>
> .   .   .   .   .   .   .   .   .
>
> But temperance ... with golden squire
> Betwixt [such passions] can measure out a meane,
> Neither to melt in pleasures whot desire,
> Nor fry in hartlesse griefe and dolefull teene.
>
> (II. i. 57. 2–58. 4)

These lines, which could be lifted from Erasmus's *Enchiridion*, betray a familiar hostility to passion as the enemy within against which reason must wage a psychomachic struggle to retain its sovereignty. Importantly, there is nothing here of Aristotle's positive passions, of pity's or anger's potential worth; no suggestion that pleasure or grief could be something other than excessive or sinful. Temperance's function, according to this description, is to manage—in effect, to suppress—both these extremes of emotion (and all the affections which fall in between) so that neither usurps control over the mind. It induces, instead, a mean-state seemingly devoid of feeling. This is not Aristotle's temperance, which is, in Bryskett's phrase, '*exercised specially* about the senses of tasting and feeling' and is confined, therefore, to moderating pleasures of diet and sexuality.[21] This temperance is a broader, but also a more austere, rationalist ideal (and it is also, incidentally, a thoroughly humanist one, an ideal of governance which puts its faith in reason without seeming to demand a visitation of grace to make that reason efficacious).

The psychomachic threat posed by the passions, the threat on which Spenser's definition of temperance hinges, is invoked repeatedly throughout Guyon's narrative. In moralizing to Pyrochles, for example, Guyon warns him that 'to be lesser then himselfe', to deny the authority of the best thing within him (his reason), is the greatest possible 'shame' (ii. v. 15. 6–9). Instead, Pyrochles should 'fly the dreadfull warre' within, using reason to purge himself of those baleful 'warriours', his passions (ii. v. 16. 1, 5). The Palmer's explicit association of temperance with a golden mean or 'squire' likewise extends across the book. Medina epitomizes just such moderation as she attempts to assuage Perissa's appetite and stimulate Elissa's (ii. ii. 14, 38); Guyon identifies with this same project, tellingly dubbed 'attempering' (ii. ii. 39. 1); and at the book's end, as Guyon and the Palmer voyage towards the Bower of Bliss, their boat steers 'an euen course' between the Rocke of vile Reproch and Gulfe of Greedinesse (ii. xii. 3. 2).

What is noticeably absent in this rationalist vision of governance, though, is any clear differentiation between continence and temperance. The two are used more or less interchangeably throughout *The Faerie Queene*.[22] For Aristotle, as previously mentioned, they are distinct things: continence or self-control is something less than temperance (a genuine virtue), since the one implies a condition in which the soul keeps to the good in face of its own passions' opposition, whereas the other implies a happy co-operation between reason and the passions, even from the very outset, in pursuing that good. Despite claiming to offer instruction 'as Aristotle hath deuised',

---

[21] Bryskett 1606: 219.

[22] Citing Jonson and Castiglione, Schoenfeldt (1999: 42–3) notes how the terms were traditionally differentiated, and argues that Spenser oscillates knowingly between them, but he does not substantiate this claim. Hankins (1971: 138–9) cites Piccolomini to the same effect, but then offers some rather loose examples of the distinction at work within *The Faerie Queene* as a whole. (It is not clear, for example, that Britomart can really represent temperance to Amoret's continence, given how powerfully Britomart herself is wounded by passion in her love for Artegall.) Morgan's implication (1986: 18) that Guyon *solus* consistently stands for continence, Guyon accompanied by the Palmer for temperance, relies on an emphatically positive reading of Canto xii which, I shall show hereafter, makes little sense of Spenser's language towards the close of that episode.

Spenser largely ignores the latter possibility. His notion of temperance reflects a Socratic, not an Aristotelian, concept of virtue, in that it amounts to no more—nothing purer—than a constant flexing of reason in opposition to incessantly rebellious passions. In fact, as Hulbert and Tuve have shown, Spenser essentially allies himself with a homogenizing tradition emanating from Macrobius and Cicero according to which: (1) temperance is a global term embracing *all* those virtues which forcibly bridle the passions under the direction of reason; and (2) continence is a species of temperance.[23] This tradition is apparent in *The Governour* (1531), for example, where Elyot, having first cited Aristotle's definition of temperance (specific to pleasures of 'taste and touching'), declares his preference for Plotinus's more general view, that temperance entails coveting 'nothynge whiche maye be repented, also nat to excede the boundes of medyocryte, and to kepe desyre under the yocke of reason'.[24] Spenser's temperance, like this one, is no more than Socrates' 'general quality of rational self-control'.[25] Its association with the golden mean suggests, of course, an Aristotelian dimension, but these two facets are commensurate, because Aristotle's mean is itself, in the abstract, only a model of rational balance.

If, however, Spenser does not differentiate between continence and temperance, he does, I suggest, distinguish between their opposites, *in*continence and *in*temperance, *akrasia* and *akolasia*.[26] For Aristotle incontinence is a mental weakness, a propensity to be diverted from the good which one knows one should pursue by the pull of contrary passions. In Plutarch's phrase it is something 'lesse than Vice' (*Moralia* 445d)[27]—just as continence is less than virtue. Intemperance, by contrast, *is* a vice, because it derives from an actual belief—the product of corrupt reasoning—that the unmoderated indulgence of sensuous pleasures is a good thing. In his *Nicomachean Ethics* Aristotle argues that the intemperate man is one who acts 'in accordance with his own choice, *thinking* that he ought always to pursue the present pleasure'. The incontinent man 'does not think so', yet still gives in to carnal desire (*NE* $1146^b22$–3). He is drawn on by the lure of degenerate affections, all the while knowing at bottom that he is erring ($1147^b10$–12), and afterwards he is therefore remorseful ($1150^b30$). There is thus a clear hierarchical relationship between these conditions: the perfection of temperance exceeds the otherwise meritorious continence, which is in turn better than incontinence, itself one step above intemperance. This hierarchical relationship reflects a causal one.

---

[23] Hulbert 1931: 190–2, 199; Tuve 1966: ch. 2.          [24] Elyot 1907: 257.

[25] Evans 1970: 113. Cf. Scodel 2002: 84.

[26] Morgan (1986: 20, 24, 28) discusses Spenser's use of this distinction, but sees it as an incidental phenomenon, whereas my aim is to show that it is integral to Book II.

[27] Plutarch 1603: 69. See *Moralia* 445b–e, 446b.

Whilst the continent man's irrational element does (reluctantly) obey his rational faculty, the temperate man's is '*still more obedient*' (my emphasis), speaking from the outset 'with the same voice as reason' ($1102^b28$). Moral progress based on a programme of educating man in 'right feelings' is possible because, precisely by being continent, repeatedly, man may learn temperance, his irrational element becoming, by habituation, evermore co-operative with reason. The effect of consistently suppressing rebellious desires is to erode the misguided disposition which produces them; and when that disposition has been thus corrected, true temperance will follow. Equally, though, and more importantly for Spenser, the same causal logic applies in reverse. Sustained incontinence will give rise, over time, to outright intemperance. The incontinent man will eventually lose sight of his sense of goodness and become accepting of the passions which at present he tries (vainly) to resist.

Sixteenth-century sources reiterate this teaching.[28] Castiglione's Bembo sharply differentiates incontinence from temperance:

... such as be incontinent ... provoked by lust ... to be ill, ... make resistance and set reason to match greedie desire, whereupon ariseth ... battaile .... Finally reason overcome by ... desire, farre the mightier, is cleane without succour .... Forthwith therefore commit they the offences with ... remorse .... [If they] without striving of reason would runne ... headlong after ... desire, ... then should they not be incontinent, but untemperate, which is ... worse.[29]

Octavian follows this passage by expatiating on the superiority of temperance over continence,[30] a theme discussed still more emphatically by Montaigne. Having initially averred that 'virtue' presupposes difficulty, and that we value it precisely for its strength in struggling against the passions, Montaigne then changes his mind. He cannot, he says, imagine anyone with a soul as faultless as Socrates' was encountering difficulty in being virtuous. Such pre-eminence points to the existence in some men of a greater form of moral achievement, a virtue of perfected habits rather than of simple continence—indeed, 'so perfect an habitude vnto vertue' in them 'that it [is] even converted into their complexion. *It is no longer* a painefull vertue ... for the maintaining of which their minde must be strengthened: It is [the soul's] ... ordinarie habite. *They have made it such, by a long exercise* .... Those vicious passions, which breede in vs, finde no entrance in them.'[31] Embedded in this passage is a distinction (analogous to that at work in *The Faerie Queene*) between the perfection that a rare few can achieve and the struggling continence which marks the limit of

[28] For instances of late medieval writers who explore the same distinction see Hulbert 1931: 186 n. 8, 188 n. 13. Aquinas discusses these issues in *ST* 2a2ae. 155–6.
[29] Castiglione 1928: 269.     [30] Ibid. 271. Cf. Elyot 1907: 257.
[31] Montaigne 1603: 245.

moral attainment for the majority. However, crucially, Montaigne's temporal phrases here also indicate that such virtue, where it does develop, does so out of continence, as a progression born of habituation. This last point is reflected in other sources too. The Latini adaptation of Aristotle's *Ethiques* explicitly indicates that man can ascend from continence to temperance as, when, and if he purifies the desiring element in his soul. Here temperance is an achievement which comes with maturity: 'Chastitie [temperance] is an habite, the whiche is fixed in the mind ... *by longe time, hauing ouercome* the desires of the flesh, so that it fealeth no assaultes of temptacions.'[32] More importantly for Spenser, where ascent is possible, so too is descent. Bryskett's *Discourse*, attuned as ever to Aristotelian habituation, charts the gradual progress of moral degradation and the absolute blindness of vice to which 'ill doing' leads once fully ingrained: 'hopelesse may they be thought ..., who by ill doing beginne euen from their tender yeares to induce an ill habit ...: for from age to age ... it increaseth and taketh roote .... [He] that is fallen into an ill habite, is ... blind to vertuous actions .... [He] liue[s] in euerlasting night of vice, after he hath once hardned himselfe to euil.'[33]

Book II of *The Faerie Queene* repeatedly reflects the view that there is a hierarchical, causal, and degenerative relationship between incontinence and intemperance. Indeed, this is another thematic framework within which Spenserian characters demonstrate their perpetual vulnerability to moral degradation. Such degeneration is apparent, for example, in the personifications of anger and pleasure which we encounter. When Furor, one of the first of these, is introduced, Spenser immediately allegorizes his capacity and blind appetite for fuelling his own condition (hence his being accompanied by the ever-provoking Occasion). Phedon (on whom Furor preys) recognizes that he has brought that Fury upon himself. Narrating his past immersion in vengeful rage Phedon recalls that as he pursued Pryene,

> ... so [Furor] me pursewd apace,
> And shortly ouertooke: I, breathing yre,
> Sore chauffed at my stay in such a cace,
> And with my heat kindled his cruell fyre ...

> (II. iv. 32. 5–8)

Anger is at first immorally but willingly—that is, incontinently—entertained, pursuant to a larger action: Phedon knows that to kill Pryene is to heap 'crime on crime', but, half-pretending that such vengeance will 'purge' his grief, harbours his fury nonetheless (II. iv. 31. 1–4). Unfortunately, as stanza 32 indicates, that anger then degenerates into something which overwhelms

---

[32] Aristotle 1547: sig. H1ʳ.        [33] Bryskett 1606: 115–16.

the soul, displacing the original purposiveness. What was a means transforms itself into an end in its own right, and the mind, caught up in a self-feeding fury (l. 8), loses its sense of self-possession. The Palmer is quick to draw the moral, an essential one for this book (and one again cast very much in the rationalist language of, say, Bryskett, rather than the Calvinist terms of Perkins):

> ... wretched man,
> That to affections does the bridle lend;
> In their beginning they are weake and wan,
> But soone through suff'rance grow to fearefull end;
> Whiles they are weake betimes with them contend:
> For when they once to perfect strength do grow,
> Strong warres they make, and cruell battry bend,
> Gainst forts of Reason, it to ouerthrow ...
>
> (II. iv. 34. 1–8)

The model here is exact: incontinence, if once indulged, will draw one into intemperance. Passions, given the chance to rule the soul, will quickly consolidate their power and then overwhelm and eradicate reason, the mind's rival and proper governing force. The waging of psychomachia, a constant suppression of passionate tendencies, is therefore a moral imperative.

If Phedon is a *reluctant* victim of rage, and in that sense (as Sirluck has noted) an epitome of incontinence, Pyrochles, by contrast, willingly embraces this affection, enjoying his fury and knowing no better ('Madman (said then the Palmer) that does seeke / Occasion to wrath, and cause of strife' (II. iv. 44. 1–2) ).[34] Pyrochles is, so to speak, habituated Furor, and therefore an emblem of intemperance rather than mere incontinence. Spenser figures this point by depicting him from the outset as absorbed in his own flames (II. v. 2. 6–7). This wilful nature is confirmed by his actions once defeated by Guyon. Given the chance, he swiftly frees the now bound Occasion and Furor—that is, aggrieved by his defeat, he unleashes fury upon himself because he knows no better. The inevitable consequence is a further fight, this time between Furor and Pyrochles. Guyon and the Palmer depart, leaving Pyrochles willingly absorbed in the company of the passion which entirely governs his soul.

The incontinence–intemperance distinction informs Spenser's treatment of pleasure as well. Acrasia, whose Greek name identifies her as Incontinence personified, dominates this half of Guyon's story. We are told at the beginning of Book II that she has already made Sir Mordant 'drunken mad' by preying on his fleshly tendencies and drawing him into 'vses bad' (II. i. 52). Under Acrasia's influence, so Amavia reports, Mordant has been reduced to a

---

34  Sirluck 1951: 84.

condition not simply of incontinence but of outright intemperance, losing all knowledge of his former self:

> ... him that witch had thralled to her will,
> In chaines of lust and lewd desires ybound,
> *And so transformed from his former skill,*
> *That me he knew not, neither his owne ill* ...
>
> (ii. i. 54. 2–5)

There remains no psychomachia in Mordant's soul, nothing of the struggle which the Palmer detects in Phedon. His faculty of reason has not simply buckled before, but has actually learned to approve, his desires. In this sense he has been reduced by—literally *by*—incontinence (Acrasia) to a condition of intemperance, a drugged state of unknowing stupor (ii. i. 54. 8).[35]

The same alluring, transformative power of 'vaine delightes' (ii. v. 27. 2) besets Cymochles, whose 'mind'—his very reason—in consequence seems wilfully to dissolve itself into the irrational side of his soul. His whole being is lost in the drift of pleasures to which it abandons itself:

> And now he has pourd out his idle mind
> In daintie delices, and lauish ioyes, ...
>
> .   .   .   .   .   .   .   .   .   .
>
> And flowes in pleasures, and vaine pleasing toyes,
> Mingled emongst loose Ladies and lasciuious boyes.
>
> (ii. v. 28. 5–9)

This liquefying of the self inevitably recalls Red Crosse, likewise 'Poured out in loosnesse on the ... grownd' as he lay by the fountain with Duessa (i. vii. 7. 2). That earlier fountain is matched here by an equally enervating, soporific stream which offers to make Cymochles 'forget / His former paine'—forget, that is, the struggles of continence on which moral self-knowledge depends (ii. v. 30. 8–9). So too, countless damsels' kisses play upon Cymochles' 'melting lips' (ii. v. 33. 6), the adjective 'melting', like stanza 28, again evoking a sense of his gradual dissolution (just as it threatens to do elsewhere when the supposedly virginal Belphœbe greets the wounded Timias with 'melting eyes' (iii. v. 30. 4) ). Since in this condition desire drowns out all other thought (ii. v. 34. 1–2, 36. 9), Atin's accusation when he comes to rouse his master, that he is '*Vnmindfull*' of his 'prowest', has an exact accuracy about it (ii. v. 36. 4). Cymochles is indeed teetering here on the edge of intemperance, about to lose his mind. Phaedria, whom he next encounters, acts as another agent

---

[35] Precisely because, according to this argument, Acrasia's role is to draw men into intemperance, to be the *mechanism* by which they reach it, I reject Morgan's view (1986: 24) that she herself stands for intemperance, insisting, rather, that she is exactly what her name suggests, incontinence, and nothing more.

of Acrasia, and she also blinds him to anything but pleasure. Hence, after a brief period with her, we discover that he has yielded up his identity (his 'martiall might') and 'of his way [has] no souenaunce' (ii. vi. 8. 3–5). This regression into sensuality is 'easie' (ii. vi. 8. 6) because he 'by kind' is 'giuen all to … loose liuing' (ii. v. 28. 2–3). Cymochles is already predisposed through habit to descend, the moment incontinence signals the opportunity of doing so, into an oblivious state of intemperance, and that fate is allegorized in his swiftly falling asleep in Phaedria's company (ii. vi. 13. 6–14.9), his somnolence demonstrating how far intemperance has taken him from the self-conscious struggles of psychomachia.

Perhaps not surprisingly, Aristotle's degenerative processes are present again, lastly, in the very home of tranquilizing pleasure, Canto xii's Bower of Bliss. Acrasia's bower is positively designed 'to keepe within' it its 'entred guestes' (ii. xii. 43. 2), blocking out all thought of the values and rationality left behind and ensuring a soporific atmosphere. The perimeter foliage beckons insidiously to the passer-by, drawing him in with the promise of a moment's delightful incontinence. Hence the pendulous vines around the porch do 'themselues into [the] hands incline, / As freely offering to be gathered' (ii. xii. 54. 5–6). All is apparently passive submissiveness as the place 'It selfe doth offer' to the eye (ii. xii. 58. 2). Inside, every aspect of the Bower is then constructed so as to prevent the intrusion of discomfort, of any pain which might stir its inhabitants into a consciousness of their condition. The fountain for one is shaded 'all the margent round, … / … thence to defend / The sunny beames' (ii. xii. 63. 1–3). The synthetic nature of its decor makes it proof against mutability—albeit that Nature, too, wantonly colludes in that evasion, ne'er suffering 'storme nor frost … to fall', 'Nor scorching heat, nor cold intemperate' (ii. xii. 51. 3–5). The 'temperate' features apparent here, though of Nature, are paradoxically unnatural in a fallen world where the mutability of the seasons should prevail.[36] The result is a false stasis which holds the occupants in the state of ignorance characteristic of intemperance.

The principal victim of this insidious environment is Sir Verdant, who is discovered slumbering in Acrasia's—incontinence's—arms, his moral awareness temporarily arrested. Acrasia hangs over him in a posture of dominance which excludes from sight any other reality but her, thereby maintaining his suspension of consciousness:

> And through his humid eyes [she does] sucke his spright,
> Quite molten into lust and pleasure lewd …
>
> (ii. xii. 73. 7–8)

---

[36] Evans 1970: 143–4. Noting these points, Scodel (2002: 85) describes the Bower as a 'parody of temperance' proper.

In sucking the martial spirit out of Verdant,[37] she drains him of the very element of the irrational, desiderative soul (*thumos*) which ought to rally to reason's cause in opposition to carnal desire. The second line here is slightly unclear, though. Is incontinence (Acrasia) able to take advantage of the youth in this way because he has *already*, hitherto, allowed his spirited side wholly to melt, transferring all its energies to man's other desire, bodily appetite? Or does 'into' in fact qualify the first verb (rather than the participle), Acrasia sucking what is at present only a 'quite molten' spirit *into* herself, transforming it into a disposition of pure sensuality? The second, if more awkward, is a more interesting reading, since it emphasizes incontinence's direct agency in reducing man to the unconscious condition of intemperance, here by attacking the *thumos* which should help to protect him. Either way, Verdant, like his predecessor Cymochles, is here being denatured, dissolved into liquefying passion. This sense of degeneration is consolidated by Spenser's subsequent comment that Verdant has become blind (II. xii. 80. 9): 'Ne for [his arms], ne for honour cared hee, / Ne ought, that did to his aduauncement tend ...' (II. xii. 80. 5–6). Verdant, then, the 'downy heare' on whose lips indicates that he is at that liminal stage of adolescence when (according to Bryskett) moral conditioning is most needed (II. xii. 79. 8), has lately been habituated into intemperance. Any hint of psychomachic struggle is absent, but there are still traces of 'grace' and 'manly sternnesse' about him (II. xii. 79. 5–8). His transition from *akrasia* to *akolasia* is not yet complete, which is why Guyon will, ultimately, be able to rescue him.

Alongside Verdant stand the animals in Acrasia's Circean farmyard. They too, more than he, symbolize a habituation to intemperance. Their bestial forms match their minds, a degradation of which they are collectively ignorant until the Palmer makes them conscious of it. When reawakened, some of them, at least, stare aghast 'for inward *shame*' (II. xii. 86. 4), an emotion which will place them back on the road towards continence. Grille, though, typifies others—'The donghill kind' (II. xii. 87. 6)—in repining at his new condition and preferring to be restored to hoggish form. Guyon interprets such perverse intransigence as the product of predisposition. A man like Grille, he imagines, 'so soone forgot the excellence / Of his creation, *when he life began*' (II. xii. 87. 2–3) that bestiality must have become second nature to him long before it became his first nature, his actual physical form. Grille, we are to conclude, chose wilfully to 'delight' in his own bestiality, to free himself from self-knowledge and its burden of psychomachia, even in youth; and such *delighting* in 'foule incontinence' precisely *is* intemperance (II. xii. 87. 7).[38] The return to human form now symbolizes a return to the self-knowledge and

---

[37] Cf. II. v. 27. 4–5.          [38] Cf. Sirluck 1951: 95–6.

self-reproach characteristic of the incontinent state, something which Grille would rather not entertain, given the alternative of intemperance's blind comforts. His negative example, then, along with other animals' positive ones, continues to enforce Spenser's *akrasia–akolasia* distinction even in Book II's very last stanza.

*The Faerie Queene* therefore gives us ample evidence that Spenser's imagination is alive to the negative aspect of the Aristotelian moral tradition, the degenerative relationship which continually draws men from *akrasia* to *akolasia*; but that being so, why does Spenser not also reflect the positive dimensions of that distinction? The answer, I suggest, lies with his underlying assumptions about the moral capacities of human nature. To judge from the evidence of his epic, Spenser's moral imagination, his core image of man, circumscribes his reading of the Aristotelian tradition, conditioning the degree to which he might accept the latter and the degree to which he gravitates, instead, towards Erasmus's or Thomas Rogers's outlook. Spenser can certainly accept the range of *depravity* delineated in Aristotle's two negative terms, but the degree of perfection to which Aristotelian *virtue* extends is, this poem seems to suggest, beyond man's reach. On Spenser's view, the maintenance of continence (envisaged by Schoenfeldt as a constructive and self-constitutive war against endless passions[39]) is all that man can hope to achieve—just as it is all that Erasmus hopes for in the *Enchiridion*. Aristotelian temperance is in truth too great a perfection for the mortal soul (albeit that the latter is capable of intemperance). That this is so can be demonstrated, first, by noting something of the general image of fallible humanity at work in Spenser's text and, second, by tracing the limits of Guyon's particular moral development.

The sense that human nature is critically flawed is a recurrent motif throughout Spenser's epic. The principal obstacle which disables men in their moral progress is original sin, the symbol of which materializes early in Book II as Amavia's helpless babe, Ruddymane. Ruddymane first appears innocently 'embrewing' his hands in his dying mother's blood (II. i. 37. 8–9). Though he is ignorant of that blood's meaning, the reader is not. The verb 'embrew' is the same one later used of the 'sugred licour' which Acrasia's damsels rain down on Cymochles' lips (II. v. 33. 5–6), and of Sanglier, who does his dishonourable hand 'in Ladies bloud embrew' (v. i. 16. 4), but it also recalls Una's remark about Red Crosse's original (and now lost) purity: 'Whose manly hands *imbrew'd* in guiltie blood / Had never bene ...'. Ruddymane's blooding also anticipates any number of other woundings—Britomart's, for example, Artegall's, or Serena's—along with the staining of Amoret's garments when Lust's wound symbolically bleeds on her. In all these cases

[39] Schoenfeldt 1999: 48–9, 53.

the bloodshed emblematizes human weakness and man's involvement in inherited corruption: 'Such is the state of men: thus enter wee / Into this life with woe, and end with miseree' (II. ii. 2. 8–9). That Guyon cannot cleanse the stains from Ruddymane's hands only reinforces this moral the more. Man's entrapment within Adam's legacy is absolute,[40] and there is thus scant hope of his rising to Aristotle's challenge, the dream of perfect self-governance.

Human fallibility peppers Spenser's poem, as when Britomart falls asleep, for example, much to her own (III. i. 58–66) or Amoret's (IV. vii. 3–31) peril; but the most striking indication that man is flawed actually comes, once again, in Book II's treatment of the passions (confirmed at the beginning of Canto v as prime authors of man's woe and bringers of 'troublous warre' within (II. v. 1)). The predicament of the House of Alma illustrated in this book brings to a head Spenser's concern:

> Of all Gods workes, which do this world adorne,
> There is no one more faire and excellent,
> Then is mans body both for powre and forme,
> Whiles it is kept in sober gouernment;
> But none then it, more fowle and indecent,
> Distempred through misrule and passions bace ...
>
> (II. ix. 1. 1–6)

The humanist vision of dignity with which this stanza begins proves transitory, a wishful ideal sustained for the course of Canto ix as the knights tour Alma's perfectly ordered body, but sustained, always, on the understanding that 'no earthly thing is sure' and that 'Soone' this Alma, like all others, 'must turne to earth' (II. ix. 21. 9). That 'turning to earth' in fact points as much to the fracturing of 'sober gouernment' as it does to mortality *per se*, and the threats to such 'gouernment' (the 'passions bace' of l. 6 above) quickly become apparent. Guyon and Arthur discover Alma's castle in a besieged, defensive posture (II. ix. 12. 6–7). On cue, a 'thousand enemie' passions then emerge from the surrounding landscape to attack the soul and, being true to their entrapping power, promptly encircle the knights. Psychomachia, graphically realized here, entails an oppressive claustrophobia. This assault is the more pernicious because the enemies, 'though they bodies seeme', are really insubstantial (II. ix. 15. 9)—this, an allegorical detail which reflects the false nature of the judgements on which passions hinge, thus recalling the Stoic aphorism, 'There's nothing good or bad but thinking makes it so'. What this canto gives us, then, is a crystallization in the abstract—these are *unnamed* 'passions bace'—of the many particular examples of corrupting passion seen elsewhere in the poem.

---

[40] Cf. II. viii. 29.

In practice, man proves to be so flawed here that every part of him is susceptible to attack. Alma is assaulted through all five senses (II. xi. 9–13), each being an avenue through which Aquinas's sensitive appetite (manifesting itself as 'strong affections') can undermine reason's 'fort' (II. xi. 1. 1–4). (Jonson saw the schematic appeal of this, annotating the passions' 'beseidging' attack on each sense as if he were abstracting the moral content most suited to the masque form and envisaging a pageant of evil passions.[41]) Granted, Spenser does present positive passions too—'the beuy of faire Ladies' who inhabit Alma's heart and represent a range of different emotional states (II. ix. 34. 2). But they are confined, impotently, to the 'Parlour' (II. ix. 33. 6) and inspire little sense of an alternative felt life awaiting realization. Similarly, although Alma offers her guests a bounteous banquet 'Attempred goodly well for health and … delight', we do not (as we will in *Paradise Lost*) *see* anything of it (II. xi. 2. 9). Spenser does not give such validated delight the same imaginative force as he does the negative passions: his lugubrious mind dwells, rather, on the threat of psychomachia (as it has done all along).[42] Once again, therefore, the resonance between Spenser's view of the passions and the moral perspective—indeed, the moral imagination—evinced in Erasmus's or Thomas Rogers's work is apparent. From this standpoint Aristotle's analysis of the negative pole of moral development would be conducive to Spenser, but the hope that Aristotle places in positive achievement seems far from realizable.

Turning to the limits of Guyon's moral development in particular, it *is* true that he does manifest virtue throughout Book II. On the one hand, he periodically succeeds in exhibiting passion when it is morally appropriate to do so. His moral worth is thus apparent in, for instance, the 'ruefull pitie' with which he responds to Amavia's plight (II. i. 44. 5), a pity which he then cultivates—'more affection to increace'—in making a sacred vow of vengeance on her behalf (II. i. 60. 8). On the other hand (and more often), Guyon also proves himself laudably capable of tempering affection. When Pyrochles first strikes at him, he is sufficiently alert, morally speaking, to evade the blow (II. iv. 46) and then, having defeated the latter, still has governance enough to 'temper' his victorious 'passion', offering mercy (II. v. 13). He has sufficient self-control, too, to ignore Occasion's goading (II. v. 21), and remains fixed in his purpose when faced with Phaedria's distracting levity, 'fairely tempring fond desire subdewd' until she eventually gives up on him (II. vi. 26. 6). Met thereafter by the still more aggravating Atin, Guyon (though

---

[41] Riddell and Stewart 1995: 180.

[42] I suggest this by way of qualification to Schoenfeldt's reading (1999: ch. 2) of Book II. The regulation in what he calls Alma's 'regulated pleasure' is much in evidence, but the pleasure is given only limited figurative form.

provoked) again masters 'with strong reason [his own] passion fraile' (ii. vi. 40. 4). *Pace* Sirluck, the knight's triumphs here (as both these latter quotations indicate) are achievements of *continence*, cases where, 'though somewhat moued' (ii. vi. 40. 3), he '[holds] his hand vpon his hart' (ii. vi. 26. 2) and keeps rebellious passions down.[43] However, there is also one limited context within which Guyon exudes true Aristotelian *virtue*: namely, in his confrontation with Mammon wherein he is tempted to be covetous of wealth. Bereft, here, of the Palmer, Guyon is forced back upon his own resources: his 'long experiment' (that is, experience) and the comforting knowledge 'Of his owne vertues, and prayse-worthy deedes' (ii. vii. 1. 7, 2.4–5).[44] He rejects the 'worldly mucke' of Mammon's treasures in the consciousness that his 'happinesse' lies elsewhere, in 'armes', 'honours', and 'atchieuements braue' (ii. vii. 10, 33). Cefalu takes his identification of honour as man's ultimate end at face value, and thinks this indicative of a moral shortcoming in the knight;[45] but Spenser is in fact at pains to emphasize that Guyon does *not* marry 'Philo-time', that is, that 'love of worldly honour' is not his aim. As an epic hero, of course he yearns, within the fiction of the poem, to excel in the service of the Fairy Queen (ii. vii. 50. 6–7); but that undertaking, interpreted allegorically according to the principle that Gloriana is Virtue personified, really amounts to a commitment to serve goodness itself. Informed by such values, Guyon swiftly identifies wealth as a 'superfluity', emphasizing rather the meagreness of man's true, natural needs (ii. vii. 15. 3–6), and then reworking that point into a formula of self-sufficiency which eschews any suggestion of greed: 'All that I need I haue; what needeth mee / To couet more, then I haue cause to vse?' (ii. vii. 39. 3–4). Guyon vilifies the passions associated with money-covetousness (ii. vii. 21–3). Though some critics seem determined to ignore the narrator and to find fault with Spenser's hero,[46] the poem emphasizes that he does not 'incline ... at all' towards Mammon's gifts, nor thereby suffer 'frayle intemperance' to corrupt his soul (ii. vii. 64. 2–3). Within the particular sphere of wealth acquisition, Guyon's passions are already rightly ordered,

[43] Sirluck 1951: 85–6.

[44] Sirluck (ibid. 79, 86, 90–1) and Hoopes (1962: 150, 154), proceeding on the assumption that the Palmer is an allegory of the faculty of reason within Guyon, deduce from his *absence* that Guyon's conduct is driven here by those habits which, according to Aristotle, engrain themselves within the non-rational part of our souls—habits which, in this context, prove temperate. Guyon, though, when faced with Mammon, articulates his own values, and responds argumentatively often enough to cast doubt on these critics' assumption, that without the Palmer the knight has no 'right reason'. Nor is Sirluck's and Hoopes's view the only viable interpretation of the Palmer's function. It is just as plausible to see him simply as a friend and teacher to this noble 'pupill' (ii. viii. 7. 5), a counsellor of the kind perennially recommended by Renaissance moralists (witness, e.g., Bacon 1985: 81–6; Burton 1989–2000: ii. 106–12).

[45] Cefalu 2004*a*: 67–8.          [46] See Evans 1970: 128–31; Cefalu 2004*a*: 68–9.

offering no resistance to reason's judgement.[47] In this context, if not in others, he exhibits perfect temperance, rather than mere continence.

However, these varying degrees of moral success aside, Guyon also manifests perhaps more than his fair share of falterings. In Mammon's company he weakens only once, 'dismay' intruding into his soul (ii. vii. 37. 7). His triumph is otherwise absolute. Yet the moment he leaves the latter's cave, he collapses into unconsciousness, becoming like Perkins's 'man in a traunce'. This happens not (Sirluck and Berger rightly insist) because he has been under the strain of some psychomachic conflict during his three-day sojourn—*temperance* entails no such conflict—but because, rather more prosaically, he has gone without food or sleep (ii. vii. 65. 3).[48] Guyon, it transpires, is no match for the most basic frailties of human nature. The result, crucially, is that during his stupor he becomes subject to attack by Pyrochles and Cymochles. Physical incapacity, Spenser hereby implies, may as easily precipitate incontinence as does its moral counterpart (a straightforward failure of will-power): such is the broken condition of man, this 'creature bace' (ii. viii. 1. 2). Under these weakened circumstances, Guyon is dependent for his survival upon 'th'exceeding grace / Of highest God' who 'with mercy doth embrace ... wicked man' (ii. viii. 1. 5–9). To that end he is protected during his trance by an angel who, even when he later devolves his defensive responsibility to the Palmer, promises 'euermore' to watch over his charge (ii. viii. 8. 3–5). Arthur's subsequent arrival to take on Guyon's assailants constitutes further 'timely grace' (ii. viii. 25. 6), and although Woodhouse and Cefalu question whether this is truly *divine* grace,[49] the *recurrence* of just such intrusions into the narrative (Arthur always bringing aid in the eighth canto of a book), together with Arthur's equation with 'heauenly grace' in Book i (i. viii. 1. 3) and his dispensing of a healing 'pretious liquour' in Book iv (iv. viii. 20. 6), indicate that his succour to Guyon should be conceived as allegorizing deific attention. Here, then, with the angel, the Palmer, and Arthur, Guyon's dependence on God is thrice emphasized (once for every day spent with Mammon). The clear implication is that he is too powerless a figure to make continuous progress in his mission without the periodic assistance of grace. That same truism is given its most absolute formulation in Book i, where the narrator insists:

> Ne let ... man ascribe it to his skill,
> That thorough grace hath gained victory.
> If any strength we haue, it is to ill,
> But all the good is Gods, both power and eke will.

> (i. x. 1. 6–9)

[47] Cf. Berger 1957: 17–18; Hoopes 1962: 155.
[48] Sirluck 1951: 91; Berger 1957: 29, 216. Cf. Schoenfeldt 1999: 50.
[49] Woodhouse 1967: 357–8; Cefalu 2004a: 71–2.

Book II opens with the related (and similarly Calvinist) observation that Guyon is 'wretched' compared to the (by then) sanctified Red Crosse, and thus stands in need of God's guidance (II. i. 32).[50] There are, of course, various respects in which *The Faerie Queene* does *not* conform to Calvinist doctrine: not least the fact that whilst Red Crosse requires initial visitations of justifying grace before he can perform any truly moral action, it is not clear that Guyon is so impotent; and the fact also that Spenser frequently invokes humanist languages of rational self-determination without suggesting, as Perkins would, that such agent-centred models of governance require the constant support of co-operating grace.[51] Nevertheless, Spenser's perspective clearly *is* Calvinist to the limited extent that the poet makes his characters intermittently dependent on divine aid. As numerous critics have observed, Spenser's conviction as to the relevance and usefulness of humanist ethics understood on its own terms is always clear (not least in Book II); but such ethics are not, in the end, sufficient.[52] Such is the fallibility and weakness of man—and of Guyon—that they require periodic reinforcement from God's grace.

This, then, is one respect in which Guyon proves less than perfect in his moral enterprise; but there are also other ways in which he falters. For all that Berger emphasizes his supposed mastery of constant temperance, at least in the first half dozen cantos,[53] Guyon in fact errs in his management of the passions, especially under the influence of precipitate pity and fury. At the beginning of the book, Archimago's tale of Duessa's suffering at the hands of Red Crosse, a tale supplemented by Duessa's own performance of 'sorrow' (II. i. 15. 2), immediately prompts in Guyon not Aristotelian anger but rash fury. Thus 'inflam'd', his first 'heroic' act is to attack Red Crosse (II. i. 25. 8). He is then caught in misguided fury again in the House of Medina, where he is drawn into combat with Huddibras and Sansloy. What begins as a 'heroick' intervention in the brothers' fight (II. ii. 25. 3) presumably degenerates under their influence, since within four stanzas Medina is appealing to Guyon as much as to them to recognize the shame and 'guiltinesse' of what he is doing: 'Is this the ioy of armes? be these the parts / Of glorious knighthood, after bloud to thrust ... ?' (II. ii. 30. 3, 29. 5–6). Fury leads Guyon astray once more in his conflict with Furor when, 'enfierced' by the latter, he attempts to wrestle him to the ground but instead overthrows himself (II. iv. 8. 6)—thereby allegorizing heroic anger's capacity to become its own worst enemy. Pity likewise sidetracks him when he proves

---

[50] These comments, together with Gless's criticisms (1994: 177–8), gainsay Anthea Hume's contention (1984: 67–8) that Guyon simply 'takes up the baton' in Book II at the same stage of moral development at which Red Crosse has left off.

[51] See also Padelford 1914; W. H. Marshall 1959.

[52] Berger 1957: 62–3; Hoopes 1962: 155; Woodhouse 1967: 369.        [53] Berger 1957: 10–13.

unduly sympathetic towards Pyrochles and must be corrected by the Palmer (II. v. 24. 7–9).[54] In all these cases Guyon's weakness is underlined. It becomes apparent that outwith the sphere of wealth-covetousness his passions lack the proper conditioning characteristic of temperance, so that in the fields of anger and pleasure management, what triumphs he displays are only ever the fleeting, unstable achievements of continence—the limited moral victories of Erasmus's soldier, not Aristotle's perfect citizen.

A crucial factor in Guyon's fluctuating efforts to achieve temperance—and another sign of his shortcomings—is his association with shame. Though a recurrent concern throughout *The Faerie Queene* (not least in the person of Turpine, whose very name denotes it), shame and its cognates play a particularly powerful role in Book II. Shame is invoked seven times between stanzas 20 and 30 in Canto i, mostly by Guyon, for whom it has a totemic value. Its potent sway over him is clear both from the manner of Medina's address to him (above) and the fact that it is a sense of his own nobility which sustains him during the Palmer's absence. The most emphatic demonstration of Guyon's attachment to shame comes, though, in the House of Alma. Alma's castle is a place of recognitions, where Arthur and Guyon learn about their own physiology, the mechanics of temperance,[55] and the past history which defines them. However, more personal recognitions are also offered: each knight meets the guiding principle of his own character in the affection with which he finds himself partnered. In Arthur's case this escort is Prays-desire, whose name reflects his 'great desire of glory and ... fame', the means by which Arthur seeks to be recognized by his beloved Fairy Queen (II. ix. 38. 7). Guyon's partner is Shamefastnesse, also a graceful figure, but one who betrays a fear of some secret ill within herself.

Shamefastness, or 'fear of disrepute', is not for Aristotle (or Aquinas) a virtue in itself (*NE* 1128$^b$11). It implies weakness, a recognition (in that aforementioned fear) that one might falter; whereas the truly virtuous, being habituated to their good disposition, no longer doubt their capacity to maintain their character (*ST* 2a2ae. 144. 1).[56] Crucially, shamefastness therefore has more in common with continence than virtue—hence Aristotle's connecting the two in passing (1128$^b$34–5). Shame is of a piece, too, with *thumos*, indignation, and heroic anger, rather than with reason *per se*, which is why Ficino associates it with the good (that is, irascible) horse of Plato's chariot in his *Phaedrus* commentary.[57] What recommends shame is that it '*disposes*' man to be temperate, encouraging virtue even though it is not itself one (*ST* 2a2ae.

---

[54] Cf. Burrow 1993: 111, 120–39; Morgan 1986: 33. Cefalu (2004*a*: 54–5) notes several instances where Guyon has failed to habituate himself into feeling proper pity and fear.

[55] Sawday 1995: 168.     [56] Cf. Morgan 1986: 19.     [57] Ficino 1981: 186–7.

144. 4, ad. 4).[58] Perhaps most importantly, Bryskett notes that shame is thus particularly useful in conditioning the young to become virtuous: 'honestie, is best induced into a yong mans mind by that true companion of vertue that breedeth feare to do or say any thing vnseemely, ... shamefastnesse .... It is euer ... carefull to keepe all disordinate concupiscences from the mind, whereby ... not onely in presence of others ... but euen of himselfe he is ashamed, if ... he fall into ... errour.'[59] Bryskett follows this by developing a contrast between shamefastness and magnanimity (Arthur's nominal virtue), the one being disposed to 'correct vs whensoeuer we shal go beyond the bounds ... of reason ... to check vs with the bridle', the other, 'to put vs forward into the way of praise and vertue'.[60] (The equation of the latter, Arthurian magnanimity, with Prays-desire, 'the way of praise', strikingly anticipates *The Faerie Queene*.) The bridle–spur distinction implicit here is, Hamilton notes, explicitly tied to Spenser's terms by Elyot in *The Governour*: 'shamefastnes' is there dubbed 'a bridell' for the *continent* restraint of wayward appetites; 'desire of prayse', a 'sharpe spurre' to actual, positive '*vertue*'.[61] Wright repeats this language in his *Passions of the Minde*, adding specifically that (in contrast to shamefastness) 'the appetite of honour ... followeth' and, causally speaking, '*is due vnto*' virtue.[62] Arthur's female partner, then, underlines *his* association with fully realized virtue, whereas Guyon's emphasizes *his* with the lesser continence.

Connected as he is to the sphere of continence, rather than to the perfection of Aristotelian virtue, Guyon is associated with a learning process which pushes towards complete habituation, but which never (as we shall see) secures it. The fearful ill which 'close lyes ... in the secret of [Shamefastnesse's] hart' (ii. ix. 42. 3–4) is precisely a reflection of Guyon's own weakness, his psychomachic propensity (recurrently apparent) to be led astray by wayward passions. Shame is essentially defensive, the self-imposed bridle of one sensitive to his enemies within and afraid of letting himself down.[63] Furthermore, this is the same defensiveness evinced by Alma's castle when the knights first discover it, besieged by perturbations. Guyon and Alma (the embodied human soul) are thus both embroiled in psychomachia, and can hope to achieve, at most, continence. Arthur, by contrast, is confident of his inner strength and self-governance; Prays-desire is, correspondingly, a more outwardly assertive figure, whose virtue has the potential to be absolute. The contrast between the two men's partners is, as such, a rare manifestation of the continence–virtue

---

[58] Cf. Cefalu 2004*a*: 20–1.     [59] Bryskett 1606: 137.     [60] Ibid. 140.
[61] Elyot 1907: 33. Cf. Spenser 1977: 255.     [62] Wright 1971: 17.
[63] To criticize Guyon, as Cefalu does (2004*a*: 55–6), for not doing more to temper his shamefastness is therefore to miss the point. Its continued presence within him is commensurate with his inability to progress beyond the achievement of mere continence.

distinction viewed in its positive aspect. It is also a contrast which makes sense of the narrative bifurcation enacted in the book's final two cantos, a bifurcation in which emphasis is again placed on the necessary limitations of mortal man's ethical capacities.

To begin, then, with Canto xii and the second of these two strands, it is clear that the faltering nature of Guyon's virtue is as clear in his last acts as in his first.[64] On the journey to Acrasia's home, Guyon is duped by the wandering islands and advocates landing there (ii. xii. 10). He is then appalled by the illusory 'fearefull shapes' which surround the Bower (ii. xii. 26. 3), and becomes captivated by both the moaning maiden and the supplicant mermaids (ii. xii. 27, 31–3). The Palmer promptly chastises his 'foolish pitty' for the former (ii. xii. 29. 2), that passion, even now, still proving a source of error. At the Bower's gates, Guyon 'disdainfully' hurls aside the mazer offered to him (ii. xii. 49. 8). Superficially, this might seem to be an act of Aristotelian anger, the knight's violence reflecting a sudden exertion of *thumos* in accordance with virtue's dictates. But there is at least a suggestion that such emphatic action is a late compensation in Guyon's mind for earlier lapses. The subsequent assurance that he suffers 'no delight / To sincke into his sence, nor mind affect' (ii. xii. 53. 2–3) may offset such anxieties, but it is juxtaposed with another burst of crockery rage as he 'violently' casts aside Excesse's cup, smashing it 'all in peeces' (ii. xii. 57. 3–4). The insecurity underlying such ostentation—that destabilizing fear of oneself embedded within shamefast man—proves its substance moments later when Guyon *is* enticed by 'secret pleasaunce' (ii. xii. 65. 9). Drawn by the sight of the damsels cavorting pornographically in Acrasia's fountain, he relents his 'earnest' pace so as to see more (ii. xii. 65. 8). As he watches, the very invisibility of the more forward maiden's pudenda, hidden beneath the waters, increases his desire. That increase, by the logic of allegory, *causes* the second, previously 'modest' woman to rise up and reveal herself (or rather not reveal herself since she sports hair by Sandro Botticelli, locks draped to frustrate as she assumes the pose of a *Venus pudens*). Having already developed the tell-tale '*melting* hart' (ii. xii. 66. 7), 'secret signes of kindled lust' now follow in Guyon, whereupon the maidens start flashing (ii. xii. 68. 6). Again the Palmer's timely intervention prevents any further disaster, and 'The constant paire' resume 'their forward way' (ii. xii. 76. 4–5), but so drastic a faltering makes emphatically clear that the most Guyon will achieve in this canto is continence (the defeat of *Acrasia*): temperance proper, at least in Aristotle's sense, is beyond him.

---

[64] Hence, whereas for Sirluck (1951: 94–6) Guyon's mere continence in the closing canto is an unexplained downturn in what has otherwise been a temperate performance throughout, I argue that it is actually commensurate with what has been a stumbling performance throughout.

When Guyon does subsequently destroy the Bower in a 'tempest of … wrath-fulnesse' (ii. xii. 83. 4), it is hard not to feel that the violence again reflects an anger with himself and, indeed, an unrealizable desire to destroy the incontinence, the seeds of intemperance, within his own soul.[65] Granted, it could be a moment where martial spirit fuses with reason and its sense of justice, *thumos* siding with the understanding to overcome sensitive appetite; and Morgan notes that in his entirely appropriate 'rigour pittilesse' Guyon does also perfect his government of that troubling emotion, pity (ii. xii. 83. 2).[66] But to insist that the destruction of the Bower is a laudable instance of Aristotelian anger, or to liken it to the divine wrath of God's law,[67] is to ignore the judgemental vocabulary of stanza 83, the felling, defacing, spoiling, burning, and razing of this tempest, all of which suggest something disturbingly intemperate and irrational.[68] Guyon's final action, like so many before it, is at best equivocal.

In line with this, there is good reason to conclude from Book ii as a whole that virtue is never fully achieved in Guyon's world. Archimago, bound by Red Crosse in the previous book, is on the loose again by the start of this one. The moral order finally achieved by Medina is palpably fractious. Guyon can bind but cannot kill Furor. Nor can he kill the irrepressible Pyrochles and Cymochles, who later return to attack his psyche at its weakest moment. Above all, Acrasia herself can only be tied up, not eliminated—a sure indication that what Guyon achieves is only continence.[69] Her future escape, like that of Archimago before her, has an air of cyclical inevitability about it. This same intractability of human nature is epitomized, too, in the book's last character, Grille, who in his resistance again demonstrates the limits of Guyon's moral force. Spenser's knight cannot save 'the donghill kind', perhaps a multitude, who acquiesce in a life of passionate indulgence, no longer knowing any better. Guyon leaves us, then, with an overriding sense of the preponderance of psychomachia in man, a resolute impression that disruptive passions cannot be quelled for long, and that the task of governance is therefore never complete. Guyon may strive through a process of repetition to habituate himself to temperance exactly as Bryskett (following Aristotle) recommends, but our actual sense, particularly after the setbacks of Canto xii, is that it is as much as he can do just to maintain continence. His repetition-compulsion is, as Greenblatt notes, both the essential, and yet

---

[65] Cf. Evans's comment (1970: 112) on the violence of Guyon's virtue.
[66] Morgan 1986: 34.      [67] Cefalu 2004*a*: 75–6.
[68] Similar vocabulary is later used of Talus's activities, e.g. at v. ii. 28; but Talus is a mechanical being compromised by none of Guyon's distracting passions: his wrath really is that of God's talion law.
[69] Cf. Evans 1970: 145–7.

also the subversive, principle of his process of self-fashioning, subversive because it presupposes a degree of recurrent failure.[70] The passions, the flesh itself, are ultimately too intransigent, too depraved, to admit of any positive conditioning of an Aristotelian kind; yet, for the same reason, they are also all too prone to give way to negative conditioning, to slip through custom from mere incontinence into outright intemperance. This conception of man, and even of regenerate (as opposed to utterly reprobate) man, obviously accords with the image of a humanity embroiled in psychomachia which the likes of Erasmus, Thomas Rogers, and Calvin all propound. The textual evidence suggests that Spenser found such a view particularly conducive, and that his taking that view therefore circumscribed the extent to which he could accept the positive threads of Aristotelian thinking.[71] But we cannot leave the matter there. To do so is to ignore Canto xi and the Arthurian narrative. It is to ignore, too, a further ramification of the Calvinist dimension within Spenser's moral vision—his interest in grace.

Arthur, as his association with Prays-desire and his special status as 'flowre of grace and nobilesse' (II. viii. 18. 4) indicate, is capable of a higher degree of moral attainment than Guyon. He appears as the agent of God's grace at the moment of Guyon's and, indeed, Red Crosse's greatest need, whereupon this type of Christ returns to each knight the powers of self-governance. Two further narrative episodes, though, also epitomize this, Arthur's superior moral power. First, whilst Guyon can only restrain Pyrochles and Cymochles, Arthur can kill them (albeit not without difficulty). Cymochles is able to injure him because, Hamilton notes, Arthur's human side, his love for Gloriana, makes him susceptible to sexual desire's wounds—this, the form of passionate bondage for which Cymochles stands.[72] In line with Arthur's divine affiliations, it is, tellingly, the Palmer's invocation of God ('great God thy right hand blesse' (II. viii. 40. 3) ) which reinvigorates the knight after these setbacks, his piety giving renewed, fatal force to his virtuous anger. Once Cymochles is dead, Arthur magnanimously offers to spare Pyrochles. Pyrochles' refusal to relent even then suggests that, to Spenser's way of thinking, man's sensitive soul is so perverse that, ultimately, it can only be obliterated. If Pyrochles is typical, the lower soul admits of no more moderate form of governance. Arthur has no choice but to cleave off the head of a power which remains unendingly defiant; he cannot simply curb or condition its force. His 'temperance', then, entails an *absolute* mortification of the flesh, something different from either Guyon's combative continence or Aristotle's gradual habituation. Being thus

---

[70] Greenblatt 1980: 177–9.

[71] Cf. Morgan 1986: 38–9. What Morgan presents as a caveat to his argument here (on the importance of Protestant attitudes) appears in fact to be a drastic modification of his thesis.

[72] Spenser 1977: 243.

absolute, it is an achievement reserved for him, not Guyon—a temperance beyond normal human power.

Arthur's lethal force is apparent again in Canto xi when he defends Alma's castle against the passions' assault. Then, too, he has the power to kill perturbations which Guyon can only quell (ii. xi. 19. 3), and of these the most significant is Maleger, the epitome of fleshly depravity.[73] With Maleger, as with Cymochles, though, Arthur struggles. Whilst locked within his merely human capacity, so to speak, the Prince cannot defeat him:

> So feeble is mans state, and life vnsound,
> That in assurance it may neuer stand,
> Till it dissolued be from earthly band.
> Proofe be thou Prince, the prowest man aliue,
>
> .   .   .   .   .   .   .   .   .   .   .
>
> That had not grace thee blest, thou shouldest not suruiue.
>
> (ii. xi. 30. 3–9)

Arthur, ordinarily the agent bringing grace to others, here lacks it in himself, and is as such reduced to Guyon's condition, that of a 'Prince prickt with reprochfull *shame*' (ii. xi. 31. 6). On this occasion Timias's intervention provides the reinforcing grace, his pugnacious intrusion into the fray reviving Arthur's 'thought of glorie and … fame' (ii. xi. 31. 8)—the confidence of Prays-desire—and prompting him to rediscover his absolute self, that which severs him from earthly limits of achievement. The intense intimacy of the confrontation which follows—like Hercules tackling Antaeus, Arthur crushes Maleger's carcass against his own breast (ii. xi. 42. 2)—emphasizes the psychomachic dimension of this conflict. Maleger, born of the earth and revivified by its every touch, is killed only when Arthur casts him into a 'standing lake' in a kind of anti-baptism.[74] To do that, in so far as it is a psychomachic action and Maleger is something inside him, is precisely to *dissolve* the 'earthly bands' within himself, and Arthur thereby attains an absolute victory, a perfection of temperance (though not exactly of an Aristotelian kind) which is beyond Guyon. Arthur can do this because he is perennially on the cusp between the mortal and the divine, and here passes from the one to the other. The ascetic temperance he represents is not, in general, a property of this world. It entails a purging of carnality which, as Calvin and Perkins argue, the receipt of grace on earth can adumbrate but cannot match. It brings a final conclusion to psychomachia which—Spenser again follows Calvinism here—regenerate man can only attain at the moment of transfiguration.

---

[73] Morgan 1986: 37; Woodhouse 1967: 366.          [74] Woodhouse 1967: 366.

## CONCLUSIONS

The two last cantos of Book II are of course reflected on a much larger scale across *The Faerie Queene*. Guyon's constant faltering, the perpetual incompleteness of his virtue (which is immediately apparent again at the beginning of Book III when he attacks Britomart), is likewise characteristic of other heroes. Red Crosse has only been before us for ten stanzas when he stumbles into Errour's den, and although he eventually wins here, the encounter is a foreshadowing of greater disasters to come. Eight cantos later, Duessa is first bound and then freed, but she cannot, it seems, be slain, any more than the witch's monster can be killed in Book III. At the end of Book I Red Crosse and Una's marriage contract is sealed, but the actual consummation of that union is deferred until such time as the knight completes his worldly service. In Book III Arthur (otherwise exemplary) and the still wayward Guyon exit smartly from Canto i in pursuit of Florimell, an 'impatient', passionate act (III. iv. 45. 7–8) which sits unfavourably alongside Britomart's 'constant mind' (III. i. 19. 1). Any impression of *her* rational constancy, though, is quickly dispelled when Spenser next reveals just how ungovernable her passion for Artegall is. That she does not find her lover in this book is another indication that Spenser's third narrative is as unsettled and inconclusive as the previous two. When the couple do finally meet, in a book about friendship, they do not even recognize each other until after each has done the other injury, and although they are betrothed, their union, too, is suspended whilst Artegall pursues his quest. He in turn, and Calidore after him, are both distracted from their missions by adulterous passions, the one for Radigund, the other for Pastorella. Ultimately, Artegall needs Britomart's help to overcome this infatuation (as he does Guyon's to 'pacify … his choler' in face of Braggadochio (v. iii. 36. 5) ), but even then political circumstances prevent Artegall from actually completing his project to civilize Irena's state (v. xii. 27). The book closes, instead, with a melancholy vision of him plodding off towards Gloriana's palace, detraction snapping at his heels as he goes. Disruption and incompleteness are endemic in *The Faerie Queene*.[75] For all that the heroes reiterate their virtues, they never realize—or seem capable of realizing—Aristotle's goal of perfect habituation. Even in the last moments of the sixth book, the Blatant Beast, previously bound, escapes again to rage through the backbiting corridors of Elizabeth's court. Yet, at the same time these many inadequacies are counterbalanced (as in Canto xi of Book II)

---

[75] This is as much a feature of structure as it is of content; see Hadfield 1996: 149–60.

by the recurrence of grace throughout Spenser's narrative.[76] Leaving aside Arthur's multiple visitations, it is also, for example, 'great grace or fortune' which brings Belphœbe to the injured Timias in Book III (III. v. 27. 3)—and there Belphœbe herself even seems to epitomize God's grace (III. v. 52). Again, grace furnishes a turtle dove in Book IV to reconcile this same pair after their quarrels. 'Gods grace' preserves Britomart in Book V (v. vi. 34. 6) and is encapsulated in the hermit in Book VI (VI. v. 36. 5). Without this power to 'vphold' him, man, Spenser insists, would be trapped within his own carnality and subject to 'daily falls' (I. viii. 1. 1–3). To the extent that the *Faerie Queene's* heroes are successful and do realize their virtues (or are at least continent), they do so, in no small degree, thanks to God's 'exceeding grace' (II. viii. 1). It is that grace which gives their quests some degree of completion at least and (as *per* Calvin) provides assurance of still more hereafter.

Spenser presents us, then, with what is primarily a humanist and rationalist vision of self-governance. Like Erasmus, Cicero, and Thomas Rogers, he places psychomachia at the heart of his ethics, casting the passions in a predominantly (if not exclusively) negative light, dwelling on their corrupting effect, and framing virtue as a conscious, rational project to suppress such forces. Man's condition is figured as an embattled one, in which the flesh (in all its aspects) serves as a perpetual catalyst for sin, but as a condition, too, in which characters are accorded a fair degree of self-determination, and thus the power to combat their rebellious affections through their own resources. There are times when Spenser's heroes certainly require the support of grace in their moral endeavours, and this is one facet of their weakness: to this degree the world of *The Faerie Queene* is Calvinist. But co-operating grace is not, perennially, a *sine qua non* of virtuous attainment. Rational autonomy—the proposition that the agent has the capacity to govern himself unaided—is the prevailing assumption, if not of Book I, at least of the later books of the poem. That said, the example of Guyon's shortcomings and those of countless others (not least the instances just noted) demonstrates how desperately fractious any achievement of reasoned self-control proves to be. Amidst a constant atmosphere of backsliding and degeneration, the most that Spenserian heroes can usually manage within the ethical sphere is a series of precariously contrived defensive postures. Thus, when Guyon secures a moral triumph, it generally amounts to no more than a temporary binding or staving off of passionate threats, the passions in question being destined to attack again at a later date. Such hard-fought victories of continence have a necessarily limited value, but are, for Spenser, the best that mortal man can hope for.

---

[76] Sinfield (1983: 45–6) does, however, note the disappearance of divine intervention in the later books, a trend commensurate with the growing disillusionment therein.

To the extent that *The Faerie Queene* offers us a vision of a notably *unstable* rationalist morality, it captures something of the anxiety which, I suggest, would come to surround psychomachic ethics by the early 1600s. Spenser's knights, though, go on fighting for their humanist cause regardless, keenly pushing themselves to improve and premissing their claim to heroism on the fact of that very struggle. Crucially, for all man's imperfections, the value of the rule of reason *per se*, of Spenser's psychomachic mission, is never challenged in this poem (even when, in the 1596 *Faerie Queene*, the *particular* inability of Elizabeth's *fin-de-siècle* courtiers to realize these ideals does become a matter of dismay (v. Pr. 1. 1–4. 4) ).[77] Indeed, the very fact that Gloriana's knights are seen to receive grace as they strive to be virtuous is itself a divine affirmation of their rationalist aspirations—or so the fiction would have us think. If God supports them in their moral efforts, it can only be because he approves their project to achieve rational self-governance. Psychomachia, the theology of the text implies, must be a worthy fight to engage in, however impossible it may be to win. Spenser, then, may not be sure of his heroes' ability ever perfectly to realize their values of temperance, chastity, and the like, but he is clearly absolutely sure that those things *are* valuable, and valuable in the particular rationalist form in which he conceives them. This is why the hermit of Book VI so firmly reiterates the Palmer's moral instruction of Book II, especially the precept to suppress all passions before they 'growe strong' (VI. vi. 8. 5). In practice, Spenser never questions these, the terms according to which he, and others such as Erasmus before him, have framed the problem of governance. He never doubts that an ascetic faculty of reason of the kind embodied in the Palmer should rule Guyon's soul, that it could do so constantly if only it could truly defeat the passions, and that in those moments when it does gain the upper hand, its first duty should be to circumscribe and suppress affections and body alike:

> First learne your outward sences to refraine,
> From things, that stirre vp fraile affection ...
>
> (VI. vi. 7. 6–7)

> Abstaine from pleasure, and restraine your will,
> Subdue desire, and bridle loose delight,
> Vse scanted diet, and forbeare your fill,
>
> .  .  .  .  .  .  .  .  .  .
>
> So shall you soone repaire your present euill plight.
>
> (14. 5–9)[78]

---

[77] See ibid. 46–7; van Es 2002: 149–63.
[78] Cf. the increasingly Stoic advice of Meliboee (VI. ix. 20–2, 29–30).

These austere goals, though, and the assumptions underlying them, are precisely the things which Shakespeare and other dramatists would proceed to interrogate, and this within just a few years of the *Faerie Queene*'s publication. In their eyes, man's imperfections would prove so great, so fundamental, as to make moral values conceived on Spenser's model intrinsically unrealizable. Hobbes would go still further, completely overturning psychomachic ideals on the grounds that their aspirations were downright delusory, the product of a misapprehension about the nature of reason and its natural relationship with the passions. It is to these and other seventeenth-century developments that I turn hereafter. Spenser's world is the world that many of my later authors became determined to reject.

# 3

---

# Hamlet 'lapsed in passion'

'Were vertue … corporeall,' remarks Montaigne, 'her pulse would beate …
stronger, marching to an assault, then going to dinner: For, it is necessarie that
she heate and move herselfe.'[1] This precept, that the vigorous performance of
actions depends upon the support of initiatory passions, has its origins in the
Aristotelian wisdom discussed in Chapter 1. I noted there the Peripatetic principle (appropriated by Castiglione and Du Plessis-Mornay amongst others)
that passions provide the necessary motive force for man's every action, and I
suggested that one of the few Thomist ideas to be accepted as commonplace in
England before 1600 was the related notion that the passions, in temporarily
altering the condition of the heart and the circulation of the spirits, thereby
dispose the body ready for exertion. To emphasize these points, though, to
insist that every vibrant act depends upon the passions' support, is inevitably
to pull against the broad thrust of the Socratic position. Whereas Erasmus,
Cicero, or Spenser would quell the bodily and emotional self, Montaigne's
idea implies the need to harness it. He departs, therefore, from the customary
emphases of the psychomachic image of man, from that ascetic outlook which
applauds transcendental reason and despises the passions as enemies within.

I want to begin this chapter by arguing that the Hamlet figure created by
Shakespeare does something similar. He craves for himself an *impassioned*
soul, one wholly inconsistent with that equable temper recommended by the
Elizabethan writers discussed hitherto. Driven by a faltering urge to avenge
his father, Hamlet strives to induce within himself the sort of overwhelming
motive passion which might drive him to murder; and when he discovers
that he cannot realize that fury, he deludes himself that assuming a pose
of passive readiness instead—as if he were a Providential agent, awaiting
God's command to strike—amounts to the same thing. In willing himself
into a condition of rage, Hamlet, in one way, challenges the rationalist norms
aspired to in Spenser's *Faerie Queene*. Yet, that said, the second half of this
chapter traces another, quite contrary tendency which Shakespeare builds
into his character: namely, the Prince's instinct precisely to embrace austere

---

[1] Montaigne 1603: 146.

ethical views, to vilify man's mortal, sensuous, sexual nature, and to push for a moral reformation both in his mother and in Denmark as a whole. This latter impulse, I argue, brings Hamlet back towards the predominantly ascetic mind-set of Spenser's Palmer or Erasmus's Christian soldier; but in doing so, it exposes a potential unnaturalness, even a madness, in that very attitude. Here again, therefore, Shakespeare's play seems to challenge the values and the image of man with which my opening chapters were concerned. *Hamlet* does not—drama in general does not—present a 'philosophy' of governance; but by staging a limit case, a study of self-governance in an extreme context, the Elizabethan dramatist could test the adequacy of prevailing norms, chip away at certainties and assumptions, and begin to fracture the precarious ideals of perfection invoked amidst the pages of works like *The Faerie Queene*. This tragedy does all those things, calling into question the very language of psychomachia taken for granted in Tudor moral discourse.

It may be objected at the outset, though, that making this case (or indeed discussing Shakespeare's Brutus and Chapman's Bussy as I do in the next chapter) involves treating dramatic characters as if they were real people rather than textual effects. To that criticism there are two answers. One is that in examining 'Hamlet's' passions or 'Brutus's' motives it is simply practical to adopt personalizing idioms in order to avoid circumlocution. One can invoke 'Hamlet's self' by way of shorthand without, in so doing, presupposing a falsely essentialist notion of selfhood or denying the author's role in fashioning this character-effect. But secondly, it is evident anyway (notwithstanding Fowler's arguments in his recent study *Renaissance Realism*) that early modern audiences *did* impute a temporary reality to the characters and scenarios which they saw portrayed on the stage. Were this not the case, were it not true that the dramatist 'bodies forth / The forms of things unknown', giving apparent substance to 'airy nothing' (*Midsummer Night's Dream*, v. i. 14–17), there would be no humour either in the mechanicals' anxiety that their lion should not be too realistic or in Bottom's interrupting the theatrical illusion of 'Pyramus' in mid-flow so as to argue with Theseus about how 'sensible' Wall should be (i. ii. 70–8; v. i. 180–5).[2] Certainly, *The Comedy of Errors* depends for its comic effect upon an audience's willingness to credit the Syracusans' sense of their own self-possession, this in face of others' attempts to 'interpellate' the strangers ('call them into being') in an alien language. The play demands that we acknowledge Antipholus's and Dromio's existence as individual selves possessed of inwardness, that we accord them (and indeed Malvolio in the exorcism scene of *Twelfth Night* (iv.

---

[2] With the exception of *Hamlet*, references to all other Shakespearean works are to Shakespeare 2005.

ii.) ) a psychological reality, this so that we can then appreciate the pathos as well as the comedy of the men's predicament. *Twelfth Night* intensifies this presumption of character realism by asserting its truth even whilst conceding that it might seem to be an 'improbable fiction' (iii. iv. 126). Shakespeare, not content with putting a 'puritan' (ii. iii. 135) on the stage to mock his sexual hypocrisy, also disrupts broader Puritan anxieties about the deceitfulness of theatrical pretence.[3] In a virtuoso display of wit, he has Olivia and 'Cesario' ring the changes on the latter's status as 'a comedian' (i. v. 175). Cesario announces that 'he' has 'taken great pains to con' his 'speech', cannot speak 'out of [his] part', has only 'poetical' words to offer, and is, by his own admission, 'not that I play' (ll. 166–7, 172, 187, 177). Yet, when Viola supposedly cross-dresses in boys' clothes and thereby attracts Olivia's (lesbian) sexual attention—when, in other words, *Twelfth Night* seems to step squarely into the territory of theatrical transgressiveness—what actually happens is the very opposite. 'Viola', the real fiction here, takes her costume *off* to become Cesario; the boy-actor resumes his own, everyday clothes. 'She' appears as what he (the actor) really is, an adolescent male, who is then desired (heterosexually) by 'Olivia', fictionally an older woman. The boy playing Cesario precisely *is* 'that [he] plays'. Shakespeare, then, teases his Puritan critics by exposing the instability of the boundary separating reality from pretence. He disrupts a distinction which would otherwise subordinate playing as something unreal. One implication of this is that, here again, fictional characters are shown to possess their own, complex kind of reality. Furthermore, that reality extends to the fact that these same characters encapsulate genuine passions, virtues, and vices, qualities which it is precisely the player's task to represent—hence Gosson's horrified observation that an actor playing the Herod of Buchanan's *Baptistes* must take the 'time to whet his minde vnto tyranny that he may giue life to the picture hee presenteth'.[4] Heywood, by contrast, positively applauds the theatrical profession for conjuring up 'portrature[s]' of 'action, passion, motion [and] gesture ... so liuely' that they 'mooue' spectators to think the characters they see are real.[5] In his revealing phrase, it is 'as if the Personater *were* the man Personated'—'*Hercules* in his owne shape', 'the true portrature of ... King *Edward* the third'.[6] Given such contemporary proofs of the realism of dramatic characters, it cannot, then, be considered illegitimate to explore the displays of emotion, introspection, and self-deception manifest in these figures. Nor does it seem unreasonable to assume that playwrights, in creating these 'personated men', used the drama as a vehicle through which to interrogate questions of moral psychology. It is in just this sense that I discuss *Hamlet*.

---

[3] On this anxiety see, e.g., Gosson 1582: sigs. E3[v]–4[r].  [4] Ibid. sig. E6[r].
[5] Heywood 1612: sig. B3[v].  [6] Ibid. sig. B4[r].

## PASSIONATE ACTING IN THE REVENGE TRADITION

Midway through his play, Prince Hamlet, guiltily noting his lack of progress in avenging his father's murder, attributes this fact to his being 'lapsed in time and passion' (*Hamlet*, III. iv. 107).[7] This ambiguous remark could support the interpretation—one which Spenser's Palmer would applaud—that Hamlet here thinks of himself as immersed in distracting passions, and consequently as incapable of fixing upon a decisive course of action; but, initially at least, I want to concentrate on the other, contrary reading of this phrase, one which brings it into line with Montaigne's precept. According to this latter reading, the Prince asserts here either that he has found no opportunity and had no motivating passion for his allotted task, or that he has let opportunities pass and allowed initial vengeful passions to cool—in either case leaving himself bereft, now, of precisely the passionate impulse which he thinks necessary to initiate action. In berating this lack of bloody passion, Hamlet implicitly wishes for the very thing which Spenser (hostile to vengeful fury if not to rationally authenticated anger) would decry, but which the Prince deems essential if he is to move himself to kill.

The paralysis of being passionless dominates this work. At the outset Hamlet exhibits a fantasy of his own charged spontaneity, determining to face the Ghost with 'artures' as blood-full as were the nerves of the Nemean lion (I. iv. 82–3). Yet that same analogy—supposedly expressive of an energized physique fired by passion—also, paradoxically, prefigures the impotence and self-abasement with which Young Hamlet tends to confront the memory of his father. He associates the latter, after all, with Hercules (I. ii. 153), and yet *he*, famously, defeated—devitalized—the Nemean lion. As if in fulfilment of that myth, Hamlet in fact senses his own nerves and the tension of his pulsing heart flagging just as the Herculean ghost leaves him, the lion within him now dying, so to speak:

> Hold, hold, my heart,
> And you my sinews grow not instant old
> But bear me stiffly up.
>
> (I. v. 93–5)

What passionate resolution the Ghost had engendered in the Prince seems already to be dissipating here, Hamlet's sinews turning phlegmatic again

---

[7] References to *Hamlet* are to Shakespeare 1985. I quote freely from the Second Quarto (Q2) as well as the Folio (F) text in what follows, because the earlier layer of the text gives explicit voice to aspects of the Prince Hamlet character-effect which remain implicit in the Folio version of the same even after revisions have taken their toll.

(just like those 'weak hams' in Polonius which, elsewhere, the Prince derides (II. ii. 196) ). Similarly, despite the initial show of eager determination when in the spectre's company ('Haste me to know't, that I ... / ... May sweep to my revenge' (I. v. 29–31) ), Hamlet's subsequent, rather book-ish idiom, his instinct to squirrel his father's commandment in the library of his brain (ll. 102–3), suggests more a man of apathetic contemplation than one of impassioned action.[8] That impression is further underlined on Hamlet's next appearance, when he enters *'reading on a book'* (II. ii. 165), again demonstrating how readily his enthusiasm for vengeance can evaporate.

It is not surprising, then, that towards the end of this same scene Hamlet launches his first attack on his own lack of fury. Confounded by his lack of an enduring sense of outrage, he attributes this failing to a physiological inad-equacy within himself: having first lamented the sluggish, 'muddy-mettled' spirits which make him so unresponsive, he adds: 'it cannot be / But I am pigeon-livered, and lack gall / To make oppression bitter' (ll. 519, 528–30). In bemoaning this dearth of choler, Hamlet may have one of two points in mind, both premissed on the observation that the anatomical locus of the passions is the heart. On the one hand, according to, say, Wright's *Passions of the Minde*, man's humours are integral to the physiological processes by which the body supports and intensifies particular passions. As previously mentioned, the passion of sorrow, for example, besides involving a cognitive dimension (a judgement), is also defined by its physiological nature as a constriction of the heart. When a sad thought strikes the imagination, the imagination responds by instructing the heart to contract, and the consequence of this, is that the flow of blood and spirits around the body is suppressed. In order to sustain this change, though, the body's temperature must be reduced, and this is effected by drawing cooling melancholy into the heart from other organs elsewhere.[9] Conversely, 'in pleasure concurre great store of pure spirits; ... in ire, blood and choller .... [More generally,] in the hunger of the heart, the splene, the liuer, the blood, spirits, choller, and melancholly, attend and serue it most diligently.'[10] It follows that a person's capacity to feel any given passion with prolonged intensity will be dependent on the humoural resources available to him at the time. If he lacks choler, his ire will not be sustainable. It will not outlast those first few moments in which the imagination alone moves the heart. On the other hand, though, just as particular humours are instrumental in *sustaining* particular passions once sensations have initiated the latter, so too the presence (or absence) of these supporting humours in the body in the first place will determine how susceptible a person is to feeling any given

---

[8] Cf. Mercer 1987: 170.     [9] Wright 1971: 35.     [10] Ibid. 45–6.

passion at all.[11] Hence, those who are by disposition choleric (and therefore abound with the choler which fuels wrath) can 'easily and often be *moued to* anger' by external stimuli.[12] Those who are melancholy are likewise peculiarly susceptible to 'griefe and heauinesse' given a suitable stimulus. When, therefore, Hamlet berates the insufficiency of his gall 'To make oppression bitter', he may simply mean—the second point here—that he wishes he were by disposition more choleric, and so more generally susceptible to wrath; or he may mean, rather more specifically, that he wishes he had bile enough within him to render his initial pangs of anger both sustainable and ever-intensifying on a physiological level—this the first point here. To do the latter would be to make his sense of Claudius's oppressive wrongs ever more 'bitter' with time.

Such physiological self-analysis is largely forgotten hereafter: Hamlet rarely probes the details of his own complexion again (except by implication, when he wonders at the perfect fusion between 'blood and judgement' which Horatio has achieved (iii. ii. 59) ).[13] But the above inadequacy, the lack of vigorous *longevity* in Hamlet's passions, is much in evidence throughout this play—even, indeed, within the very 'rogue and peasant slave' soliloquy where Hamlet first reflects on it. Disgusted by his own submissive passivity, the Prince turns here to self-abuse, imagining himself as a justly vilified poltroon and a whining whore (ii. ii. 523–7, 535–40). One of the unspoken instincts driving these remarks is Hamlet's implicit desire to energize himself, to bully himself into resolution. Hence the abuse, though it begins as a register of frustration, becomes also the means of kick-starting not merely an Aristotelian or Montaignian motive-passion, but a downright fury which might then be channelled into vengefulness. In practice, however, whilst the self-contempt is real enough, it does not prove thus transferable on to other, more outward concerns. Hamlet's Second Quarto (Q2) assault on Claudius quickly becomes tangled in its own sibilance, and peters out in a rather lame use of epistrophe: 'Bloody, bawdy villain! / Remorseless, treacherous, lecherous, kindless villain!' (ll. 532–3). There is not, here, a focused, imaginatively engaged hatred of Claudius. Within a few lines fury has given way to the breathless excitement of Hamlet's last thoughts on the Ghost (ll. 551–6) and a closing couplet which embraces a veneer of decisive action (the project to 'catch the conscience of the king' (ll. 557–8) ). By the time Hamlet next appears (to deliver his Act iii soliloquy), anger has receded further, vengeful intent giving way to the distracting escapism of suicide.

Fitful though it may be, Hamlet's longing to be possessed not simply by a vigorous passion, but by a furious, uncontrolled rage, is emphatically apparent in his evocation of the avenger, 'rugged Pyrrhus' (ii. ii. 408). That evocation

---

[11]  See Babb 1951: 16.        [12]  Wright 1971: 64–5.        [13]  See also v. ii. 95.

has something of a pornographic gaze about it. Objectively speaking, the 'hellish' character which Hamlet describes ought to be revolting (l. 421), but the Prince's words actually exude voyeuristic fascination and awestruck admiration: the rugged Pyrrhus

> Hath now this dread and black complexion smeared
> With heraldry more dismal. Head to foot
> Now is he total gules, horridly tricked
> With blood of fathers, mothers, daughters, sons,
> Baked and impasted with the parching streets,
>
> .   .   .   .   .   .   .   .   .   .
>
> ... Roasted in wrath and fire,
> And thus o'er-sizèd with coagulate gore,
> With eyes like carbuncles, the hellish Pyrrhus
> Old grandsire Priam seeks.

(ll. 413–22)

The language here, rich in tactile and visual sensations, emphasizes the heat and power of Pyrrhus's 'sable armed', physical form (l. 410). Alongside these manly signatures of a heroic presence are set transfixing eyes which hint at the fury within. Pyrrhus's very absorption in his 'Black ... purpose' (l. 411), his oblivious indifference, too, to all external judgements (moral or otherwise) and to those who might gaze upon him, lend him an impenetrable charisma which Hamlet thrills to. His is an image the Prince would like to match.

Pyrrhus's features, though, are a literary construction, and as an imaginative ideal, he and some of his precursors are worth dwelling on.[14] Pyrrhus presents the outward form of an inward disposition anatomized in the villains of Senecan tragedy—in Atreus, for example, who, over the course of *Thyestes*, successfully invokes his own furious possession and translates that frenzied, vengeful passion into bloody action. Act II of that play anatomizes the process by which Atreus acquires the characteristics (and particularly the amoral autonomy) of a hero like Hamlet's Pyrrhus, thereby rousing himself for action.[15] Atreus begins by rehearsing to himself (over some twenty lines in Heywood's translation) the litany of wrongs done to him by Thyestes. Having done so, he switches to self-exhortation, urging himself to take revenge:

> ... What stayst thou yet? at length lo now beginne.
> Take hart of Tantalus to thee, to Pelops cast thyne eye:
> To such example well beseeme, I should my hand applye.[16]

---

[14] I owe a general debt to Braden 1985 and Miola 1992 in what follows.
[15] Braden 1985: 42.     [16] Seneca 1581: f. 24ᵛ.

He then intensifies this process by banishing 'all piety' and invoking his own
further possession by fury: 'for not yet enough ... / ... rage doth burne my
boyling brest: it ought to bee repleate, / With monster more ... / ... / No guilt
will I forbeare, nor none may be enough despight.'[17] This pursuit of a totality of
possession propels Atreus towards the impenetrability and moral indifference
so manifest in Pyrrhus, and Atreus derives a reassurance, a conviction as
to his own unwavering firmness hereafter, from precisely that excess. He
is fascinated, too, by the horror he senses growing within him, viewing his
own progress towards fury through the same voyeuristic gaze with which the
passive Hamlet confronts his masterful Pyrrhus: 'I moued am and wote not
wherevnto. / But drawen I am: from bottome deepe the roryng soule doth
cry.' Both here and in succeeding lines Atreus emphasizes his submissiveness
before the fury which possesses him, a fact which allows him, implicitly,
to abnegate responsibility for future actions. Yet, paradoxically, these same
verses also betray Atreus's conviction as to his own autonomy, a new-found
'greatness' of soul which makes him independent of the world around him.
The achievement of this condition is, too, a fulfilment of the villain's family
destiny, the complexion which is (to recall one of Hamlet's words (iii. i. 84) )
'native' to him. Atreus, in invoking his father's and sister's inspiration, takes
pride in the notion that his crime will mark the culmination of his House's
bloody history.[18]

    All of these qualities combine to make Atreus, like Pyrrhus, disturbingly
transfixing. It is true that his example is partially assimilable within the
moral framework of *The Faerie Queene*. Atreus, like Phedon, resolves to
embrace outright fury—and not simply Aristotelian anger—in pursuit of
revenge, and as with Phedon the end result of that union is, morally speaking,
repugnant to the spectator. But Atreus's example does nevertheless complicate
the early modern story of wrath, at least to the extent that his fury makes
him compellingly impressive, even magnificent. The Elizabethan audience
of *Thyestes*, like Hamlet stood (as it were) before Pyrrhus, is drawn with a
strange admiration into its hero's fury. This problem, a sharp challenge to the
Spenserian moral perspective (and one of considerable relevance to *Hamlet*),
is still more apparent in Seneca's Medea, another archetype for Pyrrhus.

    When the eponymous heroine of *Medea* first appears, she, like Atreus, busies
herself excising fear and pity from her soul, inducing her own possession by
fury, and detailing the horrid crimes which she intends to perpetrate. In doing
so, though, the strains of her performance are all too apparent (especially
in Studley's fulsome rendering). In a clear anticipation of Faustus and his
neuroses, Medea oscillates sharply in her first speech between first- and

---

[17] Seneca 1581: f. 25[r].        [18] Braden 1985: 42–4.

second-person self-address, invoking (in the space of three lines) 'thy soule', 'my brest', and 'thy mynde', whilst all the time referring only to herself.[19] The testy relationship with her self which this betrays is apparent, too, in her repeated use of imperatives to try and urge herself into villainous thoughts; and those imperatives are interspersed with absurdly alliterative, anaphoric lists intended to reinforce a self-image of deep-seated criminality: 'Most hyddious, hatefull, horrible, to heare ... / Most diuelish, desperate, dreadfull deede', she says of the crime she will commit in Corinth. Since the business of rhetoric is to capture the imagination and thereby stimulate the passions, Medea hopes to use just such means to evoke from within herself a new, violent disposition. Fury, though, does not come naturally to her, a fact confirmed by her further oscillations in Act II. Besotted with Jason, she cuts a pathetic figure there as she clings to the delusion that Fortune has somehow forced her lover into infidelity against his will. Given that hopeful thought, she then begins to recant her previous vengeful 'rage'.[20] Her self-recrimination bears all the more tragic force because in Studley's (though not Seneca's) text the Act I Chorus has revealed moments before how misguided such loving devotion is. The Elizabethan Chorus laments Medea's plight as the victim of a dissembling, self-seeking Jason, one on whom the sorceress's previous criminal self-sacrifice has been wasted.[21] This moral slant (perhaps influenced by a reading of Ovid's *Heroides*) inevitably encourages a sentimental response to Medea's character, her villainy notwithstanding—this all the more so when she later recognizes (in poignantly flat prose) that 'With [Jason] now am I cleane forgot'.[22]

Medea's motive for invoking fury within herself is starkly exposed in her self-address at the beginning of Act III: 'O wretch if thou desire, / What measure ought to payse thy wrath then learne by *Cupids* fire, / To hate as sore as thou didst loue.'[23] In attempting to invest herself with a bloody passion she hopes thereby to displace her current emotional torment: fury is to be a therapy for frustrated love. In practice, though, the latter is not an easy passion to extirpate, and consequently Medea's commitment to vengeful wrath is as fitful as it will later be in Hamlet. The resultant tensions within her mind, though prominent throughout the play, are at their most emphatic in Act V. Here Medea continues to push herself into vengeance, and in so doing again vocalizes her struggle to repress the last vestiges of a love for Jason.[24] Her speeches display the familiar blend of hectoring self-questioning, inward imperatives, and second-person self-address ('in earnest ire ententiue must thou stand') by means of which she bullies herself into a constant fury.[25] When she does achieve fury, it has

---

[19] Seneca 1581: f. 120ᵛ.   [20] Ibid. f. 123ᵛ.   [21] Ibid. ff. 121ʳ–122ʳ.
[22] Ibid. f. 131ʳ.   [23] Ibid. f. 128ʳ.
[24] Ibid. f. 137ʳ.   [25] Ibid. f. 137ᵛ.

all the same characteristics as Atreus's: an indifference to public morality
('haue no respect of ryghte', 'Of godlinesse ... vsurpe the name'); a sense of
passivity and self-awe ('I know not what my wrathfull minde consulted hath
within, / And to bewray it to himselfe, I dare not'); and yet also a new feeling
of self-realization and transcendent autonomy ('*Medea* am I made'). As with
Atreus, this last, buoyant mood propels Medea towards her insane project of
infanticide. However, the more that intention and the passion supporting it
grow, the more forcefully contrary concerns turn Medea's mind away from
resolution. She takes fright at her own criminality. Contrast, for example,

> O, horrour huge with sodayne stroke my heart doth ouercom:
> With ycie dulling colde congealde my Members all benum,

with

> The hatefull heart of wife against her Spouse hath yeelded place,
> And pitious mothers mercy milde restoreth natures face.[26]

With this first and several subsequent reversals (on the one hand, 'no kith
nor kin to mee / They are'; on the other, a line later, 'holde, holde, my babes
they be'[27]) Seneca's text, far more than Euripides', directly manifests that
oscillating struggle between alternate (as opposed to coexistent) judgements
which Plutarch argues is Stoic psychology's equivalent of psychomachia.[28]
Medea articulates as much herself, desperately noting that fury and love keep
leading her in opposite directions, or that 'Wrath sometime chaseth virtue
out, and virtue wrath agayne'.

   It takes a sudden, mad hallucination to short-circuit these wavering doubts
and force Medea into butchering her children. Imagining herself surrounded
by devils, foremost amongst whom is her brother (whom she murdered), the
sorceress begins to reconceive the infanticide which they urge upon her as a
'sacrifice', one to placate her brother's vengeful right over her more so than her
own over her husband.[29] Viewed thus, the killing of Jason's offspring becomes
both a triumphant assertion of Medea's new-found autonomy and a vehicle
for expiating the guilt of former sins:

> Now, now my Scepter guilt I haue recouered once agayne:
> My fathers wronges reuenged are, and eke my brother slayne:
> The goulden cattels fleece returnde is to my natiue land,
> Possession of my realme I haue reclaymed to my hand:
> Come home is my virginity, that whilom went astray.[30]

[26] Seneca 1581: ff. 137$^v$–138$^r$.        [27] Ibid. f. 138$^r$.
[28] See further Ch. 4 below and Nussbaum 1994: 451.        [29] Seneca 1581: f. 138$^v$.
[30] Ibid. ff. 138$^v$–139$^r$.

This fantasy of purification is instrumental in helping Medea to discover an 'importunate delight' in revenge which shuts out other kinds of bad conscience: in the final analysis she aligns herself with the ecstatic fury of Pyrrhus and Atreus.[31] Yet even in these closing moments the pitiful dimension of Medea, the self-destruction to which fury drives her, survives alongside her horrific, alienating qualities. Her frantic impulse to rid herself of the last stains of Jason's love—'My bowels Ile vnbreast, and search my wombe with poking Blade'—commands as much sympathy from the audience as it does terror.[32]

It is precisely because Medea's pursuit of fury is thus also an effort to expiate old guilt, to overwhelm the pains of unrequited love, and even to implant a consoling ecstasy, that it demands extenuation. Though a criminal passion, it is not straightforwardly reprehensible. (Rather, Seneca offers us what Nussbaum calls a 'mingling of justification and horror'.[33]) Medea's struggle to achieve a resoluteness of purpose lends her pathos and even a humanity which makes her strangely charismatic—as transfixing as (and more sympathetic than) Atreus. Here again, then, the definite lines of Spenser's sketch of anger—the laudable rage of Arthur or Red Crosse on the one hand, the depraved fury of Phedon and Furor on the other—are troubled. The furious possession which eventually drives both Atreus and Medea is, of course, different in kind from the rationally authenticated anger of a Spenserian hero, but it is not unequivocally reprehensible. As Braden shows, this passion in fact imparts its own captivatingly heroic stature, partly because it adopts 'gestures of heroic arousal' also embraced by other traditions of writing about *thumos*,[34] and partly because it draws on a vocabulary of values shared with the Stoic sage. The Senecan 'heroic villain' pursues an ideal of self-possession akin to that of the Stoic wise man, each wishing to free himself from an oppressive world.[35] What makes the one (the Stoic) attractive makes the other (the villain) attractive too, thereby challenging Elizabethan assumptions about rational governance.[36] Newton, compiler of the 1581 edition of Seneca's plays, conceded as much when he worried that these tragedies, 'tending (at the first sight) ... to the prayse of Ambition, ... the mayntenaunce of cruelty, ... the approbation of incontinencie, ... can not be digested without great daunger of infection'.[37] The alluring power of passion and the twin fascinations of horror and egomania assert themselves powerfully here, and that allure (to judge by the Pyrrhus fantasy) is felt sharply by Hamlet.

---

[31] Ibid. f. 139[r].     [32] Ibid. f. 139[v].     [33] Nussbaum 1994: 446.
[34] Braden 1985: 46.     [35] Ibid. 34, 46–7.
[36] Nussbaum (1994: 463–4, 470–1) speculates that Seneca's play consciously subverts Stoic morality to a greater degree than its author was willing to entertain in his prose tracts.
[37] Seneca 1581: sig. A3[v].

Pyrrhus, Atreus, and Medea, then, as fantasy self-images for Hamlet, variously epitomize the figure which he (in one mood at least) would like to cut. As Miola notes, the Prince engages in an exercise in literary imitation, attempting to emulate Senecan heroic indignation so as to precipitate himself into committing the bloody act of regicide.[38] The larger purpose sitting behind this is Hamlet's need, in effect, to reverse the norms of Thomist governance. His killing impulse, such as it is, is *not* the product of some abiding, irrational passion, barracking a reluctant faculty of reason to support its cause (as in Medea's case). (Were it thus, the impulse might be more emphatic.) On the contrary, Hamlet sees the affront to natural justice and the proper demands of filial duty as *reasoned* grounds for justifying vengeance—as potential 'Excitements of ... reason' as well as of 'blood', stimulants of vigorous rational appetite as much as of excited passion (iv. iv. 58). (It is even 'perfect conscience' and a positive social duty to kill Claudius on such bases (v. ii. 67–70).) And it is these reasoned judgements (together with the guilt to which ignoring them gives rise) which do most to initiate what little murderous intent Hamlet does exhibit. From the point of view of early modern psychology, all of this—the fact that judgement, more than passion, is the initiating force

---

[38] Miola 1992: 40–2. The idea that the conscious imitation of literary themes provided Renaissance schoolboys with a vocabulary with which to map the extremes of human emotion has been developed by Lynn Enterline. She argues (2000: 25) that Elizabethan grammar school pupils were taught to 'discover' their own passions by identifying with Ovidian *exempla* such as Hecuba. By mimicking Ovid's use of *copia* in generating his *prosopopeia*, a boy might 'create' his own, comparable 'great emotion'. Enterline (p. 26) adduces, by way of instance, Shakespeare's Lucrece, who turns to Hecuba's example as a means of 'find[ing] voice for her own grief'. Lucrece appropriates every aspect of the world around her to reinforce her self-absorbed sorrow, reducing even morning birdsong to something 'mocking' (l. 1121). She seeks out varied screens on to which to project, and through which to articulate, her predicament: 'For more it is than I can well express, / ... / When more is felt than one hath power to tell' (ll. 1286–8). Hence she turns to her painting of Troy and Hecuba, not as a way of initiating self-expression, but as a means of varying and revivifying it, as a 'means to mourn some newer way' (l. 1365). Hecuba, as the face in that hanging 'where *all* distress is stelled' (l. 1444), is the richest 'shadow' against whose form Lucrece can 'shape' her own sorrow (ll. 1457–8). She 'lends [Hecuba] words' (ll. 1498); but in so doing she fosters in us the same thought as does Titus when *he* insists that he 'can interpret all [Lavinia's] martyred signs' (*Titus Andronicus*, iii. ii. 36): namely, the intuition that all Lucrece really does is reinscribe Hecuba's sorrow after her own fashion. As Enterline indicates though (p. 167), this is exactly the point of humanist imitation: not to replicate the original, but to use it as a model in relation to which one moulds one's own story. By these imitative means, then, Lucrece expands the vocabulary in terms of which she can frame her passion; and were she not a woman, one can imagine that, fired by that enlarged emotion, she would then do more than simply scratch out the figure of Sinon from the painting. Hamlet, of course, has precisely the opportunity to do more, to become a murderous avenger. However, the difference between Lucrece and him is that Lucrece at least has no trouble in first feeling her grief—she needs only a medium through which to articulate it—whereas Hamlet must turn to imitative models in order even to experience, to feel, any bloody passion. The passion he wants—fury—must be created *ab initio* through others' examples. He lacks, so to speak, any first text, on to which he might map others' stories.

here—might be thought a good thing; but in truth, these judgements are not excitements enough: they excite only in theory, not in practice; momentarily, not continuously. According to the Aristotelian and Thomist models of governance already discussed, reasoned impulses ought ordinarily to be met with supportive passions from the soul's subordinate, irrational faculties—at least in a well-governed mind—and those affections in turn (according to Wright) need to be *fed* by changes in the flow of humours running to the heart. Neither of the latter developments happens here: no sustained passion spontaneously reinforces Hamlet's lacklustre intent, precisely because that intent is not backed by sufficient conviction. Instead, Hamlet needs actively to demand such passions of himself, to try and elicit them forcibly, and then hope that his humoural complexion will shift so as to support them. He does this—strives to invoke lasting emotion—partly so as *retrospectively* to create the illusion that there *is* conviction and vigorous feeling behind his vengeful reasoning. In so far as he wishes to present to the world—and believe, himself, that he has—a decisive, pugnacious soul, Hamlet needs to exhibit the fiery passions and choleric humour symptomatic of such a spirit; and for this purpose, the more furious, the more Senecan he can make himself, the better, since violent feeling would seem to reflect determined judgement. Hence, lacking as he does a *conviction* in his own bloody reasoning, and failing as he does to exude vengeful passion as a result, Hamlet instead tries to generate such passions first, so that he can then thereby come to believe in his judgements. It is in an effort to induce all this that he fixes his attention on Pyrrhus.

This whole technique, as the Prince demonstrates to Gertrude in another context, has a philosophical legitimacy about it:

> Assume a virtue, if you have it not.
> That monster custom, who all sense doth eat,
> Of habits devil, is angel yet in this,
> That to the use of actions fair and good
> He likewise gives a frock or livery
> That aptly is put on.

> (III. iv. 161–6)

Hamlet makes a practical observation here: if reiterative action gradually robs the mind of any feeling for the *evilness* of sin, thereby making such sin easier to commit and allowing us to become accustomed to it, the same is conversely true of good deeds. A corrupt soul, bereft of its feel for goodness, can nonetheless force itself to perform outwardly virtuous actions, and those, too, will become customary over time, even re-establishing the agent's instinct for goodness (making inward that which was outward). Claudius craves as much when he forces his 'stubborn knees' to bow in the hope that adopting a posture of prayer will induce real piety within him (iii. iii. 70). This technique is a variation upon Castiglione's precept, 'such properties be ingendred in us, as our doings are'.[39] The mind, Hamlet advises Gertrude, can readily assume any number of garbs, and these, though initially alien, will quickly become second (or rather first) nature, for 'use ... can change the stamp of nature' (iii. iv. 169).

In saying this, the Prince draws upon a layered conception of the self according to which (elsewhere in this play) some one feature of the complexion can 'o'ergrow' the rest of the soul to become the single quality by which a person is identified (i. iv. 27); or, again, a broad condition of resoluteness may be 'sicklied o'er' and snuffed out 'with the pale cast of thought' (iii. i. 85); or 'damnèd custom' can 'braze' over the heart's surface so as to make it 'proof ... against' the very moral sense which Hamlet would have Gertrude 'assume' as 'livery' (iii. iv. 37–8). Personal identity is, in all these cases, made commensurate with man's outward face, with the uppermost amongst the many accretive layers of the self. Reciprocally, that topmost layer presses its way inward, overwriting all previous inscriptions, 'all pressures past' (i. v. 100), such that it becomes the whole person. A recurrent logic of performance and habituation is at work throughout these comments, but, crucially for my argument here, that same logic also informs Hamlet's handling of his own passions. Whatever he may protest to the contrary, he does focus upon precisely the 'forms, moods, [and] shapes' of fury, and try to 'force' his own outward 'haviour' in an effort to redefine—reinscribe from without—'that within which passes show' (i. ii. 76–86). Such is the unspoken, emulous intent underlying the Prince's description of Pyrrhus. His is the livery that Hamlet would now wear.

[39] Cefalu (2004*b*: 152–8, 194–5) argues that, intellectually, iii. iv. 161–6 is rooted in Augustine, but, to justify this claim, must assert that Shakespeare began 'sorting through' the latter's 'theological niceties in advance of the full-scale preoccupation with sinful habituation' pioneered by divines of the seventeenth century. In practice, the absence in Hamlet's comments to Gertrude of any sustained attention to the will (a central term in Augustine's moral psychology) makes this ascription dubious. Furthermore, the passages from the *Confessions* which Cefalu cites reflect, if anything, precisely Augustine's debt to *Aristotle*, and Aristotelian ideas of habituation were, anyway, so commonplace in the sixteenth century (as I demonstrated in Ch. 1) that to call upon other sources at Aristotle's expense is perverse. For Cefalu the key point in *Hamlet* (as in Augustine) is that a vicious *habit* is itself a sinful thing, quite apart from the individual vicious acts through which that habit expresses itself. However, the evidence which Cefalu adduces (p. 155) does not satisfactorily prove that Denmark's Prince was preoccupied with sin 'as a theological abstraction' or that he thought the 'habit' of sin of more concern than sinful deeds. Throughout the play, Hamlet tends to visualize particular sexual acts performed by Gertrude or specific poses which she assumes, and likewise he dwells upon particular perceptions of the flesh's corruption, this rather than musing repeatedly on the idea of her exhibiting established habits. When he does invoke habit in iii. iv, he emphasizes its fluidity, not its intractability. He makes a practical point about how easily 'habits' may be reversed—and therefore how loosely the adjectives 'sinful' and 'virtuous' attach themselves to that noun—and this sharply contradicts the *Confessions*.

The effect Hamlet is trying to achieve can be further illustrated with reference to Montaigne's 'Of Diuerting', in which the essayist notes that a good orator is typically 'mooued at the sound of his owne voyce, and by his fayned agitations; and suffer[s] himselfe to be cozoned by the passion he representeth: imprinting [upon himself] a liuely and essentiall sorrow'.[40] The imitation of passion does here precipitate 'essentiall', heartfelt feeling, and that such inner transformations are possible on stage was supposedly demonstrated to bloody (and, for Hamlet, pertinent) effect in an apocryphal story told of Julius Caesar. According to Heywood's *Apology for Actors*, Caesar, indulging his taste for acting, once took the lead role in a performance of *Hercules Furens*, but he was there so 'carryed away with … his practised fury, … to which he had fashioned all his actiue spirits', that he actually killed the servant playing Lychas in an orgy of violence.[41] As another Montaignian example, this time of hired mourners, illustrates, it is precisely reiterative habituation ('habituant'[42]) which enables performers thus to slip from the show of feeling into the reality thereof: 'For although they striue to act … in a borrowed forme, yet by abytuating and ordering their countenance[s], … they are often wholly transported into … true … melancholly.'[43] The everyday preacher, similarly, can discover an 'emotion' during the act of sermonizing which 'doth animate [him] towards beliefe',[44] and the good lawyer too, once paid his fee, will always find 'his will moved': 'Then will his reason be moved, and his knowledge enflamed withall. See then an … vndoubted truth presents it selfe to his vnderstanding; wherein he … beleeves it in good sooth, and so perswades himselfe.'[45] In this last example, just as Hamlet would wish, (temporary) reasoned conviction itself is generated by first inducing both passion and wilfulness. Something comparable happens to Kyd's Hieronimo when he 'play[s] the murderer' (IV. i. 129) in 'Soliman and Perseda', the tragedy with which *The Spanish Tragedy* concludes.[46] Hieronimo is conscience-stricken throughout the play by the anxiety that his vengeful impulses are the work of 'ugly fiends [which] do sally forth of hell, / … frame my steps to unfrequented paths, / And fear my heart with fierce inflamèd thoughts' (III. ii. 16–18). He therefore turns to the play-within-the-play not just as a Machiavellian tool for effecting revenge unnoticed,[47] but also as a way of anaesthetizing his own guilt. In absorbing himself in a script, he becomes detached from his self, side-stepping moral consciousness and surrendering himself to a bloody

---

[40] Montaigne 1603: 503.     [41] Heywood 1612: sig. E3ᵛ.     [42] Montaigne 1952: iii. 55.
[43] Montaigne 1603: 503–4.     [44] Ibid. 329.
[45] Further sources for the First Player's skills, particularly Quintilian's *Institutes* and Aphthonius's *Progymnasmata*, are discussed in McDonald 1962: 333–41.
[46] References to *The Spanish Tragedy* are to Maus 1995.
[47] See, e.g., Mercer 1987: 54–5.

passion which (in so far as he pretends that it is only a fiction) absolves him of the need to engage with the reality of murder. Carried by this prescribed role, Hieronimo, like Montaigne's preacher and lawyer, discovers the passion which temporarily reconciles him to his filial duty, automating him enough to make him avenge his murdered son.

Hamlet strives to achieve this same fluency of conduct, but remains 'unpregnant' in his cause, unable even to simulate sustained fury, let alone translate that into murderous action or a public denunciation (II. ii. 520–1). Atreus finds that he can speak at length and with assurance about his violent intent. *Hamlet*'s First Player, passionately assuming the person of Aeneas, can denounce Fortune for Hecuba's suffering (ll. 468–9). The Prince, by contrast, is conscious only of his public silence (l. 521). As Mercer says, he cannot find so much as 'a language adequate to [his] role', 'an authentic voice of woe'.[48] Hamlet's peculiar fascination with the process of acting stems from this desperate fact. He valorizes playing because in his mind it performs a purity and authenticity of feeling lacking in his own life (wherein individual passions and motivations are neither emphatic nor distinct). Thus the unnamed 'excellent play' which he invokes (l. 399) is commended for the smooth and focused singularity—the 'honesty' (an important word for Hamlet)—with which it presents the movements of man's felt life: 'I remember one said there were no sallets in the lines to make the matter savoury, nor no matter in the phrase that might indict the author of affectation, but called it an honest method' (ll. 400–3). The distaste, here, for disruptive levity and spicy humour ('savoury sallets') is ironic given Hamlet's own addiction to just such conceits, but that very discrepancy underlines the extent to which this vision of inwardness and discourse represents an idealized behaviour which Hamlet would emulate if he could. His instructions in directing 'The Mousetrap' are premised on the same ideals of purity and authenticity, the imperative to represent passions as they supposedly are in nature:

in the very torrent, tempest, and … whirlwind of your passion, you must acquire … a temperance that may give it smoothness. Oh, it offends me to the soul to hear a robustious, periwig-pated fellow tear a passion to totters … . Be not too tame neither, but let … discretion be your tutor. Suit the action to the word, the word to the action, with this special observance, that you o'erstep not the modesty of nature. (III. ii. 4–16)

Hamlet's principle of mimetic fidelity precludes any histrionics—passions are not to be buried beneath a stream of exaggerated shouts and gestures—but, importantly, it still gives full scope to vigour where vigour is appropriate. 'Temperance' is to be maintained *amidst* the torrents and tempests which

---

[48]  Mercer 1987: 191.

indicate strength of feeling, not at the expense of these things. As a dramatic virtue, it does not simply equate to 'tameness'. On the contrary, both it and the moderations of 'modesty' are variable ideals, rather than static midpoints on the volume scale. This theatrical model still leaves room, then, for Senecan fury. What must not be sacrificed in the more dynamic cases of emotion, though, is 'smoothness', a sensitivity to the way in which feelings develop—the way in which the mind moves progressively from passivity through varying degrees of passion into outright action.

In his performance of Aeneas's account, first of Pyrrhus's rage, then of Hecuba's grief, the First Player exhibits precisely this smoothness. Immersed in his role, he generates a pure, singularly focused passion which then gives the illusion of translating itself instinctively into equally focused words and gestures. As a result, somewhere along the way, the Player himself disappears, becoming in Hamlet's eyes Aeneas, 'the Personater' (to repeat Heywood's phrase) becoming 'the man Personated'. Given this transformation, Hamlet can even begin to expect that this Aeneas's passion might shortly convert into outward action. The purity of this display, a reflection of human nature as Hamlet imagines it is in others and should be in him, seems positively sacred to him. He jealously aestheticizes and idealizes the whole process. The closest he himself comes to matching it, though, is in a rare moment of 'indiscretion' (v. ii. 8) when Hamlet, having spontaneously resolved to read and then substitute Rosencrantz and Guildenstern's orders, afterwards turns to theatrical language to characterize such psychological fluency: '[Ere] I could make a *prologue* to my brains, / They had begun *the play*' (ll. 31–2). For the most part, though, he cannot achieve the automation of conduct and lack of self-consciousness in passion which seem to be second nature in the First Player. Hence the *jealous* fury with which he confronts the latter's performance (and particularly the actor's ability to exhibit those 'forms, moods, [and] shapes of grief' which Hamlet had previously professed himself indifferent to (i. ii. 82) ):

> Is it not monstrous that this player here,
> But in a fiction, in a dream of passion,
> Could force his soul so to his own conceit
> That from her working all his visage wanned,
> Tears in his eyes, distraction in's aspect,
> A broken voice, and his whole function suiting
> With forms to his conceit? And all for nothing?
> .  .  .  .  .  .  .  .
> What's Hecuba to him … ?
>
> (ii. ii. 503–11)

Try as he might to mimic this process, beginning (at l. 502) as Montaigne's preacher and lawyer begin, by unpacking his heart with words (l. 538), the ideas which Hamlet expresses nevertheless do not *capture* his imagination.[49] Though he may have a legitimate 'cue' for vengeance where the First Player has only a 'fiction' (l. 513), he is not, even so, gripped as the latter was by a forcing 'conceit'. Not being thus captivated, he necessarily fails to initiate an instinctive passion—let alone a choleric humour to fuel it—which might then become entrenched and foster a broader conviction. He is left only with his original words, words which, psychologically speaking, have taken him no further forward and are as such no more than whining verbiage—stilted, self-conscious forays into rage, rather than doorways on to Montaigne's 'liuely ... essentiall' thing.

The Prince's inability to muster a compelling vengeful passion is evidently a source of guilt to him. That much is implicit when in Act III he laments his loss of the Hamlet family's one-time '*native* hue of resolution'; but it is clear, too, from the approach he takes to staging 'The Mousetrap'. The enthusiasm with which Hamlet pursues the latter suggests that it is itself a vehicle for expiating such guilt. He can at least muster strong feelings for this bloodless (and notably cerebral) exercise in theatricality, and to do that is to create the illusion in his own mind both that this game constitutes a continued pursuit of the vengeance project and that it is a manifestation of the revenger's dangerous, potent energy. Bloody retribution is, for the moment, converted into its intellectual equivalent, a witty exercise in one-upmanship, as if to pursue the one were tantamount to pursuing the other. This delusory quality of Hamlet's Thespian scheme is particularly apparent in the way he broaches the plan to himself. The Prince first hits on the notion of staging a pointed adaptation of 'The Murder of Gonzago' *before* he commences the 'rogue and peasant slave' soliloquy (II. ii. 490–5); and yet towards the end of that soliloquy he announces the plan to himself again, as if it were, at that later moment, a sudden and new idea:

> Fie upon't, foh ! About, my brain. Hum, I have heard
> That guilty creatures sitting at a play
> Have ...
> Been struck so to the soul, that presently
> They have proclaimed their malefactions;
>
> .    .    .    .    .    .    .    .    .    .
> ... I'll have these players
> Play something like the murder of my father.
>
> (ll. 541–8)

---

[49]  Cf. Ure 1974: 36.

The speech within which this latter passage falls is perhaps the most anguished of Hamlet's several protests at his own inertia; and yet the Prince manages to close this speech on a *triumphant* note, with the celebrated couplet 'The play's the thing / Wherein I'll catch the conscience of the king' (ll. 557–8). That change of mood occurs precisely when, at line 541, the Prince rehatches his theatrical plan, presenting it to himself as if it were, only now, a new revelation. In articulating his scheme at this point, he suppresses any acknowledgement that he had actually latched on to the idea already, at lines 490 ff. Rather, he welcomes it afresh now, with a ponderous sense of self-dramatization, presumably because doing so helps to defuse those anxieties about his own torpor which had come to a head just moments before. To this comment it is worth adding another: namely, that the energy which Hamlet subsequently invests in directing the Players (typified in those meticulous instructions to them at the beginning of Act III, Scene II) also indicates the depth of his emotional involvement in the 'Mousetrap' project. That fact, too, underlines how far this scheme functions in the Prince's conscience as a substitute for bloodlust—as if, to reiterate, he had convinced himself that this enterprise is both the direct manifestation of an avenger's passion and a demonstration of his own virile dangerousness. What one Shakespearean contemporary, Daniel Dyke, called 'the mystery of self-deceiving' seems, then, to be at work here, Hamlet consoling himself with theatrical distractions as a means of evading his own shortcomings.

Certainly, once 'The Mousetrap' has done its work, Hamlet continues in this self-deluding strain. He reacts ecstatically to Claudius's flight as if, in that moment, he has actually slain the latter and thus achieved the self-realization of becoming a second Pyrrhus. The moment the usurper-king has exited, his nephew bursts into ballad metre and an otherwise unprecedented pastoral idiom (III. ii. 246–9, 255–8), betraying a frenzied pleasure in the question he now fires at Horatio, and calling repeatedly for music to accompany his revelry (ll. 250–2, 265–8). One might expect that the apparent proving of Claudius's guilt would be an occasion for sorrow, a stimulus prompting those in the know first to reflect on the sober fact of Old Hamlet's murder and then to confront anew their consequent burden of vengeance. For Hamlet it is instead a positively exhilarating proof of his own capacity to outwit his uncle. Those two contrasting responses are evident in the immediate exchange between Hamlet and Horatio, the former speaking as if (in his own mind) he had now triumphed, virtually completing (rather than just beginning) the task of revenge, the latter indicating his dissent and downplaying the significance of what has so far been achieved:

HAM. Would not this, sir, and a forest of feathers ... with two provincial roses on my
   razed shoes, get me a fellowship in a cry of players, sir ?
HOR. Half a share.

(ll. 250–3)

Absorbed in his distraction, the Prince is passionate here, more so than seems
appropriate to the occasion. To the outside observer, this premature sense of
victory is in practice another indication of his delusory disposition.

On the back of this triumph, Hamlet finally succeeds, at the close of Act
III, Scene II, in seeming Senecan to himself (if only momentarily). 'Now
could I drink hot blood,' he concludes, 'And do such bitter business as the
day / Would quake to look on' (ll. 351–3). This stagey assertion that he is at
last ready to make choler his humoural type suggests to us a figure absorbed
in his own would-be fiction, one who already thinks of himself, tacitly at least,
as a blooded killer.[50] Hamlet perpetuates that delusion by imitating, with the
'witching time' imagery of this same speech (ll. 349–51), the 'midnight weeds'
and 'Hecat's ban' previously invoked by the 'Mousetrap's' Lucianus (ll. 233–4).
He clearly places himself on the same continuum as the latter. However, such
hyperbole cannot hide the stilted, fantastical feel of this soliloquy which makes
it (for us) comic, and the one character whom Hamlet explicitly invokes here
is not, anyway, the king he should be readying himself to murder but Gertrude
('my mother' (l. 353) ). The crystallization of emotional focus which will carry
Hamlet straight past his praying, vulnerable uncle in the next scene because
his mother 'stays' him (III. iii. 95) thus begins now, and this fact demonstrates
that (hellish poses notwithstanding) Hamlet is still a figure bereft of any real
commitment to regicidal passion.

Further instances of self-deceit, always serving to negotiate the problem of
a lack of real passion, are plentiful. In Act V, for example, there is reason to
doubt the validity of Hamlet's new-found submission to 'special providence',
heaven's ordinance, and a 'divinity' that ever prevails in shaping our ends (v. ii.
192–3, 48, 10–11). The adoption of such a position in the conviction that the
soul's 'readiness is all' (l. 195) seems to constitute an assertion of will guided
by a definite rational conviction—in this case a pious submission either to
Stoicism's cosmological fatalism or to some shade of predestination.[51] Yet
all this can equally be read as no more than the discovery of a comfortable

---

[50] Ure 1974: 37.
[51] For the Stoic reading see Knowles 1999: 1062–3 (but cf. a robust counter-argument
in Monsarrat 1984: 138–9); for the Protestant reading, Matheson 1995: 390–7; and for a
juxtaposition of the two, Sinfield 1992: 226–30.

formula which renders inaction justifiable. Similarly, there is an air of evasion in Hamlet's supposedly profound reflection on the folly of Rosencrantz and Guildenstern, a reflection delivered amidst an uneasy attempt to justify his orchestration of those two men's deaths:

> 'Tis dangerous when the baser nature comes
> Between the pass and fell incensèd points
> Of mighty opposites.

> (ll. 60–2)

Hamlet's pose of greatness here rings hollow: he achieves murderous decisiveness only by way of compensation for past inertia, in a context in which the victims scarcely matter to him, and in a manner which requires that he neither perpetrate nor witness the bloody deed done at his instigation. Furthermore, the attempt to dramatize himself as something 'mighty' follows immediately upon the apologetic comment to Horatio, 'Why man, they did make love to [their] employment' (l. 57), as if he were hereby overwriting traces of guilty anxiety with a consoling distraction.[52] A similar desire for approval underlies the Prince's next speech too, where, with a series of self-consciously 'reasonable' questions, he looks to Horatio to confirm him in his regicidal intent:

> Does it not, think thee, stand me now upon—
> .    .    .    .    .    .    .    .    .    .    .    .
>         —is't not perfect conscience
> To quit [Claudius] with this arm? And is't not to be damned
> To let this canker of our nature come
> In further evil?

> (ll. 63, 67–70)

If, though, this interrogative approach is one means by which Hamlet would cajole himself into a resolute passion, the orchestration of a practical *necessity* to act and the exploitation of his own pride are others. As Horatio notes, news from England of the substitute executions will soon demonstrate to Claudius just how great a threat Hamlet is. The Prince must therefore take his vengeance before then. In creating this 'interim' (l. 73), Hamlet imposes upon himself a time frame for action, thereby trying (so we infer) to short-circuit himself into firmness of purpose. Equally, by 'agreeing' with Horatio about the *moral* need to act now (ll. 67–70 above), he also establishes an external marker to

[52] Cf. Empson 1986: 115. The impression of guilty defensiveness is strongest in F, where l. 57 is first added to the text. This addition comes against a background of other F changes earlier on which emphasize the arbitrariness of Hamlet's turn against Rosencrantz and Guildenstern (Kerrigan 2001: 7–8).

hold himself to the performance of his duty: not to take revenge now would be to lose face. Again, self-manipulation is the underlying imperative.

## HAMLET AND THE FLESH

Thus far I have emphasized Hamlet's longing to feel possessed by a villainous, irrational passion; his sense — and Shakespeare's audience's sense — that such a fury may be both an essential stimulant to overcome paralysis and something compellingly attractive, even heroic; his attempts to reverse the norms of Elizabethan psychology in an effort to induce such passion; and his parallel valorization of playing as a forum within which passions are readily invoked and smoothly transfused into actions: all this by way of a challenge to the rationalist ideals of governance outlined in my previous chapters. Secondly, I have argued that, though frustrated in these aspirations, Hamlet circumvents any direct confrontation with his own passivity by embracing a number of delusions: the belief, to take one example, that he really is pursuing his vengeful intent in staging a play and that this does allow him to realize his Senecan ambitions. How, though, are we to explain Hamlet's emotional inertia?

At least one answer to that latter question is hinted at in one of the Player King's speeches during 'The Mousetrap' when he comments that 'Purpose is but the slave to memory, / Of violent birth but poor validity' (iii. ii. 169–70). The assumption at work here is that perceptions held in the memory, in repeatedly spurring the imagination, thereby underpin the life of our motivating passions. Such passions, the basis of a lively purpose, depend upon repeated sensory stimulation for their continued vigour, and memory provides exactly that. When the Ghost first appears to Hamlet, he gives him a wealth of images on which to dwell: gnomic suggestions, first, as to the torments he now suffers in his 'Unhouseled, disappointed' state (i. v. 13–22, 77), and then a blisteringly graphic description of his actual murder (ll. 59–73). The Ghost's imperative, 'Remember me' (l. 91), is an instruction to Hamlet to maintain a vivid impression of just such perceptions at the forefront of his memory. Only thus can he keep alive the sense of outrage necessary to fuel his retributive project and fulfil the spirit's subsidiary command (to 'Revenge his foul and most unnatural murder' (l. 25) ). Indeed, it is visualization of precisely this kind which, according to Quintilian, enables the likes of Montaigne's orators to discover a passion for their cause:

I am complaining that a man has been murdered. Shall I not bring before my eyes all ... circumstances which it is reasonable to imagine must have occurred in such a connexion? ... Shall I not see the fatal blow delivered and the stricken body fall? Will not the blood, the deathly pallor, the groan of agony, the death rattle, be indelibly impressed upon my mind?[53]

Thus, within minutes of seeing *his* father's ghost, we find Marston's Antonio dwelling on the latter's degraded condition: 'By the infectious damps of clammy graves, / And by the mould that presseth down / My dead father's skull, I'll be revenged!' (*Antonio's Revenge*, III. ii. 26–8).[54] Thoughts of his father, 'Andrugio's hearse', then propel Antonio as he kills Julio, son of Andrugio's murderer (III. iii. 25). Hieronimo goes further, retaining his murdered son's bloody handkerchief as a perpetual *aide-mémoire*, a material token intended to keep the sight of Horatio's hacked corpse fresh within his memory lest he stray from his purpose (*Spanish Tragedy*, II. iv. 113–14). Hamlet, by contrast, evades such preoccupations, fixing his attention elsewhere, rather than rehearsing images which might prove passionately provocative.

The almost complete absence of a return to the spirit's words throughout Hamlet's many speeches is striking. His reference, for example, to 'the motive and … cue for passion' which he bears as 'son of the dear murderèd' (II. ii. 513, 536) is typical of the curiously flat, abstract manner which characterizes his allusions to the injustice done to Old Hamlet. In the same soliloquy from which that first comment derives, Hamlet describes himself as '[peaking] / Like John-a-dreams' at the thought of his father's 'damned defeat' (ll. 519–20, 523). 'Peak' is usually taken as meaning 'to mope or languish', but it was also at this time a variant of 'peek', and the image could therefore refer to the dim half-vision of a sleepy figure. If so, Hamlet would be drawing attention here to his failure acutely to visualize the deep damnation of his father's taking off, his failure to maintain a sharp and constant impression of the Ghost's revelations in his mind's eye. Only when he watches Claudius praying does he actually recall Old Hamlet's uncertain 'audit' and the grossness of the moment of his assassination (III. iii. 80–2), and even then the recollection is short-lived. The Prince's thoughts swiftly turn, instead, to his mother awaiting him in her closet, just as earlier, having instructed the First Player to dwell upon 'Priam's slaughter' (II. ii. 406) so that he might stir himself with the image of Pyrrhus's fury, Hamlet nonetheless then urged his actor not to linger over the Old King's death but to continue and 'come to Hecuba' (ll. 458–9). Not surprisingly, therefore, when the Ghost returns to his son in Act III, Scene iv, his first command is 'Do not forget' (III. iv. 109). It is evident that Hamlet has been doing exactly that, focusing his imagination elsewhere. His memory's 'validity' is indeed transient, and in the absence of reiterative ruminations on the details of his father's suffering,

---

[53] Quoted in McDonald 1962: 339.    [54] References to this play are to Marston 1978.

this young lord simply cannot discover a passion to motivate his vengeful 'purpose'.

Hamlet's enthusiasm to 'come to Hecuba' and to press on to Gertrude's closet betrays why it is that Old Hamlet's fate never commands his son's lasting attention. Bluntly, it is always the idea of the passive mother, not of the dying father or the warrior son, which truly *captures* the Prince's attention. I began this chapter with the observation that one meaning behind the idea of Hamlet's being 'lapsed ... in passion' was that he was bereft of (real) passion. But that phrase also commands another, quite contrary interpretation: the recognition that Hamlet *is* in fact powerfully possessed by emotion, but by emotions so distracting that they prevent him both from concentrating on the outrage of his father's murder and from holding to any vengeful fury. These distracting feelings are passions *into* which Hamlet lapses; passions, equally, which render him lapsed (or paralysed) with respect to any other concern but their own. Hamlet's passion for his mother—his desire to come to Hecuba—is precisely one such affection; his associated distaste for the flesh, another; and his moral and religious compulsion to reform both Gertrude and Denmark, a third. All these things repeatedly draw his attention away from regicide and the burden of filial obligation.

On the first of these emotions, Hamlet's preoccupation with Gertrude, ample critical comment already exists. Of more relevance here is the second obsession which Shakespeare implants in his Prince, a disgust, repeatedly demonstrated, for human sinfulness, fleshliness, and corporeality, for the general phenomena of sexual and moral corruption, and even for himself as one implicated in such failings.[55] This is expressed in various ways throughout the play. One instance is Hamlet's own reaction to his spontaneous display of emotion at Ophelia's graveside. In Act v, Scene i, in a rare moment

---

[55] Both Adelman (1992: 11–37) and Greenblatt (Gallagher and Greenblatt 2000: 152–62) offer compelling accounts of the reasons why 'enfleshment' is a source of corruption in this play. Adelman (p. 24) argues that Shakespeare's narrative of fratricidal rivalry is only 'a cover for the ... primal story' which really informs Hamlet's 'unweeded garden' speech: viz. the story of sexualized woman's introduction of corruption into the world. This deeper narrative, which makes woman the origin point of man's material being, and thus of his mortality too, identifies Gertrude's sexuality as the root poison which infects the world and the self of both father and son Hamlets (ll. 27, 30). On this interpretation Hamlet's loathing for sex, death, and the flesh derives from a revulsion against his mother, and Adelman, who reads that nexus of associations psychoanalytically, as an 'infantile fantasy' (p. 35), traces it back to Shakespeare's own vision. Greenblatt (pp. 160–1) prefers to interpret Hamlet's 'elemental nausea' at the vulnerability of matter and his 'obsession with a corporeality' that 'reduces everything to appetite and excretion' as an expression of contemporary Protestant anxieties about the flesh, particularly as reflected in eucharistic controversies. My own reading of this facet of the play favours that same historicist (as opposed to psychoanalytic) approach, not least in that I see Hamlet's vilification of the flesh (as discussed hereafter) as continuous with that which is evident in *The Faerie Queene*.

of pugnacity, the Prince suddenly reasserts his 'expertise' on the subject of authentic human passions—something he had previously lectured the Players on. Faced with Laertes' histrionic lament for Ophelia, he claims for himself the right to specialize in passion:

> What is he whose grief
> Bears such an emphasis? whose phrase of sorrow
> Conjures the wandering stars ...
> ... This is I,
> Hamlet the Dane.

(v. i. 221–5)

Accusing Laertes of only mouthing and whining shallow sentiments (ll. 244, 250), he takes for himself, exclusively, the burden of true grief, and in that moment of resolute assurance also finds himself publicly laying claim to his kingship. So complete is Hamlet's realization of his heroic status at this juncture that he also affirms his willingness to outdo Hercules. Miola observes that Laertes' grief-stricken imagery (ll. 218–21) recalls the language of the eponymous hero in *Hercules Furens*.[56] Hamlet, in appropriating that imagery and redoubling it (ll. 247–50), places himself beyond Hercules and thus beyond a figure who was previously a byword for his own father. There is in all this more than a hint that the Prince has been stung by a competitive impulse. In a repetition of Collatine's and Lucretius's 'emulation in ... woe' (*Lucrece*, l. 1808), he indicts Laertes for 'outfacing him', and with that verb reveals how far the focus of his feelings lies with his pride and public reputation, more so than with any grief (v. i. 245). The 'dangerous' pose, though, quickly collapses (l. 229), Hamlet losing conviction in the role he has stumbled into. His parting couplet, 'Let Hercules himself do what he may, / The cat will mew, and dog will have his day' (ll. 258–9), whilst it is darkly threatening, nevertheless cedes the Herculean identity back to Laertes in favour of a more demeaning self-image. Hamlet, the animal images imply, must work out his destiny more prosaically. Crucially, the failure of nerve implicit in this retreat reveals a sudden (one might say Spenserian) uncomfortableness with passion. In the next scene Hamlet confides to Horatio that he positively regrets this moment of genuine fury: such 'towering passion' (v. ii. 80) constitutes, in his eyes, an undignified loss of self-control. In private contexts he can occasionally thrill to spontaneous self-surrender (as when his brain sets itself aplaying without need of a prologue from him (ll. 30–1)) but publicly, when on the royal stage, 'Th'observed of all observers' (iii. i. 148) cannot brook such impassioned lapses in decorum. Furthermore, the Prince, looking back on

---

[56] Miola 1992: 43–4.

this whole episode, must also be aware that in outranting Laertes (v. i. 251) he has transgressed his own idealized vision of the impassioned state, the very image which he had earlier so carefully expounded to the Players (III. ii. 4–16). In transgressing this ideal, Hamlet in fact exposes it as a fiction: genuine emotion is not, it transpires from this ugly fracas, as smooth, neatly confined, and downright aesthetic as his fantasy would suggest. Behind such disillusionment the underlying impression conveyed to the audience is that Hamlet cannot accept the reality of being genuinely passionate (for all that he might wish to be vengeful or furious). This antipathy is one expression of a broader, markedly ascetic outlook which prevails in the Prince—an outlook which draws him back towards Spenser's ethic. Emotion, with all its fleshly and corporeal associations, is ultimately unpalatable to him.

The same disgust with fleshliness also manifests itself more directly in Hamlet's revulsion for his own, corrupt physicality—this, a theme apparent even in his first soliloquy, where it is interwoven with his larger distaste for Elsinore's moral environment:

> O that this too too solid flesh would melt,
> Thaw and resolve itself into a dew,
> Or that the Everlasting had not fixed
> His canon 'gainst self-slaughter. O God, God,
> How weary, stale, flat and unprofitable
> Seem to me all the uses of this world!

> (I. ii. 129–34)

The longing for dissolution, for an escape from fleshliness, is realized here in a series of concrete images which tend towards limpid purification: 'solid', 'melt', 'thaw', 'resolve' (an alchemical term), 'dew'. Hamlet, feeling his every thought with this same exactitude of sensation, figures the ennui of the world as both tangible ('weary'), saporous ('stale'), and visible ('flat'), before capturing its sickness in the first of the play's numerous horticultural metaphors, that of an 'unweeded garden' (ll. 135–7). Like Eliot's perfect 'metaphysical poet', Hamlet experiences his revulsion for corporeality not merely intellectually but also graphically. Such sensuous consciousness of corporeality is a perennial feature of his imagination.[57] It is present in the Prince's praise for honest theatre (theatre which lacks 'savoury sallets') and in his similarly gourmet resolution to kill Claudius only at a time which has 'no *relish* of salvation in't' (III. iii. 92).[58] He dismisses flatterers as 'candied tongues' who 'lick absurd pomp' (III.

[57] Honigmann 2002: 68.
[58] The preponderance of saporous language in *Hamlet* is reminiscent of Florio's Montaigne, which frequently celebrates the 'taste' or 'savour' of tranquillity, death, and beauty, or of one's own life, temperance, and contentment (e.g. Montaigne 1603: 31, 354, 358, 381, 661–2).

ii. 50)), assures the king that he will soon 'nose' out Polonius's body (IV. iii. 33), and makes mock self-deprecating reference to his own 'rawer breath' (v. ii. 115). It is presumably the suffocating totality of just such perceptiveness, the awareness that every moment of consciousness is saturated with earthy impressions, which drives Hamlet to thoughts of suicide. At the same time, crucially, this obsessive sensitiveness underlines how slight the boundary is between asceticism and madness, how easily the one shades into the other. To sense this is to begin to doubt the value of the former, that asceticism which, I demonstrated earlier, is so much a feature of sixteenth-century moral thought.

Hamlet's passionate distaste for all things visceral is informed, above all, by his idealization of his father. 'Canonized' in his son's mind (I. iv. 47) as the measure of all things ('a man...all in all' (I. ii. 187)), Old Hamlet is invoked at the heart of the Prince's first soliloquy as 'So excellent a king, that was to this [other man] / Hyperion to a satyr' (ll. 139–40). A controlling force over nature, rather than a cancerous growth within it, the former king epitomizes the transcendent brilliance of a Titan alongside Claudius's earthly satyr. Hamlet appropriates this perfected image of his father in order to help construct and reinforce his own loathing for corporeality. He does, therefore, remember his king; but he remembers him as he was when alive and potent, rather than during the long moments of his death or subsequent purgatorial sufferings (the memories which might provoke vengeful sentiments); and he remembers him less as a person and more simply as a gauge against which to measure and berate the awful present.[59]

What Hamlet feels most of all is the pollution of original sin, that same principle which cuts into the heart of Spenser's *Faerie Queene*. The first hint of this comes amidst the talk of 'swinish' Denmark's failings (I. iv. 19) when he notes just how inescapable the taint of moral imperfection is. A single 'vicious mole of nature' will always (in Hamlet's estimation) prove sufficient to corrupt 'all the noble substance' of the self (l. 37). The inward application of this otherwise abstract comment becomes apparent when the Prince confronts Ophelia in Act III, Scene i. At that point, his ascetic passions, and especially his distaste for the flesh, come to a head. Though the fact is rarely noticed, the emphasis in Hamlet's first words to Ophelia is on his own corrupt soul, not hers: 'Nymph, in thy orisons / Be all *my* sins remembered' (III. i. 89–90; my emphasis). Ophelia is to beseech God's grace, but for Hamlet's sake, not her own. Likewise, in this same vein the Prince applies the doctrine of original

---

'Relish', especially, becomes a favoured word in Shakespeare's vocabulary from the time of *Hamlet* onwards.

[59] Cf. Greenblatt 2001: 213–14, 222. Greenblatt (p. 222) notes that 'the metamorphosis of a particular man into a painted combination of ... deities' amounts more to a 'way of forgetting' than of truly remembering.

sin specifically to himself, deploying in so doing a typically sensuous image (and another image which presupposes a layered conception of the self): 'You should not have believed me, for virtue cannot so inoculate our old stock but we shall *relish* of it' (ll. 116–17). Here again an ever-sensitive imagination *tastes* its own fleshliness. It is against this backdrop and in recognition of his own 'offences' (ll. 120–6) that Hamlet first advises Ophelia to get to a nunnery (so as to protect herself from him). Only latterly does he turn vicious, attributing the source of earthly corruption more to womankind than man. In the meantime he achieves a quiet humility during which he visualizes himself as but a helpless fellow 'crawling between earth and heaven' (l. 125). This, then, is the condition to which his passionate moral consciousness reduces him, and it is one so unforgiving towards the corporeal part of the self that it must again call into question the value of ascetic idealism.

Hamlet's asceticism, his revulsion in the face of human bodiliness, is complemented by another ruling passion, his impulsive desire to effect moral and religious reform. To some extent the Ghost positively invites him to undertake as much, to reform the royal household, but also, by extension, the character of Denmark *per se*: 'Let not the royal bed of Denmark be / A couch for luxury and damnèd incest' (i. v. 82–3). Hamlet embraces this sentiment in its largest sense when he resolves to 'set ... right' the times (l. 190). The subsequent drive to protect Ophelia from himself, and then mankind from Ophelia, is (to take one example) of a piece with this fantasy. More poignantly, though, Hamlet also conceives of himself as a sometime priest and confessor, and it is in that role that he most emphatically strives to bring purity to the corrupted. Besides discovering and playing upon a 'confession' in Guildenstern's looks (ii. ii. 265), he also devotes the entire closet scene to urging his mother to 'Confess' and 'Repent' (iii. iv. 150–1). Furthermore, this latter scene, undoubtedly the most disturbing in the play, marks the Prince's one true moment of fluency and self-assurance in the tragedy as a whole. It constitutes, in a sense, the climax of the action,[60] after which the rest is Providence.

Viewed in confessional terms, the closet scene inevitably begs questions about the denominational character of *Hamlet*'s world.[61] That the Ghost is a purgatorial (and therefore Catholic) creature parachuted into an otherwise Protestant dramatic world—Protestant in that Hamlet himself, like Spenser,

---

[60] On this point and the idea that Hamlet aims, in the closet scene, to 'remake his mother', cf. Adelman 1992: 31.

[61] Shakespeare's own religion and the combination of Catholic and Protestant threads which his works have been seen as embracing are discussed in general terms in Collinson 1994; Devlin 1963; Dutton, Findlay, and Wilson 2003a, b; Honigmann 1998b; G. K. Hunter 1996; Milward 1973; Mutschmann and Wentersdorf 1952; Schoenbaum 1987: 45–62; Taylor 1994: 290–5; and R. Wilson 2004.

evinces such a sharp distaste for flesh and matter—is a critical commonplace.[62] These dual possibilities persist even at the particular level in the closet scene's confessional rhetoric. Mutschmann and Wentersdorf have cited a wealth of instances of confession in Shakespeare's works as evidence of the playwright's Catholic understanding of that subject.[63] Yet it is clear that a commitment to confession in particular, and to penance more generally, actually retained the same powerful position in Reformed spirituality as it had long done in Catholic traditions, Calvin for one claiming the precedent of James 5: 16 in support of such practices (*Institutes*, 3. 4. 12).[64] In his *Babylonian Captivity* Luther (though no fan of the Epistle of James) also encouraged the custom of making auricular confessions—in this case to friends, elsewhere to a pastor—as a way of relieving oneself when burdened with a sense of sin: 'a man's secret sins are forgiven him when he makes a voluntary confession before a brother ... asks for pardon and mends his ways .... Christ manifestly gave the power of pronouncing forgiveness to anyone who had faith in Him .... [Hence] one who has done wrong [may] lay bare his sin ... and beg absolution ... from the mouth of his neighbour.'[65] Calvin, similarly, advised Christian brothers, 'we sholde laye our weakenesse one in an others bosome to receiue mutuall counsel, ... compassion and ... comforte' (*Institutes*, 3.4.6).[66] Auricular confession was advocated accordingly by Tyndale, Cranmer, Latimer, and Ridley.[67] For the Protestant auditor, they argued, it was a work of charity first to hear such confessions and then (in Jewel's words) to offer one's afflicted brethren 'godly advice and earnest prayer'.[68] Indeed, Reformed faiths really only differed from Catholicism in their approach to confession in that they insisted that it was neither a sacrament nor the exclusive preserve of ordained priests. Hence, in practice, in so far as the vocabulary of Act III, Scene iv of *Hamlet* resonates with confessional and penitential idioms, it has as much in common with Protestant texts on this theme as it does with Catholic ones.

Hamlet opens the closet scene by announcing his intention to 'set ... up a glass' wherein Gertrude may 'see the inmost part' of herself (III. iv. 19–20),

---

[62] Traces of Catholicism in *Hamlet*, especially in the treatment of the Ghost, are discussed in Devlin 1963; Dutton, Findlay, and Wilson 2003*b*: 143–60; and Greenblatt 2001: 232–7; 244–8. Hamlet's nonetheless Protestant temperament is explored in Matheson 1995: 390–7, Gallagher and Greenblatt 2000: 152–62; and Greenblatt 2001: 240–4. Hankins (1941: 197–9) resists the common assumption that Old Hamlet's dying 'Unhouseled, dis-appointed, unaneled' (I. v. 77) should be taken to indicate that he died bereft of *Catholic* last rites, this on the grounds that Protestantism accorded the priest a similar healing role at his parishioners' deathbeds. Greenblatt (2001: 252–4), meantime, offers an attractive explanation for the co-presence of Catholic and Protestant forces within the play.

[63] Mutschmann and Wentersdorf 1952: 218–21.    [64] Calvin 1561: ff. 141$^{r-v}$.

[65] Luther 1961: 321.    [66] Calvin 1561: f. 139$^r$.    [67] Frye 1963: 159–62.

[68] Quoted in ibid. 160.

and after the interruption of a brief stabbing, he proceeds with that purpose. The emphasis in much of what follows is then on ocular experience. He urges his mother to 'Look' on the images of his father and uncle (l. 53) and to 'See' the discrepancy between them (l. 55), albeit that the contrast he then develops is only halfway realizable in the mind's eye. Old Hamlet's ethereal qualities (to which he turns first) are all intangible, demanding imaginative idealization. He is said to have had the hair of Hyperion, the forehead of Jove, eyes 'like Mars', qualities none of which can be visualized in *objective*, concrete forms, any more than one could really *see* the 'grace' on the late king's brow (ll. 55–9). According to this retrospective portrait, Old Hamlet, even in life, assumed the characteristics of a transcendent being, one who existed above the reach of fleshly corruption. Hamlet images Claudius, by contrast, with all the graphic particularity of the mutable world. The usurper is likened, with vivid precision, to a 'mildewed ear' of corn rubbing against its neighbour and spreading—'blasting'—contagious influence all around (ll. 64–5). Later he is figured as a common thief filching the royal diadem 'from a shelf' (ll. 99–101). More immediately, though, he also becomes a barren 'moor', this in contrast to his brother's 'fair mountain' (ll. 66–7). It is with this last image that the moralizing gaze turns inward, the Prince suddenly forcing Gertrude to visualize herself as the dumb quadruped which once fed on fair Old Hamlet and now fattens itself on that moor (ll. 66–7). With this inward turn, Hamlet drives home his earlier imperative to the queen to take up a mirror and see herself: 'Have you eyes? / ... / ... Ha, have you eyes ?' (ll. 65–7). By such means—and not least through a shrill censuring of her sexuality—he tries to propel her towards confession.

In Q2, this same kind of analysis is also given an abstract inflection, Hamlet supposing from Gertrude's extraordinary behaviour that she must have suffered an apoplexy (ll. 71–6), a wide-ranging failure of the senses of the sort elsewhere described by Falstaff (*2 Henry IV*, i. ii. 109–24). More specifically, she is imagined to have lost the use of all the senses bar taste (the most bestial of the five), since if she still had even one of the other four at her disposal, she would surely be unable to tolerate Claudius's intimacy:

> Eyes without feeling, feeling without sight,
> Ears without hands or eyes, smelling sans all,
>
> .    .    .    .    .    .    .    .
>
> Could not so mope.
>
> (iii. iv. 78–81)[69]

---

[69] The mention of '*hands* or eyes' in the second line here suggests that the first line's 'feeling' refers to touch in particular.

Hamlet's subsequent Q2 attempt to blame 'custom' for Gertrude's current predicament, since, as noted earlier, it 'all *sense* doth eat, / Of habits devil' (ll. 162–3), reinforces again the sensuous focus. The word 'sense' here means consciousness, but it also retains more specific connotations of the five senses because 'custom' (or bad habit), adopting the lowliest of these five (taste), '*eats*', by implication, precisely the other four. Critics generally assume that Hamlet's comments here about apoplexy, feeling-less eyes, and eaten senses were cut from the Folio (F) version of iii. iv because they were deemed to be either prolix or ungainly.[70] However, they may actually have been excised because their intellectual tone distracted from a feature which Shakespeare or his company wanted to accentuate to the full: namely, the otherwise predominantly graphic, sensuously engaged nature of Hamlet's language. After all, the one thing left behind when the lines cited above (ll. 71–6 and 78–81) are cut is an *image* of Gertrude playing at blindman's buff (ll. 76–7)—an intensely visual realization of the psychological concepts expressed either side of it in the Q2 text. Clearly, Hamlet's primary purpose throughout the first half of this scene is to re-engage his mother's apoplexed senses (partly so that she may despise Claudius; partly so that she may learn to view the world with the same distaste as Hamlet himself does: in sum, so that she may confess to herself her sin and repent of it); but given that engineering such re-engagement is his aim, there would be an obvious appropriateness in adapting his idiom, excising it of all abstract content, to make it as intrusively vivid as possible. That the Prince's language does indeed have this stimulating effect is clear from Gertrude's reaction to his first rant:

> O Hamlet, speak no more.
> Thou turn'st my eyes into my very soul,
> And there I see ... black and grainèd spots ...
>
> .     .     .     .     .     .     .     .
>
> Oh speak to me no more.
> These words like daggers enter in my ears.
>
> (ll. 88–95)

Hamlet's impact is registered precisely in terms of reactivated senses. He achieves here what seemed to him the impossible goal of Act ii, Scene ii, to 'amaze indeed / The very faculties of eyes and ears', 'cleaving' those ears 'with horrid speech' (ii. ii. 514–18).

Returning the sinner to a true sight of herself is a common theme in both Catholic and Protestant confessional literature. Hence, for the former, Wynkyn de Worde's *Ordynarye of Crystyanyte* argues that the devout, in

---

[70] Shakespeare 1985: 12–13; John Jones 1995: 85.

embarking on their confessions, should use the Commandments 'as ten myrrours' against which to measure the spiritual health of their souls.[71] Equally, for the latter, Frye quotes various Protestant divines all of whom figure the moral law as a mirror which reveals 'the spots in our faces'—this, Gertrude's own idiom.[72] Erasmus's *Lytle Treatise* on confession and Arias's *Litle Memorial* push this theme further, Erasmus urging the 'ghostly father' to '[set] the whole man ... forthe before his owne iyes leauynge none of all the secrete corners of his mynde ... vnsearched'.[73] Catholic spiritual manuals such as Roye's *Doctrinal of Sapyence* and Myrc's *Instructions for Parish Priests* also advise the confessor to devote a section of the confession to inspecting ways in which each of the five senses may have induced the parishioner to sin. As Myrc puts it, 'Hast thow spende thy wyttus fyue / To goddus worschype? telle me blyue.'[74] Richard Greenham offers, in his repeated efforts to bring his brethren to 'the sight' of their sins, a more sophisticated approach to this same focus.[75] He argues in his *Meditations on Proverbs 4* that the senses are subservient to the heart: whatever the latter is preoccupied with, the senses will also focus upon, this to such an extent that they may lose their true sensory capacity (their ability to register the realities of the world): 'hence ... there be oftentimes great sounds & much noyse: yet because our eares doe attend vpon our hearts ... we heare not the sounds .... Wee see not goodly sights ... when they bee ... offered ... because our eyes are set vpon that thing, about which the heart is occupied.'[76] Greenham's comment in particular resonates with Hamlet's description of Gertrude's problem, but it is clear from much of the foregoing material that, in a wider sense, Hamlet the confessor's sensuous focus is not without its precedents.

What the Prince himself does not *see* amidst these proceedings is Polonius's corpse bleeding all over the stage. As he stands over his mother, haranguing her to open her eyes, it is tempting to imagine the blood lapping at his ankles. That he is oblivious to this is a measure of his own blinding passion, the zeal—indeed, the madness—with which he sets about 'wringing' his mother's 'heart' (III. iv. 35). What Hamlet implicitly interprets as moral fervour within himself seems more like a vicious, frenzied passion to Gertrude and the audience, especially so when the son replies to his mother's pleas to relent (ll. 88, 94) with such excited intensifications of his attack as the following:

> Nay, but to live
> In the rank sweat of an enseamèd bed,

---

[71] Anon. 1502: sig. X2ᵛ. Cf. Hankins 1941: 206, 208.       [72] Frye 1984: 164.
[73] Erasmus 1535: sigs. E1ᵛ–2ʳ. Cf. Arias 1602: 103.
[74] Myrc 1902: 40–1. Cf. Duffy 1992: 59–61.
[75] Greenham 1599: 257. I am grateful to Jason Yiannikkou for alerting me to this source.
[76] Ibid. 194.

Stewed in corruption, honeying and making love
Over the nasty sty.

(ll. 91–4)

Where Gertrude complains that her eyes *have* now seen into her soul (ll. 89–91), he responds here with perhaps the most vivid, visceral imagery of the entire play—imagery which highlights his interest in his mother's sexuality. The aim of such language, couched in minute particulars, seems to be to force her into perceiving fleshliness in the same disgusted terms as does Hamlet, to foist his ascetic way of viewing things upon her. Further to this, when Gertrude pleads again for release, he replies by renewing his attack on Claudius (ll. 96–101). The Prince seems positively to *feed* on his mother's shame, enjoying the feeling of bringing her to self-knowledge and purgation. In his own mind, though, all this is presumably an objective process of lancing bodily sores before Gertrude loses all touch with heavenly 'grace' (l. 145). Indeed, for her to dismiss Hamlet's actions as mere madness is—in another layered image of the self—

... but [to] skin and film the ulcerous place,
Whiles rank corruption, mining all within,
Infects unseen.

(ll. 148–50)

Once again language of this kind finds its counterparts in confessional handbooks. Erasmus casts the confessor as a 'surgean' to whom the sick must present the 'boyles' and 'botches' which afflict even their bodies' most 'priuie partes'.[77] Hankins, similarly, cites Hooker, for whom proper contritional suffering 'renteth the heart'.[78] Greenham, still more so, relishes this, the violence of his clinical task. In *Sweet Comfort for an Afflicted Conscience* he urges ministers to tent, purge, and sear the wounds of sin in preference to merely offering 'sugred consolations' which will 'for a while ouer-heale the conscience'.[79] Just as

we are loath to haue ... our sores rifled ... and lanced; ... so we are hardly brought to haue ... our sinnes ... ripped vp; but would still haue them plaistered with sweet promises.... [S]ome sores may seeme to close and skin vp apace, yet they proue worse, and being rotten still at the core ... haue aboue a thin skinne, and vnderneath dead flesh. In like manner, we would cloake ... our sinnes ... but it is more sound Chirurgerie to ... pearce our consciences with the burning iron of ... Law ... least that a skinne pulled ouer ... , we leaue the ... corruption vncured vnderneath.[80]

---

[77] Erasmus 1535: sig. B7ʳ.      [78] Hankins 1941: 207, 209.
[79] Greenham 1599: 255–6.       [80] Ibid. 245.

To that medical idiom Greenham adds the hint of a sexual one, more pronounced than in Erasmus: this invasive surgery is a 'touching', 'boring and pearcing' of 'our most priuie' parts.[81] However, close though Greenham's language is to Hamlet's talk of 'filming ulcerous places', my suggestion is not, here, that Shakespeare is alluding to him. The point is, rather, that Hamlet mimics a general discourse,[82] and does so because he conceives of himself as Gertrude's moral and religious reformer. In so doing he aligns himself with the most ascetic dimensions of *The Faerie Queene*. Red Crosse's crucifixion of the fleshly principle within him is, after all, constructed using this same confessional rhetoric. As a festering sore 'Close creeping twixt the marrow and the skin', the knight's sin-encrusted, 'superfluous flesh' must be dieted until it rots enough to be plucked out 'with pincers firie whot' (*Faerie Queene*, I. x. 25. 4–26. 9). During this same process Penance also whips Red Crosse, Remorse nips at his heart, and Repentance drenches his body in salt water so as to cleanse it of 'filthy blots' (27. 1–7). Just how much 'flesh' is deemed 'superfluous' here remains nicely ambiguous, but the phrase clearly parallels Hamlet's own anti-corporeal outlook.

Greenham, then, and Spenser would seem to endorse the Prince's moral project, and certainly critics like Hankins and Frye credit Hamlet's supposedly Lutheran claim that he is being 'cruel only to be kind' in forcing his mother to face herself (III. iv. 179).[83] In reality, though, any audience watching the play will find it hard to see Hamlet as anything other than frenzied and passionate at this juncture. Rather than being endorsed by the likes of Greenham, his conduct actually brings the *latter*'s moral outlook into question, exposing not the lucid rationality but the potential madness of that ascetic extremism to which discourses founded on a vilification of the flesh lend themselves. Not surprisingly, one need look no further than Florio's Montaigne to find confirmation that sceptical awareness of such follies was commonplace in Shakespeare's period. In 'Of Drunkennesse', for instance, Montaigne follows Plutarch in speculating that the impulse which prompted Brutus and Torquatus mercilessly to kill their own children was not, as they imagined, some high rational principle of 'virtue', but rather 'some ... passion'.[84] Metrodorus, Anaxarchus, and more recent Christian martyrs' positive enthusiasm to suffer torture at tyrants' hands is likewise said to denote 'furie' or madness, a displacement of the mind from its 'wonted seate', rather than wisdom. In Montaigne's view the ascetic impulse 'to lie vpon the hard ground, ... pull out [one's] eyes, ... cast ... riches

---

[81] Greenham 1599: 247, 261.

[82] It is striking in this context that Sidney describes Senecan tragedy as the form which characteristically 'openeth the greatest wounds, and showeth forth the ulcers that are covered with tissue' (quoted in Sinfield 1992: 215).

[83] Frye 1984: 164.          [84] Montaigne 1603: 202.

into the sea, [or] seeke for paine'—the very impulse exhibited by Isabella in *Measure for Measure*—is always 'the action of an excessive virtue'; and all such actions '*beyond [man's] ordinarie limits*' provoke '*sinister interpretations*' more readily than they do rational ones.[85] Hence, musing on those pious figures who stress the 'violent' combats which they endure against 'provocations of the flesh', Montaigne observes wryly that he 'admires' the (to him) 'vnknowne strangenesse and vnfelt vigor' of the temptations apparently felt by these great men just as much as he 'admires' their 'constant resistance' to these torments.[86] Those wedded to the mind in opposition to their bodies and the most humane of feelings hope, of course, to transform themselves into angels—Hamlet will later see a 'cherub' at his shoulder (IV. iii. 45)—but more often, Montaigne avers, 'they transchange themselves into beasts: in lieu of advauncing, they abase themselves'.[87] Hamlet's conduct in the closet scene—like Guyon's in the Bower of Bliss—invites precisely such uneasy considerations, and in doing so, chips away at the wider moral confidence which works like *The Faerie Queene*, Erasmus's *Enchiridion*, or Thomas Rogers's *Anatomie* might otherwise command.

The Prince, though, far from registering such reservations, pursues his instruction to its logical end, advising Gertrude how to refuse Claudius's body. Crucially, he then concludes his discourse by remarking that it has been his providential destiny to be, throughout this scene, heaven's 'scourge and minister' (III. iv. 176).[88] Here, in fact, perhaps more than at any other point in the play, Hamlet discovers a role for himself which he can confidently (and passionately) act upon—a role as confessor and moralist rather than as murderer-in-waiting. That Hamlet embraces this role with assurance is clear from the loquacity and linguistic fluency to which it provokes him. In III. iv as a whole he rises to his most sustained and systematic elaboration of themes originally broached in the Act I, Scene ii soliloquy. Thus his troubled sense of the flesh's sullied nature, a preoccupation first introduced in that initial monologue and often touched upon thereafter, positively crowds into this later scene. The 'too too *solid* flesh' of the Folio speech (I. ii. 129) reappears in III. iv as the equally wretched '*solidity* and compound mass' of the Earth itself (l. 49). Act I, Scene ii's 'flat' landscape becomes the aforementioned 'moor'. Again, in one scene as in the other, Gertrude is said to *feed* on her lovers. Act III, Scene iv, brings to a head, too, Hamlet's earlier horticultural metaphors. The 'unweeded garden' of I. ii. 135, together with the later sprig of virtue fruitlessly grafted on to 'old stock' (III. i. 116–17), prefigures the Prince's III. iv attack on Claudius as mildewed and infectious (ll. 64–5) and

---

[85] Ibid. 121, 202.　　[86] Ibid. 620.　　[87] Ibid. 664.
[88] Again the idiom is reflected in Greenham 1599: 261.

on Gertrude as one who first robs love of its rose (replacing it with a blister (ll. 42–4) ) and then (in denying her own corruption) 'spreads … compost on the weeds' of her garden-soul (ll. 152–3). Most important of all, though, past recollections of Old Hamlet likewise find their focus at this point in the action. The Hyperion of I. ii. 140 reappears as the Hyperion of III. iv. 56. The comparison between old and new kings first developed in Act I, Scene ii (ll. 139–42), and by the Ghost in Scene v (ll. 47–52), is given its most intense articulation here (III. iv. 53–71, 96–101, 136), as if previous iterations had been but rehearsals for this moment. I noted earlier that Hamlet does remember his father during the play, in a living, idealized form at least; but in practice he remembers him only long enough to remember him, here, *to* Gertrude. In reminding his mother of the man, Hamlet presents him as the symbol of an ideal but irretrievable past. His absence, now, robs the carnal present of any value and reduces the flesh to a worthless appendage better mortified than nurtured. The Prince invokes him to enforce this lesson, to exemplify, by a process of contrast, the corruption of these times. Once Old Hamlet has fulfilled that rhetorical function, once he has been displayed to Gertrude as the principal illustration in a lecture which Hamlet feels a burning need to subject her to, the old king is largely forgotten. His purpose served, Hamlet has no further reason to remember him, and does not.[89]

All these various ideas, then, are directed at Gertrude in III. iv with the aim of coercing her into seeing the world—and rejecting it—as Hamlet does. In practice, her son has been waiting, since he first lashed out at his mother in the I. ii soliloquy, to say these things to her face—to which end he has been rehearsing the various elements of this lecture (whether to himself, Ophelia, or Polonius, Rosencrantz, and Guildenstern) throughout much of the foregoing play. It is this fact which makes the last scene of the third act, with all its tempests of passion, seem like a point of culmination in the action as a whole. Yet this scene is significant, too, because in tracking Hamlet's efforts to reform Gertrude, one gets the impression that larger issues are at stake. Both the Prince's undefined sense of his own sinfulness and his general desire to save a Denmark otherwise so 'out of joint' (I. v. 189) line up behind the specific purpose to redeem his mother. The process of bringing her to repentance thus has a synecdochic value: in part, it offers Hamlet a compensation for his own sinfulness and for his inaction on other fronts; in part, it promises a wider salvation, this because Gertrude is so potent a presence in her son's consciousness that he cannot imagine any change taking place in her without

---

[89]  Greenblatt (2001: 226–7) is one of several recent critics who have charted Hamlet's process of forgetting, but his explanation for *why* it happens is insufficient. I have sought to elaborate on that question here.

that change also impacting on the world around her. To save her is to begin to save himself and Denmark—or so Hamlet implicitly imagines.


## CONCLUSIONS

In the closet scene Hamlet's ascetic passions intersect with his love for his mother to stimulate him into action: action in the sense that the Prince makes strenuous efforts both to communicate his austere sensibility to Gertrude and to secure her participation in the cleansing of her soul. Having done this (remembering his father to her along the way), Hamlet has accomplished by the end of Act III the one thing which it has most been on his mind to do since Act I, Scene ii—the one thing, perhaps, which he really wants to do.[90] Endless jockeying and self-coercion notwithstanding, Hamlet never hereafter elicits any other ruling passion from himself. He neither renews nor otherwise reinvigorates his desire for, and interest in, vengeance. Once III. iv is over, he simply falls back into inactivity, particularly in F, where the removal of the anxious Act IV, Scene iv soliloquy leaves him seeming all the more acquiescent. In both Q2 and F the Prince does retain enough guilt about this torpor (his failure to take vengeance upon Claudius) to need to justify it, but the form of justification which he adopts—identifying himself as one privy to, and the subject of, heaven's ordinance (v. ii. 48)—is merely continuous with the earlier Act III fantasy of casting himself in a religious role. That pose, comforting because it keeps alive the pretence of vengeful 'readiness', now becomes an excuse for passivity, so that Hamlet's experiment with Senecan passion simply ossifies and turns dormant. Even in the final, shambolic moments of the play, it is not a brooding, long-invoked fury for his father's loss which drives Hamlet to kill Claudius, but rather a moment of impetuous jealousy on his mother's behalf. If, then, the Senecan pose stagnates, what of the Prince's other, more truly passionate obsession (his contempt for the tawdry inadequacies of the flesh)? On the face of it, this at least receives more frequent, overt attention in Acts IV and V, catalysed as it is by thoughts of Polonius's putrefaction. Hamlet ghoulishly reflects that the counsellor's corpse, 'compounded ... with dust' (IV. ii. 6), will now be food for worms (IV. iii. 19–29), and this time it is the body's sebaceousness which attracts his prurient attention: 'we fat all creatures else to fat us, and fat ourselves for maggots. Your fat king and your lean beggar

---

[90] Whilst it is overstating the matter to say that this scene *entirely* 'liberates' Hamlet 'from the burden of ... outrage that has weighed him down since the [play's] beginning' (Mercer 1987: 227), there is a broad truth to Mercer's point. The Prince is indeed 'now in some measure returned to himself'.

is but variable service' (ll. 21–2). Yet, as before in Act III, Scene iv, there is nothing new in this disillusionment: it only reiterates earlier preoccupations. Polonius's 'dust' recalls man's 'quintessence of dust' (II. ii. 290). The equation of kings and beggars repeats Hamlet's previous comparison of the same (II. ii. 250–1). The podgy Prince's[91] talk of fatness likewise chimes with earlier sniping at 'the fatness of these pursy times' and their 'bloat King' (III. iv. 154, 183). Furthermore, what Polonius's corpse provokes, the graveyard scene then regurgitates. The corruptibility of the flesh is brought closer to home as Hamlet recoils from the stench of Yorick's skull, but otherwise he simply reiterates his 'dust and worms' thought pattern, this time imagining how the dust of Alexander the Great (a man notably *sweet*-smelling in life) might one day form the loam stopper of a beer barrel. The overriding impression generated by these reveries is of Hamlet simply working new material into familiar conclusions.[92] A morbidity which began as something urgent and passionate—tied, not least, to suicidal impulses—becomes (after its airing in III. iv) the product, rather, of an automatic, even flippant wit. Put another way, where previously Hamlet had turned his wit to the task of expressing his anti-corporeal passion, in Acts IV and V the opposite is just as likely to prove true, the Prince making the motifs of that passion simply the vehicles for indulging his wit. Horatio is rightly sceptical about such 'curious' thinking (V. i. 174). In this context too, then, as with the pursuit of vengeful fury, the intensity and sense of dramatic movement of the closet scene give way to stasis and downright repetition. Indeed, it is tempting to reflect (in light of such repetitiousness) that if Spenserian heroes *do* the same deeds time and again, the Prince of Denmark devotes his energies to just *saying* the same things *ad nauseam*. Watching *Hamlet* is consequently rather like watching a series of rehearsals: rehearsals for a vengeful murder which (as an act of vengeance) never quite happens, and rehearsals for a conversation which, once completed, leaves the hero with nothing more (or at least nothing new) to say.

In Q2's Act IV, Scene iv, Hamlet finds himself trapped between admiration for the heroic pugnacity of Fortinbras and a lingering suspicion that the Norwegian's cause, a fight over 'a little patch of ground' (IV. iv. 18), is absurd. On the one hand, to 'debate the question of this straw' (l. 26) is, for Denmark's ascetic Prince, a distinctly fleshly vanity, one which Hamlet instinctively figures in corporeal terms as an 'impostume' (l. 27). On the other hand, this would-be avenger sees that 'Rightly to be great' is precisely to find quarrel even 'in a straw / When honour's at the stake' (ll. 53–6). By that light Fortinbras is

---

[91] See V. ii. 264–5.

[92] In saying this, I disagree with those who detect in the graveyard scene a transformation in Hamlet's sensibility. See, e.g., Hunt 1992: 188–9.

the man that Hamlet must emulate. As he himself puts it, 'Examples gross as earth exhort me' (l. 46). Yet therein lies the problem: the very earth does exhort Hamlet to fight, and he feels it; but at the same time matter '*gross as earth*' is also, always, what most disgusts him, what he would least heed. In the long run disgust for grossness triumphs over honourable pugnaciousness. The loathsome mutability of the flesh made so graphic in the graveyard scene reduces even the greatest of heroes, Alexander, to something worthless ('To what base uses we ... return' (v. i. 171) ). Viewed against so absolute a perspective, the heroism of Fortinbras loses its value. Hamlet, overwhelmed by a distaste for corporeality, can thus no longer credit the heroic ideals of reputation and greatness of soul on which anger and vengeance hinge. He cannot be both ascetic and a Senecan villain, and ultimately he favours the former. However, in first struggling between the two for most of the play, he exposes, at both ends so to speak, the limitations of Elizabethan moral thought. If Hamlet echoes much of the revulsion for the flesh and its passions already seen in Erasmus, Rogers, or Perkins, that traditional moralizing nevertheless seems, in his hands, more mad than rationalist, more disturbing than laudable. An otherwise commonplace vilification of the flesh becomes, in the half-light of this tragedy, something unhealthily oppressive (rather than morally uplifting). And yet Hamlet also aspires to be possessed by passion, by the kind of Senecan fury which makes violent action possible and lends it its own peculiar magnificence, and that aspiration issues its own challenge to contemporary ideals of governance. It is not one with which the audience straightforwardly identifies. On the whole, few of us long to be bloody avengers, and Hamlet's predicament, like those of most Renaissance tragic heroes, is a limit case. But the feeling he taps into and epitomizes at an exaggerated extreme is simply the more general inclination to act in ways which may be passionate and emphatic (and which thus do not conform to the norms of psychomachic ethics), but which nevertheless seem proper and fulfilling to the agent. In this respect Hamlet plays upon the desire precisely *not* to be rational, but rather, to be something never dreamt of in Spenser's philosophy. That *indulgence* of the passions (together with Shakespeare's implicit critique of ascetic moralizing) will play its way out throughout subsequent chapters of this book.

# 4

---

# Renaissance Tragedy and the Fracturing of Familiar Terms

*The Faerie Queene* devotes considerable attention to the struggle which man faces in conforming to the rationalist values of humanist ethics, but for all that, it nevertheless affirms the worth of engaging in that struggle. *Hamlet*, by contrast, calls such assumptions into question. My aim in this chapter is to demonstrate that three other late Elizabethan and early Jacobean tragedies did likewise, staging a still more searching interrogation of the norms of Elizabethan governance as they resonated against the changing cultural circumstances of the new century. Thus *Julius Caesar* is read here as a study in the power and complexity of self-delusion, one which casts doubt over man's capacity ever truly to know himself, and thus to govern himself according to rational principles. Shakespeare's Roman play acquires this force, I suggest, against the wider background of a growing taste for Montaignian introspection, a trend which began with the circulation of Florio's Montaigne and was stimulated, not least, by the rediscovery of ancient scepticism in the later 1500s. Chapman's *Bussy D'Ambois*, though, challenges Tudor moral ideals on quite another axis. Refracting the turn-of-the-century interest in humoural psychology and physiology, it presents as wholly ungovernable some of the very things which Spenser would quell: man's humours, his corporeal passions, and his viscerally felt sexual instincts. These bodily powers are (such is Bussy's tragedy) simply too potent to contain. A third concern which again sapped confidence in psychomachic ideals is given dramatic expression in *Troilus and Cressida*, the final play analysed in this chapter (and one which strikingly anticipates Hobbes's thought). *Troilus*, which is read here as a resonant accompaniment to the cupidity of Elizabeth's *fin-de-siècle* court, probes the influence wielded by self-interest and subjectivity in shaping human actions (this again in defiance of principled self-governance). This play illustrates, too, the colonizing and levelling effect which new idioms of mercantile capitalism were exerting over other frameworks of evaluation at this time.

These, then, are some of the axes on which Spenser's model of governance came to be challenged in the early 1600s, some of the bases on which Renaissance drama paved the way for a reconfiguration of the moral imagination in the next generation. In a sense, later university playwrights and devotional poets would each recognize the desirability of according the passions a positive role in their ideals of moral consciousness, precisely because the irrepressibility of those affections—and thus the inadequacy of Stoicism, for example—had first been demonstrated in plays such as these. Likewise, Hobbes's generation would find themselves able to reimagine human psychology in terms diametrically opposed to the psychomachic assumptions of their Elizabethan predecessors, in part because the likes of Chapman had first figured the body as an eruptive, volcanic presence capable of tearing through the soul and realigning the latter on its own terms. My point is not to insist that, say, Herbert or Hobbes was directly influenced by the particular playwrights discussed here, but simply to suggest that, in fashioning new idioms within which to construct accounts of human nature, these dramatists made it possible for others to surpass their achievement and to reconstruct man's moral psychology in yet more radical ways. This, then, is the broad significance of the works discussed below.

## SELF-DELUSION AND THE CORRUPTION OF REASON'S AUTHORITY

Even in an essay otherwise as consistently Stoical as his 'Taste of Goods and Evilles' piece, Montaigne makes room for some Ciceronian[1] scepticism about the integrity of Posidonius's constancy. If the gravely ill Posidonius is so indifferent to pain, Montaigne asks, why, in mid-conversation, does he stop to exclaim, '*Paine, do what thou list, I shall never be drawne to say ... thou art an evill*': 'if the pangs thereof move him not ..., why breakes he off?'[2] The Stoics, of course, allowed that their sage might feel initial physical 'agitations' or mental shocks (*De Ira* 2. 3–4).[3] He might sigh, cry, or get an erection. But the true Stoic's mind would never 'assent' to these promptings. No sustained, passionate impulse would be generated from them, since these 'first motions' would be dismissed as responses to 'things indifferent'.[4] Reason's governance of the self would not, therefore, be disrupted.[5] This subtlety,

---

[1] Montaigne 1991: 57 n. 18.    [2] Montaigne 1603: 130.    [3] Seneca 1620: 531.
[4] Ibid. 532.    [5] Nussbaum 1994: 374, 380–1; Sorabji 2000: 66–75, 375–84.

registered in Lipsius's *De Constantia*,[6] was understood, too, by Montaigne: he cited blinking, blushing, and other such instincts as 'light marks' of Nature's ineradicable 'aucthoritie', yet made 'staying ... [the] first motions of [his] perturbations' (such that the soul would continue to know itself, even in pain) an important tenet of his ideal of governance.[7] The point here, though, in the *Essayes*' attack on Posidonius, is that the latter does not merely blink, as it were, but implicitly—unwittingly even—'assents' to his pain. Pain becomes a real preoccupation within his consciousness; hence his outburst which affirms precisely what it seeks to deny, and thereby undermines the integrity of the philosopher's Stoic pretensions. Posidonius's Stoicism is, as Montaigne puts it elsewhere, 'more verball then essentiall', the product of self-delusion rather than pure reason.[8] Not only that; the same is also true of Seneca. For all that the Roman philosopher aspired to Stoic tranquillity and, in that spirit, presented himself as viewing death with equanimity, Montaigne detects a contrary tendency buried within his physical bearing and literary style: 'To see the strugling endevours which *Seneca* giveth himselfe, to prepare ... against death; to see him sweate with panting ..., sheweth that himselfe was fervent and impetuous ..., that hee was pressed by his adversary.'[9] 'What wee beleeve', Montaigne notes of such self-contradictory cases, we simultaneously 'beleeve it not'.[10]

Driven by their sometime commitment to scepticism,[11] the *Essayes* brim with examples of delusions at work in human nature, delusions which needs must undermine man's every effort at self-governance. Montaigne notes, for example, that the general aspiration to 'make a good end' is checked by each dying man's perpetually self-deceiving hope that in fact his last hour has not yet come (when in truth it has).[12] Or again, men unwittingly allow their own beliefs to be led by the desire to please their leaders.[13] So too, contrary to what we might like to imagine, the fact that we so fiercely resent being accused of lying is a measure not of our integrity, but of our secret guilt that the allegation is true. By being so properly horrified by the taint of the accusation, 'we in some sort discharge our selves of the ... imputation'.[14] Thus man 'defends himselfe' from the reality of his defects. Montaigne's interest, though, in such instances of self-delusion is really symptomatic of a larger (and again sceptical) preoccupation with motivation in the essayist's mind. He admires Plutarch, for example, primarily because the latter, more than any

---

[6] Lipsius 1939: 75.     [7] Montaigne 1603: 201, 607.     [8] Ibid. 283.
[9] Ibid. 619–20.     [10] Ibid. 360.
[11] The standard accounts of early modern scepticism remain Popkin 1979 and Schmitt 1972. On Montaigne's interest in this, see Popkin 1979: ch. 3; Tuck 1993: 45–64.
[12] Montaigne 1603: 352.     [13] Ibid. 605–6.     [14] Ibid. 386.

other ancient bar Tacitus, emphasized motives before actions.[15] Plutarch's inward turn provides the starting point for a similarly introspective focus in Montaigne's own work, one of which the Frenchman became increasingly conscious as he drafted successive editions of the *Essais*. In the A Text of 'De l'Exercitation', for instance, having recorded in meticulous detail a near-death experience occasioned by his being thrown from his horse, Montaigne is then content to append to that description some conventional instruction on the art of dying. So pleasant was it to languish ('m'alanguir') on the edge of mortality, he says, that afterwards he found himself inured ('s'aprivoiser') to all fear of death and ready to embrace it when it should come.[16] By the time he came to revise this passage for the C Text though, after years of brooding on Sextus Empiricus and Lucretius (and thus on the limits of rationality and self-understanding), the personal significance of this episode had clearly changed. On subsequent reading, Montaigne finds himself struck more by the subtle introspection in his A Text description of the instant of apparent death than he is by any instructive moral which that event might convey, and it is therefore the virtuous complexity of that introspective activity itself which C emphasizes:

Nous n'avons nouvelles que de deux ou trois anciens qui ayent battu *ce* chemin .... Nul depuis ne s'est jetté sur leur trace. C'est une espineuse entreprise, et plus qu'il ne semble, de suyvre une alleure si vagabonde que celle de nostre esprit; de penetrer les profondeurs opaques de ses replis internes; de choisir et arrester tant de menus airs de ses agitations. Et est un amusement nouveau et extraordinaire .... Il y a plusieurs années que je n'ay que moy pour visée à mes pensées, que je ne ... estudie que moy .... Il n'est description pareille en difficulté à la description de soy-mesmes, ny certes en utilité.[17]

This late addition articulates what was clearly an emergent interest as the *Essais* evolved: namely, Montaigne's growing preoccupation with the theatre of self-consciousness. That focus took him further into the soul's 'replis internes'—what Florio termed the 'winding cranks' of inwardness—than Plutarch had ventured. But, crucially, the awareness of psychological complexity which it brought with it made the ideals of rationalist governance seem increasingly unrealizable.[18] How could one achieve mental autonomy if one had to contend with such a murky web of motive forces?

---

[15] On Plutarch see ibid. 240; on Tacitus, ibid. 563.     [16] Montaigne 1952: ii. 46, 50.

[17] Ibid. ii. 50–1. A similar shift of focus away from particular themes to a broader methodological point is apparent in the contrast between the A and C Text versions of 'Of Democritus and Heraclitus' (1991: 337–40).

[18] Montaigne 1603: 219. For an account of the limits of Plutarch's treatment of interiority, latterly in contrast to Montaigne's, see C. Marshall 2000: 74–80, 83–7.

'Of the Inconstancie of our Actions' and the 'Apologie for Sebond' expand
on this problem. In both Montaigne, sketching the vagaries of the soul,
comes to realize that man is physiologically and psychologically incapable of
virtuous constancy. Hence, in the former essay he notes that our deeds—our
own as much as other men's—are often mutually contradictory, guided by
incompatible beliefs. Willingly or not, most individuals vacillate so much that
it would be fanciful to identify any one principle as the ruling force of a given
person's self, to frame him into 'a constant ... solide contexture'.[19] The more
honest method by which to judge a man's conduct is in its detail, 'part by
part', inferring motives and intentions only from a contextual understanding,
from a sense of the 'next circumstances' either side of each act.[20] This nuanced
approach to the measuring of inwardness is necessary because man is in truth
driven by fluctuating 'humours' and ever-shifting passions:

> Our ordinarie manner is to follow the inclination of our appetite, this way and
> that ... according as ... occasions doth transport-vs: we never think on what we would
> have; but at the instant we would have it: and change as that beast that takes the colour
> of the place wherein it is layd .... He whom you saw yesterday so boldly-venturous,
> wonder not if you see him a dastardly meacocke to morrow ...: for either anger or
> necessitie, company or wine, ... might rowze-vp his hart .... It is [not] so framed by
> discourse or deliberation.[21]

The 'Apologie' supplements these arguments with the consciously sceptical
observation that though, at a given instant, we may hold rigorously to
individual judgements, we later find ourselves holding with similar conviction
quite contrary views; and these too, in turn, we may come to judge as false.
Reason in man is nothing more than that 'shew of discourses, which every
man deviseth or forgeth in himselfe: That reason, of whose condition, there
may be a hundred, one contrarie to another, about one selfe same subject.'[22]
Again, the cause of such cognitive mutability is the body's 'motions',[23] each
of which by turn 'possesseth' the individual, shaping reason in line with the
current moment's passions and humours.[24] Hence magistrates, when incensed
by a private jealousy, tend to judge the accused more harshly than they would
otherwise do, and Montaigne himself concedes that Michel 'fasting ... finds
[his] selfe' to be quite different from Michel 'full-fed'.[25]

The conclusion to draw from this is that since the self is harlequin in nature,
'framed of flappes and patches, ... of [a] shapelesse and diverse ... contexture';
since, too, 'there is as much difference found betweene vs and our selves' over
time 'as there is betweene our selves and others', the man who would discover
'by what ... springs [his] motions stirre' must commit himself to constant,

---

[19] Montaigne 1603: 193.      [20] Ibid. 193–4.      [21] Ibid. 194–5.      [22] Ibid. 328.
[23] Ibid. 327.      [24] Ibid. 328.      [25] Ibid. 327–8.

probing introspection.[26] It is not sufficient to finger the surface of the self (as Screech's creative translation puts it), or to look upon the latter in exclusively approving terms, as those do who view 'themselves as a third person'.[27] Rather, man must thoroughly search the fluxive qualities of his nature, moment by moment, for human constancy (even at its best) can never be more than '*a languishing ... wauering dance*'[28] —just as human virtue, far from being pure, must always encompass 'sundry byasses, ... bendings and elbowes' in order to accommodate itself to our 'imbecilitie'.[29]

Montaigne's critique of those who view themselves approvingly and in the third person provides an apt framework with which to approach *Julius Caesar*, a play wherein the lead character figures himself as a republican rationalist and, latterly, as a Stoic. Brutus, like Hamlet, suffers 'hideous dreams' and an 'insurrection' within as he traverses the 'interim' between 'the first motion' and the 'acting' of his dreadful task (II. i. 63–9); but where Hamlet fails, Brutus succeeds, temporarily at least, in rationalizing his action as the fulfilment of an ideal. He finds such idealism motive enough to press ahead with Caesar's stabbing.[30] Plutarch, focusing on that rational inspiration, takes it at face value. 'The Life of Brutus' begins by venerating its subject as one who 'framed his manners ... by the rules of vertue and studie of Philosophie'.[31] Plutarch applauds the respect for 'contrie and common wealth' which guided Brutus's conduct and makes of him someone universally esteemed, 'never ... in ... rage, nor caried away with pleasure', but driven only by such rational considerations as justice.[32] Shakespeare, by contrast, presents a more searching view of his assassin's inward 'contexture'.[33] He exploits for dramatic effect the gap between Brutus's own, at times 'third-person' self-image—that which Plutarch endorses—and the audience's impression of other 'springs' stirring him to motion. The product of that disparity of perceptions is a turn-of-the-century play which suggests that Stoicism and other rationalist philosophies are all too prone to delusion.

Shakespeare's Cassius gives us a firm grasp on the rational, political ideals at stake in Brutus's philosophy. Sounding out Casca at the end of Act I, he berates the Roman people for lacking the ancient spirit of republican *virtù*, that blend of masculine strength, courage, and civic virtue—a commitment to the furtherance of the public good—on which the health of any republic depends (I. iii. 57–8, 81–3).[34] Lamenting the prodigious growth of Caesar's

---

[26] Ibid. 197.     [27] Montaigne 1991: 426; 1603: 220.     [28] Montaigne 1603: 483.
[29] Ibid. 593. Florio's 'elbowes' (Fr. 'couddes' (Montaigne 1952: iii. 230) ) is nicely suggestive of the all too human, imbecile constable who polices the inconstant world of Shakespeare's Vienna.
[30] For further comparisons see Honigmann 2002: 54.     [31] Bullough 1957–75: v. 90.
[32] Ibid. v. 91, 101, 110.     [33] See further C. Marshall 2000: *passim*.
[34] See Skinner 1978: i. 175–80, 182. Cf. Kahn 1997: 83.

power, he asserts the need for Romans to defend themselves against tyranny (ll. 75–7, 97–9), emphasizing that to be truly 'Roman' one must uphold the rights of liberty and equality even to the point of self-sacrifice. Such talk amounts, on Cassius's part, to little more than a ventriloquizing of *Brutus*'s idealist discourse. Indeed, Cassius has a knack of alighting upon ideas inchoate in Brutus's language and giving them sharper articulation than Brutus himself can manage. He does this, for example, throughout Act i, Scene ii, when, in conversation with the Praetor, he attempts partly to tease out, partly to flesh out, the latter's idealized self-image (a self-image which will ultimately make tyrannicide seem justified). Coaxing Brutus into conceding that self-knowledge comes only by reflection, Cassius figures himself as the 'glass' which 'Will modestly discover to yourself / That of yourself which you yet know not of' (i. ii. 70–2). In doing exactly this, uncovering Brutus's 'hidden worthiness' (l. 59), Cassius has little to go on. Besides asserting his devotion to the general good (l. 87), Brutus also lets slip simply that he 'fears' the people will make Caesar king (ll. 81–2), a fear symptomatic of an aristocratically slanted, republican egalitarianism, and of a loathing of demagogy. These hints, though, are information enough for Cassius, who infers from them Brutus's preferred self-image, and promptly reflects this back to him.[35] Hence Cassius seizes on the 'honour' invoked by Brutus at i. ii. 88 and makes it his theme too, protesting that he (like Brutus) was born as free and equal as Caesar, and that the two of them dishonour themselves in submitting to Caesar's megalomania (ll. 97–8, 139–40). Such subservience is indicative of an age in which Rome has 'lost the breed of noble bloods' (l. 152), the aristocracy forgetting their ancestral commitment to republican *virtù*, just as Brutus has forgotten Lucius Junius Brutus's dedication to the same (ll. 160–2). Cassius foregrounds the principles, therefore, of an aristocratic, republican ideology, and Brutus affirms his approval of this in noting that, faced with a monarchy, 'Brutus had rather' become a rustic villager than remain a Roman citizen (ll. 173–6).[36] Brutus would never *really* countenance such self-effacement: the illocutionary force of his statement is simply to indicate that he regards embracing monarchy as even more sordid than becoming a peasant. The latter is so repellent a thought that he phrases it in Montaigne's third-person voice ('Brutus had rather')—this, a form of self-description which dramatizes and aggrandizes the self even whilst announcing its supposed abasement, but which also distances the speaking voice, the first-person 'I', from what is described, as if holding this would-be rustication in the pincers of another's grammatical personage.

---

[35] Leggatt 1988: 142.

[36] On the adequacy of this republican ideology to serve the future political needs of Rome at this moment in its history (i.e., that history as Shakespeare here presents it), see Hadfield 2004: 137–49.

Behind all of this, Cassius's actual motivation, unquestionably, is envy, not reasoned conviction: *he* espouses republican ideology only as a manipulative tool. It is less clear, though, what motivational significance the same principles have for Brutus—how far Brutus is driven by high-minded political idealism, how far, perhaps, by envy or an ambition which it is beneath his dignity to admit to himself. When he speaks of being 'Vexèd' by 'passions of some difference' (ll. 41–2), it is unclear whether he is hinting, confessionally, at an ambition which prompts him to kill, but about which he feels guilty; or is lamenting the conflict he faces between his friendly love for Caesar and his disgust for the latter's monarchical ambitions, a conflict which drives him reluctantly towards tyrannicide; or whether, on the contrary, he is saying nothing at all about motives, but is aiming, rather, just to *intimate* that his mind harbours murderous thoughts (being no more definite than that, lest Cassius prove to be a spy). Is his tellingly third-person comment, 'poor Brutus, with himself at war' (l. 48), indicative of one who would prefer only to finger the surface of his soul and is unhappy to find himself, now, having to confront complex, more inward motives; or is this just the gnomic language of someone suspicious of the figure who is seeking a confidence from him, but who is nonetheless eager to give some indication of rebellious intent? When Brutus responds to Cassius's question, 'can you see your face?', by affirming that 'the eye sees not itself / But by reflection' (ll. 53–5), Leggatt and Miles assume that he is conceding a dogma about the impossibility of achieving self-knowledge unilaterally, and is thus surrendering himself to others to define.[37] But one might equally say that Brutus here simply matches a provocative question with an evasive reply, implicitly daring Cassius to speak *his* bloody thoughts before he likewise implicates himself in rebellion.

In Act I, then, Brutus's mental state is ambiguous: his few speeches leave unspecified the degree to which his murderous intent (such as it is) is driven by republican idealism or by envy and ambition. Equally, it remains doubtful whether his reticence is the product of outward wariness or inward tension. The soliloquy at the beginning of Act II brings clarification to this, Brutus confirming to himself for the first time that Caesar must die, but swiftly adding the self-reassurance, 'I know no personal cause to spurn at him, / But for the general' (II. i. 11–12). Self-interested motives are dismissed here in the name of republican *virtù*, a rational dedication to furthering the good of the polity (or so Brutus tells himself). In the lines which follow, he struggles to reinforce this conviction. He does so, as is often noted, not by propounding

---

[37] Leggatt 1988: 142; Miles 1996: 138–9.

rational inferences, but by resorting to metaphors and comparisons.[38] Hence, having first hypothesized that Caesar, once crowned, '*might* change his nature' for the worse, Brutus next observes, by way of a supposed analogy, that bright days habitually *do* 'bring forth' adders, and then collapses these two distinct premises—possibility and probability—into one, simply asserting that the act of crowning necessarily puts a serpent's 'sting' into a man and that therefore, by implication, Caesar no longer 'might' but certainly 'will' turn poisonous once newly empowered (ll. 13–17).

In the second half of Brutus's soliloquy the frictions in his would-be rationalism are still sharper. 'Caesar may' learn to scorn others, he begins;

> Then lest he may, prevent. And since the quarrel
> Will bear no colour for the thing he is,
> Fashion it thus: that what he is, augmented,
> Would run to these and these extremities;
> And therefore think him as a serpent's egg,
>
> .   .   .   .   .   .   .   .   .
>
> And kill him in the shell.

> (ll. 27–34)

Here, as before, Brutus acknowledges that he knows not if his prophecy be true ('So Caesar *may*') but will do as if for surety. Now, though, he works harder to persuade himself of the reasonableness of such a course. Logical connectives abound in the above quotation, accentuating its putative rationality ('Then', 'since', 'thus', 'therefore'). Likewise, as if to prove to himself his own honesty, Brutus concedes that his prudence defies surface appearances, depending upon rhetoric for its appeal (ll. 28–30). More tenuously, he also skates over Caesar's exact crimes with his vague and hurried 'these and these', implicitly allowing himself to come back to such details later on the understanding that he has already grasped them in his mind's eye but must now, as a matter of urgency, push forward with the bigger picture. Such vagueness seems wilful: one suspects that if Brutus imagined exactly what atrocities Caesar was supposedly going to commit hereafter, he could not *really* reconcile these images with his own impression of Caesar's character. He could not *really* believe that his friend (whom he loves (i. ii. 84)) would be capable of such things. This last point, though, is a relatively slight indication of the process of self-outwitting underlying this speech. More significant is the preponderance of imperatives. Brutus batters himself into conviction here in a tense sequence of commands: 'prevent', 'think him', 'kill him', 'fashion it'. The last of these is

---

[38] Palmer 1970: 403–4; Vawter 1976: 215–16. For further reservations, highlighting traces here of Brutus's emulous ambition, see Kahn 1997: 91, 96, and Rebhorn 1990: 88.

as much an instruction to his own imagination, an order about how he himself must visualize Caesar, as it is a command to shape other people's perspectives. The use of the imperative is telling, because it points, again, to a mind viewing itself in the third person (as an external figure to be pushed around). Such a mode encourages the mere fingering of the soul's surface, disrupting any more searching introspection, and certainly Brutus here evades all close inspection of the adequacy of his arguments, straining, rather, to rationalize murder as a just, politically necessary act. Why this is a strain though—whether because he is evading a hidden ambition, incommensurable with his high-minded self-image, or because he faces an impossible contradiction between his ancestral conviction that all monarchs are corrupt and his loving faith in Caesar's personal nobility[39]—remains opaque. What is clear is that the soliloquy's rational pose is only superficial. In reality, the speech is fraught with tension, prone at any moment to expose the evasiveness on which Brutus's reasoning hinges.

The one thing which secures Brutus in his volatile frame of mind and eventually prompts him to embrace the conspiracy is the apparent endorsement of others. To that end, Cassius forges letters to him in which citizens affirm their faith in the Praetor's 'greatness' and urge him to live up to his name (I. ii. 315–20, II. i. 46). It is to these that Brutus turns immediately after his soliloquy, finding there the means to bolster his nerve, and having thus consolidated his sense of purpose, he then asserts with renewed conviction the rational probity of his cause. Brutus fosters his own confidence over two subsequent orations, neither of which betrays any measure of the earlier, stilted, third-person self-address. Only initially does the first of these speeches reveal any tension as Brutus reproves any notion that the conspirators might bind themselves to one another with an oath (ll. 113–39). Whereas Plutarch had simply noted that none of the murderers felt the need to swear allegiance to their cause,[40] Shakespeare dramatizes this as Brutus's particular demand. To swear a resolution would be, the Praetor argues, to imply that the abuses of the time and the sufferings of every good republican's conscience in face of Caesar's tyranny are not 'motive' enough to make men go through with

---

[39] Caesar, of course, strikes most audiences as repellent—a vain figure addicted to third-person self-dramatization ('Caesar shall forth' (II. ii. 10), 'Caesar will not come' (l. 68) ) and to an all too proud Stoicism ('I am constant as the Northern Star' (III. i. 60) ). As such, audiences might view Brutus's vision of a dangerous serpent as thoroughly prescient. Honigmann (1998a: 35–6) collates plentiful evidence to demonstrate that Caesar does threaten the republican ideal. But on the second of the two interpretations of Brutus's motivation adumbrated here, what would matter more is that *Brutus* cannot accept this fact, cannot quite believe his own rhetoric enough to relinquish his sometime admiration for the man, and therefore to embrace *whole-heartedly* his own murderous intent.

[40] Bullough 1957–75: v. 97.

the assassination (ll. 113–16). Taking an oath would amount to conceding that another stimulus was needed besides: namely, fear—each man's fear, in face of his oath, of what might follow from his letting the faction down. And to concede this would be to betray a doubt about the probity of the conspirators' purpose, a doubt about the rationality, virtue, and sufficiency of the republican cause as a justification for murder. Brutus *needs* to believe that he acts for reason's sake alone. Swearing an oath could only pollute this image of his own integrity, 'stain[ing] / The even virtue of [the] enterprise' (ll. 131–2) by betraying the principle that a Roman requires no 'other bond' than his 'honesty' and honour to make him act (ll. 123, 126).

Brutus begins this speech, then, defensively, combating an idea which threatens the composure of his self-image; but as he makes his case, he grows in confidence (like Montaigne's lawyer talking his way into robust conviction). He shifts from broken, hesitant syntax (ll. 113–18) to a defiantly interrogative mode (ll. 118–27) and then a confidently imperative one (ll. 131–5). By the end of this oration he implicitly regards himself as unassailable in his supposed rationalism, and that air of self-belief persists in his next speech on the need to make the mob understand that assassination is a medicinal purgation born of necessity, not a butchering born of envy (ll. 166, 177–80). The creature that Brutus intends to destroy is Caesar's 'spirit', the unrepublican, megalomaniac impulse within him, not the man himself, whom the Praetor still admires and would yet be friends with:

> O, that we then could come by Caesar's spirit,
> And not dismember Caesar! But, alas,
> Caesar must bleed …
>
> (ll. 169–71)

In Brutus's mind, Caesar is the necessary victim of a sacrificial process whose real target is the poison within the latter's soul (just as Desdemona is also 'sacrificed' lest, despite herself, she should 'betray more men' (*Othello*, v. ii. 70, 6) ). By such means, Brutus sanitizes the murder for himself, making it seem rationally sustainable as an act both of absolute goodness (since Rome will benefit) and of individual love (since the freshly purged Caesar will too).[41] (Again there is an anticipation of Othello, who would kill Desdemona 'and love [her] after' (ll. 18–19).) One can interpret all this (with Anson) as an act of envy which Brutus makes tolerable to himself with a saving lie.[42] However,

[41] Rebhorn, whilst underlining these motivations, identifies also an implicitly self-punitive dimension to this process (1990: 90–2, 96).

[42] Anson 1966: 27–8. Anson's suggestion that Brutus spares Antony so that he may later become the avenging hand which kills Caesar's murderer, and that Antony therefore functions in Brutus's mind as the displaced focus of Brutus's own conscience, is especially appealing.

whilst Brutus does undoubtedly delude himself, it remains plausible to imagine that he does so not on grounds of envy, but because his engrained admiration for Caesar makes the idea of killing him just as intolerable as letting him live to subvert the republic. Given such an impasse, Brutus is forced into some form of delusion which will sustain both his rational commitment to *virtù* and his desire to do good by his friend (to go on loving him even as he hates him (iv. ii. 160) ).

It follows from this that Brutus must also frame the physical action of killing as a rationally controlled process. He envisages it as driven by boldness, not wrath (ii. i. 172); as the product of an impulse which, though a passion, is nevertheless closely allied to virtue and consciously circumscribed:

> … let our hearts, as subtle masters do,
> Stir up their servants to an act of rage,
> And after seem to chide 'em.
>
> (ll. 175–7)

Brutus concedes here that he must engage in an exercise of self-outwitting.[43] He bows to the Aristotelian principle that decisive action relies on a prior passion to give it motive force.[44] The heart, determining organ of all men's passions, must induce a degree of rage in each assassin both to motivate his bloody act and to predispose his body (its organs, blood and humour supplies, and muscles) to support pugnacious action. But although this accommodation to the body may be necessary to initiate aggressive movement, the heart and soul, far from acknowledging the resultant passion as their own, must quickly check it after the fact, reasserting rational autonomy. By implication, Brutus regards even the briefest concession to the passions as a precipitous threat.

Armed with these rationalizations, Brutus urges his fellow conspirators to 'carve [Caesar] as a dish fit for the gods, / Not hew him as a carcass' (ll. 173–4). Remove but the giblets of his wicked 'spirit', and the rest of this noble joint will be fit for deific company. This final contrast, though, is surely one nice distinction too many for any audience. Brutus may dispel his own doubts with such subtleties; but for us the very extremity of his self-belief here assumes the air not of virtuous purpose, but of madness. *Pace* Levitsky,[45] there is a sense of fantasy in the idea that such boundaries—between sacrifice and butchery, rage and wrath, carving and hewing—could be observed at all (mentally speaking)

---

[43] On the broader context of this self-fashioning see Drakakis 2004: 213.

[44] An Aristotelian context seems more pertinent than the Stoic one invoked by Miles (1996: 131). In the use of the master–servant analogy amidst a discussion of controlled rage there is an echo of *NE* 1149$^a$26–31 and its textual progeny—Aristotle's comment that anger, like a hasty servant, listens to reason's command but rushes off to execute it before hearing the full order. Whereas Aristotle recounts a lapse in rational governance, though, Brutus's imagery highlights that same possibility only to affirm the reimposition of rational control.

[45] Levitsky 1973: 242–3.

in the instant of action. Brutus seems in fact to bear out, throughout Act
II, one of the few dubious aspects of his character which Plutarch *does* note:
namely, his tendency to follow 'honest' causes with a 'forcible ... vehement
perswasion that calmed not, till he had obteyned his desire'.[46] '[V]ehement
perswasion' inevitably pulls against the sobering demands of rationality. As
Montaigne observes, 'We may so seize on vertue, that ... embrac[ing] it with
an over-greedie ... desire, it ... becomes vitious': there is clearly something of
that 'savage' goodness in Brutus's project.[47] To an audience, his 'virtuous'
presentation of the assassination acquires precisely the flavour of 'passion',
'furie', or madness which Montaigne (as already noted) saw in Torquatus
and Junius Brutus's killing of their own children, and for which Plutarch also
attacked the latter in the opening words of his 'Life of Brutus'.[48]

This problem of tone persists throughout Acts II and III. Brutus seems
more bossily wilful than rational when he excludes Cicero from the conspiracy
simply because the latter is too opinionated (II. i. 149–51).[49] Likewise, his
admiration for Portia's bizarre act of self-harm only underlines the more
how distant his outlook is from any common understanding of rationality (ll.
301–2).[50] If Portia is, as she claims, the mirror-image of her husband's self (ll.
273, 281), this self-mutilating reflection (so aptly illustrative of Braden's point
that there is a structural homogeny between the Stoic ideal self and Tacitean
imperial derangement)[51] hardly augurs well for Brutus. Again, although when
killing your friend with kindness it is always hard to know how far you can feel
good about it, Brutus does seem just too complacent in addressing Antony.
He figures his recent deed as an act of noble 'pity' for 'the general wrong of
Rome' (III. i. 171) and as one of 'love' for Caesar (l. 183)—the latter, an idea
which grows on him the more he uses it, so that later he will tell the mob
that he loved Caesar as much as Caesar did him and slew him 'not that I
loved Caesar less, but that I loved Rome more' (III. ii. 21–2). These idealist
cries sit oddly alongside a frenzied orgy of stabbing—twenty-three wounds in
all—which looks distinctly more like butchery than sacrifice, and which ends
in an awkwardly primaeval blooding ritual (III. i. 106–8).

By the mid-point of the play, then, the fractures in Brutus's self-styled
virtuous rationalism are already apparent. Further indications of troubling
pressures then follow in the later acts. Act IV, first, is dominated by two
events: news of Portia's death, and Brutus's and Cassius's argument. The
latter is sparked by Brutus's accusation that Cassius has been ruling unjustly,

[46] Bullough 1957–75: v. 93. Cf. Leggatt 1988: 143–4; Palmer 1970: 405.
[47] Montaigne 1603: 97–8.        [48] Bullough 1957–75: v. 90.
[49] Honigmann 2002: 33; Leggatt 1988: 144; Rebhorn 1990: 89. Shakespeare departs from
Plutarch's account here in order to make this point of characterization.
[50] Cf. Vawter 1974: 185–6.        [51] Braden 1985: 13–15, 21–6.

a transgression significant because in Brutus's mind it brings into doubt the idealism of the assassination itself:

> Did not great Julius bleed for justice' sake ?
> What villain touched his body, that did stab,
> And not for justice ?

(IV. ii. 71–3)

This question clearly has an inward as well as an outward application. There is a sense (albeit an irrational one) in which Brutus seems to feel that his own integrity is retrospectively threatened by Cassius's conduct. He is provoked to doubt himself, and the wish not to have his thoughts prompted in that direction is, I suggest, a major factor behind his chastisement of his friend and his all too shrill reassertion of his own probity. In part at least, Brutus turns on Cassius's alleged choleric pride precisely so as to create the pretext for affirming his own constancy:

> There is no terror, Cassius, in your threats,
> For I am armed so strong in honesty
> That they pass by me as the idle wind ...

(ll. 121–3)

Cassius's choler is certainly a given in Plutarch's narrative,[52] but it is rather less evident in Shakespeare's cool Machiavellian. In this scene Brutus's pomposity and testiness are actually no less apparent than his fellow conspirator's ('Go to, you are not, Cassius' (l. 85), 'Away, slight man' (l. 90) ).[53] Indeed, a now somewhat *Caesarian* self-approval[54] comes through in Brutus's ripostes, labouring as they do the first-person pronoun. Just how fractious Brutus actually is, his pose of constancy notwithstanding, is clear from his caustic reaction to the poet who interrupts the generals (ll. 186–90, 195). Brutus's humour even prompts from Cassius a Stoic reprimand, challenging his friend to maintain his supposed rationalism: 'Of your philosophy you make no use, / If you give place to accidental evils' (ll. 197–8).[55]

One explanation for this, Brutus's tension, is that it reflects his grief for his wife. Latent agony is apparent in the terseness of this usually articulate man's riposte to Cassius: 'No one bears sorrow better. Portia is dead' (l. 199).

---

[52] Bullough 1957–75: v. 94–5, 110.

[53] *Pace* Miles (1996: 144), for whom Brutus is 'rigidly self-contained in ... face of Cassius's passion'. Levitsky (1973: 243) is surely right to discover a passionateness even in Brutus's IV. ii. 71–3 'justice' speech.

[54] Anson 1966: 29.

[55] Monsarrat's stricture (1984: 143) that we should not regard this sentiment as necessarily inspired by Stoicism, whilst strictly accurate, nonetheless seems churlish: the ideal expressed here was, in Shakespeare's time, primarily associated with Stoic *apatheia*.

But despite carrying such a burden of feeling, Brutus remains determined to present a public show of Stoic equanimity. The price he pays for that performance is to be disputatious in other contexts and on other themes; to vent, in private, the passionate intensity otherwise restrained. This first explanation, though, does not do enough to account for Brutus's crucially suggestive comment at the beginning of Act IV, Scene ii, that Cassius's unjust behaviour 'Hath given me some worthy cause to wish / Things done undone' (ll. 8–9). The idea that Brutus momentarily regrets the assassination itself points, I suggest, to a larger crisis of conscience reaching beyond the trauma of marital bereavement. Cassius's corrupt behaviour is insufficient to justify such a thought: it might be disappointing, but should not impinge on Brutus's estimation of his own motives or the probity of his own actions. The fact that, even so, it does, indicates not that Brutus now doubts the virtue of his republican cause and regicidal act, but that he does nevertheless find himself oppressed by guilt. Hints of regret are apparent in the indignation with which he contemplates mere 'villains' '*touching*' Caesar's body for their own ends (IV. ii. 72). Such language illustrates the reverential, protective instinct with which Brutus looks, still, upon Caesar—this, an instinct which, by implication, he himself has violated. Guilt comes through, likewise, in his reference to the dead man as 'Julius' (l. 71), a first-name intimacy which Brutus never otherwise demonstrates. Brutus also dubs Caesar at this point as still 'foremost man of all this world' (l. 74). It is against this background of flickering guilt that the tensions in Act IV, Scene ii, make greatest sense. Brutus must defend the image of his own moral constancy precisely so as to keep his conscience at bay. He must attack Cassius's irascibility because that anger draws out his own fear, the thought that he might lose his grip over his own passions. If Brutus's defence of his rationality thus grows shriller, it does so in proportion as his self-confidence grows thinner.

The appearance of Caesar's ghost marks a sharper sign still of the guilt suppressed in Brutus's consciousness. The spectre, Leggatt observes, has no identity of its own, calling itself rather 'Thy evil spirit, Brutus' (l. 333)—a mirror, therefore, of the latter's conscience.[56] Brutus construes it as a '*monstrous apparition*', a fiction shaped by the weakness of his own eyes (ll. 327–8) which troublingly recalls the one-time '*monstrous* visage' of conspiracy itself (II. i. 81). Tellingly, this ghost surfaces in Brutus's mind when news reaches him of *Cassius*'s death—when, in short, he finds himself bereft of a figure against whom he had hitherto tensed himself in an effort to sustain his own self-image:

---

[56] Leggatt 1988: 159. Honigmann (1988a: 34) notes that it is Shakespeare, not Plutarch, who makes the spirit resemble Caesar in particular, thereby making it indicative of Brutus's inner guilt. For an illuminating Oedipal reading of this point see C. Marshall 2000: 82.

O Julius Caesar, thou art mighty yet.
Thy spirit walks abroad, and turns our swords
In our own proper entrails.

(v. iii. 93–5)

Brutus perceives Cassius's demise as an act of vengeance on Caesar's part, implying (since the death was by suicide) that Caesar has inveigled his way into his killer's mind. This vengeance is presented, furthermore, as justified (a pushing back of hostile swords upon themselves), an image again illustrative of Brutus's sense of guilt.

Two scenes later, in Act V, Scene v, Brutus is still dwelling on this guilt-stirring ghost, and now the thought of it propels the Praetor himself into suicide. That preoccupation is, I want to argue, a new departure for Shakespeare's character at this late juncture. In discussing Cato's suicide with Cassius earlier in the act, Brutus shuns that celebrated example: 'I do find it cowardly and vile / For fear of what might fall so to prevent / The time of life' (v. i. 103–5). In a change to Plutarch, he shuns this precedent absolutely: immediately after this earlier comment there is then no instantaneous reconsideration of suicide's merits in light of present political 'dangers' (as there *is*, immediately, in the Greek source).[57] When, in Shakespeare's text, Cassius responds to Brutus's V. i resilience by threatening him with the prospect of his being led captive through Rome's streets, Brutus replies that he 'bears too great a mind' to let that happen (l. 113). Critics generally take this to be a volte-face after the criticism of Cato, a sudden concession that he will, after all, take his own life if needs be;[58] but just as obvious and more consistent a reading is that Brutus implies here only that he will be sure to fall in battle if defeat looks inevitable. Brutus, I suggest, indicates with this remark that he will die with harness on his back, not that he will play the Roman fool.

The implication of interpreting Brutus's 'too great a mind' remark as a reference to death in battle is not, obviously, that Shakespeare does *not* match Brutus's reconsideration about suicide (reported by Plutarch), but rather that in Shakespeare's version of events that reconsideration comes later—specifically with the return of the ghost and of Brutus's oppressive sense of guilt in V. v. It is then that Brutus suddenly and explicitly fixes upon the idea of self-slaughter. In part, this decision constitutes his last effort to sustain something of his Roman, rationalist self-image. He confronts suicide as the only course to take once faced with 'vile conquest' by the enemies of republicanism (v. v. 38). However, primarily, the suicide is presented not in such political terms but with reference to Brutus's wish to settle his

[57] See Bullough 1957–75: v. 119–20.      [58] e.g. Miles 1996: 114.

conscience—witness his dying words (which invoke nothing of Stoic or republican rationalism):

> Caesar, now be still.
> I killed not thee with half so good a will. [*He dies.*]
>
> (v. v. 50–1)

There is no precedent for these words in either Plutarch's 'Life of Caesar' or his 'Brutus'. Clearly, they introduce at the last a formal element of repentance, a near-explicit recognition that Caesar's murder was (though it did not seem so to Brutus at the time) the work of a corrupted 'will'; and they confirm, too, the ghost's symbolic status as an index to Brutus's bad conscience, a conscience which will now, at the eleventh hour, be stilled. Truths previously evaded, only fleetingly or half acknowledged, or suppressed under the pressure of rationalization and in pursuit of 'savage' virtue, are now finally confronted. Brutus looks, briefly, into the 'winding cranks' of his soul.

Yet, in general, such introspective honesty has always eluded this, 'the noblest Roman of them all' (l. 67). The tragedy with which Shakespeare presents his audience is the harsh fact that even this good, honest Praetor's powers of reason prove, over the course of the action, insufficient to sustain his would-be moral rationalism. Brutus is drawn unwittingly into the mystery of self-deceiving, persuading himself for a time that he kills in the name of goodness; but when that self-deception unravels, and he is forced to call what he thought a sacrifice a murder, he finds himself exposed instead to the inadequacies of his own nature—afflicted by a guilt brought on by his blindness. After *Julius Caesar* the ideals of governance and the veneration of man's supposedly transcendental reason need must seem less tenable than ever. Reason's governing authority begins to be eclipsed.

## ACCOMMODATING THE BODY

If Brutus's supposed grip on reason and virtue is delusory, we need only look to Chapman's *Bussy D'Ambois* for another example of the same phenomenon.[59] Bussy first appears as one who has turned his back on a corrupted world because its so-called great men are, to his eyes, empty Colossi, 'Heroique … without' but jugglers within (i. i. 8–9, 16–17, 87, 102–3).[60] His distaste for such characters is apparent proof of his integrity, and in both styling himself as one 'for honest Actions, not for great' (l. 124) and then ostentatiously embracing

---

[59] I focus, here, mainly on the 1607 edition of *Bussy D'Ambois* (Q1).
[60] References to Chapman's plays are to Chapman 1987.

poverty he certainly seems to assume that virtue is already his. Monsieur, though, casts doubt on this self-image, glossing the latter's withdrawal from court as the action of a melancholy malcontent who, being 'discontent with his neglected worth', has learned to scoff at others so as to console himself (ll. 47–8, 52). This proud reclusiveness sits uneasily alongside what Monsieur takes to be Bussy's *other* temperament, his choleric propensity 'to take / Fire' if once offered the opportunity of worldly advancement (ll. 49–50). According to this description, D'Ambois's supposed 'philosophy' should be viewed as an attitude 'spawned of misfortune', not as the product of principled conviction; as 'the grudge' of one who would actually prefer to set himself amongst (not against) the Colossi.[61] And indeed, there are traces of this latter, unspoken attraction in Bussy's initial remarks. His judgements that those who 'flourish' at court are as 'Cedars beaten with incessant stormes' (ll. 5–6) and that every courtier is but 'a Torch borne in the winde' (l. 18) are, for example, as heroizing as they are derogatory, suggesting resilient nobility as readily as they do folly. Even in this play's first scene, then, the virtuous pose of Chapman's hero looks questionable, and it remains so in what follows. For all that Bussy's vigour and 'great spirit' (II. i. 2) are affirmed by others, it is far from clear, given what *we* actually see of him, that we should share in this view. There is little sign of greatness of soul, for example, in Bussy's squabble with Maffé, in which each party is as haughty and choleric as the other. In the subsequent dispute with Guise, D'Ambois is more provocative than noble, deliberately stirring Guise's matrimonial jealousy so as to create a pretext for exercising his own defiance of the court's 'great ones' ('Hee's iealous by this light: are you blinde of that side Sir? Ile to her [the Duchess of Guise] againe for that' (i. ii. 94–5) ). Similarly, although the moral fervour in Bussy's Act III reverie on court hypocrisy (with its image of his hawking self 'thump[ing]' into the liver of a fat cat (iii. ii. 37) ) may be stirring, that magnificent tone quickly collapses when Guise interrupts this speech to accuse his rival of pride. Rich oratory gives way to a familiar scrap over who is the noblest of them all, and when this nerve is touched, the most that Bussy can manage is lines such as 'He is not, I am noble' (l. 76) or 'Thou liest proud Guiserd' (l. 80), squawks which would have seemed the more puerile coming from the boy-actors of St Paul's.[62] No moral principle dignifies such exchanges. Rather, D'Ambois's pugnacity betrays only an irrational and largely pointless *compulsion*, a vestige, Ide demonstrates, of Homeric heroism, but one which no longer has a place in the tawdry culture of Henry's court.[63]

Monsieur, at least, reflects accurately upon these various contradictions, demystifying Bussy's character and anatomizing its sources in a way that has

---

[61] Ide 1980: 79–80.    [62] See also Florby 1982: 147–8.    [63] Ide 1980: 81–5.

more to recommend it than most critics realize.[64] Monseiur correctly observes
in Act iii, Scene ii, that D'Ambois positively *craves* opportunities to demonstrate his *virtù*[65] ('to feede / The rauenous wolfe of [his] most Caniball valour'
(ll. 336–7) ). This is a man who will happily betray his ideals, turning 'Hackster
to any whore' in accommodating himself to King Henry's degraded court (l.
339), simply so as to have the chance of vaunting his valour. Monseiur's
further assertion that D'Ambois is blessed with 'strange gifts' by nature but
has 'no soule / Diffus'd quite through, to make them of a peece' (ll. 347–8) is
also incisive. Bussy demonstrates only a limited capacity to exercise rational
self-control. For the most part he is driven by his passions, vainglory especially
(l. 357). Crucially, though, motivating 'passion' is only an implicit term here:
the king's brother identifies the deeper motive force in Bussy as his 'humours'
(l. 349), since these, in so far as humoural temperaments have the power to
influence the heart's activity,[66] may actually initiate passions such as vainglory, and thereby induce, for example, combative behaviour. Ultimately, then,
Monseiur makes corporeal complexion the root cause of all Bussy's actions:

> Thou eat'st thy heart in vinegar; and thy gall
> Turns all thy blood to poison, which is cause
> Of that Tode-poole that stands in thy complexion;
> And makes thee (with a cold and earthie moisture,
> Which is the damme of putrification,
> As plague to thy damn'd pride) rot as thou liu'st.

(ll. 361–6)

Bussy's blood, on this analysis, is overwhelmed by the excessive quantities
of choler emitted from his gall bladder. This choler, though, evidently dena-
tures itself, since it in turn produces a 'Tode-poole' in the 'complexion'. The
toadpool is predominantly 'colde and earthie', indicating that it is melancholy
in nature (albeit with an admixture of phlegmatic 'moisture'). This is not
surprising. According to early modern pathology, when choler accumulates to
excess (as it does in Bussy), it is prone to spontaneously combust. As a result
of this development, known as adustion, the choler converts into the more
putrefying humour of melancholy.[67] Monseiur puts this phenomenon at the
heart of Bussy's identity:[68] his boundless excesses of choler are perpetually
degenerating into melancholy, in which respect his very life is an endless

---

[64] Montuori (1988: 292), e.g., considers that this speech and Bussy's riposte are 'interchange-
able', ignoring the fact that the first (as I demonstrate here) presents a kind of pathology of the
soul, whilst the second simply moralizes.

[65] Here meaning possession of courage and manly spirit, not necessarily in a republican or
other specifically virtuous sense.

[66] See the discussions to this effect in Chs. 1 and 3 above.

[67] See, e.g., Burton 1989–2000: i. 167.          [68] Cf. Bamborough 1952: 102.

process of self-rotting. Choler kindles passions of spirited pugnacity, competitive ambition, and pride, one facet of D'Ambois's observable behaviour; but melancholy, by contrast, stimulates the more negative passions of the malcontent, envy, spite, and resentment. These, too, play their part in shaping Bussy's conduct, precisely as 'plagues' to which his 'pride' must respond with violent acts of self-assertion. Monsieur, then, produces here an acutely accurate account of his subject's psychopathology, one, incidentally, which invites comparison with Chapman's Duke Byron, who also 'Flowes with adust, and melancholy choller' (*Conspiracie of Byron*, II. ii. 43–4).

In offering so precise and (for its day) so plausible an anatomy of the soul, Monsieur delivers a fatal blow to the pretence that Bussy is governed by 'honest' virtue. Indeed, he raises a serious question as to whether D'Ambois can be said to govern himself at all, or whether he is merely the passive agent of bodily (and particularly humoural) impulses. That such questions were a frequent refrain in the early modern period is a well-documented fact.[69] In *The Anatomy of Melancholy*, for example, Burton cites Galen's contentious treatise *Quod animi mores corporis temperaturas sequuntur* to support the proposition that the body, working on the imagination 'by mediation of humours and spirits', thereby 'so forcibly inclines [the soul] that we cannot resist'.[70] Huarte's *Examination of Men's Wits* makes a comparable case,[71] as does Ford's Giovanni, who argues in *'Tis Pity She's a Whore* that 'the frame / And composition of the mind doth follow / The frame and composition of the body' (II. v. 15–17).[72] At the heart of this argument lies the assertion (explicit in Wright and implicit in Hamlet's reference to his lack of gall) that each man's humoural complexion periodically prompts him to be overwhelmed by such passions as are commensurate with that humour. Hence Burton again: 'Sanguine are merry, Melancholy sad, Phlegmaticke dull, by reason of abundance of those humours, and they cannot resist such passions which are inflicted by them. … How should a man choose but be cholericke and angry, that hath his body … clogged with … humours?'[73] Bright goes still further in his *Treatise of Melancholie*, enumerating the various mental alterations which 'diuersitie of complexion, & excesse of the foure humours … do procure, not only to the affections, as sanguine cheerefulnesse, melancholicke sadnesse, fleume heauiinesse, & choler anger: but to the wits, and such faculties as approch … the soueraigne … mind it selfe: as choler procureth rashnesse … & vnstablenesse of purpose: melancholie contrarily, pertinacie, with aduised deliberation: … fleume flat foolishnesse'.[74] Here then, as in some of the passages from Montaigne quoted earlier, the

[69] For discussions of the body's suasive influence over the soul see Introduction, n. 6.
[70] Burton 1989–2000: i. 372.      [71] Schoenfeldt 1999: 9.
[72] References to Ford's plays are to Ford 1995.      [73] Burton 1989–2000: i. 373.
[74] Bright 1586: 52–3.

soul is made helplessly subject to corporeal forces, and this factor, as much as any Shakespearean doubt over reason's capacity to circumvent self-delusion, clearly challenges the Tudor humanists' discourse of governance. The body is accorded a power and intrusiveness here more determinist than anything conceived of in *The Faerie Queene*, and that same notion resonates with Chapman's view in *Bussy*.

Any full consideration of the *corporeal* force of the passions in *Bussy D'Ambois* needs must focus, though, less on Monsieur's taxonomy of Bussy's humours and more on the weather, a feature of the play ignored by critics. The common discourse of humoural psychology is largely sidelined in *Bussy*, Chapman cultivating instead a nexus of meteorological idioms with which to index the irresistible force of man's body-soaked passions. When D'Ambois kills Barrisor in Act II, Scene i, the mixed emotions of sorrow and fury with which L'Anou and Pyrhot greet that act are likened to 'two opposite fumes / Met in the vpper Region of a Cloud' (ll. 110–11). Chapman, Evans notes, alludes here to Aristotle's *Meteorologica*, the work which informed Renaissance interpretations of a wide range of 'meteorological' phenomena.[75] According to Aristotle, man's terrestrial environment is constantly producing two kinds of excrescence, one a predominantly hot, dry, windy 'exhalation', the other a predominantly cold, moist 'vapour' ($341^b6$–12). Both of these, when warmed by the sun, are drawn aloft towards the aether. However, as they rise, the solar heat imparted to the 'vapour' evaporates, dispersing upwards and leaving the moister part of that 'vapour' to condense into clouds. These clouds are densest at their upper limit where the processes of heat dispersal and condensation are at their most intense. Because they are so dense, though, it is not always possible for the hot, dry 'exhalations' also ascending from the Earth to break through the obstructions which they form, and thus to reach the aether towards which these 'exhalations' incline. On the contrary, these latter fumes may be repulsed and forced downwards from the clouds, like pips squeezed from a lemon. In such cases this ejected wind will catch fire, forming lightning ($369^a10$–$^b11$). This theory (put to spectacular use in Herbert's 'The Answer') is pithily captured in Chapman's simile, and its explosive implication is also borne out in the violence which Barrisor's surviving companions later perpetrate as, like thunderbolts, they 'surcharge' Brisac (II. i. 115).

Tamyra, beset by an adulterous passion for Bussy to which she dare not confess, suffers under the blows of her own 'meteor'. Hers is 'a fume'

---

[75] Chapman 1965: 84. For instances of the importance of Aristotle's theories in Renaissance meteorological writings, see Heninger 1960: 8–9, 14–15, 17, 21, 25, 37. On the early modern meaning of 'meteor' see ibid. 3–4.

> Hot, drie and grosse, within the wombe of earth
> Or in her superficies begot:
> When extreame cold hath stroke it to her heart,

which, 'The more it is comprest, the more it rageth' (II. ii. 34–8). Brooke
suggests a connection between the understanding of earthquakes and volcanoes
in play here and Seneca's *Naturales Quaestiones* 6. 17–18.[76] In fact, though,
the primary source is again the *Meteorologica* ($365^b21-7^b7$).[77] On Aristotle's
theory, the hot, dry, windy 'exhalation' produced by the terrestrial world is
brewed within the Earth itself, partly by the Earth's own inner fire, partly by
the Sun's calorific action working from without. Ordinarily, this exhalation
is simply vented through the soil and forms the winds. However, sometimes
it may find itself shut in—for example, during heavy rainfall, or when the
midday sun's heat, beating downwards, blocks the *upward* passage of any
lesser heat. Equally, at night-time (having flowed outward for much of the
day), the exhalation may suddenly turn 'like an ... ebb tide' ($366^a20$) and rush
inwards again. In these cases the initial result of such compression may be
an earthquake around the area where the inflow was induced; but where the
suppressed winds find a lateral passage through the Earth, they may burst
out into the air elsewhere on the planet's surface, catching fire as they do
so: this, a volcanic eruption. Aristotle does not identify 'extreame cold' (l. 37
in Tamyra's speech) as a cause which might drive the fumes into the Earth
(though it equates to the effect of nightfall). This one detail may therefore echo
*Naturales Quaestiones* 6. 13, which invokes Strabo's theory that earthquakes
are due to the action of hot and cold winds compressing each other within the
Earth.[78] Alternatively, it may recall Pliny's idea that the cause of earthquakes
is akin to that of lightning: a cold surrounding presence forcing a hot wind
into violent motion.[79] Whatever the case, though, the essential model behind
Tamyra's thinking remains Aristotelian.

More important than the specific learning displayed is the expressive function of the image. Here, as in the example of fury's lightning, the imagery works
to emphasize the (literally) eruptive, overwhelming force not of Tamyra's
humours but of her sexual emotions, earthy impulses which come from deep
within. Just as seismic movements are beyond human control, so too (the
analogy implies) is her 'wombe'-bred erotic passion. Chapman's figurative
language, then, bodies forth the irresistible force of corporeal desire; but the
connotations of the *Meteorologica* extend still further. The guiding conceit
throughout that treatise is one of fluidity: excrescences flow from the Earth
and waters to the air, and from thence back towards the terrestrial or up to

[76] Chapman 1964: 42.    [77] Chapman 1965: 86.    [78] Seneca 1620: 873.
[79] See Heninger 1960: 128.

the aetherial spheres; 'vapours' and 'exhalations' mingle, seeping in and out of each other's substances and natural spaces; the rain is but 'a river flowing up and down in a circle' (347ª2–3), falling as precipitation, then later streaming upwards towards the firmament like Marvell's 'Drop of Dew'; and the same stuff 'is wind on the earth, … earthquake under it, and in the clouds thunder' (370ª26–7). Chapman exploits precisely this imaginative possibility of fluidity in Tamyra's language as she contemplates initiating an adulterous affair. The raging fume within her, she reports,

> Exceeds his prisons strength that should containe it;
> And then it tosseth Temples in the aire,
> Alle barres made engines, to his insolent fury:
> So, of a sudden, my licentious fancy
> Riots within me: not my name and house
> Nor my religion to this hour obseru'd
> Can stand aboue it: I must vtter that
> That will in parting breake more strings in me,
> Than death when life parts: and that holy man
> That, from my cradle, counseld for my soule,
> I now must make an agent for my bloud.
>
> (ii. ii. 39–49)

One key suggestion embedded here is that 'barres' become 'engines': in a single, *fluid* transfer, a reversal, the forces which before suppressed lust now support it and flow into it. Those sometime 'strings'—literally heart-strings, but also the moral ties of 'sex, … vertue, [and] Renowne' (l. 174) enforced by right reason—do not merely retreat into the background now; rather, they 'breake' altogether, the energy once invested in them becoming subsumed, instead, in the passion which they previously smothered. Bars transform themselves into engines. Crucially, with this idea Chapman comes closer than any of his contemporaries to imagining the mind in terms of the so-called monistic psychology of Chrysippan Stoicism. Unlike Cicero, most ancient Stoics maintained that in the mind there is no faculty division between our rational and irrational powers.[80] Rather, there are only different kinds of reasoned judgement: 'the part of the soule … subject to passions, sensuall, brutish and unreasonable, differeth not from reason by any essentiall difference …. The very part [called] reason, … being wholy turned, … becommeth … vice …. [The Stoics] would have that … passion it selfe to be reason, howbeit depraved, … taking her force … from false and perverse judgement' (*Moralia* 441c–e).[81] Right reason, then, on the one hand, and the combination of

---

[80] Long and Sedley 1987: i. 321.       [81] Plutarch 1603: 65.

passion and false opinion, on the other, are here conceived as opposite poles
on a *single* mental continuum, wise and foolish dispositions respectively of the
same one, judgement-forming faculty. As Lipsius puts it in his *Manuductio*,
'Unus animus atque una Rationalis pars, modo ad *melius* tendit et *Ratio* dicitur;
modo ad *peius*, et est *Affectus*.'[82] This theory denies the possibility of *akrasia*,
identifying psychomachia instead as a process of oscillation, 'an alteration ... of
one & the ... same thing to wit, reason both waies; which we our selves are not
able to perceive, for that ... it changeth suddenly and with ... celeritie' (*Moralia*
447a).[83] Reasoned and passionate judgements may invert at a moment's notice,
either one submerging itself into the other; and because passion as much as
reason commands the force of cognitive 'judgement' (albeit in a 'perverse'
form), it can easily rationalize itself, villainy dressing like goodness simply
by donning the 'reasoned' garb conventionally thought more characteristic of
virtue. Although not widely cited in a Renaissance culture for which Pauline
*akrasia* was a given of experience, Chapman could have encountered this
monistic psychology in Plutarch's *Moralia* (the dramatist's familiarity with
which is well documented[84]), in Seneca's *De Ira* 1. 8. 3,[85] or in Lipsius. Certainly
Tamyra, visualizing her mind in terms sympathetic to such views, has difficulty
conceiving of her passion of the 'bloud' and her rational sense of virtue as
separate, coexistent things. If sexual appetite (born of the blood in her liver)
constitutes the volcanic force now rumbling within, the bars to that—both
the general 'strings' of morality and the specific ties of priestly counsel and her
once-pure imagination (her 'fancy')—are here, 'of a sudden', dramatically
reversed: her priest becomes, in her mind, the *means* to lechery, and her fancy
turns 'licentious', now rioting *with* the 'bloud'. Again, forces which once held
passion at bay thus become subsumed within the latter. The result is that
Tamyra's volcanic self explodes. The 'Temples' which once stood atop her
moral probity—her 'name', 'house', and 'religion'—are 'tossed' aside. Once
more then, though now with subtler psychological connotations, corporeal
passion's obliterative power is evoked. The forces of rational self-governance
literally melt away amidst hot blood from the liver. Furthermore, in the First
Quarto (Q1) at least, Tamyra appears pitifully aware of her impotence before
such influences: 'See, see the gulfe is opening, *that will swallow / Me*' (II.
ii. 176–7).[86] Tamyra seemingly imagines herself, here, disappearing into the

---

[82] Quoted in Levi 1964: 72.    [83] Plutarch 1603: 71. See Nussbaum 1994: 383–5.
[84] Schoell 1926: ch. 4 (esp. 76–83), 197–247.    [85] Seneca 1620: 517.
[86] Though literally a reference to the now opening trapdoor through which Bussy will shortly
enter her closet, Tamyra's lines here (as phrased in Q1) also punningly convey the larger moral
connotations of what is about to happen. Those connotations are lost in Q2's amendment to
this passage (Q2: II. ii. 127–31). However, that particular alteration is commensurate with Q2's

cratered landscape left by her volcanic passion. Her rational, virtuous self sinks, so to speak, into her rapacious body. Sexuality overtakes her whole being.

This same haemorrhaging of the self is apparent in *The Revenge of Bussy D'Ambois*. When Clermont's protégé, Guise, receives prophecies of his death, he (like Tamyra) describes a sudden, absolute collapse in his powers of governance, a dissolution of the higher self amidst the encroachments of its own body:

> ... these [prophetic] words, this imperfect bloud and flesh
> Shrincke at in spight of me; their solidst part
> Melting like snow within mee, with colde fire:
>
> . . . . . . . . . . .
>
> ... Would any spirit
> Free, manly, Princely, wish to liue to be
> Commanded by this masse of slauerie,
> Since Reason, Iudgement, Resolution,
> And scorne of what we feare, will yeeld to feare?
> While this same sincke of sensualitie swels,
> Who would liue sinking in it?

> (v. iv. 7–17)

Guise's rational self 'sinckes' into—and thus simultaneously gives body to—his 'swel[ling] sensualitie', passion increasing in proportion as 'Reason' diminishes (as if the latter were making a fluid transition across a continuum). Similarly, resolution (manifest in a physically tense body, the flesh's 'solidst part') melts into a condition of irresoluteness, a virtuous disposition liquefying into the passion of fear, just as 'snow' turns to water (another state of the *same* substance). Guise's subsequent invocation, 'O Clermont ..., wert thou here to chide / This softnesse from my flesh, farre as my reason, / Farre as my resolution' (ll. 20–2), reinforces this impression, the hope here being that Clermont might chide fear back towards, back *into*, the original condition of courageous resolution. That hope is not, though, fulfilled. Guise, like his predecessors Tamyra and the Bussy figure anatomized by Monsieur, remains sunk within his own corporeality, impotent before the sway of passions and humours alike.

Tamyra reflects again on her paralysis in her second soliloquy, where the conviction that her rational identity is imperilled by the imperialism of the body's passions receives fuller treatment:

> We cannot keepe our constant course in vertue:
>
> . . . . . . . . .
>
> ... euery houre and minute:

more drastic removal of the first fifty lines of this scene since, as Tricomi (1973: 291–2) notes, the various changes systematically rob Tamyra of her pathetic dimension.

> I, euery thought in our false clock of life,
> Oft times inuerts the whole circumference ...

> (*Bussy D'Ambois*, III. i. 53–7)

Here again Chrysippus's idea of a mirror-reversal in the orientation of reason and the body's impulses predominates. Tamyra, alive to the 'inversion' of her whole psyche, envisages her destiny, now, as one of ongoing oscillation between reason and passion's opposing imperatives—this, precisely that *oscillatory* process which Plutarch associated with monistic psychology. Besides exploiting this Stoic vein, though, Chapman also returns to meteorology to underline the pathos of his heroine's plight. Hence Tamyra, thinking of herself as at once the mote before some greater sun and a sun herself, figures herself in the latter respect as a radiant soul (rational and virtuous) which finds itself immersed amidst 'thicke clouds' (adulterous passions) of its own body's making (l. 59):

> When all the starres, and euen the sunne himselfe,
> Must stay the vapors times that he exhales
> Before he can make good his beames to vs:
> O how can we, that are but motes to him,
>
> .   .   .   .   .   .   .   .   .   .
>
> Disperse our passions fumes, with our weake labors,
> That are more thick and black than all earths vapors?

> (ll. 61–7)

Tamyra, then, harbours within herself her own troubling vapours—*literally* so in so far as she suffers from melancholia, since Burton (following Galen) makes the passage of precisely such fuliginous vapours from corrupted organs within the body, upwards, into the imagination, essential to the pathology of that condition.[87] If, though, these asphyxiating smoke trails within *seem*, to Tamyra, alien to her 'true' (ideal) self, one scientifically accurate detail of Chapman's meteorology corrects this impression. It is the Sun—'he' himself—which originally 'exhales' (draws up (l. 62)) the hot, windy exhalations from the Earth, those vapours which then occlude that same Sun's light. Likewise, the soul (man's *anima*, or life principle) in a sense *makes* the body what it is, drawing out the latter's passions through its own thought processes. (There is a parallel here with Marvell's 'Dialogue between the Soul and Body', where it is the *soul* which suffuses man's 'nerves ... arteries, and veins' with the tensile force of life (l. 8), thus creating for itself the robust *corporeal* prison of which it then complains. The soul is complicit in its being 'hung up, as 'twere, in

---

[87] See Burton 1989–2000: i. 413, 418–19; Tilmouth 2005: 529.

chains' by the body (l. 7).[88]) The implication of Chapman's nuance in line 62 (as of Marvell's) is that the sexually passionate body and rational soul are more interdependent than the soul might like to imagine, and the registering of this fact emphasizes all the more that there is no easy solution to the problem of accommodating the body.

Friar Comolet, certainly, is far from hopeful in his estimation as to what rational governance can achieve. He takes it for granted that reason simply cannot quell 'affections storme' (II. ii. 186–7), and this impression is confirmed, not least, by Montsurry, Tamyra's jealous husband. Montsurry sees in *his* uncontrollable passion a pollutant force which promises to invade and 'drowne' Tamyra (IV. i. 157), and this threat of inundation is, latterly, an emergent motif of the play. From Act IV onwards, passions and even the body itself threaten to break free of the bounds of their host soul and to invade—to haemorrhage into—*other* characters' very beings.[89] In both lightning flashes and volcanic eruptions, one element, fire (the essence of the Earth's hot exhalations), thrusts its way through another—through the water of the stratosphere's moist vapours in the case of lightning; through the Earth itself in the case of volcanoes. Sexual passions here promise to do the same, eroding, certainly, the autonomy of those individuals whose minds they possess, but also invading the bodies of *other* protagonists in the surrounding landscape. Comolet, spotting this danger, warns Montsurry against doing worse than even lightning ('The stony birth of clowds' (v. i. 13) )[90] would do, by striking *into* his wife. Montsurry, for his part, imagines himself as a Titan,[91] whose fury manifests itself in fuming exhalations and volcanic emissions vented from the Earth ('my hot woes / (Vented enough) I might conuert to vapour, / Ascending from my infamie' (ll. 45–7)). He then envisages an Armageddon-like destruction stemming, implicitly, from his own eruptive passions as they invade and overwhelm the world around him (ll. 48–9).

Montsurry (like Tamyra) identifies with the forces of plate-tectonic violence here as a way of articulating his own *loss* of autonomy, his sense of being overrun by corporeal passions which he cannot govern. By contrast, Bussy (who has previously immersed himself in bloody haemorrhaging processes [92] and has led the

---

[88]  Marvell 2003: 61 ff. See Leavis 1986: 190.

[89]  Besides the examples discussed here, other instances of haemorrhaging and the interfusion of separate bodies include v. i. 65, 110–11, and 129–30.

[90]  The reference to lightning as a '*stony* birth' exploits the same idea touched upon by Donne (1985: 250 ff.) in 'The Storme' (ll. 13–16), when he refers to a hot, earthly 'winde' meeting resistance 'at th'ayres middle *marble* roome' and being thrown backwards again as lightning. 'Stony' and 'marble' both emphasize the cold, impenetrable nature assumed by moist vapours by the time they have reached the stratosphere, and this is the matrix from within which Comolet's 'wild seed' of lightning (v. i. 16) is born.

[91]  See Chapman 1965: 100, 109–10.        [92]  See II. i. 45–7, 77, 134.

way in purporting to embody elemental powers) uses that same meteorological language precisely to *assert* his autonomy. Meteorology is the idiom by which he signals his consciousness of his own presumed greatness. Hence in Act IV he imagines himself embodying an earthquake's destructive power (IV. i. 87–90); becomes, in his own eyes, a greater force even than lightning (nature's 'hot surfets' thrown from the clouds (IV. ii. 15–17) ); and then figures his 'heart' as a mine set beneath Monsieur which will, when detonated, 'rush into [the latter's] bloud'—this, a haemorrhaging, a bodily fusion, in which Bussy will master his nemesis (ll. 156–7). He casts himself, too, both as an oppressive heat issuing in lightning strikes and as the emergent thunderbolt itself which will lance into Monsieur and melt his bones (ll. 162–9). By now, though, unbeknownst to D'Ambois, the weather has turned. Henry has already sighted the gathering clouds (IV. i. 109–11) which issue in real thunder in the play's last scenes, thereby stressing the reality of those forces to which even Bussy must become subject. In keeping with this, Act V charts the passions' progress in overwhelming Chapman's hero and undermining his presumption of autonomy.

Even at the end of Act IV Bussy's supposed virtue and valour are exposed as mere 'rage' (IV. ii. 138). It is that passion, humoural in origin, which (according to Behemoth) really governs the hero's soul. Likewise, it is 'will' (here meaning sexual, not rational, appetite) which draws Bussy back towards Tamyra's closet and his death (v. ii. 70–1).[93] Emotion then overpowers him for a third time when he receives a letter from his mistress. Whereas previously Bussy had envisaged himself as the active agent rushing upon *another*'s (Monsieur's) blood, the reality of this latter incident is that *he* becomes the passive victim of such haemorrhaging and intermingling. Chapman, mirroring the Paracelsian idea of the weapon-salve,[94] imagines the dried blood-stains on Tamyra's letter emitting some of the very 'elixer' of her blood, and that essence then strikes into D'Ambois's heart, 'Command[ing] the life confinde in [his] vaines': 'O how it multiplies my bloud with spirit' (ll. 91–5). Infused thus with another's vital spirits, D'Ambois is rendered subject to the invading force of Tamyra's body. He thereby falls victim, albeit willingly, to the very mechanism which he previously conceived of as a means of mastering Monsieur. In these various respects, then, D'Ambois's dangerous susceptibility to the encroachments of passion (and to the loss of autonomy which that entails) become increasingly clear—clear, that is, to all except D'Ambois. Initially, at least, his response to his impending death indicates, rather, that he remains oblivious to the forces corroding his illusion of self-possession.

---

[93] See further Montuori 1988: 296.

[94] For an exposition of the theory behind this method of medical treatment, see the Second Member of *Doctor Fludds Answer unto M. Foster* (Fludd 1992: 191–213).

Shot in the back, Bussy's first thought in his final scene is to contrast the pusillanimity of his unseen opponents with his own greatness. The 'coward Fates', he is pleased to reassure himself, have 'maim'd' their own honour with this spineless action (v. iii. 120–1). He can take pride from his assailants' evident fear of confronting him head-on (ll. 124–5). This moment of mortality thus reinforces (rather than undermines) Bussy's presumption of his own magnificence, and that same preoccupation persists throughout this first, long death speech. Dissatisfied with his fall, D'Ambois determines to complain directly 'to heauen' about his treatment (l. 135)—this in contrast to Comolet's earlier Stoic instruction that the 'great mind ... submits to all' whilst only 'the small / ... carps at [Earth's] foundation shaker' (ll. 71–3).[95] Bussy's next, equally self-approving thought is to die standing up, 'like a Roman Statue' (l. 140). The nobility of such a posture, testimony to his irrepressible autonomy, positively cheers him up. To assume this 'marble' form (l. 141) is to render himself permanently resistant to the melting and haemorrhaging which overtake other characters. It also allows him to play the impassive Stoic once more: 'The equall thought I beare of life and death, / Shall make me faint on no side' (ll. 138–9). The manifest pride of this gesture, the self-consoling passion underlying it, in fact undermines its supposed Stoicism, but Bussy presses on with such rhetoric nonetheless. Here, even at the last, the figure with which I began this discussion—D'Ambois the great—keeps on reaffirming himself, and yet, as at the beginning, so at the end, his performance betrays its own delusory status.

That said though, there are some signs, in this initial death speech, of Bussy *consciously* faltering in his commitment to his own heroic pose. He does, for example, recognize that his body is but 'penetrable flesh' (l. 126) and, as if affronted by that truism, concludes that the fact of *his* being capable of death needs must imply that life generally is 'nothing but a Courtiers breath' (l. 132).[96] (What value could 'life' have if it does not preserve the being of one such as him?) To that he adds the more searching question, 'And must my minde / Follow my blood?' (ll. 126–7). Throughout the play the experience of other characters has affirmed that the answer to this key enquiry is yes, and D'Ambois, too, now begins to comprehend as much. Furthermore, the very form of his question (the choice of the verb 'follow') re-emphasizes the point that one should think of soul and body, reasoned and passionate cognition, as things connected on a single continuum, not as things dualistically opposed. The critical moment in this process of disillusionment comes, though, only

---

[95] Monsarrat 1984: 194. Monsarrat sees no evidence of true Stoicism anywhere in this scene.

[96] Montuori (1988: 297) emphasizes the irony of Bussy's choosing the 'courtier' image as a way of expressing this point: it is a nuance which underlines his ultimate identification with the very court world which he had previously professed to despise.

when Bussy turns away from meditations on his own portentousness and reflects, instead, on the 'killing spectacle' of the wounded Tamyra (l. 177). It is then that his mind gives way to—'follows'—his blood; then that his heart is literally 'broken' by grief (l. 174):

> My sunne is turnd to blood gainst whose red beams
> Pindus and Ossa (hid in endlesse snow),
> Laid on my heart and liuer, from their vains
> Melt like two hungrie torrents, eating rockes,[97]
> Into the Ocean of all humane life,
> And make it bitter, only with my bloud.

(ll. 178–83)

The literal sense of these lines is that Tamyra, in seeming to bleed from her otherwise snow-white breasts (perhaps because in a previous gesture she had pressed her wounded arms against her bosom (ll. 171–2) ), now haemorrhages blood on to Bussy's recumbent torso. Bussy, taking his cue from the Titanic volcanoes Pindus and Ossa, thinks of Tamyra's melting, bloody torrents as lava which eats into his own stony body, fuses with his blood, and turns it (along with all 'life') into something 'bitter'. This hard-felt emotion cuts through D'Ambois's statuesque, Stoic pose, the rock-like impermeability of his 'marble' form. In an instant he is thereby subjected, passively, to the very haemorrhaging and invasive process which he had previously thought to impose upon others, or which, when he last perceived it as something visited upon him by Tamyra (v. ii. 91–5), he could only conceive as exhilarating. Likewise, in the same instant, and by the same volcanic metaphor, Bussy is here subjected to a kind of meteorological assault identical to that which he had elsewhere imagined himself embodying or visiting upon others. In these senses the imagery which was once a signature of his own supposed *virtù* becomes, at this moment, an index to the eruptive, irresistible force of passion, a corrosive blood-force which Bussy's mind cannot help but 'follow'. Bodily powers at last overwhelm him, crushing all vestige of autonomy as emphatically as they had already done in Tamyra and Montsurry.

Faced with this terrible reality, Bussy's dying gesture is to imagine himself as 'a falling starre' testifying to the frailty of 'strength, valure: vertue' (v. iii. 187, 184), goals of rational self-governance which cannot be sustained under the impress of emotion. This last meteor, though, is supposedly to be but 'Silently glanc't' (l. 188), scarcely noticed amidst the larger backdrop of the cosmos. Given the story of his follies and miscalculations, one might think this a fair judgement, but D'Ambois does not actually lose all claim to grandeur.

---

[97] I follow Evans's punctuation in this line. See Chapman 1965: 75.

Whether or not critics are right to find nobility specifically in his struggle to die in the posture of *homo erectus*,[98] Ure's general observation that Bussy's person remains larger than the moral framework within which Chapman strives to contain it is surely correct.[99] Bussy acquires a tragic stature if only because the massiveness of the corporeal passions ranged against him is made so unfairly apparent from the outset. His acknowledging their triumph over him lends him, at the last, a moving and redeeming degree of humanity, the more so because the seismic imagery of the play indicates that that defeat was always inevitable. According to this tragedy's perspective, the bodily passions and humours constitute, quite simply, an irresistible force, one destined to possess the soul absolutely.[100] Such is *Bussy D'Ambois*'s challenge to contemporary moral assumptions, and any rationalist mode of governance which ignores as much, refusing to find an indulgent way of accommodating the body, will ultimately (on Chapman's description) prove unsustainable.

## SELF-INTEREST AND THE MARKET

Man as presented in *Caesar* and *Bussy* is a figure driven by delusions, humours, corporeal passions, and inner impulses unknown to himself. These are forces which defy rational governance, and do so more absolutely than Spenser envisaged. But by the early seventeenth century the little world of man had also become one of markets, commodities, and a perpetual round of trafficking—this too a world of values which challenged the priority of moral rationalism.[101] Wheeler declared in his 1601 *Treatise of Commerce* that there was '*nothing* in the world so ... naturall vnto men, as to contract [and] truck ... one with an other.... All the world ... runneth & raueth after Marts, Markets and Merchandising, so that all thinges'—men themselves included—'come into Commerce, and passe into traffique'.[102] *King John*'s Philip the Bastard affirms as much in his set piece on 'tickling commodity', 'That smooth-faced gentleman' whose influence is felt everywhere (*King John*, ii. i. 574). 'Commodity' connotes here the goods and merchandise for which late Elizabethan London had such an appetite; but in tandem with that commercial sense it also means 'profit', 'expediency', and, above all, 'self-interest'—hence Burton's references to the 'string of commodity' in each of us, a chord which, if

[98] Ide 1980: 94; Ure 1974: 174.        [99] Ure 1974: 168–76.
[100] On this theme cf. Paster 2004: 19–20, 155–6.
[101] On London's conspicuously consumptive taste for commodities, see Bruster 1992: 40–3; R. J. Fisher 1948; Peck 2005; Thirsk 1978.
[102] Wheeler 1601: 6.

plucked by another, provokes us to fury.[103] In Shakespeare's England there was seemingly a natural correlation between these two facets of 'commodity', the pursuit both of commerce and self-interest, and it is man's taste for the latter which Philip emphasizes. Commodity is cast here as a 'purpose-changer' who happily 'breaks the pate of faith' and draws men away from 'all indifferency' (all impartiality) whenever advantage so demands (ll. 568–9, 580). Yet, if the Bastard vilifies 'commodity' for this, he does so only because it has not, thus far, 'wooed' him (l. 589); and to say as much is to underline that his own commitment to self-interest is as strong as that of any other character in this play. In John's immoral kingdom, commodity, the craving for profit and self-interest, overrules and erases every other motive (in particular, right reason's language of moral duties).

The culture of ruthless egotism which pervades *King John* resonates with a broader cupidity and moral indifference observable in Elizabeth's actual polity. It is, for example, a notorious fact of the Elizabethan state that whilst Burghley was happy to complain about others' tax evasion, he led the way in such corruption, minimizing his contributions by maintaining the same income assessment (£133. 6*s*. 8*d*. per annum.) throughout his life. Likewise, those who obtained Crown licences and monopolies at this time typically used such rights to garner personal profit at the commonweal's expense. Raleigh benefited thus by exercising a monopoly over the manufacture of playing cards; Sir Edward Dyer used his patent for searching out concealed wardships as a tool of blackmail; and Leicester, being granted all concealed Crown rights in the Forest of Snowdon, 'discovered' an amazing number of royal claims on the land there.[104] Ultimately, Elizabethan England's most successful monopolists became the subject of furious parliamentary debate, because their profiteering had prompted a doubling of steel, a tripling of starch, and an elevenfold rise in salt prices. Such fostering of 'commodity' extended, too, to court jockeying for royal offices. Given Elizabeth's well-known impecuniousness, these were inevitably in short supply: there were no more than 1,200 variously lucrative posts to be shared amongst the gentry. Consequently, there was much exploitation and trading of offices. Russell notes that Leicester, for example, accepted multiple bribes from figures wanting to be proposed for the Denbighshire bench.[105] Essex, the inheritor of Leicester's patronage network, but also a self-appointed spokesman for malcontent militarists within the court,[106] exploited his privilege as commander in the field to create an entourage of knights for himself—twenty-one in 1591, sixty-eight in 1596, eighty-one in 1599, all of

---

[103] Burton 1989–2000: i. 51, iii. 19.     [104] See C. Russell 1971: 206.     [105] Ibid. 249.
[106] See Mallin 1995: 31–2.

them, by implication, his placemen.[107] His chief rival, Cecil (the successor to Burghley's patronage network), matched Leicester's conduct by selling wardships at extortionate prices, and in the struggle to win control of the office of Attorney General, he also vigorously promoted his own man, Coke, so as to defeat Essex's candidate, Bacon. Such precedents underline the realism of Middleton's character, the Black Knight (*alias* Count Gondomar, the Spanish ambassador), who claims in *A Game at Chess* to have 'sold the groom-o-the-stool six times [over]' by trading on his influence at court (IV. ii. 42).[108]

I emphasize the rapacious force of self-interest and its capacity to reduce human beings to tradeable commodities, because the emerging mercantile culture which fostered these values during Elizabeth's reign challenged, in so doing, the ethical and rationalist aspirations of late Tudor ethics. Increasingly in this period, moral languages of evaluation threatened to be overwritten by utilitarian ones, a fact particularly apparent in contemporary usury debates, for example.[109] Market thinking placed profit and egotism at the centre of its value system, argued for subjectivity and relativism in contrast to ratio-nalist moral authoritarianism, and promoted Machiavellianism as the model of self-fashioning which could best preserve the individual within such an environment. Here again, then, was a new set of idioms which contested right reason's supposed monopoly over the language of self-governance. Although *Troilus and Cressida* is commonly read in political terms, as a meditation on Essex's contention for power in his struggle with the Cecils and Elizabeth,[110] it is equally profitable to see it as reflecting upon the colonizing power both of mercantile values and of a principle of self-interest which has the capacity to invade and suffuse every corner of consciousness. Shakespeare's satire offers a taxonomy of the means by which self-interest, passionate wilfulness, and market imperatives distort man's rational processes, superseding right reason's judgements—this, so much so that *Troilus* also illustrates something of the origins of Hobbes's moral thought.[111]

[107] On Essex's attempts to revive feudalism for his own benefit, see Shapiro 2005: 285–9; Womersley 1991: 341.

[108] References to this play are to Middleton 1966.

[109] Thus Sir John Wolley argued in Parliament's 1571 usury debate that, since 'men are men, no Saints', it would be better to 'permit a little' usury than 'utterly to take away ... Traffick' (the consequence of *not* allowing it), 'for to have any man lend ... money *without* Commodity, hardly should you bring that to pass' (Tawney and Power 1924: ii. 155). Similarly, when Bacon wrote 'Of Usurie', he framed his discussion so as to emphasize not biblical law but 'the *Incommodities*, and *Commodities*' of this practice, its utilitarian value (Bacon 1985: 125). See further N. Jones 1989.

[110] Honigmann 1988a: 114–17; H. James 1997: 85–118; Mallin 1995: 25–61.

[111] My approach to *Troilus* thus complements those of Bruster (1992: 97–117), and Engle (1993: 147–63). For Engle especially, the play is a drama about the opposition between feudal and market ethics. I depart from his view in so far as I focus, here, on the particular role played by self-interest in the action, emphasize Shakespeare's anatomization of the psychology

The importance of these latter themes is immediately apparent in Act II, Scene ii, where the Trojans debate Helen's value. Troilus responds to Hector's misgivings about Helen by hypothesizing that the action of valuing is a purely subjective affair ('What's aught but as 'tis valued?' (ii. ii. 51) ). He then posits a test case in which one's selection of a consort is indeed thus superficial. Invoking the word 'will' in its Thomist sense—this, an otherwise rare usage for Shakespeare—Troilus first reconstructs the psychology by which such a selection might be made. 'Will and judgement', he argues, may be 'dangerous shores' to our senses, but the latter are skilful at navigating their way around them (ll. 62–4). The senses know how best to approach our rational powers so as to avoid being wrecked; they know how to get their own sensuous whims—the stuff of narrow self-interest and concupiscible appetite—accepted without will or judgement detecting that they are thereby being corrupted. Once accepted, these sensitive judgements will 'enkindle' a now hoodwinked 'will' to crave for *their* goal—in this hypothetical example, the 'election' of an attractive (but ultimately inappropriate) wife (ll. 60–2). All these, though, are academic preliminaries. Troilus's end-purpose is to insist (this erring psychology notwithstanding) that, even though the husband will eventually rue his decision, he cannot then relinquish his bride without also sacrificing his honour (ll. 66–7). If Helen were to be thought of as a comparable case, still it would be wrong for the Trojans to abandon her; but Troilus's actual view is that keeping Helen is *not* such a mistake: the woman herself remains what she always was, a prize of 'Inestimable' worth and intrinsic value (l. 87).

It is this last point, the estimate of Helen's inherent worth, which Hector contests. He, too, differentiates between a thing's actual value and its value as apprehended in the 'particular will' of the 'prizer' (ll. 52–5); but in his view Troilus is driven by the latter to overestimate the former, to misconstrue Helen's objective worth because his (Troilus's) 'discourse of reason' (l. 115) is swayed by 'pleasure' and 'the hot passion of distempered blood' (ll. 167–73). On *this* account, Troilus's 'hypothetical' scenario of a will being driven to distraction, surreptitiously, by the senses applies precisely to Troilus's own judgement, and of such cases Hector notes:

> the will dotes that is [attributive]
> To what infectiously itself affects
> Without some image of th'affected merit.
>
> (ll. 57–9)

underlying that impulse, and enumerate ways in which this work anticipates that of Hobbes. Where Engle (p. 148) maintains that *Troilus* situates 'philosophical debate in an attenuated atmosphere *without established positions*', I argue, rather, that the play *presupposes* rationalist (and particularly Thomist) models of ethicized psychology, and then challenges these.

'Image' here stands for that objective picture of a thing's value—as Engle puts it, of its use (as opposed to exchange) value[112] —which, in the example of Troilus's estimation of Helen, Troilus supposedly lacks. Instead, says Hector, the latter is swayed by wishful thinking, by a will which 'attributes' to the valued object—adds *from within itself*—the value which it then purports to discover in that external object. The play's recent editors, Bevington and Dawson, have preferred Folio's 'inclineable' to the Quarto's 'attributive' quoted above, but Q is surely superior here, neatly encapsulating a crucial theme.[113] Hector's argument is that the will *adds* something from itself to that which it values, attributing to the external object a quality which really only exists in the will's own apprehension. 'Attribute' (in this sense) resonates elsewhere in *Troilus*, recalling this passage: namely when Pandarus's servant plays on Cressida's 'attributes' (III. i. 36), and when Agamemnon notes, ominously, that 'much attribute' is *currently* 'ascribe[d]' to Achilles (II. iii. 115–16). Besides this, Q's 'attributive' also has the virtue of anticipating the pun on 'affects' in Hector's next line here, where the will 'affects' its valued object both in the traditional sense that it admires the latter and in the (here new)[114] sense that it alters—indeed, 'infectiously' attaints—that object, *attributing* its own properties to the latter.

Hector's judgement here is clearly accurate. Throughout this scene Troilus does indeed 'attribute'—add—the preoccupations of his own passionate interests to his estimation of Paris's cause. He has already, by now, declared his actual indifference to the 'starved ... subject' of Troy, dismissing Helen's 'painted' value (I. i. 90–3). When (in II. ii) he advances the contrary view (that she is priceless) by hypothesizing a marriage (II. ii. 60) or dubbing her a 'pearl' (l. 80), it is clear that, really, he is contemplating his own union or transposing the Trojan scenario on to his own 'pearl' (I. i. 100), Cressida, and only then and on *those* bases drawing conclusions about how his family should act. Thinking from that interested perspective, driven on by his infatuation for Cressida, he would indeed have all Troy fall in defence of such a woman. We also see just how inclined Troilus is subjectively to inflate the value of things when he reflects, later, on Cressida's imminent approach:

> Th'imaginary relish is so sweet
> That it enchants my sense. What will it be
> When that the wat'ry palates taste indeed
> Love's thrice-repurèd nectar?
>
> (III. ii. 17–20)

---

[112] Engle 1993: 159.
[113] Shakespeare 1998: 193, 361; 2003: 120.
[114] *OED* gives this example as the first instance of 'to affect', $v^2$, 1.

The very word 'repurèd' demands an exaggerated, trisyllabic reading, and in line with that indulgence, the lover's will here clearly attributes to the beloved treasures culled from its own stock of fictive anticipations. By extension, in so far as the Trojans are all lovers of Helen, we are invited to conjecture that they all similarly inflate *her* value. Troilus's saporous idioms,[115] so redolent of Hamlet's, reveal the same over-refined sensibility as that manifested by Denmark's Prince, but in this play that trait is common to all, not peculiar to one.[116] This is important, because the more active men's imaginative sensibilities are, the more 'attributive' they will be (the more they will allow their own preoccupations to infect their estimations of outward things). The supersensitivity of the combatants at Shakespeare's Troy, their penchant for 'delicate palate' imagery, points to their being especially 'attributive', especially prone to wishful, self-interested thinking.

If Hector's own conclusions were as rational as is his analysis of Troilus's self-delusions, we might conclude that Shakespeare's play endorsed Thomist psychology; but in fact the sensibility shared between Troilus and other Trojans extends even to Hector, and Shakespeare's larger purpose in II. ii is to demonstrate as much. For Hector, just as for Troilus, it transpires, there is no escape from self-interest and the attributive effect of the subjective will. Aquinas's rationalist goal is therefore unrealizable. In part, Shakespeare makes this point bluntly by introducing a notorious volte-face in Hector's reasoning at the end of the scene. Having won his arguments about morality and moral psychology (II. ii. 172–87), having 'proved' that Helen should be returned, Hector nonetheless concludes by affirming that she should be retained to uphold Trojan dignity (l. 192). He does so, clearly, out of a vain concern for his own reputation, a 'commodity' which has an 'attributive' effect in reshaping his estimate of this cause's value. The transparency of this emphasizes just how emphatically irrational men are, in the end, prone to be, how little rationality need matter when narcissism is at stake. In fact though, as Bradshaw demonstrates, the true aberration here is not the last-minute volte-face, but Hector's making a rational case for surrendering Helen in the first place: it is, after all, he who, prior to II. ii, had already declared himself bored of the truce, and he who has issued a new challenge to the Greeks (motivated, in so doing, by a desire to erase the shame of his earlier defeat at Ajax's hands (I. ii. 32–4): motivated, therefore, by passion and interest more than by public

---

[115] By this point Troilus has already used the verb 'distaste' twice (II. ii. 65, 122), and he will use it again at IV. iv. 47.

[116] The Grecian, Diomedes, e.g., later chastises the Trojans for 'Not palating the taste of [Helen's] dishonour' (IV. i. 61).

good).[117] To this blunt demonstration of the prevalence of egotism can be added a subtler one. When Hector invokes an impersonal measure to set against the attributive will's impression of a thing's worth, he describes this absolute gauge as (to reiterate) an '*image* of th'affected [party's] merit'; but the word 'image' here betrays, somewhat unwittingly, the actual inaccessibility of this imagined standard. 'Images', being only representations, fall short of that which they portray, and are themselves tainted by the subjective gaze of their creators.[118] They may pretend to objectivity, but are actually relative. In the end, therefore, despite reassurances to the contrary, Hector too butts up against the irreducible partiality of our attempts to determine the absolute value of things.

Act II, Scene ii, presents a particularly subtle picture of the mechanisms of psychology and reveals, in a more sophisticated fashion than other plays of the period, the incorrigible influence of self-interest and subjectivity in shaping human conduct. As such, it is illustrative of a moral imagination which stands at odds with that of Spenser or Erasmus. What is true of *Troilus*'s Trojan scenes, though, is also true of its Greek ones. These, likewise, dramatize the processes by which the will and Philip the Bastard's 'commodity' inform acts of evaluation. Ulysses, for example, like Hector, tries to present 'degree, priority, and place' (I. iii. 86) as clearly discernible absolutes. The plausibility of this position, though, is doubtful. After all, the Trojans have some difficulty in identifying Agamemnon amidst the Greek crowd (ll. 222–32), still more in recognizing Menelaus (IV. vii. 60). Furthermore, as Ulysses and Nestor acknowledge, nominal degree tends, anyway, to be overwritten by shifting public opinion (and here the market forces to which I alluded at the beginning of this discussion begin to play their part). Nestor knows that the Trojans' aim in issuing Hector's challenge is to 'taste our dear'st repute / With their fin'st palate' (I. iii. 331–2), so that whichever side triumphs in this contest will, in the eyes of both, win a stronger 'opinion' for itself hereafter (l. 347). The combat will only be between two individuals, and so will not really measure the full worth of the conflicting camps; but it will be *perceived* as if it does (to the detriment of one of them). Ulysses responds to this risk in market-minded fashion, by first 'show[ing] our foulest wares' to see if they will 'sell' (ll. 352–3). By putting forward Ajax, a combatant whom the Trojans know is not the Grecians' greatest hero, the Greeks (Ulysses notes) can insure themselves against the damage of defeat, protecting their valuation on the international market by keeping back their best asset. Simultaneously, this strategy will signal to the all too conceited Achilles the apparent collapse

---

[117] Bradshaw 1987: 133. Heather James (1997: 98, 102–5) relates Hector's shift between his ethical and chivalric selves to the play's larger process of 'characterological instability', and develops this point through a case study of Achilles' multiple selves.

[118] Cf. Shakespeare 2003: 39.

of his standing *vis-à-vis* Ajax *within* the Greek camp (i. iii. 353–77). It suits the Greek commanders' interests that Achilles should see his virtues thus 'lose their gloss' in other Grecians' 'eyes' (ii. iii. 118), since that decline in his popular standing, a deflation which will overwrite his intrinsic worth, will render him more compliant—or so they hope. They therefore determine falsely to inflate public appreciation of Ajax so as to accelerate Achilles' fall from vanity. Here again, then, vested interest disrupts the processes of judgement, superseding supposedly objective evaluations of men's worth.

Ulysses' 'degree' and 'priority' emerge from *these* exchanges as tradeable commodities determined by market forces. Interest judgements—the various interests of Agamemnon, Ulysses, and Nestor which constitute 'demand' within this market—become the real determinants of their value. The play thus moves us from a focus on the attributive will and its preoccupations viewed simply in themselves (the theme inside Troy's council chamber) to a study of these same phenomena as they operate in larger, more public, more interactive contexts (the theme within the Greek camp). This latter emphasis on the relationship between the self and the market forces which shape it receives its fullest treatment in Ulysses' Act III, Scene iii conversation with Achilles, just after the latter has been spurned by the other Greeks. Faced with an Achilles who conceives of his own worth as intrinsic, Ulysses presents him with two propositions which challenge this assumption (and therefore contradict the essentialism of Ulysses' 'degree' speech). No matter how richly endowed with inward qualities a man is, he cannot, Ulysses maintains,

> ... make boast to have that which he hath,
> Nor feels not what he owes [i.e., owns], but by reflection.
>
> (iii. iii. 93–4)

The first claim here is the strongest, implying (with its emphatic 'have') that our very *possession* of our inner qualities is somehow deferred until acknowledged by or in others. The second claim argues more simply that we do not *perceive* our own powers and virtues until we witness them exerting their effect upon others and/or witness those others' recognition of them. This latter point would later be echoed in King James's *The Peace-Maker*. There, honour is defined as 'the Rumour of a beautifull ... vertuous Action; which redoundeth from our Soules to the view of the World, and by Reflection, into our selues, bringing to vs Testimonie of that which others beleeue of vs'.[119]

Ulysses follows up the first iteration of his argument with a second, subtler one:

[119] James VI and I 1619: sigs. D4^{r–v}.

> ... no man is the lord of anything,
> Though in and of him there be much consisting,
> Till he communicate his parts to others.
> Nor doth he of himself know them for aught
> Till he behold them formèd in th'applause
> Where they're extended.

(ll. 110–15)

Again, the first proposition here asserts that man's potential qualities only become distinct entities when they are actualized as activities or processes. Self-command only becomes genuine, man can only be said to be 'lord' of himself (or truly 'to *have* that which he hath'), when he can produce from the muddled terrain of his soul the deliberate actions which constitute powers and virtues. Things which only exist *in potentia* may as well not exist at all: it is their actualization which demonstrates the lordship of the self over its own matter. This amounts to a performance of self-definition, the individual displaying to others the distinct 'parts'—the particular capacities—which he can create from his 'much consisting'. The second proposition, following from this, is again that the individual himself only *perceives* his powers through that same process of exercising them, extending them to others; but on second iteration Ulysses takes this point further. Now, he makes the more radical claim that *what* exactly these virtues and capacities are to the individual, *how* he himself sees them (as opposed to merely the fact that he does see them), depends upon the context which receives *and constructs* them. According to Ulysses' argument, it is the recipients of man's actions who 'form' them (l. 114). This audience, in other words, draws the boundaries between the individual's various qualities, deciding on the moral and utilitarian value of his different actions and labelling some as expressions of virtue, some as powers, some as neither, all according to their—this audience's (or market's)—interests at the given moment. Such, then, is the 'applause' (or otherwise) which puts 'form' upon each man's parts and actions, and thereby determines *in what way* he will 'know' himself. Achilles provides a famous instance of this process. In commonplace sketches of the Trojan landscape, he is valued ('applauded') for his powers as a warrior. In keeping with this fact, the communicable 'part' into which others 'form' him—the only part by which they see him—is his arm. In the painting of Troy which bedecks Lucrece's apartments, Achilles is only partially depicted, represented solely by his 'armèd hand' gripping a spear (*Rape of Lucrece*, ll. 1424–8). This same synecdoche creeps in at the edge of *Troilus*: Agamemnon swears 'With surety stronger than Achilles' arm' (I. iii. 219), again demonstrating how far this one part of the Myrmidon has been assimilated into colloquial consciousness.

If man's self-knowledge is formed in the applause of others, that medium is, inevitably, a distorting reflector. Ulysses likens it to an 'arch' reverberating back the voice which strikes it, or to 'a gate of steel' which mirrors the Sun's image and heat (III. iii. 115–16). As Bowen notes, though, neither of these is a perfectly reflective surface, and Shakespeare avoids the one thing which would be, the analogy of a mirror.[120] The audience, these exactly chosen similes imply, actually shapes the viewed spectacle according to its own image—and certainly in relation to its own passions and interests. In short, to quote again that illuminating Quarto phrase, the audience is 'attributive / To what [it] itself affects'. As Achilles has by now discovered, once the preoccupations of these spectators change (as they will keep on doing, perpetually), the figure 'formed' by them will, by implication, dissolve. On this description of the world—a far cry from Ulysses' other vision, where 'degree' is absolute—Achilles' valued self does not merely go out of fashion, but, in a phenomenological sense, ceases to be, to have form. Thus Ajax, being as yet unappreciated, '*knows not* what' he has (l. 122): he will not 'know' his powers 'for aught' until 'tomorrow' (l. 125), when they will be 'formed' in applause. Meantime Achilles, Ulysses hints, should recognize that *he* is disappearing: Ajax even now 'eats into' him (l. 131). In a phenomenological sense his very existence is threatened. To the extent that his parts and virtues can only exist *to* him in proportion as they are shaped *for* him by others, his inwardness becomes here something externalized. It becomes a self which is constructed (and perpetually reconstructed) outside the self, or which resides within, but which is eternally dependent upon interpellation from without.[121] *The Peace-Maker* again echoes such vertiginous scepticism:

Reputation is but another mans Opinion, and Opinion is no substance for thee to consist of: For how canst thou consist of a thing that is without thee? ... [C]an there bee any thing more delusiue? ... a stranger ... separated in the Ayre from him that is honoured: ... it does not only, not enter into him, nor is inward and essentiall vnto him, but it does not so much as touch him.[122]

Ultimately, what Ulysses really hints at in arguing that men's persons are formed by the market of public opinion is the possibility that Achilles may shortly find himself deconstructed; and, having made that ugliest of postmodernist threats, he moves on to impress upon Achilles the appropriate response to make to this new, market-orientated idea of selfhood. Since good deeds 'are devoured as fast as ... made' (III. iii. 143) and actions of the present, 'Though less than [those] in past', will (simply by virtue of being present) 'o'ertop' their predecessors (l. 158), Achilles, Ulysses says, has no choice but

---

[120] Bowen 1993: 108.     [121] Cf. ibid. 108–9.     [122] James VI and I 1619: sigs. D3ʳ, 4ᵛ.

to embrace an ethic of constant, forward 'motion' (l. 177). Rather than relying on past achievements to secure present credit he must persistently reassert his virtues. At present, he has begun to 'entomb [himself] alive' (l. 180), since in keeping to his tent he shuns the processes on which his name and self depend for life. Now he must commit himself anew to life's perpetual race, for if he once slackens his pace, the thousands behind him, driven on by ambitious 'emulation' (l. 150), will surge past, at best 'rush[ing] by / And leav[ing] [him] hindmost' (ll. 153–4), at worst leaving him ignominiously 'O'errun and trampled on' (l. 157). Fates as ugly as the latter are possible because the glory market fosters the violently competitive passions of envy (l. 168) and emulousness (ll. 150, 183).[123] If Achilles himself does not embrace such self-regarding affections, he will become victim to others who do—and indeed every character in the play, even Thersites (and especially Ajax), does exude these same passions.[124] This entire lecture is of course improvised to induce in Achilles a paranoia which might push him back on to the battlefield. The race image, especially, crystallizes the fear which Ulysses would foist upon him. But this 'wisdom' is also, as it happens, expressive of the play's larger ethos. Cressida, for example, muses in Act I on the dangers of ever reaching love's finishing line, and therefore determines to postpone that moment of fruition—to keep the chase going—for as long as possible:

> Things won are done. Joy's soul lies in the doing.
> .    .    .    .    .    .    .    .    .
> Men price the thing ungained more than it is.
> That she was never yet that ever knew
> Love got so sweet as when desire did sue.
>
> (i. ii. 283–7)

Similarly, towards the end of the Folio text Agamemnon affirms that only each 'extant moment' is alive and significant (iv. vii. 52). 'What's past and what's to come' (l. 50), the larger meanings of history, subside into formless oblivion as the self-regarding heroes of Troy concentrate, instead, on the present instant and the competition to preen themselves before one another's eyes.

---

[123] Kahn (1997: 15–17, 88–96, 113–17, 125–7, 134–7) discusses at length the troubling centrality of emulation within Shakespeare's concept of republican Rome. Cf. Mallin 1995: 34–5; Rebhorn 1990: *passim*, esp. 97–9.

[124] Ulysses himself is the first to exhibit just such feelings. Disgusted that Achilles dismisses his own penchant for strategic planning as mere 'closet war' (i. iii. 205), Ulysses casts his rival as a figure who threatens to 'overbulk us all' (l. 314). He replicates his own sense of affront in Agamemnon and Nestor by mimicking before them Patroclus's demeaning game of acting out *their* greatness. Implicitly, therefore, the project of disciplining Achilles is in part Ulysses' exercise in vengeance and a reassertion of his own 'priority' as much as it is one of furthering Greek state interests. On Thersites' emulousness see Bradshaw 1987: 140–1.

The honour market produces, then, an ethic of constant forward motion and a preoccupation with competitive, emulous passions. The Greek generals encourage these tendencies amongst Ajax, Achilles, *et al.* because they are necessary to the promotion of the Achaean military cause; but inevitably, as Achilles' proud resistance demonstrates, such ambitions are equally prone to turn in upon the state. The same forces which, when directed into the race for prestige, galvanize competitive individuals to pursue civic achievement, may just as easily work to tear a society apart, propelling it backwards into a bellicose state of nature. This is the vision with which Ulysses terrifies his fellow commanders in Act I:

> Strength should be lord of imbecility,
> And the rude son should strike his father dead.
> Force should be right—or rather, right and wrong,
> Between whose endless jar justice resides,
> Should lose their names, and so should justice too.
> Then everything includes itself in power,
> Power into will, will into appetite,
> And appetite, an universal wolf,
> .   .   .   .   .   .   .   .   .   .
> [Must] last eat up himself.

> (I. iii. 114–24)

If in other parts of *Troilus* Shakespeare presents the 'particular will' as circumscribed by putative measures of absolute value (Hector's lecture to Troilus) or as fostered within the restraining environment of 'forming' applause (Ulysses' to Achilles), here the playwright imagines that same will as something wholly untrammelled—self-interest running riot. Ulysses makes three distinct points about man's degeneration into such a state of nature. First, and most straightforwardly, in such a scenario moral terminology loses its currency. Second, the categories of moral psychology also fragment: will (understood as a special form of desire, subservient to reason) simply dissolves into animal appetite, because the psychomachic relationship between Aquinas's different orders of appetition, a relationship driven by conflicting measures of interest (social versus bestial self), ceases to apply. Third, this ethos of unchecked indulgence needs must end in the destruction not just of others, but also of the aggressive agent himself, because rapacious hedonism can never satisfy its desires and so descends into self-torment. This, of course, is yet another vision of tasting and eating, but where Ulysses' Act III, Scene iii race ends only in localized bouts of cannibalism—the odd Ajax 'eating into' the odd Achilles—this other possible future presents a catastrophe in which every man feasts on every other. Such is the end-point of a world driven by 'particular wills' instead of by wills formed within the constraining applause of public opinion.

The philosophical aspects of *Troilus* emphasized here—the pervasiveness of self-interest and subjective evaluations, the market conception of the self, the ideal of constant motion, the anatomization of a bellicose state of nature—are important because they carry us forward from the tawdry cynicism of late Elizabethan disillusionment to the defining precepts of Hobbes's moral philosophy. In this regard *Troilus* demonstrates how far that Hobbesian thought (a subsequent concern of this book) was the natural outgrowth of a turn-of-the-century critique of Tudor ethics, more so than critics preoccupied with Hobbes's place in the history of natural law or contract theory, for example, have allowed. But *Troilus* is important, too, more immediately, because it brings together a third set of terms and values which again prove resistant to the morality celebrated by Spenser or Erasmus. It underlines, along with the other works discussed here, how far Shakespeare's theatre made a point of challenging the moral assumptions of its day. As I have argued throughout the first part of this book, received wisdom at the beginning of the 1590s championed the sovereign authority of man's faculty of reason, casting the latter as a beacon of ascetic values and making it the driving force in a psychomachic project to crush the passions. *Hamlet*, though, and the tragedies of this chapter can be read as works which directly question the practicability of such goals; as works, too, which interrogate the adequacy and even desirability of so austere a set of aspirations. In that sense, in so far as they exemplify the gradual undermining of established assumptions, these plays chart a crucial step in the story of passion's triumph over reason. However, in order to trace the next stage in that same narrative, we need, now, to shift our ground, to move away from the predominantly secular ethos of the drama and turn instead to some theological (and thereafter poetic) responses to precisely the challenges outlined here.

# 5

## Augustinian and Aristotelian Influences from Herbert to Milton

One way in which moralists could respond to the challenges outlined in Chapter 4 was to identify a model of the mind which would give the emotions *moral* validation. If the affections could once be given a socially constructive mandate, they could then be indulged and cultivated with proper justification. Within academic and theological circles two approaches developed in the early 1600s which offered a solution of this order. The first of these marginalized previous talk of reason and psychomachia, elaborating instead upon Augustine's thesis that the Pauline spirit–flesh dichotomy provides a framework on to which to map a distinction between two different categories of feeling, one laudable, one not. This approach was favoured by English Protestants keen to deepen their understanding of Calvinist theology, but it was an outlook adopted too by Counter-Reformation writers eager to steal a march on the Reformers by capturing the ground of pious affectivity for themselves. These theological stances are congruent with, and to some extent informed, the devotional verse of Herbert and Crashaw, poetry in which the disposition of the heart is of pre-eminent concern and which celebrates the latter for the sanctified affections which it exudes. The other approach which again valorized certain passions as morally admirable is one which I have hinted at before: namely, the seventeenth-century extension of that Aristotelian tradition which had initially received only limited treatment during the Tudor period. The 1600s witnessed the publication of various, sophisticated Thomist and Aristotelian treatises on the passions which systematically reflected Aristotle's desire to rehabilitate the latter. These had a direct impact upon university drama of the time, but their outlook (along with that of the Augustinian tradition) also resonates with Milton's treatment of the passions in *Paradise Lost*. This is true, not least, in so far as Milton capitalizes in his poem on the complex analyses of self-delusion originally executed in such Thomist works as Wright's *Passions of the Minde* and Reynold's *Treatise of the Passions*. These, then, are the lines of argument sketched here.

## VARIETIES OF AUGUSTINIANISM

The distinction between spirit and flesh derives, as is well known, from Paul's separation of those in whom the spirit of God dwells from those of a 'carnal mind' who rather stand against him (Rom. 8: 7, 9). What this means in practical terms is laid out in Galatians 5: 19–26 and Colossians 3: 5–17, where Paul enumerates the works of both the flesh and the spirit. The former—lasciviousness, concupiscence, hatred, vainglory, envying, and a host of other passions—must be mortified if man is to put off the old man (the earthly Adam) and put on the new (Christ). The Christian must embrace instead spiritual actions of love, kindness, temperance, and forbearing. At root this amounts to distinguishing between those who 'live unto themselves' and those who 'be in Christ', living 'unto him which died for them' (2 Cor. 5: 15, 17). The spiritual man, remembering whose creation he is, devotes himself to the good of mankind, 'turning to his neighbour in order to use rightly' what he has been given.[1] In doing this, he demonstrates his love for others, a love premissed on the recognition that his neighbours share with him a place in God's world and therefore demand the same veneration which he himself does (hence 'love thy neighbour *as thyself*' (Gal. 5: 14) ). Charity is simultaneously an imperative to recognize others' value and to do homage to God by serving his creation. It is the core principle by means of which spiritual man lives in and through Christ's example. Carnal man, by contrast (forgetting that he is God's creature, utterly dependent upon the latter's grace), directs all his actions towards satisfying his own 'peruerse desire' of exaltation (*Citie of God*, 14. 13).[2] He lives according to his own, not God's, idea of morals, and proudly places an absolute value upon his own person, rather than seeing it as derivative of and dependent upon the 'vnchangeable good' of a higher being (14. 4, 13).[3] Carnal man's falsehood thus consists in his electing 'not to liue as hee was *made* to liue'—that is, according to the principles of charity and self-sacrifice which he was designed by God to serve (14. 4).[4] Instead, he lives a selfish, self-centred life. The spirit–flesh distinction is thus one between two different mind-sets—as Augustine puts it, two different cities, 'Gods loue swaying in the one, ... selfe-loue in the other' (14. 13).[5] In the Heavenly city men worship God, looking for reward only 'in the society of the holy'; in the earthly one they exalt themselves, pursuing only 'goods of the body' and their own 'minde' (14. 28).[6] In both cases, though, the prevailing disposition is, Augustine insists, a disposition of man's *will*. It

---

[1] Dihle 1982: 84.      [2] Augustine 1610: 514.      [3] Ibid. 500, 514.
[4] Ibid. 500.     [5] Ibid. 515.     [6] Ibid. 531.

is the *will*'s prerogative (working under grace's influence) to choose whether to live according to spirit or flesh, and *it* therefore determines man's moral character. The capacities of reason and understanding so prized by Socrates and the Stoics are comparatively unimportant in Augustine's way of imagining the mind. The will is presented as a faculty prior to and independent of them,[7] and as the independent point of origin for all impulses within the soul.[8]

For Augustine, though, as for Calvin, Perkins, and others, the experience of Christian life is not one in which the will *definitively* assumes either one disposition or the other, spirit or flesh. On the contrary, just as Paul lamented that the law of his members perpetually warred against the law of his mind (Rom. 7. 23), so Augustine notes that 'the flesh' constantly 'contend[s]' against the spirit', the will being pulled in two directions at once as it resists its own efforts to adopt a true Christian ethic (*Citie of God*, 13. 13).[9] This, man's 'disobedience to himselfe', is the subject of abstract comment in *Citie of God* 14. 15[10] and of graphic discussion in Book 8 of the *Confessions*. There, Augustine looks back to the moment when, though his will was predominantly carnal, he nonetheless sighted another, better disposition nascent within himself:

the new *will* which I began to haue [with which] to serue ... and ... enioy thee, O God, ... was not yet in termes to maister that other, which had beene established by ... long continuance. Thus did my two *Wills*, ... one carnall and another spirituall, fight one against the other, and ... diuide ... my soule asunder .... I had, I say, experience in them both; but now there was more of me in that, which I approued, then in that which I misliked .... For in this [the latter, carnal will] I was not then so much, because ... I did ... but suffer that vnwillingly, which before indeed I had done willingly. (*Confessions*, 8. 5)[11]

This psychic conflict, which becomes for Augustine the essence of spiritual life, is different from the psychomachia of, say, Platonic tripartition. Augustine (like Perkins after him) describes in effect 'the fragmentation of a *single* principle' within himself,[12] a fight between the heart and the heart, not between two allegorically separable entities. His condition is one in which the mind is possessed of two wills 'neither of which is intiere' and neither of which can command in 'full and perfect' fashion (8. 9).[13] Instead, time and again he finds his intentions (indeed his very selfhood) 'dissipated' by that same self, even against his own wishes (8. 10)—this because 'the violence of custome' (8. 5), his long-habituated taste for carnality, refuses to relinquish its grip.[14]

Augustine insists that the troubles of man's internecine conflict are of his own making. 'Custom' (or sinful habit), he notes in the *Confessions*,

---

[7] Dihle 1982: 127.          [8] Dillon and Long 1988: 257.
[9] Augustine 1610: 475, alluding also to Gal. 5: 17.          [10] Augustine 1610: 517–18.
[11] Augustine 1620: 361–2.          [12] Dillon and Long 1988: 257.
[13] Augustine 1620: 382–3.          [14] Ibid. 384, 364.

'had grown ... importunate against me, by myne own fault, because by ... ill gouernement ... I was come thither willingly' (8. 5).[15] By contrast, the solution to this problem stems primarily from God. Books 2 and 3 of *De Libero Arbitrio* prioritize grace as the primary agent responsible for our regeneration: 'since man cannot rise of his own will as he fell of his own will, the right hand of God ... is outstretched to us' to help us on our way (*Free Choice of the Will*, 2. 20. 54).[16] According to the *Retractiones*, though, the means through which grace exerts its influence is by regenerating man's power of self-determination. God 'predestines His elect' precisely by 'making ready [our] wills', whereupon it is incumbent on us to respond in kind, *willingly*, by 'embracing' his 'outstretched' hand (*Retractions*, 1. 9. 2, 4).[17] Regeneration is thus the product of co-operation between grace's efforts and our own,[18] but with first place going to grace. In *Ad Simplicianum De Diversis Quaestionibus* Augustine exemplifies this by explaining that grace first moves man to faith, but that thereafter inspired faith attracts further grace; faith and grace then combine, prompting man to do the good works indicative of a renewed spirituality (*To Simplicianus*, 1. 2. 2).[19] This same point is also put negatively: 'Unless ... the mercy of God in calling [us] precedes, no one can even believe, and so begin to be justified and ... receive the power to do good works' (1. 2. 7).[20] All this is also reflected in Book 8 of the *Confessions*, where Augustine repeatedly marries the efforts of his own agency to the greater redeeming influence of God's grace. On the one hand, Augustine now finds within himself the impulse to turn to his Lord and tread a spiritual path; yet on the other, he figures his soul as *initially* incapable of rousing itself without grace's assistance (*Confessions*, 8. 5).[21] It is God, the majority partner in this enterprise, who must first release him from being 'streightly bound' by lust; he then responds positively by pouring out his heart in penitence (8. 6).[22] As God forces him to look upon himself, so he takes the cue to 'whip on' his soul and translate 'a lame ... halfe wounded' spiritual will into 'an entire & strong' one (8. 7, 8).[23] The fact, though, that self-will is always the subservient, respondent partner in this relationship is scarcely surprising. As Paul puts it, 'What hast thou that thou didst not [first] receive?' (1. Cor. 4: 7).

It is into this framework of Pauline ethics that Augustine fits a more particular discussion of the moral value of the emotions. The crucial observation which he makes for this purpose is that the will, whatever its disposition may

---

[15] Augustine 1620: 362.     [16] Augustine 1968: 163.     [17] Ibid. 235, 239.
[18] Hence Augustine notes of Paul's spiritual acts, 'it was neither grace alone nor [Paul] himself alone' which produced them, 'but the grace of God and himself together' (*De Gratia et Libero Arbitrio* 5. 12 (Augustine 1968: 264) ).
[19] Augustine 1953: 386.     [20] Ibid. 391.     [21] Augustine 1620: 363–5.
[22] Ibid. 365.     [23] Ibid. 373, 376, 379.

be, whatever God may inspire it to 'delight' in and be 'stirred' to (*To Simpli-cianus*, 1. 2. 21–2),[24] will always manifest itself in and through the affections. Thus the worth of the latter will depend upon that of the will which informs them: 'if *it* be bad, so are all those motions, if good, they are … praise-worthy: for there is a will in them all: nay they are all direct wills: what is desire, and ioy, but a will consenting to that which wee affect: and what is feare, and sorrow, but a will contrary vnto what we like?' (*Citie of God*, 14. 6).[25] Above all, the quality of the will will determine what particular things man chooses to love and hate. Indeed, Augustine defines each of his cardinal passions—desire, joy, fear, and grief—with reference to love, arguing that where the latter is spiritually based, the derivative feelings will also be good, and where carnal, bad (14. 7).[26] Given this basis of validation, Augustine is inevitably as sup-portive of the cultivation of right feelings—feelings arising 'from the loue of good' and holy charity (14. 9)—as Aristotle and Aquinas are.[27] For him the operative question is 'not whether one be angry, but *wherefore*? *Why* he is sad, not whether he be sad?' (9. 5).[28] For a Stoic the very presence of an emotion would be enough to render the mind vicious, but for Augustine what counts is intention and the quality of willing. Rightly directed, these make passions virtuous. 'For anger with an offender to reforme him: pitty vpon one afflicted to succour him: feare for one in daunger to deliuer him, these no man, not mad, can reprehend.'

Augustine devotes a substantial chapter to this theme in *The Citie of God*, the fulsomeness of his text underlining both the significance of this point for his conception of governance and his sense that in advocating passion he is arguing against the grain. He begins chapter 9 of Book 14 by citing numerous emotions which Christians positively ought to feel: fear of eternal punishment, desire for eternal life, fear and pain about their sins, gladness in their good works, fear and pain or (if they are more confident) desire and gladness in face of temptation, etc. Grief too is accorded a place in this catalogue in light of Paul's commendation of the Corinthians 'for that they were Godly sorrowfull' (14. 8).[29] Indeed, the value of each of these affections is confirmed by biblical citations.[30] Augustine, though, endorses his position further by emphasizing the various passions which moved Paul in particular. 'Behold him', he urges us, as he '*Weepe*[*s*] *with them that weepe, and reioyce*[*s*] *with them that reioyce*, fightings without, and terrours within, *desyring to bee dissolued and to be with* CHRIST, … beeing iealous ouer the Corinthians, … hauing great sadnesse, and continuall sorrow of heart for *Israell*' (14. 9). Furthermore, Augustine celebrates Christ for his emotions. He notes the extent to which Jesus, in

---

[24] Augustine 1953: 405–6.  [25] Augustine 1610: 503.  [26] Ibid. 504.
[27] Ibid. 508.  [28] Ibid. 343.  [29] Ibid. 506.  [30] Ibid. 508.

his Incarnation, chose to exhibit feelings: sorrow *'for Ierusalems hardnesse of heart'*, tears for Lazarus, grief at the approach of his own Passion.[31] Given this divine endorsement, there can be no doubting the affections' virtue. Indeed, the corollary of all this is that *not* to feel emotions in this life—to attain to the supposed ideal of *apatheia*—is morally reprehensible. *Impassibilitas* is bought at too high a price, the price of 'stupidity of bodie, and barbarisme of minde' (and of pride too, the characteristic carnal failing of the Stoics).[32] In sum, then, *The Citie of God* insists that the Christian who manages (with God's grace and through his own efforts) to render himself spiritual, will also be one who exhibits holy affections, and his doing so constitutes, in Augustine's view, the realization of an ideal well worth aspiring to.

This view is directly reflected in Calvin's *Institutes*. Calvin refuses to condemn man's natural desires per se, because they were implanted in him by God (*Institutes*, 3. 3. 12).[33] (The fault lies, rather, in their becoming unbridled.) Like Augustine, he therefore applauds Christ's earthly affections, his 'sorrow ... and fearfulnesse', because they retain an intrinsic moderation characteristic of man's prelapsarian state which makes them morally valuable (2. 16. 12).[34] Calvin also rehearses the numerous biblical passages in which Christ's weeping and quaking for his own and others' adversities is cast as exemplary (3. 8. 9).[35] In the same vein, Bouwsma notes, Calvin reiterates Augustine's condemnation of the stone-hearted Stoics as figures who 'put off all nature of man'.[36] More importantly, the French theologian emphasizes that grace's principal role is to exert so inward an influence that man learns to obey God 'from his very heart' (2. 3. 14).[37] The conviction of justification, in other words, when it comes, should register immediately as a birth of new 'affections' within the will (3. 3. 8).[38] The elect should experience their regeneration through an eruption, within the heart, of those same emotions identified by Augustine as indicative of the spiritual will. (The *difference* between the two theologians here is that whereas Augustine attributes regeneration to a co-operation between God's grace and a certain amount of responsive, self-willed impetus in man, Calvin's explanation for the same phenomenon gives overwhelming emphasis to the force of grace, man being simply the passive recipient thereof.) The new feelings born in the heart include, in the first instance, godly sorrow and an abhorrence of sin (3. 3. 7).[39] These impulses extend to such holy affections as shame, self-indignation, fear of God, a zealous 'Desire for diligence in oure dutie and redy cherefulnesse to obeye', and even vengefulness towards one's past sins

---

[31] Augustine 1610: 509.       [32] Ibid. 509–10.       [33] Calvin 1561: f. 130$^v$.
[34] Ibid. f. 100$^r$.       [35] Ibid. f. 166$^v$.       [36] Ibid. f. 166$^r$, and Bouwsma 1975: 39.
[37] Calvin 1561: f. 24$^r$.       [38] Ibid. f. 129$^r$.       [39] Ibid. f. 128$^v$.

(3. 3. 15).[40] More consolingly though, the same scheme encompasses love of
God (3. 3. 11) and spiritual joy (3. 8. 10).[41] This, then, is the 'feeling faith', the
display of devout emotions (more important than the activity of any faculty
of reason), which Calvin makes intrinsic to his ideal of Christianity.[42]

As Calvin realized, the Augustinian ideal of affectivity offered an alternative
to the humanist language of psychomachia and its inbuilt hostility to the
emotions. It acknowledged, rather, the power of such feelings, and offered a
positive assessment of affectivity for those (symbolized by Hamlet or Tamyra)
who sought a way of incorporating the passions, in *some* form, into moral
life. Unsurprisingly, English Protestant theologians began to reflect this same
ideal from the late 1590s onwards, their prior concentration on psychomachia
notwithstanding. Traces of Augustine's ethic are apparent, for example, in
Greenham's *Meditations on Proverbs 4*, where Greenham argues that the best
way to gauge one's spiritual state is to observe what one's joy, grief, hope, and
fear are focused upon. Those who find themselves inclined to probe their own
state of salvation, and who feel joy or grief when they do so, may be sure of their
election; those who find their affections turned towards self-advancement, and
who 'reioyce more in [their] owne gaine, then [they] canst be sorrowfull for
[their] brothers harme', may take that for evidence of reprobacy.[43] The
experiencing of all this, though, is, for Greenham, a matter of absolute
passivity: man cannot shape his destiny or, therefore, his emotions; he can
only read off that destiny by weighing the morality of the affections which he
observes himself exhibiting. Perkins builds on Greenham's point, emphasizing
all the more those good 'motions ... and desires' which the spirit begets in
a regenerate will.[44] He notes (as per Augustine) that in mortal man such
affections are characteristically divided against themselves, partly embracing
and partly eschewing God's purposes. His treatise *The Estate of a Christian
in this Life* matches *The Citie of God* by enumerating twenty-two scriptural
texts which applaud Christian passions. Perkins then anatomizes man's four
most 'Sanctified affections': zeal, fear of God, hatred of sin, and joy at the
approach of Judgement Day.[45] Again, a Christian animated by these emotions
is told that he may be sure of his spiritual worth. Donne signals another step
in the development of this argument. The ethical value of holy affections
is the principal theme in his 1623 sermon on the text 'Jesus Wept'. There
he insists that Christ's tears—and Christ's emotions generally—were never
uncontrolled. He may have 'ungirt himselfe, and give[n] more scope ... to his

---

[40] Ibid. ff. 131$^v$–2$^r$.     [41] Ibid. ff. 130$^r$, 166$^v$.

[42] For broader comment on the part played by 'devout affection' in sixteenth-century
Continental Protestantism, see Bouwsma 1975: 38–9 and Strier 1983: 144–5.

[43] Greenham 1599: 200–1.     [44] Perkins 1603: 567–8.

[45] Ibid. 442–3. Cf. Perkins 1604: 413, 416, 442 ff.

passions, then ... other men', but always, Donne says, Christ's passions were 'in his own power', sanctified, and forever pure: 'as in a clean glasse, if water be stirred and troubled, though it may conceive a little ... froth, yet it contracts no foulenesse in that clean glasse, [so] the affections of Christ were moved, but so: in that holy vessell they would contract no foulenesse.'[46] Christ's tears signify his pity for man, and our task is to weep likewise. Those who, like sponges dried into pumice stones, cannot come to 'that melting, ... thawing, ... resolving of the bowels which good soules feele', are to be condemned.[47] It is man's duty to foster holy affections within himself, to feel sorrow for men's sins and a desire to avert human calamities.[48] Crucially for the development of moral thought later in the century, Donne figures this growth of sensibility as an expansion of the self. Just as God chose to 'draw a Circumference about [his] Center, Creatures about himselfe, and to shed forth lines of love upon all', so man's expansive soul should throw out lines of love to others.[49] To do this is, Donne notes, to follow Augustine's explicit moral instruction.

These examples notwithstanding though, the most important of England's Protestant treatments of the passions is William Fenner's *Treatise of the Affections*, a book published in 1641 and reprinted six times in the next seventeen years. The treatise comprises several sermons on the Pauline theme 'Set your affections on things that are above, and not on things ... on the earth'. Fenner's thesis is that because man's affections are never idle and, left unguided, will always be 'running out and bringing into the soul' sometimes 'healing' but often 'hurtful objects', it is imperative that they should be directed to spiritual goals.[50] Man's aspiration should be to see his heart overwhelmed by affections of love and fear for God, and of grief for his sins. Strictly speaking, it is, anyway, his duty to set his emotions upon godly things because the affections by their nature crave the good and the only true good is God.[51] Hence Fenner urges man to make his heart *'engaged for'* and *'quite given up to'* God, to love only Christ as his spouse and eschew all other goods.[52] Carnal affections, though, exert a bewitching hold over the heart such that the latter develops a 'sympathy' with the things of this world.[53] Erasing this is no easy matter.

Pursuant to this larger aspiration, Fenner does allow the individual a degree of personal agency in the management of his affections. Although the latter are seated in the heart, Fenner insists that they are not simply the dumb motions of Aquinas's sensitive appetite (whose existence he also acknowledges). The Pauline 'affections' (like Aquinas's rational 'affections')

---

[46] Donne 1953–62: iv. 328–9.        [47] Ibid. iv. 339.        [48] Ibid. iv. 343.
[49] Ibid. iv. 330.        [50] Fenner 1651: 1.        [51] Ibid. 48–51.
[52] Ibid. 17–18.        [53] Ibid. 62.

are something more than Thomism's sensitive passions, because (as is clear in the case of something like shame) they are directly responsive to such *rational* considerations as disgrace and esteem.[54] The will's affections can stimulate the lower, sensitive passions, but Fenner is scrupulous in discriminating between these two because the Scriptures would not, he says, command us to set the latter, animal motions upon God.[55] Given their connection with rationality, Fenner's 'affections' are, then, susceptible to the techniques of governance of humanist philosophy, in which respect carnal man can (by his own agency) raise them up *towards* goodness and *towards* Christ. He may possess enough '*embers of right reason*' to moderate his affections exactly as Spenser's Palmer had hoped, making himself 'morally humble', chaste, and just.[56] However, the crux of Fenner's typically Calvinist argument is that this will not be of absolute, theological value until *after* grace has reorientated the soul, investing it with a spiritual disposition. Then indeed such everyday self-governance will become a pressing obligation as the agent works with the Holy Spirit to defeat his flesh; but in the meantime that same display of self-control can do nothing to solicit the regeneration of his will which is God's work alone. Fenner therefore announces early on that 'If ye be not risen with Christ' already, 'ye cannot mortifie your affections, nor raise up your affections to God'.[57] Here, as in Augustine, a visitation by grace is the *sine qua non* of truly virtuous attainment; yet in procuring that, the individual is himself impotent. That said, those who do have grace visited upon them quickly discover that '*the affections are good channels for* [it] *to run down in*'.[58] In other words, grace (here, just as in Calvin) is felt *as* an eruption of valuable, holy affections within the heart. Fenner thus urges his audience to search for signs of those within themselves and to treasure any such experiences.

Besides making these points, Fenner takes pains to emphasize the usefulness of man's sanctified affections. He describes them as both the hands and the handles of the heart: hands because (as per Aristotle's argument about desire) man would not be *moved* to 'take hold' of any good, any worthy object or moral opportunity which might be before him, if he were bereft of these activating impulses; handles because, reciprocally, nothing (the Word included) can take hold of the heart except by first stimulating its affections, its capacity to love and take delight in things.[59] The affections, then, are the vital medium through which regenerate man interacts, morally, with his environment, and Fenner emphasizes that fact by invoking some familiar analogies. Without the affections we would be but 'senselesse stones'.[60] Deprived of any stimulus to act, we would be like Plutarch's pilot stranded at sea awaiting a wind, or like St

---

[54] Ibid. 4. Cf. Fiering 1981: 160.   [55] Fenner 1651: 4–6.   [56] Ibid. 18–19.
[57] Ibid. 2.   [58] Ibid. 59.   [59] Ibid. 39–40.   [60] Ibid. 57.

Bernard's chariot without wheels.[61] In Cicero's familiar phrase, just as anger is 'the whetstone to valour', so we should recognize that all the affections are '*whetstones to good*', love promoting obedience; grief, repentance; pity, charity; and anger, zeal.[62] It comes as no surprise to find Fenner supplementing these judgements with the observation that such impulses cannot be sinful because prelapsarian Adam and Christ Incarnate both felt them.[63] Here again, then, is the familiar portfolio of Augustinian arguments recycled for Caroline audiences.

Theological claims for the moral value of the affections were not, though, the preserve of Puritans. After the Council of Trent, Counter-Reformation voices intent on matching the emotive appeal of Protestantism also set to work putting this case. Their texts, too, could thus meet England's need for a new ethical language. St François de Sales's *Traité de l'Amour de Dieu*, for example, a work translated by Herbert's friend Miles Pinkney in 1630, and Jean-François Senault's *L'Usage des Passions*, translated in 1649, are both built upon the proposition that Christianity's distinctive experience is one of relinquishing the passions of the flesh and embracing those of the spirit. These treatises appropriate the same Augustinian sources as their Protestant counterparts, but differ in fusing Augustinian with Thomist moral psychology. According to François and Senault, once grace has first rejuvenated the heart, Aquinas's intellectual powers of reason and rational will kick in, resuming their autonomous government of the self.[64] Where Calvinism emphasizes the perpetual impotence of the human agent, his dependence on recurrent infusions of grace, these Catholic authors follow Aristotle in allowing, instead, that man has considerable power to define his own nature through his rational faculties (once, that is, grace has set him on the right affective path, teaching him spiritual love). The Counter-Reformation moralists thus meet their opponents on the latter's own ground, but with an argument which, enticingly, gives men more reason to have faith in themselves.

The Catholic popularization of holy affections is still clearer, though, in another work by François, his *Introduction to a Deuoute Life*.[65] First published in English in 1613, and reprinted eight times during the remainder of the century, the *Introduction* is not a treatise on self-governance but a guide to François' meditative practice, the purpose of such meditation being to 'roote

---

[61] Fenner 1651: 507–8. On St Bernard's theory of the passions and his chariot imagery, see Tilmouth 2000.

[62] Fenner 1651: 58.        [63] Ibid. 54–5.

[64] For a full description of these theologians' arguments, the subtlety and contradictoriness of which I cannot do justice to here, see Levi 1964: 114–22, 213–24.

[65] On Ferrar's and Herbert's particular interest in this, see Clarke 1997: 72–4.

out of [the] hart all sinne' and induce an 'abundance of good motions in our will'.[66] François begins by offering some commonplace instruction in the kinds of carnal inclination which man must purge from himself (Part I, chapters 5–8, 21–4). Against this is set another, more positive command to engage in intensely visualizing meditations upon Christ's Passion.[67] It is these contemplative exercises which produce the 'pour[ing] out' of 'good motions' into the heart, an overwhelming 'loue of God & our neighbour; the desire of Paradise, and eternall glory; zeale ... compassion, ioye, feare of iudgement ...; hatred of sinne; confidence in the ... mercy of God; shame ... for our naughty life passed'.[68] In a mirroring of Donne's vision of self-expansion, the primary effect of these 'affects' is to 'dilate', 'amplify', and 'extend' man's spirit, to transform him into a larger, (literally) magnanimous being, charitably connected to the world around him. More prosaically, François also urges his reader to translate such emotions into action: so if meditation upon Christ's first words from the Cross (Luke 23: 34) provokes in the devotee a desire to pardon his enemies, he must then frame that impulse as a specific resolution to forgive or placate some particular individual.[69] Searching out the day-to-day opportunities to execute these good purposes becomes an immediate obligation.[70] Admittedly François, having made these points, does immediately return to dwelling upon the ecstasy of emotions produced by meditation—'Many times ... thy affection wilbe ... fired ... with deuotion to God: and then ... thou must lett go the bridle ... that they may runne freely after the inuiting of Gods spirit'—but even here he concludes by re-emphasizing the actions into which these feelings must flow.[71] As with the Calvinists, then, there is a clear purpose to such affectivity. But if François matches Calvin on this point, he departs from him in his understanding of how these experiences are brought about. The very fact that this form of ethical growth emerges from a series of spiritual exercises, consciously undertaken, underlines how far the devotee himself is, according to this Catholic writer, the agent of his own transformation. François allows the latter far more autonomy than would, say, Fenner. The meditative process is fuelled by God's grace (for the support of which one must pray)[72] but throughout the *Introduction*—for example, in the discussion of how to cope with a spiritual crisis, and in the twin descriptions of Christ and God's love for mankind[73]—François emphasizes that since grace is infinitely forthcoming, one may be confident of receiving

---

[66] De Sales 1613: 63, 143.
[67] For further explication of this technique, see Martz 1962: 250–4.
[68] De Sales 1613:143.  [69] Ibid. 144.  [70] Ibid. 148–9.
[71] Ibid. 151–3. On this practical element cf. Clarke 1997: 94, 96.
[72] De Sales 1613: 63, 146.  [73] Ibid. $^{2}$67–79, $^{2}$118–124.

it.[74] Like Augustine, in fact, he describes an experience which is essentially one of co-operation between divine intervention and self-willed agency; an experience, therefore, which purports to be more accessible than the affectivity offered by Calvinism, but which is every bit as invigorating.


## HERBERT AND CRASHAW

The fact that Caroline England provided both a Puritan and a High Anglican audience eager to embrace the new language of holy affections outlined here has been emphatically demonstrated by Thomas Healy,[75] and further to Healy's own work the obvious place to turn to to locate a literary analogue for this same development is the poetry of Crashaw and Herbert. My aim now, though, is not to identify any relationships of detail or direct allusion linking the theological works discussed above with the lyrics of these poets. Rather, my focus is on tracing some of the imaginative presuppositions which connect the one with the other: their common emphasis on the heart (or spiritual love), for example, as the centripetal presence within the soul; their emphasis, too, not on psychomachic confrontation but on fissile self-division; and, above all, their common concern with affectivity.[76]

The Pauline dynamic which puts affectivity at the heart of man's selfhood is immediately apparent in Herbert's parallel lyrics, 'Love I' and 'Love II': [77]

| | |
|---|---|
| Immortal Love, author of this great frame, | Immortal Heat, O let thy greater flame |
| Sprung from that beauty which can never fade; | Attract the lesser to it: let those fires, |
| How hath man parcelled out thy glorious name, | Which shall consume the world, first make it tame; |
| And thrown it on that dust which thou hast made, | And kindle in our hearts such true desires, |
| While mortal love doth all the title gain! | 5 As may consume our lusts, and make thee way. |
| Which siding with invention, they together | Then shall our hearts pant thee; then shall our brain |

---

[74] Bertonasco (1971: 59–60, 67–8) particularly emphasizes François' encouragement to us to trust in divine benevolence.

[75] Healy 1986: 31–9, 67.

[76] Tuve (1970) and Strier (1983: pp. xviii–xix, ch. 7) both discuss the last of these, affectivity, but in the earlier part of this chapter I have sought to provide a less Lutheran background for my analysis of this theme than that employed by Strier in particular.

[77] Herbert and Vaughan 1986: 46 ff.

Bear all the sway, possessing heart and
brain,
(Thy workmanship) and give thee share
in neither.
Wit fancies beauty, beauty raiseth
wit:
The world is theirs; they two play out
the game,
Thou standing by: and though thy
glorious name
Wrought our deliverance from
th'infernal pit,
Who sings thy praise? only a scarf or
glove
Doth warm our hands, and make them
write of love.

All her invention on thine Altar
lay,
And there in hymns send back thy fire
again:
Our eyes shall see thee, which before
saw dust;
10 Dust blown by wit, till that they both
were blind:
Thou shalt recover all thy goods in
kind,
Who wert disseizèd by usurping
lust:
All knees shall bow to thee; all wits shall
rise,
And praise him who did make and
mend our eyes.

These two sonnets portray contrasting loves, each oriented around a different axis. Working as a pair, they dramatize a single soul divided against itself, heart against heart, affection against affection. The frustration of unity which that dichotomy implies is evident at a verbal level within the text of 'Love I'. In this first sonnet, a picture of one whose 'heart and brain' are 'possessed' by worldly passions, the antimetabole of a line like 'Wit fancies beauty, beauty raiseth wit' might suggest that carnal souls enjoy a peculiar autarky, that they are somehow complete unto themselves. But that rhetorical trick is an illusion. In practice there is an air of superficiality about the Cavalier poetaster conjured in this poem. Life, according to his values, is reduced to a 'game', and pleased though he is with his inventiveness, the most that *his* muse can rise to is the praise of some lady's 'glove'. Tellingly, Herbert imagines here a garment which warms only the hands, a bodily extremity: the imagined Cavalier may purport to possess the heart, but he does not probe it; rather, he gravitates *away* from it. The same carnal mind presumes that it can 'parcel out' God's share of the world and cast that aside, yet that verb 'parcel' is reminiscent of another parcelling out in Herbert's 'Offering'.[78] There, the fleshly heart is portrayed as a perforated organ (l. 4), one devoid of integrity and unity because ruptured by divergent passions—

> so oft divisions
> Thy lusts have made, and not thy lusts alone;
> Thy passions also have their set partitions.
> These parcel out thy heart.
>
> (ll. 14–17)

[78] Ibid. 133 ff.

The Cavalier of 'Love I' suffers just such a fate. The dust (the frippery) blown before his eyes by his own wit blinds both eyes and wit alike ('Love II', ll. 9–10). Where two powers imagine themselves co-operating in the pursuit of sensuous pleasure, they actually succeed only in disabling themselves and dividing away from each other.

By contrast, the conceits of 'Love II', Herbert's vision of a love expressive of spiritual affection, underline the centripetal effect of this kind of emotion. With its opening image of God, 'O let thy greater flame / Attract the lesser to it', this lyric both acknowledges the overwhelming magnetism of grace and declares a longing for the unity which that grace promises. In fulfilment of that hope, the body parts—eyes, brain, and heart—of the new, spiritual lover sketched in 'II' are all imagined as focused upon God, and this lover's 'true desires', the new order of affections born in him at the moment of his justification, likewise gravitate towards the Lord. The ambiguities threaded into one of the clauses expressive of this point—'our hearts pant thee'—further intensify this impression of cohesion. The divine 'thee' here is the entity *for* which our hearts pant, but in so far as it is also *what* they breathe out, that 'thee' must already be inside the heart, and it must, too, be the agent *through* which (thanks to which) our hearts pant.[79] Furthermore, if God is already within us, and yet makes the heart pant *for* him, he thereby exerts a centripetal force. The heart, in yearning for God and finding him within, is pulled, as it were, towards itself, pulled into greater unity with itself (in contrast to the 'Offering's' dilemma). Likewise, 'Love II's' 'true desires', which (the persona tells God) now 'make thee way', are also locked by Herbert's pun on 'way' into a double process. Of course, these affections make God their way in that his spiritual ideal, his way, shapes their goals. However, as powerful registers of the Lord's weighty substance, these affections also make God *weigh*, both in this agent's own soul and in the souls of others who bear witness to the new, God-filled emotions animating this regenerate man. At every level, then, the language of love draws Herbert, in these sonnets, towards images of division, dissipation, cohesion, and concentration. Such are the terms within which Augustine's two spheres of affectivity are here experienced.

The 'Love' sonnets invoke a variety of body parts which testify to the Pauline transformation of the will. Ordinarily, though, Herbert imagines that process as a regeneration of the heart in particular—a thing now 'sapless grown' which, like a dead branch, 'drops away' until such time as God 'pours' in his love and refreshes its 'pulse'.[80] This focus is especially clear in

---

[79] Cf. Fish 1972: 193.

[80] 'Nature', l. 16; 'Repentance', l. 29; 'Mattens', l. 11; 'Gratefulness', ll. 31–2 (Herbert and Vaughan 1986: 38, 41 ff., 54, 111). The variety of ways in which Herbert exploits the language

'The Altar'.[81] The heart sits at the literal centre of this lyric where Herbert declares,

> A HEART alone
> Is such a stone,
> As nothing but
> Thy pow'r doth cut.
>
> (ll. 5–8)

The initial point made here is that, of all created things, only the human heart 'alone' is so intransigent as to be impervious to all influences but God; but quite *why* this is so, why man's heart is so hardened, is revealed in the other meaning of 'heart alone', the suggestion that in abandoning the way of the spirit man has isolated his heart from God, and thereby petrified it until such time as grace revivifies it. The further implication of these lines is that God's regeneration of this protagonist will be akin to the work of a stonemason, cutting a new sculpture from resistant rock. On this, Fish's reading, to 'cut' is to form.[82] But to 'cut' is also to wound, in which respect Herbert alludes in line 8 (the centrepoint of his poem) to the paradox at the heart of Christian experience: namely, that it is exactly wounding and bleeding which does re-form us. Christ's blood, 'Dropping from heav'n, ... doth ... cleanse and close / All sorts of wounds' ('An Offering', ll. 20–1), but the wounds must be made first: the Christian must *feel* his brokenness in order to be healed. Herbert feels just this in the opening couplets of 'The Altar'. He presents the altar of his own 'heart'[83]—as opposed to the altar that is his poem[84]—as indeed 'broken' and inadequately repaired:

> A broken ALTAR, Lord, thy servant rears,
> Made of a heart, and cemented with tears:
> Whose parts are as thy hands did frame;
> No workman's tool hath touched the same.
>
> (ll. 1–4)

Knowing that his whole being was originally God's workmanship (l. 3), he recognizes that at present its 'parts' retain that signature, but that 'parts' are all he has: the spiritual integrity which once bound these elements into a unity has gone, sacrificed through his own indiscretion. The heart / altar

---

of love and the motif of the heart is sketched, along with the diverse roles played by the heart in seventeenth-century emblematic literature, in Lewalski 1979: 292–9, 309–11, 193 ff.

[81] Herbert and Vaughan 1986: 22.

[82] Fish 1972: 213. Lewalski (1979: 205) notes the relevance of Cramer's emblem, 'Mollesco', which shows God hammering his way into a heart.

[83] On the biblical sources of this analogy see Lewalski 1979: 309, 312.

[84] See Strier 1983: 192.

which Herbert *now* 'rears' (turns upwards) to God is one which he has hastily 'reared' (constructed) from those shattered fragments by 'cementing' them together with penitential tears. This new heart cannot erase the traces of its past fracturing—only the cement of Christ's blood could, as the 'Offering' puts it, truly 'close' such scars—but then again nor should it, because, as the poet realizes, to hide such faultlines and feign perfection would be to sacrifice what little integrity he has now recovered (l. 4).

The first half of 'The Altar' records, then, Herbert's—mankind's—history of spiritual degradation and his dependence on grace if his heart is to be healed. The second half moves on to praise and pray to God, but, crucially, without losing sight of these prior truths. As we progress into the third quarter of the poem, the heart remains 'hard', tainted by carnality, but over and against that fact, it also now carries the touch of justification, making it simultaneously spiritual (and thus capable of sincere praise):

> Wherefore each part
> Of my hard heart
> Meets in this frame,
> To praise thy Name.

(ll. 9–12)

The word 'wherefore' here indicates, partly, that *because* man recognizes his dependence upon God (ll. 5–8), he now 'praises' him in a mixture of supplication and gratitude; but more than that, the 'wherefore' also suggests that Herbert's new-found ability to praise, now, is itself *the direct effect* of God's work, of God's having acknowledged man's dependence and chosen to 'cut' a new heart for him (ll. 7–8). Either way, the centrifugal tendencies of this shattered soul are, for an instant, arrested. Its disparate, self-dividing 'parts' contract and collect (in l. 11) around a new 'frame', the regenerate organ cut for man by God. Just as in 'Love II', a turn to the spirit brings unity. And this momentary convergence upon a centre point is enacted, too, in the poem's other 'frame', the visual frame of the work itself. Herbert's *mise en page* places the dimeters of lines 5–12 at the centre of the lyric, so that the verse itself seems to contract at its midriff, thoughts crowding together in the narrowest part of the textual frame. Since the two couplets before and after this section are first pentameters followed by tetrameters (ll. 1–4), and then the opposite (ll. 13–16), the result is a visual representation both of a perfect classical altar and of the letter 'I'.[85] However, it may not be too fanciful to add that the same *mise en page* also depicts (at a pinch) a single systole of the heart itself, and that Herbert squeezes into his text the oscillating spiritual states, the divergent

---

[85] See Schoenfeldt 1991: 165–7.

reflections, which typically pulse through the Christian soul with each beat of Harvey's cardiac muscle—that beat itself being a miniature moment of death and rebirth. Whatever the case, though, the '*hard* heart', the '*broken* Altar', does not go away amidst line 11's moment of distilled wonder and regeneration. (Justification brings a beginning, not an end, to the combat between spirit and flesh.) Herbert may, in short, 'chance to hold [his] peace' again, to stop celebrating God and revert to carnality hereafter (l. 13). However, even if he does so, the fact that it was *God* who brought the poet's parts together to 'Meet' in praise here, guarantees for all time the integrity of *this* spiritual moment recorded in *this* poem. 'These stones', the visually perfect altar which Herbert's *text* forms, will provide eternal testimony of God's power whatever the author's subsequent fate (l. 14), and in the meantime their demonstration of the sincerity of Herbert's spiritual gesture persuades the poet to dare a further prayer. He ends by praying that Christ may deign to 'SACRIFICE' himself upon 'this ALTAR' (Herbert's broken yet penitent body) and thereby 'sanctify' his charge as one of the elect (ll. 15–16).

'The Altar' underlines the centrality of the heart, of images of self-division, and of a craving for unity in its author's spiritual consciousness. Visually, it invites us to contemplate the heart's very pulse, which for early modern readers like Digby was the corporeal signature of the passions[86] and for Herbert was thereby a physical trace of one's love of God ('Gratefulnesse', ll. 31–2). 'The Altar' ends, though, by inviting a bodily connection with Christ, praying that the Son should die upon the poet's own torso in order to redeem it. This impulse to establish a physical basis for emotional connection is particularly important, because it informs several lyrics. In 'Repentance', for example, Herbert begins by conceding the minimalness, the insignificance, of mankind ('Each day doth round about us see' (l. 8)); but he nevertheless then urges God to 'Compassionate short-breathèd men' (l. 14), his verb meaning not merely 'to pity' but 'to share passions with' man.[87] The full, two-way sense of this idiom, which is underlined in *The Faerie Queene* when Priscilla and Aladine 'Each others griefe with zeale affectionate … compassionate' (VI. iii. 12 .1–7), is drawn out by Herbert in a poem like 'The Dawning'.[88] That work ends with a note of advice for the grieving, penitent soul. Such a man is urged to 'dry' his eyes with Christ's 'burial-linen' (l. 14), a material medium which facilitates intimate contact between Saviour and sinner. The implicit evocation of the Passion here reminds tormented Christians that Christ has already suffered the perturbations which now afflict them, that he has already shared in *their* affections. Reciprocally, Christ now offers the afflicted the chance to share in

---

[86] 'Physitians do tell us, that euery passion hath a distinct pulse' (Digby 1645: 365).
[87] Herbert and Vaughan 1986: 41 ff.     [88] Ibid. 99.

*his*. Herbert's persona thus urges his own 'sad heart' to 'Awake' and participate in Christ's affection of 'mirth', now available to him (ll. 1, 4). Importantly, Herbert, like Donne and François, figures this new affectivity as an expansion of the self, the curing of a spiritual headache and a blossoming into joy—hence 'Unfold thy forehead gathered into frowns' (l. 3). It is this bursting forth of new affections which God's compassionating, his willingness to share his mirth, offers at the end of 'Repentance', 'That so [thy] broken bones may joy, / And tune together in a well-set song' (ll. 32–3). The promise here is that such emotions will finally close the fissures scarring the surface of man's broken altar.

In this latter case the glory of infusing sacred affections into the regenerate is God's alone; Herbert's man is, as Tuve emphasizes,[89] too impotent in his own will to be anything but the passive recipient of God's undeserved, unrequitable compassion. But if this is predominantly the case, it is not always so. The protagonist of 'The Dawning' may be told that he need only choose 'not [to] withstand' (l. 9), and that grace will do the rest in granting him new emotions; but set against that instruction are multiple imperatives urging him actively to 'awake' himself, to 'take' Christ's comforts, and to take up the latter's 'grave-clothes'. The poem turns upon a mingling of active agency and passive receptiveness. Likewise, there are other cases where God's affection for man, his impulse to compassionate, does no more than promote *self-willed* imitation in the recipient of that sympathy. In 'Ephes. 4. 30', for example, it is God who first 'puts on sense' (l. 16) and grieves for man's sins (ll. 1–4),[90] but when the persona urges himself to respond compassionately, and imitate God's feelings, he figures this as a volitional act ('Then weep mine eyes ... / Weep foolish heart' (ll. 7–8) ) rather than as the consequence of God simply creating a penitential affection within him. That autonomy intensifies in the fourth stanza, when Herbert, now addressing himself in the second person, determines to redouble the process of imitation. He turns to the medium of lute-song not to reinvigorate his mimicking of *God's* grief, but to help imitate his own:

> Oh take thy lute, and tune it to a strain,
> Which may with thee
> All day complain.
>
> (ll. 19–21)

He then uses a pun to internalize his grief for himself still further. If the marble slabs of 'The Church-Floor' can sweat moisture in the heat, 'surely strings / More bowels have, than such hard things' as that stonework (ll. 23–4). 'Bowels', here, is the biblical idiom for affections, and it is those which

---

[89] See Tuve 1970: 177–8, 187, 194–6, to which my subsequent comments offer qualification.
[90] Herbert and Vaughan 1986: 121 ff.

Herbert's lute 'strings' must capture; but the 'strings' are also his heart-strings, in which sense the larger demand he makes upon himself is directed to his own heart: it must demonstrate, of its own accord, the depths (the great bowels) of its emotional sensibility. The heart can never be sufficient in this, never cry enough for its own faults, but the implication nonetheless is that there is much *self-induced* emotion in the protagonist's response to God's grief. Herbert's man can generate his own moral affections as well as benefiting from those bestowed upon him by grace, and thus the dynamic in the process of compassionating is as often reciprocal and mutually responsive as it is linear.[91]

What Herbert's poems do not offer us, though, is any triumphant, outward *displaying* of moral emotions; and nor does the poet give much emphasis to the turning of holy affections towards others. For the most part his preoccupation in his *Private Ejaculations* (if not in his *Priest to the Temple*) is with the personal *struggle* of turning his soul to face God (and with the struggle of then keeping it there). It is largely to that end that he devotes his meditations on sacred affectivity. In Crashaw's verse the story is rather different.

Crashaw, too, places sacred affections at the centre of man's spiritual life,[92] but his poetry differs from Herbert's, first, in presenting a more absolute, graphic realization of such experience. Christian moral emotions become, in his hands, confident, animated, and dynamic. 'On a Prayer Booke', for example, begins by figuring the spirit of God (once it is internalized in the 'close couch' of Mrs M. R.'s bosom) as 'loves great Artillery' (ll. 9–11).[93] Rather than simply washing through R's heart, this amorous principle lurks there, coiled and 'contracted', a ballista always ready to fire, and its living force is subsequently felt throughout the poem. Crashaw's constantly shifting stanza forms seem to chart pulses of emotion on a large scale but, equally, within individual verses modulations in pace suggest bursts of ecstasy:

> Amorous Languishments, Luminous trances,
> > Sights which are not seen with eyes,
> Spirituall and soule peircing glances.
> > Whose pure and subtle lightning, flies
> Home to the heart, and setts the house on fire;
> And melts it downe in sweet desire.

(ll. 63–8)

Shifts from Latinate to plain diction; sudden accelerations into strings of monosyllables, fuelled by enjambement (ll. 64, 66–8); an increasing use of polysyndeton ('and … / … and … / … and … ') in an otherwise paratactic

---

[91] On Herbert's sometime presentation of the heart as an active character, cf. Lewalski 1979: 311. On the mutual relationship between man and God's affections, cf. Strier 1983: 184–8.
[92] See Roberts 1990: 57.     [93] Crashaw 1957: 126 ff.

sequence: all these things vivify the divine love which here 'flies to' and through the heart. That same intensity is also apparent in 'Lady Madre de Teresa' where the '*full* joyes' (l. 121) which invest Teresa's will are again more absolutely possessive and more animating than comparable affections in Herbert:

> loe [her heart] beats
> High, and burnes with such brave heats:
> Such thirst to dye, as dare drinke up,
> A thousand cold deaths.
>
> (ll. 35–8)[94]

Crashaw also gives texture to his Saint's passion as Love possesses her, figuring it as 'a sweet and subtile paine' (l. 98). The specific suggestion of orgasm here is a constant motif. Even at Love's first approach, as Teresa's ecstasy begins, the idiom is erotic: her breast 'heaves with strong desire' (l. 40). Thereafter the connotations become phallic too: as the seraphic dart penetrates her, the blow itself seems to 'taste' her reflex exhalation, and her heart in turn then 'kisses' that instrument (ll. 80, 105–6). So 'delicious' is the stroke that the two lovers, angel and Saint, die over and again until 'at last' they 'dye into one', whereupon Teresa, transfigured, comes before Christ in a post-coital glow (ll. 108, 101, 112, 154). Crashaw inherited such metaphors as much from the Spanish mystics as from his own metaphysical contemporaries,[95] and he uses their mingling of death and love (otherwise suggestive of the little deaths which punctuate sexual love) to denote that mortification of flesh and self which must accompany union with the spirit.[96] But clearly his erotic medium (like that of Bernini's sculptural rendering of the same scene) is also intended first to grab the attention of an increasingly libertine public and then to *sanctify* corporeal sexuality, drawing it back into a spiritual realm whilst nonetheless exploiting its physical nature. Sexual coition is characteristically so intense that it obliterates all other consciousness, making it the most absolute of unions. It is that absolute quality which Crashaw here usurps in order to emphasize both the incontrovertibility of Teresa's union with God (so different from Herbert's shaky encounters) and the power of the love which overtakes her. Here again, then, the heart's holy affections are, in Crashaw, a potent, self-confident force.

Teresa's attainment of a spiritual soul is bound up with her martyrdom, and it might therefore be thought that Crashavian affectivity is principally a thing of the next world. In practice, however, this hymn ends with an instruction that men should 'learne *in life* to dye like [Teresa]' (l. 183). Her womb has already proven fruitful in bearing forth the order of Barefooted

---

[94] Crashaw 1957: 131 ff.    [95] See Young 1982: 14–16, 81–90.
[96] Cf. Bertonasco 1971: 77–8.

Carmelites (ll. 169–70), and both in them and in others her example has the capacity to 'strike fire' in hard hearts even here, on earth (l. 161). Similarly, although the ecstasy promised to M. R., bearer of the 'Prayer Booke', is reserved for death, something of its passions can be anticipated now. In contrast to Calvinist emphases on the impotence of the will, Crashaw (more than Herbert) impresses upon his addressee her ability to propel *herself* into this new experience, and to do so now. She herself has the power to ensure that her hands are pure, her eyes wakeful (ll. 21–5); and tempting though it may be 'To dance in the Sunneshine of some smiling / but beguiling / Spheare of sweet, and sugred lies' (ll. 48–50)—the sibilance and double rhyme are as entangling as the pleasures themselves—R. must find it in her will to forgo such Cavalier loose living. If, though, she does this and labours to 'improve' (turn to good spiritual account[97]) the 'precious houre' of Matins,[98] she will catch at an 'early Love' and 'every day', even in this world, seize on Christ 'All fresh and fragrant as hee rises' (ll. 94–102). A good deal of Teresa's sensual delight is available immediately, then, to the devout Christian.

Crashaw pursues this same point again in 'To … Countesse Denbigh', shifting the focus there still more on to the individual will.[99] In this case the Love which waits to unlock and animate Denbigh's 'close heart' (l. 34) is the Roman Catholic Church as well as the Holy Spirit, but Crashaw is emphatic that the Countess's is a 'self-shutt' soul (l. 36):

> So when the year takes cold, we see
> Poor waters their owne prisoners be.
> Fetter'd, & lockt vp fast they ly
> In a sad selfe-captiuity.
>
> (ll. 21–4)

The poet deploys here what Ricks calls self-inwoven imagery (l. 22), in order to underline that Denbigh is kept from liberty purely by her own will. The inability to flow forth from herself, and thus connect with others, reinforces an earlier suggestion that her 'free Heart' is currently deprived of the use of its 'hands' (l. 20). Fenner's notion that the affections constitute the hands of the heart, the very means by which man relates to his world, provides an illuminating gloss here. Viewed in that light, Crashaw's images suggest a woman unable either to move herself or be moved (hence unable to flow); a figure starved of those very affections via which the heart translates its impulses into outward action and connects with others. 'Allmighty Love', we are told,

[97] *OED v*², 2f.
[98] On the liturgical reference here and scriptural allusions in the surrounding verse, see Roberts 1990: 57–9.
[99] Crashaw 1957: 236 ff.

stands ready to bestow just such emotions upon her (ll. 27–9). But Love can only realize his intent if Denbigh is willing to '*Meet* his well-meaning Wounds' (l. 45), matching her free will to God's grace in a co-operative union akin to that envisaged by François and Senault in their models of self-governance. Crucially, Crashaw figures this process and the affectivity it would bring as an expansion of the self, hence his imperative to the Countess: 'Vnfold at length, vnfold faire flowre' (l. 43). The promise in the 'Prayer Booke' is of the same order. It will be M. R.'s destiny to partake of God's 'roseall spring of ... rare sweets, / ... / Boundlesse and infinite' (ll. 110–13). Just as François sought in meditation a 'pouring out' of 'good motions' which would 'amplify' and 'extend' the spirit; just as Herbert in 'The Dawning' and Donne in 'Jesus Wept' envisaged unfoldings and a shedding forth of lines of love: so here, Crashaw foresees the same for his spiritual charges if they can once turn their wills to meet God's freely given love.

These same themes—the animating force and rich variety of affections available to man; the generosity of God in bestowing his love; the emphasis on an amplification of the soul which accompanies such experiences—can also be seen in one last hymn, 'To the Name ... of Jesus'.[100] A reflection on the effect worked by Christ when he binds himself to man, this poem again betrays no doubt that, when invited, the Son *will* 'giue [himself]' to 'humble Soules' (ll. 120–1). In contrast to the diffident Herbert, Crashaw matches the self-assurance of François. There is an implicit certainty behind his hymn that God will prove his love for his creation by filling out the poet's meditation with a real spiritual presence: Christ will answer when called.[101] Being confident of this fact, Crashaw concentrates less on weighing his own merits and more on tracing his Lord's transformative influence over the soul. One aspect of the latter is the Son's impact on the body and the full spectrum of human senses. When Christ comes upon men's souls his immediate effect is to '*fill* our senses' (l. 170). His recalibrating influence is such that all past measures of olfactory pleasure, for example, are instantly erased. Instead, the Son's 'Nectareall Fragrancy' becomes the defining standard of such delights, and no perfume may thereafter 'passe for Odoriferous' which does not derive its sweetness from him (ll. 173–82). This language (derived from the Song of Songs[102]) is metaphorically expressive of the purity of soul which Christ's

---

[100] Crashaw 1957: 239 ff.

[101] Cf. Bertonasco 1971: 59, and Healy 1986: 31. On the broader question of Crashaw's engagement with François' thought, see Allison 1948: 295–6, 301–2; Bertonasco 1971: 62–3, 70, 77–8; and Roberts 1990: 183–8.

[102] Healy 1986: 112–14.

touch and our 'tast' of him (l. 188) bring; but to the extent that it can be taken literally, it also suggests how pervasive an impact such purity has on man's everyday sensibility. It is reasonable to suppose that, once regenerate, man's *physical* experience and appreciation of the world should indeed diverge (if only subtly) from that of his reprobate counterparts. According to Crashaw, his *emotional* experiences will certainly be different. The hymn records a predictable list of sanctified affections—hope, 'Bright Ioyes', 'a Bosom big with Loues' (ll. 145, 164, 160)—which grace confers on man's heart, and those new sources of self-animation have, too, a practical import. They provide present-day Christians with a means of imitating those martyrs of the early Church who once turned just such emotions to moral effect as they 'Fought against Frowns *with smiles*', turned '*Bold* BRESTS' upon a hostile world, gloried in resisting persecution, and '*durst* [be] *Braue*' in face of death (ll. 199–204). Here again, then, are Augustine's moral affections.

All these experiences are fruits of man's spiritual union with God, but to them we should add one other. Where humans are typically 'Narrow, & low', Crashaw's Christ bears an 'vnbounded NAME' (ll. 22, 12). The hymn, an 'vnbounded All-imbracing SONG', offers man a chance to hold his heart 'wide ope' whilst the Son 'Vnfolds' before him a 'compacted / Body of Blessings' (ll. 91, 126, 163, 165–6). It provides him, in short, with a chance to expose himself to an infinitude which (as with François *et al.*) will amplify his very being. Again, the martyrs provide exemplary proof of this. The wounds inflicted upon them, Crashaw claims, served only to 'Inlarge [Christ's] flaming-brested Louers' so that they might 'More freely… transpire' the fires of passion within their hearts (ll. 212–15). They, truly, endured not yet a breach but an expansion, their wounds of persecution becoming sources of growth, weapons by which to wound others, and thus a means of *spreading* holy affections. On this account, the wounded is a wounding heart: 'Loue's passiues'—partly meaning its 'passions'—are indeed here 'his actiu'st part' ('The Flaming Heart', ll. 73–4).[103]

Such is Crashaw's closing vision of affectivity. In overflowing 'the Bounds' of hatred ('Name of … Jesus', ll. 223–4), Pauline love and its derivative emotions become, for the Peterhouse poet, sources of *boundlessness*, the media by which Christian souls can transcend their own narrow confines. But if this was the largest, most positive vision to which the Augustinian mind-set could reach, what can be said of the other academic tradition prevalent at this time which also accorded moral value to the passions? What did Aristotelianism contribute to this same narrative of passion's triumph over reason?

---

[103] Crashaw 1957: 326.

## VARIETIES OF ARISTOTELIANISM

From the late sixteenth century onwards, Britain (and Oxford particularly[104]) witnessed a considerable revival of interest in Aristotelian philosophy. As a result, both Aristotle's works and medieval commentaries thereon (Aquinas's, not least) received renewed, ever more detailed attention. One effect of this movement (which culminated in the Laudian statutes of 1636 whereby Aristotelianism was enshrined at the heart of the Oxford curriculum[105]) was to separate Aristotle from the restrictive, somewhat ascetic context within which he had previously been understood. This shift made room for a more substantial recognition of his validation of the passions. Hence, from John Rainolds's ground-breaking lectures on the *Rhetoric* in 1570s Oxford, to the 1609 *Treatise of Anger* by Cambridge's John Downame, to Pemble's *Summe of Morall Philosophy* printed in Oxford in 1632, a succession of theologians and philosophers, each in turn, began to emphasize the moral worth of rationally approved affections. It was a recognition which must have rendered Aristotle's thought particularly amenable to Jacobean readers eager to embrace any ethic that would accommodate (rather than vilify) the passions. Two works in particular helpfully illustrate this trend. One is the Dominican bishop Nicolas Coëffeteau's *Tableau des Passions Humaines*, which was translated into English by Chapman's friend Edward Grimestone in 1621. The other is Bishop Edward Reynolds's *Treatise of the Passions and Faculties of the Soule* (1640), which became, in the latter part of the century, one of the standard Oxford textbooks on Aristotelian ethics.

Both these treatises are premissed on models of the mind derived from the *Summa* and the *Nicomachean Ethics*.[106] Coëffeteau waivers between identifying the common sense or the imagination as the faculty which passes immediate judgement on the desirability of sensuous objects.[107] However, either way he argues (as per Aquinas) that the judgement thus reached stimulates the sensitive appetite, which appetite then pursues or rejects what is 'pleasing or troublesom ... vnder the *forme of Good* and *Euill*' and through the medium of the passions.[108] Meanwhile, the understanding also makes a judgement about the object which has provoked this sensitive response: the *apparent* 'forme' of that object (as registered in the imagination) suddenly finds itself set against

[104] See Schmitt 1983: 26–7, 43–4, and *passim*; Sorell 1995: 53–4.
[105] For accounts of the place of Aristotelian texts in the Oxford curriculum, see McConica 1986: 176–9; Schmitt 1983: 43–5; Tyacke 1997: 389–404.
[106] The Neoplatonic account of love incorporated into Coëffeteau's treatise is not discussed here. See Levi 1964: 148–51.
[107] See Coëffeteau 1621: sigs. a1$^{r-v}$ and a6$^r$, 15.          [108] Ibid. sig. a6$^r$.

the *true* form of the same thing, its form when purged of sensible qualities and 'singular conditions'.[109] This true measure of the object's goodness or evil is, in its turn, represented to the will which desires or eschews the object accordingly. Ideally, the sensitive appetite (being promptly subservient to the soul's higher powers) then executes not the imagination's but this, the will's recommendation—*she* being '*Queene* of the ... soule' (to the understanding's kingship).[110] Too often, though, things actually proceed differently. The twin powers of '*reason*' cease to control the sensitive appetite, and man simply abandons himself to the latter, 'So as suddenly when ... fantasie offers to the *Appetite*, the *formes* which shee receiues from the *Sences*, vnder the shew of *Good* or *Euill*; [man] without stay to haue them iudged by the discourse of *vnderstanding*, and chosen by the *will*, commands of himselfe the mouing *power*.'[111] The implication here (contrary to Aquinas's account of sin) is that when man transgresses, not even the will, let alone the understanding, need authorize the course of action which he takes: the sensitive appetite alone has sufficient power to determine the mind so to act.[112] In better times, though, when the sensitive appetite *does* bow to the will and allow its sensuous inclinations to be redirected from above, that same appetite also performs a further duty: it 'quickneth all the powers and *passions* ouer which [it] commands, and sets to worke those which are necessary to ... action'.[113] It produces, in short, new, morally valuable emotions subservient to reason's interests. Reynolds, picking up on this point in his *Treatise*, imagines that there is not merely a qualitative but a categorical distinction between purely sensitive passions (motions induced in the sensitive appetite by the imagination alone) and rational passions (motions produced, rather, as a result of the 'immediate subordination' of the sensitive powers 'unto the government of the *Will* and *Understanding*').[114] The one is typical of animals, the other distinctive to humans.

If these works did no more than invoke, in passing, a scholastic model of psychology, though, they would scarcely differ from numerous other Renaissance analyses of the little world of man. What makes them distinctive (and indicative of a seventeenth-century reappraisal of Aristotelianism) is the extent of their arguments in favour of the moral role to be played by the passions. Coëffeteau and Reynolds argue for that role on three bases, the first a naturalistic and teleological one.

Self-evidently, the existence of passions is a given of human nature, and since such motions are irresistible realities, it follows that man must engage with

---

[109] Ibid. sig. a6$^r$.    [110] Ibid. sig. a6$^v$.    [111] Ibid. sigs a7$^{r-v}$.
[112] Levi (1964: 144–5, 148, 153–7, 164–5) observes in this context that, in denying the understanding a role in the mental processes which lead man to act sinfully, Coëffeteau reveals his neo-Stoic sympathies and undermines a crucial principle of scholastic psychology.
[113] Coëffeteau 1621: sig. a6$^v$.    [114] Reynolds 1640: 38.

them, tempering them by whatever means he can muster. Equally, if viewed teleologically, the sensitive appetite and its motions constitute 'a present of *nature*, which God ... hath freely bestowed vpon vs'.[115] In Reynolds's words the passions are '*ordained* for the perfection or conservation of the Creature', 'Creature' here reminding us of the Creator who fitted us with these feelings.[116] Man's aim, therefore, neither can nor should be to destroy these passions, or to leave such naturally endowed powers idle (the Stoic goal), but, rather, to 'adde vnto [them] the perfection which [they] want'.[117] The passions in themselves have no moral value, good or bad, but they gain such value according to 'the quality of the will that gouernes them'.[118] When that will is laudable, it 'adds' to the passions, which issue from it the same 'perfection'. As Coëffeteau realizes, though, to say this is really to concede another, profoundly Aristotelian point: namely, that the moral virtues actually derive their existence and nature, their 'content', from the challenge of governing the emotions.[119] This fact is variously registered in the *Table of Humane Passions*. First, Coëffeteau echoes the *Nicomachean Ethics* 1104$^b$4–5$^a$16 in noting that rightful pleasure (a passion) is an integral component of—a thing to be managed within—every virtue: 'What iust man but feeles certaine pleasure and sweetnes in the effectes of Iustice? what sober man but receiues content in the actions of sobriety? what valiant man but suffers himselfe to bee transported with the *loue* of braue exploits?'[120] Secondly, since courage is nothing but a mean-state moderating between excessive fear and boldness, both it and the other virtues derived from it—fortitude, magnanimity, patience, perseverance—can only exist as functions of those same two passions ('Take ... feare and hardiness from fortitude, and it is no more a vertue').[121] Thirdly, temperance and its train (modesty, abstinence, sobriety, chastity) are equally dependent on the pleasures of taste and touch and on the griefs and sorrows associated therewith.[122] Passions, on this analysis, are not merely the raw materials of virtue, but become virtuous in themselves.

A second argument made by Coëffeteau and Reynolds in defence of the value of affections is premised on another Aristotelian proposition. This is the principle that just as desire is blind without knowledge, so knowledge must be impotent without desire.[123] Sensitive appetite and its passions are essential for the motive force which they provide: they are 'the armes of reason'.[124] Our passions provide the 'liuely sparkes which inflame ... our soules' and drive or 'carry' us to virtue. As such, they become 'so many incouragements to

---

[115] Coëffeteau 1621: 63.      [116] Reynolds 1640: 47.      [117] Coëffeteau 1621: 63.
[118] Ibid. 55.      [119] Ibid. 59.      [120] Ibid. 59–60.      [121] Ibid. 60–1.
[122] Ibid. 61–2.      [123] Ibid. sigs. a3$^v$–4$^r$; Reynolds 1640: 32.
[124] Coëffeteau 1621: 69. (Compare Fenner's analogy of the affections as hands.)

piety, temperance, and other vertuous actions'.[125] Coëffeteau exemplifies this point by turning to the irascible faculty and stressing its moral effect. That passionate power both pushes man to perform dangerous but virtuous actions when the concupiscible passions are resistant and aggrieves and punishes the self if one gives in to desires which ought to be resisted. As if deliberately confirming Aquinas's source for 1a. 81. 2, Coëffeteau cites instances of both of these phenomena in the *Republic* (439e–40c).[126] Reynolds makes this same case by turning instead to Cicero and the idea that the passions are whetstones of virtue;[127] but here, as elsewhere in his *Treatise*, he also cites epic material to support his view:

Thus Anger, Zeale, Shame, Griefe, Love, are in their severall orders the Whetstones, whereon true Fortitude sharpneth its Sword ...

Aeneid. lib.
10

A noble shame boyl'd in his lowest breast,
Rage mixt with griefe suffer'd him not to rest;
Love and a conscious Valour set him on,
And kindled furious Resolution.

So, Love and Compassion are the inciters of Bountie; Hope, the stay and anchor of Patience ... ; Feare, the sharpener of Industrie; and Caution an antidote in all our actions.[128]

This, then, is the second argument in favour of the passions, one best encapsulated in Boyle's *Aretology* (a work influenced by Reynolds's *Treatise*). As Boyle puts it, the affections are 'Excellent instruments for the Bettering of Moral Vertu; whose motions wud be ... dull and languishing, were they not, ... enliuen'd by these Sprihtly Passions, stirring vp the Spirits and quickning the Fancy'.[129]

The third argument for the passions is one of common experience. It is a matter of everyday intuition, Coëffeteau notes, that right feeling is a part of virtue. What, he asks, could be more reasonable than to be moved with compassion for another's suffering; to feel grief for the misfortunes of one's children; to be indignant when criminals are honoured; to wish to emulate the great; to feel love for a friend?[130] These are passions which, in Boyle's words, 'euery where pass current for Good with the Stamp of Generall Approbation'.[131] But 'experience' in a different sense also underlines this point. Every Christian intuitively grasps the truth of the Augustinian observations that Adam was 'subiect to ... Passions before his Fall',[132] and that Christ 'who was neuer subiect to sinne' nevertheless 'had *Passions* and humane

---

[125] Coëffeteau 1621: 59.     [126] Ibid. 8–10.     [127] Reynolds 1640: 45.
[128] Ibid. 58–9.     [129] Boyle 1991: 17.     [130] Coëffeteau 1621: 57–8.
[131] Boyle 1991: 17.     [132] Ibid. 17.

affections'.[133] The latter must therefore be capable of goodness. Reynolds turns to the imagery of Donne (and to Isa. 57: 20) to express this truism:

our Saviour himselfe sometimes loved, sometimes reioyced, sometimes wept, sometimes desired, ... [though] these were not *Passions* that violently ... troubled him; but he, as he saw fit, did with them *trouble himselfe* ... The *Passions* of sinfull men are many times like the tossing of the Sea, which bringeth up *mire and durt*; but the *Passions* of *Christ* were like the shaking of pure Water in a cleane Vessell, which though it be thereby *troubled*, yet ... is not *fouled* at all.[134]

Such are the arguments in favour of the moral value of the passions, and in making them so assiduously Coëffeteau and Reynolds prove themselves more rigorous Aristotelians than their predecessors. That said though, they also recognize that to admit that man should utilize his sensitive appetite is not to say that the affections are easily governable. On the contrary, even 'the most excellent soules' cannot always subject their appetites to reason.[135] Coëffeteau quotes, in recognition of this fact, Aquinas's favourite commonplace from the *Politics*, the precept that man's rational powers rule their lower counterparts not as slaves but as citizens (figures capable of periodic dissent).[136] Governance hinges not on tyranny or indeed Spenserian psychomachia, but on a constitutional monarchy, a negotiated relationship between ruler and ruled. It was this precept (and, with it, the accompanying emphasis on rehabilitating the passions) which particularly informed one last group of scarce-studied works, the university plays of the Jacobean and Caroline periods which made Aristotelian moralizing their stock-in-trade. Of these, two—Strode's *The Floating Island* and the anonymous *Pathomachia*—merit particular attention, because they provide a striking measure of changing attitudes to governance in the seventeenth century.

## PASSIONATE DRAMA IN THE UNIVERSITIES

*Pathomachia: Or, The Battell of Affections*, though not printed until 1630, was probably performed in Cambridge in the mid-1610s.[137] One of its characters, Curiosity, refers to a Parliamentary plot by the nobility to 'kill all the Kings ... Minions, which comming out of a poore and hungry Countrey were

---

[133] Coëffeteau 1621: 56.          [134] Reynolds 1640: 48–9.          [135] Coëffeteau 1621: 72.

[136] Aquinas several times cites Aristotle's *Politics* 1254^b3, but does so in the particular context of self-governance at, e.g., *ST* 1a. 81. 3 ad. 2.

[137] For questions of dating and attribution see Bentley 1941–68: v. 1225, 1390–2, and Moore Smith 1908: 149–50.

thought to … sucke vp the iuice of the fertile … Land'.[138] Curiosity reports, too, that, though 'The King craued a Subsidie', this was denied by the Commons, 'whereupon the Parliament brake vp', the King having to make do instead with 'a Beneuolence' from the Convocation House. These passages seemingly recall both the 1610 Parliament which heard a petition to exclude all Scots from court[139] and the 1614 'Addled Parliament' (perhaps the 'Nullitie Parliament' referred to in the play[140]) which, in the few weeks for which it sat before James dissolved it, denied him a subvention,[141] leaving the Convocation of that same year to grant him a clerical subsidy instead.[142] *Pathomachia* reproduces such Crown / Parliament antagonisms, but on a political rather than just an economic plane. It charts the struggle for power between three parties: a Royalist faction commanded by King Love and Queen Hate, whose supporters include the eleven virtues who sit in the House of Convocation; a rebellious Parliamentarian grouping led by four peers, Fear, Grief, Hope, and Joy (Boethius's version of the Stoic tetrachord of principal passions),[143] whose number also includes a further nine passions from the Commons, all intent on 'reduc[ing] the Kingdome to a Senate, or popular State';[144] and a Banditti of sixteen other affections (captained by Pride and Self-Love) who were banished from society long ago but now plan to capitalize on the Parliamentary rebellion to launch their own assault on Pathopolis, Love's stronghold. In dramatizing a resolution of this conflict, *Pathomachia* (and indeed, Strode's *Floating Island* after it) exploits precisely the aforementioned Thomist analogy between reason's co-operative government of the passions and a good monarch's constitutional government of his polity. The result is thus a play which expresses a moral, but also by extension a political, ideal.

In examining *Pathomachia*'s moral ideal, we need not be concerned with the dramatist's endless tabulations of virtues, vices, and passions (the comprehension of which must have been rather a chore for an audience yet to discover the joys of the flip-chart). It may suffice to note some illustrative subtleties embedded within the play. The identification of Love, for example, as king of the passions is probably an Augustinian touch, alluding to the principle that the orientation of that affection, good or bad, determines the moral quality of the will as a whole. Queen Hate may not in name seem the most sympathetic of figures, but she is partially redeemed by the Thomist pedagogic point that she is only a function of her husband:

why doe we hate Euill, but that we know that Goodnesse is to be beloued?[145]

---

138 Anon. 1630: 6.     139 C. Russell 1971: 280.     140 Anon. 1630: 11.
141 C. Russell 1971: 282–3.     142 Hill 1956: 195.     143 Soellner 1958: 550.
144 Anon. 1630: 2.     145 Ibid. 17.

what is Loue, but a turning of the mind to Good? And what is Hatred, but a turning of it from Euill? That is a suspension ... of Loue .... [A]ll Affections issue from [Love] extended, or contracted.[146]

Another subtlety worth noting is the fact that amongst the tetrachord of rebel passions, not all seem reprehensible. In so far as Fear and Grief turn against Love, we may side with the latter; but when Lords Hope and Joy resist Hate, we are more likely to applaud those pleasant-sounding peers than Her Majesty. There is, then, merit on both sides in the play's constitutional struggle. And there is potential merit, too, amongst the Banditti. Their leaders, Self-Love and Pride, are described (in a Pauline gesture) as twin brothers, the one an 'inward', the other an 'outward', manifestation of the same corrupt principle;[147] but it is clear that Self-Love, a figure now fallen from grace, was once a positive passion. Reynolds describes a proper self-love governed not by *cupiditas* but by *charitas*, this the legitimate self-love of one who worships himself as one of God's created things. It is natural for every creature to 'delight in the simplicitie of its owne being: because the more *simple* and *One* it is, the more it is like [God] .... [T]his *love* of Man unto *himselfe*, if *subordinate* unto the *love* of God, ... is ... a necessarie Debt' to be paid to 'Nature'.[148] It is also a debt which promotes a love of thy neighbour since 'as we *love* our *selves*, ... so, wheresoever we find any *similitude* to our *selves*, ... upon that also doe the beames of this Affection extend'. Self-love of this rational kind is therefore integral to virtue; yet *Pathomachia*'s figure of the same name has degenerated into an egotistical, bastardized version of himself.

It is, though, in the play's conclusion that the passions' positive moral potential is best elaborated. In a pithy illustration of paradiastole, the Banditti (emotions long since banished from Love's city) attempt to infiltrate Pathopolis by disguising themselves as cognate passions. Jealousy, for example, dresses himself as Zeal, Envy as Emulation, Pride as 'Monsieur Magnanimitie', each pretending to be no different from the affection it simulates. Justice, though, who keeps the gates, sees through them all and apportions a suitable fate to each. Malice, Pride, Envy, Jealousy, Lust, and Curiosity are all cast 'into the deepest Dungeon'[149]—Lust because a catalogue of recent outbreaks of syphilis is laid at his door, Curiosity because he is singled out as the root of all the Church's troubles.[150] On the other hand, Enmity and Friendship (which had also become bandits in this cynical Jacobean age) are redeemed and placed under the care of the Virtues, whilst Self-love, having first been instructed in the merits of that form of self-love described by Reynolds, is then confined to a comfortable cell—that is, accorded a carefully circumscribed role, but

---

[146] Anon. 1630: 46. Cf. *ST* 1a2ae. 25. 2, 29. 2.  [147] Anon. 1630: 3.
[148] Reynolds 1640: 84–5.  [149] Anon. 1630: 31.  [150] Ibid. 35.

a role nonetheless, within the soul. These affections, at least, acquire a new moral purpose. The subsequent attack by the Parliamentarians fails because Fear, appropriately enough, betrays them. The other rebels then capitulate, craving 'to be reduced to a setled order'.[151] Love's response, though, far from punishing his fellow passions, is simply to give a lecture on their proper order, and then to relate most of them to one or other of the eleven Virtues. Thus Hope and Fear, for example, are tied to the virtue of Fortitude, Desire and Pity to Charity. The virtues themselves are then arranged as a series of Aristotelian means, each with an excessive vice on either side of it. Clearly, the pedagogic intent of all of this is to foster a sound understanding of moral excellence, and that all of this is done in so rationalized and categorizing a fashion inevitably betrays the influence of Thomism. The result, though, is to advocate just as firmly as in Coëffeteau and Reynolds what part the passions should play in the good life. Such is *Pathomachia*'s theme.

Strode's equivalent to *Pathomachia*, *The Floating Island*, was performed before the King (along with Cartwright's *Royal Slave*) in Oxford's most loyal and Laudian of colleges, Christ Church, in 1636.[152] Laud himself took an active role in producing this 'very well penned' work (though alas, according to George Evelyn, it was 'generally misliked of the Court, because it was so grave').[153] The occasion of the royal visit was the presentation to the University of its new (and markedly Aristotelian) statutes; so it is apt that, in contrast to *Pathomachia*'s Augustinian monarch, Strode's kingdom is ruled by the straightforwardly Aristotelian figure of Prudentius (the *Nicomachean Ethics' phronēsis*). Prudentius, too, faces a rebellion on the part of the passions, who dub him a Stoic because he curtails their liberty and makes them all equals (this contrary to Irato, Malevolo,[154] and Audax's various appetites for dominance). The restraint which Prudentius demands deprives them, so they claim, of their very essence:

> IRATO. For what's a Lord ... but his anger?
> MALEVOLO. Or what's a great man but oppression?[155]

Strode's rebels gather instead around an agreed leader, Fancie, a pretender to the throne who 'neerest is / To unyoak'd Passion' and will (the others hope) prove less tyrannous 'to our Commonwealth'.[156] Sure enough, when Prudentius retires and Fancie is crowned, she does indeed decree that each passion may from now on follow 'His proper humour, be it Vice or Vertue, / Inordinate

---

[151] Ibid. 39.   [152] Havran 1962: 143–4.
[153] Trevor-Roper 1988: 291–2; Evelyn 1906: i. 354. Cf. Sharpe 1981: 151; Tyacke 1997: 652–3. Sharpe notes that the King, at least, approved of the play.
[154] Malevolo is thought to represent William Prynne (Trevor-Roper 1988: 291).
[155] Strode 1655: sig. B2$^{r1}$.   [156] Ibid. sig. B4$^{r1}$.

or stay'd'.[157] The inevitable chaos then ensues. Irato, for example, attacks Sir Timerous-Fearall 'cause tis [his] humour' and therefore (according to Fancie's ruling) legal.[158] Malevolo, pursuing his own will to power, leads a murderous assault against Livebyhope, recently the beneficiary of Fancie's preferment. Amidst a raft of such squabbling, Sir Amorous speaks for all in declaring, in Act IV, 'I have not pass'd / One hour in those delights whereof I dream't'.[159] Desperato is the only affection who triumphs, in so far as Fancie and the others all eventually adopt *his* mood: they assemble at his banquet, where each is 'served' with an appropriate weapon for committing suicide. This, though, is the moment when Intellectus Agens enters to make a case for Prudentius's restoration.

Prudentius had insisted, earlier in the play, that, far from Stoically eradicating the passions, his aim was to accord them the opportunity of realizing themselves effectively:

> ... this ungrateful Rout ... I ... taught
> Both how to Feare and Love, and what to Loath,
> Wherefore to Grieve and Joy, and in what place
> To rouse their anger and audacity
> By Rule and Circumstance.[160]

His Aristotelian governance (to which the passions now return) provides each passion with the proper degree of indulgence, in the absence of which restraint they would all descend into chaos, contrary to their own ends. The implication of this allowance is that all moral virtue does (and should) encompass a measure of right feeling as well as of moderate action. Prudentius confirms as much when he subsequently applies the concept of the mean not to action but to the degree of passion which should be felt in virtue:

> Oft have I bore them [the passions] under both these wings,
> One under each, when they, inclin'd to Fury,
> Would push each other down a Precipice ...
> There on a narrow ridg, an edg, a Thrid,
> (Such is the meane, so plac'd betwixt two Gulfes)
> I bore them in their Strife.[161]

This ideal is realized anew at the play's close when Prudentius (thinking in Thomist classifications) instructs the passions to rank themselves with their opposites, Amorous alongside Malevolo, Livebyhope beside Desperato, Audax beside Timerous, etc. True to Aquinas's template, Irato (odd one out amongst the five irascible passions) stands alone, bearing the monarch's sword. Given this orderly arrangement, the body politic is able to love the

---

[157] Strode 1655: sig. C2[v1].        [158] Ibid. sig. C3[v1].        [159] Ibid. sig. E4[r2].
[160] Ibid. sig. B4[r2].        [161] Ibid. sig. B4[v1].

good and hate evil, hope for true peace, strive boldly for just ends, fear what is unfit, and so forth. In what Strode calls a 'Model of Self-policy', each passion is marshalled for a moral purpose, and the result, they then realize—paradoxically, given the restraint involved—is that 'No souls so Passionate as we'.[162]

So much, then, for the moral message of these two plays, but what of their political ramifications? Both works, clearly, drive home the stabilizing political implications of Aristotle's ethic of self-governance. They dramatize the widely-held belief that men rebel in a political context (just as they sin in other contexts) when and because they allow themselves to be led astray by misdirected passions. Thomas Sprat's characterization of the civil wars as a time when rampant passions governed human behaviour is a late reflection of this belief, but the same view can also be found earlier, in Browne's *Religio Medici*.[163] It follows that, if order is to be maintained, reason must govern effectively both within the individual soul and from without (in the person of the monarch and other political structures). Beyond this, though, the two playwrights' Aristotelian tales carry a larger, more challenging political message. They imply that monarchs make themselves and their states stronger to the extent that they harness and indulge (as well as circumscribe) their subjects and their subjects' passions. If, politically, the Stoic and Platonic models of governance were straightforwardly authoritarian and repressive, the Aristotelian view demands that reason allow its subject-passions, its citizens, a greater (though still constrained) liberty. Such an accommodation (which abandons psychomachic oppositions) is shown here to generate a happier, stronger body politic. Granted, this settlement depends upon the passions being prepared to serve reason, but, equally, it depends upon reason being willing to make use of the passions (not merely to oppress them). Performed as it was at the height of the King's period of personal rule, *The Floating Island* was presented to Charles at a time when his own 'Isle [was] setled, rage of Passion laid', but at a time also when he was denying his Commons (the citizenry represented by the passions) any role in the governance of the land. Politically, it might be said that Charles's manner of ruling did not exemplify that which Strode was gently recommending, any more than James epitomized *Pathomachia*'s ideal of governance in 1614 when he preferred to dissolve Parliament rather than hear its grievances. Far, then, from being the commonplace endorsement of royal authoritarianism which Trevor-Roper and Havran assume it to be,[164] *The Floating Island* is actually more like its companion piece, Cartwright's *Royal Slave*, the critical slant of which has been

---

[162] Ibid. sig. F4[v2].    [163] Sprat 1959: 53–6; Browne 1977: 65–6, 68–9, 138–9.
[164] Trevor-Roper 1988: 291; Havran 1962: 144.

analysed by Butler and Sharpe.[165] Strode's play is as much a political work which advocates constitutional *rapprochement* as it is a moral one arguing for the passions' ethical value, and much the same can be said of *Pathomachia*.

## *PARADISE LOST*

Inevitably, the one text in which the various threads of this chapter most obviously cohere is Milton's *Paradise Lost*. That poem provides at once both an epitome of the Augustinian moral sensibility (in Adam and Eve) and an argument for the relevance of Thomist ethics, replete with their validation of the passions. Just as importantly (in light of my discussion of *Julius Caesar*), *Paradise Lost* exudes a sophisticated understanding of the mechanisms of self-deception, and like the university plays, it also probes all these themes with reference to what Milton saw as the political needs of the moment.

What Fish identifies as the unified moral consciousness of a mind which knows no other course than to be at one with God is intrinsic both to Augustine's spiritual will and to Milton's depiction of his prelapsarian couple.[166] God is a reference point in the latter's every sensation and affection, and thus a guarantor of the sanctified value of these things. These mental qualities—gifts in Adam's eyes—are presented, on the one hand, as so many proofs of the Father's beneficent love for man. On the other, Adam and Eve, in demonstrating their appreciative enjoyment of them, thereby demonstrate their grateful piety. Milton measures this two-way dynamic in relation to three topoi: the sensuous beauty of Eden, Adam and Eve's management of natural appetite, and the pleasures of sexual congress. To begin with the first of these, it is clear that the paradisal environment stimulates a heightened yet pure sensuous response (like Crashaw's 'tast' of Christ) in all those who encounter it. Adam's wonder-filled eye delights in every detail of the garden, every bee that sits on bloom (*Paradise Lost* (*PL*), 5. 24–5).[167] In his company, Eve likewise savours each glistering dewdrop or the earth's 'fragrance' after 'soft showers' (4. 645–6, 653). A sense of 'sweetness' brackets her every sensation, just as the word 'sweet', belaboured in her double deployment of epanalepsis (ll. 641–56), brackets her paean to Nature.[168] The landscape inspires

---

[165] Butler 1984: 44–9; Sharpe 1987a: 47–51.

[166] Fish 1997: 143–6, 159–60. In Augustine's spiritual man, all impulses of the will issue from, contribute to, and therefore express, a love of God and his creation.

[167] References to *Paradise Lost* (*PL*) are to Milton 1998.

[168] The paean begins with the line 'Sweet is the breath of morn, her rising sweet', and 'sweet' is also the word on which this period concludes in l. 656.

'Vernal delight and joy' even in Satan, as 'gentle gales / Fanning their odoriferous wings dispense / Native perfúmes' before his twitchy snout (ll. 154–8).
Milton, like the equally 'Odoriferous' Crashaw ('To the Name ... of Jesus', ll.
173–82), makes no apology for this sensuous revelry.[169] A divinely sanctioned
enjoyment of Paradise, and particularly of its hospitable plants (trees which
hang 'amiable' with fruit; the vine which 'Lays forth her purple grape' (ll.
250, 259) ), is for him simply the corollary of man's obligation to tend this
garden. Eden, though, is a source of food as well as of beauteous sensations,
and that second sphere of desires is another on which Milton concentrates.
One reason why the regimen of work provided by gardening is important
is because it augments the pleasure which Adam and Eve then derive from
culinary delights. Toil makes 'wholesome thirst and appetite / More grateful',
giving depth but also balance to such indulgences (ll. 327–31). Within the
moderating framework which a well-regimented day prescribes, there is no
danger in relishing the very textures of pleasant foods—the 'savoury pulp'
of the nectarines on which the couple chew, for example (l. 335)—because
these things have no opportunity to become the focus of decadent over-
consumption. On the contrary, Adam and Eve, who have taken symbolic
'instruction' from Nature in the twin merits of bountiful provision and 'frugal
storing', know how to satiate (without burdening) their stomachs and yet
how, also, to order their diet such that 'Taste after taste' brings 'kindliest
change' (5. 316–28, 451–2, 304–6, 332–6).[170] Implicitly, in thus respecting
their bodies, these Epicurean gourmets respect, too, God's creation; so again
the idea conveyed is of validated appetites taking their place within a coherent
and unified moral demeanour.

What is true of dietetics is true also of sexuality. Whilst distinguishing
them from the libertines of his own day (for whom 'Casual fruition' was
the be-all and end-all of coition), Milton nevertheless accords to his first
couple all the physical pleasures and excitement of intercourse (4. 767).
As Adam presses Eve's lips 'With kisses pure', her '*swelling* breast'—the
poet imagines her arousal—presses back against him (ll. 494–502).[171] Cupid
'revels' and shakes his 'purple wings' for these two as much as for the Earl
of Rochester (ll. 764–5). Yet *their* passion is apparently 'unlibidinous' (5.
449), not an inexhaustible, self-enslaving desire, but one 'Founded in reason'
(4. 755)—circumscribed therefore, for all that it is intensely pleasurable.[172]
Furthermore, as the source of offspring, such wedded love is both the origin
of, and model for, all subsequent charitable relations between men (ll. 754–7).

---

[169] On the eroticized function of Eden's odours, see Turner 1987*a*: 240–1.
[170] On Milton's interest in bounding dietary pleasures, see Schoenfeldt 1999: 136–8; Scodel
2002: 236–45, 257–63.
[171] Cf. Turner 1987*a*: 236–7.       [172] See further ibid. 270–2.

The reverence for, and delight in, another which connubial love epitomizes, and which makes such love a form of mutual worship, is the same as that which the law of charity requires between men generally. Hence what is partly a gift of sexual pleasure from God also assumes, for Adam as for Paul, a spiritual significance. Loving union is a vehicle via which each human may revere others amongst God's creations and a means, too, by which to worship God himself *in* and *through* those other creations. Such is the wider implication in Milton's framing the couple's marriage as a doorway on to 'rites / Mysterious' (ll. 742–3). Here again a prelapsarian passion is simultaneously validated in moral terms and sanctified as a form of piety.

Adam and Eve lead 'the richest possible emotional life',[173] but it is one which flows from a love of God and his creations, and is therefore saturated with spiritual resonances. This is especially clear in the couple's morning and evening prayers, wherein God is exalted as the maker of that world which so much delights them (5. 153–5; cf. 4. 720–5). He stands at the centre of their consciousness, 'Him first, him last, him midst, and without end' (5. 165). Importantly though, the impression that one forms from all *this* is that Adam's and Eve's moral sensibility is a largely intuitive affair. If Adam governs himself well, he does so because he is driven by the instinctive impulses of a good will, not because an analytical faculty of reason supplies him with codified moral principles.[174] Likewise, when hostess Eve is 'on hospitable thoughts intent', she ponders the practical question of which dish goes best with which rather than preoccupying herself (as Guyon might) with the imperative to 'be temperate' (l. 332). Adam has no abstract concept of the freedom of the will before Raphael teaches it to him (ll. 548–9), and his own talk of 'reason' sometimes seems to presuppose an instinctive rather than a self-conscious mental faculty, one fluidly indistinguishable from the passions with which it interacts ('for smiles from reason *flow*, / To brute denied, and are of love the food' (9. 239–40) ). These observations are commensurate with the judgement in *De Doctrina Christiana* that prelapsarian man had 'the whole law of nature ... so ... innate in him that he was in need of no command', no precept, to enforce its observance (1. 10);[175] and they also contribute to a sense that Milton's understanding of moral psychology is close, here, to Augustine's. (Augustine, too, downgraded the significance of rational self-determination, emphasizing instead the prior effect of the will's disposition, its loves and inclinations.)

And yet, having said this, it is clear that there is, besides, another moral language at work in *Paradise Lost*, a much more Thomist one which distributes

---

[173] Turner 1987a: 235.     [174] See Fish 1997: 159–60.
[175] Milton 1953–82: vi. 353.

the responsibility for self-determination equally amongst several mental faculties (the 'passions', 'will', 'sensual appetite', and 'sovereign reason' of 9. 1122–31). This Thomist language underpins, for example, Adam's warning to Eve:

> … God left free the will, for what obeys
> Reason, is free, and reason he made right,
> But bid her well beware, and still erect,
> Lest by some fair appearing good surprised
> She dictate false, and misinform the will.
>
> (9. 351–5)

When Adam speaks here, or when Raphael speaks in Books 5 (ll. 519–43) and 8 (ll. 635–7) of a will free to determine its own course, yet dependent on the direction of a rational power prone to be misled by passions, each has in mind not an intuitive but a self-consciously deliberative faculty of reason. This 'reason' is also that invoked by Milton's Arminian God[176] in Book 3 when he announces, doubtless reading from a signed copy of *Areopagitica*,[177] that 'reason … is choice' (3. 108). The point distilled into that aphorism is that man is free to choose his own fate precisely because he is equipped with a power of *analytical* reasoning which enables him, at any given moment, to make informed decisions. His 'reason' empowers him to cogitate and deliberate in weighing the merits of divergent options. The sceptical reader, though, may doubt just how far Milton's prelapsarian Adam could, on *these* terms, make any meaningful choices, since *his* moral ratiocination seems destined to be lopsided. Adam, not yet having eaten of the tree, must lack that clear understanding of the nature and extent of possible vices which man needs if the negative side of his deliberative calculations is to be sufficiently informed. Inexperienced as he is, the first man has yet to learn to recognize all the dangers which might 'misinform the will'. Satan may, then, have a point when he questions the worth of a prelapsarian condition in which men 'only stand / By ignorance' (4. 518–19) and asks instead whether evil might not be 'easier shunned' if its nature were first known (9. 699).[178] The suspicion must be that

---

[176] On the relevance of Arminianism in dictating this moral psychology, see Danielson 1982: chs. 3–5.

[177] See Milton 1953–82: ii. 527.

[178] Cf. Donne's comment to the Countess of Bedford, 'ignorance of vice, makes vertue lesse' (Donne 1985: 276). The counter-argument is made by Fish (1997: 144). If, though, Satan's arguments *do* have validity, it may be a reflection of unresolved guilt on Milton's part that he nonetheless channels them through the devil's voice—just as he makes *Eve* articulate his own view of *Areopagitica*, that a 'fugitive and cloister'd vertue' is worthless (Milton 1953–82: ii. 515), when he has *her* question the value of a 'virtue unassayed' (9. 335). Such a conjecture about repressed theological anxieties within Milton lends itself to Stachniewski's thesis (1991: ch. 8)

Raphael and God, in depending upon a humanist notion of reason—that is, one which conceives of reason as a faculty which thinks in terms of binary oppositions, between evil and good, appearance and truth, etc.—are urging prelapsarian Adam to defend himself with a tool better suited to repairing the soul *after* it has fallen. The post-lapsarian utility of just such contemplative reasoning is certainly much emphasized in *Areopagitica*:

Good and evill we know in the field of *this* World grow up together ... inseparably; ... the knowledge of good is ... interwoven with the knowledge of evill .... As therefore the state of man *now* is; what wisdom can there be to choose, what continence to forbeare without the knowledge of evill? He that can apprehend and consider vice with all her baits and seeming pleasures, and yet abstain, and *yet distinguish*, and *yet prefer* that which is truly better, he is the true warfaring Christian .... [T]hat which purifies us is triall, and triall is by what is contrary. That vertue therefore which is but a youngling in the *contemplation* of evill, and knows not the utmost that vice promises ... , is but a blank vertue.[179]

Strikingly, the implication here is that *Areopagitica*'s muscular, distinctly rationalist version of virtue might actually be more admirable than its intuitive, prelapsarian counterpart.[180] That impression, a variant of Milton's dalliance with the idea of the Fortunate Fall (12. 473–8), is reinforced in a passage of *De Doctrina* which asks, 'where does virtue *shine* ... if not in evil?' (1. 10), the implication being that it thus shines brighter after the Fall.[181]

   We are faced, then, with a second moral paradigm alongside that with which I began, one which encourages Adam to be more self-conscious and scientific about his ethical thinking, which may therefore be better adapted to the mental capacities of fallen man, and which yields a more splendid (because harder-fought-for) form of virtue. *Perhaps*, though, the coexistence of two such discourses need not amount to a contradiction in Milton's thought. If, generally, the conduct of the prelapsarian couple appears to be guided by the intuitive impulses of their good wills (the Augustinian model), it is equally true that when they encounter new challenges, one can imagine them

that in his characterization of Satan the poet tried, and failed, to lay to rest the ghost of Calvinism past, otherwise a haunting force within his imagination.

[179] Milton 1953–82: ii. 514–16. Burrow (1993: 277) uncovers another manifestation of this same phenomenon of contrariety when he notes Milton's tendency to examine valued emotions through their opposites.

[180] Poole (2005: 138–40) offers similar observations on the passage quoted here, and notes that, later in *Areopagitica*, Milton extends the idea of moral struggle backwards in time, attributing it to the prelapsarian Adam too, so as not to denude him of real virtue. However, though Milton may do this in *Areopagitica*, it is less clear that *Paradise Lost*'s prelapsarian couple is similarly equipped with *effective* powers of ratiocination. How far they are is a problem which I investigate here.

[181] Milton 1953–82: vi. 353.

resorting to a more consciously deliberative form of judgement in order to establish how best to proceed (the Thomist model). Furthermore, Blackburn and Danielson defend the practical utility of that latter, rationalist approach even within a prelapsarian context, by arguing that from the outset Milton's couple *are* sufficiently informed about evil to make full moral calculations. Blackburn contends that before the Fall they possess a 'conceptual' knowledge of evil without being tainted by sin in practice.[182] Danielson, similarly, invokes Irenaeus's account of Paradise to demonstrate that the 'matter of sin' exists there even though sin itself does not, and is thus known to Adam and Eve.[183] That 'matter' comprises their own passions and appetites—hunger, thirst, and desire for rest, for example—all of which could be carried to excess, in which context (Blackburn maintains) the couple would recognize such impulses as evil.[184] The example of Eve's dream and Adam's analysis thereof bears out this point. Although Satan steals into Eve's imagination to dangle there the 'pleasant savoury smell' (5. 84) of the fruit of knowledge and the temptations of hubris (ll. 77–8), Eve does not—or so Fish assumes[185]—take the bait. In the cold, rational light of day, she 'abhors' what she dreamt (l. 120), and Adam recognizes it as an evil appetite to be rejected by the will: for such 'Evil into the mind of god or man / May come and go, so unapproved, and leave / No spot or blame behind' (ll. 117–19).

Adam's powers of reason do, then, have some idea of evil on which to work even before the Fall, and Fish regards his confession of his own passion for Eve (8. 521–59) as another demonstration of this point (because Fish imagines that Adam fully understands and overcomes that feeling as he discusses it with Raphael).[186] In fact, however, I want to suggest that this episode does more to expose the precariousness of prelapsarian powers of self-comprehension than to affirm them. It shows, *pace* Blackburn and Danielson, and in line with the implications of *Areopagitica*, that prior to his transgression Adam does not know enough about the temptations that lie within—enough about 'evil'—to muster anything more than 'blank vertue' in face of his own uxoriousness. Adam frames his obsession for Eve as a contrast. He tells Raphael that, though he delights 'in all enjoyments else' (delicacies of taste, sight, and smell), none of these provokes a desire 'vehement' enough to displace his power of rational self-command (ll. 524–32). But with Eve things are different. The sight and touch of her body 'transport' him; 'Commotion strange' overwhelms his

---

[182] Blackburn 1971: 126.        [183] Danielson 1982: ch. 6.
[184] Blackburn 1971: 130 ff.; Danielson 1982: 181–2, 189 ff.
[185] Fish 1997: 222–4. Cf. Blackburn 1971: 131; Danielson 1982: 193. Milton's description of the moment of possible ingestion (5. 85–7) is actually more ambiguous than Fish allows, and neither lover chooses to spell out whether or not Eve really did bite the apple in her dream.
[186] Fish 1997: 229–30.

mind (ll. 529–31). Although, crucially, Adam himself does not articulate as much, one can readily deduce the 'libidinous' nature of this passion (for all that the narrator may elsewhere deny the presence of such perturbations in Eden (5. 449) ). Eve, then, exercises 'absolute' sway over Adam's consciousness, usurping his own reason's sovereignty there and making her (inferior) 'will' the determinant of his (8. 546–56). 'All higher knowledge in her presence *falls*', and with that illuminating verb Milton signals the prior inner transgression—the fall within the will—which makes possible Adam's later, outward fall.[187] Raphael naturally condemns this collapse, urging Adam to respect the authority of his own faculty of reason and to love Eve not for her appearance but for what is 'higher in her society'—qualities the contemplation of which will make of Adam's earthly love a Neoplatonic 'scale / By which to heavenly love' he may ascend (ll. 570–92). It is Adam's reply at this stage which reveals most about the shortcomings of his own self-understanding. He responds defensively by insisting that neither Eve's fair outside nor the touch of her body

> So much delights me, as those graceful acts,
> Those thousand decencies that daily flow
> From all her words and actions, mixed with love
> And sweet compliance, which declare unfeigned
> Union of mind, or in us both one soul.

> (ll. 600–4)

Schoenfeldt construes this speech as primarily an attempt by Adam to affiliate his love to heavenly harmony; Turner, as primarily a defence of the value and complexity of eroticism.[188] These contentions are not incompatible, but they underline the inexactness of Adam's description. The 'graceful' words and actions which the latter now says claim his particular admiration are proffered to Raphael as Adam's proof that he does indeed love the 'higher' things in Eve; and it should be equally to Raphael's satisfaction, he implies, that Eve comports herself in a way that is compliant with Adam's wishes and best judgement. Yet at the same time Adam's emphasis on 'gracefulness' and the 'sweetness' of Eve's complaisance leaves open the possibility that what he most admires in such conduct is still precisely its sensuous qualities. Furthermore, in saying only that this deportment 'delights' him *more* (l. 600) than does Eve's body which he first said transported him, he is not exactly *negating* his previous speech. Although he seems, here, to 'correct' that earlier description of his 'passion', it is tempting to suspect that, actually, he simply shifts his ground.

---

[187] For an exposition of theological meditations on the two-stage Fall, see Poole 2005: 15–19, 26–9. Milton's comment here reflects the Augustinian nicety quoted by Poole: 'in secret they began to be evil, and this enabled them to fall into open disobedience'.

[188] Paster, Rowe, and Floyd-Wilson 2004: 55–6; Turner 1987*a*: 277–8.

Further to that impression, Adam's next words (after praising Eve's grace and compliance) are little clearer:

> Yet these subject not; I to thee disclose
> What inward thence I feel, not therefore foiled,
> Who meet with various objects, from the sense
> Variously representing; yet still free
> Approve the best, and follow what I approve.

(ll. 607–11)

The referent of 'these' (l. 607) may be *both* that initial sexual allure which Adam said sent him into raptures at the sight of Eve and those matters of which he has just spoken, her enticingly 'graceful acts'. It is more probable, though, that 'these' refers solely to the latter. Similarly, the 'inward' feelings of the next clause may encompass both these things, or again only the 'graceful acts'. If Adam does have just the latter in mind here, as he insists upon his capacity for self-control, that restriction would seem to leave open the possibility that the basic touch and sight of Eve *do*, by contrast, 'foil' and subjugate his soul. If, on the other hand, the more inclusive sense is the right one, lines 607–11 must amount to a flat contradiction of lines 546–56, in which he had confessed that his every sensual apprehension of Eve did overwhelm him. Perhaps there is also something a little too glib, too evasive, in Adam's twofold use of the word 'various' in lines 609–10: it hints at a voice eager to brush over this difficult matter and move on to more comfortable themes. The word 'sense' may not be sufficiently discriminating either, given the ambiguous status of Eve's every 'graceful act'—at once both a sensuous and a 'rational' good. And what, finally, is 'the best' in line 611? If Adam's thought processes are as subtly shifting and ambiguous as I have suggested, then the answer cannot be entirely clear. In the matter of his love for Eve, 'the best' for Adam would seem to be something over which reason's grip is at the least precarious. Perhaps all this is due to the fact that Adam does not understand the exact nature of his 'Commotions strange'. Perhaps, rather, he does not want to confront an emotion which he senses is dangerously complex. Either way, we are left with a figure whose comprehension of the potential evils within him is a good deal less clear-cut and a good deal more perilous than Blackburn and Danielson imagine. Prelapsarian Adam cannot, it seems, fulfil the demands which Raphael's Thomist language of governance puts upon him.

Adam's difficulties of self-comprehension are illustrative of Milton's wider interest in the many 'wily suttleties and refluxes' of human thought.[189] Milton, even more than Spenser, remains preoccupied throughout his epic with

---

[189]  Milton 1953–82: i. 817.

the business of *anatomizing* human degradation. Drawing on seventeenth-century Thomist models for assistance, he charts (in Adam, Eve, and Satan) 'sensual appetite's' progressive usurpation of the authority of 'sovereign reason' (9. 1129–30). In particular, he charts the processes of self-delusion which accompany that usurpation.[190] Milton tries, in other words, to unravel those same mysteries of self-deceiving which so confounded Brutus and Bussy.

The first of Thomism's degrees of mental malfunctioning is a simple weakness on reason's part. For Aquinas it is a biological fact that the soul's power is limited. Consequently, when all its 'energy' is focused in some particularly vigorous impulse of the sensitive appetite—a passion such as lust, for example—the voice of the understanding, being left with 'little ... force for its own activity', will be 'overwhelmed' (*ST* 1a2ae. 77. 1). As Reynolds puts it, 'the *Soule* is of a limited and *determined Activitie* .... [I]t cannot with perspicuitie and diligence give attendance unto diverse Objects. And therefore, when a *Passion* in its fulnesse ... doth take it up, the ... brightnesse of Truth [will be] suspended.'[191] 'For lacke of spirits', then, the intellect may want the stamina 'exactly [to] consider the reasons which [should] *disswade*' the soul from attending to its passion (Wright).[192] When thus debilitated, reason will be unable to register what Reynolds calls a '*Negative Determination*',[193] and where *it* offers no negative counsel the will (being reason's appetite) will not resist either. On the contrary, the will will allow itself to be co-opted by the sensitive appetite. As such, passion will triumph unchecked, yet (in this case) *without* corrupting reason's core judgement, without fostering any self-delusion. The power of understanding will retain throughout, if only at a deep-seated level, an accurate grasp of where its duty lies. The soul will thus find itself in a state of *akrasia*, doing wrong even whilst knowing, residually, that that is what it is doing.

All this is precisely the position of Milton's Adam at the moment of his fall. The pull of love and the horror of loneliness make him certain that he must die with Eve. Passive before his own passion, he allows the 'link of nature' to 'draw' him in (9. 914). But there is scant pretence here that this course is one which right reason could recommend. Adam tries to lessen the significance of the troubles to which the couple will hereby expose themselves, but he does so without conviction, witness the half-hearted ploche of '*Perhaps* thou shalt not die, *perhaps* the fact / Is not so heinous now' (ll. 928–9). Clinging to the idea that the serpent 'yet lives' having eaten God's fruit, he presses that point upon himself with an incessant use of polyptoton ('he yet lives, / Lives ... and gains

---

[190] I differ from Hunter (1994: 83–5), who also discusses Milton's account of self-deception, in proposing that *Paradise Lost* presents, across these characters, a systematic anatomization of sinful psychology and its different delusions.

[191] Reynolds 1640: 69.     [192] Wright 1971: 50.     [193] Reynolds 1640: 68.

to live ... / Higher degree of life' (ll. 932–4) ); but such hope will not stick, and the best that Adam can then do is to speculate on 'likely' fates for Eve and himself (ll. 935–7). This sequence of would-be self-deceptions ceases at line 952 not with a 'Therefore' but with a 'However' ('However I with thee have fixed my lot ...'), that conjunction signalling Adam's lurch away from any attempt to convince himself that things may yet be well. Instead, he reverts to simply conceding the irresistible pull of passion, 'So forcible' now that it has become not a 'link' but a 'bond of nature' (ll. 955–6). Burrow suggests that a 'magnetism' draws Adam to Eve.[194] Gilbert thought that magnets worked by reinvigorating a magnetic form latent within the iron on which they acted, thus making the latter akin to the former's own nature. Once thus alike, the two materials became *mutually* attractive, each gravitating towards the other. Adam's rhetoric captures this same point. Line 956 ends with the idea of his being drawn '*me* to *my* own', like a loadstone searching out its mirror-image in other entities. Sure enough, in a Donnish trick of anadiplosis, this line is then drawn immediately towards that very same phrase, 'My own', at the start of the next, and on this *second* iteration the 'My own' is indeed the 'My own' (the identical magnetic force) '*in*' Eve: '... me to my own, / My own in thee ...'. The two identical phrases thus rush to meet each other, 'compassionating' at the line-break between 956 and 957. With this trick Milton reinforces the point that amorous passion overwhelms an Adam who stands passive before it; an Adam, too, who knows he *should* resist what in practice he cannot govern. When he falls, then, it is in a moment of *akrasia*, not self-deception:

> he scrupled not to eat
> Against his better knowledge, not deceived,
> But fondly overcome with female charm.

> (ll. 997–9)

The 'charm' here is a pointed resurgence of that 'charm of beauty's powerful glance' which Adam acknowledged to Raphael in Book 8 (l. 533). His *akrasia* now is rooted in his incomplete confrontation with such passion then, a fact also reflected in Adam's uxorious 'compliance' now (9. 994), which recalls and overwrites Eve's alleged 'compliance' towards him back at 8. 603.

The *De Doctrina* (1. 11) insists with 1 Timothy 2: 14 that, whilst Adam was not deceived at the moment of the Fall, Eve was, and here again Thomism provides an explanatory structure.[195] According to Wright, passion may prove so pervasive an influence over us that when reason 'looks into the imagination' it will find there no other ideas, memories, or perceptions with which to think except those which 'mother & nurse' the prevailing sensitive

---

[194] Burrow 1993: 284.     [195] Milton 1953–82: vi. 382.

appetite.[196] Under these circumstances the intellect, being thus steered towards the sensitive appetite's goals, will become deluded such that it gives '*Affirmative Consent*' to the passions' demands.[197] Furthermore, this process will be self-sustaining: over time the mind will find more 'reasons to confirme [passion's] purpose' until finally it judges 'all things that occur in fauour of' the latter to be 'agreeable with reason'.[198] Once the intellect is thus bastardized, *its* appetite (the will) will also follow suit, affirming passion's course. Eve epitomizes such processes as she eats from the tree. The pressure of appetite is a constant presence beneath her verse here, her recurrent use of words like 'taste', 'want', 'fair', and 'fruit' reminding us what really drives her thinking. However, reason also furnishes a growing list of inferences to support Eve's act: inferences from the name of the tree (the acquisition of '*Knowledge*' could surely only be good (9. 750–5, 758–9) ); from its positive effects (the fruit gives elocution to the serpent and makes it benevolent (ll. 748–9, 769–71) ); and from the absence of negative effects (the serpent does not die (ll. 762–4) ). Whereas Adam's parallel rationalizations never gain traction, Eve's conviction grows—witness her comment on the last of these points: 'He hath eaten and lives, / And knows, and speaks, and reasons, and discerns' (ll. 764–5). The crescendo of polysyndeton here (five 'and's' in thirteen words) tracks her increasing will to believe, the fruit of which is her acceptance of sophistries such as the proposition that what one does not *know* the nature of, one does not 'know to fear' either (l. 773). So successfully does Eve deceive herself, and so relaxed is she afterwards, that she subsequently finds 'bland words at will' to justify her action (l. 855).

Satan, who of all Milton's characters owes most to the Shakespearean theatre's deluded villain-heroes,[199] completes this trilogy of self-deceivers. To some extent his psychology is akin to Eve's, save that whereas she is first drawn into self-deception passively, Satan actively wills deceit upon himself. We infer early on that he effectively commands his 'Wit ... to finde out ... perswasions that all the appetite demandeth ... is lawfull', this so that he may 'think his hatred and ire ... most iust & reasonable'.[200] Thus, when he frames the angels' rebellion as a libertarian struggle against an autocrat's arbitrary legislation (5. 788–802), it is clear that his speech is forcibly directed at himself as much as others, its aim being to ingrain a conviction as to the rationality of his cause. Satan's actual motive (he elsewhere admits) is 'pride and worse ambition' (4. 40), but he finds it more dignifying to dress himself, even for the benefit of his

---

[196] Wright 1971: 51.        [197] Reynolds 1640: 67. The source here is *ST* 1a.2ae. 77. 1.

[198] Wright 1971: 48–9.

[199] In an earlier incarnation Satan's Book 4 soliloquy was, supposedly, to have been the opening speech of a tragedy on the 'paradise lost' theme. See further Stachniewski 1991: 340.

[200] Wright 1971: 53, 49.

own eyes, in the clothes of Milton's scrupulously rational republicanism.[201]
To Milton, such wilful self-delusion was all too familiar a feature of political
life. He traces it in *Eikonoklastes*, where the 'unself-knowing' Charles (as if
swallowing the ideology of the university plays whole) is said to have deluded
himself 'that wisdom and all reason came to him by Title, with his Crown;
Passion, Prejudice, and Faction ... to others by being Subjects'.[202] In reality this
king's intellectual powers were 'maistred long agoe by his sense and humour',
and when he 'insist[ed] upon the ... Plea of ... *Reason*', what he really wielded
was his 'fantasie' and passions stemming from that.[203] According to Milton,
though, the Long Parliament's 'blinde' Presbyterians were no better, since,
though they too imagined '*Scripture*' and '*reason* ... [did] halt with them for
company' (*Tenure*), their opposition to Charles's execution was actually driven
not by the logic of the common good but by resentment, resentment both that
'the Independent parties ... carried more weight in Parliament' than did they
and that the regicide was the latter's policy, not one 'performed' by their 'own
faction' (*Second Defence*).[204] In his superficial commitment to republicanism,
Satan epitomizes this latter breed of false republican, a breed who professed
a commitment to 'public reason just' (4. 389) but who, in practice, were
driven by passionate self-interest, and therefore harboured false images of
themselves. *Paradise Lost*'s discussion of self-deception thus hints, subtly, at a
wider explanation for the failure of the Commonwealth.[205]

Satan, of course, busies himself keeping his passions at bay as early as
Book 1, and here too speeches nominally directed at others are also a form
of wilful self-inflation. Desperate to sustain an approving sense that he is
'still the same' (1. 256), the archangel steels his mind to search out glories
in his own character: hence the driving anaphora of lines 106–9, which
discover an 'unconquerable will', 'And ... immortal hate, / And courage never
to submit ... / And what is else ... ?' For Satan, as for Iago, such delusion is
best served by cultivating epigrams, figures the very form of which—terse,
symmetrical, incisive—seems to epitomize a mind's command over its world:
hence, 'Better to reign in hell, than serve in heaven' (1. 263). In the same

---

[201] See Sharpe and Zwicker 1987: 222–3; Loewenstein 2001: 203–26. Loewenstein extends
the argument to suggest that Satan ventriloquizes multiple different parties, Milton's point being
to expose the treacherous ambiguity of all political rhetorics.

[202] Milton 1953–82: iii. 435, 356.     [203] Ibid. iii. 456, 459.

[204] Ibid. iii. 256, iv. 626. On the background to Milton's opposition to the Presbyterians, see
Loewenstein 2001: 180–90.

[205] Cf. Hill 1977: 366–7; Norbrook 1999: 442, 444, 446, 454–5. The false republicans denoted
by Satan were, in Milton's view, representative of a broad absence of republican virtue amongst
the English people, a shortcoming which necessitated the Commonwealth's transformation into
a Protectorate. On Milton's disillusionment with England's public, see Hill 1977: 160–2, 184–6,
194–5, 198–204, 347–51; Norbrook 1999: 189, 202–3, 335–6, 412–14.

vein, Satan gradually practises his chiasmus (for instance, in ll. 159–60 and
163–5) until finally he rises to the perfection of antimetabole: 'The mind ...
in itself / Can make a heaven of hell, a hell of heaven' (ll. 254–5). Here the
rhetorical figure gives the illusion of performing its own meaning, the second
iteration of the nouns deftly inverting these two metaphysical kingdoms
through the very act of word transposition. Satan's discovery that he can do
this—switch heaven for hell—with ease in language implicitly encourages
him in the delusion that he can do the same with equal ease in reality, so it is
hardly surprising that chiasmus subsequently becomes his figure of choice.[206]
The grimmest example of antimetabole, though, is reserved for another voice,
Adam's, as he counsels Eve about man's nature:

> *within* himself
> The danger *lies*, yet *lies within* his power:
> Against his will he can receive no harm.
>
> (9. 348–50)

Adam's surface protestation of autonomy is undercut here by his use of Satan's
figure, a subtext which emphasizes the insistent presence of 'lies'—Milton
puns here—inside man's mind. Such self-delusions are the greatest threats to
the will, and like the rhetoric of lines 348–9, they do *not* lie entirely within
Adam's power—this because Adam does not seem to be a fully conscious
architect of his language here: rather, Satanic chiasmus is an unwitting presence
within his speech, *haunting* his words. Nor, though, does antimetabole lie
wholly within Satan's power. His use of it, too, rings hollow once juxtaposed
against divine iterations of the same trick. When God predicts that one day
we will see 'earth be changed to heaven, and heaven to earth' (7. 160), we are
bound to conclude that this really will happen; not so, Satan's transformation
of hell into heaven. And nor can Satan ever hope to match the ultimate act of
chiasmus, that fortunate fall which 'good of evil shall produce, / And evil turn
to good' (12. 470–1).[207]

Within the larger format of Milton's text, then, the figure which the Devil
uses to seal shut his passionate delusions runs away from him; but it also directly
attacks him when the narrator uses it in Book 4 to refute the heaven–hell
proposition of 1. 255: 'troubled thoughts ... stir / The hell within him, for
within him hell / He brings' (4. 19–21). Satan's self-deceptions collapse at the
start of this book, now that he is bereft of that pressuring audience whose
presence had hitherto forced him into performances of resilience. Instead, the

---

[206] Cf. 2. 39–40, 453–5; 4. 108, 377; 9. 710–12.

[207] It is a moot point whether the narrator's own taste for antimetabole (e.g., 'though fallen
on evil days, / On evil days though fallen' (7. 25–6) ) places Milton with God or the Devil.

passions which he has kept at bay in deference to pride—guilt, self-disgust, a longing for lost delights (ll. 37–57)—burst forth. However, the collapse of delusion goes further than this, bearing out the full implications of that narratorial chiasmus which introduces Satan's soliloquy. Satan, here as yet poised midway between divinity and pure evil, recognizes that he cannot recover the former (ll. 79–83, 93–104); but he also accepts the inevitability of his descent into the latter, the inevitability that a hatred of God, and a desire to destroy those heavenly things the sight of which torments him, will draw him into greater crimes: hence 'myself am hell',

> And in the lowest deep a lower deep
> Still threatening to devour me opens wide,
> To which the hell I suffer seems a heaven.
>
> (ll. 75–8)

In acknowledging this predicament, Satan turns back to his original self-deception of 1. 255 and discovers a warped truth in it. He will indeed make a heaven of his present hell, it now transpires, but only in the relative sense of line 78 here (in so far as his *future* hell will make the present one seem pleasant by comparison); not, then, in the absolute sense which he had originally envisaged. Such disillusionment does not spell the end of Satan's glibness. Within minutes we again find him assuming that thoughts and passions can be juggled as easily as words ('So farewell hope, and with hope farewell fear' (l. 108) ). However, the Book 4 soliloquy does signal a new departure, one which takes Satan into a more corrupt condition than mere self-deception. He begins, here, to will his fall, to *will* the depravity of his own will.

For Aquinas this third, most desperate stage of sinning arises when the will (through its own perversity) decides deliberately to 'suffer the loss of spiritual goods in order to acquire temporalities … e.g. riches or pleasure' (*ST* 1a2ae. 78. 1). A depraved will of this kind will knowingly choose evil and offend God (regardless of subsequent consequences), all for the sake of what Reynolds calls 'some instant-conceited Good'.[208] Craving the 'little bribe of pleasure' to be had immediately in scratching an itch, this will will not stop to pretend that such actions are rational.[209] Milton's Satan, once he starts pursuing this state of mind, begins by striving to dispel from himself all contrary passions. He thus frames his sympathetic feelings for man in the conditional tense, telling himself that he 'could love', 'could pity', Adam and Eve, but will not (4. 363, 374); that under other circumstances he would 'abhor' his own actions, but does not (l. 392). These half-acknowledgements help him pretend that his villainy is absolute, and thereupon will himself into a disposition of outright

[208]  Reynolds 1640: 521.     [209]  Wright 1971: 58.

malice, but in his forays into the latter his sarcasm is undercut by a genuine 'solicitude' for Adam and Eve and by a desire, even, for kinship.[210] The venom of lines such as 'my dwelling *haply* may not please' (4. 378) or 'hell shall unfold, / To *entertain* you two' (ll. 381–2) is offset by both a real longing for 'league' and 'amity' with man behind Satan's feigned one (ll. 375–6) and a clear sense of guilt implicit in the contortions of his syntax: 'Thank him who puts me loth to this revenge / On you who wrong me not for him who wronged' (ll. 386–7). Those anxieties are still present in Book 9 when Satan continues to delude himself, for example, that he has always been the 'Patron of liberty' (4. 958; evident in 9. 140–2); but this need for self-justification notwithstanding, he does now, in this later book, manifest the depraved will imagined by Aquinas. Emphasizing that the paradisal pleasures before him create torments within him (9. 119–23), he determines to destroy them solely so as to scratch that itch, to gain immediate relief, this full in the knowledge of what will 'thereby worse ... redound' upon him: 'For only in destroying I find ease / To my relentless thoughts' (ll. 128–30). The complete absence of self-deceit here is chilling:

> Revenge, at first though sweet,
> Bitter ere long back on itself recoils;
> Let it; I reck not.
>
> (ll. 171–3)

A vigorous reworking of *Comus*, line 592, these mangled pentameters give aural form to their own sense. The very syntax of each phrase in verses 171–2 is reversed, and the crucial terms 'Bitter' and 'back on ... ' are both (like 'Let it') trochaic, the iambic metre coiling back upon itself at these most caustically alliterative of moments. Twisted verse, then, for a now twisted will; and the devils' subsequent metamorphoses into snakes are the predictable corollaries of such willed denaturing.

The passions stand at the root of all this vice and delusion, but for Milton, as for Coëffeteau and Reynolds, they provide, too, the stuff of virtue. 'Wherefore did [God] creat passions within us, pleasures round about us,' *Areopagitica* asks, 'but that these rightly temper'd are the very ingredients of vertu ?'[211] One might expel sin by eradicating 'all objects of lust', but by the same operation one would expel virtue, 'for the matter of them both', the passions, 'is the same'. As Danielson notes, the authority underlying this text and mediating what is essentially an Aristotelian perspective is Lactantius,[212] the same Lactantius whom Thomas Rogers had toyed with but then sidelined in his *Philosophicall*

---

[210] See Stachniewski 1991: 349; Burrow 1993: 271–2.  　　　[211] Milton 1953–82: ii. 527.
[212] Danielson 1982: 174–6.

*Discourse*. Milton, unlike Rogers, pushes through the idea that passions may be virtuous, here as before following two tracks in doing so.

On the one hand, Raphael urges Adam to 'love, but first of all [to love] / Him whom to love is to obey' (8. 633–4), and in saying so he points to the Augustinian tradition which sets love of God at the centre of a circle of virtuous affections. After the Fall, though, this emotion is not in either spouse's looks, 'either to God / Or to each other' (10. 111–12), and the initial story of Adam and Eve's rehabilitation is essentially one of rediscovering such affection. Eve is the first to do this, reaffirming her 'love sincere' (l. 915) and, in that spirit, proposing herself as the sole sacrifice to expiate both their sins: 'Me me only just object of [God's] ire' (l. 936). Her repetition of 'me' / 'my' as she does so—twelve times in twenty-three lines (ll. 914–36)—recalls (as is often noted) the same ploche deployed by Christ as he announces his willingness to die for man's transgression (3. 236–53, 11. 32–44). To that extent (if not in her specific plan to commit suicide) Eve feels her way towards the kind of 'martyrdom' which can redeem Christian life (9. 32). Crucially, her submission and distress also provoke in Adam an intuitive understanding of the obligations of Pauline charity—to 'strive / In offices of love, how we may light'n / Each other's burden in our share of woe' (10. 959–61).[213] Perhaps too, though the thought goes unspoken, it is then Adam's awareness of this, his reaction to Eve's supplication, which prompts him to reflect anew on the 'mild / And gracious temper' (ll. 1046–7) shown by Christ as he judged them earlier in Book 10. Pondering that, and receiving in the meantime an infusion of prevenient grace, Adam rediscovers both his faith and his love of God. God, reciprocally, inspires new 'motions in him' (11. 91), those holy affections of the regenerate charted by Calvin *et al.* The latter are, in Christ's view, 'Fruits of *more* pleasing savour' (l. 26) than any which preceded the Fall (this, another variant of the *felix culpa* motif). Indeed, the Son responds by so 'compassionating' with this human 'savour' that he in turn radiates 'The smell of peace towards mankind' (l. 38). This deliberate recovery of the sensuous idioms of Paradise signals, just as in Crashaw, a rebirth of man's moral life, a life measured, once again, specifically in terms of intuitive affectivity.

On the other hand, though, Milton's closing books also perpetuate a more consciously rationalist approach to the fashioning of virtuous passions. We are told in Book 9 to expect not the heroic wrath of pagan epic, but 'the better fortitude / Of patience' (9. 31–2), and that is indeed the ideal which Michael impresses upon Adam in teaching him 'to temper joy with fear / And pious sorrow' (11. 361–2).[214] In Books 11 and 12 Adam's heart thus learns

---

[213] See also Paster, Rowe, and Floyd-Wilson 2004: 64–5.
[214] Cf. Fish 1997: 274–80, 293–4, 324; Paster, Rowe, and Floyd-Wilson 2004: 65–6.

new depths of dismay, grief, and compassion as he witnesses Cain's crime, the victimization of Enoch, the great inundation; but he learns, too, the joy of the new covenant and Christ's triumph, perceptions which teach him to circumscribe his emotions within rational calculations ('Far less I now lament for one whole world / Of wicked sons destroyed, than I rejoice / For one man found so perfect' (11. 874–6) ). Likewise, though initially he weeps for the occupants of the seeming lazar-house (ll. 477–95), Adam, once taught that their affliction is the reward of serving 'ungoverned appetite' (l. 517), revises his passion in favour of an acceptance of God's justice. Again, where first he delights in the decadence of Seth's descendants, Michael's instruction never to judge the good by pleasure prompts him, subsequently, to abhor their 'shame' (l. 629). But perhaps most importantly, when provoked by the sight of Nimrod, Adam immediately senses the need to rationalize his *political* passions, in this case justifying a disgust for tyranny on the principle that monarchical authority is contractual, not patriarchal (12. 64–71). At each stage, then, Milton's first man learns a lesson in how rightly to temper the ingredients of virtue; how, indeed, to generate those intrinsically 'rational passions' envisaged by Aquinas and Reynolds.

As will be clear from these last two paragraphs, Milton's account of man's positive emotions does not amount to a vision of vibrant moral sentiments such as would be seen a few generations later. Rather, he offers a relatively muted sketch both of those affections which emanate from the spirit of charity and of a number of rationally conditioned passions (mostly associated with Christian sufferance). Standing behind the latter is a concept of 'Rational liberty' (12. 82) which, as in the university plays, is at once moral and political. Such men as fail in the task of self-governance and allow 'upstart passions' to 'catch the government' of their souls subject themselves (as Satan did) to an inner 'servitude', an enslavement to the tyranny of their own appetites (ll. 88–90). These libertines (Restoration rakes by implication) surface sporadically throughout *Paradise Lost*, as Book 1's 'sons of Belial', for example (ll. 501–2), a sobriquet for the Cavalier faction,[215] or as 'Bacchus and his revellers' in Book 7 (l. 33). Their presence—or rather *fate*—is felt too, metaphysically, in the 'boundless ... deep' of Chaos, an infinite nothingness just beyond the 'appointed bounds' of Earth (ll. 167–8). This 'Illimitable ocean without bound' (2. 892) is mirror both of the libertines' present inward state and of their perpetual future, one in which a parodic 'wide womb' is eternally 'swallowing' them up, rendering them 'Devoid of sense ... motion', and autonomy (ll. 149–51). However, as Milton argued in the *Tenure* and *Second Defence*, and as he argues again here, it is the destiny of the

---

[215] Davies 1991: 63.

self-unbounded to find themselves bounded, politically speaking, by God.[216] Michael, looking to contemporary England, tells Adam that those nations whose citizens depart so far from republican right reason that they permit 'unworthy powers to reign' within themselves are thereupon subjected 'from without to violent lords', Providence depriving them of 'outward' exactly as they have squandered 'inward' liberty (12. 90–101).

In contrast to these libertines, individuals who do discipline themselves according to reason's rule retain their mental and political freedoms. But more than that, precisely in thus bounding themselves, they in fact discover a greater kind of release—and it is in this context that Milton's thinking about virtuous passions is suddenly less muted. For one thing, he who confines his passions to rationally prescribed models thereby protects himself from the self-delusion otherwise suffered by Milton's characters. He remains 'self-knowing' (7. 510), particularly in so far as he recognizes, and would preserve through rational self-governance, 'the dignity of Gods image upon him'.[217] Given that knowledge, this agent can lay claim to the *objective* passion of self-love applauded by Reynolds, the same 'self-pious regard' and 'reverence toward [one's] own person' of which Milton speaks so passionately in *The Reason of Church Government*:

this … just honouring of our selves … may be thought as the … fountain head, whence every laudable and worthy enterprize issues forth. And although I … name [it] a liquid thing, yet it is not incontinent to bound it self … but hath in it a most restraining … abstinence to start back, and glob it self upward from the mixture of any ungenerous … motion … wherewith it may … stain it self.[218]

Milton captures in this extraordinary imagery an emotion which is at once bounded—both modest and self-preserving—and yet also fluid, the latter because it promotes an interplay of affections between men as each is moved by 'generous and Christianly reverence one of another' to love his neighbour as himself. This, then, is the potent principle which underpins Raphael's advice to Adam to 'weigh [Eve] with'—that is, with and by—himself, and to profit in so doing from a 'self-esteem, grounded on just and right' (8. 570–2); but it also feeds, secondly, into another crucial Miltonic concept towards which the above use of the word '(un)*generous*' points: namely, magnanimity. Magnanimity, literally meaning 'greatness of soul', and thus signifying a feeling of mental expansion (self-imposed boundaries notwithstanding), is a quality which Milton rather hopefully attributes to the Rump Parliament in both his *Tenure* and the *Readie and Easie Way*; a quality, too, which he looks for in

---

[216] Milton 1953–82: iii. 190, iv. 684.      [217] Ibid. i. 842.
[218] Ibid. i. 841–2. For the background to this text, see McEachern and Shuger 1997: 264–8; Scodel 2002: 269–75.

*Areopagitica*, where any magnanimous Parliament ought to understand that uncensored liberty '*enlarges* ... our apprehensions'.[219] Likewise, in the *Second Defence* and *Readie Way*, he expects it from the English people, who should be 'magnanimous' enough to need no king, recognizing rather the 'generositie of minde' which a 'free Commonwealth' fosters.[220] But above all he demands a continued 'mighty spirit' from Cromwell, whom he pictures as one already 'well-versed in self-knowledge' and possessed of the rational liberty which careful 'subjection' of the perturbations yields.[221] Should Cromwell cease thus to 'honor [himself]', give way to his passions, and turn tyrant, he will not only sacrifice the liberty of England (which he now protects) but will also, Milton warns, 'lose his own liberty', becoming 'slave' to his appetites.[222] Here again, then, rationality, freedom, and the sense of greatness of soul which stems from justified self-esteem are all interrelated. Consequently, whilst Eve may imagine that her spirits 'dilate' and her heart grows 'ampler' once she has eaten of the tree (9. 876), and whilst the 'transported' Adam may think that he finds 'Greatness of mind' in a luscious Eve (8. 557), the reality for both is rather different. *Paradise Lost*'s true experiences of amplification, those analogous to the enlargement of self envisaged by Donne, François, Herbert, and Crashaw, are reserved for others: first, for Raphael's ideal, rational lover who discovers, through *his* passion, that his 'heart *enlarges*' and connects with 'heavenly love' (ll. 590–2); second, for Michael's agent of rational liberty who, through his own self-governance, grows 'thence / *Magnanimous* to correspond with heaven' (7. 510–11).[223] It is these parties whose union with God in the great republic at the end of time will be absolute. Then, when Christ puts by his 'regal sceptre' (3. 339–40), the magnanimous, enjoying the ultimate enlargement of their own beings, will become incorporate with him. God, as Christ puts it, 'shalt be all in all, and I in thee / For ever, and *in me* all whom thou lov'st' (6. 732–3).

*Paradise Lost* stands as a fitting conclusion to this survey chapter because it provides, if not quite a synthesis, at least a diptych of the Augustinian and Thomist perspectives on governance. At once sensuous and austerely disciplined; focused (implicitly) on the purity of the good will, yet also a study in reason; preoccupied with man's relationship to God, but preoccupied, too, with the worldly connection between politics and ethics, Milton's epic unites the threads which run through Herbert, Crashaw, *The Floating Island*,

---

[219] Milton 1953–82: iii. 237; vii. 355; ii. 488, 559.          [220] Ibid. iv. 684, vii. 382.

[221] Ibid. iv. 667–8.

[222] Ibid. iv. 673. On Milton's equivocal attitude to Cromwell, cf. Hill 1977: 189–94; Norbrook 1999: 335–6.

[223] For further comment on magnanimity in Milton, see McEachern and Shuger 1997: 274–6; Norbrook 1999: 129–35, 414.

and *Pathomachia*. It responds vigorously to Spenserian and Shakespearean interests in the anatomy of sin and self-delusion, but also answers broader, turn-of-the-century challenges to the psychomachic tradition which hoped to eliminate the passions. Milton adumbrates instead a new ethic which would deliberately cultivate the affections under the twin banners of Pauline charity and Aristotelian moderation. Furthermore, in doing so, this epic arrives at a vision of self-reverence and magnanimity which resonates with earlier writers' desires to find spiritual ways of amplifying the self. *Paradise Lost* completes, then, two traditions which can be traced back through such preachers as Donne and Fenner, amidst theologians from Greenham to Reynolds, and in the works of two rival universities' orators, Herbert and Strode: all of these, writers who bore witness to the increasing moral and practical value accorded to the passions between 1600 and 1660. These traditions testify to the erosion across the seventeenth century of an image of man grounded on ideas of psychomachia and the dangerousness of emotions. They testify, too, to the replacement of the latter by an image which emphasizes the spiritual worth of the heart, the rational worth of moderated passions, and the broad value of affectivity as a means of connecting humans to their environment. However, though both Augustinianism and Thomism, thus interpreted, would go on to exert a powerful influence over the moral culture of Williamite England, their history was a disrupted one. It was broken by the impact—the rise and fall—of another outlook, a philosophy which opposed not merely the ethos of psychomachia but also the very principle that the mind was ruled by a transcendent Reason or Will; a philosophy which, instead of making the passions servants of reason or expressions of a love of God, made reason the servant of the passions, and those passions measures of naked self-interest. This alternative perspective, which put fear and power at the centre of human nature, was to grip the imaginations of a generation of Restoration courtiers, those same libertines whom Milton so vilifies in his poem. It is to this philosophy that I now turn, and its story begins with Thomas Hobbes.

# Part II

# The Rise and Fall of Libertinism

# 6

## Hobbes: Fear, Power, and the Passions

The Augustinian and Aristotelian models of governance resonant within the works of Crashaw, Herbert, and Milton constitute one riposte to England's turn-of-the-century theatre, one distinctly moral answer to which imaginations challenged by a new, more cynical, more corporeally focused vision of man could turn for comfort. To this intellectual force one can add others: the narrative of later seventeenth-century Cartesian ethics, for example, of the Caroline renegotiation of Stoicism, or of theological ideals of right reason.[1] But in the second part of this book I want to concentrate on a different tradition, a response to Jacobean scepticism which capitalized upon (rather than resisted) that human reality emphasized by Tacitus: namely, man's habit of prioritizing self-interest over all other goods. Hence my story, now, charts the rise and fall of an unapologetically egotistical view of self-governance, in so doing, striking to the heart of Restoration England's taste for libertinism. The works of Hobbes play an important part in this narrative, first, because (arising as they partly do from an engagement with Tacitus and Bacon) they are especially illustrative of egoism and its assumptions; second, because they illustrate a very different approach to the passions from those discussed hitherto; third, because the 'Malmesbury Apostle's' books were, besides, notoriously influential in shaping Restoration sensibilities. Hobbes (a writer who scarcely speaks that language of Pauline spirituality so prevalent in my previous chapter) thus takes centre stage here. I examine in this sixth chapter his efforts not merely to undermine, but completely to overturn, the idea of rationalist psychomachia, this (1) by casting the passions as, properly, the primary determinants of behaviour; (2) by relating them to a new, kinetic model of happiness in which fear, self-interest, and lust for power play critical roles; (3) by reconceiving reason, from one perspective at least, as an instrumental, not a transcendental faculty; and (4) by representing morality from that same perspective as a social construct, not an absolute. In elaborating upon these themes, Hobbes constructed what

---

[1] On the English reception of Cartesian ethics, see Tilmouth 2007; on Stuart Stoicism, Barbour 1998: 114–19, 144–94, 245–64; and on seventeenth-century rationalism, Beiser 1996.

he thought of as a new, empirically validated moral psychology, in contrast to which the ascetic aspirations of the Tudor rationalist project were simply delusional—a denial of the ineluctable realities of human nature. Hobbes's own forthright literary manner was characteristic of a man determined not to expose himself to like-minded self-delusions (yet ironically, as I note in an addendum to this chapter, personal passions and interests *did* exert a distorting influence over the construction of Hobbes's supposedly objective, 'scientific' arguments). These, then, are my major concerns here, but before turning to them I begin by outlining the Tacitean and Baconian traditions via which the cynicism and anti-rationalism of the early 1600s extended forward into Hobbes's own time.

## HOBBES'S IMMEDIATE BACKGROUND

The preoccupation with egotism graphically captured at the turn of the century in plays like *Troilus* remained a dominant theme in Jacobean and Caroline drama.[2] However, this same attitude also found expression in the English tradition of Tacitean scholarship which emerged in the early 1590s. As is well known, Tacitus's *Annals* themselves place an aggressive form of egotism at the heart of human nature. Charting the history of imperial Rome, they lament the demise of republican virtue and of the republican constitution (in all but name) under the influence of an array of egotistical passions. Tacitus presents that erosion as a development engineered by Augustus and Tiberius, both secret advocates of monarchical power who appropriated the rhetoric of republicanism in support of their autocratic purposes. Hence he attributes Tiberius's treatment of Silius, for example, to a mixture of imperial vanity and paranoid concern to maintain power. The Emperor is said to have viewed Silius's military triumphs and consequent popularity as 'embasing to his [own] greatnes' and as too splendid to be safely requited.[3] In imperial Rome such 'good turnes are no longer well taken ... then they may be recompensed: when they grow greater ... then hope of requitall', in place of thankfulness they 'breede hatred'. Where he expected to be feted for his victory, the triumphant leader therefore finds himself tried, instead, for misconduct. The true motives behind this attack are imperial fear and envy, but Consul Varro prosecutes Silius in the name of protecting 'the common-wealth' (that is, under the auspices of republican rhetoric), it being 'a common tricke with *Tiberius* ... [thus] to

[2] The discomforting moral vision prevalent in Jacobean tragedy is surveyed in Lever 1987 and Ornstein 1960.
[3] Tacitus 1598: 95.

cloake new coyned mischiefe with old words', old ideals.[4] The *Annals*, filled as they are with episodes like this, present the story of successive reigns of terror ('For what daie was past free from executions ... ?'[5]) in which right and wrong lose their names, all things include themselves in power, will degenerates into appetite, and Rome, in effect, eats itself in bloody emulousness. 'The scope of our discourse', Tacitus dryly comments, 'is streight, and our labour inglorious: ... we heape vp bloodie commaundements; continuall accusations; deceitfull friendships; the ouerthrow of innocent persons.'[6] In all this, over and again, ungoverned, self-interested passions come to the fore, but always under the guise of promoting the republic's interests.

The Renaissance reception of this Tacitean vision has attracted much commentary in recent years.[7] A brief summary cannot do justice to this scholarship; but it is clear, for example, that readers in Shakespeare's time could extract three kinds of lesson from the *Annals* and *Histories*. For the likes of Casaubon, Tacitus's sketches of an age 'enraged against all Vertues' could only be infectious, imbuing young minds with all too intuitive a grasp of 'the Principles of *Tyranny*'.[8] For Lipsians, by contrast, the *Annals* provided statesmen with a handbook of sobering lessons in how a polity and its citizens might disintegrate; a sheaf, too, of 'Similitudes' which reminded the reader of 'Evils too well known in [his own] times'. Tacitus's books also presented moving examples of integrity and Stoic endurance in face of such affliction, edifying conclusions with which to redeem otherwise tawdry material.[9] For a third kind of student, foremost amongst whom was the new school of 'politic' historians emergent around 1600, Tacitus offered what Bradford calls 'a clue with which to thread the labyrinth of power politics'.[10] These last partakers, who included Bacon, read him not with any moral judgement in mind, but simply to imbibe insights into historical causation and human motivation.[11]

English readers, especially, were tacitly encouraged by the Essex faction to favour the latter two approaches. Henry Savile's 1591 translation, for instance, which brings together Savile's own composition, *The End of Nero and Beginning of Galba*, and his renderings of the *Histories* and *Agricola*, begins with a preface (putatively by Essex) emphasizing the utilitarian political wisdom and Machiavellian *arcana imperii* to be gleaned from Tacitus.[12] Lest it should seem too seditious in propagating such knowledge, the work also

---

[4] Ibid. 95–6.    [5] Ibid. 114.    [6] Ibid. 100.

[7] See Bradford 1983; Butler 1985: 140–6; Morford 1993; Peltonen 1995: 124–36; Salmon 1989; Sharpe and Lake 1994: 21–43, 76–89; Tuck 1993: 39–45, 65–119; Womersley 1991.

[8] Quoted in Bradford 1983: 129.    [9] Ibid. 128. See also pp. 145–6 and Tuck 1993: 47.

[10] Bradford 1983: 130.    [11] Ibid. 132.

[12] For examples of such precepts see Sharpe and Lake 1994: 28 and Tuck 1993: 105.

alludes to the merits of the peace maintained by Elizabeth.[13] Superficially, this book therefore deflects any suggestion of criticism of the English polity. Yet behind that guise, so Smuts and Womersley argue, sits a more radical intent. Savile's *End of Nero* effectively *heroizes* Vindex, the man who rebelled against Nero. It celebrates Vindex as the possessor of a distinctively Machiavellian kind of republican *virtù* (this, a quality singularly lacking in Nero himself),[14] and as a patriot driven not by ambition but by a longing 'to redeeme his cuntrey from tyranny'.[15] Likewise, Savile's Tacitus as a whole exposes how weak monarchical states (of which Elizabeth's would surely be one) disintegrate under pressure.[16] The entire work is provocatively bracketed by its portrayal of two strong figures—Vindex at the beginning, Agricola at the end—these (Smuts suggests), ancient counterparts for Sidney, the contemporary most beloved of the Essex faction.[17] Add to that Tacitus's emphasis on the petty jealousies of the Roman court, and you have a book which tacitly prompts English readers to criticize their own court and its ailing monarchy's weaknesses. It prompts them, too, to seek out edification in reaction to such tawdry matter, and invites them to find that in the magnanimous figure of Essex.[18] Two respondents did exactly that. Hayward dedicated his 1599 *Reign of Henry IIII*, a history saturated with quotations from Savile, to Essex.[19] Camden, in chronicling the Essex revolt, likewise indicated his admiration for the Earl by identifying him with Germanicus, the fated but totemic figure towards whom opponents of Tiberius gravitated.[20] Furthermore, this same, pointed use of Tacitean material continued well into James's and Charles's reigns. In 1615 Sir John Holles constructed his critique of Somerset's fall precisely in terms of Tacitean examples.[21] In 1626 Sir John Eliot was quick to satirize the Duke of Buckingham as a new Sejanus, and two years later two translations of a biography of Tiberius's favourite both made that same equation.[22]

Tacitism, then, provided a language through which to attack contemporary authoritarianism, egotism, and cupidity. By way of preparing the ground for Hobbes, though, it is worth emphasizing two particular passions—fear and unremitting appetite—to which Jacobean authors drew attention in

---

[13] Sharpe and Lake 1994: 26.          [14] Womersley 1991: 320–7.
[15] Quoted in Bradford 1983: 146. Womersley (1991: 318–20, 326–9) demonstrates that the argument used to justify rebellion against Nero's tyranny matches Huguenot theories of resistance developed under the Valois monarchy.
[16] Sharpe and Lake 1994: 26.          [17] Ibid. 26–7.
[18] Cf. ibid. 83–4; Womersley 1991: 341–2.
[19] See Sharpe and Lake 1994: 22; Tuck 1993: 106–7.          [20] Bradford 1983: 153 n. 22.
[21] Sharpe and Lake 1994: 35.
[22] Salmon 1989: 225. For further examples of the Sejanus–Buckingham analogy, see Butler 1985: 143–6.

scrutinizing Tacitus's Rome. Jonson's *Sejanus* (1603), a study of Tiberius's reign, is perhaps most remarkable for its gradual, chilling evocation of fear. That passion builds exponentially across the play. Beginning with a few intimations of anxiety (I. 419), Jonson traces the rise, first, of an unfocused caution amongst the Germanicans; then, of a more desperate insecurity ('Was Silius safe? Or the good Sosia safe? / Or was my niece, dear Claudia Pulchra, safe?' (IV. 20–1) ).[23] In the later acts paranoia spreads amongst the whole Senatorial class (l. 238), eventually producing an outright reign of terror:

> This man receives his praises of Sejanus;
> A second, but slight mention; a third, none;
> A fourth, rebukes. And thus he leaves the Senate
> Divided and suspended, all uncertain.
>
> (ll. 419–22)

This last state, especially, complements Tacitus's own description of Tiberian Rome: 'The citie was neuer in greater perplexitie and feare, then at [this] time; euery man estranging himself euen from his neerest kindred ... : they auoided all meetings, ... eschuing as well knowen friends, as strangers.'[24] Fear, though, exists even amongst those whose megalomania is the source of others' terror. In managing Tiberius, Sejanus gives to him with one hand and takes with the other, encouraging his master to turn his fear against potential enemies without taking thought for the public hatred he will thereby foster (II. 165–85), yet simultaneously urging the Emperor, 'Be not secure: none swiftlier are oppressed / Than they whom confidence betrays to rest' (ll. 206–7). Like Ulysses lecturing Achilles, Sejanus impresses upon Tiberius the imperative to pursue infinite motion, instilling in him the very anxiety he also encourages him to heal through violent action. Tiberius, though, responds in kind, reminding his servant how far he, too, is hated (III. 564), and frightening him with the thought that he also might not be 'safe' (l. 550). As will become clear hereafter, this preoccupation with fear was to prove essential to Hobbes's moral thought.

The anonymous *Tragedy of Nero* (1624) illustrates another important Tacitean impulse, man's ceaseless appetite for power and the pleasures of power. Here, for example, naked ambition drives Nimphidius, Nero's would-be successor. For him the people are no more than a seething arena of living passions to be exploited for his own ends. Both their hatred of the Emperor and Poppæa's private desire for Nimphidius himself become, in the latter's mind, valuable simply as ladders to the royal throne (his single-minded obsession).[25]

---

[23] References to this play are to Jonson 1990.  [24] Tacitus 1598: 114.
[25] Anon. 1624: sig. B2^r.

Nero, the occupant of that throne, can of course climb no higher, but the same unending appetite for power nonetheless persists in him, diverting itself into ever more perverse pleasures expressive of his supremacy. Nero already does, by his own admission, whatever he pleases:

> Kings must vpon the Peoples headlesse courses
> Walke to securitie, and ease of minde.
> Why what haue we to doe with th'ayrie names
>
> .    .    .    .    .    .    .    .    .    .
>
> Of *Iustice*, and ne're certaine Equitie[?][26]

Yet since, nowadays, this tyranny meets no resistance which he could enjoy overcoming, nor is therefore entirely gratifying, his itch for satisfaction turns instead to mass destruction. Cursory executions being no longer sufficient, Nero craves instead a more apocalyptic entertainment, the incineration of Rome and its entire population. He imagines himself as a salamander 'bathing ... / In the last Ashes of all mortall things'; figures his planned crime as an act of cosmic creation (as splendid as the creation of a star); and casts himself as both Priam supposedly delighting in the death of his own Troy and Pyrrhus finally sating his fury with the same spectacle.[27] This contradictory pose of triumphant avenger and infanticidal father (the latter enjoying the demise of his own creation) exemplifies, incidentally, Braden's description of imperial derangement as the product of a classical competitive ethos which turns in upon itself once it lacks external opponents.[28] Again, this ceaseless search for new expressions of power and new pleasures will recur as a vital principle of Hobbesian psychology hereafter.

The obsessive promotion of self-interest which, in the aforementioned tragedies and in Tacitus, precipitates so much immorality is apparent too, if more subtly, in the work of another precursor to Hobbes, Francis Bacon. Attuned as he is to Christian obligations, Bacon repeatedly stresses in his *Essayes* the value of charity;[29] yet that pious tendency is conflated with an equal and somewhat contrary emphasis on the care of the self, the impulse to 'Divide with reason betweene *Selfe-love*, and *Society*: And be so true to thy *Selfe*, as thou be not false to Others' ('Of Wisedome for a Mans Selfe' (1612) ).[30] This slant is applied, for example, in the very midst of 'Of Goodnesse' (1612) when Bacon, tempering the idealism of the Gospels (Mark 10: 21), puts worldly limits upon charity: 'beware, how in making the Portraiture, thou breakest the Patterne: For Divinitie maketh the Love of our Selves the Patterne; The Love of our Neighbours but the Portraiture. *Sell all thou hast, and give it to the poore* ... : But sell not all thou hast .... For otherwise, in feeding the Streames,

---

[26] Anon. 1624: sigs. C2$^v$–C3$^r$.    [27] Ibid. sigs. D4$^v$, E2$^v$.    [28] Braden 1985: 14.
[29] Bacon 1985: 8, 33, 38–41, 81 (ll. 17–20), 112.    [30] Ibid. 73.

thou driest the Fountaine.'[31] An essay such as 'Of Simulation' (1625) exhibits these same tensions. It begins morally enough, Bacon discriminating between the ablest men, who demonstrate 'an Opennesse ... of dealing', and a 'weaker Sort', who resort to dissimulation because they lack the others' strength of mind.[32] But midway through his argument Bacon concedes, in contrast to this initial distinction, that the great statesman's sometime need to observe secrecy may lead him into that very dissimulation earlier dubbed 'a Poorenesse' of character. By the end of the essay he goes further, asserting that the politician should always 'have ... *Dissimulation* in seasonable use' and cultivate 'a Power to faigne, if there be no Remedy'.[33]

The imperative standing behind these shifts in Bacon's argument is his fixation upon the art of making or 'pressing' one's fortune.[34] In pursuit of the latter, the two *Advancements of Learning* (1605, 1623), together with numerous pieces in the *Essayes*, systematically anatomize the means by which to 'get on' in life (in commerce and court), and that focus inevitably pulls against more pious lines of instruction. 'Of Honour' (1597) and 'Of Ambition' (1612), for example, contribute to Bacon's more worldly brand of wisdom, as does 'Of Fortune' (1612), perhaps the most Machiavellian of all the discourses given its precept 'there be not two more *Fortunate* Properties ... then to have a *Little* of the *Foole*; And not *Too Much* of the *Honest*'.[35] Granted, amidst such trimming comments the moral voice does persist in certain judgemental touches, witness the vaguely ominous 'All Rising to *Great Place*, is by a winding Staire' ('Of Great Place' (1612) ),[36] but the appeal of the easy life of self-interest remains ever-apparent. Hence when Bacon tries to write *against* the evil of Machiavellian techniques of self-advancement, his argument is tellingly unemphatic, petering out in a half-hearted extenuation of good morals: 'certainly with [such] dispensations from the laws of charity and integrity, the pressing of a man's fortune may be more hasty and compendious. But it is in life as it is in ways, the shortest way is commonly the foulest, *and surely the fairer way is not much about*.'[37] In passages like these Bacon falls far short, of course, of the depravities of Jacobean tragedy, but his *Essayes* nonetheless position themselves a long way, too, from the moralizing of Erasmus or Thomas Rogers. They demonstrate how far arguments centred on interest, commodity, and policy—idioms hostile to *The Faerie Queene*'s world—had begun to take their place within civil discourse even before Hobbes set to work.

Some at least of these sources must have exerted an influence over Hobbes's early thinking. His interests in humanist rhetoric, in Grotius's and Selden's

[31] Ibid. 40.    [32] Ibid. 20–1.    [33] Ibid. 22.
[34] Bacon 1973: 187.    [35] Bacon 1985: 123.    [36] Ibid. 36.
[37] Bacon 1973: 203.

political thought, and in the Mersenne circle's efforts to answer sixteenth-century scepticism, have all recently been documented.[38] With respect to the last of these, for example, Tuck has interpreted Hobbes's preoccupation with motion (especially those seemingly external motions which have a percussive impact upon our consciousness) as the outcome of his endeavour in the 1630s to outflank the solipsistic tendencies of Continental scepticism. However, as Bacon's amanuensis and a sometime translator of his *Essayes* into Latin, Hobbes must also have developed an intimate acquaintance with the latter's writings, and not least with their moral equivocations.[39] More significantly, he was certainly acquainted with the Tacitean tradition. Indeed, it is in precisely the 1620 'Discourses' on Tacitus and Rome associated with him[40] that Hobbes's interest in motion is first observable. In his 1629 translation of Thucydides' *History* Hobbes describes the Peloponnesian War as 'the greatest motion' in Greek history; the Athenians are characterized as perpetually in motion, 'seldom enjoying their possessions because they are always adding to them'; and Alcibiades is quoted as arguing that states must never 'rest' if they are to avoid decay.[41] But this last, Machiavellian point is foreshadowed in the earlier 'Discourse of Rome' in which Hobbes (assuming he is the author) berates all 'ease ... of life', protesting that 'a continual working of the mind, ... if it should be suffered to rest, would soon degenerate'.[42] More significantly, constant motion—a fixation upon *future* attainments—is also the theme in the accompanying Tacitus 'Discourse': 'desire and hope of good more affects [men] than fruition: for this induces satiety; but hope is a whetstone to ... desires, and will not suffer them to languish.'[43] Again, Hobbes (the presumed author of this essay) continues to think kinetically when he describes the jockeying for power in Augustan Rome as a race: 'the emulation of those that are in the way to authority [is such that they] often labour not so much to outrun each other ... as ... to trip up one another's heels. And the same emulation, when they once draw near the race's end, makes them snatch at the prize.'[44] Likewise, the ambitious Tiberius is figured as one willing to destroy those 'before him' in hope to supersede them, and those 'behind' out of fear.[45] Inevitably, such imagery recalls (for us) the mind-set put before Achilles by Shakespeare's Ulysses. Hobbes further emphasizes man's obsession with motion by arguing that passions like anger and lust actually thrive on adversity (when it is 'such as [men] expect to overcome') because frustration only augments the more

---

[38] See, respectively, Skinner 1996; Tuck 1993: 154–221, 302–11; and Leites 1988: 235–63, and Rogers and Ryan 1988: 11–41.

[39] Sorell 1996: 18, 200–1. See also Collins 2005: 52–4.

[40] For the question of attribution here, see Reynolds and Hilton 1993.

[41] Quoted in Rogers and Sorell 2000: 123–4.          [42] Hobbes 1995: 73–4.

[43] Ibid. 55.          [44] Ibid. 66–7.          [45] Ibid. 58.

the excitement of anticipated pleasures: 'men please their ... fancies ... with the conceit of what they will execute ... hereafter, when they shall have the power'.[46] The human mind, then, constantly leans towards the future.

In these various respects the Hobbesian Tacitus essay develops an image of man which figures at its centre a competitive interest in motion. As the above reference to 'power' indicates, though, other Hobbesian themes are also nascent in this early text. Honour is measured here (as in Ulysses' marketplace rhetoric) not according to intrinsic qualities but rather 'by the acceptance that [men's] persons find in the world'.[47] States dominated by an authoritarian magistrate are preferred to 'factious ... Commonwealths' because what corruption there is in the former (on the ruler's part) is as nothing compared to that in the latter.[48] These points find echoes in later Hobbesian thought, as do early remarks (reminiscent of Tacitus's reflections on Silius) on ingratitude:

benefits received are pleasing so long as they be requitable. When once they exceed that, they are an intolerable burden, and men seldom are willing to acknowledge them .... Princes ... like not to have such great Creditors in their eye .... [G]reat services procure ... rather ... hatred than ... love.[49]

The comparable passage in *Leviathan* (1651) has often been noted:[50]

To have received from one ... greater benefits than there is hope to Requite, disposeth to counterfeit love; but really secret hatred; and puts a man into the estate of a desperate debtor, that ... tacitely wishes [his creditor] there, where he might never see him more. For benefits oblige; and obligation is thraldome.[51]

Both these extracts emphasize the essential Tacitean message, that man's conduct is dominated by self-interest and a concern for power. It is this assumption and the accompanying focus on endless forward motion and future expectations which is carried across from these early readings of Tacitus and Bacon into Hobbes's mature articulations of his *own* moral thought; and it is to the latter that I now turn.

## *THE ELEMENTS OF LAW*: 'A VIEW OF THE PASSIONS REPRESENTED IN A RACE'

In his *Elements of Law* (1640) Hobbes purports 'to put men in mind of what they know already ... by their own experience', to provide simply an empirical

---

[46] Ibid. 66.   [47] Ibid. 65.   [48] Ibid. 48.   [49] Ibid. 51.
[50] e.g., Rogers and Sorell 2000: 104; Wootton 1997: 215–16.
[51] Hobbes 1996: 71.

description of man 'considered ... by himself, without relation to others'.[52] He stages an archaeology of the self, stripping away the surface accretions of social being and presenting the foundational elements constitutive of 'human nature',[53] elements from which a more complex psychology then evolves. The first 'observation' of this anatomy lesson is that the passions—varied manifestations of man's ceaseless appetite for pleasure—are the primary motivators, initiators, and determinants of action, an undeniable part of our being. They *are* our motions. Where the Aristotelian tradition concedes that desire and passion are certainly essential, because theirs is the motive force behind our actions, yet immediately suspends these forces amidst a nexus of controlling soul functions, Hobbes instead isolates them. Imagining (for the moment) that the passions are prior to the psyche's other elements, and that they remain ineradicably present beneath other, apparently more sophisticated impulses, he resolves to describe them in and of themselves. His opening survey of the affections is therefore free of moral and civil considerations. *Elements* presents the passions as they had not been seen before, as pre-social, morally indifferent urges. Where the Stoic and Platonist moralists of my previous chapters had thought of the passions from the outset as forces to be suppressed or eliminated; where Aristotelians and Augustinians subordinated them within a circumscribed role, as assistants to moral conduct or as the functional expressions of a good or bad will, Hobbes simply embraces them as the natural, proper life forces of humanity. To deny that, to hide from the visceral realities of human nature and pursue, for example, a psychomachic agenda, is, in his view, to foster a delusion. Such is the new perspective which Hobbes's approach brings to this book's narrative.

Part 1 of *Elements* is consequently dominated by a descriptive catalogue of the passions. According to this, man's every thought or perception is communicated as an impulse from his imagination to his heart, there either to 'help or hinder that motion which is called vital; when [the impulse] helpeth, it is called ... PLEASURE, which is nothing really but motion about the heart, ... and the same ... with reference to the object, is called LOVE: but when such motion weakeneth ... vital motion, then it is called PAIN; and in relation to that which causeth it, HATRED'.[54] The association of man's passions with the motions of his vital spirits and with the heart's dilations and contractions was, as noted in Chapter 1, a commonplace by Hobbes's time. Hobbes's innovation is to insist that this impulsive motion—in the imagination, in the heart, and between those two—*is* man's passion (in its entirety). That material, percussive movement (continuous with the motion first imparted to the senses by the object perceived) is all that is 'felt' by the agent. Man has no separate Cartesian soul,

⁵² Hobbes 1969: 1, 64.		⁵³ Ibid. 1.		⁵⁴ Ibid. 28.

no forum of consciousness within which the body's mechanistic operations suddenly assume the intangible, immaterial quality of subjective experience.[55] Hence further passions are also defined materialistically, as cardiac motions (or 'solicitations') 'either to draw near to [a] thing that pleaseth, or to retire from [what] displeaseth'. '[T]his solicitation is the ... internal beginning of animal motion, which when the object delighteth, is called APPETITE; when it displeaseth, ... is called AVERSION, in respect of the displeasure present; but in respect of the displeasure expected, FEAR.'[56]

One might ask here why, if Hobbes differentiates between a revulsion for displeasurable objects currently present ('aversion') and a like revulsion for such objects when expected but not yet present ('fear'), the same temporal distinction does not apply to the equivalent *positive* passion, 'appetite'. However, the *Elements'* description of 'felicity' does much to account for this asymmetry (and to define the passions' broader function). In a move which signals a remarkable imaginative departure from previous traditions Hobbes rejects the idea that man has any 'utmost end' or *summum bonum*: 'for while we live, we have desires, and desire presupposeth a farther end.'[57] Since all pleasures give way to new appetites, 'there can be no contentment but in proceeding': 'as men attain to more riches, honours, or ... power; so their appetite continually groweth ... ; and when they are come to the utmost degree of one kind of power, they pursue some other, as long as in any kind they think themselves behind any other .... FELICITY ... consisteth not in having prospered, but in prospering.' This is obviously a critical, 'empirical' judgement within the *Elements* which draws directly upon the comments already cited from Hobbes's Thucydidean *History* and the two 'Discourses' ('Upon Tacitus' especially).[58] For Hobbes, as for Shakespeare's Ulysses, it is an essential fact of the moral imagination that man is engaged in constant forward motion, reaching always towards a better future rather than settling upon the present. His passions are the particular measures of this self-interested process. To return, though, to my previous point, such comments on felicity are of further importance because they account for Hobbes's otherwise asymmetrical sketch of the emotions.

The definition of felicity indicates that Hobbes's 'appetite' should really be considered in opposition to 'fear', not 'aversion', because, like 'fear', Hobbesian 'appetite' is always solely concerned with *future* goals. Whether a beloved object has just been or is yet to be enjoyed, the reciprocal response of the *appetite* is always only focused upon the future. Man's perpetual desire is for 'more of this, more of this' hereafter. If a given pleasurable object is yet to be obtained, appetite focuses on procuring it. But if it has been

---

[55] Cf. S. James 1997: 128–31.    [56] Hobbes 1969: 28–9.    [57] Ibid. 30.
[58] Cf. Rogers and Sorell 2000: 103–4; Wootton 1997: 215.

obtained, there is no desire to continue experiencing that *present* pleasure, which would be the appetitious equivalent of 'aversion' (the desire to escape *present* pain); rather, there is only a desire to obtain a second, additional pleasure—to move on. On this model each source of pleasure is consumed and exhausted the moment it is felt, such is man's insatiable nature. Present pleasure may be real, a heartfelt experience, but it is ephemeral, and man's attention soon shifts back to the future. This view is confirmed in *De Homine*, in which a constant (and in some sense always forward) momentum again defines appetite: 'Even the enjoyment of a desire, when we are enjoying it, is an appetite, namely the motion of the mind to enjoy by parts, the thing that it is enjoying. For life is perpetual motion that, when it cannot progress in a straight line, is converted into circular motion.'[59] Hobbes's Calliclesian man, then, will scratch and scratch and scratch again, even if this means resorting to the trivialiest of passions for diversion. (In an acute recollection of Bacon's 'Of Empire', Hobbes thus notes that Nero and Commodus, having reached the height of political power, transferred their appetite to the pursuit of mastery in other arts: music and poetry, and gladiatorial combat, respectively.[60]) For these reasons, then, there is no 'appetitious' equivalent of 'aversion'—only of 'fear'—hence the asymmetry of *Elements*' analysis.

One further point is bound up with these observations. As is implicit in the reference above to man's thinking himself 'behind any other', and as we shall see in detail later, Hobbes figures the pursuit of 'FELICITY' as a competitive race against others. But it is also a race against oneself, each man continually aspiring to exceed his previous achievements. For Cornwallis this amounts to a process of perverse self-torment: 'when ... the determined contentment approcheth, we flie from, not the enioying, but the opinion we had. Another contentment is set vp; that obtained, another. So doth our ... liues runne after contentment, but neuer ouertake her.'[61] Cavendish, Hobbes's pupil, commenting on the self-enslaving habits of the ambitious, laments the same 'Continual proiectinge without stop'.[62] Such endless endeavours of self-propulsion could be thought to constitute a vertiginous neurosis, but for Hobbes (like Plutarch's Caesar, who delighted to engage in 'an emulation with him selfe as with an other man'[63]) the processes of constant momentum and self-variation are but plain

---

[59] Hobbes 1978: 54.

[60] Hobbes 1969: 30. Bacon (1985: 58–9) argues that when kings, 'being at the highest, want Matter of desire, ... and Lack ... some predominant desire, that should marshall ... all the rest', they '*make* themselves Desires, and set their Hearts upon toyes: Sometimes upon a Building; Sometimes upon Erecting of an Order; ... Sometimes upon obtaining Excellency in some Art .... As *Nero* ... , *Domitian* ... , *Commodus* ....'

[61] Cornwallis 1946: 119–20.

[62] Wolf 1969: 139. On the question of attribution here, see Malcolm 1981: 319–21.

[63] Bullough 1957–75: v. 79.

facts of nature, matters for neutral report. Images of perpetual motion and of the individual's struggle constantly to exceed his past self are, in Hobbes's eyes, simply reflective of the way man is.

These, then, are some of the considerations—motion within the heart, relationship to felicity and to constant momentum—with reference to which Hobbes catalogues man's seven aboriginal passions: pleasure, pain, love, hate, appetite, aversion, and fear. However, as he descends to more particular emotions such as shame and anger, another factor, power, is increasingly brought to bear in his description. 'Power' embraces, for Hobbes, any instrumental capacity to satisfy one's appetites: it includes both immediate capacities such as strength and knowledge and 'such farther powers, as by them are acquired'—for example, wealth or public authority.[64] In so far as it conveys to its possessor a sense of his own potency and productivity, power is inevitably a source of pleasure; but it is also, by its nature, a relative term keyed to the competitive character of the Hobbesian world. For Hobbes it has, ultimately, no meaning other than as 'the excess of the power of one above that of another'. Each individual thus measures himself against his peers to see whether or not he is the frontrunner—the only position which matters—in the race for superiority. Where he finds that he is, the experience of power becomes valuable for its own sake, as a source of felicity in itself. Power viewed in this light ceases to be simply an instrumental means by which one can obtain *other* objects (those other objects being the things which satisfy one's appetite). It becomes, rather, a quality the possession of which is desirable and delightful in itself, specifically because it promotes a sense of glory, of excelling over others 'that contendeth with us'.[65] Having developed this point, Hobbes adds, crucially, that the appetite for this particular pleasure of dominance is in fact stronger than any other. Glory, the passionate regard for power, is, he says, pre-eminent amongst our emotions as a source of felicity. As 'C. C.'s' translation of *De Cive* puts it, 'all the mindes pleasure is either Glory, (or to have a good opinion of ones selfe) or referres to Glory in the end'.[66] Power, then, emerges from these comments as a defining feature of man, a dominant term in the—to Hobbes's mind—'empirical' sketch of human nature which underpins the *Elements*' moral programme.

According to Hobbes, the particular motive forces which propel our search for felicity, moment by moment, are the passions; but the more general dynamo driving this mechanism is the ceaseless momentum of our hunt for power. For that reason, power informs our various affections. Self-evidently, it shapes the definition of glory and its cognates, but power is also implicit, for example, in the idea of shame (the grief of one who, whilst harbouring 'a good

---

[64] Hobbes 1969: 34.     [65] Ibid. 36–7.     [66] Hobbes 1983: 43.

opinion of himself', suddenly discovers some defect within, 'the remembrance whereof dejecteth him') and in the idea of courage (a 'contempt of wounds and death, when they oppose a man in the way to his end').[67] Each of these passions is defined as a reaction to a challenge to one's standing. So too is anger. Leo Strauss, aiming to demonstrate the *Elements'* dependence upon Aristotle, noted the initial comment in the 1640 work that

Anger ... hath been commonly defined to be grief proceeding from an opinion of contempt.[68]

and aligned this with Hobbes's definition of anger in his 1637 *Briefe of the Art of Rhetorique* (a translation of Aristotle's *Rhetoric*):

*Anger* is desire of revenge, joyned with greefe for that He, or some of his, is, or seemes to be *neglected*.[69]

In the *Elements*, though, the Aristotelian opinion is actually invoked only to be discarded. Hobbes continues the first of the above two quotations by stating that 'common' thinking is

confuted by the often experience we have of being moved to anger by things inanimate and without sense, and consequently incapable of contemning us.[70]

He then offers, by way of the *Elements'* last word on anger, the distinctly non-Aristotelian definition that it is 'nothing but the appetite ... of overcoming present opposition' of any kind, a 'sudden courage' and thus a bursting assertion of one's power.[71] There is no hint here of anger being privileged above other passions (as there is in the *Nicomachean Ethics*). Discussed as it is from a pre-covenanting, pre-moral point of view, its worth is measured solely with reference to power, not to Aristotle's ethical criteria.

What is true of anger is also true of envy and emulation. These are defined in the *Elements* with self-interest very much in mind:

EMULATION is grief arising from seeing one's self exceeded ... by his concurrent, together with hope to equal or exceed him in time to come, by his own ability. But, ENVY is the same grief joined with pleasure conceived in the imagination of some ill fortune that may befall him.[72]

There is certainly a clear comparison here with Hobbes's treatment of the same affections in his *Briefe*.[73] However, again neither the *Briefe* nor, more importantly, the *Elements* reflects the evaluative dimension which characterizes

---

[67] Hobbes 1969: 38.       [68] Ibid. 38–9.
[69] Hobbes 1986: 69. See Strauss 1952: 37; cf. S. James 1997: 133.
[70] Hobbes 1969: 39.       [71] Ibid. 38.       [72] Ibid. 41.
[73] Strauss 1952: 39. Cf. Hobbes 1986: 83–4.

Aristotle's original analysis of these passions. The original *Rhetoric* continues in moral tones as follows:

[Emulation] is ... a good feeling felt by good persons, whereas envy is a bad feeling felt by bad persons. Emulation makes us take steps to secure the good things in question, envy makes us take steps to stop our neighbours having them. (*Rhetoric* 1388ᵃ34–6)

Envy, then, is specifically condemned in the *Nicomachean Ethics* as a passion which, by definition, can never be virtuous, its name implying extremity (*NE* 1108ᵇ1–6). The absence of such moralizing in Hobbes's work is indicative of his desire—so different from that of other moralists discussed thus far—to present the passions in pre-covenanting terms, as impulses which precede ethical considerations. Instead, each emotion is related only to the passionate individual's estimate of his own power *vis-à-vis* others. In tandem with that, Hobbes builds into each of his two descriptions here a positive feeling of expectation. The *Elements*' definitions of envy and emulation incorporate within them the endeavour of a constant, forward momentum in pursuit of future felicity, a 'hope to equal or exceed [others] in time to come'. (This is implicit in Hobbes's envy in so far as the relativity of power ensures that any diminishment of another's fortune must simultaneously imply improvement in one's own.)

Power and Hobbes's egotistical conception of felicity also inform the *Elements*' account of pity. Here, though, Hobbes can afford to stick closely to Aristotle, since, as every reader of the *Poetics* knows, pity is, for the latter, intimately related to fear and self-preservation. The Aristotelian position on this issue is reflected in Hobbes's *Briefe*, where pity is cast as

a perturbation of the mind, arising from the apprehension of hurt ... to another that doth not deserve it, and which [a man] thinkes may happen to himself ...
... it appertaines to *Pitty* to thinke that he, or his may fall into the misery he pitties in others.[74]

Such pity, clearly, is peculiarly expressive of what Hobbes takes to be the essential self-centredness of man:

PITY is imagination ... of future calamity to ourselves, proceeding from the sense of another man's present calamity; but when it lighteth on such as we think have not deserved the same, the compassion is the greater, because then there appeareth ... more probability that the same may happen to us.[75]

Hobbes's own pity was a matter of comment in this regard, Aubrey citing an occasion when the philosopher was seen to give 6*d*. to a beggar.[76] A passing divine, one Jasper Mayne, was quick to ask Hobbes whether he would have

---

[74] Hobbes 1986: 80.    [75] Hobbes 1969: 40.    [76] Aubrey 1960: 157.

acted so had it not been Christ's command, to which the latter reputedly replied, 'Yea .... Because ... I was in paine to consider the miserable condition of the old man; and ... giving him some reliefe, doth ... ease me.' Here, then, egotism is again the primary impulse, but considerations about power also prevail in so unexpected a passion as laughter. For Hobbes, even laughter is a 'sudden glory arising from sudden conception of some eminency in ourselves': a mixture, in short, of delight as to one's own capacities and derision as to others' weaknesses.[77] Again, lust is conceived as another such self-celebration. The sensual pleasure of lust may be one of delighting in corporeal titillation, but that affection is also accompanied by the mental pleasure of recognizing one's own power to please, 'the delight men take in delighting'.[78] Lastly, this self-affirming structure also drives Hobbes's account of charity. 'There can be', Hobbes says, 'no greater argument to a man of his own power, than to find himself able, not only to accomplish his own desires, but also to assist other men in theirs.'[79] On this account, charity pleases us, primarily, as an expression and extension of our own power, and only in a secondary, derivative sense because we are satisfied to see others benefit.

So much, then, by way of the *Elements*' comments on various particular passions, comments which underline how absolutely Hobbes's approach to this subject departs from contemporary norms. The *Elements*' catalogue of affections culminates in a 'comparison of the life of man to a race', an extended conceit which centres every human passion on that competition.[80] The race comparison has a long Christian history. Man's life is likened to such a contest in 1 Corinthians 9: 24, Galatians 5: 7, 2 Timothy 4: 7, and Hebrews 12: 1. Perkins preached to the theme[81] and Spenser alludes to it.[82] More tellingly for Hobbes's purposes, Fairfax's Tasso (like Shakespeare's *Troilus*) relates the same figure—in distinctly less Christian, more pagan terms—to the competition for glory: 'Thine elders' glorie herein see and know, / ... / Whom thou art farre behind, a runner slow / In his true course of honour, fame and praise' (*Gerusalemme Liberata*, 17. 65).[83] Above all, though, the *Elements*' comparison draws directly upon the race imagery used in the Tacitus 'Discourse' to figure the rapacious nature of man's world. The goal of this human race is to excel all others in one's power—that pre-eminence, a source of felicity. The virtue of such figurative language is that it provides Hobbes (and the reader) with a remarkable imaginative purchase on the Hobbesian theory of the emotions. It illustrates in a single conceit the synthesizing force which power and self-interest exert in determining all—or almost all—passions. 'For all joy and grief of mind [consists] ... in a contention for precedence with them to

---

[77] Hobbes 1969: 42.      [78] Ibid. 43.      [79] Ibid. 44.      [80] Ibid. 47.
[81] Cited in A. Hume 1984: 64.      [82] *FQ* ii. i. 32. 7, 34. 7.      [83] Tasso 1981: 483.

whom [men] compare themselves.'[84] Hobbes shows considerable acumen in adapting his image to express the essence of the various passions in terms of competition, hence:

> To consider them behind, is glory.
> To consider them before, humility.
> To lose ground with looking back, vain glory.
> To be holden, hatred;

as also:

> To be in breath, hope.
> To be weary, despair.[85]

Hobbes's conclusion, too, is brutally emphatic, as much a message for those who deny his account of psychology as it is a judgement on those—like Achilles 'entombed' in his tent—who abandon the race:

> Continually to be out-gone, is misery.
> Continually to out-go the next before, is felicity.
> And to forsake the course, is to die.[86]

This conceit is, furthermore, more inclusive than Hobbes's critics allow. Herbert complains that fear is incompatible with the race image, since it must surely encourage one to give up.[87] In fact, the analogy includes several such negative passions: for example, humility and repentance. Hobbes's assertion that power provides a core value against which all passions are measured does not imply that all passions feed one's impulse to win the race. Rather, the point of a passion is that it is an affective response to the individual's sense of how he is faring, a response defined by the circumstances affecting his performance at any moment, which may or may not be encouraging in its nature.

The race conceit serves as an epitome of human nature, an account of the passions which makes power and the appetites surrounding it essential to man; which emphasizes the self-interested aspect of all passions; and which posits only one (distinctly amoral) evaluative distinction between those various passions, the question of how far each supports man's race to exceed his fellows. According to the Hobbes of 1640, this rapacious vision of man is the basis on which any civic morality would have to be built, but which such morals could neither change nor destroy, only temper. This broad (and very Jacobean) thesis, that the competition for precedence is the guiding principle of human action, is of course proven here only in so far as it is shown to provide an interpretive framework within which the full range of human

---

[84] Hobbes 1969: 169.     [85] Ibid. 47–8.     [86] Ibid. 48.
[87] G. B. Herbert 1989: 93.

feelings can be understood. Whether or not it is validated in any deeper sense, as a true description of the way things are, is a matter to be proven on the pulse of each individual reader; and certainly it is clear that by 1651 Hobbes himself had changed his mind on this issue. The account of the passions offered in *Leviathan* is noticeably different from that of the *Elements*, principally because Hobbes, at some stage in the intervening decade, abandoned the idea that all men pursue power as an end in itself in favour of the more moderate claim that all pursue it, at least, as the *means* of satisfying their wants (but perhaps not as an end per se). Since Hobbes is best remembered for *Leviathan*, and since it was the heresies in that work more than anything in *Elements* which attracted the animadversions of seventeenth-century critics fishing for trouble, it is worth examining this development (and the account of the passions which follows from it) in detail, this before turning to the next layer in Hobbes's archaeology of the self (his idea of the faculty of reason).

## *LEVIATHAN*

*Leviathan*, too, has its catalogue of passions, but a very different one from the *Elements*. Power no longer provides an overarching conceit for the analysis; emotions are not now defined according to their relationship to one's standing within a race; and glory, hitherto the foremost passion, assumes only a subordinate place within the survey. In this later text, appetite alone is accorded pre-eminence—though since it remains unquenchable (as in the original model of felicity), life remains a struggle. The Gestalt used in the new catalogue is an associationist one. Hobbes starts from a definition of a particular passion and runs through all the other affections whose definitions associate them with that first one. Having once exhausted that line of thought, he then isolates a new one and begins afresh. Consequently, the list itself admits of only loose divisions, forming blocks of cognate passions. The first of these threads starts from hope and runs through despair and fear to courage, newly defined as fear combined 'with hope of avoyding... Hurt by resistence'.[88] Anger is still sudden courage, and other derivatives of these first emotions also follow. The second cluster, mostly composed of new material, lists our 'desires of' various things. Amongst these affections are benevolence, good will, and charity, all of which amount to '*Desire* of good to another'. Whereas the *Elements* had emphasized charity's egotistical aspect, its value as an expression of power, the toning down of such points here is indicative

[88] Hobbes 1996: 41.

of a shift in direction. Hobbes's third group of passions concentrates on varieties of love and lust, two affections which (like charity) are themselves now given less polemical definition. (Whereas the *Elements* had stressed the delight of recognizing one's power to please more than that of being pleased, lust is now given the innocuous meaning '*Love* of Persons for Pleasing the sense only'.) The fourth group lists various desires *to do* certain things; the fifth (again wholly innovative), species of fear. Only with the sixth group, a discussion of species of joy, does Hobbes revert to his 1640 analysis of glory, breaking into much the same sequence of passions of honour already familiar from the *Elements*: glory, shame, pity, emulation, envy, etc. Within this group laughter born of the observation of *others'* imperfections is now condemned, but only because it is commonest in those 'conscious of the fewest abilities in themselves', and thus betrays their impotence.[89] Laughter born of delight in discovering one's own abilities remains laudable (because it is an index to power), as does pity for 'the Calamity of another', which is still said to arise 'from the imagination that the like … may befall [oneself]'. Hobbes then, despite revising his definition of charity, does not here abandon his egoistic psychology. The feel of his analysis is changed by virtue of abandoning the race conceit and the obsession with power which that implies, but the sixth group of passions continues to play a dominant part in the catalogue, comprising the whole of the second half of it.

Another of *Leviathan*'s innovations is chapter 10's laborious anatomy of power;[90] but as with the catalogue of passions, Hobbes nowhere reiterates in this his central claim of the *Elements* that love of power as an end in itself (a source of glory) is man's universal obsession. In *Leviathan*'s world, not everyone is intent (solely or even principally) on demonstrating his supremacy in life's race. Indeed, chapter 10 begins with the assertion that power is a 'present means to obtain some future apparent Good', an 'Instrument' which 'procureth' and 'draweth', serving simply as the *means* for satisfying other appetites. In line with this, the definition of power differs from that in *Elements*. Whereas in *Elements* Hobbes had argued that an individual measures his own potency by weighing, equally, both his own and other people's estimates of it, in *Leviathan* all the emphasis is placed on the latter. Since power is conceived as a means for obtaining other things, it is only buyers' valuations of that power—the market price they put on the qualities one possesses—which is now said to matter.[91] That being so, one's actual power is mutable, subject to changing external circumstances:

---

[89] Ibid. 43.　　[90] Ibid. 62 ff.

[91] Brown 1965: 227, 230–1. Keith Thomas argues here that 'dignity' at least, the value which the sovereign (as opposed to general populace) puts on an individual, is not market-orientated. However, whilst this is true, that valuation of the person is still determined wholly from

The Value ... of a man, is ... his Price; ... so much as would be given for the use of his Power: and therefore is not absolute; but a thing dependant on the need and judgement of another. An able conductor of Souldiers, is of great Price in time of War ... ; but in Peace not so.... And ... not the seller, but the buyer determines the Price. For let [men] rate themselves at the highest Value they can; yet their true Value is no more than it is esteemed by others.[92]

Again this text echoes comments on honour in the Tacitus 'Discourse',[93] as well as spelling out the attitude behind the marketplace rhetoric of Shakespeare's Ulysses. More importantly, though, it reduces power to a tradeable commodity, not an absolute end in its own right.

Additional comments on power support the view that, often at least, this quality is coveted solely for its instrumental value. In chapter 11, for example, Hobbes begins by '[putting] for a generall inclination of all mankind, a perpetuall and restless desire of Power after power, that ceaseth onely in Death'; but he then adds,

And the cause of this, is not always [1] that a man hopes for a more intensive delight, than he has already attained to; or [2] that he cannot be content with a moderate power: but because [3] he cannot assure the power and means to live well, which he hath present, without the acquisition of more.[94]

The second of these three 'causes' clearly points to a pursuit of power as an end in itself. The first, the hope for more 'delight', *may* also imply this if the further 'delight' sought is the glory of power per se; but it may equally imply a case of power being accumulated simply as a *means* to obtaining other delights. This latter idea is definitely the one at work in the third option, which makes power purely an assistant in pursuing other concerns. In support of this last emphasis, the context within which this whole sentence falls is in fact that of a recapitulation of Hobbes's views on felicity (unchanged from the *Elements*). Hobbes has already emphasized by this point that man is prone to seek not only immediate goods but also the means to 'assure for ever, the way of his future desire'. Human actions 'tend, not onely to the procuring, but also to the assuring of a contented life'. Living (even within civil society) in a competitive world, men, we infer, therefore accrue power so as to provide themselves with such assurance, in which respect that power is again valued as a means, not an end.

There are, of course, instances where Hobbes does allow power the status of end-in-itself. In admitting glory (self-exaltation) into the *Leviathan* catalogue of passions at all, he acknowledges the possibility that some will desire power

without—it is not an intrinsic quality—and it remains contingent upon the needs of the sovereign and his commonwealth at any particular moment.

92  Hobbes 1996: 63. Cf. ibid. 105.
93  See above, and cf. Rogers and Sorell 2000: 104–5.          94  Hobbes 1996: 70.

in its own right. Likewise, here (as in the *Elements*) glory is listed among the factors which propel men in a state of nature into one of war, because 'every man looketh that his companion should value him, at the same rate he sets upon himselfe: And upon all signes of contempt ... endeavours ... to extort a greater value from his contemners.'[95] In this context reputation is again valued for its own sake. Yet even here that love of power is not presented as either *the* dominant passion in man or one with which we are *perpetually* concerned. Furthermore, the claim of universality here ('*every* man looketh ... ') sits uneasily alongside Hobbes's specific observation, moments before, that only '*some*' men 'take pleasure in contemplating their own power in ... acts of conquest', the rest preferring to keep themselves 'within modest bounds'. In sum, therefore, these exceptions aside, power in *Leviathan* is generally only a serviceable commodity, not the *Elements'* end in itself.

Quite why Hobbes made this change is difficult to determine. Certainly, though, in thus softening the aggressiveness of his account of human nature, Hobbes presented a kind of man more *capable* than his *Elements* figure had been of demonstrating lasting deference towards sovereign authority. Perhaps this emollient gesture, removing some of the dangerousness from Hobbesian man, was of a piece with the philosopher's wider project to make *Leviathan* more palatable to the Cromwellian authorities.[96] In any event, his shift away from the leading assumption of the *Elements* implied a need to find other terms (besides that of the race conceit) with which to analyse the passions, hence *Leviathan*'s stark change of approach to the classification of the emotions.

Having said this, it would be misleading to overemphasize the differences between the *Elements* and *Leviathan*. Much of what is distinctively 'Hobbesian' in the former survives in the latter, and where there are changes, they often introduce improving nuances. In *Leviathan*, more so than *Elements*, Hobbes stresses that *natural* man would not be bound by, but would predate, any form of morality: 'The Desires, and other Passions of man, are in themselves no Sin. No more are the Actions, that proceed from those Passions, till they know a Law that forbids them.'[97] Hobbes now concedes, too, that 'It may ... be thought, there was never such a time, nor condition of warre' as the phrase 'state of nature' implies, and he then affirms that 'it was never generally so, over all the world'. However, the latter's historical reality is not the issue: what counts, and what Hobbes continues to assert in *Leviathan*, is that the egoistic, asocial mentality associated with the state of nature is still to be

[95] Ibid. 88.
[96] In addition to Skinner 1972, see, for the latest account of Hobbes's *rapprochement* with the republic, Collins 2005: esp. ch. 4. For an alternative explanation for the textual changes discussed here, see Rudolph 1986: 87.
[97] Hobbes 1996: 89.

regarded (from an empirical perspective at least) as the essence of human nature, the ineradicable foundation on which all other, acquired characteristics (civic morality included) rest. Though in 1651 Hobbes renounces the race for power, he does not renounce this egoistic view of man. The supposition that all actions are done for the benefit of the self—a supposition equally active in *both* works—is after all logically independent of the *Elements*' further assertion that all humans specifically desire to outrun their fellows, to assert their superiority. Nor does Hobbes alter in his later work his accounts of felicity or appetite, with their emphases on the constant forward motion of desire—witness the fact that in *Leviathan* he rejects the Stoics' idea of 'perpetuall Tranquillity of mind' on the grounds that 'Life it selfe is but Motion, and can never be without Desire'.[98] Life remains, in his 1651 text, a struggle, requiring man to engage in a constant pursuit of new commodities to satisfy his own insatiability. It is still, in that sense, a race against one's own self. Finally, and above all, what *Elements* and *Leviathan* share are their accounts, first, of deliberation and the nature and role of reason, and, second, of the pre-eminent place accorded to fear in man's felt life. In both works that fear emerges as the driving force behind civil society and its structures. I turn next, therefore, to these concerns, and first to deliberative reason.

## *LEVIATHAN* AND *THE ELEMENTS*: THE 'BEGINNINGS OF OUR ACTIONS'

The majority of conceptions which strike man's mind prove, on first intuition, to be either pleasant or painful, whereupon they give rise to appetite or revulsion. That reaction, an endeavouring towards or away from the object, constitutes 'the first unperceived beginnings of our actions'.[99] However, man commonly tests such first endeavours—his initial impulses to act—before responding to them, and he does this by deliberating upon them. Deliberation is the practice whereby reason casts about to identify all the *probable*, future consequences of a given course of action, thus determining whether or not the latter is as beneficial as it appears to be.[100] In this cognitive process—what

---

[98] Hobbes 1996: 46.     [99] Hobbes 1969: 61.

[100] How far the mind will foresee a particular action's consequences will depend on the degree of worldly experience, and therefore 'prudence', which the given agent has garnered hitherto (Hobbes 1996: 36, 46; 1969: 16). Whatever his experience, though, the *rational* individual will base his conclusions only on probabilities. Hobbes argues in *Leviathan* that a person should not quietly transgress the laws of his society, hoping not to be caught, because he cannot '*reasonably* reckon upon' thus getting away with his crime. On the contrary, the *probability* is that he will be detected, and even to attempt to transgress is therefore 'against the reason of his [own] preservation' (Hobbes 1996: 102–3).

James terms a 'rhythm of embracing and denial'[101]—fear (as much as, if not more than, appetite) is of the utmost importance: 'for either the action immediately follow the first appetite, ... or else to our first appetite there succeedeth some conception of evil to happen unto us by such actions, which is fear, and withholdeth us from proceeding. And to that fear may succeed a new appetite, and to that appetite another fear, alternately.'[102] The mechanism of deliberation, then, is one in which successive rational conclusions about options each resolve themselves into passions, and these passions succeed and displace one another according to their relative strengths. Sir Robert Howard dramatizes precisely this economy of the emotions in his 'Duel of the Stags' as he allegorizes the already once defeated Buckingham's ongoing attempts to challenge Charles II's power: 'T'other that saw his Conqueror so near, / Stood still and list'ned to a whisp'ring fear; / From whence he heard his Conquest, and his Shame; / But new-born Hopes his ... Fears o'recame.'[103] This alternation of appetites, fears, and modified conceptions suggesting new courses of action, and consequently prompting new appetites, only ceases when circumstances intervene to make action impossible anyway, or when a modified appetite presents itself to which there are no objections. In this second case deliberation therefore culminates in a specific resolution to act in a given way, which resolution ends our potential liberty to choose one way or the other. That last appetite—or last fear, if the conclusion is not to act—is precisely man's settled 'will';[104] and will, for Hobbes, has no other sense than that: it is not, as it is for Aquinas, a distinct faculty, but rather, just as in the degree speech of *Troilus*, resolves itself into appetite.

A crucial point follows from this theory, again separating it from most of the traditions discussed hitherto. Clearly, for Hobbes there can be no such thing as *akrasia* or psychomachic conflict. In his model of deliberation passions, each in combination with a reasoned judgement, succeed and displace one another, one by one. There is no direct confrontation or conflict between these impulses (as there would be according to some Platonist and all Aristotelian accounts of the mind), or any possibility that two categorically distinct inclinations, one rational and one emotional, could simultaneously vie for authority in a psychomachic struggle.[105] Psychomachia is not part of Hobbes's psychological vocabulary. The psyche is, to him, a single, unified entity, not the partitioned bundle of distinct faculties imagined by (for example) Aquinas. Indeed, as Hobbes's alternative explanation for the alleged phenomenon of *akrasia* makes clear, his account of the mind compares, if anything, with the monistic

---

[101] S. James 1997: 273. The phrase was coined by Nussbaum (1994: 384).
[102] Hobbes 1969: 61.     [103] Howard 1695: 78.
[104] For Hobbes's further comment on the freedom of the will, see Hobbes 1969: 62–3.
[105] Cf. S. James 1997: 272, 284.

psychology of Chrysippan Stoicism (that psychology also dramatized by Chapman).[106] Hobbesian deliberation is akin to that rapid and imperceptible process of oscillation described by Plutarch in *Moralia* 447a, where the mind alternates between its twin aspects of right reason and passionate reasoning, each advocating a contrary impulse.

With this account, then, Hobbes seems to overturn the model of human psychology accepted by Erasmus, Spenser, and their kind—that same model which had already been interrogated by Shakespeare *et al.*, and which Calvinists and other Augustinians were also, at this time, resisting on a different basis. On Hobbes's theory (at least as examined so far) the passions now *use* reason, and reason, reciprocally, adopts in its various cognitions the ends of the passions: it '*directs*' men '*in the way to* that which they desire to attain'.[107] The passions therefore take priority in this process, but they are not *opposed* to reason as such, because reason's natural function, Hobbes argues, is precisely to ensure that the passions' demands are fulfilled to the maximum. Empirically examined, the task of reasoned deliberation is simply to optimize man's ability to satisfy his appetites, a process which certainly involves calculating the best *means* by which to achieve passionate ends, but which will often also involve denying or qualifying some desires because their long-term consequences are wont to prove counterproductive—not pleasurable but painful. From this point of view, then, there would seem to be no transcendental or right reason in the Hobbesian mind intuiting its own values, manipulating the affections to its own ends, and governing behaviour, as it were, from above. Guyon and the Palmer's fantasy psychology has no bearing here. On the contrary, and in direct contrast to the philosophies discussed in Chapters 1 and 2 above, the voice of practical reason now subordinates itself to the passions' best interests. It works to optimize man's pleasure and survival and to support the passions' own natural values. This perspective is beautifully summarized by Noel Malcolm, who comments,

The reduction of 'reason' to instrumental reasoning was an important part of [Hobbes's] psychological picture. Reason, on this view..., did not intuit values, but found the means to ends that were posited by desire; desires might be various, but reason could also discover general truths about how to achieve the conditions (above all, the absence of anarchic violence) in which desires were least liable to be frustrated.[108]

Such is Hobbes's account of instrumental reasoning, that next layer of the psyche which, when added to man's passionate substrate, creates an empirically accurate model of human psychology. Alternative models of the mind which

---

[106] Cf. S. James 1997: 272–3.     [107] Hobbes 1969: 75.     [108] Sorell 1996: 27.

posit the existence of a transcendental faculty of reason or imagine a soul perpetually engaged in psychomachia are, according to Hobbes's empirical description, fictitious, the product of a deluded, implicitly self-aggrandizing asceticism. Yet it is worth reiterating by way of conclusion here that this new, Hobbesian idea of psychology is shaped by fear. It is fear which repeatedly checks and redirects the deliberative process: fear not of moral condemnation, but of adverse material consequences, fear that what an individual hopes will put him ahead in life's race may actually put him behind. This emotion dominates Hobbes's image of human nature, compelling man to rethink the value of the state of nature and persuading him to embrace both civil society and an absolute sovereign instead. Fear, then, is the next focus to turn to in examining Hobbes's idea of governance.

## FEAR

Whilst men exist in a state of nature, prior to the institution of civil society, they are characteristically unable to agree on the meaning of key moral terms. There being no absolute standards, moral terminology functions, rather, as a measure of individual passionate interests:

the diversity of our ... different constitutions of body, and prejudices ... gives every thing a tincture of our different passions. And therefore in reasoning, a man must take heed of words; which besides the signification of ... their nature, have a signification also of the ... disposition, and interest of the speaker; such ... are the names of Vertues .... For one man calleth *Wisdome*, what another calleth *feare*; ... one *cruelty*, what another *justice* ...

... whatsoever is the object of any mans Appetite ... ; that is it, which he ... calleth *Good*; And the object of his ... Aversion, *Evill* .... For these words ... are ever used with relation to the person that useth them: There being [no] ... common Rule of Good.[109]

Besides, though, being unable to agree between themselves as to the exact nature and application of man's moral ideals, individuals cannot achieve consistency in this even on their own. Hobbes, like Montaigne, notes that because the body is in 'continuall mutation', every individual's desires will vary over time: 'man in divers times, differs from himselfe'.[110] This, then, is one source of fractiousness within the state of nature, but there is also another.

The second (and greater) problem is that, on Hobbes's account of psychology, men are bound to come into competition, and thus conflict with one another. If the struggle for precedence which follows from this continues

---

[109] Hobbes 1996: 31, 39. Cf. 1969: 23, 29.     [110] Hobbes 1996: 39, 110.

unchecked, the state of nature will inevitably degenerate into a state of war. There are three reasons for this. One of these emphasizes man's interest in acquiring power for its own sake; the other two, his need to acquire it as a means of preserving himself and satisfying his desires.[111] First, all men, thinking well of themselves, being sensitive to the slightest suggestion that others do not recognize their quality, yet disliking such self-approval in other people, will constantly provoke one another for glory's sake "till at last they must determine the pre-eminence by strength'.[112] Secondly, many men's appetites driving them towards a pursuit of the same commodities, they will inevitably compete for such goods, especially since in Hobbes's state of nature 'every man' has an equal right 'to every thing'.[113] Thirdly, a few who are especially vainglorious will forever be prosecuting their claim to precedence by attempting to subdue others: all men must therefore guard against the aggression of such upstart crows, predicting the worst and acting pugnaciously on that assumption. In this hostile world there will always be 'a necessity of suspecting ... anticipating' and guarding against the rapacity of the few whose quest for precedence knows no limits, especially since 'we cannot distinguish them' in advance.[114] That this is true even in civil society, let alone in the state of nature, and that it implies that fear threatens to be pervasive in either condition, is sharply demonstrated in *De Cive*: 'Wee see ... men travell not without their Sword by their sides, ... neither sleep they without shutting not only their doores against their fellow Subjects, but also their ... Coffers for feare of domestiques. Can men give a clearer testimony of the distrust they have each of other, and all, of all? How since they doe thus, ... they publiquely professe their mutuall feare.'[115] The message here and in the *Elements* is that even those moderate folk who desire 'no more but equality of nature' cannot risk being diffident in the state of nature for fear that any sign of weakness will encourage others to overrun them.[116] Because some insist on competing at all times, all must do so, hence the continued dominance of the appetite for power, whether just as a means or as an end as well.

Under these conditions it is every man's right of nature to 'do whatsoever action is necessary for the preservation of his body', and that needs must include preventative warfare.[117] However, so long as all men have a natural

---

[111] Spragens 1973: 182–3.          [112] Hobbes 1969: 71.          [113] Ibid. 72–3.
[114] Hobbes 1983: 33.          [115] Ibid. 32–3.
[116] Hobbes 1969: 71. This, Hobbes's sudden reference in the *Elements* to the existence of certain moderate-minded individuals, is not incompatible with the assertion that nevertheless *all* men compete for power—so long as that power is viewed, in *their* case, as a means only: viz., a means of inspiring preventative fear in others so as to ward off those who would attack them. However, the gist of the *Elements* is that *all* men pursue power as an end in itself, as a source of glory and hence delight, and in this respect Hobbes here momentarily contradicts himself.
[117] Ibid. 72. On the 'blameless liberty' of such behaviour, see Spragens 1973: 178–9.

right to all things, the effective consequence is that none will have the power consistently to exercise that right. Often man's efforts to meet his desires will be frustrated by others; 'he therefore that desireth to live in such an estate, as is the estate of liberty and right of all to all, contradicteth himself. For every man by ... necessity desireth his own good, to which this estate is contrary.'[118] Deliberative reason thus protests against the 'contradictions' of such a condition, because the state of war proves to be one in which man's appetites will not be satisfied consistently. (Reason, in making this judgement, is still, of course, ministering to the passions and their interests.) However, more important than this frustration of desires is the fear of death which will accompany it, a fear induced by the further recognition that 'no man is of might sufficient, to assure himself... of preserving himself... whilst he remaineth in [this] state of hostility':[119] 'consider how brittle the frame of our ... body is, ... how easie a matter it is, even for the weakest ... to kill the strongest'.[120] All too often bloody instructions, being taught, return to plague th'inventor. This, too, is a fact identified by reason as it discharges its deliberative function. Acknowledging the immediate pleasure of living in a world where each is free to do as he pleases, reason then examines the long-term consequences of that conception, and finds that chief amongst them is the probability of living a life nasty, brutish, and short. According to these calculations, the state of unchecked nature will indeed end in the destruction prophesied by Shakespeare's Ulysses, and ultimately it is this fear that checks man's appetite for such an unrestrained life. Fear is in this respect the negative side of man's concern for power. Whilst the race image emphasizes his positive desire to outgo all others, the real determining passion turns out to be the desire not to fall behind them (by suffering injury or worse). In Hobbes's Tacitean vision, much as in Jonson's *Sejanus*, fear is in the end a greater drive than ambition.

If, however, deliberation identifies the fearful consequences of living in a world of unchecked self-indulgence, it also proceeds to identify other ways in which the appetites could be satisfied whilst accommodating the imperative of self-preservation—furnishing, then, what Watkins terms 'doctor's orders'.[121] The prerequisite of any successful attempt to satisfy an appetite must be sustained peace, since only in a state of peace can man be certain that his achievements will not bring violence upon him. Reason therefore dictates that the only means by which to ensure man's prosperity in the pursuit of at least *some* of his desires is to seek this peace. It teaches, further, that the latter initiative must be built upon the consent of all those whose deliberation

---

[118] Hobbes 1969: 73.    [119] Ibid. 74.    [120] Hobbes 1983: 45.
[121] Watkins 1973: 59.

brings them to the same conclusion. Fortunately, reason predicts that this consent *will* be forthcoming. In recognizing their shared need for security, men will also come to acknowledge the 'laws of nature', those principles logically deduced from the fact of their common fear, their common awareness of the state of nature's self-defeating contradictions, and their common concern to develop a social arrangement immune to such problems. The laws of nature constitute the ground rules which all would have to observe if a peaceful society were to survive. They are the dictates of a Hobbesian brand of 'right Reason ... conversant about those things which are either to be done, or omitted for the constant preservation of Life'.[122] They include a recognition of the need for '*every man [to] divest himself of the right he hath to all things by nature*'; an agreement as to the binding nature of covenants; an undertaking that '*every man do ... endeavour to accommodate each other, as far as may be without danger of their persons, and loss of their means*'; and a resolution that '*Whatsoever right any man requireth to retain, he allow every other man to retain the same.*'[123] If they could live by these principles, all citizens alike would maximize their capacity freely to indulge their appetites whilst avoiding any action likely to provoke self-destructive conflict. Such is instrumental reason's first solution to the problem of conflict.

Fear, though, does not stop here. Further deliberation prompts a recognition that, even if all men agree to abide by the laws of nature, that act of covenanting will prove insufficient to ensure the stability of the society thereby created. The laws, as recognized by reason, are only generalities, and require interpretation in particular situations. However, man's enduringly egotistical nature—his propensity always to be 'blinded by self love, or some other passion'—is such that he will forever be prone to interpret the laws in his own favour, misconstruing and misapplying them, even without knowing it, under the influence of self-interest.[124] These delusions and errors will then provoke fresh acts of *unwitting* lawlessness, the perpetrators thereof rationalizing those short-sighted acts as lawful deeds. On top of that problem, the usual, more conscious motives for contention already seen in the state of war will not disappear either with the formation of a covenant. Such motives will persist behind the collective façade of sociability, and under their influence men (despite foreseeing the benefits of concord) will continue to infringe nature's laws as they vie for precedence. Thinking that their crimes will go unnoticed, or that they will get away with them anyway, villains will continue to 'aim at

---

[122] Hobbes 1983: 52. For a discussion of the difference between traditional ideas of *recta ratio* and Hobbes's purely methodological definition, see Skinner 1996: 294–6.

[123] Hobbes 1969: 75–89 *passim*. I quote from *Elements*, but these laws have their equivalents in *Leviathan*.

[124] Hobbes 1996: 190–1. Cf. 1969: 90.

dominion ... and private wealth'.[125] Via these two means, then, unconscious and conscious, passions will persist in warping human behaviour, rekindling the conflicts which the supposed collective adherence to the laws of nature was intended to quell. Deliberative reason's acknowledgement of this fact needs must reignite men's fears.

Again though, that same reason identifies the means which men must determine upon in order to guard against such corruptions whilst still catering for their own interests. Since, given the problem of man's partiality, natural law must forbid 'us to be our own judges',[126] reason dictates the need to create disinterested arbitrators instead, tasked with resolving disputes. Beyond that, a measure is also needed to counteract in advance man's propensity to break the law: a measure, that is, which will exert its policing effect over an individual's deliberation even when the allure of powerful passions makes transgression *seem* worthwhile. Ultimately, the only means of achieving this is precisely to perpetuate the very fear which brings society into being in the first place—that is, to institutionalize it. Deliberative reason deduces that men can best do this by instituting a sovereign who commands absolute power. This sovereign, by utilizing his power, can so frighten his citizens that, whenever an individual countenances indulging an appetite in a situation where he *knows* that to do so would be contrary to natural law, he will quickly be overcome with fear. The fear of 'some punishment, greater than the benefit' to be expected from his transgression will coerce said individual into remaining law-abiding.[127] And if the sovereign is sufficiently frightening, then the problem of transgressing the law *unwittingly* will also be eradicated, because citizens will choose always to err on the side of caution in governing themselves lest they accidentally provoke the leviathan's wrath. Reason dictates, then, that the sovereign must have 'so much Power and Strength conferred on him' that his authority is absolute; only thus will he induce the sheer 'terror' necessary to ensure that citizens perpetually 'conforme' their wills to his.[128] Ideally, this sovereign should also establish a series of civil laws which further guard against misconstrual of nature's laws by defining how the latter apply in practice. These statutes, in carrying the sovereign's authority, will be invested with all his fearsomeness, so that under no circumstances will men ignore them in favour of other interests. Hence, by all these means the simple anxiety of self-preservation can be made to negate those affections which might otherwise advocate antisocial behaviour. The individual will learn instead to circumscribe his every effort to satisfy his own appetites, thereby guaranteeing the long-term stability of the body politic. Such are the conclusions which instrumental reason comes to in

[125] Hobbes 1969: 102.  [126] Ibid. 92.
[127] Hobbes 1996: 101.  [128] Ibid. 120.

determining upon the best means of stabilizing the human condition, and the model which it endorses is one in which the self-governance imposed by man upon himself is, ultimately, as much the product of terror as of more positive kinds of self-interest.

As noted earlier, an empirical inspection of the state of nature presents no 'common Rule of Good and Evill', no transcendental criterion of morality. Nor can the deliberative process offer such an absolute. But it does, nonetheless, identify an unequivocal practical criterion of goodness. In so far as fear and reason establish self-preservation as 'the end [of] every one', that at least must be one universal goal which can serve as the first principle for morality: '[for] he that foreseeth the whole way to his preservation ... must also call it good, and the contrary evil. And this is that good and evil, which not every man in passion calleth so, but all men by reason.'[129] In so far as right reasoning also identifies the laws of nature as principles which all must observe to be sure of achieving this primary end, it follows that those principles too, backed by an absolute sovereign, must act as the foundation for a universal morality. Laws, then, which began simply as pragmatic requirements for bringing society into being, end up assuming the status of moral imperatives. Indeed, according to Hobbes, they express the very essence of moral virtue: namely, 'to be sociable with them that will be sociable, and formidable to them that will not'.[130] The natural laws, though, are only a bare minimum, sufficient to lift men out of the state of war and maintain peace in its most basic form. In practice, morality will extend into other areas, embracing, for example, the civil laws, those *particular* 'measures' whereby subjects may determine whether their actions be 'right or wrong'.[131] Such is the province of Hobbes's newly founded morality, a morality premised on the understanding that it is a social construction rooted in self-interest, not a transcendental absolute rooted in eternal verities. On this description, morality is no more than a set of prescriptions which each individual agrees to abide by because it provides a secure environment within which to satisfy most, at least, of his own wants—a set of prescriptions made binding by their being grounded in fear.

One consequence of an individual's grasping all this is that he will re-evaluate his various passions according to whether or not they serve the interest in peace arising from his terror of death. For example, the law of nature asserts that vengeance is justified only where it is likely to yield future benefit. Revenge which disrupts the peace to no profitable end other than present triumph falls foul of this criterion. In the new social condition, such vengeful affections must be dismissed by the Hobbesian citizen. Here, therefore, as in any other

---

[129] Hobbes 1969: 94. Cf. 1996: 111.     [130] Hobbes 1969: 95.

[131] Ibid. 188–9.

ethical system, the governance of passions of this kind remains an obligation. In a further appropriation of past traditions—this time, another element of Aristotelianism—Hobbes also maintains that that governance will become a matter of habit. The production of socially compliant impulses will become automatic as men develop the prior 'proneness … affection, and inclination of nature' to perform only such actions as Hobbesian deliberation would, anyway, approve.[132]

If, however, the Hobbesian civil condition thus changes the behaviour of natural men, moderating their egotistical impulses, those impulses do nonetheless remain dominant within the psyche. On Hobbes's argument, men do not so much admit as submit to the premiss of universal equality. They do so because that equality allows citizens of the leviathan to carry on indulging a certain proportion of their appetites, and because it sets limits on the *Elements'* race for precedence *without* requiring them to abandon that race altogether. Indeed, the whole point of the citizens acknowledging a set of common laws is to allow that race to persist *ad infinitum*, each continuing to pursue his appetites (particularly the appetite for power) in a form which is socially sustainable, not prone to degenerate into war. Traces of this fact are observable in *Leviathan* and *Elements*. In both, Hobbes imagines the polity as one in which a culture of complaisance and sociability emerges from (and as a function of) blatantly self-interested motives. For example, in civil society man becomes willing to give to another merely on trust, but he does so in the confidence of then 'obtaining the … favour of that other', so that he (the benefactor) will ultimately 'procure a greater … benefit or assistance to himself'.[133] And if the giver thus hopes in due course for a material reward, he also gets, in the meantime, the additional honour of the recipient's thanks, earning what the Earl of Rochester called 'the after Bribe of Gratitude' for his benevolence.[134] Reciprocally, though, that same show of gratitude can be (on the *recipient*'s part) 'retribution' enough for what he has received.[135] At least in the short term, the beneficiary may be 'revenged' precisely in 'confessing' thanks for his gift, Hobbes's point being that gratitude *graciously* enough delivered is itself an expression of power: namely, of the magnanimity of the receiver who feels strong enough to acknowledge his debt *without*—as in Tacitus's example of Tiberius's response to Silius—feeling compromised by it. From all of this there emerges, then, 'an Emulation of who shall exceed in benefiting; the most noble and profitable contention possible'. The obligations of morality and complaisance become, themselves, opportunities for self-advancement. This

---

[132] Ibid. 83.     [133] Ibid. 84. Cf. 1996: 105.

[134] Rochester 1999: 187. Schoenfeldt (1991: 184–5) shrewdly discovers the manipulative force of supplicatory gestures even in Herbert's devotional verse.

[135] Hobbes 1996: 71.

is so far true that whilst the *Elements'* fourth law of nature (the requirement for men to '*accommodate each other, as far as may be*') may entail a downplaying of 'those passions, by which we strive to ... leave others as far as we can behind us',[136] it is also, in Hobbes's view, a direct expression of charity as defined in chapter 9 of that same work—charity there being an extension of one's own power over others. Again, whilst civil society may demand the quelling of passions characteristic of the race for power such as vengefulness, Hobbes emphasizes that it also provides formal structures which *expand* the parameters of that competition. The sovereign will establish 'titles of Honour', an 'Order of place, and dignity', and 'signes of respect', by which to measure the 'publique rate of ... worth' of his citizens, and such structures will facilitate natural competitiveness as much as they circumscribe it.[137] The state, then, does not aim to arrest the motion of its people. Rather, its actual purpose is 'to direct and keep them in ... motion', but in such a way as they 'hurt [not] themselves by their ... desires'.[138] Motion, albeit circumscribed, remains the abiding characteristic of human nature. Power and felicity maintain their place amidst the atmosphere of institutionalized fear.

## SUMMARY

In *The Advancement of Learning* Bacon complains that although moralists have written at length on the particular 'forms of virtue', they have never 'stayed ... upon the inquiry concerning the roots of good and evil': they have never defined the essential nature of goodness.[139] Hobbes sees it as his unique contribution to science to have done precisely this, to have studied 'wherein consisteth [virtue's] Goodnesse'—a process involving the overturning of some key moral assumptions of his day.[140] Like Bacon, he objects to those Peripatetics, for example, who concentrate on defining individual virtues according to the dogma that virtue consists in mediocrity, vice in extremes, this without stopping to ask *why* the doctrine of the mean should be the determining property of moral excellence.[141] Hobbes offers three examples to counter this particular creed:

Courage may be virtue, when the daring is extreme, if the cause be good; and extreme fear no vice when the danger is extreme. To give a man more than his due, is no injustice, though it be to give him less; and in gifts it is not the sum that maketh liberality, but the reason.[142]

---

136 Hobbes 1969: 85.      137 Hobbes 1996: 126.      138 Ibid. 239.
139 Bacon 1973: 155.      140 Hobbes 1996: 111.
141 Cf. Hobbes 1983: 75; 1996: 111.      142 Hobbes 1969: 94.

In practice, of course, Aristotle would agree with the first and third of these propositions: his mean is by its nature flexible, not a static mid-point but a shifting quality determined by *phronēsis*. Hobbes's core objection, though, is not to such details, but to the point underlying this argument: namely, that Aristotle's views 'concerning virtue and vice' were 'no other than those' which constituted 'received' opinion in his own day. His complaint is that Aristotle offers no explanation as to why courage is a virtue in the first place, or what makes a quality morally valuable. The Athenian's implied position is that reason simply intuits that courage is valuable, an impression which he can confirm by appealing to popular opinion because his fellow citizens did in fact number courage amongst their cardinal virtues and assumed that it was 'rational' to do so. Aristotle conceives of reason as the highest, most divine thing in man, a transcendental faculty whose values we should live up to. It follows that, if he takes it for granted that courage is recommended by this faculty, he need do nothing more to prove courage's worth. As with courage, so with any other 'virtue', it is enough to assert that reason applauds it. Such is Aristotle's rational ground for morality, his justification for urging us to do good. Hobbes, by contrast, is determined to offer a more elaborated explanation for *why* we should be virtuous. He presents a pragmatic case as to why morality is useful, and what it must consist in to be thus useful. On his argument man must act virtuously so as to evade death. All those qualities which reason identifies as assisting this self-preservation will therefore constitute virtues. But these virtues will not, for Hobbes, be valuable simply because reason recommends them. They will be valuable, rather, because they serve the best interests of man's passions. 'Their Goodnesse'—the quality which Hobbes thinks himself unique in defining—lies in the fact that these qualities are the *'means'* to peace, to 'sociable, and comfortable living'.[143]

On Hobbes's model of governance, then, the passions are tempered solely for passions' sake: such is the function of instrumental reasoning and of virtue. Man remains, at root, self-seeking and appetitive, the artificial superstructure of laws and virtues resting uneasily atop this somewhat frustrated animal. Crucially, there is therefore no sign in this philosophy of the Greek assumption that man is, *by nature or design*, a sociable being, 'a Creature born fit for Society'.[144] For Hobbes, civil society is the product of mutual fear, not of any instinctive sociability or a belief that man is and ought to be a political animal:

men would much more greedily be carryed by Nature, if all fear were removed, to obtain Dominion, then to gaine Society. We must therefore resolve, that the Originall of all ... Societies, consisted not in the mutuall good will men had towards each other, but in the mutuall fear they had of each other.[145]

[143] Hobbes 1996: 111.    [144] Hobbes 1983: 42.    [145] Ibid. 44.

For who would lose the liberty that nature hath given him, of governing himself by his own will and power, if they feared not death in the retaining of it ?[146]

With this judgement Hobbes establishes a new set of priorities, a new imaginative framework, within which to structure ethical reflection. He presents a radical alternative to the received, rationalist model of moral psychology built around images of psychomachia. The traditional antagonism between the passions and rational virtues which so preoccupied Hobbes's predecessors, Spenser not least, is on this view overstated. The true relationship between reason and the passions is not, for Hobbes, one of historical parity traced out in an eternal psychomachia, each power forever struggling to eliminate the other. Nor is it an Aristotelian story of coercion and co-operation, reason repeatedly seeking to appropriate the passions to the service of its own, higher ends. These images of the mind, and the often ascetic ideals which attach to them, are no more than delusions. The truth is, rather, that instrumental reason raises the edifice of justice and civic virtues on the back of, and for the sake of, the aboriginal passions. It is because this is so that the *Elements*' dedicatory epistle promises a work which will indeed reduce the doctrines of justice and policy 'to the rules and infallibility of reason', but in a way which 'passion not mistrusting, may not seek to displace'.[147] That personifying turn of phrase indicates Hobbes's desire to take 'Passion' with him in building his account of civil society. The focus of his imaginative effort is an attempt to conceive of moral psychology in terms other than the straightforwardly oppositional dynamic of previous moralists. To that end, he instead figures man as a creature driven by power, self-interest, and an unwavering commitment to kinetic pleasures; as one for whom felicity 'consisteth' in constant, forward motion. The dynamo, though, at the centre of this new psychological model is fear. This, according to Hobbes, is the passion on which, more than any other, civil society—civilization itself—rests.


## ADDENDUM: HOBBES'S PASSION FOR ORDER

It is perhaps unsurprising that fear played so instrumental a role in Hobbes's philosophy. Several sources intimate that, though courageous in print, Hobbes accorded fear a particular significance in his personal life. Certainly, his verse autobiography announces that the philosopher's mother, having gone into labour at the shock of hearing that the Armada had reached British waters, brought 'forth Twins at once, both Me, and Fear'. Hobbes also confessed

---

[146] Hobbes 1969: 79.     [147] Ibid. p. xv.

elsewhere to a fear 'of "Nights darkest shade", ... of persecution by his enemies, [and] of death, ... [that] ... "Leap in the Dark" '.[148] His poem 'De
Mirabilibus Pecci', exudes a phobic fear of heights and darkness,[149] and in his
day it was also murmured abroad 'that he was afrayd to lye alone at night',
not (Aubrey insists) for fear of '*Sprights*', but because he was 'afrayd of being
knockt on the head for five or ten pounds, which rogues might think he
had' about him.[150] Tuck and Zagorin conclude, following another hint from
Aubrey, that it was also fear which prompted him to flee England in 1640,
shortly after completing his *Elements*, as Parliament impeached Strafford.[151]
Fear, then, may owe its importance in Hobbes's work to these autobiograph-
ical resonances, and if so, that fact should remind us of the need to ascertain
not just how his philosophy shaped the passions, but also how the passions
shaped it. It is to this issue that I turn by way of an addendum to this chapter,
focusing in particular on the influence which Hobbes's own *desire* for order
and obedience exerted over the formulation of his argument.

The Hobbesian account of 'the Civill Right of Soveraigns' and 'the Duty
and Liberty of Subjects' is presented as a series of deductions derived from
an inspection of 'the known naturall Inclinations of Mankind'—inclinations
'known' from everyday 'Experience'.[152] This empirical process re-enacts the
theoretical development of aboriginal man who is led by reason to infer
the utility value of the so-called laws of nature. In his pre-social condition
(the hypothetical condition which Part I of *Leviathan* reconstructs) this figure
embraces the 'dictates of Reason' as egoistical 'Theoremes concerning what
conduceth to the conservation' of his own being.[153] These dictates are, to him,
'Precepts, or generall Rules'—in Kantian terms, hypothetical imperatives of
governance which the principle of self-preservation would oblige him to act
upon if external circumstances were right.[154] For now, though, they oblige
only *in foro interno*, at the level of intention rather than practice; they manifest
themselves simply as 'dispositions of the mind' which render the primitive
predisposed to co-operate should a social covenant arise.[155] As Hobbes notes,
these precepts are certainly not, in any proper sense, laws, since Law is 'the
word of him, that by right hath command over others'.[156] The term 'law'
carries connotations of formality and of an external edifice of commands
exerting a ruling influence over the individual, associations which can have
no political application for aboriginal man since his world is as yet bereft of
any state authority. Only 'when a Common-wealth is once settled', we are
told, will reason's precepts of governance become 'properly' and politically

---

[148] Mintz 1962: 1.       [149] Ibid. 15.       [150] Aubrey 1960: 156.
[151] Tuck 1993: 314.       [152] Hobbes 1996: 489, 255.       [153] Ibid. 111.
[154] Ibid. 91.       [155] Hobbes 1983: 73–4. Cf. 1969: 93 and 1996: 110.
[156] Hobbes 1996: 111.

laws; 'not before'.[157] And yet, from the outset Hobbes calls them exactly this, *laws* of nature. Even in his earliest discussions of these *lex naturalis*, Hobbes tacitly conceives of them in a legalistic sense, as political imperatives. As Taylor first noted, such laws are figured as 'Fundamentall', 'commanding', and 'forbidding', as if they were already enshrined in a sovereign state.[158] Man becomes a passive agent before them (he is 'obliged' to do one thing, 'ought not' to do another); 'DUTY', a concept more meaningful in a developed social context, is precipitately invoked; and the laws are even personified ('where no other Law ... forbiddeth ... '). Hobbes argues too, in a telling image, that man must '*devest* himselfe' of his rights, making himself naked before a greater order to which he does obeisance.[159] These idioms are deployed in what is otherwise, for the purposes of the argument, a pre-social (or only rudimentarily social) context. The use of legalistic idioms thus introduces into that argument social and political connotations—premises—which do not as yet belong to it. Whilst it is true that in a pre-social situation I am in one sense 'obliged' by my reason's calculations about how best to promote my self-interest, that obligation is only self-imposed, not determined (as the word 'law' suggests) from without. I simply *choose* (for now) to regard myself as obliged. I am not literally, not absolutely, bound to my principles. ('For he is free, that can be free when he will: Nor is it possible for any person to be bound to himselfe; because he that can bind, can release.'[160]) And yet the intonations of Hobbes's language, the references to commanding and forbidding, suggest otherwise. They betray the fact that Hobbes *imagines* the laws of nature, right from the outset, as *absolutes*, political imperatives with their own external authority independent of the deliberating agent who has supposedly formulated them. Even as Hobbes writes in the relativist terms of the individual's passions and interests, his imagination (and with it his language) is drawn towards the absolutism which, I suggest, he himself *craves*, and which is the predestined conclusion of his political theory. My argument, then, is that Hobbes's precipitate introduction of the language of law reveals a passion—the desire for order and obedience—at work behind his thinking, a passion which distorts the purity of his empirical method. The same 'interference' effect can be seen operating, too, amidst his discussions of the Bible and God's laws.

The relativist perspective which confines Hobbes to deriving morality from the most minimal of truisms (men's common commitment to self-preservation) also prompts him to emphasize the contested nature of

157 Hobbes 1996: 185.
158 Brown 1965: 40–1; Hobbes 1969: 92; 1996: 91–3, 96–8 *passim*.
159 Hobbes 1996: 92.    160 Ibid. 184.

scriptural interpretation. Hobbes notes in *De Cive* that successful interpretation of any text presupposes a Skinnerian analysis of the speech acts involved in producing it. 'It sufficeth not ... that a man understand' just the 'language', the vocabulary, 'wherein [Scriptures] speak'; he must also weigh 'the living voice' behind them.[161] Interpretation hinges, too, upon an intertextual knowledge of the Bible, since the apparent clarity of the simplest commandment can always be called into question by setting it against other parts of the text—as is done in *De Cive* 17. 10.[162] Recognition of these facts needs must prompt as much controversy in the field of scriptural studies as do attempts to settle the 'signification' of virtue terms in the field of ethics. In *De Cive* and *Elements* the determination of biblical meaning is therefore arrogated to the Church.[163] In the more Erastian *Leviathan*[164] it is the sovereign alone who decides which Scriptures are canonical and how they should be understood.[165] In both cases the assumption is that the Bible presents instabilities which can be tamed only by authoritarian, somewhat arbitrary means. Yet elsewhere Hobbes writes as if his *own* interpretation of that same Bible were unequivocal. In *Elements*, *De Cive*, and *Leviathan* he lists a series of scriptures which, he asserts, unambiguously endorse his empirically derived laws of nature, especially the precept that sovereigns should command our unconditional obedience.[166] Thus Psalm 15's exchange, '*Lord who shall dwell in thy tabernacle, ... He that sweareth to his own hindrance, and yet changeth not*', is apparently straightforward confirmation of the law that 'men ought to stand to their covenants', whilst the injunction, '*Give to Caesar that which is Caesars*', constitutes biblical confirmation that men ought indeed 'to pay such taxes'—ship-money, perhaps—'as are by Kings imposed'.[167] Hobbes seems certain of the accuracy of his interpretations here; he does not trouble to couch his readings as conditional upon a sovereign's imprimatur. On the contrary, putting his Erastianism to one side, he presumes to authorize his conclusions himself: 'I am sure they are Principles from Authority of Scripture.'[168] Again, these methodological inconsistencies—visible only at the edges of his argument—bespeak an appetite for orderly certainty in this writer which is prone to override his reason's sceptical reserve.

[161] Hobbes 1983: 233.     [162] Ibid. 227–8.

[163] Ibid. 233–4, 245–9; 1969: 58–9. See Tuck 1992: 122–3. There are, though, hints of an Erastian subordination of the clergy to the sovereign even in *Elements*: see Hobbes 1969: 145, 160–1, 164–7.

[164] On *Leviathan*'s Erastianism, see Hobbes 1996: 268, 321, 373–4; Tuck 1992: 125–8; Collins 2005.

[165] Hobbes 1996: 260, 269, 324.

[166] See Hobbes 1969: 96–9, 146–7; 1983: 76–84; 1996: 143–4, 342–3.

[167] Hobbes 1969: 96; 1996: 144.     [168] Hobbes 1996: 233.

If, though, there are problems with Hobbes's general use of the Bible, his particular attention to divine law raises further difficulties. For the believer it is a truism that the ancient Jews had first-hand experience of God because he governed them directly, by 'Positive Lawes' given them 'by the mouths of his ... Prophets'.[169] For them, the authority of the Old Testament was therefore axiomatic. For Christians now the situation is different: they cannot '*know*', in the same empirical sense, that the Scriptures 'are Gods Word'.[170] The Bible is only taken as such as a matter of 'faith', and since faith is a different order of knowledge from that of 'infallible science', its doctrines cannot command or oblige us in the way that Hobbesian prudential reasoning can.[171] Hobbes, though, circumvents this reservation by arguing that some, at least, of the Bible's imperatives—those of the Decalogue's second table—are simply reason's scientifically deduced laws of nature masquerading under another name.[172] He explains this equivalence by asserting that it was God (whom deductive logic identifies as the 'author' or first cause of all things in the world) who first placed instrumental reason in man.[173] Furthermore, God apparently did this so that such reason might be 'a light unto [us]'.[174] We are to assume, then, that God *intended* man to think egoistically (in just the way that Hobbesian 'deliberation' does); that he intended man to deduce from his own interest in self-preservation the *subjective* worth of those very laws whose *objective* worth the Bible then also proclaims in the second table.[175] Reason being God's gift to man, it is inevitable (if God is a consistent workman) that reason's 'dictates' should prove commensurate with the positive laws elsewhere advocated by God in his Scriptures. Reciprocally, the fact that the Scriptures' moral teachings so closely reflect those of 'naturall reason' authenticates those biblical precepts—otherwise accepted only on grounds of faith—as, indeed, truly God's laws.[176] Ultimately, then, there is an exact equivalence between God's laws as reported in the Bible and the moral and political imperatives deduced by deliberative reasoning, and this is why Hobbes actually tends to slide back and forth between these two idioms, divine and natural. At one moment, in describing aboriginal man, he terms the rational precepts at work in the latter as 'Theoremes'—avowedly not 'Lawes', because this individual is not yet bound to any temporal authority. Yet in the next sentence Hobbes inverts his perspective, for 'if we consider [these] same Theoremes,

---

[169] Hobbes 1996: 246. Cf. 262, 266, 280–4, 322–31.　　　[170] Ibid. 267.

[171] Hobbes 1969: 58.　　　[172] Hobbes 1996: 357. Cf. 1969: 187–8.

[173] Hobbes 1969: 53–4, 93, 95, 99. Cf. 1996: 77, 255.　　　[174] Hobbes 1969: 99.

[175] Cf. Martinich 1992: 135: 'God commands that people act in their genuine self-interest.'

[176] 'As far as they differ not from the Laws of Nature, there is no doubt, but [the Scriptures] are the Law of God, and carry their Authority with them, legible to all men that have the use of naturall reason' (Hobbes 1996: 268).

as delivered in the word of God, that by right commandeth all things; then are they properly called Lawes': 'Lawes' in so far as they *are* now conceived as impressed upon (or inserted into) man from without—not, admittedly, by a temporal authority, but by a spiritual one.[177] I suggested earlier that Hobbes's use of the phrase 'laws of nature' in a pre-social context often carries inflections more appropriate to a post-covenanting condition; but for the reasons just given we *also* find him describing those laws—again in a supposedly purely prudential context—as 'Immutable', or expressive of 'the Eternall Law of God'.[178]

The problem with this argument, though, is that, if we set aside the faith-based evidence of the Bible and confine ourselves to empirical science, experience offers no proof that God did insert deliberative reason into man specifically so that man might discover Hobbes's laws of nature. Indeed, empiricists might question whether the divine first cause was benevolent or purposive at all in its creative act. The correct model of the universe may actually be the Lucretian one, in which case the laws of nature would not be God's teleological gift to man; rather, those laws would simply be the tools which man generates within himself so as to create order out of chaos. My point is that Hobbes has no *empirical* basis for asserting either that reason's prudential maxims are 'lights' provided by God, or that they mirror the divine laws of God's own reasoning. Empirical science can never know the latter. It is scriptural faith alone which prompts the philosopher to assume an equation between divine and natural law. In making that equation, Hobbes again seems eager to discover as much *absolute* order and authority in the world as possible. Indeed, he seems almost to reassure himself in drawing the conclusion that the relativist's egoistical 'Theoremes' can, after all, be reconceived as universal 'Lawes'. Here then, as elsewhere, Hobbes reveals an inclination to revert back to that transcendental moral absolutism which his model of psychology otherwise seemed intended to supersede.

The tensions evident in Hobbes's treatment of divine law are evident also in his comments about what motivates the sovereign. Since the latter is to have absolute, irrevocable power, there must be a risk that he will rule tyrannically. The people's intention in creating him is that he should govern them through civil laws which enshrine, in everyday legislation, the spirit of the laws of nature. The parity between natural and divine law should thus be mimicked in the civil law too,[179] so that society is ruled in accordance with the principles for the protection of which it was first established. Hobbes hopes that all this will happen because it is in the sovereign's interest that it should. Straightforwardly, the 'strength and glory' of any ruler (whether a monarch

---

[177] Ibid. 111.    [178] Ibid. 110, 192.    [179] Ibid. 185.

or democratic or aristocratic assembly) will depend upon the 'vigor' of its subjects; so the furtherance of the sovereign's good should go hand in glove with the furtherance of the people's.[180] More particularly, though, Hobbes matches the claim of the Tacitus 'Discourse' and of Bacon's 'Of Wisedome for a Mans selfe'[181] that this relationship is especially strong in monarchies. That is why citizens should choose to create a monarchy rather than any other kind of sovereign power:

whosoever beareth the Person of the people, or is one of that Assembly that bears it, beareth also his own naturall Person. And though he be carefull in his politique Person to procure the common interest; yet he is ... no lesse carefull to procure ... private good for himselfe ... and ... if the publique interest chance to crosse the private, he preferrs the private .... From whence it follows, that where the publique and private interest are most closely united, there is the publique most advanced. Now in Monarchy, the private interest is the same with the publique. The riches, power, and honour of a Monarch arise onely from the riches, strength and reputation of his Subjects .... Whereas in a Democracy, or Aristocracy, the publique prosperity conferres not so much to the private fortune of one that is corrupt ... as doth ... treacherous action, or ... Civill warre.[182]

In theory, then, self-interested monarchs should rule justly. The fact that they do not always do so clearly makes Hobbes uneasy. His acknowledgements of this awkward truth generally take the form of brief caveats or hesitant phrases, hence 'whatsoever a sovereign doth, *if* it be not against the law of nature ... ', or, 'the Intention of the Legislator is always *supposed* to be Equity'.[183] In more forthright moments he confesses that sovereigns may commit outright crimes (David's killing of Uriah, for example),[184] and he lists the various kinds of bad government which may have a degenerate effect upon the polity;[185] but even here Hobbes is quick to extenuate. He downplays the significance of such matters by terming them 'incommodities' or 'Inconveniences'; blames the man, not the office ('This inconvenience ... must be derived, not from the power, but from the ... passions which reign in every one, as well monarch as subject'); quibbles that, though a sovereign 'may commit Iniquity', he cannot, technically, be convicted of 'Injustice'; and argues that, anyway, however irksome these iniquities may be, they are as nothing compared to the 'horrible calamities' of civil war and a return to the state of nature.[186]

Such, then, is Hobbes's nervous posturing in face of the problem of tyranny. The striking thing is that he again assuages this anxiety by turning

---

[180]  Hobbes 1996: 128–9. Cf. 240 and 1969: 137–8.          [181]  Bacon 1985: 73–4.
[182]  Hobbes 1996: 131.          [183]  Hobbes 1969: 187; 1996: 194.
[184]  Hobbes 1996: 148.          [185]  Hobbes 1969: 141–3; 1996: 131–3.
[186]  Hobbes 1996: 128, 145; 1969: 141; 1996: 124, 128, 144–5. On 'iniquity' see Brown 1965: 37.

to the language of moral absolutes. Hobbes finds in that language at least a *rhetoric* of subjection with which to curb bad rulers. So we are reassured that a sovereign, for all his power, is actually 'as much subject, as ... the meanest of his People' to the laws of nature, and natural law apparently '*commandeth* [every leader] to procure peace, and ... maintain the same'.[187] Hobbes devotes a substantial chapter in each of his three political treatises to enumerating the duties which sovereigns are—and should see themselves as being—obliged to perform. They are, for instance, 'bound by the law of nature to make ordinances' which promote public 'commodity'.[188] It is not clear, though, that sovereigns really *are* 'as much subject as' their people. The latter are bound to natural law both in the weak sense that they will themselves so to be (for self-interest's sake) and in the strong sense that they surrender themselves to the commands of a higher temporal power. The sovereign, by contrast, *is* that higher power, and is therefore bound only by the first of these considerations, a fragile source of obligation in practice ('For he is free, that can be free when he will ... '). Hobbes counters this problem by suddenly insisting that all 'Soveraigns are ... subject to the Lawes of Nature; *because* such lawes be Divine, and cannot by any man ... be abrogated'.[189] Although the natural laws' simultaneous status as divine commands is often noted, Hobbes generally emphasizes that the *compulsive* force of these *lex naturalis* stems, rather, from their prudential worth. His thesis is that God himself turned deliberative reason's precepts into divine law precisely *because* those rational theorems were conducive to self-preservation; and therefore men too should embrace these precepts primarily because of their utility value. The fact that the natural laws are also divine commands is one reason which obliges us to obey them, but usually Hobbes does not emphasize this; he emphasizes, instead, the other factor which makes them obligatory, their prudential value in ministering to the imperative of self-preservation.[190] *Here* though, in order to bolster his claim that even sovereigns are *absolutely* bound by natural law, Hobbes shifts

---

[187] Hobbes 1996: 237; 1969: 136.    [188] Hobbes 1969: 180–1.

[189] Hobbes 1996: 224.

[190] In arguing this I, like Martinich, steer a middle course amongst the combatants preoccupied with the Taylor–Warrender thesis. Taylor (Brown 1965: 40–53) and Warrender (1957: 98–100, 212–13, 279) both concluded from the claim that 'Soveraigns are ... subject to the Lawes of Nature *because* such lawes be Divine', and from Hobbes's habit of recasting nature's laws as immutable, that it was the divinely commanded status of these edicts (not their prudential utility value) which constituted the ground of men's *obligation* to obey them. Skinner's riposte, though (1964: 328), was more accurate: 'Hobbes's *description* [of the *lex naturalis* as God's laws] is independent ... of any suggestion that it is *in virtue of* their character as the commands of God that Natural Laws are said to oblige: such a claim, moreover, Hobbes himself never makes.' Yet the phrase above ('*because* such lawes be Divine') constitutes one exception to Skinner's last assertion here, and it contradicts, too, Tuck's comparable statement (1989: 79) that Hobbes

his ground. Here at least, he does insist that it is 'because' the *lex naturalis* are divine commands that they oblige rulers. So the sovereign, though he is not bound by any temporal authority, is bound by a spiritual one. It is striking that Hobbes, in pursuing this same vein, also qualifies *Leviathan*'s Erastianism. One might think, given that Erastianism, that rulers would be authorized to interpret their way around any biblical commandments which proved inconvenient, but Hobbes actually limits this process: 'For though it be not determined in Scripture, what Laws every Christian King shall constitute in his own Dominions; yet it *is* determined what laws he shall *not* constitute.'[191] Finally, Hobbes also insists that all leaders must, eventually, 'render an account' of themselves 'to God', and should therefore 'stand in fear' of divine retribution if they ignore their duties now.[192] Again, the idea is that sovereigns are obliged by God to be law-abiding. The shiftiness of all this, though—the move from emphasizing one source of obligation to emphasizing another; the sudden qualification of *Leviathan*'s Erastianism; the equally sudden invocation of eschatological considerations so as to bind the sovereign—is surely telling. It points to Hobbes's *desire* to ensure order, and to his tendency to depart from strict argumentative transparency when that desire is under threat.

Most Hobbes commentators think it 'implausible' that he could have been 'inconsistent' in formulating his argument or could even, at times, have failed wholly 'to understand what he was doing'.[193] Hence they either strive to impose complete coherence upon his thought or maintain that he adopted certain contradictory idioms simply to make his philosophy sound compelling to 'all sorts of believers'.[194] The tensions discussed here, though, may make more sense if we do allow for the possibility that Hobbes's own convictions and passions 'were not at every point compatible with the logical implications of his argument'.[195] The history of ideas should include a history of just such tensions and confusions; it cannot be simply a story of the cold march of logic. Hobbes certainly began his argument from an empirically observed position of relativism according to which no two individuals could agree on what things are 'good'; and doubtless he then moved deductively, logically, to the conclusion that men would, under pressure of self-interest, embrace an authoritarian polity and its constructed morality. But my suggestion is that from the moment he started to develop this thesis, an underlying preference for a world of absolute, eternal moral values began

'*never* advanced the view ... that the *reason* for doing what the laws prescribe is that they are the commands of God'. Hence my own interpretative suggestion here.

[191] Hobbes 1996: 260.      [192] Ibid. 231, 221. Cf. 1969: 179.
[193] Brown 1965: 33; Skinner 1964: 324. Cf. Martinich 1992: 105–6.
[194] Watkins 1973: 56, 65.      [195] Brown 1965: 60.

influencing the composition of the argument. So it is that the slightest of phrases early on in his works reveal his personal feel for the charisma of law, his penchant for a force which commands, forbids, and dominates over the populace. Likewise, we find him appropriating for himself the cultural authority of the Scriptures, this regardless of the interpretative problems associated with so doing. And again, in discovering the supposed reciprocity between divine and natural law (and thus transferring the transcendental associations of the one on to the other), Hobbes seems to indulge a latent passion for order. He indulges his desire—despite starting out from relativism—to impose a form of *immutable* moral absolutism upon man. This same taste, surely, propelled him towards structures of unconditional power in formulating his political theory. Another theorist faced with Hobbes's account of the state of nature might well have concluded that men should 'commission' a sovereign-representative to rule over them, but with the caveat that they *should* 'limit him' in his powers (as Hobbesian authors of representatives can do): this, notwithstanding Hobbes' objections to such limitations.[196] Such a theorist—call him John Milton—would have constrained the sovereign so as to ensure that he promoted 'all ... Contentments of life' for the benefit of 'the people in general'.[197] It is difficult to imagine that a community, if deliberating *ab initio* with reference to their own interests, would *not* wish to put some such parliamentary limitation upon their monarch. And yet to Hobbes, drawing such an inference when faced with the belligerent state of nature was unimaginable. He preferred to embrace autocracy and thereby run the risk of courting tyranny, a decision which was surely driven as much by passion and instinct—an admiration for absolute power, a desire to obey, a distaste for disorder—as by deductive reasoning. Those very inclinations are, after all, evident even at the level of his prose style, dominated as it is by orderly, enumerative lists, and by conjunctions which pin down every last cause, consequence, and logical relationship.

It is a bitter paradox of history, though, that these cruces in the political grammar of Hobbes's work—the motifs of divine law, order, and obedience so important to the author himself—were largely ignored by those who read his writings in the 1660s. Granted, scholarly commentators such as Bramhall picked up on the equivocation surrounding the status of the divine and natural laws.[198] But, for the most part, Hobbes's audience consisted of more rakish readers, and they remembered him neither for the authoritarian structures which he prescribed to contain man's egotism nor for his interest

[196] Hobbes 1996: 114. For the objections see pp. 121–9.
[197] Ibid. 231; 1969: 179.  [198] Rogers 1995: 163–6.

in God's law. They remembered him, rather, for the discourse of fear, power, and self-interest, and the kinetic image of man, with which I concluded the previous section of this chapter. It is therefore to that legacy, and the phenomenon of Restoration libertinism associated with it, that I turn next.

# 7

## The Restoration Ethos of Libertinism

By 1666 fear, rather like the plague, was catching, and nothing was more frightening than so-called Hobbism.[1] Anti-tolerationists within the Commons, hostile to the Independency advocated in the ecclesiological sections of *Leviathan*, were by now straining to have Hobbes labelled an atheist.[2] Indeed, the publication of his works was cited in Parliament as a probable cause of Great Fire and Great Plague alike.[3] Hobbism, then, numbered amongst the ghastly spectres which arose from London's chemic flame and stood eager to terrify even the most spirit-friendly of Cambridge Platonists. This disfigured beast had been sighted as early as 1657, lurking amidst the pages of Lucy's *Observations, Censures and Confutations of … Hobbes His Leviathan*, and it was momentarily caught again by Bishop Bramhall in 1658; but in the mid-1660s it kennelled itself in the familiarly sinful womb of Charles's libertine court, since from there it could bark and howl unchallenged.

The exposition of this Hobbism is my first concern in Chapter 7. I examine it here in conjunction with a series of other intellectual traditions prevalent in the 1650s, 1660s, and 1670s, showing how Hobbism coalesced with the sexual rapacity in early Cavalier poetry, with the ideals of governance expressed in the poetry of France's *libertins érudits*, and with popular perceptions of Anglo-French Epicureanism. I show, too, how, after the Restoration, those various threads fed into a mode of dissolute, aristocratic 'libertinism'[4] which was particularly cultivated by Charles's 'Court Wits' circle,[5] but which also

---

[1] *OED* records early uses of the words 'Hobbist', 'Hobbian', and 'Hobbism' in 1681, 1687, and 1691 respectively, all in disparaging contexts. Skinner (1966: 296–7) cites other examples, again disparaging, from the 1670s and as early as 1658. The neutral 'Hobbesian' is a later coinage.

[2] Tuck 1993: 333–9.     [3] Mintz 1962: 62.

[4] R. D. Hume (1983: 144, 160, 163–6), Turner (1987*b*), and others have rightly emphasized that 'libertinism' is not a static, organized, universal philosophy: its meaning and philosophical bedfellows shift repeatedly between 1660 and 1800. In particular, its association with Hobbism and the court wits during Charles's reign gives way in the 1690s to a more temperate notion of libertinism associated with neo-Epicureanism.

[5] In using the phrase 'Court Wits' I follow J. H. Wilson's nomenclature (1967: 5–10, 206–17). On his definition, this group included the Duke of Buckingham, the Earls of Carbery and Rochester, Lord Buckhurst (latterly Earl of Middlesex and Dorset), Sir George Etherege, Sir

became an object of imitation amongst followers of court fashion.[6] The libertinism which emerges from these materials rests, I argue, on a conviction that the best sort of governance is a lack of governance, and that man is, *and ought to be,* driven by an idea of self-interest identified with the riotous pursuit of pleasures; this, a conviction, too, which rejects any notion of a transcendental, Christian morality or divinely sanctioned law of nature, and which subordinates reason to appetite even to the extent of eschewing prudent deliberation. This same ethic also minimizes the importance of fear in human nature, discounting the structures of containment associated with that passion which Hobbes had made central to his notion of governance. Instead, the libertine, embracing (consciously or otherwise) the account of man given in the *Elements'* race analogy, pursues his desire for self-assertion up to (and beyond) the limits set by law, this safe in the knowledge that King Charles will not exercise that punitive tyranny which the leviathan should wield. The libertine thus adopts an ideal of felicity constructed in much the same terms as was Hobbes's, identifying happiness with a continuous forward motion in pursuit of desires. The result is a dissolute lifestyle which constantly breaches the covenant on which society is based. The confidence underlying this attitude derives from the presumption of self-honesty on which libertinism is grounded. Building on Hobbes's sense that in overturning psychomachic ethics he was overturning something delusory, the libertine styles himself as starkly realistic. He confronts the visceral realities of body and appetite, refusing to delude himself by harbouring rationalist or ascetic pretensions. Such is his claim to authority.

Besides outlining all this, this chapter offers, secondly, some explanations as to *why* libertine perspectives acquired such currency amongst the Buckingham–Rochester coterie (the effect of their doing so being that others then followed, if with less conviction and consistency, the example of these fashionably rebellious aristocrats). In this context I examine Royalist attitudes to the Interregnum, the Restoration, and post-Restoration politics, and discuss the

Charles Sedley, Sir Fleetwood Sheppard, Henry Bulkeley, Henry Guy, Henry Killigrew, Henry Savile, and William Wycherley, though the Duke of Monmouth and Earl of Mulgrave also matched the raucous manners of this coterie. It is clear (1) from contemporary testimonies, (2) from Love's analysis of manuscript circulation amongst this anti-Yorkist, anti-Church-party group (Love 1993: 242–53), that Buckingham's wits did indeed constitute a distinct social circle. Marvell (1971: ii. 355) dubs Buckingham, Rochester, Buckhurst, *et al.* as 'the merry gang'; Pepys, as 'the counsellors of pleasure' (quoted in Keeble 2002: 99); Clarendon, as the 'men of mirth' (quoted in J. H. Wilson 1967: 5).

[6] As Skinner, for one, has demonstrated (1966: 294–5), Hobbist and libertine manners achieved an extensive popular purchase in the 1660s and 1670s amongst both young students and gentlemen of the coffee-houses, which is why Hobbes's works attracted such bitter criticism from those alarmed by this trend.

part played by those factors in shaping the moral attitudes prevalent amongst court wits in the 1660s and beyond.

Further to that, the third part of the chapter concentrates on some specific social and literary manifestations of the libertine outlook. Here the focus shifts to that culture of manners which played so significant a role in Carolean England. I argue that the libertine ethic, for all its egotism, was compatible with the collectivist ideal of a highly mannered society precisely because that culture provided a controlled forum within which men could exercise their appetites (not least for power) even whilst maintaining a show of civility. This constraint to be complaisant reimposed a form of governance on Charles's courtiers through the back door. So, too, did both the imperative to exercise power through wit and machinations (not through acts of violence) and the parallel concern to avoid displays of passion lest one should thereby expose one's weakness. Conduct was therefore controlled, but for strategic, not moral, reasons. There is ample evidence of these phenomena in Etherege's *The Man of Mode*, a play particularly associated with the court wits circle because its hero, Dorimant, was proverbially equated with the Earl of Rochester. In 1924 Dobrée argued that, as a genre, Restoration comedy 'said in effect, "Here is life lived upon certain assumptions; see what it becomes" '.[7] In *The Man of Mode* those assumptions are libertine, and we do indeed see what kind of life they produce—one dominated, not least, by an obsession with repartee, courtly manners, and the cultivation of power through such avenues.

These, then, are the themes of this chapter, but at the outset it is worth asking what proof there is that the wits, Marvell's 'Ministers of Pleasure',[8] really indulged in the kind of bawdy lifestyle commensurate with the libertine ideals outlined here. Writing with reference to Rochester, Greer has questioned how far Charles's court was actually the 'supercharged bordello catering for all kinds of sexual preferences' which anti-Stuart propagandists made it out to be.[9] Contemporary sources substantiate the fact that Rochester was belligerent, but not, Greer contends, the idea that he was a 'sexual athlete'.[10] Even her minimalist account of Rochester's libertinism, though, still allows that he kept Elizabeth Barry as his mistress; that in 1675 he, Buckhurst, Henry Savile, and others destroyed the priceless sundial in Whitehall Privy Gardens; and that the following year Rochester, together with Etherege and one Captain Downs, was involved in a brawl with the Epsom watch which left Downs dead.[11] Furthermore, the letters between Savile and Rochester published posthumously as *Familiar Letters* testify to the latter's taste for various kinds

---

[7] Dobrée 1924: 23.    [8] Marvell 1971: ii. 355.    [9] Greer 2000: 3.
[10] Ibid. 19, 5.    [11] See Pinto 1935: 184–5; J. H. Wilson 1967: 38.

of 'sweet sin'.[12] Greer discounts these printed documents as being suspect;[13] but the same features are equally apparent in the more reliable Harleian and Portland manuscripts of the Rochester correspondence. In a letter in the first of these collections Savile refers to the two friends' involvement in an attempt to import dildos into England, an attempt which floundered when customs officials seized and burnt the consignment. Savile urges Rochester to return to London to prosecute the 'revenge due to $y^e$ ashes of these Martyrs' for '$Y^r$ $L^p$ is chosen Generall in this war betwixt the Ballers & $y^e$ [tax] farmers'.[14] Another letter, this by Rochester himself, alludes to his own role as a go-between in supporting Savile's simultaneous seduction of the Countesses Falmouth and Northumberland.[15] A Portland manuscript from John Muddyman to Rochester refers, similarly, to the Earl's sexual involvement with one Foster, an unknown 'damsell of low degre'; another, from Savile, encourages Rochester to 'carry away [the] maydenhead' of a new, 15-year-old actress; and a third makes knowing reference to the vices of seduction which Savile is aware '$y^r$ $L^p$ is given to'.[16] Allusions such as these pull against Greer's conclusions, betraying signs of precisely that dissolute living the extent of which she wishes to question; but even if one accepts her argument, and puts Rochester to one side, there is good evidence that others amongst the wits pursued a libertine lifestyle.

Even in 1659 Evelyn could describe England as a country beset by 'popular Libertinism', and by a tavern culture where the 'chanting [of] Dithy-rambicks' was commonplace and it was 'esteem'd a piece of wit, to make a man drunk'.[17] Gangs of what Evelyn called 'a sort of perfect Debauchees, who stile themselves Hectors' had in fact existed amongst the gentry's decommissioned officers since the early 1650s, and these 'Knights of the Blade' were wont to pursue a loutish lifestyle of 'gaming, ... whoring, swearing, and drinking'.[18] Throughout the 1660s 'the great bawdy house at Whitehall'[19] offered further instances of debauched conduct, making it an inviting environment within which to cultivate a Hobbist or libertine mentality. Both Marvell and Pepys touch, for example, on the infamous affair between the King's mistress, Lady Castlemaine, and Henry Jermyn, which fired such jealousy in Charles that he refused to acknowledge the bastard which Castlemaine was then carrying as his own.[20] The same authors describe, too, the Duchess of York's alleged poisoning of her

---

[12] See, e.g., Rochester 1980: 91–2, 138, 201–2.     [13] Greer 2000: 4.

[14] Rochester 1980: 63. 'Ballers', as Pepys's use of the word to describe 'young blades' with a penchant for 'dancing naked' makes clear (1987: 919 (30 May 1668)), was the collective name taken by Rochester, Savile, *et al.*

[15] Rochester 1980: 67.     [16] Ibid. 71, 175, 218.     [17] Evelyn 1995: 78, 83–4.

[18] Graves 1923: 409–11.     [19] Pepys 1987: 895 (25 Mar. 1668).

[20] See 'The Last Instructions to a Painter', l. 102 (Marvell 2003: 360 ff.); Pepys 1987: 815 (30 July 1667).

husband's mistress, Lady Denham, and her own adulterous passions for Savile and Henry Sidney (her Master of Horse).[21] Pepys also records the revenge which the Earl of Southesk reputedly took when he learned of his wife's affair with the Duke of York—namely, to contract the pox from 'the foulest whore he could find' and then pass it, via his wife, to York himself.[22] The 1670s offer a list of comparable incidents, the Duke of Monmouth embarking on an affair with Lady Grey, for example, whilst Lord Grey meantime took up with his own sister-in-law; or Monmouth, again, murdering a beadle during a public brawl over a prostitute.[23] The wits pursued their indulgences against this background of royal lusts. In 1666 Buckingham followed Henry Killigrew and several others in becoming lover to the Countess of Shrewsbury.[24] Two years later, having fatally wounded her husband in a duel, he took her under his roof, blithely banishing his own wife to her father's house.[25] In an implicitly competitive move, 'Lying Killigrew' defamed the Countess by circulating a paper, supposedly signed by her, which testified to his magnificent virility during their sometime affair.[26] Just as outrageously, in 1671 (so Muddyman reports to Rochester) Savile broke into the bedroom of the widow, Lady Northumberland, intent on raping her.[27] Sex aside though, the wits also embroiled themselves in breaches of the peace, acts of hostility against society in general. (The importance of this antisocial aggression will become clear later.) Pepys recorded on 26 October 1668 Sedley and Buckhurst's 'late story of [their] running up and down the streets … all night' until they were taken in a fight with the constable.[28] Still more notorious were the same men's drunken antics five years before, when they appeared naked on the balcony of the Cock in Covent Garden, whereupon Sedley (so Pepys was told) mimed 'all the postures of lust and buggery', indulged in a little blasphemous sermonizing, and then washed his prick in a glass of wine before drinking the King's health from the same.[29] Inevitably, most of the surviving records for these scandals take the form of gossip (as in Pepys's diary) or lampooning satire. However, as Love has shown in a masterly study of Hamilton's *Memoirs of Grammont*, the persistent overlapping between such sources, and the survival of certain, tellingly exact details within them, indicates that they must have been based in partial fact.[30] That impression is only reinforced by the intersection of these documents with other, more formal or personal ones (court records,

[21] 'Last Instructions', ll. 65–8, 75–6; Pepys 1987: 556, 570–1, 681 (17 Nov. 1665, 9 Jan. 1666, 15 Oct. 1666).
[22] Pepys 1987: 901–2 (6 Apr. 1668).
[23] See Spurr 2000: 197; Marvell 1971: ii. 323; Lord *et al.* 1963–75: i. 172–6.
[24] Keeble 2002: 173–4. [25] Pepys 1987: 866, 911 (17 Jan., 15 May 1668).
[26] Spurr 2000: 200. [27] Rochester 1980: 68–70. [28] Pepys 1987: 951.
[29] Pinto 1927: 61 ff.; J. H. Wilson 1967: 40–2. [30] Love 1995.

state papers, private correspondence, etc.). Clearly, then, the beliefs and self-perceptions with which this chapter is concerned had, to some significant degree, a grounding in material reality.

## BELIEFS: FROM HOBBISM TO LIBERTINISM

Although scholarly interest in the full range of Hobbes's works was extensive, it was inevitably *Leviathan* (or accounts of Hobbesian thought derived therefrom) which attracted both the most criticism and the greatest popular attention in the 1650s and 1660s,[31] so much so that Pepys commented on 3 September 1668: 'Hobbs's *Leviathan* ... is ... mightily called for; and what was heretofore ... 8s. I now give 24s. at the second hand, and is sold for 30s., it being a book the Bishops will not let be printed again.'[32] Needless to say, for all that it moderates the *Elements'* earlier account of power, *Leviathan* provides no shortage of contentious points. Most relevant here are its continued emphasis on the primacy of appetite and self-interest in determining governance; its sometime rejection of any transcendental moral standard, of traditional right reason, or any notion of a *summum bonum*; the definition of felicity in terms of continuous forward motion; and the continued reliance on the premiss of a state of nature underlying man's social condition. Initially at least, the last of these points caused the greatest offence, because it seemed to assume an atheistical perspective. In the natural part of his account of man, Hobbes, it was thought, denied what Anglicans like Lucy and Clarendon wished to assert: namely, the assumption that there is, *ab initio*, 'in the heart *of* every man *a* thought *of* a GOD' (that is, a fully Christian God) which entails 'secret consent to that great Axiome, *such measure as you mete shall be meted to you againe*'.[33] For Hobbes, at least as Parts I and II of *Leviathan* present matters, that summary law is only recognized and becomes binding when man deduces that it is in his interests to enter into society, and then only *in foro interno* until such time as there is 'sufficient Security' to justify obeying the law outwardly.[34] For his critics, by contrast, there could be no pre-moral, pre-covenanting state (or state of mind), because 'every man', no matter how primitive, 'is borne a Citizen of the world, and ... must submit to that great ... *Lawmaker* ...,

---

[31] For details of the attention which Hobbes's work received, see esp. Skinner 1965–6 and 1966.

[32] Pepys 1987: 942.

[33] Lucy 1663: 146. On the broader motives propelling Anglican opposition to Hobbes, see Collins 2005: ch. 7.

[34] Hobbes 1996: 110.

God', whom he recognizes within his conscience the moment he begins to think.[35] The moral law is, on this perspective, transcendental, and should be recognized as such from the outset. Given this critical perspective, it is not surprising that both Lucy and Clarendon overemphasize the depravity of Hobbes's state of nature. The latter is a view of humankind, Clarendon insists, which makes man more of a beast than those animals over which he was appointed to rule.[36] Hobbes is said to present men as, universally, 'full of jealousie and malignity'; and given this account of his proposition, his arguments are then found wanting, hence Clarendon: 'Nor is ... wariness to prevent the ... injury that ... Robbers may do to any man, an argument that Mankind is ... disposed to commit those out-rages. If it be known that there is one Thief in a City, all men have reason to shut their doors.'[37] In fact, Hobbes concedes precisely this point: men are diffident not for fear of 'Mankind' *en masse* (Clarendon's précis of Hobbes), but for fear of a minority. He does add that, not knowing who the unreliable few are, it is prudent to mistrust all; but to say this is not to say that one should believe all men actually to be evil. Lucy and Clarendon are, though, prone to misread Hobbes thus—and to ignore all that he says about the actual divinity of the laws of nature—because, reacting against his initial emphasis on self-interest, they see him as a thinker who 'makes [man] seeme to act those things justly which we abominate in them'.[38] They see him as one who sanctions (in any situation where civil society is absent) actions which they regard as damnable under *all* circumstances.

It is a short step from this last, 'seditious Principle'[39] to the general assertion that Hobbes simply encouraged wrongdoing. Not surprisingly, therefore, that claim became a defining feature of 'Hobbism' as it was understood by critics and proponents alike in the 1660s, another such feature being the claim that Hobbes crudely identifies sensuous appetite and self-interest as man's primary motivations. Both these points are implicit in Samuel Parker's 1670 harangue against those 'Apes of Wit' who, pretending 'no other ... Learning but a few shavings of Wit gather'd out of ... Comedies; ... huffingly will ... assert ... that Power is Right, and justifies all actions ... and that the Laws of Nature are nothing but Maxims ... of meer self-interest!'[40] Eachard has the same perception in mind in his *Second Dialogue* (1673), which is addressed to that 'company of easy, giddy ... gentlemen who swagger that ... Hobbes hath said more for a bad life and against the other life after this, than ever was

---

[35] Lucy 1663: 155.   [36] G. A. J. Rogers 1995: 195.
[37] Ibid. 196–7. Cf. Lucy 1663: 153, an awkward passage, but one which seems to match Clarendon's point.
[38] Lucy 1663: 138.   [39] G. A. J. Rogers 1995: 182.   [40] Quoted in Mintz 1962: 135.

pleaded ... to the contrary'.[41] Hobbism, then, according to these Anglican critics, actively affirms wrongdoing. As will be immediately apparent, it comprises a reading of Hobbes's works—a reading based more on coffee-house hearsay than on textual scrutiny[42]—which ignores all that the author said about natural, civil, and divine law; one which ignores all that he advocated to counteract the problems associated with men exercising, uninhibited, their right of nature. Where Hobbes had sought, initially, simply to anatomize human motivation, to observe man as he at bottom is (a passionate and appetitious being), Hobbism construed that empirical analysis as if it were a positive recommendation in favour of libertinism, casting aside in so doing the political and religious philosophy which Hobbes constructed to suppress self-indulgence. Hobbism was a reading, therefore, which emphasized Hobbes's *supposed* renunciation of Christian ethics and which actively promoted a lifestyle of lawlessness.

As Mintz has shown, numerous Restoration sources testify to these perceptions and damn Hobbism accordingly.[43] Charles Wolseley, for instance, comments in his *Reasonableness of Scripture-Belief* (1672) that ''Tis but of late that men ... defend ill living and secure themselves against their own guilt, by an open defyance to all the great maxims of Piety and Virtue.'[44] In his view, most such 'bad Principles ... are of no earlier date then one very ill Book, ... Leviathan'. In writing this, Wolseley probably had in mind figures like Daniel Scargill, sometime brawler, flasher, Fellow of Corpus Christi, Cambridge, and would-be defender of such Hobbist theses as 'rationes boni et mali non sunt ab aeterno', who in 1669 sought to recant his former ways and, to that end, confessed that Hobbism had indeed been the root of all his lawlessness: 'I gloryed to be an *Hobbist* and an *Atheist* .... Agreeably unto which principles ... I ... lived in great licentiousness; swearing rashly; drinking intemperately; boasting ... insolently; corrupting others by my pernicious principles ... to ... the just offence of mankinde.'[45] So too, the author of the 1671 satire 'Upon the Beadle', in ventriloquizing the Duke of Monmouth's

---

[41] Quoted in Bowle 1951: 150.

[42] The Town-Wit is described in *The Character of a Coffee-House* (Anon. 1673: 4–5) as one who has read but 'two leaves of *Leviathan*', whose discourse turns about the twin poles of '*Atheism* and *Bawdry*', who 'boasts ... that he holds his *Gospel* from the *Apostle of Malmsbury*', and yet who 'it is more than probable [has] ne'r read, at least understood *ten* leaves of that *unlucky Author*'. Similarly, the *Character of a Town-Gallant* (Anon. 1675: 7), which refers to 'the Rattle of [the *Leviathan*] at *Coffee-houses*', reports of the gallant: 'he Swears the *Leviathan* may supplly all the lost Leaves of *Solomon*, yet he never saw it in his life, and for ought he knows it may be a *Treatise* about catching of Sprats'.

[43] See also, for other examples, Skinner 1966: 295–7.       [44] Quoted in Mintz 1962: 134–5.

[45] Quoted ibid. 50–1. For examples of Scargill's debauchery, see Axtell 1965: 103–4.

efforts to justify his infamous killing of a Holborn beadle, ascribes to him the Hobbist's nostalgic preference for a pre-moral outlook:

> 'Curs'd be their politic heads that first began
> To circumscribe the liberties of man,
> Man that was truli'st happy when of old
> His actions, like his will, were uncontroll'd,
> Till he submitted his great soul to awe
> And suffer'd fear to fetter him with law—
> This law that animates with partial looks
> One saucy watchman to oppose two dukes.'
>
> (ll. 45–52)[46]

The poet here, in dubbing Monmouth's action as one of 'gen'rous fury' (l. 9), emphasizes the fate of Aristotle's noble-minded anger in this Hobbist age—the fact that, for this generation of 'heroic' spirits, rage could only be a tawdrily self-regarding passion. The noble ideals of Spenser's era stand beyond the imaginative reach of the Carolean Hobbist.

Hobbism was not, of course, the only mid-century tradition which emphasized the determining importance of self-interest, developed a cynical understanding of mankind, or otherwise laid the foundations for Restoration libertinism. The next place to turn to for such ideas is the work of England's first generation of Cavalier poets (particularly those poems which fostered a lusty celebration of sexuality), and foremost amongst these was Thomas Carew's 'Rapture'.[47] In the latter Carew gives strident voice to man's corporeal imperative, valuing it on its own terms and revelling (with a notably generous spirit) in the titillations of sexuality. There, as the Cavalier poet vaunts man's sexual act which 'shoot[s] ... fresh fire' into our veins (l. 53), the sheer exuberance of his imagery reveals how far a corporeal imagination has, at this moment, been set free. Carew's fancy as much as his hand is 'enfranchiz'd' as his fingers slide over his beloved's 'naked polish'd Ivory', touching on her breast, a 'warme, firme Apple, tipt with corall berry' (ll. 29–30, 66). If this last is a comic image, the comedy only adds to an air of luscious self-indulgence in which the persona can delight even in his testes, first as a bee's honey-sack which 'swells' as he rifles the 'sweets' of this Paradise; then as a 'Rudder' by means of which his partner may 'guide / [His] Bark into Loves channell', there to 'Dance, as ... bounding waves ... rise or fall' (ll. 59–61, 87–90). This exuberance is matched by the movement of the verse itself. Where a later Cavalier poet like Suckling clips and end-stops his couplets, Carew softens his. He offsets his rhyming words by deploying extensive enjambement in

[46] Lord 1963–75: i. 174 ff.    [47] Carew 1949: 49 ff.

combination with mid-line caesuras, thereby generating what Lennard has termed rocking lineation (something more characteristic of a conversational idiom than of formal verse):

> Come then, and mounted on the wings of love
> Wee'le cut the flitting ayre, and sore above
> The Monsters head, and in the noblest seates
> Of those blest shades, quench, and renew our heates.

> (ll. 21–4)

If the anaphoric use of 'and' here creates a pulsing motion, the caesural effect which precedes its every iteration nevertheless renders the verb 'quench' momentarily intransitive, as intransitive indeed as is the experience of orgasm itself for each lover. Pace is reimposed after such suspension both in the repetitive use of such emphatic auxiliaries as 'shall' (ll. 45–8), in the doubling of conjunctions like 'till' (ll. 51, 54), and in the constant reiteration of 'Then' and 'Thence' (ll. 55–78). The resultant modulations between motion and stasis, 'faint respites' and 'active play' (l. 40), add to the mood of rapture in which Carew here parades sexuality's enchantments.

As Lovelace would later do in his lyric 'Love Made in the First Age', Carew sets his ecstasy in an Elysian field, a paradise where the 'hated', unnatural categories 'Of husband, wife, lust, modest, chaste, [and] shame' have no meaning (ll. 107–10). In this lotus land, 'All things … that may delight / … unrestrained Appetite' are lawful (ll. 111–12). It would be a mistake, though, to abstract the 'Rapture' from its contemporary culture. When Sharpe casts it in 'a world apart from society', he robs the work of its small but significant satiric force.[48] Carew, for example, begins his poem by emphasizing that the Colossus of conventional sexual morality is no more than a 'stalking Pageant', an oppressive fiction whose very legs are 'borrowed' from his audience, and who is thus '*made*' precisely by such people as choose to believe in him (ll. 15–17). To say this is to mount a direct assault upon those figures with whom I began this book, those moralists who believed that their truths were eternal verities. Carew, pursuing this same iconoclastic vein, subsequently reimagines the Renaissance favourite, Lucrece, as a keen student of Aretino's postures (ll. 115–16), and then recasts Penelope as a nymphomaniac eager to devote some 'gamesome nights' to Ithaca's fittest lads (ll. 125–30). Far from emulating the metaphysical aspirations of Charles's Neoplatonist court, Carew rejects pious talk of souls embracing one another, delighting instead in the fact that such souls may 'taste'—the sensuous idiom is instructive—'the embraces of our bodyes' (ll. 43–4). Most tellingly of all, he

---

[48] Sharpe 1987a: 118.

plunges, in his raptures, straight into the very same 'Bower of blisse' which for Spenser was the epitome of all things menacing (ll. 68, 27). In doing all this, Carew disrupted the halcyon calm and moral rigour of a court famously policed by the monarch himself (for which reason the 'Rapture's' author duly earned his reputation as 'a great libertine').[49] Nonetheless, though he thus positioned himself as something of an iconoclast, we do well to remember the limits of Carew's libertinism. He lacked, in his libertine poetry, both the aggression and the edge of social and political vengefulness which I will argue hereafter characterized later, Restoration strains of the same outlook. Furthermore, his lusty pieces always coexisted alongside a host of idealizing works (not least *Coelum Britannicum*), as if the former were momentary indulgences of an impulse otherwise repressed beneath official court ideology.[50] Carew's is not, then, an exclusively (or even predominantly) libertine performance; but that part of it which is, is a display, a blazon, which was vibrant enough to bolster a growing sense, in Caroline England, of the body's perhaps ungovernable, certainly delightful potency.

Carew seems to have belonged to the so-called Order of the Bugle, a society whose members devoted themselves to bibulousness, whoring, and fighting the watch.[51] According to Graves and Raylor, loutish drinking societies like this were as much a feature of London life in the 1620s and 1630s as their hectoring counterparts were in the 1650s, and as such, they provide a context within which to set the emergent libertinism of the late Jacobean / early Caroline period.[52] Raylor hypothesizes that the so-called Tityre-tu orders provided a focus for the young, angry, and ambitious who felt excluded from positions of influence in 1620s society, and thus sought a forum within which to vent their rebellious instincts.[53] In line with that judgement, the author of one 1641 broadside regarded John Suckling (perhaps a member of the Order of the Fancy)[54] as the epitome of every type of antisocial vice. Members of what this author called 'The Sucklington Faction', a group of 'joviall roaring Boyes' and 'Gallants' all too prevalent in 'these … loose-living times', were apparently variously guilty of 'intemperate voracity, delicate luxury … [and] wastfull prodigality', thereby rendering themselves very 'Puppet[s] on the stage of vanity'.[55]

---

[49] On the halcyon reputation of Caroline England, see Anselment 1988: ch. 1; Wilcher 2001: ch. 1. On Charles's enforcement of moral decorum, see Sharpe 1987*b*: 232, 236. On Carew's libertine reputation see Carew 1949: pp. xlvii–ix.

[50] See Corns 1993: 211. Further to this point, Momus articulates Carew's libertine voice in the opening speeches of *Coelum*'s anti-masque, but then becomes complicit in the play's work of moral instruction, endorsing, e.g., Mercury's Spenserian dismissal of the five senses.

[51] Graves 1923: 402 n. 22.     [52] Ibid. *passim*; Raylor 1994: 69–110.

[53] Raylor 1994: 81–2, 102–4, 110.     [54] Ibid. 92–3.     [55] Anon. 1641: *passim*.

Suckling's libertine verse certainly supports this view of its author, at least
to the extent that it is more aggressive, snide, and self-consciously rebellious
than is Carew's. 'A Candle', for instance, presents a masturbatory fantasy
which gestures at the carnival of human sexuality and, as such, gives rein to
the bodily imperative within man; but where Carew might accord this impulse
free, relaxed expression, Suckling prefers to deploy the half-statements of
innuendo. Thus the candle, when applied to a candlestick holder *or some other*
'hole', is said to 'spend' itself, yet leave behind a residue of 'moisture thick
and thin' (ll. 7–10).[56] Whilst entertaining fellow libertines, this innuendo also
bites at the polite sensibilities of those who find the poem distasteful, goading
them to articulate a cloaked but obvious meaning which is intended to affront
them. The same antagonistic, demeaning attitude is still more apparent in
'Upon my Lady Carliles walking', Suckling's mock-dialogue between himself
and Carew in which Carew figures Lady Carlisle platonically, as a symbol of
spiritual perfection, only to be debunked by Suckling who replies, caustically,
'I had my Thoughts, but not your way'.[57] 'Alas! *Tom*', Suckling continues,

> ... I am flesh and blood,
> And was consulting how I could
> In spite of masks and hoods descry
> The parts deni'd unto the eye.
>
> (ll. 22–7)

Suckling's visceral aim is to venture '*hard* to drink' of the fountain between
Carlisle's thighs and then 'with ease [to] go in and out' there (ll. 45, 49). There
is nothing here of the lyricism which aestheticizes Carew's raptures, and all
hint of the latter's Platonist idealism is likewise belittled. Suckling (in a manner
which anticipates much Restoration verse) is brutally forthright in reducing the
woman to an object of animal appetite. Again therefore, what Parker terms the
latter's 'plain-dealing' is indicative of a roaring boy's rebellious, antagonistic
stance,[58] and that stance also informs the two letters which apparently passed
between Suckling and Carew on the subject of the latter's marrying a widow
(both of which Clayton in fact attributes to Suckling[59]). These documents,
too, are primarily concerned to shock their audience with a show of staged
flippancy. 'Carew' matches 'Suckling's' accusation that a widow is a kind of
'*chew'd-meat*' with the ripostes that an old shoe is more easily put on than
'a *strait-boot*', and a 'well-wayed horse' more easily ridden than any '*unbackt
Filly*'.[60] The innuendo implicit in this talk of easy riding is obvious, the more
so when both letters end by musing, once more, on the filling of holes. Such

[56] Suckling 1971: i. 19.      [57] Ibid. i. 30 ff.      [58] Parker 1982: 350.
[59] Suckling 1971: i, pp. lxxxvi, 331–2.      [60] Ibid. i. 156–8.

bluntly prosaic language again paves the way for a later culture of libertinism, a libertinism more violent than that imagined by Carew, yet commensurate (for that very reason) with a Hobbist view of human relations.

English Cavalier poetry constitutes one source, then, which contributed to the literary ethos of Restoration England; but to that we should add another, the French *libertin* tradition.[61] Cowley, Waller, Davenant, and Buckingham certainly came into direct contact with the culture of *les libertins érudits* whilst the court pursued its life of exile in Paris during the Interregnum.[62] At a later stage, Wycherley spent the second half of the 1650s in Angoulême as a member of Madame de Montausier's salon, whilst Buckhurst and Rochester journeyed through France in the late 1650s and early 1660s as part of their Grand Tours. Rochester, Buckhurst, Savile, Sedley, and Buckingham would all travel to Paris again in subsequent years on embassies for the King.[63] It is therefore reasonable to suppose that Restoration opinion was influenced by some, at least, of the libertine literature native to the Continent.

One such celebrated author whose works may have made a lasting impression upon Englishmen was Théophile de Viau, leading light amongst a libertine group gathered around Queen Anne of Austria in the early 1620s. Théophile's 'Satyre Première' presents man as a creature dominated by Nature, bound, therefore, to submit to the sway of his own passions and humours in all their inconstancy:

> Comme Saturne laisse et prend une saison,
> Nostre esprit abandonne et reçoit la raison.
> Je ne sçay quelle humeur nos volontez maistrise,
> Et de nos passions est la certaine crise;
> Ce qui sert aujourd'hui nous doit nuire demain,
> On ne tient le bonheur jamais que d'une main.
>
> (ll. 55–60)[64]

Importantly, though, those who trust in (rather than resist) these corporeal imperatives will supposedly discover in such a life of self-compliance both pleasure and equanimity:

---

[61] This tradition is most fully explored in Pintard 1943.     [62] See Smuts 1996: 178, 189–92.

[63] In light of these connections several critics have sought to link later seventeenth-century English poets to French precursors. Crocker (1937) makes this case with reference to Rochester. Farley-Hills (1978: 13–14, 150–68) then connects the same Earl's writings with those of de Viau, Régnier, and Boileau, noting that the Boileau satires in which Rochester was most interested belonged to the French poet's early, libertine period when he frequented the Croix-Blanche literary club (and thus interacted with Des Barreaux and La Mothe le Vayer). Griffin (1973: 173–82) hypothesizes a *direct* connection between Des Barreaux's verse and Rochester's. Thormählen (1993: 198–201, 362) adds Dehénault and Mme Deshoulières to the list of possible influences upon the Earl. See also Quaintance 1963.

[64] Adam 1964: 56 ff.

> J'approuve qu'un chacun suive en tout sa nature;
> Son empire est plaisant, et sa loy n'est pas dure.
> Ne suivant que son train jusqu'au dernier moment,
> Mesmes dans les malheurs on passe heureusement.

(ll. 85–8)

Hence Théophile's ode 'Heureux tandis qu'il est vivant' celebrates the idea that submission to Nature is a liberating experience, one which gives the libertine (in his consequent detachment from worldly anxieties) a peculiar autonomy and stability of self.[65] Any man who, by contrast, resists 'les mouvemens de ses affections' ('Satyre Première', l. 139) and disregards the instruction never to bridle his passions, will find that such efforts are counter-productive: 'Si tu veux résister, l'amour te sera pire' (l. 141). Indeed, Théophile pushes home this point by allegorizing Adonis's death as the most extreme consequence of self-denial. In a further blow to prevailing values, he also demystifies the Church's rationalist ethics as but so much delusion and hypocrisy, a denial of man's visceral nature made by those no longer capable of feeling it:

> Un vieux père resveur, aux nerfs tout refroidis,
> Sans plus se souvenir quel il estoit jadis,
> Alors que l'impuissance esteint sa convoitise,
> Veut que nostre bon sens révère sa sottise,
> Que le sang généreux estouffe sa vigueur,
> Et qu'un esprit bien né se plaise à la rigueur.
> Il nous veut arracher nos passions humaines,
> Que son malade esprit ne juge pas bien saines.

(ll. 75–82)

This, then, is the unrepentant naturalism which led Garasse, celebrated critic of the early *libertins*, to identify as one of their guiding maxims that 'Il n'y a point d'autre divinité ... au monde que la NATURE, laquelle il faut contenter en toutes choses sans rien refuser à nostre corps ... de ce qu'ils désirent de nous.'[66] To cite only this judgement, though, and Théophile's more philosophical verse, would be misleading, since such abstractions ignore de Viau's more raucous, even blasphemous, cabaret poetry. In a sonnet such as 'Qu'un avare désir amasse la richesse', Théophile is positively jubilant in rejecting all other worldly pleasures in favour of the sexual satisfaction to be gained from some one mistress.[67] A single 'gaillard appétit' (l. 14) is there vaunted over all other pleasures. In 'On m'a dit que ma soeur chevauche', meanwhile, he rails against man's mortal fate and against a God who would seemingly have us *sleep* 'Dans

---

[65]  Viau 1984: i. 286–7.
[66]  Adam 1964: 42. On Garasse's possible influence upon Rochester, see Turner 2003: 265.
[67]  Viau 1981: 62.

le commun lict des humains' (l. 37).[68] Théophile's preference is to keep alive the 'mouvement' (l. 40) of man's body, to maintain that perpetual motion elsewhere so much emphasized by Hobbes and other *libertins*. Precisely that preoccupation also animates the lyric 'Marquis, comment te portes-tu?', which aims to galvanize a friend back into libertine revelry on the grounds that *'Dieu nous veut conserver / Les nerfs souples et le vit roide'* (ll. 19–20).[69] Here, too, the maintenance of vitality would seem to imply a commitment to constant motion.

As these texts demonstrate, Théophile emphasizes an ethic of self-indulgence, even of bodily determinism, but he does not depict that hedonism as something self-centred or aggressively acquisitive. For the development of *that* emphasis, which brings French libertinism closer to the Hobbist egotism already discussed, we need to look forward twenty years, first to Vauquelin des Yveteaux's celebrated sonnet 'Avoir peu de parens, moins de train que de rente' (*c*.1645).[70] During the mid-century Vauquelin reigned as an *arbiter elegantiarum* in France, and his 'Avoir peu' sonnet was a defining document of that image. On the one hand, it prescribes the pursuit of *easeful*, decorous pleasure, 'l'honneste volupté' (l. 2). Hence man is to satisfy his every desire but without compromising his health (l. 3). He may cultivate public honour but always 'sans peine' (l. 13)—only to the point of convenience. He should enjoy music, poetry, fine art, gardens, hospitality; but all this whilst maintaining only 'une table ... de peu de couverts', a table, therefore, which is intimate and exclusive rather than extravagant and expansive (ll. 9–10). On the other hand, man should also preserve his autonomy, his detachment from the world. He should exempt himself (so far as possible) from business and vice, from both less for moral reasons than because they involve untold aggravations. Likewise, the poet recommends not that one should have no bastards but that one should have only a few (l. 13), again more because they are a practical burden than because of any moral objection. Stanza 2 advises man to evade all external commitments likely to prove onerous, to eschew ambition, and to preserve 'sa liberté' (l. 7). To this Vauquelin adds the precept, 'Estre estimé du Prince et le veoir rarement' (l. 12): patriotism thus takes a backseat within an outlook which is predominantly self-centred. As the most telling (and typically cool, unapologetic) line of the sonnet puts it, this perfect libertine is to have 'bien plus d'amour pour soy que pour sa Dame' (l. 11). Self-interest comes first, and a clear limit is put on outward obligations.

This, Des Yveteaux's libertinism, was matched, though, and surpassed by that of his long-lived contemporary (and friend of Théophile), Jacques Vallée des Barreaux. An admirer of Descartes, Des Barreaux's unique contribution

---

[68] Ibid. 84 ff.    [69] Ibid. 63.    [70] Adam 1964: 202.

to French freethinking was to unite the social and material dimensions of libertinism emphasized by the lyric poets with the more philosophical concerns pursued by Cyrano de Bergerac *et al.* This latter tendency is reflected in his pessimism, the product of a disillusionment with reason. In sonnet after sonnet Des Barreaux mocks man's pretension that possessing a faculty of reason makes him the 'petit Roytelet' over all nature ('Maistre sans contredit de ce globe habité', l. 7).[71] Possession of that attribute, he complains, cannot erase the corporeal reality that our bestial functions are always paramount: 'Toujours moucher, cracher, éternüer, tousser, / ... manger et boire, / Et puis roter, dormir, peter, chier, pisser' (ll. 11–13). Nor does it obscure the fact of our addiction, as a species, to criminality and self-imposed suffering ('L'Homme a dit en son coeur', ll. 11–14).[72] Indeed, Des Barreaux devotes a whole sonnet—'Ce n'est qu'un vent furtif ... '—to boggling at the perversity of man's capacity for self-torment, not least the fact that 'la ... raison' itself (precisely in feeding our passions with fresh thoughts) 'le rend irraisonnable' (ll. 5, 8).[73] In that context Vallée (like Montaigne) admires, instead, animals who manage to be oblivious to such worries (ll. 9–14). Trapped by a desperate sense that life is only a dream wherein our passions and aspirations (seemingly so important) are in truth irrelevancies;[74] by the knowledge, also, that in the march towards death, past and present are constantly streaming away from us ('la suite du temps qui fuit sans retourner');[75] trapped, lastly, by an intuition that nothingness (the Epicurean void) brackets our existence and waits to re-embrace us,[76] Des Barreaux concludes that we should really study pleasure rather than understanding, 'Et nous servons des sens plus que de la raison'.[77]

Viewed in the context of his cynicism, Des Barreaux's hedonism (his preference for 'sens' over 'raison') might seem to be only a reflex response, an act of self-consolation. And certainly, in a sonnet such as 'Toy qui braves la mort', Vallée, when faced with the fact of mutability, resorts to debauchery as an act of pure escapism ('Jette-toy comme moy dans le sein des plaisirs' (l. 14) ).[78] However, he is equally prone to turn to the *carpe diem* ethic in a consciously enthusiastic fashion (witness the opening lines of another poem, 'Il faut prendre pendant la vie, / Tout le plaisir qu'on peut avoir'[79]); and at such times that acquisitive outlook, far from being merely consolatory, a

---

[71] Lachèvre 1911: 243.     [72] Ibid. 244.     [73] Ibid. 245.

[74] See 'Tout n'est plein icy bas que de vaine apparence', *passim*, and 'Que la condition de notre sort est dure', ll. 9–14, ibid. 248, 252.

[75] 'Que la condition de notre sort ...', l. 4.

[76] See 'Mortels qui vous croyez, quand vous venez à naistre', ll. 1–5, 9–11, in Adam 1964: 194 ff.

[77] 'Mortels qui vous croyez', ll. 7–8, 12.     [78] Adam 1964: 197.     [79] Ibid. 195.

distraction from otherwise negative perceptions, assumes a positive inflection in its own right. In 'Que ta condition, Mortel, me semble dure' the background established is (as in the reference, elsewhere, to 'la suite du temps qui fuit sans retourner') one of perpetual motion, life constantly fleeing from the self into an ever-receding past;[80] but here the imperative to counterbalance that movement by lunging forward towards new pleasures—'employons bien le temps pendant qu'il dure./ Prenons tous les plaisirs que permet la Nature' (ll. 4–5)—becomes its own delight, a source of regenerative exhilaration:

> Bien que j'aye douleur qu'il [la mort] me faille mourir,
> Cette douleur en moy de plaisir est suivie.
>
> (ll. 10–11)

What began, then, as a consolation becomes an ethic valued for itself. This same forthright vigour is also apparent in Des Barreaux's imitation of the Des Yveteaux sonnet already discussed. Des Barreaux recasts Vauquelin's self-centred ideal in absolute, downright egotistical terms:

> N'estre ny magistrat, ny marié, ny prestre,
> Avoir un peu de bien, l'appliquer tout à soy.
>
> (ll. 1–2)[81]

*This* libertine would have no ties or responsibilities whatsoever ('ny maistresse, ny maistre', l. 5), seeing Court and King, for example, only by appointment (l. 6). He would turn everything ('tout') towards himself and (in a line echoing Des Barreaux's 'Mortels qui vous croyez') would again use such resources to study 'bien plus à jouir qu'à connoistre' (l. 4). Above all, his watchword would be to

> Posséder le present en pleine confiance,
> N'avoir pour l'avenir crainte ny espérance;

to thrust forward, then, in pursuit of immediate pleasures and new motions, secure in the conviction that self-love should indeed be the determining principle of conduct (ll. 12–13). With such precepts—a blend of constant motion and bold self-interestedness—the French 'tradition du libertinage' abandons Théophile's philosophical naturalism to embrace something more akin to Hobbes's aggressive egotism. It is, for example, only a short step from Des Barreaux to La Rochefoucauld, who, in Hobbist fashion, coolly reduces all friendship to 'un ménagement réciproque d'intérêts ... où l'amour-propre se propose toujours quelque chose à gagner';[82] and this in turn is

[80] Lachèvre 1911: 253.   [81] Adam 1964: 203.   [82] La Rochefoucauld 1965: 39.

precisely the ethos of Etherege's *Man of Mode*, wherein Dorimant explains his association with Bellair by announcing, 'It is our mutual interest to be [friends]; it makes the women think the better of his understanding, and judge more favourably of my reputation; it makes him pass upon some for a man of very good sense, and I upon others for a very civil person' (i. i. 467–71).[83]

Kay Smith, though, argues that it was Montaigne's and Gassendi's Epicureanism (rather than *libertin* verse) which had the greatest influence on Cavalier poets, and certainly in weighing up the forces which shaped Restoration libertinism the Anglo-French Epicurean tradition also demands discussion.[84] The so-called Epicurean Revival of this time,[85] which (like Hobbism) encouraged an unapologetic valorization of bodily pleasure, began in earnest in France with Montaigne's *Essais*. In one of the many C Text additions to Book 1 thereof, bending the emphasis of that book towards Epicureanism, Montaigne argues that man has lost touch with nature's instinctive law embedded within the body: 'If in our members we did not trouble the jurisdiction, which ... belongs vnto them ... we should be the better for-it; ... nature hath given them a just ... moderate temperature toward pleasure and ... paine .... But ... we have ... alienated our selves from her rules, to abandon our selves vnto the vagabond libertie of our fantasies.'[86] An ill-disciplined, overly inventive imagination (aided by too much 'learning')[87] has disrupted the process of governance which once kept man—and still keeps the cannibal or 'day-labouring swaine'—in good moral order, this with the result that to recover, now, a 'moderate temperature toward pleasure', man must make conscious nature's principles of self-control and deliberately reimpose them on himself.[88] Montaigne's aim, therefore, is to restore this lost sensibility, and especially to overturn lingering ascetic assumptions. (Psychomachic ideals dismissive of the body are misguided, because ours is a 'commixt condition' in which the soul ought willingly to 'cherish' her bodily companion.[89]) Further to these objectives, Montaigne claims neither to correct nor to resist his own natural complexion and inclinations.[90] He looks to them, rather, for the same kind of guidance as does the humble ploughman, and this practice proves morally productive, because in fact man naturally apprehends virtue as admirable. Any 'sound iudgement', Montaigne avers, cannot help but find vice ugly and greet every virtuous action with 'generous jollitie'.[91] Indeed, according to this analysis, pleasure—or, in Florio's translation, 'voluptuousness'—is

---

[83] All references to Etherege's plays are to Etherege 1982.      [84] Smuts 1996: 192–200.
[85] For scholarship on this theme, see Barbour 1998; Fleischmann 1964; H. Jones 1989; Joy 1992; Kargon 1964 and 1966; Kroll 1991; Mayo 1934; Osler 1991; Røstvig 1954.
[86] Montaigne 1603: 131.      [87] See ibid. 283–4, 313–14.      [88] Ibid. 284. Cf. 625.
[89] Ibid. 535, 659, 371.      [90] Ibid. 631.      [91] Ibid. 484.

the absolute end of virtue, the benefit which we attain from being good.[92] Rightly conceived, virtue is also (for Montaigne) assiduous in *nurturing* bodily pleasure. It transforms corporeal delight from something ephemeral into something enduring: 'in making [pleasures] just and vpright, [Virtue] makes them sure and sincere. By moderating them, shee keepeth them in vse and breath. In limiting and cutting them-off, whome she refuseth; she whets-vs-on toward those she leaveth vnto vs.'[93] Virtue, in short, ensures us a happy degree of satisfaction without engendering satiety (an indulgence which would kill the very pleasure it seeks to foster). It is an ideal of governance which does, therefore, entail a degree of temperate self-discipline, but the *value* of that temperance lies in its restraining pleasure solely in order to make it sustainable,[94] in order to perfect its relish or '*seasoning*'.[95] Ultimately, the cultivation of just such relishing stands at the heart of Montaigne's Epicurean vision, particularly as expressed in his concluding essay, 'De l'Experience'. Montaigne's purpose in life—God's purpose for man[96]—is to 'taste' every minute in its entirety, 'to runne it over againe, and take holde of it', and, where that minute is pleasurable, to 'sound' such 'contentment' to its very bottom (for 'There is a kinde of husbandrie in knowing how to enjoy' life properly).[97] Where others let their lives slip away from them, Montaigne would delay his, compensating for the haste of time's fleeing by maximizing 'la vigueur de l'usage' of every moment, making each instant always 'more profound and full'.[98] Whilst Des Barreaux, then, counters the constant dissipation of experience by grabbing at successive delights ('Prenons tous les plaisirs'), his more reposeful predecessor would rather *stay* the passage of time, at least in so far as consciousness can—this, the difference, perhaps, between making the sun run and arresting it at the brave clearness of midday.

Useful though they are for my purposes in establishing the parameters of Epicurean ethics, these Montaignian Epicurean manœuvres were of course only a prelude to Gassendi's greater act. It was he who *systematically* reconstructed Epicurus's thought in a manner fit for Christian audiences of the mid-seventeenth century, and he from whom the English revival most directly stemmed.[99] Evelyn, one of England's early scholars of Epicureanism, was a frequent visitor to Paris between 1649 and 1652, and if Sharp's conjectures are correct, the other, Walter Charleton, was probably also there during the same years.[100] Then, if not before, Charleton came into contact with Gassendi's work: his own atomistic physics, *Physiologia Epicuro-Gassendo-Charltoniana* (1654), confesses to such an influence in its very title, and his *Epicurus's Morals*,

---

[92] Ibid. 30.    [93] Ibid. 78.    [94] Ibid. 663.    [95] Ibid. 661.
[96] Ibid. 662–3.    [97] Ibid. 661–2.    [98] Montaigne 1952: iii. 368; 1603: 662.
[99] See H. Jones 1989: 198 ff.    [100] Sharp 1973: 324–7.

a sympathetic account of Epicurean ethics which followed two years later, likewise opens with 'An Apologie for Epicurus' indebted to Gassendi. Both Charleton, though, and Evelyn were hesitant Lucretians, anxious about the atheism and materialism of their sources. For a more confident English-language exegesis of this creed, we do better to look forward to 1660 and the publication of the third volume of Stanley's *History of Philosophy*. That text merits further attention in illuminating the intellectual precedents of English libertinism.

Stanley's 'Thirteenth Part' of his *History* offers a panoramic outline of the Epicurean school's philosophy, not least its ethics. Epicurus, of course, like Montaigne after him, identified pleasure as the good; but in so doing, he distinguished between two different kinds of pleasure, 'one in station or rest, which is placability, calmness, ... immunity from ... grief; the other in motion, ... a sweet movement, as in gladness, mirth, and whatsoever moveth the Sense delightfully, ... as to eat and drink out of hunger and thirst'.[101] Only the first of these, 'Indolence of Body, and Tranquillity of Mind', constitutes true felicity. This distinction between static and kinetic pleasure is an integral feature of the natural world:

Nature tends to no other Pleasure primarily ... but ... the stable, which followeth upon removal of pain .... The Moveable she proposes not as the end, but ... only as a means conducing to the stable, to sweeten ... that operation of hers which is requisite to the extirpation of pain .... For Example, Hunger and Thirst being things troublesom ... , she ... seasons with a sweet relish the action of eating and drinking, that the Animal may apply himself more readily thereto .... Hence also it comes, that the highest pleasure terminated in privation of pain may be varied ... , but not increased.

The last point here is crucial. Once hunger has been satisfied, further consumption of food (according to Epicurus) can bring no additional felicity. Variety is 'not necessary' to pleasure. Assuming that one's basic hunger has been assuaged, or that there is sufficient food available to allay it, the insistence on having some specific, elaborate dish can only be a 'vain' desire grounded on a misguided conception of happiness. Desires 'which infer no damage ... though not satisfi'd, yet are accompanied with ... vehement instigations, are such not by necessity, but vain opinions, and though they have some beginning from nature, yet their ... excess they have ... from the vanity of opinions .... [S]uch desires, ... never to be satisfi'd, ... are ... justly esteemed causes of harm.'[102] Epicurus, clearly, was never pregnant.

Rightly understood, Epicureanism is not, then, a luxurious philosophy: 'we are far from meaning the pleasures of luxurious persons ... as considered in the motion or act of fruition' (that last, a word which will be important

---

[101] Stanley 1701: 608.      [102] Ibid. 615. See Long and Sedley 1987: i. 113–14.

later in this book).[103] 'For it is not perpetual Feasting, and Drinking; not the Conversation of beautiful Women; not'—and this is surely the most contentious point—not even 'Rarities of Fish, ... that make a happy Life; but Reason, with Sobriety, and a severe Mind, searching the causes, why this Object is to be preferr'd, that to be rejected'.[104] Those who think otherwise (like Des Barreaux, perhaps, or Hobbesian man), and who seek happiness in the restless pursuit of endless different desires, suffer the affliction of a heart which, resembling a vessel 'full of holes, can never be filled'.[105] Stanley repeatedly stresses the need for man to 'be satisfi'd with a little', to understand the 'just bounds of our Desires'.[106] (His emphasis on boundaries chimes with Milton's, and anticipates a major theme of Rochester's poetry discussed hereafter in Chapter 8.) Epicurus's sober reason, which is equated with a 'general prudence',[107] much as in Hobbes's instrumentalist account of reason, judges how to bound desire according to four 'Canons of Affections'.[108] These state that simple pleasure is to be pursued, simple pain shunned, and, conversely, that pleasure which either hinders a greater pleasure or procures a greater pain is to be shunned, pain which dispels a greater pain or procures a greater pleasure to be embraced. But if prudence is therefore necessary to felicity, so are fortitude and (as in Montaigne) temperance, because these counteract the disruptive perturbations of fear and desire, respectively. Justice, too, is to be fostered because it 'calms ... the mind', where a bad conscience would stimulate anxiety.[109] The virtues, in short, guarantee man's pleasure, whereas a life spent trying to appease endless appetites remains vulnerable to the vagaries of fortune. Moral excellence of a familiar and predictable kind is, therefore, as much recommended by genuine Epicureanism as by any Christian or Stoic ethic. The one crucial difference is that Epicureanism, in identifying the good with pleasure, recommends virtue on grounds of self-interest—that is, not for its own sake, but because it maximizes one's delight.

In mid-century England, though, there were plenty who chose to recognize little of the above, and who propagated a popular image of Epicureanism as distorting as Hobbism was of Hobbes's philosophy. Just as Platonists like Henry More and John Smith condemned those in 'the stie of *Epicurus*' as a 'herd' who 'drowned ... their ... sober Reason in the ... *Lethe* of sensuality',[110] so too Thomas Creech, in the preface to his 1682 translation of *De Rerum*

---

[103] Stanley 1701: 608.
[104] On fish see Davidson 1997: 3–35, 139–47, 186–90, and Middleton's Black Knight, who is keenly aware of their association with Epicureanism (*Game at Chess* v. iii. 6–21).
[105] Stanley 1701: 605. Cf. *De Rerum Natura* 6. 17–23, and *Gorgias* 493a–c.
[106] Stanley 1701: 605, 548.   [107] Ibid. 610.   [108] Ibid. 554.   [109] Ibid. 626.
[110] Quoted in Gabbey 1982: 199, and Patrides 1969: 140, respectively. The swinish phrase derives from Horace ('Epistle', 1. 4. 16).

*Natura*, happily asserted that in Epicureanism 'Providence is deny'd' and 'the notion of a Deity thrown out' solely in order 'to make room for *Pleasures*, such often as a Beast would disdain to stoop to'.[111] Continuing in this vein, Creech justified his book, England's first complete, printed translation of Lucretius, with the argument that 'the best Method to overthrow the *Epicurean Hypothesis* ( … as it stands opposite to *Religion*) is to expose a full System of it to publick view'.[112] He insisted in his preface that Epicureanism's atheism and alleged licence were intrinsically related: '*Ease* is the *study* of the *Atheist*, *Sense* … the *Reason*, and *Pleasure* the *Argument*.' In the prefatory life of Lucretius, Epicurus was thus attacked as 'a most loose and dissolute Voluptuary',[113] and this portrait was reinforced in the new dedication to the 1683 edition, in which Creech claimed that Epicurus deliberately 'baited his hook with Pleasure' so as to appeal 'to the loose affections of the debauched'.[114] In none of Creech's remarks in this work is there a recognition of Epicurus's distinction between mental / static and bodily / kinetic pleasures. Indeed, he, like most readers in this period, misconstrues Epicureanism as akin to Cyrenaic philosophy, this despite Stanley's meticulous reiteration of Diogenes Laertius's efforts to dissociate the two. Stanley outlines the work of Aristippus and 'The Cyrenaick Sect' in the second part of his *History*: 'They assert corporeal pleasure to be our ultimate end, … not catastematick, permanent pleasure, which consisteth in privation of Grief and a quiet void of all disturbance, which *Epicurus* held.'[115] Perpetual motion, Stanley says, the constant succession of '*particular pleasures*', is the characteristic image and ethical ideal of Aristippus's sect; not stasis. Furthermore, for Aristippus, 'Pleasure is good, though proceeding from the most sordid dishonest thing.'[116] Such an outlook, the *History* repeatedly emphasizes, is philosophically and ethically a world away from true Epicureanism:

> The Cyrenaicks *admit not pleasure, to consist in rest, but in motion only,* Epicurus *allowed both, as well that of the Soul as of the Body …, expressly thus; Of pleasures, indolence and imperturbation consist in rest; and delight, in motion.*
>
> *Moreover … the* Cyrenaicks *… conceived the pains of the Body to be worse than those of the mind …. But* Epicurus *held, that the pains of the mind are the greatest, for … no ill can afflict the Body longer than whilst it is present; but … the past and future also torment the Mind; and by the same reason, the pleasures of the Soul are the greatest.*[117]

If Creech though, unlike Stanley, insists on collapsing the distinction between Epicureanism and Cyrenaic libertinism, he is explicit, too, in connecting such hedonism with both the court and Hobbes's philosophy. Hence,

---

[111] Lucretius 1682: sigs. b2$^{r-v}$.    [112] Ibid. sig. b2$^r$.    [113] Ibid. sig. $^\pi$A4$^v$.
[114] Lucretius 1683: sig. $^\pi$A4$^r$.    [115] Stanley 1701: 134.    [116] Ibid. 135.
[117] Ibid. 633.

his description of Epicurean atheists contains a veiled criticism of Charles's court wits: these atheists are men who harbour 'a setled Fancy that all … are their secret Rivals in *Pleasure*', and for them 'the *height* of … perfection [is] a little readiness in profane *Buffoonery*, their *Wit* like *Fish* … never shining but when it stinks or rots'.[118] He then adds to this an attack on those who describe '*the rise of Man out of the ground, like a Pumkin*', this an allusion to *De Cive* 8. 1, and thus a criticism of Hobbes. Creech goes on to assert that 'admirers of … *Hobbes* may easily discern … his *Politicks* are but *Lucretius* enlarg'd': Hobbes's state of nature, his account of the beginning of society and laws, and his criteria of justice are all apparently 'natural *Consequents* of the Epicurean Origine of Man'.[119] The translation of *De Rerum* 5. 958–61 is slanted so as to underline this equation. Lucretius's state of nature is rendered thus:

> No fixt *Society*, no steddy Laws,
> No *publick* good was sought, no *common* Cause:
> But all at war, each rang'd, each sought his food,
> By Nature taught to seek his *private* good;[120]

but there is actually no precedent in the source-text here[121] for Creech's thoroughly Hobbesian 'war', and if Lucretius does 'imagine men springing out of the *Earth*, as from the teeth of *Cadmus*', nonetheless they are not '*fierce, and cruel*' in a Hobbesian sense (that is, with respect to other men) as Creech implies in his notes.[122]

Creech's hostility to Epicureanism stems from his eagerness to display his Tory credentials. He may have been compiling the notes to this edition in Oxford at precisely the time that the third 'Exclusion Parliament' was meeting there. In his *De Rerum* he condemns covenanting theories such as Hobbes's and Lucretius's—the kind of theories favoured by Whigs—because they maintain that a governor derives his authority from public consent, whereas he argues instead (with Filmer) that '*Power* descends from *above*', bestowed directly by God.[123] In Creech's mind this patriarchal outlook promises a degree of political stability absent in the philosophies of those Hobbists and Lucretians who attribute the rise of society to 'leagues and combinations':

Now if *Societies* began thus, tis evident that they are founded on *Interest* alone, and therefore *self preservation* is the only thing that obliges Subjects to Duty; and when they are strong enough to live without the protection of their *Prince*, all the bonds to *Obedience* are cancell'd, and … *Rebellion* will … break forth; for

---

[118] Lucretius 1682: sig. b2ᵛ. [119] Ibid. sig. b3ᵛ. [120] Ibid. 169.
[121] Lucretius 1937: 408. [122] Lucretius 1682: Notes, 39. [123] Ibid. Notes, 41.

we all know, how ambitious every man is of Rule .... And why should his *Conscience* startle at wickedness, that is attended with pleasure? since all *Epicurean* vertues are nothing but *Fear*, and *Interest*, and the *former* is remov'd, and the latter invites.[124]

Against a background of 'Exclusion Crisis' politics, the contemporary pertinence of this argument must have been clear; and if Creech opposed Lucretius's work because he associated it with Whig political theory, he may well also have associated it with dissolute, unchecked libertinism precisely because it was the Whiggish, anti-Yorkist wits who, amidst the court world of the 1670s, most commonly appeared as debauched voluptuaries. Whatever the explanation for his hostility, though, the perception which Creech's last comment above reveals is his awareness that Hobbists and Epicureans alike make self-interest man's primary motive. That principle (which takes us right back to Bacon, *Troilus*, and a host of Jacobean tragedies) provides, therefore, an apt note on which to conclude this sketch of the textual traditions which furnished the intellectual background to English libertinism.

I began this chapter by outlining something of the rioting and bed hopping which went on amongst the privileged classes in Charles II's court and which was intrinsic to Restoration libertinism. Granted, Buckingham's 'merry gang' exercised some degree of self-restraint: crimes as serious as the Downs affair were infrequent, and Rochester, Savile, and others were, besides, good enough to flee the court when propriety demanded it. Nevertheless, such Falstaffian abuse of 'cobweb laws',[125] all in the service of appetite and self-interest, did amount to a re-creation of something like the state of nature within, and against the grain of, society,[126] and Charles, far from checking this tendency, lent the Rochester circle his protection. At least one line of inquiry which so extraordinary a development provokes is the question of how the court wits (and those who followed their fashionable example) represented such behaviour to themselves. Under what descriptions did they present their actions in the literature of the day? And how did that literature relate to the various earlier, often Continental traditions outlined hitherto in this chapter? These are awkward questions to answer, since the recorded evidence celebrating *English* libertine ideals is generally either satirical (and thus implicitly hostile to its material), or is cast in a voice which mingles mockery, self-criticism, even penitence, with an air of amused (indeed

---

[124] Lucretius 1682: Notes, 39–40.

[125] The phrase comes from another satire on Monmouth's murderous assault on the Holborn beadle, 'On the Three Dukes Killing the Beadle', l. 42 (Lord 1963–75: i. 174).

[126] Mintz 1962: 139–40, 142; Chernaik 1995: 24.

'cavalier') insouciance. The anonymous 'I Rise at Eleven, I Dine about Two' and Radcliffe's 'The Ramble' offer two blunt examples of the latter.[127] They present *images* of a dissolute life—*poses* rather than an exact reality—which seem both to expose their tawdry visions for derision and to celebrate their extravagance, this as if the author in each case were inclined at once to relinquish and reassert his hedonistic addictions. On either reading, though, these poems are relatively slight. More lavish and more informative, for all their equally parodic exaggeration, are Shadwell's *The Libertine* (again a work which only half-heartedly satirizes its protagonists) and Oldham's 'Ode' of 1676, 'A Satyr Against Vertue'.[128] The latter, especially, reveals a good deal about how English libertinism portrayed itself.

Oldham's persona, 'a Court-Hector' (implicitly Rochester, since this persona, like the real Earl, has a taste for breaking sundials), is quick to rail against conventional morals, psychomachic and otherwise. Besides quipping at contemporary 'sniveling Puritan[s]' (this via an attack on Socrates (l. 99) ), he also derides divines of the established Church, calling them 'gown'd Impostors' and moral hypocrites (l. 150). He reserves particular vitriol for the school of Aristotelian virtue ethics propounded at the time even in latitudinarian works like Henry More's *Enchiridion Ethicum*. Such morals, he claims, are designed 'to fetter free-born Souls' (l. 2) and destine men to a life of self-torment akin to that berated by Des Barreaux (ll. 58–63). Reflecting on the fact that the goal established by this Christian scholastic tradition is 'an hard unpracticable Good' (l. 53), Oldham's libertine responds by inverting such received moral idioms. 'No *prudent* Heathen ere *seduc'd* could be / To suffer Martyrdom' for such an ethic (ll. 95–6), he avers, thereby wittily figuring Christian 'Vertue' as a loose seductress (l. 56). Martyrs to her cause are said to bleed '*prodigally*' for her (l. 93). Aristotelians, in a similarly delicious attack, are accused of 'debauch[ing] the World with their Lewd Pedantry' (l. 12). Over and against this, only the libertine heathen should be reckoned truly 'prudent'—prudent in the same functional sense in which Hobbesian instrumental reasoning makes man prudent. The Christian ascetic ideal is (as it was in *Bussy d'Ambois*) 'Too difficult for Flesh and Blood' (l. 54). 'Were [man] all Soul' (l. 55), it might be realizable, but since, true to Montaigne's wisdom, his is a 'commixt condition', it is not. Oldham's persona therefore celebrates instead 'we, whose active Pulses beat / With lusty Youth and vigorous Heat' (ll. 111–12), appetitious heroes who 'have not yet the Leisure to be Good' (l. 119). Here (again as in Théophile's 'Satyre') the constant, imperative momentum of the body's desires override any other principle of governance. To be a libertine is thus to live naturally, according to the 'Rule of Sence' and forceful, corporeal

---

[127] Rochester 1999: 274 ff., and Love 1968: 47 ff.    [128] Oldham 1987: 56 ff.

instincts (l. 20). To be a libertine is also, though, to be forever 'unconcern'd at Epithets of Ill or Good, / Distinctions, unadult'rate Nature never understood' (ll. 24–5). This Court-Hector, like the Monmouth character in 'Upon the Beadle', regrets losing touch with the Hobbesian state of nature. He regrets that individual 'Pow'r', 'Will', and 'primitive Liberty' have given way to collective slavery before 'each caprichious Monarch's Tyranny' (ll. 13–19), and in his own mind he reverses that social contract.

The libertine assault on conventional virtue takes one further step though: Oldham's Court-Hector (like Théophile in his 'Satyre', Rochester in his 'Epilogue' to *Circe* (ll. 14–16),[129] or Nemours in *The Princess of Cleve* (IV. iii. 14–19) )[130] attacks the *hypocrisy* of conventional moralists. Man, so the persona argues, should not lose sight of the fact that ascetic 'virtuousness' is but 'a fair Pretence' claimed by the agèd once 'sprightly Vice' has retreated from their bodies (ll. 125–7). Being no longer capable of good living, and feeling jealous of those who still are, they artlessly cheer themselves up by condemning that naturalism and calling their own sapless condition 'virtue'—this, an act of self-deception of the kind to which the libertine now thinks himself impervious. The Christian conscience is, in a more general sense too, said to be founded on delusion. Far from being an inner measure of God's transcendental values, it really registers only cowardly fear, man's fear of punishment by the authorities should he break the law (ll. 142–9).[131] As part of his larger strategy of inversion, the Court-Hector counterbalances this accusation of pusillanimity with an affirmation of his own heroism. Appropriating and implicitly redefining a key term in the vocabulary of moral approbation, the persona figures himself as the bearer of Aristotelian *megalopsychia* ('greatness of soul'):

> A true and brave Transgressor ought
> To sin with the same *Height of Spirit* Caesar fought.
> *Mean-soul'd* Offenders now no Honour gain,
> Only Debauches of the nobler Strain.

> (stanza 7, ll. 167–70)

The Hector matches, therefore, the 'gen'rous fury' satirically attributed to Monmouth in 'Upon the Beadle'. Indeed, he will be moved to just such 'gen'erous Fire' a hundred or so lines later (l. 251). In the meantime, though, three increasingly outrageous stanzas (8–10) present a hagiography of supposedly libertine 'sinners'—Herostratus, Nero, Guy Fawkes, Lucifer—whose 'glorious Mischief' the persona seeks to transcend (ll. 257, 290). There is an

---

[129] Rochester 1999: 122.    [130] References to this play are to Lee 1955: vol. ii.
[131] Don John *et al.* pursue this same Hobbesian vein at the beginning of *The Libertine* (I. i. 1–14). References to this play are to Manning 2001.

obvious parallel here with *The Libertine*: that play's Don Antonio would also emulate Herostratus (v. i. 54–8), and Shadwell's libertines end their tragedy in an inverse apotheosis, being absorbed (Faustus-like) into a company of devils whilst revelling in their rejection of Christian values.

The 'Ode's' hagiography, though, and, still more, the absurd exaggerations of stanza 11—'We're the great *Roya'l Society* of Vice, / … / … I, the bold Columbus … / Who must new Worlds in Vice descry' (ll. 269–73)—make clear a problem of tone in the poem, hints of which are already apparent as early as line 51 ('haughty scornful I') or in the absurdly portentous line 88 ('the Manhood and Discretion of Debauchery'). Oldham's 'Satyr' is built around some sort of genuine belief that the self should attend to its own 'Flesh and Blood', to the individual, passionate, and self-centred body; but the *limits* of that ethic become crucially unclear as the poem develops and its tone evolves. Over time, the persona's hubris and his increasingly frenzied contemplation of a career in sin grow ever more comical, underlining the fact that Oldham's satire is not, straightforwardly, a versified declaration of a sincerely held doctrine so much as it is a rhetorical gesture. Its truest function—and the same could be said of several Rochester poems—is simply to represent daringness of vision, to launch a deliberate assault on moral norms, the intention being more to repel the conventionally minded and weak-spirited than to proselytize for some elaborate atheists' creed. If the poem exudes a sense of ease and delight at its own outrageousness, this points more to Oldham's Suckling-like pleasure in repelling the majority—a pleasure shared as an in-joke with the Buckingham circle[132]—than it does to any sense of conviction. Conviction must, anyway, be in doubt in Oldham's case, since in 1681 he claimed to have written this piece solely to satirize the attitude it ventriloquizes,[133] besides which he also wrote 'A Counterpart to the Satyr' and 'An Apology', investing the last dozen lines of the latter, especially, with as much wit and intensity as were present in the original 'Ode':

> Had he [the reformed poet of this 'Apology'] a Genius and Poetique Rage,
> Great as the Vices of this guilty Age;
>
> .    .    .    .    .    .    .    .    .    .    .    .
>
> He'd shoot his Quills, just like a Porcupine,
> At Vice, and make 'em stab in ev'ry Line.

(ll. 63–70)[134]

If we were to 'believe' *these* poems, we could not 'believe' in the original 'Satyr'. It would have to be read, like Creech's Lucretius, as a sketch to help us know

---

[132] Buckingham *et al.* challenged Oldham (through his patron, Sir Nicholas Carew) to write a poem *against* virtue to match one he had already written for it (Burns 1995: 188–9).
[133] Oldham 1987: 4.          [134] Ibid. 68 ff.

our enemy. But then again, there are lines in the 'Apology' which cut against its pious argument. Of his here allegedly reformed Muse, Oldham notes dryly that she has turned 'a modest civil Girle' once more (l. 15); and if that seems coy, bathetical, or downright demeaning, the poet's self-declared intent 'never' again 'to make his End Delight' (l. 55) also invites suspicions of irony (presumably he 'hopes' his future work will be plain boring). Nor can Oldham suppress the urge to indulge in a little innuendo here: the idea that lewd poets '*spend* at Quill' (l. 42) is hardly the image of a reformed imagination.

The point, I think, of these oscillations and instabilities is really to underline Oldham's sense that performance, and the possession of a 'labile psyche'[135] *capable* of performing conflicting poses, are themselves integral features of libertinism (whether in Oldham's own poetry, Rochester's, or indeed Marlowe's). The ability to assume divergent positions (including those which are anathema to the moral majority) is, after all, a natural product of freethinking, itself an implicit part of libertinism. It is precisely this 'negative capability' which the dogmatist cannot rise to: he cannot imagine the world from the hedonist's point of view; he cannot—as Lucy and Clarendon could not do—make sense of Hobbes on Hobbes's own terms. If Oldham's tone, then, is shifting, this is surely part of his purpose, a quality intrinsic to the libertine stance (at least as English writers interpreted it). The great social danger posed by the libertine is that, outside his own intimate circle, others do not know how far he will go. They do not know when (and when not) to take him seriously. To say this is not to *deny* that the naturalist ethic avowed in Oldham's 'Satyr' accurately represents the outlook of English court libertines. (I do not mean to imply, in light of the poem's hyperbole, that the 'Satyr Against Vertue' is all humour and no substance. On the contrary, the exaggeration masks a bedrock of substantive beliefs.) Rather, to say that one cannot quite detect where polemical argument ends and ludic self-parody[136] begins, is simply to emphasize that the extent of libertine attitudes—the limits of 'immoral' action to which libertines might really go in the service of their beliefs—was known only to the coterie of initiates for whom Oldham wrote. For others, the boundary between robust self-assertion and a simply teasing exaggeration designed to rile conservative opinion—the boundary, too, between self-assertion and self-mockery—was forever unclear.[137]

---

[135] Selden, in Burns 1995: 202. My comments here are inspired by Selden's stimulating essay.

[136] Both Vieth and Selden note how far Rochester, Buckhurst, and others enjoyed playing up to their popular image as debauchees. Selden further observes (Burns 1995: 190–1) that, whilst that aristocratic pose may have been beyond schoolmaster Oldham's reach in social terms, his 'Ode' nevertheless exudes all the *frisson* of one abandoning himself to wickedness—or at least (in Barthesian fashion) to the signifiers thereof.

[137] On the performance of libertinism, see also Webster 2005: 1–36. On the relevance of class dimensions to this question, see Turner 2002: 232–4.

Oldham's 'Satyr Against Vertue' thus raises the specific problem of limits. In toying with the boundary between the fashioning of libertine myths and the description of libertine realities, in 'blurring the distinction between irony and sincerity',[138] it dramatizes an essential theme in the self-representation of English libertinism. But another of Oldham's poems, his 'Dithyrambique on Drinking',[139] points to a further idea also relevant to the Restoration libertine's self-image. The persona of the 'Dithyrambique' ('Suppos'd to be ... Rochester') determines not to waste a minute of his existence but to put all time to use in pursuit of bibulous pleasure (l. 10). Life's journey being tedious, he aims to make it seem shorter by reaping every joy he can (ll. 20–1). Inevitably, this *carpe diem* mentality, arising as it does from an anxious sense that every minute lost is 'Slipt by and ne're to be retriev'd' (l. 56), promotes a corresponding preoccupation with forward motion. 'Life with standing [still] ... is pal'd' (l. 59). The libertine must 'Push on' with his drinks 'And never rest, till his last Race be done' (ll. 61–8). The pattern of thought here, shifting from what has ebbed away to what must be grasped now, and the specific sentiment articulated in line 56, are immediately reminiscent of Des Barreaux's poetry. The 'Race' image likewise recalls Hobbes. In keeping with those precursors, this libertine embraces the ideal of constant forward momentum. He founds his Cyrenaic notion of 'governance' on this 'brisk' principle (l. 94), and in so doing eschews traditional ideas of 'tottring Reason' prone to 'check' our motion (ll. 89, 93). Charles Cotton's 'Clepsydra'[140] (another ventriloquizing performance) presents a further, more subtle meditation on this same ideal. In the opening lines of his lyric, Cotton's persona immediately relativizes the passage of time, arguing that whilst for some it 'creeps away' in the monotonous turning of the water clock, for his own drinking circle it 'posts' forward in endless rounds of sack (ll. 3–4). Urging his addressee to 'set thy foot, brave Boy, to mine' (l. 9), he indicates that again the prevailing image here is one of racing ever forwards, making the sun run, so to speak. That said, though, Cotton then introduces a paradox. Traditional 'temp'rance' may be unable to 'stay' such motion (l. 44), but those who 'love good time' (l. 25) and post forward with him, matching his fast pace with their own (l. 17), can, in a relative sense, make time wait upon them (l. 21). The root idea here, as in Oldham, is of living each moment and its pleasures to the full, but Cotton (sometime translator of Montaigne's *Essais*) turns precisely to 'De l'Experience' for an idiom in which to express this point. His ideal is that time 'lives' (in every sense of that word) with those 'That *husband* it, and *taste* it' (l. 32)—this (as we have already seen), Montaigne's vocabulary for savouring, and (so far as consciousness can) arresting, the relish of life. *Time*, on this understanding,

[138] Burns 1995: 190.    [139] Oldham 1987: 260 ff.    [140] Love 1968: 41 ff.

becomes 'the *space* / That men enjoy their being' in (ll. 37–8), and what form that space takes is theirs to define. For his part, Cotton imagines a pivotal moment in which Epicurus's static and kinetic pleasures coincide in a single sensation, an ideal that few other libertine personae will manage to emulate. But this aside, what Cotton and Oldham both stress is that, for libertines, hurtling motion is always a vital component in the moral imagination.

These, then, are some of the terms in which English wits and libertines articulated their lifestyle, but the next question which this material provokes is why it was that a coterie amongst Charles's courtiers came to espouse these beliefs or fashion themselves in such terms—this, the second major theme of this chapter.

## THE SOCIAL AND POLITICAL ORIGINS OF RESTORATION LIBERTINISM

In 1660 Charles and his courtiers re-established the court in London in the face of an Interregnum dominated by religious idealism and Puritan morals. Given that truism, historians of the Restoration have traditionally interpreted the rise of libertinism as a knee-jerk reaction against Cromwellian asceticism.[141] However, the court was re-established, too, against the background of an exposure to Hobbism, a range of French *libertin* writings, and various emergent forms of Epicureanism. These diverse influences (along with more long-standing traditions of court rivalry reaching back to Tacitism and beyond)[142] offered a doubtless exaggerated picture of the part played by self-interest in shaping human actions. And yet these textual traditions, coming to the fore as they did within the context of events of the 1650s and 1660s (in particular the Royalist experience of exclusion and economic hardship[143]), were bound, thereby, to appear all too applicable to recent facts of life. To the mind of a Restoration Royalist resentful of recent history, accounts of human nature emphasizing egotism and a cynicism about motivations must have seemed peculiarly reminiscent of reality itself. If we concentrate for a moment just on such attitudes to history as were current in the early 1660s, it is clear that contemporary reflections on both the Interregnum and the management of the Restoration settlement resonated with precisely those sketches of psychology to be found in Hobbes, Des Barreaux, and others.

To begin, first, with reflections on the Interregnum, it is clear that recriminations and accusations of past disloyalty were commonplace in the years

[141] See, e.g., Bryson 1998: 256–7; Keeble 2002: 172.
[142] See, e.g., Whigham 1984: *passim*, esp. 48–9 and chs. 4–5.
[143] On the latter, see Smith 2003: 71–2, 93–114.

immediately after 1660, particularly amongst those Royalists who now dressed themselves as ever-faithful supporters of the King. In the 1650s these same individuals had responded all too variously to defeat. According to Clarendon, some young men at that time had 'inherited their [late] fathers' maligni-ty' and were 'impatient to revenge their death[s], or ... be even with their oppressors'.[144] The loyalty of Cavaliers of this hue, Clarendon implies, was based less on principle than on an impassioned, personal concern for vengeance; but the discovery of those rebellious activities in which such men participated (not least the disastrous 1655 conspiracy) gave Cromwell's Major-Generals the occasion 'to exercise greater tyranny upon the *whole* par-ty, in imprisonments, ... sequestrations', and (especially in 1655) decimation taxes. Consequently, a different kind of Royalist, men who 'desired to be quiet, and ... abhorred ... rash ... insurrection', were made to 'pay their full shares of the folly of the [former sort]'. Those of this latter, 'wiser and more sober part' (who 'had yet preserved or redeemed enough of their fortunes to sit still and expect some hopeful revolution') therefore inveighed against the others who had 'disturbed their peace'; whilst those others in their turn reviled these trimmers as 'men who had spent all ... stock of allegiance, and meant to acquiesce with ... tyranny'. Even in the midst, then, of the Interregnum, Royalists invested their energy in mutual recrimination, conservatives accus-ing insurrectionists of imprudence, whilst insurrectionists cast conservatives as self-serving—and that the latter charge had some force is apparent in the testimonies of those who advocated compounding. The guilt is palpable in Buckingham's voice as he urges Newcastle to make his own peace in England: 'for certaynly your Lordship's suffering for the K. has beene great enough to excuse you if you looke a little after your self now, when neither hee is able to assist you, nor you in a possibility of doing him service'.[145] Looking a little after oneself had uncomfortable implications for the Royalist's sense of identity and reputation. Buckingham himself returned to England prematurely, in 1657, and as a result was haunted in later life by balladeers who accused him of treason—'the Papers of Old Oliver ... can tell when and where'.[146]

After the Restoration, recriminations grounded on just such accusations multiplied. According to Clarendon, those who made their way in Charles's court during succeeding years were 'full of bitter reflections upon the actions ... of [each] other, or of excuses ... for themselves for what they thought might be charged upon them',[147] and this was the more true because in 1660 itself there was a flurry of self-interested activity by relatives and well-wishers seeking indemnity for selected republicans. As Hutton observes, Colonel

---

[144] Clarendon 1978: 377.     [145] Quoted in Tuck 1993: 323.
[146] Quoted in Buckingham 1985: 338.     [147] Clarendon 1978: 378.

Hutchinson escaped with his life 'through the efforts of friends',[148] whilst his fellow regicide, Heveningham, was also safeguarded by the Privy Council 'out of respect for his grandfather-in-law'. The Act of Indemnity and Oblivion was designed to foreclose reflection on such matters, 'extinguishing … Fear' and creating 'kindness in us to … our joynt … security'.[149] In September 1660 Clarendon warned of severe penalties for any who 'presume malitiously to … object against any other person … names, or … words of reproach, any way leading to revive the memory of … late differences'.[150] These sentiments, though, were scarcely heeded. Butler's 1661 ballad 'The Turn-Coat' cast its spotlight on precisely those faceless many who had 'loved no King since forty-one' but were now eager to 'pray for any' in order to 'gain / The people's admiration'.[151] True to libertine assumptions, then, the recent past was full of murky corners in which passion and self-interest had overruled principle. No courtier could ignore that fact.

If reflections on the Interregnum provoked a cynicism about human nature, though, so did perceptions of the management of the Restoration settlement itself. Whereas many expected 1660 to provide an opportunity for vengeance, the actual settlement, far from monopolizing power in the hands of loyalists, gave twelve seats in Charles's new Privy Council to Cromwellians.[152] Five ministerial and royal household offices also went to the Crown's former opponents. Only about half of the Army's regiments were transferred back to old Royalist commanders, and at most levels of administration, from county benches down to constables, the same even-handed approach prevailed. As Hutton shows, numerous Royalists did receive baronetcies, knighthoods, or pensions, but, equally, the greatest beneficiaries of the Restoration were the Cromwellians who had brought it about, Monck (made Duke of Albemarle) and Mountagu (made Earl of Sandwich).[153] Between these two extremes lay a host of impoverished King's-men who received nothing, whilst their sometime opponents profited. For them, one of the most contentious sources of resentment was the question of land ownership.

In 1660 the Parliamentary Convention quickly restored to the royal family all Crown lands confiscated during the Commonwealth, and it also muddled its way towards a settlement concerning alienated Church property.[154] Yet at the same time parliamentarians avoided legislating to redress the losses which private individuals had suffered—the losses of Royalists, for example, who had had their lands confiscated or sold by the Interregnum authorities

---

[148] Hutton 1985: 133.     [149] Quoted in Scott 2000: 410, 424.     [150] Ibid. 394.
[151] Mackay 1863: 231–2.     [152] On this and subsequent points, see Hutton 1985: 127–31.
[153] Ibid. 137–8.     [154] Ibid. 139–42.

because they had been convicted of delinquency or treason.[155] Equally, the
Convention decided to accept as legally binding all voluntary sales made under
the Commonwealth even if the only reason why a given Cavalier had sold
his property was because he needed to pay composition fees and decimation
taxes or was funding the King's war effort. Granted, as Morrill and others
have demonstrated, a substantial proportion of those who initially lost out in
these ways were able to recover their lands (often through indirect repurchase)
before the Restoration.[156] However, even for these lucky parties, 1660 brought
no reparation for the trouble they had been through, no compensation for
the memory and indignity of their having had to submit to a new class of
bureaucrats whom the sequestration process threw into prominence.[157] Nor
was there government help, now, for those who had *not* hitherto succeeded in
making good their losses. The latter were forced either to seek redress through
individual lawsuits or to submit petitions and private bills to the Commons
and Lords (as, for example, Lord Newport did in arguing before the Lords
that his family had only sold their Shropshire assets to pay a £10,000 fine, and
should not now see past 'loyalty' treated as if it were a 'crime'[158]). In practice,
eleven key figures did prevail in getting their estates restored in 1660;[159] but
success in this matter depended upon individual claimants' influence. The Earl
of Derby's several efforts to push through a Lords bill returning to him lands
that he had previously sold, met with repeated failure (eventually because the
King himself refused assent).[160] The opposition to Derby came especially from
Clarendon and a collection of ex-Presbyterians and ex-Cromwellians, the very
people whose continued prosperity Cavaliers most resented, and who had a
vested interest in resisting restitution.[161] In sum, then, whilst the Crown and
assorted magnates won back past losses, the rank and file of Royalists (and
some peers besides) either did not or had to suffer trials and indignities before
they prevailed. The very people who had put their own funds towards the
King's war effort lost out in 1660 at the moment of anticipated vengeance. In
their eyes, notoriously, the Act of Indemnity and Oblivion was one of oblivion
for Charles's friends and indemnity for his enemies.

   Evidence of immediate Cavalier discontent at the settlement was widespread.
Lord Bristol complained that 'the wickedest ... people' had been 'rewarded
for their treasons', resting 'triumphant in [their] spoils' whilst 'the blood
of ... virtuous ... Peers [cried] loud for vengeance'.[162] In 1661 Roger L'Estrange
described in his 'Caveat to the Cavaliers' a court now 'dangerously throng'd
with *Parasites: Knaves* represented ... for *Honest* men, and *Honest* men for

---

[155] J. R. Jones 1978: 135–6.   [156] Morrill 1992: 97–9.
[157] On this class, see Hirst 1986: 259–60.   [158] Feiling 1924: 100–1.
[159] Hutton 1985: 142.   [160] Ibid. 142, 163.   [161] Seaward 1989: 202–3.
[162] Quoted in Feiling 1924: 99.

*Villeins*.[163] Such protests, directed against the still powerful Presbyterian interest, were audible even in 1664;[164] and these same themes are pressed home in the Restoration songs, 'The Cavaleers Litany', 'The Cavalier's Complaint', and Brome's 'The Cavalier'. Royal pardons now 'entitle thieves to keep our goods', so sing the malcontents of these texts; Parliament denies even 'one tax' to compensate the 'Cavaleers'; the King lacks the judgement to divine who amongst his followers join for love, who 'for fear, or … design', but those who 'on their bodies bear the markes / Of … integritie' dare not, anyway, appear at court 'For want of coyne and cuffes'.[165] So the ballads continue. A pamphlet such as the *Humble Representation of the Sad Condition of … the Kings Party* (1661), written specifically for Royalist soldiers,[166] sounds the same notes. It begins by anatomizing the losses suffered by Cavaliers, protesting that martyrdom deserves a better reward, and hinting at the collapse to come if such grievances are not heeded: 'How will it discourage our tender Plants of Loyalty, to be Spectators of … Ruine ! How will it multiply Neuters to observe noble Families extirpated, and their Estates possessed.'[167] The pamphlet then pleads for a vengeful programme of restitution, one which will exclude from His Majesty's party those who have previously 'betraied' him, and which gives the King the right to command that 'Vacant Employments' within the kingdom should be filled by those of his loyal servants who are currently destitute.[168] The fantasy pursued is thus one of a special, exclusive relationship between King and King's-man, one which sets the latter apart from the majority. Such aspirations were not, of course, heeded. In 1665 Sir James Bunch could still complain to Pepys, 'Aye … this is the time for you … that were for Oliver heretofore; you are full of imployment, and we poor Cavaliers … can get nothing.'[169]

These, then, were two of the preoccupations exciting a mood of cynicism amongst Royalists of the early 1660s, this at the very moment when most of Wilson's 'court wits' stepped, for the first time, on to the political stage. Buckingham excepted, the wits themselves were but youths during the Commonwealth, witnesses to, rather than participants in, the events of the Interregnum; yet they certainly cultivated a consciousness of others' past self-interestedness in their writings. Sedley's *Mulberry Garden* (1668), for example, makes comic capital out of those same Cromwellians-turned-monarchists on whom Butler had focused in his 1661 'Turn-Coat'. Whilst the play's Cavalier exiles, Eugenio and Philander, are eulogized for their sincere patriotism (I. iv. 34–49), the turn-coat, Puritanical Sir Samuel Forecast, is satirized, first, as one

[163] Quoted in Keeble 2002: 82.     [164] Seaward 1989: 211.
[165] Mackay 1863: 205–12, *passim*.
[166] On their fate, see Seaward 1989: 208–9; Smith 2003: 193–5.     [167] Anon. 1661: 3, 6, 7.
[168] Ibid. 10.     [169] Pepys 1987: 562 (15 Dec. 1665).

whose past support for sequestration was driven by petty vengefulness (II. i. 24–30), and second, as one who, at the moment of the Restoration, capitalized on chance occurrences to repaint himself as a loyal Cavalier of old (IV. ii. 190–200; v. iii. 43–59).[170] Rochester's protagonist in 'Timon' (1674) likewise glances caustically at the gap between his dinner host's proclaimed past loyalty to the Royalist cause and the man's actual loyalty to his own interests. Since 'mine Host'

> Had beene a Collonell, wee must heare him boast
> Not of Townes won, but an Estate he lost,
> For the Kings service; which indeed he spent,
> Whoreing and drinking, but with good intent.
>
> (ll. 95–9)[171]

Again, Wycherley, writing as late as 1676, can still satirize the self-proclaimed Royalist Oldfox as one 'for the king and parliament: for the parliament in their list and for the king in cheating 'em of their pay and never hurting the king's party in the field' (*Plain Dealer*, III. i. 698–701).[172] Such remarks, coming more than a decade after 1660, indicate how potent a thought the recognition of past egotism could be in the minds of court wits.

Those same writers had some reason to be conscious, too, of the impact of Interregnum sequestration on their family fortunes. Buckingham's estates were sequestered in 1645, and his mansion at Burley burned by Parliamentary troops. He sustained himself during the 1650s by selling artworks from York House and by borrowing heavily. Lady Sedley, Charles Sedley's mother, likewise became 'ingulphed in the usurer's books'.[173] Repeatedly during the 1640s she and Charles's elder brother had to defend themselves before Parliament's Committee for Advance of Money, further to which her Ladyship was arrested at least once.[174] Like Rochester's mother,[175] Lady Sedley also had to petition the Committee of Sequestration for the return of seized properties, this both in 1645 and probably also in 1651. There were then further trials for the family in 1657 when the young Charles Sedley, now living in Kent, seems to have had his movements restricted by the Protectorate.[176] In practice, though, the tribulations scarring the family memories of Charles II's future rakes should not be overestimated. Buckingham actually recovered much of his property by way of a dowry when he married Fairfax's daughter in 1657, and the rest of his estates were restored to him in 1660. Hence he personally had no reason to lament the Restoration settlement. Nor did Buckhurst,

---

[170] References to this play are to Sedley 1928.    [171] Rochester 1999: 258 ff.
[172] All references to Wycherley's plays are to Wycherley 1981.
[173] Quoted in Pinto 1927: 33.    [174] Ibid. 30–5.    [175] Greer 2000: 10.
[176] Pinto 1927: 46–7.

whose parents seem not to have suffered during the Interregnum and whose own biography after the King's return is, anyway, one of prosperity, often courtesy of Charles himself.[177] Lady Rochester, too, was modestly successful during the early 1660s, soliciting financial favour for her children from both Charles and Clarendon.[178] If, then, the cynicism which propelled Rochester *et al.* into libertinism was provoked by a feel for the tawdriness of England's recent past, we can hypothesize that the wits' consciousness of this was at least as much the product of an imaginative identification with the sufferings of Royalist aristocrats in general as it was of their own first-hand experience. Buckhurst, for instance, might have had difficulty highlighting ways in which he personally suffered during the Interregnum, but he could certainly sense the affront, the indignity, done to his class as a whole. Hence his drinking catch 'When rebels first push'd at the Crown' bespeaks the shame not of himself but of an entire class of Royalists, all of them reduced to impotence under the Commonwealth: 'Both prick and prelate then went down. / No men to fucking were inclin'd' (ll. 2–3).[179] A whole natural order has, by implication, been violated here with Parliament's intrusion into the proper rights of birth and privilege. For Buckhurst it is the generic affront, not an individual experience, which haunts the mind in its cups.

   If, though, distaste for past hypocrisies and political compromises was more an abstract idea than a concrete memory in the minds of the wits, there is one other factor which *was* directly experienced by all of them, a consideration which again helps to explain their turn towards libertinism. According to Clarendon, ever the Malvolio amidst Charles's belching, cavorting courtiers, the disruption to the moral upbringing of the young which the fractures of civil war produced had a determining influence upon Rochester and his kind. The collapse of the parent–child relationship in the absence of fathers allowed adolescent Cavaliers to get into the habit of doing whatever was 'good in [their] own eyes' (there being no king in Israel).[180] Their subsequent taste for libertine literature and its licensing of self-indulgence followed from that. This may seem like a dubiously high-minded explanation for later behaviour, but it is true that the fathers of Henry Savile and Fleetwood Sheppard, for example, were killed (or died) in arms, and that Etherege and Rochester, being brought up in England, could scarcely have known their exiled fathers (who died abroad in the 1650s). Furthermore, Evelyn, Dorothy Osborne, and even Buckingham himself offered explanations for the contemporary growth of dissolute habits which closely complement Clarendon's own.

---

[177] See, e.g., Harris 1940: 20, 36–42, 50–2, 65–6.
[178] J. W. Johnson 2004: 55–7.          [179] Dorset 1979: 49.
[180] Clarendon 1978: 380. Clarendon is alluding to Judg. 17: 6 and 21: 25.

Osborne observed that the 'want of a Court to govern themselves by' was one 'cause of [young gentlemen's] ruin' in the 1650s.[181] Buckingham ascribed his debauchery to his being 'banishd' from England during the very years of his life which should have been 'the cheif time of strict Education', years when a young man 'can hardly resist ... dangerous impressions' which it is 'difficult ... afterwards to get rid of'.[182] Hence it was, he said, that he 'learnt ... customes and qualities ... not agreeable to the ... modest temper of the English Nation'. Evelyn, meantime, attributed the inadequacies in the self-governance of *domiciled* English aristocrats to their 'having no standard at Court', indeed no domestic royal court at all, 'which should give Lawes, and do countenance to ... fashion'.[183] Writing in 1659, he further lamented that 'most of these great persons'—the aristocracy—'are in their minority, ... the age wherein they should be furnished with the noblest impressions', but are instead 'taught onely to converse with their servants'.[184] To minds schooled in ideas of habituation, it was self-evident that the Court's proper function was to provide a guiding structure within which children of the nobility could learn to emulate their elders' decorous, virtuous habits. During the Interregnum, though, the court-in-exile provided limited opportunities for service even for those who could afford to attend upon it. Many exiled fathers left their families behind in England. Compounding Royalists, meanwhile, lived a retired life at home. In both these cases children were thus deprived of their traditional social forum. Sons were left to mark time amidst the security of taverns instead, environments which encouraged 'the liberty of vice, without reprehension or restraint'.[185]

If these sources are correct, then, social dislocation played some part in shaping the attitudes of Rochester *et al.*, since amongst the latter's peer group the lawlessness and egocentrism of youth were not checked as they might have been. The 'merry gang's' later libertinism can thus be read as a continuation of bad habits, of that rebellious, self-indulgent manner adopted by young Royalists in the 1650s when their age and political affiliations rendered them excluded, and when it therefore seemed appropriate to assume a devil-may-care attitude to the world. Socialization within the restrictive environment of the Court might have sublimated this adolescent disposition, turning it to better things; but in the absence of such a Court we may assume that young Cavaliers found themselves feeling conscious only of their detachment from society—indeed, of their detachment from a world rudely indifferent to their ancient birthrights and privileges. Such a predicament was bound to encourage them to turn in upon themselves. The habits of egotism formed

---

[181] Quoted in Bryson 1998: 256.   [182] Buckingham 1981: 169–70.
[183] Evelyn 1995: 85.   [184] Ibid. 86.   [185] Clarendon 1978: 378–9.

thus, at this stage, were afterwards, we may conjecture, too ingrained (and too gratifying) to drop. So it is not surprising that the tendency to do what was 'good in [one's] own eyes', which Clarendon attributed to alienated Royalists of the 1650s, can be seen again in the 'discontented Cavaliers' observed by Robert Blackburne in 1663: they too went about 'swearing ... cursing and stealing', each only 'looking after himself'.[186]

The wits' libertinism was more, though, than just the perpetuation of youthful rebelliousness. On to the latter was mapped a consciousness—perhaps deliberately cultivated—of those other factors which I have previously discussed. The story of Interregnum compromises and recriminations offered young Royalists an object lesson in the realities of motivation. It impressed upon them the primacy of self-interest in determining human conduct. And what the Interregnum taught, the Restoration emphasized still more acutely, since the structure of that settlement, too, was so obviously shaped by the vested interests of the moment, not by past loyalties. A young Savile or a young Rochester could fix upon these truths as proofs, justifications, for their own underlying sense of alienation. Since recent history itself seemed positively to *invite* cynicism, these rakes-in-the-making could see in that history an endorsement of such Hobbist attitudes as they had already developed in growing up fatherless and bereft of a royal court. Adolescent egotism thus became, under the influence of a wider post-Restoration cynicism, something altogether more intense: more hostile, resentful, and aggressively competitive; a mentality, therefore, of just the kind we associate with 'libertinism'. In an age when self-interestedness was suddenly so much in evidence, the decision mentally to shun political society, always to put one's own interests before others, must have seemed only natural. Furthermore, the perception that England had offered neither sufficient reparation nor sufficient penance in restoring its peers to their traditional position of primacy could only exacerbate underlying feelings of resentment. Aggrieved at such a fact, and yet consoled by the notion that egotism was now thoroughly justified, the wits could persuade themselves that the commonweal in fact owed them more than they owed it—even, that it was *right* to step outside the social covenant and exact for themselves vengeance and restitution from a society unworthy of respect. This intuition, I suggest, is the foundation of that unilateral permission of the will (and also of that edge of spiteful aggression and vengefulness) at the heart of court libertinism. It is the source, too, of that attitude which endorses a Hobbist disregard for political good order, indulging, instead, bodily appetites and competitive passions. The drunken Sedley was defiant when he taunted the mob from the balcony of the Cock tavern. So, likewise, was Buckingham when

---

[186] Pepys 1987: 320 (9 Nov. 1663).

he appeared at the première of Etherege's *She Would if She Could* just days after so seriously wounding Lord Shrewsbury. In both cases what is implicit in the men's actions is a vengeful contempt for society at large, a desire to provoke and punish, yet also remain aloof. In their libertine moments the wits' overriding impulse became one of living, in Rochester's phrase, 'chiefly out of spite',[187] and that disposition, I suggest, was born of bitter reflection upon the experiences of recent history.

Here, then, were the social and political conditions which triggered the rise of libertinism amongst the wits (and once that trend was established, other followers of fashion could delight in imitating it, if with less vim); but what, in the longer term, sustained this mood, particularly amongst the Buckingham coterie? One answer to that is certainly pleasure and the protection which the King afforded his 'counsellors of pleasure'; but another explanation lies in the fact that the sense of marginalization which originally produced libertinism became, thereafter, a recurrent feature of the Buckingham circle's experience. In the first place, Clarendon's and Arlington's domination of government between 1660 and 1667, latterly to the exclusion of Villiers, could only reinforce the wits' disenfranchised, separatist perspective. Clarendon had been blamed for the fact that the initial Restoration settlement favoured Cromwellian and Presbyterian interests, and he continued to be attacked in office as the perception grew that he was protecting his own interests at others' expense.[188] Hence, in his 1667 satire 'Clarendon's Housewarming' Marvell connected the alleged profiteering surrounding the construction of Clarendon House with accusations that Hyde had mismanaged the Indemnity Act to the detriment of loyal subjects' interests:

> Bulteel's, Beaken's, Morley's, Wren's fingers with telling
> > Were shrivelled, and Clutterbuck's, Eager's, and Kipp's;
> Since the Act of Oblivion was never such selling,
> > As at this benevolence out of the snips.
>
> (ll. 69–72)[189]

Line 71 here may refer to the illicit selling of pardons at the Restoration, or it may point to the fact that, because the 1660 Oblivion Act had for the time being endorsed all voluntary property sales made during the Interregnum, those who had acquired estates under those circumstances took this unexpected opportunity to sell up before any Parliamentary volte-face could deprive them of their gains. Either way, the insinuation is that just as a loyal majority had lost out at the Restoration, thanks to Clarendon, so now he was again

---

[187] Rochester 1980: 114.    [188] See Keeble 2002: 83, 97, 101.
[189] Marvell 2003: 355 ff. A 'benevolence' is a voluntary tax; 'snips' are perquisites; Bulteel *et al.* are Clarendon's underlings, here counting the profits from the Chancellor's exchequer dealings.

serving his own interests at others' expense. Crucially, Marvell juxtaposed this, Hyde's egotism, with the selfless 'sacrifice' of 'Great Buckingham' ('House-warming', l. 100). Though nominally a Privy Councillor from 1662 onwards, Buckingham showed little interest in Parliamentary politics during the early 1660s, but in 1664 Ormonde (Clarendon's ally) frustrated his attempt to become President of the North.[190] The following year the Chancellor himself blocked York's proposal (endorsed by Buckingham) to elevate George Savile to a peerage, this because the latter was of 'very ill Reputation amongst Men of Piety and Religion'. Hyde attacked, too, the 'Presumption' of Henry Savile, whom York had made a gentleman of his bedchamber.[191] For Buckingham, the Saviles, and their like, the price of Clarendon's ascendancy was thus their own marginalization, a marginalization akin to that already suffered by Cavaliers at the Restoration. Libertinism became appealing in this light, because it offered a means of resisting such treatment. It was, as Oldham's 'Satyr' demonstrates, a medium through which to mock the ruling forces of society, a way of asserting a threatening, unassailable separateness from the latter. In 1666, though, Buckingham also took more directly political action, in Marvell's words, '[daring] to ... rebel' against Hyde ('Last Instructions', l. 357). He did so by openly criticizing mismanagement of the Dutch war and by supporting the Irish Cattle Bill (to which Clarendon and the bishops were opposed).[192] He quickly paid the price, though, for crossing Clarendon, Arlington contriving a plot to convict him of treason and send him to the Tower.[193] Hence Marvell's reference above to the Duke's 'sacrifice'.

Eventually Buckingham proved his innocence, was returned to favour, and took a lead role in putting 'my Lord Chancellor upon his back, past ever getting up again'.[194] (So, incidentally, did Rochester, who attended debates on Hyde's impeachment and was a signatory on the Demurrer of November 1667 which advocated the latter's immediate arrest.[195]) However, although Buckingham now went on to enjoy prosperity as a minister of the cabal, events from 1673 onwards brought this to an end, propelling him and his circle back into exclusion and thus refuelling that resentful, separatist outlook to which, again, libertinism gave expression. In March 1673 Charles, finding himself under pressure from an anti-tolerationist Commons, and yet in need of fresh finances, was forced to rescind his Declaration of Indulgence (a measure guaranteeing religious liberty). The Commons, sensing that the initiative was theirs, determined to put into law a Test Act which would force Catholics out of office. They also held up the government's supply bill, and in the autumn

---

[190] J. H. Wilson 1954: 48.     [191] On both incidents, see Treglown 1982: 99–100.
[192] J. H. Wilson 1954: 49–50.     [193] Ibid. 58–77.     [194] Quoted in Keeble 2002: 99.
[195] Greer 2000: 15; J. W. Johnson 2004: 99.

revolted over the news that York had chosen a Catholic wife. Amidst this fractious atmosphere, the collapse of the cabal became inevitable: Buckingham was the third of its ministers to fall. In January 1674 the Lords heard a petition against his cohabitation with Countess Shrewsbury, and ordered the couple to separate. Meantime other charges were brought against the Duke in the Commons.[196] In order to defend himself, Villiers not only deigned to appear before that House, but also violated royal prerogative by openly discussing details of foreign policy and the Privy Council's deliberations. Charles quickly stripped him of (or forced him to sell) his various offices,[197] initiating the period of Buckingham's opposition which would last until his death.

Danby now took over as the King's leading minister, and rapidly calculated that the best way to advance Parliamentary business was to pander to the appetite for religious intolerance. Hence he set about building an alliance between Anglican bishops and the Crown. That process issued in an attempt, in April 1675, to push through the Lords a new, vigorously discriminatory Test Act, the Disaffected Persons Bill, requiring members to swear never to 'endeavour any alteration of government either in church or state'.[198] The initiative prompted Buckingham, Shaftesbury, and others to record their formal dissent to the majority votes secured by Danby at each reading. This 'Bishops' Bill', Shaftesbury reflected, constituted an attempt to concentrate all 'Power and Office of the Kingdom', in perpetuity, in the hands of 'High Episcopal Men', to the detriment of England's ancient rights and liberties.[199] Like earlier steps in the 'Clarendon Code', the new bill was (in Shaftesbury's view) a measure which prioritized obedience over understanding and tolerant, rational enquiry.[200] Certainly, the threat to liberty was real enough for those who saw in such clerical tyranny a return to Laud's Episcopal authoritarianism. They attacked this development on grounds of a general Erastianism, and as a matter of principled support for Dissenters. But religious principles aside, Shaftesbury and others also had another reason to resist Danby's proposal: namely, the fact that a spirit of aristocratic *hauteur* made these opponents simply indignant at the thought of kowtowing to clerics. A bill, Shaftesbury argued, which threatened to bar selected Lords from sitting in Parliament necessarily constituted 'the highest Invasion of the Liberties and Priviledges of the *Peerage*'.[201] It was 'destructive of the Freedom, which they ought to enjoy ... by Birth' as an 'inherant' right 'that nothing can take ... away'. Buckingham was happy to step forward as 'General' of a 'partie' committed to this theme, 'the *English* Interest'.[202] He responded to the Disaffected

---

[196] See Spurr 2000: 53.    [197] J. H. Wilson 1954: 205.
[198] Quoted in Goldie 1990: 82.    [199] Shaftesbury 1675: 1.    [200] Ibid. 2.
[201] Ibid. 10.    [202] Ibid. 31.

Persons Bill by proposing, in November 1675, a Bill of Indulgence which would benefit all Dissenters. Yardley has fairly questioned the authenticity of Villiers's commitment to toleration, casting him, rather, as an opportunist;[203] but it is difficult to see why Buckingham would have produced his earlier, 1672 publications, arguing both for the primacy of a 'free ... uncontroul'd use of ... REASON' in establishing 'true faith' and for the moral importance of 'Liberty of Conscience', unless because, at some level, he actually believed in such goals.[204] His 1675 speech in favour of an Indulgence Bill certainly recapitulates just such latitudinarian principles.[205] However, of more relevance to the present discussion is the fact that this same speech also reveals another motive. In it Buckingham contemplates with horror England's Dissenters being 'divested of their Liberties and Birth-rights, ... miserably thrown out of their Possessions and Free-holds'. As he does *this*, it is clear that he is recalling the other side of Shaftesbury's attack on the bishops, Ashley's much more self-interested criticism of the latter for their impertinent violation of aristocratic privilege and birthright. There is, I suggest, a connection between this kind of political concern and Buckingham's attachment to libertinism. Libertinism itself is essentially the *assertion*, the parading, of a separatist attitude. The libertine revels in being at odds with the moral majority, and despises those who would intrude upon his independence. For this reason he is bound to feel an affinity with the Dissenter, and to relish the opportunity of using the latter's cause as another stick with which to beat the established Church.

Charles faced deadlock in November 1675, and dealt with it by proroguing Parliament, instructing that it should not reconvene for fifteen months. When it did so, in February 1677, Buckingham immediately renewed his attack by arguing that since (so he alleged) the prorogation had been unconstitutionally long, Parliament was now automatically dissolved. As previously, he found reason in the course of making this case to claim that privileges of birthright were being abused (this time by a Commons insufficiently 'respectful to your Lordships'): 'They do not think ... they are an Assembly that are due to return to their own homes ... but ... look upon themselves as a standing Senate, ... pickt out to be Legislators for ... their whole lives .... [T]hey ... believe themselves our Equals.'[206] Buckingham's insistence, here, on asserting the peer's right to consider himself above the common man again correlates with his libertinism, since libertinism functioned as an exaggerated expression of that very attitude, playing upon the licence of aristocratic privilege. But such privilege did the Duke little good. Danby's

---

[203] Yardley 1992: *passim*, esp. 331. For the counter-argument, see Buckingham 1985: 8, 10, 15–16, 19–20, 24–5, 41–2.
[204] Buckingham 1985: 87–90. Cf. 1981: 168.          [205] Buckingham 1985: 102–3.
[206] Ibid. 105.

supporters in the Lords (the bishops especially) voted to commit the peer to the Tower for contempt of the House. When later pardoned (partly through Dorset's efforts), Buckingham immediately petitioned the King to be made Lord Steward. In a sentiment reminiscent of the fantasy relationship driving the1661 *Humble Representation*, he told Rochester that his aim was to make the monarch 'distinguish that his [i.e., the King's] interest is different from the interest of some about him'.[207] The implication was that Charles's true interest lay with Buckingham, who was trying to draw his King into the same position of antagonism *vis-à-vis* the Court which the Duke himself occupied. Charles, though, saw things differently, and rejected the petition. His one-time counsellor of pleasure was left to live out his days in isolation.

Buckingham, then, was held in a position of opposition for much of the 1670s. The same was true of his associates. Sedley, who seems to have enjoyed royal support in the late 1660s, had ceased to do so by the middle of the next decade.[208] He became, instead, one of the translators of the Coleman letters (crucial documents used by Shaftesbury to expose the Popish Plot), and indeed Shaftesbury listed him in 1677 as a 'doubly worthy' man. Dorset, likewise a sometime beneficiary of the Crown, used his 1680 poem 'On the Young Statesmen' to cite as disastrous a catalogue of recent royal ministers from Arlington to Danby and Sunderland (ll. 18–25).[209] These 'madmen', Dorset wrote, threatened 'freeborn' man's 'right', 'from *consent*'—note the Whiggery—'and custom draw[n]', to be 'ruled by law' (ll. 26–35). Given such signs of antagonism, it is not surprising that the textual traces of Rochester's political opposition, too, date to this period. As Johnson has shown, Rochester did maintain constructive if mutually self-interested exchanges with Danby through to late 1675, and there were also positive episodes at this time in his relations with Charles—so much so, in fact, that the Earl initially defended the Disaffected Persons Bill.[210] Amidst such co-operation, though, spikes of hostility became increasingly frequent. During Christmas 1673, for example, when Charles had already begun his drift away from the cabal, Rochester handed the King his notorious 'Satyr', 'In the Isle of Brittain', in which he accused the latter of being ruled by whomsoever had 'sway' over his sceptre-prick.[211] *Timon* followed the next year, and there the dominant impression is of a persona who feels isolated from the world around him. Furthermore, this satire alludes darkly to the difficulty of restoring national honour once it has been tarnished (ll. 163–4) and to a play (Crowne's *Charles the Eighth*) about a careless 'young Monarch' who allows 'Forreigne

---

[207] Rochester 1980: 149.     [208] Pinto 1927: 177. Cf. 148.     [209] Dorset 1979: 50 ff.
[210] See J. W. Johnson 2004: 201, 209, 223–5, and 212, 246, 217–19.
[211] Rochester 1999: 85 ff.

Troopes, and Rebells' to 'shock his State' (ll. 135–6)—this whilst the speaker longs to flee from everyday society into the consoling company of 'Sidley, Buckhurst, [and] Savile' (l. 34)—that is, the Buckingham circle. In 1675/6 Rochester then wrote his mock 'Dialogue' between the various royal mistresses in which he voiced anxiety over the power of '*Paris* Plotts, and Roman Cunt' to influence 'our *Faiths Defendor*' (ll. 13–14).[212] Crucially, this caustic poem, like the sceptre-prick 'Satyr' before it, presupposes the speaker's own sense of exclusion from the determining processes of English politics. From 1675 onwards, that impression increasingly drove Rochester towards Country Party interests, so that, although he did not stand with Buckingham in 1677 in *publicly* challenging the prorogation, he did subsequently petition for the Duke's release from the Tower.[213] He was also listed by Shaftesbury as another of the 'worthies'.[214] These examples aside though, the most telling sign of Rochester's newly oppositional mentality needs must be his destruction of the royal sundial in the Privy Garden in 1675. Viewed against the broader background outlined here, that action begins to look like a gesture expressive of political frustration; expressive, too, of the poet's rebellious hostility towards his monarch.[215] Equally, as a *lawless* act, it underlines the intrinsic connection between feelings of political marginalization and the impulse to embrace libertinism. Lawlessness here is premissed upon (and justified by) the individual's indignation at his own, and his kind's, exclusion.

The argument, then, underlying this sketch of the 1660s and 1670s is that the pulsing episodes of exclusion to which Clarendon and Danby exposed the Buckingham circle mapped on to habits of cynicism, resentment, and self-assertion which were already established in the latter by the early 1660s. These later experiences aggravated attitudes of egotism and hostility to the world (attitudes constitutive of libertinism in this period) which were nascent in the wits at the time of the Restoration. The effect of this was to make the appeal, the relevance, of Des Yveteaux, Des Barreaux, or La Rochefoucauld, of Hobbism, and of Cyrenaic hedonism, *enduring* rather than simply transitory. Those diverse textual traditions had all staked their claim to authority on the basis that they demystified old, usually delusory values, undercutting dignified rationalist pretensions in favour of acknowledging man's visceral realities. This same avowal of intellectual sophistication was ideally suited to the self-image of a modern coterie whose members regarded themselves as having won a hard-fought maturity, first, in suffering the upheavals of the Interregnum and the indignities of the Restoration, then in facing the disappointments of

---

[212] Rochester 1999: 91.

[213] See J. W. Johnson 2004: 222–5, 232–3, 266–7, and on the petition, Rochester 1980: 145–6.

[214] Greer 2000: 22.        [215] Cf. J. W. Johnson 2004: 219–20.

later political developments. Indeed, this ongoing *synthesis* of grim, real-world experience with Hobbist/libertine thinking came to constitute what one might call the collective faith of the Rochester group (and of the Restoration court more generally): a faith precisely in the lack of faith of others; a faith, too, which understood that there are no moral absolutes; which valued appetite and allowed it unrestricted expression; which insisted, cynically, on the prime importance of self-assertion; and which therefore—as will become clear hereafter—valued the cultivation of power and control over others as a means of surviving. This, the defining knowledge of a community (even of a single generation), was an object of pride, an achieved collective wisdom which marked out the insight of this age—at least so far as members of the 'merry gang' were concerned. So too, the fact that courtiers confronted these truths was supposedly a token of their uncompromising honesty, a quality which distinguished them from previous generations. Cassio, in short, now spoke with the tongue of Iago.

Rochester, Wycherley, Etherege, even Oldham on the periphery, all wrote according to these premisses. Lucy, Bramhall, Clarendon, Dryden too (in his representation of Achitophel), wrote against them. But though its exponents regarded this libertine outlook as knowledge, knowledge of the way things truly were, had been, and must always be, it was really only a faith, an image of the nature of man to which they were imaginatively and emotionally committed. It was (to repeat an earlier phrase) life lived upon certain assumptions, and in the comedy of Etherege, in the poetry of Rochester, we will see what became of it.

## THE MANNERED WORLD OF THE RESTORATION COURT

Halifax's retrospective 'Character of King Charles II' (*c.*1690–5) presents an image of Charles and his court commensurate with the idea of human nature which I have suggested prevailed amongst the wits. According to Halifax's sketch, Charles was as self-interested as any other politician of his day, as complicit as the rest of his court in its processes of flattery, dissembling, and mistrust. His apparent bounty could not be trusted, since its true 'Motive ... was rather to make Men less uneasy to him, than more easy to themselves. ... It was throwing a Man off from his Shoulders, that leaned upon them ... so that the Party was not gladder to receive, than he ... to give.'[216] Nor were Charles's words any more reliable: 'Those who knew his Face' instead 'fixed their Eyes there; and thought it of more Importance to see, than to hear

[216] Halifax 1989: ii. 500.

The Rise and Fall of Libertinism

what he said.'[217] Charles was a Hobbesian monarch in a Hobbesian world, an environment in which others' intentions were inscrutable unless one could read the 'signes of Passions present ... in the countenance'.[218] The combined facts that the King trusted no man 'entirely', felt 'forced to dissemble in his own Defence', and developed a peculiarly rapid gait as if he were desperate to seek 'Sanctuary' from his own people, all underline what must have been his tremendous sense of isolation.[219] Yet the fact that he secured his authority by '*hearing every body against any body*' ensured that all those around him shared in this isolation, none ever knowing what others might be saying in order to curry favour.[220] Halifax justified Charles's dissembling practices by arguing that they constituted a necessary defensive strategy, not merely a means of furthering aggressive self-interest; a strategy, too, which 'ceaseth to be foul play, having an implied Allowance by the general Practice'.[221] However, in saying this, he only emphasized the more how close this court came to mimicking the Hobbesian state of nature in fostering so universal an atmosphere of suspicion.

Such, then, was Halifax's shady vision of court life. And yet we need to set this alongside the very different image of the same culture put forward by Dryden in his 'Epilogue' to *The Second Part of The Conquest of Granada* and in his 'Defence of the Epilogue' (1672). These texts exude the self-confidence of a community assured of its own witty, cultured refinement:

> Wit's now arriv'd to a more high degree;
> Our native language more refin'd and free.
> Our ladies and our men now speak more wit
> In conversation than those poets writ.
>
> (ll. 23–6)[222]

Poetry, the measure of a culture's achievement, is said now to have 'arrived to its vigour and maturity'.[223] What passed for humour in Jonson's 'narrow' comedic imagination, the follies of the low, has become a 'meanness of thought' beneath the true poet.[224] The contemporary dramatist focuses, rather, on courtly manners, the conversation of gentlemen, wherein gallantry, generosity of spirit, and genuine wit are most often manifest. Courtiers have, of late, become 'easy and pliant to each other in discourse', and it is that conversational idiom which the playwrights favoured by Dryden imitate now, because it is one expressive of both a linguistic and a social ideal.[225] Jonson had

---

[217] Halifax 1989: ii. 490.　　[218] Hobbes 1996: 46.　　[219] Halifax 1989: ii. 494, 504, 493.
[220] Ibid. ii. 494.　　[221] Ibid. ii. 504.
[222] Dryden 1962: i. 167. 'Those poets' are 'the writers of the last age', principally Shakespeare, Jonson, and Fletcher (ibid. i. 170).
[223] Ibid. i. 172.　　[224] Ibid. i. 148–50, 180.　　[225] Ibid. i. 182.

no choice but to look beneath him for subject matter, because in his age poets 'wanted the benefit of converse' with a refined audience—that is, an audience capable of elegant conversation and sharpness of conceit.[226] Such a body exists today, in the 1670s, and since 'Greatness [is] ... easy of access', it is the poet's function to write for it and of it.[227] Indeed, gentlemen are eager to see their manners imitated on stage. They 'will ... be entertained' even with 'the *follies* of each other'.[228] Their culture is 'vigorous and mature' enough to suffer such criticism lightly. Both polite society and the poetic art attendant upon it have, then, come of age, but the crucible which produced this refined 'maturity' of wit is precisely the mannered world of the court: a world a good deal more noble in Dryden's eyes than in Halifax's, and a world whose self-confidence is, in the laureate's view, unassailable.

What, then, is the meeting point between these two commentators' dissonant voices? Given what the Buckingham literary circle, like Halifax, had 'discovered' about morality and egotism, given their indifference to the post-covenanting elements of Hobbes's philosophy, why was it that they (as much if not more than other courtiers) placed such emphasis on manners—this even to the point of cultivating a Drydenesque drama designed to celebrate politesse and repartee? Manners, ordinarily at least, take their meaning from a belief in man's sociability, the very thing dismissed in the wits' Hobbist outlook. This paradox is integral to the structure of life in Charles's social circle and, as such, demands explanation.

At least one function of what one might call the Restoration court's game of manners is immediately apparent. The cultivation of elaborate manners met a political need in this period for a publicly visible, brilliant court lifestyle. The emphases on lavish fashions, repartee, and extravagance (whether with respect to eating and drinking, gambling, or sexual activity) all contributed to an aesthetic of conspicuous refinement in the 1660s which obliterated all thought of past austerities. Manners, in this sense, manifested the collective belief that opulence and sophistication could now beautify court society, this irrespective of how base the appetites were which those forms served. There was a patriotic dimension to this too: where Evelyn had despaired in 1659 that English culture lagged behind that of the French, such despair could now be overcome.[229] However, alongside this first, political purpose the Restoration game of manners can be seen to have served two other functions.

Manners, secondly, satisfied the collective need for an easeful form of coexistence—this, a requirement which needs must persist in some form even where man does think of himself as predominantly antisocial.[230] Hobbes, as

---

[226] Ibid. i. 172.    [227] Ibid. i. 181.    [228] Ibid. i. 182.
[229] See Evelyn 1995: 85, 87.    [230] Cf. Underwood 1957: 39.

already mentioned, made such 'COMPLEASANCE', the judgement that '*every man* [should] *strive to accommodate himselfe to the rest*', *Leviathan*'s fifth (and the *Elements*' fourth) law of nature.[231] Man, he argued, has an 'aptnesse to Society' as well as being independent and self-seeking: his task is to balance the two impulses, albeit in the latter's favour. The same 'aptnesse' prompts Milton's surprisingly cavalier gent., Adam, to tell the 'sociably mild' Raphael that he longs for the 'complacence' of another (*PL* 11. 234, 8. 433); and Hamilton also makes complaisance an informing ideal throughout his *Memoirs of … Grammont*. There, prudence and decorum alike require that Lord Chesterfield be 'so complaisant as not to express [his] sentiments' when the Duke of York makes love to Lady Chesterfield.[232] La Rochefoucauld too, though otherwise so critical of human nature, emphasizes the value of this disposition, his 'honnête homme' consciously minimizing the offence he gives to others. 'Les vrais honnêtes gens', La Rochefoucauld avers, 'sont ceux qui … connaissent [leurs défauts] parfaitement et les confessent', and likewise, 'Le vrai honnête homme est celui qui ne se pique de rien.'[233] Every such gentleman must be willing to be 'exposé à la vue des honnêtes gens' at all times and, reciprocally, must contrive to ignore what he knows about others' motivations, since 'Les hommes ne vivraient pas longtemps en société s'ils n'étaient les dupes les uns des autres.'[234] Again, the honnête homme is, in Maurice Magendie's words, 'celui qui manifeste dans le monde, avec ce minimum de vertu indispensable aux relations sociales, les qualités de politesse, d'esprit, de conversation, de grâce, qui … observe "cette civilité apparent qui se pratique dans le monde, au milieu de la haine et de l'envie" '.[235] In line with these judgements, the satiric effect in Rochester's so-called Mulgrave poems does *not* depend on what the persona says—when Bajazet announces in his 'Very heroical epistle', 'In my dear self, I center every thing, / My Servants, Friends, … Mistress, … King' (ll. 7–8),[236] his declaration is, after all, no more than a libertine commonplace. The satire depends, rather, on the *graceless* way in which Bajazet says all this, so charmlessly pronouncing to his mistress's face beliefs which might better be served by being hidden. What is exposed for ridicule is the gauche hubris of this Mulgrave figure, one who lacks the wit to see the value in assuming a complaisant demeanour.

On this second analysis of manners, then, all parties are involved in a game which yields to its players the pleasures of sociability, but only if the show of complaisance, of collective graciousness, is maintained. Hence 'La galanterie de l'esprit', for example, 'est de dire des choses flatteuses d'une

[231] Hobbes 1996: 106.     [232] Hamilton 1905: 207.
[233] La Rochefoucauld 1965: 56.     [234] Ibid. 57, 39.
[235] Quoted in Underwood 1957: 37.     [236] Rochester 1999: 96.

manière agréable',[237] and the agreeable manner is what counts: mutual flattery is enjoyed not because it is believed but because it bespeaks a degree of respect on the part of each flatterer for the other. Amidst the performance of sociability, as each interlocutor goes to the trouble of displaying 'politesse' before the other, each party thereby derives an egotistical pleasure from the show of deference made to his own person. Even in this simple sense, therefore, the game of manners does appeal to self-interest: the latter is still the primary motivation. As I noted in Chapter 6, Hobbes confirms this in the *Elements* version of his discussion of complaisance. There he links complaisance to charity, but charity conceived as an 'argument to a man of his own power', not as a self-sacrificing disposition. For La Rochefoucauld, likewise, 'La civilité est un désir d'en recevoir et d'être estimé poli', a desire therefore grounded in an interest in one's own standing.[238] The outcome of such 'civilité' is a kind of equilibrium wherein all parties benefit from one another's deference, but only, it should be added, if they all cultivate civility to the point where it appears natural and spontaneous, rather than the product of laboured artfulness. Civility which carries the taint of effort ceases to be civility. What is required is *sprezzatura* or, better, a Horatian ease, a manner of bearing analogous to the Horatian plain style. The latter gives the impression of a natural spontaneity, but that impression is founded on the utmost endeavours of an invisible artifice. When that artifice becomes apparent, the pretence of spontaneity—and with it, the pleasure—is lost. The moment complaisance seems forced, the illusion of mutual deference, which it is manners' second role to maintain, will be shattered.

Manners, though, also assumed a third and more important function in this period, one which strained against the show of unity intrinsic to the first two. They provided a framework—albeit, in light of these first two factors, a necessarily circumscribed framework—within which to pursue Hobbist impulses (including both the aggressive desire for power discussed in my previous chapter and the more straightforward carnal appetites celebrated by the libertines).[239] Under the guise of sociability, therefore, manners provided an outlet through which men might express and satisfy competitive passions. In Chernaik's words, 'the rituals of society' became precisely 'covert *expressions* of a state of war', thereby fostering that mutual fear which civil society was supposed to suppress.[240] What seemed charming might really be at bottom

---

[237] La Rochefoucauld 1965: 41.       [238] Ibid. 66.

[239] Where Underwood argues (1957: 38) that 'life became a ruthless and self-seeking battle for survival, conquest, power, conducted beneath an urbane veneer of "politesse"', I prefer to substitute 'through' for his 'beneath', the point being that manners ('politesse') assumed an exaggerated significance precisely because they provided a conduit through which to fight that battle.

[240] Chernaik 1995: 35.

aggressive or malicious. Chernaik invokes the Hobbesian race simile in this context[241]—appropriately so since when, for example, Etherege's Freeman threatens to start courting Lady Cockwood, Courtall replies, 'I am not such a jade, but I should strain if another rid against me' (*She Would if She Could*, IV. ii. 166–8). Hobbes's analogy is apposite, because the practices of formal civility did indeed stand in for the regulatory structure of a race's rules. If, then, in so far as they fostered complaisance, manners yielded roughly equal delight to all parties, it was also true that, in so far as the same practices made room for competition and acquisitiveness, they could yield differential levels of pleasure, this depending upon how different parties fared in the contest to reap profit from seeming civilized. Thus it was that Dryden's image of a court arranged in various poses of refinement could intersect with Halifax's idea of a bear pit full of conflicting parties on the make.

Mannered competition understood in this third sense of the word took a variety of forms in the Restoration court, the most obvious being the practice of courting, wherein men attempted, by means of charm, conversation, actions, and appearance, to conquer their chosen women of the week, and the business of witty repartee, wherein each party strove to demonstrate that his was the greater wit. However, the world of manners provided other opportunities besides. In *The Man of Mode* the aptly named Lady Townley prides herself on the fact that her house is the focal point for polite society, because she is the foremost provider of gossip, these triumphs, assertions of authority which she cultivates by serving and exploiting the conventions of social interaction. The same can be said of Lee's Lady Tournon in *The Princess of Cleve*, whose breadth of acquaintance makes her the chief procuress, and thus the chief manipulator, of the French Queen's court.[242] In a different context Wycherley's Novel (*Plain Dealer*), albeit that he unwittingly speaks more for fops than for wits, insists that 'a man *by his dress* ... shows his wit and judgement, nay, and his courage too' (II. i. 665–7). Sir Fopling Flutter, in deeming himself a most absolutely fabulous man of mode, likewise presumes that a good frizz atop a modish peruke brings its own particular authority. His French vocabulary, his sartorial elegance (nothing but 'originals of the most famous hands in Paris' (*Man of Mode*, III. ii. 247–8) ), his revulsion for tallow candles ('How can you breathe in a room where there's grease frying!' (IV. i. 308–9) ), and his entourage of baladines ('the best in France' (ll. 314–15) ) are all, in their way, indices to his good manners, and therefore assertions—so he hopes—of his superiority. These devices fail because they are too obviously affectations. Fopling's vain Frenchification marks him out, like Dryden's Melantha before him (*Marriage*

---

[241] Chernaik 1995: 34–5.          [242] See, e.g., II. i. 1–9; II. ii. 150–6.

*A-La-Mode*), as the butt of the comedy. However, even Dorimant, for all his apparent naturalness, takes seriously such contrived testimonies of worth. Though he purports to lament the fact 'That a man's excellency should lie in neatly tying of a ribbond, or ... cravat' (I. i. 385–6), he is happy to be complimented on his own 'fancy in ... clothes' (ll. 392–3), and is always careful to don 'a mighty pretty suit' (l. 389).[243]

In all these cases a struggle for power between two or more individuals, one which also affects their public reputations, is acted out within the parameters determined by social decorum. Man must govern his actions so as to appear complaisant whilst still pursuing his own interests, and—at least when his victim is a social equal or superior—those interests are to be satisfied by means of wit and machinations, not through violence or other indecorous acts. Satisfaction of one's own appetite, though, rather than any shared fulfilment, is the prize which motivates this governance, and the Hobbist individual exploits any means available to him (within the bounds of decorum and his ability) to win that prize. These concerns are powerfully evident in the subplot of Dryden's *Marriage A-La-Mode*. There, the two friends, Palamede and Rhodophil, each try to seduce the other's wife / fiancée without being discovered. In reality all four lovers quickly become aware of their respective appetites, but each couple nonetheless shrouds their affair in a show of pretence. When Rhodophil and Melantha (Palamede's betrothed), having arranged to meet secretly in a close walk, stumble across Palamede and Doralice (Rhodophil's wife) engaged in a like assignation, all four feign innocence. In a show of mannered exchanges, they excuse their appearing in public, each with the other's ostensible lover. Palamede speaks for them all in his aside, emphasizing the furtive power struggle which lingers beneath their game of sociability: 'Now am I confident we had all four the same design: 'tis a pretty odd kind of game this, where each of us plays for double stakes: this is just thrust and parry with the same motion; I am to get his Wife, and yet to guard my own Mistris' (*Marriage*, III. ii. 139–42).[244] A similar manipulative contest is played out between Etherege's Lady Cockwood and Courtall, the latter striving to frustrate the former's advances even whilst carrying things 'so like a gentleman, that [Cockwood] has not ... the least suspicion of unkindness' and thus remains under Courtall's spell (*She Would if She Could*, I. i. 263–5). Again Harcourt, one of the heroes of Wycherley's *Country Wife*, demonstrates the superiority of wit which empowers him by engaging Sparkish and his betrothed, Alithea, in a conversation intended simultaneously to compliment the couple, yet make advances towards the

---

[243] Cf. Brown and Harris 1965: 67; J. H. Wilson 1967: 13–14.
[244] References to this play are to Dryden 1956–2002: vol. xi.

latter (III. ii. 228–388). Although Alithea realizes that she is being flagrantly courted, Harcourt persuades Sparkish to interpret such advances as but Harcourt's friendly affirmation of Sparkish's own taste.

The great connoisseur, though, of such complaisant games, the man ever adept at exploiting good manners as a vehicle for his own self-assertion, is Etherege's Dorimant. He is the master both of conversational and of practical wit, witness his ability to manipulate and outwit those around him so as to maximize the satisfaction of his own desires, not least his appetite for power. To this end Dorimant delights in dissembling; for example, in conversing with Lady Woodville, when he pretends to be Mr Courtage and plays to Woodville's humour:

DOR. All people mingle nowadays madam. And in public places women of quality have the least respect showed 'em.

LADY WOOD. I protest you say the truth, Mr. Courtage.

DOR. Forms and ceremonies, the only things that uphold quality and greatness, are now shamefully laid aside and neglected.

(*Man of Mode*, IV. i. 11–18)

The latter is partially true, in so far as the egoism of Hobbism implies a universal disrespect, but Dorimant is in fact assiduous in observing and capitalizing upon the 'forms and ceremonies' of love, the game of amorous manners, albeit solely for his own purposes. He knows, for example, the proper course a lovers' argument must take, and knows that Mrs Loveit will follow that script to the letter:

She means insensibly to insinuate a discourse of me, and artificially raise her jealousy to such a height, that transported with the first motions of her passion, she shall fly upon me with all the fury imaginable, as soon as … I enter; the quarrel being thus happily begun, I am to play my part, confess and justify … my roguery, swear her … ill humour makes her intolerable, tax her with the next fop that comes into my head, and in a huff march away. (I. i. 253–62)

Having anticipated this attack, he is ready to meet it with a calmly philosophic argument (justifying his recent, adulterous absence as due to 'business'). His purpose is to antagonize Loveit and give him the upper hand in their power relationship: 'We are not masters of our own affections, our inclinations daily alter; now we love pleasure, anon we shall dote on business; human frailty will have it so, and who can help it?' (II. ii. 160–3). The predicted fury which this provokes in her sanctions his expressing some irritating home truths in return, thus reinforcing for Dorimant his own (Hobbist) sense of domination over her:

DOR. Constancy at my years! 'tis not a virtue in season ...

.   .   .   .   .   .   .   .   .

LOV. Dissembler, damned dissembler!

DOR. I am so I confess, ... good manners corrupt me. I am honest in my inclinations, and would not, wer't not to avoid offence, make a lady a little in years believe I think her young ... and seem as fond of a thing I am weary of, as when I doted on't in earnest.

(ll. 203–17)

Loveit's fury provides, too, a rare but here justified (rather than graceless) opportunity for Dorimant to voice his own libertine beliefs: he dismisses love (which 'makes us show fine things to one another for a time' (ll. 221–2) ) as a gilding which soon wears away to reveal the native brass, the brute appetite, lying beneath it. Oaths sworn in its name are only as good (and as durable) as the present passion of which they are a symptom. The delight in all of this is plainly egotistical: 'next to the coming to a good understanding with a new mistress, I love a quarrel with an old one, but ... I have not had the pleasure of making a woman so much as break her fan, to be sullen, or forswear herself these three days' (I. i. 216–21).[245] (Dorimant echoes here Wycherley's Horner, for whom 'next to the pleasure of making a new mistress is that of being rid of an old one' (*Country Wife*, I. i. 175–6).) Dorimant's 'these three days' speaks volumes as to the scale on which such pleasures operate. He seeks some such confirmation of his power over others' affections on a daily basis. In this respect Harriet alone has the full measure of his character: 'He's agreeable and pleasant I must own, but he does so much affect being so, he displeases me' (*Man of Mode*, III. iii. 28–9). Belinda, by contrast, is as trapped in the power of this egotistical grip as Loveit is. Such is her genuine affection for the man, she is drawn further and further into Dorimant's conspiracy to deceive Loveit—this because she wills herself to believe in the pose which he assumes for her benefit, that of self-sacrificing lover. Here again Dorimant is adept at the game of manners in question, and when Belinda questions his constancy, he simply plays out the list of appropriately passionate responses:

BEL. ... You shall swear you never will see her more.

DOR. I will! a thousand oaths—by all—

BEL. Hold—you shall not, now I think on't better.

DOR. I will swear—

---

[245] On the vanity of these lines and the sterility of the society here dramatized, see Underwood 1957: 91–3; Brown and Harris 1965: 60–8.

BEL. I shall grow jealous of the oath, and think I owe your truth to that, not to your love.

DOR. Then, by my love! no other oath I'll swear.

(IV. ii. 39–47)

The impression one gets from this exchange is that no matter what Belinda had said, the outcome would have been the same: no real assurance for her, no real challenge to Dorimant. He remains invulnerable, because he has no passionate attachment to Belinda, nothing more than a gilded love. She remains vulnerable precisely because she, by contrast, has made an investment in him.

Dissembling, though, is not a capacity exclusive to Etherege's hero, and Loveit's use of that same practice is one thing which *does* threaten Dorimant's self-assurance. Contrary to the latter's orchestration of events, she appears too fond of Sir Fopling. Despite Dorimant's having tired of her as a sexual partner, he clearly remains interested in her not so much as an object of affection but as a creature whose heart he commands. He takes pride in the fact that her emotions are tied to his will, and it is surely for that reason that he begins to be 'jealous in earnest' at the thought of her actually biting on the bait he has put before her. The fact that she seems so easily to have found consolation, and to have found it in so slight a coxcomb as Fopling, gives the impression that she actually invested little significance in her attachment to Dorimant: a blow, therefore, to the latter's public reputation. Although Dorimant insists that he 'knows she hates Fopling, and only makes use of him in hope to work me on again' (III. iii. 358–9), the fact that he has to reassure himself (and Medley) of as much, to announce and confirm it to himself, indicates that the incident has a little dashed his spirits.

When, though, Dorimant's power seems to be at its weakest, he is able to restore it and satisfy his pride by again playing the game of manners. Loveit declares herself wise to his ploys, particularly his periodic tendency to make a quarrel so as to win a week's freedom. She identifies, too, his motive: 'You take a pride of late in using of me ill, that the town may know the power you have over me. Which now … expects that I … must love you still' (v. i. 185–9). Dorimant, though, maintains the pose of lover (here of wronged lover), protesting that she, in indulging Fopling's advances, has made his (Dorimant's) love look ridiculous, so that now he 'begin[s] to think you never did love me' (l. 191). When Loveit does initially give way to these arguments and seek to settle their disagreements, he then takes up her point about his concern for reputation as if it were, to him, a secondary consideration, but one the significance of which he intends to insist upon by way of demanding some gesture of recompense from her for the slight she has put upon their love. Hence: 'Should I be willing to forget it, I shall be daily minded of it, 'twill be a commonplace for all the town to laugh at me, and Medley ... will ever be declaiming on it in my ears' (ll. 245–9). Dorimant's concern regarding this issue is genuine, but the *simulated* tone is that of the peevish, aggrieved lover who demands that his beloved repair his reputation (of which she has been so careless) not for its own sake but by way of a sacrifice, to reaffirm their love: ''Tis necessary to justify my love to the world' (ll. 256–7).

At this point Dorimant miscalculates. Loveit sees all too clearly how real his concern over his reputation is, how far he in fact values it for its own sake, and she is consequently unwilling publicly to snub Fopling 'to please your vanity' (ll. 269–72). But again the lapse in power is only momentary. Dorimant persists in the role of aggrieved, faithful lover, and when Loveit discovers his supposed plans to marry Harriet, immediately implies that the marriage (which was for money only) is now unlikely to take place. He leaves Loveit to conclude that this is because she (Loveit) proved so destructively suspicious of his secret business, that mask which kept him from her:

DOR. To satisfy you I must give up my interest wholly to my love, had you been a
  reasonable woman, I might have secured 'em both, and been happy—

. . . . . . . . . . .

LOV. Was it no idle mistress then?
DOR. Believe me a wife, to repair the ruins of my estate.

(v. i. 315–28)

This explanation not only apparently accounts for Dorimant's absences from Loveit, but also convicts her for her lack of faith in him, a betrayal of their love to which he (she is now given to suppose) has indeed remained true. Loveit's suitably penitential response is to do as Dorimant had originally asked, but now of her own free will rather than under coercion. She does indeed publicly snub Fopling. The moment she disappears, Medley concludes that Dorimant's reputation has been cleared, 'and henceforward when I would know anything of woman, I will consult no other oracle' (v. ii. 448–9). This is clearly the great triumph of the play. The hero's manipulative wit is confirmed, and his egotistical appetite satisfied, satisfied through an apparently unremitting adherence to the manners and conventions of dutiful love which leave him vindicated and free of Loveit, but also assured of her submission. She announces that she will lock herself up hereafter, being too humiliated even to seek consolation in another love. Dorimant's power over her is absolute.

It remains, though, to account for Dorimant's relationship with Harriet, a part of the plot which adds further qualification to the libertine ethic dramatized by Etherege. Loveit and Belinda fall foul of Dorimant because they are victims of their own love, an exposed emotion which reduces them to manipulable objects amidst the power struggles of a predatory society. Self-control is a critical value in this Hobbist-libertine world. A wit like Dorimant is celebrated precisely for his *cool* pursuit and indulgence of appetites; but in order to maintain his power, he must never suffer, or at least be seen to suffer, under the influence of feverish passions. On the contrary, artful and obsessive though he may be in creating the means to satisfy his appetites, he must remain, on the face of it, a casual indulger of those desires. The moment he visibly becomes a slave to them, he exposes a weakness, a passionate dependence, on which others could prey. This is the very threat which Dorimant faces (but then faces down) when Loveit detects his real concern for public reputation. For the wily Hobbist, passions are acceptable only if feigned for manipulative purposes. Under other circumstances they become vulnerabilities. Libertinism does, then, value a kind of rational autonomy (if not right reason per se): namely, an imperviousness to what Underwood calls the 'problem of passion'.[246] It advocates governance of the passions just as Elizabethan and Jacobean moralists had done, but for strategic, not moral, reasons, and always in the service of (not to the disadvantage of) one's appetites. Dorimant, in his passion for Harriet, threatens to betray this principle and succumb to the very loss of autonomy which elsewhere affects his admirers. His Hobbist dominance seems endangered.

Etherege repeatedly emphasizes this point. Dorimant is genuinely unnerved by his first encounter with Harriet, who matches his every witticism with cool ripostes: 'she has left a pleasing image of herself behind that wanders in my soul—it must not settle there' (III. iii. 143–5). Their second meeting begins more propitiously, the hero venturing some acute observations about Harriet's expression and outwitting the muffled sarcasm of her reply with a compliment. Where she asserts that she cannot affect the languishing facial expressions then *à la mode*, he responds to the hint of aggression with a tender charm: 'You need 'em not, you have a sweetness of your own, if you would but calm your frowns and let it settle .... Put on a gentle smile and let me see, how well it will become you' (IV. i. 127–43). But here again, if this sounds like the customary dalliance of the master of manners, its seriousness quickly emerges: 'DOR. [*aside*]. I love her, and dare not let her know it, I fear sh'as an ascendant o'er me and may revenge the wrongs I have done her sex' (ll. 164–6). Dorimant attributes to Harriet his own usual motivations, fearing lest her intention be to conquer and then abandon him.[247] Faced with that anxiety, he loses control of the conversation. Harriet succeeds in disrupting his attempts to test her affection for him, and just when he seems set to risk

---

[246] Underwood 1957: 64–5, 75–80.     [247] Chernaik 1995: 13.

revealing his passion, she interjects, taunting him by revealing what affectation she is capable of:

> ... but now I must speak—
>
> HAR. If it be on that idle subject, I will put on my serious look, turn my head carelessly from you, drop my lip, let my eyelids fall, and hang half o'er my eyes—thus while you buzz a speech.
>
> (ll. 184–9)

Harriet defends herself against Dorimant's advances because she suspects his motives, but in truth she shares his passion (witness v. ii. 104–5). Eventually the latter, detecting as much, defeats one of her repulses with a brilliantly incisive maxim: 'You wrong your own, while you suspect my eyes' (l. 146). Dorimant finally wins Harriet, though, only with the promise that he will 'make a journey into the country' (l. 161). Metaphorically, that gesture represents an undertaking to abandon his appetitious ways (and thus to negate the kind of triumph he has lately won over Loveit). Hitherto, Dorimant confesses, High Park, the rapacious world of town and court, 'has been the utmost limit of my love—but now my passion knows no bounds, and there's no measure to be taken of what I'll do for you from anything I ever did before' (ll. 167–70). Clearly, Etherege here makes a concession to the romantic topos, one demanded of him by his comedic plot; but that concession, the step away from Dorimant's otherwise absolute status as the 'oracle' of libertinism, is less emphatic than it at first appears to be. The assurance which Dorimant offers to Harriet is at best ambivalent. The sense in which the word 'now' ('now my passion') should be qualified remains nicely indeterminable. So too, there is an implication that Dorimant recognizes that it is safe to give way to passion 'in the country', when beyond the reach of the town's closely competitive social circle. Once safely rusticated, he can indulge his fancy, this without compromising his town reputation or breaching the wits' decorum. Crucially, there is nothing in Dorimant's promise to indicate that, when he returns to London, he will not resume precisely the appetitious lifestyle in which he has excelled of old. Hence, the future of the couple's relationship and of Dorimant's love remains open to question. The court wits, at least, are free to persist in imagining him as the epitome of libertinism, whilst doe-eyed lovers delight in the happy ending.

J. H. Wilson was surely right to emphasize that in this play 'Etherege seized upon ... not the ... day by day life of Whitehall, but the life which Whitehall was pleased to imagine it led.'[248] *The Man of Mode* is representative neither of Restoration comedy *en masse*[249] nor of the whole culture of its time; but it

---

[248] J. H. Wilson 1967: 164.       [249] See R. D. Hume 1983: 146, 158, 160, 162–3, 166.

does bear out a fantasy life particular to the court wits' circle and those keen to emulate them, a life expressive of the Hobbist ethos. That fantasy was clearly extraordinarily compelling (even amongst those for whom the pleasure of the play lay only in its titillating shock value). To Etherege's hearty supporters, Dorimant was the man they would be, and his egotistical triumphs certainly represent the summation of the trends and ideas examined throughout this chapter. Viewed against that background, it seems questionable that in 1676 libertine-minded audiences would have thought of *The Man of Mode* (as modern commentators like Powell do[250]) as critical—disapproving of the perversity of the Restoration game of manners, or of the sense of isolation to which it gave rise. Yet that latter response is not as anachronistic as it might at first seem. For Dorimant's real-life equivalent, Rochester, the merits of Hobbist libertinism were by no means unequivocal. Indeed, in his own work Rochester developed just such a questioning perspective, and it is therefore to that probing, often hostile engagement with the traditions and beliefs described in this chapter that I wish to turn next.

[250] Brown and Harris 1965: 60–8.

# 8

---

# Rochester: The Disappointments of Hobbism and Libertinism

According to Gilbert Burnet, the pattern of the 2nd Earl of Rochester's short life was one of perpetual oscillation, an endless alternation between licence and learning, spells of 'woful Extravagancie' in the town and 'fits of Study' in the country.[1] In this chapter I want to argue that those divergent moods are reflected in Rochester's works, his poetry especially revealing a scrutinizing engagement with the Hobbist-libertine outlook already discussed. Some of Rochester's lyrics, whatever the degree of insincerity and outrageous performance in them, do celebrate this libertine ethos (just as Etherege had done); others present a critique, one the more important because it was subsequently endorsed by developments in the history of moral thought after 1680. This chapter traces those two tendencies and, with them, the decline of the court wits' Hobbist ethos.

Rochester is (in one guise at least) very much the poet of appetite, his lifestyle and lyrics seeming to reflect a sometime belief that felicity 'consisteth not in having prospered, but in prospering', proceeding ever forward from the indulgence of one appetite to the next. In that mode of performing, Rochester is, too, the guardian of self-interest, the diviner of fear in human nature, and a writer who subordinates reason to the appetites (thus escaping the psychomachia associated with the old right reason). Considered on such terms, he is, clearly, the Hobbist poet *par excellence*, one whom Robert Parsons reported in his funeral sermon had been '*undone*' by the '*absurd ... Philosophy ... propagated by ... Mr.* Hobbs'.[2] (Anthony à Wood, similarly, claimed that frequenting the court 'not only debauched [Rochester] but made

---

[1] Burnet 1680: 6. Cf. 25. Burnet's report is confirmed by manuscripts from the Rochester–Savile correspondence in which Savile fluctuates between urging his friend, on the one hand, to put his 'leasure' at Woodstock to good use and produce poetry illustrative of his 'abilities', and imploring him, on the other, to return 'to towne' lest the latter, already dull without him, become so boring that 'Dutch men thinke themselves in Holland and goe Yawning about as if they were att home' (Rochester 1980: 136, 164 vs 157–8).

[2] Parsons 1680: 26.

him a perfect Hobbist'.[3]) Twentieth-century commentators, drawing on such testimonies, have constructed Rochester as Hobbes's 'professed disciple',[4] sometimes to the extent of measuring his writings as exact responses to the Malmesbury Apostle's own.[5] In presenting Rochester, though, as a critic of Hobbism and libertinism, my own argument does not take as its premiss this model of detailed Rochesterian engagement with Hobbesian texts. I do not construct Rochester's approach to Hobbism as one of allusions to, and direct criticisms of, Hobbes's works. Rather, the relationship between Rochester and Hobbes is understood here in terms of shared imaginative premisses. If Rochester seems sometimes to echo Hobbes, this is more because he starts out from the same image of man, the same assumptions about human nature, as does the latter, than because he busies himself studying the leaves of *Leviathan*. What specific debts Rochester does owe, he owes to what Russell calls his 'philosophic landscape', 'the spectrum of views' prevalent in Charles's court;[6] but even these—the loose synthesis of perspectives described in Chapter 7—are treated in the Rochesterian canon less as abstract ideas academically expounded than as attitudes assimilated into the very patterns and outlooks of different speakers' lives. Hence Rochester's poems are examined here as records of what it *feels* like to imagine oneself (and one's life) on Hobbist and Cyrenaic terms.[7] Rochester himself is seen not merely as a spokesman for Hobbism and libertinism in the way that Oldham was, but as one who lived out this philosophy (albeit in a series of performances), and in living it, reached disparate conclusions about its merits. Rochester's poetry records less a pattern of reading than one of living—a life, indeed, lived upon certain assumptions, recorded in such a way that we may see what becomes of it.

With this broad approach in mind, I begin the present chapter by analysing the lyrics. Focusing on the most representative of appetites, sexual desire, Rochester explores in his short poems assorted attitudes to the libertine model of governance. Some poems endorse it. Others, particularly those keyed to the tradition of poems 'Against Fruition', reveal its inadequacies, the inevitability of disappointment which such a view of felicity entails. Still others present questionably successful, alternative patterns of relationship—patterns, incidentally, also expressive of the poet's fascination with pain and Christian experience.

The 'Satyre against Reason', the major concern of the latter half of this chapter, enlarges upon the second of these three attitudes. Rochester develops

---

[3] Wood 1813–20: iii. 1229.        [4] Chernaik 1995: 24. Cf. Pinto 1935: 29; Vieth 1988: 206.
[5] See, e.g., Fujimara's contribution to Vieth 1988.        [6] F. Russell 1986: 248.
[7] Mayo (1934: 165) was the first to suggest (albeit without taking the matter further) that, 'though he probably thought of himself as an Epicurean, [Rochester] was in fact a good deal of a Cyrenaic'.

there an ideal of governance poised between latitudinarian theological models centred on traditional right reason, on the one hand, and the Cyrenaicism typical of libertinism, on the other. Rochester's satirist characterizes both of these positions as threatening dissolution and loss of autonomy. His own ethic, by contrast, whilst still giving primacy to the appetites, affords reason a stabilizing, moderating role. This is one aspect of the 'Satyre's' critique of that libertine culture played out at court by the wits and their imitators. But beyond that, the poem also attacks the atmosphere of mistrust and isolation which the parallel Hobbist obsession with power (typified in a figure like Dorimant) fosters. A coterie social structure dominated by this ethic is shown to engender not contentment, but fear and paranoia. Rochester highlights the need, instead, for a collective faith in some less cynical notion of human nature, for an ideal of governance supportive of a more generous-minded society. He does so against the background of his own disillusionment with an English court by then more favourable to Danby and Mulgrave than to Buckingham's circle.

These conclusions inform two further works of the later 1670s, with a discussion of which this chapter ends. *Lucina's Rape* (Rochester's reworking of Fletcher's *Valentinian*) matches the 'Satyre's' twin concerns, dramatizing a criticism of both the libertine ethic of self-indulgence and the dysfunctional polity to which that ethic lent itself. Meanwhile, the so-called 'Lovesey' Preface to the projected 1679 edition of the 'Satyre' recasts the vision of moral and social governance at the heart of the latter as a testament to Rochester's own moderate reasonableness. The poet emerges from that document as one who, though Whiggish in inclination, nevertheless opposes the extremism of both sides jockeying for power at the height of the Popish Plot; as one, also, who speaks instead for such 'freeborn Englishmen' as see the merit in binding themselves to a principle of governance so long as the limits of their obedience remain clear. This last, generous-minded Rochester stands a world away from the aggressive, egotistical figure of the most libertine lyrics, anticipating new departures which were to shape the English moral and political imagination from the 1680s through to 1700.

## IMAGINATIVE PREOCCUPATIONS

Although his engagement with Hobbism and libertinism is my main concern here, it is worth registering first another of Rochester's imaginative preoccupations. Throughout his poetry Rochester exhibits an anxiety about oblivion and self-dissolution, and this was evidently a lifelong obsession. On his deathbed he described to Burnet an incident which occurred in 1665, when he was 18, and which stayed with him ever after. Aboard ship, taking part in the disastrous Bergen expedition, the young Earl one day found himself stood on deck beside one John Windham, Gent., brother of his former Wadham classmate Thomas.[8] John Windham confessed to Rochester a premonition that he would soon be killed. Perhaps in youthful imitation of Canius Julius,[9] perhaps with an eye on the *libertin* physician Gui Patin,[10] he promised the Earl that he would return after death to declare his soul's fate. Moments later he was indeed sliced in half by a cannon ball, but, gentleman or not, Windham did not keep his promise. Rochester remembered this and another comparable episode, Burnet claimed,[11] because they indicated 'that the Soul … had a sort of Divination' unknown to the body, thus underlining the distinctness of these two substances.[12] Perhaps, though, Rochester remembered the Bergen episode too, because the separate soul did not return, because its fate after death's oblivion was unclear.

Certainly, it is the Epicurean idea of dissolution which Rochester alighted on in selecting an excerpt from Seneca's *Troades* to translate.[13] Two parts of his selection follow their original closely:

(1)  After Death nothing is, and nothing Death,
The utmost limit of a Gasp of Breath.
Let the ambitious Zealot lay aside
His hopes of Heaven; …
Let slavish Souls lay by their Fear.

(ll. 1–5)

(2)  Devouring Time swallows us whole;
Impartial Death confounds Body and Soul.

(ll. 11–12)[14]

The translation here adopts two characteristically Rochesterian images (to which I shall return hereafter). One is the notion of limits and boundaries: in all his poses the Earl is perennially fascinated by the idea of an 'utmost limit',[15] here the fixable boundary which the moment of expiring constitutes between

---

[8] Burnet 1680: 16; Rochester 1980: 12; J. W. Johnson 2004: 73, 364.

[9] See Montaigne 1603: 215.

[10] Patin claimed to have asked one dying patient to return to him after death and report on the afterlife. The patient did supposedly return, but, alas, remained mute (Spink 1960: 21).

[11] See Burnet 1680: 19–20.    [12] Ibid. 18, 20.

[13] On the popularity of the same excerpt amongst French *libertins*, see Spink 1960: 22–3; Adam 1964: 259–61.

[14] Rochester 1999: 45 ff.

[15] Compare, e.g., his figuring of Corinna's vagina as the 'balmy *brinks* of bliss' (l. 12) in 'The Imperfect Enjoyment' (ibid. 13 ff.).

a life lost in boundless desires and a death lost in boundless dissolution. The other is that of consumption (l. 11), here the loss of self within an infinite something.[16] It is this latter image which Rochester develops in the intervening lines, a significant expansion of Seneca's 'quaeris quo iaceas post obitum loco? / quo non nata iacent',[17] which comes, anyway, at the end of the extract in the original (as if by way of afterthought) but is here made central:

> Nor be concern'd which way, nor where,
> After this Life they shall be hurl'd;
> Dead, we become the Lumber of the World:
> And to that Mass of Matter shall be swept,
> Where things destroy'd, with things unborn are kept.
>
> (ll. 6–10)

Man's absorption here into an infinite other is figured in two images of vigorous movement, his being 'hurl'd' through a void and 'swept' away. Again, these motions are recurrent features of Rochester's poetic imagination, here implying a loss of autonomy, bearings, and even self. The (thoroughly Epicurean) argument, of course, is that the soul should not be perturbed by these thoughts, since it will not survive to be conscious of them. Rochester reinforces that perspective in lines 8–9 (for which Seneca offers no precedent): 'Lumber' refers to the doctrine that all matter (the soul included), once dismantled into its atomic parts, is reused to form new objects; but man should be indifferent to this because he will feel none of it. Erskine-Hill has observed that Rochester 'transforms the calm … quiescent tone of his original, … [giving] it a contemptuous … hostile spirit; Seneca pities those who hope for immortality, Rochester … despises them'.[18] In fact, though, the transformation goes further: the *personal resonance* of the images which Rochester deploys to describe the process of annihilation belies the dogma in question, betraying his own degree of emotional *involvement* in these reflections precisely where Epicureanism teaches that such involvement is inappropriate. Rochester cares deeply about his fate after death, and even where he tries to experiment with the belief that after death nothing is, he still finds himself visualizing that nothingness in personally significant idioms (idioms to which he turns time and again in his poetry, and which are therefore indicative of his concern here). Blount was closer to the truth than he realized when he commented, 'I cannot but esteem the translation to be … a

---

[16] Compare the imaging of arguments as arrows shot upwards but then lost 'in the Bosome of the *boundlesse* Aire' (*Lucina's Rape*, ii. ii. 129–31). (References to this play are to Rochester 1999.)

[17] Seneca 1917: i. 156.     [18] Erskine-Hill 1966: 58.

confutation of the original .... [The] hand that wrote it may become lumber, but ... the spirit that dictated it can never be so.'[19]

Assuming one accepts the attribution,[20] Rochester's imaginative preoccupation with the theme of dissolution is evident again in 'Upon Nothinge', the third stanza of which prophesies as follows on the fate of 'Somethinge' (created matter) after its brief existence:

> Somethinge, the Generall atribute of all,
> Sever'd from thee [i.e., from Nothinge] its sole originall
> Into thy boundless selfe must undistinguish'd fall.

> (ll. 7–9)[21]

The 'boundless' infinitude of Nothing which 'had'st a beinge ere the world was made' (l. 2)—its 'boundlessness' is, for Rochester, its most transfixing quality—will ultimately *re*absorb all the stuff which Something has created out of it (and against its will). Despite Something's having differentiated its newly generated matter into 'men, Beasts, birds, fyre, water, Aire, and land' (l. 12), those parts will nevertheless end their life by returning, *'undistinguish'd'*, to Nothing, their non-existent point of origin, wherein they will be dissolved and lost without trace.[22] What seemed to be Something's absolute 'Command' (l. 10) over its parent (Nothing), and over the world, thus proves only transient. Nothing has the power to destroy this 'short liv'd Raigne' of Something 'And to [her own] hungry woombe drive backe [her] slaves againe' (ll. 19–21), rekennelling them in the matrix whence they were wrenched. (This 'hungry woombe' compares, of course, with the 'Devouring Time [which] swallows us' in Rochester's *Troas*; with 'le sein du Néant' which Dehénault adds to his version of that same work;[23] and with the 'devouring *Cunt*' in 'A Ramble in St. James's Park' (l. 119)[24] whose capacity to 'gorge' itself (l. 117) is simultaneously a source of exhilaration and terror.) Here, Nothing's inexorable absorption of all living things is not, though, viewed with quite the horror one might expect, given the example of *Troas*. For instance, tedious debates which have 'wract the Polliticians Brest' (l. 34) are, 'when Reduc'd to [Nothing,] ... least unsafe and best' (l. 36): Nothing renders these questions harmless, either in so far as time obliterates them or (reading 'Reduc'd to thee' another way) because it exposes their trivial irrelevance. Likewise, numerous worthless, worldly goods, 'The Greate mans Gratitude ... , / Kings promisses, whoores vowes, towards thee

---

[19] Rochester 1980: 234.

[20] See Rochester 1999: 371–2. On the Rochester canon generally, see Vieth 1963.

[21] Rochester 1999: 46 ff.

[22] There is an obvious parallel here with Des Barreaux's sonnet 'Mortels qui vous croyez', which likewise dwells on 'le néant' (l. 10) bracketing human existence (Adam 1964: 194 ff.).

[23] Ibid. 260.

[24] Rochester 1999: 76 ff. On the ambiguities of Corinna's 'devouring *Cunt*', see Burns 1995: 29.

[Nothing] ... bend, / Flow swiftly into thee and in thee ever end' (ll. 49–51). To the extent that it devours these things, Nothing is downright beneficent. Disillusioned as he here is with the Restoration polity and its court society, Rochester would be happy to see those things destroyed. In this regard, then, and in so far as it focuses on *others'* elimination, 'Upon Nothinge' testifies to the positive promise of death's nothingness. *Troas*, by contrast, in fixing on the persona's own individual fate, points rather to the horror of that void. But in both cases Rochester remains transfixed by the ideas of devourment and absolute loss of autonomy.

Rochester's images of boundlessness, obliteration, and sweeping precipitation through a void have, of course, a long heritage quite apart from the Epicurean tradition. To a Christian readership such language recalls, for example, both Lucifer's fall and the 'boundless' ocean of Chaos in *Paradise Lost* (another Restoration work which I have suggested is particularly concerned with boundaries). Milton's fallen angels are driven 'to the bounds' of heaven (*PL* 6. 859) and either throw themselves 'headlong' into the deep (ll. 860–6) or are 'Hurled headlong flaming' by the Almighty (1. 45). The void they fall into is an 'unreal, vast, unbounded deep' (10. 471) but also, simultaneously, a 'womb of Nature' and its 'grave' (2. 911).[25] Clearly, Rochester may have had Milton in mind as he wrote *Troas* or 'Upon Nothinge', but what this connection also emphasizes is the ethical and religious inflection of some of the key figures which shaped the Earl's imagination. The motifs of hurling motion, utmost limits, and boundless spaces were all imbued, whether Rochester liked it or not, with connotations of governance and Christian theodicy, two languages which return at unexpected moments throughout even this writer's most libertine poems (those poems to which I now turn).

## ROCHESTER'S LOVE LYRICS: THE POETRY OF APPETITE

Rochester's lyric performances frequently construct felicity in terms akin to Hobbes's—that is, as an experience which (far from terminating in a single attachment) demands the acquisitive pursuit of one conquest after another, each becoming valueless the moment it reaches fruition. These poems draw upon the libertine ideal of governance, focusing on man's foremost appetite, sexual desire. Such is the spirit, for example, of 'Against Constancy', a reworking of a commonplace theme given earlier expression in Donne's Elegies 'Change' and 'The heavens rejoice in motion', his lyric 'Confined

[25] Cf. *PL* 2. 180–2, 373–4; 10. 476–7; 12. 370–1.

Love', and Jonson's song 'In Defence of... Inconstancy', but which here assumes a new inflection under the pressure of the Hobbist context. 'Against Constancy' opens with a strident imperative:

> Tell mee noe more of Constancy,
>      The frivolous pretence
> Of Cold Age, narrow Jealouzy,
>      Disease, and want of Sense.
>
>                    (ll. 1–4)[26]

This explosion contrasts sharply with the aptly wavering syntax of the next two stanzas, stanzas which describe characters so weak that in advocating constancy they only make a virtue of necessity. These men '*Ought*, to bee constant Lovers' (l. 12), the persona remarks scathingly, because the latter is the virtue of the impotent, those too witless to manipulate circumstances so as to maximize their own satisfaction. Such 'Duller Fooles' are dependent on 'chance' alone for the one 'easy Heart' (ll. 5–6) which they gain (and dare not then be unfaithful to); but they lack the honesty to admit as much, instead deluding themselves that constancy is an asset. By contrast, libertines like Rochester's, knowing 'how [they] in Love excell', revel in their own visceral forthrightness and 'Long, to bee often try'd' (ll. 15–16). The persona's 'try'd' implies less the passivity of being chosen by numerous women than the idea of being oft tested (and found triumphant) by fate itself. There is thus a mock inversion here of the practice of habituation and self-testing put to work in a poem like Spenser's *Faerie Queene*. The result in this case is a hedonistic (not an Aristotelian) repetition-compulsion, one which equates felicity with corporeal pleasure, and corporeal pleasure with a constant momentum of change. Happiness for this persona (as for Hobbes) consists not in having prospered but in prospering, now and hereafter. But happiness clearly also consists in the possession and assertion of power. Rochester's Dorimant-like character, unrepentant in face of his own egotism, reassures himself that his heart does '*justly* swell / With noe vaineglorious pride' (ll. 13–14). He is conscious of the social supremacy which his sexual triumphalism accords him, and this brusque complacency, a more deep-seated version of Suckling's bluntness, extends even to the last stanza where he avows his intention to pursue Cyrenaic motion to his dying day: 'I'le change a Mistresse, till I'me dead, / And Fate change mee to Wormes' (ll. 19–20).

This last reminder of time's chariot hurrying near 'As each kind Night returnes' (l. 18) recalls the mentality informing Des Barreaux's *carpe diem* ethic or Oldham's 'Dithyrambique', the consciousness of 'la suite du temps qui fuit',

---

[26] Rochester 1999: 34.

for which aggressive acquisition of new joys is but a balancing compensation. The same consciousness animates 'To Love', Rochester's translation of Ovid's *Amores* 2. 9, in which the ageing persona first entertains and then rejects the notion of retiring from the sexual chase on the grounds that 'There's time for rest when fate has stop'd your breath' (l. 46).[27] The images with which this figure describes the renewal of appetite's grip are familiar:

> When e're these flames grow faint, I quickly find
> A fierce black storm, pow'r down upon my mind,
> Headlong I'm Hurl'd like Horsemen who in vain
> Their fury-foaming Coursers wou'd Restrain.
>
> (ll. 31–4)

I have already noted the significance of the verb 'Hurl'd' (Ovid's 'rapit'[28]) in Rochester's *Troas*, and it will recur in the 'Satyre against Reason', where, in addition, a metaphysician will fall '*headlong* down / Into doubts boundless Sea' (ll. 18–19)[29] just as the persona is here hurled 'Headlong' ('in praeceps') by the horse. In 'To Love' this self-renewing appetite is figured in line 32 as a storm which invades and drowns the mind. In this case, though, the loss of autonomy and dissolution of self intrinsic to that experience (and to appetite's hurtling motion generally) are welcomed as exhilarating sensations, not threats. The same is true of 'My dear Mistris has a heart', where, speaking of his mistress, the persona thrills to the fact that 'Melting Joys about her move' (l. 9), as if to be drawn into the dissolving vortex of *this* pudenda were a positive pleasure.[30]

'Upon his leaving his Mistresse', an obvious counterpart to 'Against Constancy', is another sensationalist poem which celebrates libertine appetite. An exercise in wit and a manœuvre within the game of manners, the poet's sport here is to cast the announcement of his departure from a lover as an elaborate compliment to her, a testament to her supposed divinity:

> Tis not that I am weary growne,
> Of being yours, and yours alone;
> But with what face can I design
> To damn you to be only mine?
>
> (ll. 1–4)[31]

The exaggerated *diminutio* of line 4 here anticipates the reference to Cælia's having been made by 'some kinder Pow'r' (l. 5) and the closing imperative that she should live up to her 'mighty Mind' (l. 20). Whatever the exact tone of this song—and the clumsy, colloquial quality of the line 'The joy at least of one

---

[27] Ibid. 12 ff.     [28] Ovid 1914: 408.     [29] Rochester 1999: 57.     [30] Ibid. 32 ff.
[31] Ibid. 17 ff.

whole Nation' (l. 7) certainly sounds a note of wry irony—it is surely too easeful
to achieve the 'wavering between heartbreak and savage sarcasm' which Ellis
finds in it.[32] The opening couplet signals a witty, sophistical intent indicative of
the persona's wish to sustain the *impression* of loving concern for his beloved
(a Mrs Loveit figure). Stanzas 2 and 3 are cast as a friend's benevolent advice.
The persona can maintain some sincerity in this performance because he here
purports to be coaxing his mistress into adopting what is in fact his own ideal
of conduct. The 'meaner Spirits' whom she must abandon, for example, are
the female equivalents of 'Against Constancy's' 'Duller fooles':

> Let meaner Spirits ...
> Contrive to make one happy Man,
> Whilst mov'd by an Impartiall Sense
> Favours like Nature, you dispence,
> With Universall Influence.
>
> (ll. 8, 11–14)

This looks more like an instruction for the future than a sarcastic reflection
on this woman's current actions. At the end of the poem she is still, for now,
'*my* Cælia' (l. 19), and it is as his supposed beloved that the persona advises
her (ostensibly for her own sake, so that she might fulfil her 'mighty Mind's'
potential) to become 'the Mistresse of Mankind' (l. 21). We are confronted,
then, with the manipulative argument of a Dorimant who feigns a gentle,
loving disposition but has no real passion for his sometime mistress—only
an appetite now satiated and eager to move on, but without retrospectively
revealing its true indifference for fear that the lover might thereby lose his power
over his admirer. The ethic which lies behind the poem is, as such, familiar.

The same sophistical wit employed in the service of the libertine's ever
predatory appetite and lust for power also informs 'Love and Life' (a Rochesterian reworking of Waller's 'To Phyllis' and of the opening of Lovelace's
'The Scrutiny').[33] 'Love and Life' has long been taken as positive proof that
Rochester engaged in detail with Hobbes's philosophy, and that assertion
merits some comment. Treglown has matched the lyric's opening stanzas to
the sketch of prudence/foresight in *Leviathan*:[34]

(1)                     All my past Life is mine no more,
                          The flyeing houres are gone

[32] Rochester 1994: 353. Farley-Hills's judgement (1978: 62–3) that, though there are 'menacing' moments, the organizing mood is one of 'anti-platonic playfulness', is more plausible.
[33] Such is its ambiguity, 'Love and Life' admits of other, less cynical interpretations than that
advocated here. It could indeed be read as arguing 'that love can provide moments of enrichment
that snatch meaning out of meaninglessness' (Farley-Hills 1978: 42).
[34] Treglown 1973: 44.

Like Transitory dreams given o're
Whose Images are kept in store
By memory alone.

What ever is to come is not:
How can it then be mine ?
The present moment's all my Lott ...

(ll. 1–8)[35]

(2) ... by how much one man has more experience of things past, than another; by
so much ... he is more Prudent, and his expectations the seldomer faile him. The
*Present* only has a being in Nature; things *Past* have a being in the Memory onely,
but things *to come* have no being at all; the *Future* being but a fiction of the mind,
applying the sequels of actions Past, to the actions that are Present.[36]

The parity between these two texts is clear, but at most proves only that
Rochester read chapter 3 of *Leviathan*. A harsh judgement, perhaps, but the
details of his literary life suggest (as Treglown concedes)[37] that Rochester
was never a stayer, too protean a character to be willing to study a book
like *Leviathan* from cover to cover. Besides, if the Hobbes extract is indeed
Rochester's source, 'Love and Life' constitutes a significant distortion of that
original. Rochester's speaker, Treglown notes, far from being interested in
Hobbesian 'foresight and prudence', would be using Hobbes here (were that
his inspiration) 'to provide an eloquent excuse for ... infidelity' and precisely
to deny the possibility of foresight.[38]

There is, though, another, equally plausible source for 'Love and Life', one
which would entail no such inversions: namely, the centre-piece of Stanley's
discussion of Aristippus and Cyrenaicism:[39]

... neither the remembrance of past goods, nor expectation of future[,] compleat
pleasure .... Pleasure, according to *Aristippus*, ... *consisteth only in one part of time*,
the present: for the remembrance of past pleasures, or expectation of the future, is
vain ... and nothing appertaineth .... [T]hat only is good which is present. With those
pleasures which he received heretofore, or shall receive hereafter, *Aristippus* said, he
was nothing ... moved, the first being gone, the other not yet come, and what it will
prove when it is come ... uncertain. Hence ... Men ought not to be sollicitous either
about things past or future .... He ... advised to take care only for the present day,
and in that day, only of the present part thereof ... for ... the present is only in our
power, not the past or future, the one being gone, the other uncertain whether ever it
will come.[40]

[35] Rochester 1999: 25 ff.    [36] Hobbes 1996: 22.    [37] See Rochester 1980: 31.
[38] Ibid. 13.    [39] This *pace* Griffin 1973: 171.
[40] Stanley 1701: 135.

Clearly, this doctrine is itself a source or analogue for *Hobbes's* definition of appetite, a fact highlighted by Stanley's use of the word 'power' here. That aside, though, Stanley's text is directly and unapologetically concerned not with prudence but with the nature of bodily appetite, precisely the theme of 'Love and Life', and as such it squarely maps on to the latter, foregrounding the mind-set which that lyric and others dramatize.

To the Stanley one can add other analogues, casting further doubt over *Leviathan*'s status as the assumed source for Rochester's poem. Des Barreaux's sonnets, Oldham's 'Dithyrambique', and Cotton's (then unpublished) 'Clepsydra' all insist upon the immediate perishability of the present moment. So does Philips's 'Lucasia *and* Orinda *parting with* Pastora *and* Phillis *at* Ipswich' (published in 1667):

> How perish'd is the joy that's past,
>     The present how unsteady!
> What comfort can be great, and last,
>     When this is gone already?
>
> (ll. 5–8)[41]

In Philips's lyric too (as in l. 5 of Rochester's 'Love and Life'), 'memory' is invoked (l. 10) as the one store in which past joys *are* kept; but now (since their present absence is noted more than is their original pleasantness) those recollected delights function only as sources of pain. This detail of content presages Rochester's work, but so, likewise, do some of the linguistic qualities. The preponderance of terse indicative forms, of imperatives and interrogatives in Philips's ballad, foreshadows the similar grammatical structuring in 'Love and Life'. Likewise, her use of a phrase like 'we'll not grieve' (l. 13) anticipates the conversational ease of Rochester's customary style, the slight slouchiness of his idiom (witness 'wee'l not disagree' (l. 18), for example, in 'How perfect Cloris').[42] Here, though, the similarities end. As with the Hobbes extract, the argument of Philips's poem ultimately takes a different course from Rochester's own. In 'Lucasia *and* Orinda' Philips prays for a reversal of fortune, hoping that the parting of friends which first induced her sense of transience will be rectified by some future reunion. Rochester, by contrast, having voiced the same thoughts about time's perishability, offers his mistress only the following promise:

> The present moment's all my Lott
> And that as fast as it is gott
>     *Phillis* is wholly thine.
>
> (ll. 8–10)

---

[41] Philips 1990–3: i. 228.      [42] Rochester 1999: 23 ff.

The argument in Rochester's poem is—to return to my main theme—a sophistry designed to circumvent any questioning of the persona's own fidelity, and thus to give him power over his mistress. The speaker seeks to allay her demands for constancy by claiming that such an undertaking would be philosophically unsustainable (the future being as resistant to appropriation as the past is to retention). Lines 9 and 10 above imply that what attachment he can offer will be intense but volatile, and though he purports to emphasize the former aspect, there is, woven within his language, a witty acknowledgement of the latter. The persona's claim is that as quickly as each present moment is realized, it will be devoted entirely to Phillis; but 'fast' can also mean 'secure', and the implication of that is that only in so far as each present moment is secured within his grasp, only in so far as he has control over what he does with his life, will it be devoted wholly to Phillis. What could he do if some vile seductress possessed him, robbing him of his autonomy? Such a moment would not be fast got under his control. Such a moment would not, alas, be Phillis's.

The abdication of responsibility which the Cyrenaic argument entails is pursued in the final stanza:

> Then talk not of Inconstancy,
>     False hearts and broken vows:
> If I by miracle can be
> This livelong Minute true to Thee
>     Tis' all that Heaven allowes.

(ll. 11–15)

Heaven alone, and its kind miracles, will, so the mock-pious hyperbole goes, determine the extent of the man's fidelity. Within those parameters he can offer the devotion of a 'livelong Minute', but whether that means a Platonizing eternal now, an idealized union of lovers' souls transcending the rags of mortal time; or whether it be, following out preceding stanzas' logic, a minute in which the lover invests his whole being (his 'life') because past and future are non-existent; or simply an intense and therefore seemingly long minute; or just the 'lucky' or 'happy' minute of orgasm, 'livelong' because ending in a little death, remains nicely ambiguous. This equivocation matches the ambiguity of the attachment presented here. We remain uncertain as to whether the persona is addressing only a fleeting mistress, an enduring one, or even his wife. Part of the point is that the imagined addressee is presumably left equally uncertain as to her status, that anxious doubt being another reflection of the persona's power. This Dorimant figure, without ever fracturing his pose of good manners, without ever presenting himself as anything less than 'reasonable', holds his Belinda in his grip, but at arm's length—under his control, certainly, but never in a way which imposes reciprocal obligations upon him.

Having said this, though, there is another dimension to the experience recorded in this lyric. The persona achieves his abdication of responsibility on the back of an argument which, if he believes it, destabilizes his own identity. As with Hume's critique of personal identity in his *Treatise*, the sense of self here is tied primarily to the present moment of consciousness. Past life amounts to only a series of 'Transitory dreams given o're' (l. 3), seemingly abandoned. Though also 'kept in store', this personal history is kept 'By memory *alone*' (ll. 4–5), the adjective reminding us that memory is fallible and suggesting that this form of relation to one's past is, anyway, inadequate: there is something missing, some process of recall and review, without which the 'memory *alone*' cannot shore up the sense of self. The absence of any such effort to build connections between past and present is an inevitable corollary of the *carpe diem* ethic, which lives only for the here and now, draining each moment of its delights and then consigning it to the brain's homogeneous mass of memories. This past is, for the rake, a distraction of no emotional value; and nor should his mistress value it: the fact of its supposed *lack* of connection to the present implies that she would be wrong to infer any lessons for the present from it, wrong to use it in the prudential manner advocated by Hobbes. But the effect of insisting upon that supposed lack of connection is to generate the potential for instability in the persona's own sense of self.[43] His relationship to his past is, as described here, insufficient to induce the impression of continuity which Locke, in the 1694 edition of his *Essay*, was to make essential to personal identity. Nor is this vertiginous interpretation of 'Love and Life' conceivable only to those schooled in British empiricism: Browne[44] and Montaigne[45] were concerned with the perpetuity of identity long before Rochester wrote. Plutarch's 'On Tranquillity of Mind', too, provides a gloss to this effect:

... such as are foolish ... , doe ... let go the ... good things ... they have, and never care to enjoy them, so ... earnestly bent are their mindes ... to that which is comming.... [The] senselesse oblivion of many ready to catch and devoure al good things as they passe by, yea and to ... cause to vanish away every ... notable action ... and pleasant pastime, ... will not permit, that ... life be one and the same, linked ... by the coppulation of things passed and present; but deviding yesterday from to day, and this day from the morrow ... bringeth in such a forgetfulnesse, as if things ... past had never beene.... [These] for fault of memorie not able to reteine ... those things that are done ... , but suffer every thing to passe away ... through a sieve, doe ... in ... effect, make themselves voide and emptie ... , depending onely

---

[43] Cf. Treglown 1982: 10–11.

[44] See Browne 1977: 107. Browne's wish to associate identity with some sense of personal 'history' prefigures Locke's idea of consciousness.

[45] See *Essais* 2. 1, 2. 6, and 3. 2.

upon the morrow, as if those things which were done the yeere past, of late, and yesterday, nothing appertained unto them, nor ever were at all.[46]

The significance of this threatened loss of self-possession, the making oneself 'voide and emptie' which the fantasy self-image of 'Love and Life' adumbrates, is clear: it tallies with the images of self-dissolution touched upon positively in Rochester's Ovid translation and 'My dear Mistris has a heart', ambivalently in 'Upon Nothinge', and negatively in *Troas* and the 'Satyre against Reason' (discussed below). But if this threat is underlined by the ease with which each 'present moment' of the second stanza slips backwards into the disappearing 'houres' of the first, that same relationship also highlights another problem: the instability of the felicity that the persona is here seizing upon. Each appetite is only a source of pleasure for a single minute. In a life lived according to Hobbist premises, each such delight, the moment it has passed, loses its value and must be replaced. And yet, 'What ever is to come is not': there is no certainty in this happiness, no guarantee of continuity (no matter how adept a wit is at creating his own opportunities). Consequently, this felicity is as inherently unstable as the sense of self which accompanies it. The word 'fast' in the phrase 'as fast as it is gott' thus has a third, still larger connotation, one which has worrying implications not for the addressee but for the lyric voice. The adjective registers the ambivalent nature of the persona's lifestyle, the fact that he lives life as a continuous, hurtling race, potentially either exhilarating or exhaustive, a source of assertion or of self-enslavement. As Spragens argues, this truism is crucial to the legacy of Hobbes's moral thought:

[Man's] life is one of... endless striving, without any *telos* to fulfil his quest. He must run, but... has no resting place for his goal. While in one sense it is accurate to say... that the seventeenth century destroys the tension that characterized the Aristotelian cosmos—the tension of the dialectic between potential and actual—in another sense it universalizes tension; for what is destroyed is not the striving, but the *telos* which made the strife resolvable .... [T]he proximate anxiety of the finite human organism generated from its not-yet-fulfilled condition turns into the ... unresolvable anxiety of the racer who is condemned to run continually after a nonexistent fulfilment.[47]

If, though, the racer faces the anxiety of having no ultimate goal, he is trapped, too, by the thought that he cannot afford to stand still. The paranoia that somehow pleasure is always ahead of him, always threatening to escape, drives the libertine forward. This enslaving fear, the negative corollary of 'Against Constancy's' positive appetite, is pithily captured in Rochester's song

[46] Plutarch 1603: 156.
[47] Spragens 1973: 190. Cf. Vieth 1988: 15–16; Weil 1993: 148–51.

'Phillis, be gentler I advise', with the sentiment 'Your pleasure, ever comes too late, / How early ere begun' (ll. 7–8).[48]

'Love and Life', then, as a sketch of the imagined reality of the rake's life, invites either a celebration or a critique of the libertine ethic, depending on how one interprets it. As a lyric of the critical sort, it is not alone in the Earl's canon. For instance, at least one implication of Rochester's suggestion that even the triumph of a sexual 'Victor' may be one of only '*Empty* Pride' ('While on these Lovely Lookes I gaze', l. 15[49]), is that coital fruition need not, in the final event, prove physically satisfying. On the contrary, it may disappoint our expectations. To make sense of this phenomenon, though, which is also integral to the critique of libertinism enacted in 'The Fall' and 'The Platonick Lady' (discussed hereafter), we need first to invoke a wider tradition of works which argued 'Against Fruition' in this period. The earliest lyric poem to do this was Jonson's translation of 'Foeda est in coitu et brevis voluptas', 'Doing a filthy pleasure is, and short' (before 1619); but to that one can add Shakespearean examples. Cressida, to reiterate, determines to postpone the moment of Troilus's fruition for as long as possible in the fear that 'Things won are done, joy's soul' lying only 'in the doing'. Cleopatra provides a fantasy counter-argument to this same anxiety. Her corporeal presence is so absolute that it transforms her every passion, bleak or joyous, into something alluring (*Antony and Cleopatra*, i. i. 50–3). In keeping with this fact, she is thus a *perpetual* source of sexual fascination to her lovers: 'Other women cloy / The appetites they feed, but she makes hungry / Where most she satisfies' (ii. ii. 242–4). Cleopatra's 'infinite variety' (l. 242) renders her, uniquely, an endless source of erotic delight, so that in her 'fancy outworks'—keeps ahead of—'nature' and its satiating limits (l. 208). In contrast to this ideal, though, stand numerous other poems 'Against Fruition', all following in Jonson's vein. These include Oldham's own 1683 paraphrasing of 'Foeda est in coitu'; Donne's 'Farewell to Love' (before 1635); Suckling's 'Upon A. M.' (between 1626 and 1632), and his two songs 'Against Fruition' (1632–7), which occasioned replies by Waller and Henry Bold; King's 'Paradox. That Fruition destroyes Love' (between 1641 and 1648); Cowley's 'Against Fruition' (1656); Philips's 'Against Pleasure' (1664); Creech's and Dryden's translations of Book 4 of Lucretius (1682, 1685); and the two poems, Alexis's 'Against Fruition' and Behn's 'Answer', both printed in *Lycidus* (1688).[50]

These works draw on a common sequence of themes. First, they attack sexual intercourse for its physical disappointments, the ephemeral nature

---

[48] Rochester 1999: 19 ff.

[49] Ibid. 26 ff. 'While on these Lovely Lookes' is fiendishly ambiguous, and the particular protest quoted here bears other interpretations besides that which I put upon it.

[50] On this genre, see Hartle 2002.

of its pleasures. The most vigorous such portrayal of fruition's sensuous inadequacies is Lucretius's, which emphasizes how far bodily cravings are left unquenched by sex. Intercourse needs must be (according to the *De Rerum*) an imperfect enjoyment, because it is always undercut by a contrary, hostile motive which makes it aggressive. Man

> ... strains at all, and fastening where he strains,
> Too closely presses with his frantic pains;
> With biting kisses hurts the twining fair,
> Which shows his joys imperfect, unsincere:
> For stung with inward rage he flings around,
> And strives t'avenge the smart on that which gave the wound.
>
> (4. 39–44)[51]

This expectation of vengeance is constantly frustrated: 'Repletion is to love denied' (l. 56). The beauties of the beloved enjoyed by the lover do not fill a space as food fills the stomach. The lover finds nothing in his 'deluded grasp' (l. 61) and 'no real drink to quench his thirst' (l. 64) either in the first or subsequent acts of coition. Lucretius worries this theme, reiterating his argument with increasing (and increasingly graphic) intensity, as if imitating the repetitious actions of lovers themselves:

> When both press on, both murmur, both expire,
> They gripe, they squeeze, their humid tongues they dart,
> As each would force their way to t'other's heart—
> In vain; they only cruise about the coast,
> For bodies cannot pierce, nor be in bodies lost.
>
> (ll. 74–8)

The Donnish tendencies of lines 76 and 78 here are reinforced by Creech's translation, in which the lovers 'cannot mix their Souls'.[52] The image in line 77, recalling Spragens's notion that appetite's race is never done, is Dryden's own addition. The point in both translations is that the *pleasurable* dissolution of self, the interanimation whereby each might endure not a breach but an expansion, is always frustrated.[53] Though man 'dissolves in [the] excess of joy' (l. 82), he does so only momentarily and in a physical sense which does not, or ever will, satisfy his larger, metaphysical aspiration. Worse still, that physical dissolution is not, even on its own, purely corporeal terms, a lasting source of contentment (in which respect it is a world away from Carew's erotic raptures).

---

[51] Dryden 1995–2005: ii. 332 ff.    [52] Lucretius 1682: 134.
[53] Cf. Hammond 1983: 20.

Man's tendency, faced with initial disappointment, is to persevere. The first 'full possession does but fan the fire' (l. 51), a feverish need for fulfilment which propels the lovers into re-enactment: 'Again they in each other would be lost, / But still by adamantine bars are crossed' (ll. 89–90). This second theme of *perpetual, repeated* frustration is common in poems against fruition. Suckling argues in 'Against Fruition [1]' that with repetition fruition 'cloyes' (l. 8).[54] King offers another striking distillation of this point, asking, witheringly, 'After Fruition once, what is Desire / But ashes kept warm by a dying fire?' (ll. 73–4).[55] Such repetitive hankering after intercourse is no more than a diseased condition:

> For when the *Heat ad Octo* intermits,
> It poorly takes us like Third Ague fits;
> Or must on Embers as dull Druggs infuse,
> Which we for Med'cine not for Pleasure use.
>
> (ll. 77–80)

Third-day ague is a fever characterized by the occurrence of a paroxysm every third day (hence 'intermit'). The suggestion here is that the sexual urge for fruition possesses man in all its intensity ('*Heat ad Octo*') on a periodic basis, but now as a fever rather than some pleasant inclination. Correspondingly, the dying fire of dwindling love comes to depend less on fresh fuel and more on its own embers' heat (the remnants of its first, now corrupted and spent fuel) for its survival—just as man's desire, after the first disappointment, focuses increasingly on re-enacting memories of what was and might have been, instead of on capturing new pleasures. In this poem's bleak vision coition therefore becomes a medicine to relieve man's feverish itch, to satiate the addictive need for intercourse, rather than a source of new delights. Here, as in *Troilus*, the desire is boundless, the act a slave to limit.

One response to this dilemma is to postpone indefinitely the shift from desire to spasm, filling out the intervening time with endless kissing. The measured, rhythmic grace of that act is neatly captured in Jonson's metre:

> But thus, thus [Sed sic sic ...] ...
> ... Let us together closely lie.
>
> (ll. 6–7)

> This hath pleased, doth please, and long will please
> [Hoc iuvit, iuvat et diu iuvabit].
>
> (l. 9)[56]

---

[54] Suckling 1971: i. 37 ff.     [55] King 1657: 75 ff.
[56] Jonson 1985: 432; Buecheler and Riese 1895–1926: vol. i (pt. ii), p. 171. Cf. Hartle 2002: 79.

What makes *this* pleasure truly ideal is the fact that it never will decay, 'but is beginning ever' (l. 10). Kissing is allegedly a delight secure from the disappointment of closure. Another, less physical solution to the problem, though, is simply to languish in the delusional pleasures of anticipation: hence King's preference for holding 'Lovers joyes … in Reversion' (ll. 81–4). The paradise lost with knowledge is a delicate 'sweet dream' (Suckling, 'Against Fruition [1]', l. 5) from which the over ardent lover too readily wakes himself. Suckling maintains that this pleasure is dependent on ignorance and expectation, and on the fantasies which thrive where those factors 'leave us room to guesse' (l. 27). For Montaigne this 'room to guesse' is a veritable 'stately pallace' which we should allow to detain us: better to linger over its 'diuers porches … pleasant galleries, and well contriued turnings' than to snatch immediately at 'absolute possession'.[57] Philips's lover, similarly, postpones the disillusioning moment of 'approach' ('Against Pleasure', l. 8),[58] whilst Cowley's bluntly privileges distant fantasy over close reality, affirming the self-interest which underpins his predilection for dreams even whilst conceding their unnaturalness:

> Thou in my *Fancy* dost much higher stand,
> Then *Women* can be plac'd by *Natures* hand;
> And I must needs, I'm sure, a loser be,
> To change *Thee*, as *Thou'rt there*, for *very Thee*.
>
> ('Against Fruition', ll. 17–20)[59]

Restraint, then, in Suckling's words, must 'Hold up' delight ('Against Fruition [1]', l. 28), both in the sense of holding back enjoyment (that is, orgasm) and of *supporting* a more moderate, sustainable delight, that of the fancy. Women enjoyed 'Are like Romances read, or sights once seen:/Fruition's dull, and spoils the Play … / … / 'Tis expectation makes a blessing dear' (ll. 20–3).

Rochester's 'The Fall' and his 'Platonick Lady' both assess the failure of sensuality to satisfy even on its own terms. They present fruition (as in so many of these other poems) as an experience which does not begin to quench man's amorous flame. Written against the background of an Augustinian tradition of commentary on paradisal sexuality,[60] 'The Fall' (like Donne's 'The heavens rejoyce in motion' and Lovelace's 'Love Made in the First Age') laments the lost sexual blessings of man's 'Created state' (l. 1).[61] Back then, intercourse was no source of shame:

---

[57] Montaigne 1603: 528.    [58] Philips 1990–3: i. 137 ff.    [59] Cowley 1993: 58.
[60] See Turner 1987a: ch. 2.    [61] Rochester 1999: 26.

> Naked beneath coole shades they lay:
> Enjoyment waited on desire.
> Each member did their wills obey
> Nor could a wish sett pleasure higher.
>
> (ll. 5–8)

In his *Citie of God* (14. 24) Augustine reiterates the truth of line 7 here: that in the prelapsarian state 'Man ... should haue sowne the seede, and woman ... receiued it, as neede required, without all lust, ... as their wills desired', and this with the perfect co-operation of their bodily members.[62] Whilst Augustine's Adam cannot be said to experience the voluptuous kind of 'desire' referred to in Rochester's poem (l. 6), it is true at least that his fulfilment will 'wait on', and be immediately responsive to, his mind's impulse. As Augustine puts it, the first man, 'beeing laid in his wiues lap', was able to move his member 'without concupiscentiall' (or the 'exorbitance' of any 'hotter') 'affect', and 'without corruption' of his own or Eve's 'integrity' (14. 26).[63] Rochester, by choosing the sexualized vocabulary of 'Enjoyment' and 'desire', modifies Augustine's vision (rather as Milton had done), including within it a perfect *sensual* pleasure absent from the *Citie of God*'s Adam; but his prelapsarian ideal, that of a harmonized body and mind working together to provide unfailing delight, is otherwise still akin to Augustine's. Hence, its fleeting ambiguities aside, the primary sense of Rochester's eighth line, 'Nor could a wish sett pleasure higher', is clear. There is a perfect correspondence in his antediluvian couple between their hopes and the reality of their fulfilment, and hence no disappointment in this fruition.

In man, now, the condition is different:

> ... we poore slaves to hope and fear
> Are never of our Joys secure:
> They lessen still as they draw nere
> And none but dull delights endure.
>
> (ll. 9–12)

The delight of fruition, on this account, begins to diminish even before coition takes place. Sexual pleasure may be, for Rochester, ' "false" because it does not last and ... is based on lies, the delusion of fidelity',[64] but it is also false because it peaks even before coition begins, and wanes with the latter's approach. The very concerns expressed by the writers 'Against Fruition' blight the moment of orgasm in advance, the lover fearfully anticipating, before he has even made

---

[62] Augustine 1610: 526.      [63] Ibid. 529.      [64] Chernaik 1995: 67.

his conquest, the disillusionment which will attend it. Joys, then, 'lessen still as they draw nere'.[65]

Besides emphasizing this envisaged disjunction between sour pleasures actually felt and sweet wishes frustrated, 'The Fall' also suggests (especially through its second stanza (ll. 5–8) ) that fallen man, in contrast to prelapsarian Adam, can expect to suffer the disobedience of the body too. He will experience an asymmetry between 'desire' and 'will', on the one hand, and the actual 'Enjoyment' which his 'member' proves capable of yielding, on the other. In this respect 'The Fall' gestures towards another favourite Restoration topos, the 'Imperfect Enjoyment' poem exemplified by Etherege, Behn, and Rochester (in his own 'The Imperfect Enjoyment'). This tradition focuses not on the purely psychological disappointments which precede and succeed achieved fruition, but on the feelings associated with bodily failures—impotence, premature ejaculation—which also thwart consummation. The concerns of this latter tradition are clearly uppermost in Rochester's closing stanza, where the lover betrays an anxiety that his 'frayler part' (l. 16) may not stand up to his mistress's expectations. Nevertheless, that the *third* stanza (ll. 9–12) amounts to a critique of the psychological pleasures of coition, that 'The Fall' therefore contributes to the 'Against Fruition' tradition as well as the 'Imperfect Enjoyment' one, remains clear.

Alongside 'The Fall', 'The Platonick Lady' makes a still more obvious contribution to this genre. Written in the persona of a lady whose tastes are anything but Platonic (a world away from Donne or Castiglione's Bembo), and written too (like Suckling's 'Carlile' poem) as a mocking inversion of the cult of Platonic love practised in Henrietta Maria's court,[66] Rochester's lyric reworks the bluntly corporeal theme of 'Foeda est in coitu'. The pun in the first line, 'I could Love thee till I dye',[67] is instrumental in focusing the poem's sense, which argues that because fruition (the little death) destroys the sexual pleasure it should consummate, because it fails to satisfy even on its own, purely sensual terms, it must be postponed for as long as possible whilst the lovers eke out the interim with the genuine, untainted delights of foreplay. Clearly, in this respect, the poem is one of several Rochester lyrics which explore provisional 'solutions' to the problem of fruition, the solution here being simply to stall the moment of surrender in favour of pleasures

---

[65] It is worth noting that the generality of the language in this third stanza of 'The Fall' indicates the extent to which this poem invites a broader interpretation. Sexual appetite is used here synecdochically for appetite in general. Human desires of every kind are, the lyric implies, prone to the kind of disappointment identified in the 'Against Fruition' poems, and for that reason the libertine-Cyrenaic ethic in general is flawed.

[66] See Orgel and Strong 1973: i. 49–75; Sharpe and Zwicker 1987: 134–41.

[67] Rochester 1999: 35.

(in Oldham's phrase) 'fresh, and always but begun'.[68] The Lady's lover must therefore 'Love ... modestly' (l. 2). Enjoyment (orgasm)

> ... cutts of [i.e., cuts off] all thats Life and fier,
> From that which may be term'd desire;
> Just like the Be whose sting being gon,
> Converts the owner to a Drone.
>
> (ll. 9–12)

The second couplet here alludes to the ending of Cowley's 'Against Fruition', whilst lines 9 and 10, if not an allusion, do evoke the argument of King's 'Paradox', 'cutts of' implying a removal of the fuel supply similar to that which leaves the dying fire to feed only on its embers' warmth. The persona is clear in her mind that the pleasures she will permit herself—gently 'pressing' some youth's body, taking the chance 'to kisse, / ... sigh and looke with Eyes that wish' (ll. 15–16)—are infinitely preferable to those of fruition. The boyish lad in turn is allowed the 'Liberty to toye' (l. 19) with her, but his are the freedoms afforded to the lover by Cowley's mistress: 'Such *freedoms* give[n] as may admit *Command*' (l. 9). Here, as in Suckling and Cowley, the greater part of both parties' pleasures stems from fantasy and expectation, themselves sustained by the couple's mutual ignorance each of the other's body. As in other 'Against Fruition' poems, it is precisely restraint which holds up such delight.

Another way of 'solving' the fruition problem is to cultivate jealousy deliberately. Lovers who thereby invest their relationship with tension, making their enjoyment of each other 'a little less easie, ... a little more unlawful' (*Marriage A-La-Mode*, iii. i. 77–9), provoke in so doing renewed pleasure (the pleasure of excitement and uncertainty) and thus overcome the cloying effect of familiarity. Such is the scenario developed to resolve *A-La-Mode*'s subplot, to the writing of which Rochester contributed. In Act v both Rhodophil and Palamede are reconciled to monogamy, because each is driven by jealousy to rediscover the value of his own betrothed. As Rhodophil puts it, '*Palamede* has wit, and if he loves [Doralice], there's something more in [my wife] than I have found: some rich Mine' (v. i. 323–4). The innuendo of digging into mines which follows from this is appropriate, since coition is destined to assume new value under the influence of these rekindled loves. This same jealousy-fuelled rekindling is celebrated by Rochester in 'The Mistress', another lyric based on a kinetic model of pleasure, but one which suffuses that model with complex strains so as to make it more lasting.

'The Mistress' opens in devotional mood, its persona lamenting both the celerity with which time advances when he is in the company of his beloved and

---

[68] 'A Fragment of Petronius Paraphras'd', l. 24 (Oldham 1987: 216).

the sense of torpor which accompanies her absence.[69] Despite such torment, though, the lover (at least in the 1691 printed text) is quick to round on those who despise his raving. He counsels them (with grim sarcasm) that 'Short Ages live in Graves' (l. 16);[70] that is, that they will be dead a long time and ought themselves to seize the day rather than sniggering at the troubles of those who do.[71] The real weight of the poem follows from this defiant attitude. Those who take the lovers' arguments at face value are deluded:

> ... tis sacred Jealousy,
> Love rais'd to an extream,
> The only proof twixt her and me
> We love and doe not Dream.

(ll. 25–8)

The embracing of 'extreamities' and intensity of experience is typical of Rochester. He uses it here to reach beyond the writers of the 'Against Fruition' tradition for whom the indulgence of appetite could only end in the demolition of a dream. Extremity is developed as something necessary to a life of appetite—necessary, that is, to maintain the vibrancy of a particular desire. The proposition of 'The Mistress' is (to quote Thormählen) that, 'If what we have is disappointing, we can reduce our dissatisfaction by pretending that we do not have it after all, [or] by worrying that we might not be able to keep it'. [72] The persona thus insists that, in order to feed appetitious love such that it continues to appeal rather than cloying, each party must embrace a degree of torment. This is partly a repetition of Cowley's argument in 'Against Fruition' that even hope, unless checked by purgative fears, becomes another kind of surfeit. The point there, as here, is that to sustain the pleasurableness of indulging a sexual passion there must be an element of unpredictability about it, a fear in each lover[73] that future allowances might not be forthcoming. This fear, fuelled by jealousy, prevents coition from becoming familiar, forcing each lover to reaffirm the worth of those occasions when he or she *is* able to take pleasure in the other. By invoking the threat (or reality) of infidelity, jealousy reminds the couple of the delights of love precisely in interrupting

---

[69] Rochester 1999: 27 ff.

[70] The Longleat Thynne and Yale Osborn MSS (ibid. 28, 359, 528) read 'Short Ages, Living Graves' here, making l. 16 simply the persona's summary of his own previous ravings: ages made seemingly short amidst too much pleasure; life protracted into death during the beloved's killing absences.

[71] For another, less muscular interpretation of this same phrase in the 1691 text, see Vieth 1988: 186.

[72] Thormählen 1988: 221.

[73] The focus in stanzas 6–9 of 'The Mistress' is mutual, referring equally to both protagonists ('us', 'we', 'our', etc.), but it is true that the closing line of the Longleat Thynne text (l. 40) does, uniquely, accord a controlling and dominant influence to the mistress.

them. But the implication of this stance is that the persona must *willingly* allow his mistress to strew his path with upheavals, so much so that every renewal of their love will, sooner or later, find itself frustrated. That disruption gives the successful moments of indulgence their intensity precisely because it cuts them off before they have yielded all their pleasure. By such means, each party's appetite is kept alive.

These, then, are what the persona terms love's 'sacred' pains (l. 25). They are also, strikingly, pains which 'can ne're deceive' (l. 32), a proposition that has the air of a Cartesian *cogito* about it. In one sense such pain cannot deceive because it promises nothing. In an environment in which fortune is against man, every aspect of material reality is mutable, and human affections are fickle, pleasure—the invitation to relax and imagine that all is right with the world—must be a kind of delusion. Pain, in confronting what that pleasure ignores, carries with it the force of truth. This is certainly the view taken by Des Barreaux when he insists 'Que nos maux sont réels et nos biens qu'en peinture'.[74] However, pain cannot deceive, secondly, because it is also unmistakably real: real in that its experiential intensity makes its presence undeniable, and real because that intensity is all the more emphatically experienced if felt as *masochistic* ecstasy. Intensity (extremity) is clearly a feature of the pain in 'The Mistress', but it is at one remove from the *erotic* masochism in, say, Rochester's 'My dear Mistris has a heart' (in which 'Killing Pleasures' and 'wounding Blisses' abound (l. 10) ). The masochism *here* is closer to that mystical (though still sexual) torment which so thrills Crashaw's (or Bernini's) Teresa as she embraces the 'delicious wounds' and 'sweet ... subtile paine' of divine love. Rochester dubs the agonizing jealousy behind his poem as 'sacred' too, thereby appropriating this category of divine pain and suggesting that his lovers imagine themselves achieving a similar transcendence in their agony.[75]

These are some of the senses in which pain is too brilliant to be deceitful, but that proposition has one other, still more important application. The lovers in 'The Mistress' contrast their torment with the 'Fantastick fancys' and 'fraile joys' of others who take 'false pleasure for true love' (ll. 29–31). In choosing to persevere in pain, rather than abandon their attachment, Rochester's lovers prove just how much they value the pleasures which *succeed* such torment. They also demonstrate that the continuation of their affair is not merely a consequence of automatic habit, but something more considered. They affirm, in short, the authenticity of their union precisely by what they are prepared

---

[74] 'Que la condition de notre sort', l. 7 (Lachèvre 1911: 252).
[75] On Rochester's use of Crashaw, see Burns 1995: 211.

to sacrifice to maintain it.[76] It is a commonplace of Restoration comedy that jealousy is 'the only infallible sign' of love (*Country Wife*, II. i. 261–2), and here, too, 'Anxious cares (when past) / Prove our Hearts Treasure fixt and Dear / And make us blest at last' (ll. 34–6). Rochester's hearts, 'proved' thus by jealousy, are *proof against* adversity, their strength confirmed by the ordeal which they surmount. Nevertheless the 'at last' here will only ever be a temporary fiction. The dynamic at work throughout the poem implies that the blessings of line 36 will not persist. Tormenting fears needs must intervene again at some later stage to revivify the affections.[77]

Pain, then, is to be actively solicited on a recurring basis, and celebrated as a beacon of truth and certainty. This fact underlines how far 'The Mistress' has carried us from any ordinary notion of Epicureanism. The latter, Thormählen notes, takes it for granted that man's first concern should always be to *eliminate* pain.[78] Rochester presents us, rather, with a paradoxical, uneasy, and downright perverse solution to the problem of appetite. Indeed, for all its apparent honesty, 'The Mistress' cannot help but stand out, for us, as the portrait of a remarkably tenuous, rather baroque strategy of self-outwitting. Nor is it alone in this respect. The same can also be said of one final, celebrated lyric, 'Absent from thee I languish still'.[79]

In 'Absent from thee' the infidelity is real and is the man's only. It is he who protests:

> Then ask me not when I return,
> The straying fool twill plainly kill
> To wish all day, all night to mourn.
>
> (ll. 2–4)

Exactly when the persona's straying from his beloved takes place remains vague: line 1 may refer to a specific absence and languishing which occur now, or at some future point; or it may state a more general precept applicable on countless occasions. The timing, though, is unimportant. What counts is the sequence of events: departure from the beloved, regret, return—and the absence of specificity is further significant in that it contributes to Rochester's overall implication (reinforced in the final stanza) that this sequence is eternally recurrent. The sense of regret in this cycle is expressed in line 4.

---

[76] Rochester makes the same point in a darker context in *Lucina's Rape*. There Chilax argues that a boy's love for a man will always be more 'sincere' than a woman's, because he suffers 'Paine' to give sexual pleasure to his lover, whereas the woman gains as much satisfaction as she gives (II. ii. 181–8).

[77] On this 'restlessness' and 'nervous mobility' at the heart of Rochester's poetry, see N. Fisher 2000*b*: 27.

[78] Thormählen 1993: 77.    [79] Rochester 1999: 29.

The wishing and mourning there could be predicated of the beloved, but their principal referent is clearly the poet-lover himself. As Barton notes, he recognizes that at the first moment of his every straying, both now and for evermore, he will foresee all the pain to which that self-imposed exile must lead, and even his return 'wearied with a world of woe' to a place he should never have left.[80] Assuming that the beloved allows him unchecked freedom, the promiscuous fool within him (compulsively hankering after the pleasure of others' bodies 'all day', finding only a sense of lack in the coition which follows at 'night') will soon burn out—that is, 'plainly kill' off *itself*. His fate is thus depressingly clear:

> Dear from thine arms then let me fly
> That my fantastick mind may prove,
> The torments it deservs to try
> That Tears my fixt heart from my love.

> (ll. 5–8)

Tied to a slavish impulse which implicitly goes against his better judgement, he needs must stray, and suffer for so doing.

The 'torments' he undergoes are precisely those apparent sexual pleasures on the other side of the fence which actually 'prove' miserable. They are, though, 'deserved', a fact which goes to the heart of the 'fantastick mind'–'fixt heart' distinction. 'Fantastick mind' invites two interpretations. First, it suggests that the mind identifies itself solely with the fancy, specifically with the imagination's exaggerated expectations about the pleasures of straying, which fruition cannot then appease.[81] But secondly, 'mind' also implies a 'cerebral'[82] (as opposed to heartfelt, intuitional) element. The persona is seduced by the *idea* or mental habit of playing out the libertine role, a role supposedly ordained by 'Nature', but actually ordained by Hobbes and other libertine sources. Thinking that he must cultivate a wide-ranging sexual appetite, and that maintaining such perpetual motion will bring him felicity, these compulsive *thoughts* and the desire raised upon them persuade him to 'fly' from his mistress. What he loses in thus detaching himself from her (but will subsequently regain) is a genuine satisfaction which answers to the '*heart's*' needs and is thus stable ('fixt'). The torment of that loss is 'deserved', because the persona merits the punishment of dissatisfaction for wilfully supposing that another might satisfy him as well as would his beloved. Nature, then, 'serves' this figure justly: given his compulsion to stray, he 'deservs to try'—needs must experience—the alternative, a giddy chase which ends in disappointment.

---

80 Righter [afterwards Barton], in Vieth 1988: 24.
81 Cf. 'The Mistress': 'Fantastick fancys'.
82 Thormählen 1993: 73. Cf. Vieth 1988: 182.

In these respects, then, the lover languishes still (that is, always) whilst absent from one in whose bosom he finds a satisfying locus for his desire. Hence what follows:

> When weary'd with a world of woe
> To thy safe bosome I retire
> Where love and peace and truth doe flow,
> May I contented there Expire
>
> Least once more wandring from that heav'n
> I fall on some Base heart unbles'd,
> Faithless to thee, false, unforgiv'n
> And loose my everlasting rest.

(ll. 9–16)

The beloved must set the persona free precisely so that he can, as here, rediscover his need for her. Straying is his way of periodically refounding his loving attachment for this woman. Lines 9–12 thus evince the tempered satisfaction which the return to the beloved fosters. The 'everlasting rest' which she offers is presumably twofold (in line with the ambiguity of 'Expire'). It signifies the contentment of a peaceful life which will last until death itself (a literal expiring) parts the couple, but it also encompasses the 'everlasting' qualities of 'Love and Life's' 'livelong Minute' with all *its* connotations, ranging from Platonic transcendence (another kind of 'rest') to earthy orgasm (a metaphorical expiring). Quite which of these pleasures the persona most craves remains nicely ambiguous. There is a double meaning, too, in the words 'May I' and 'Least' (that is, Lest). Their principal tone is that of a *prayer* for expiration, in which sense these words express a wishful thought provoked by *fear* of the alternative (philandering's futile destiny). On this interpretation lines 12 and 13 signal the man's near-*desperate* desire for the safety of his beloved's bosom. However, in a contrary reading, the same words may also constitute a warning to the woman that she must be forgiving (l. 15) and sexually accommodating (l. 12), since otherwise this poet-lover will not *condescend* to reconcile himself to her. If she is not thus emollient, so the warning goes, her lover will 'wander' off immediately.

Clearly, if expiration in the sexual sense is denied him, the persona is like to stray again, whereas if that want is satisfied, stanza 3 expresses some hope that a more durable contentment might follow: the lover's quest to find happiness in moderation, untroubled by fantastic aspirations, could then, perhaps, be resolved. Nevertheless, the clear implication of lines 13–16, and of the poem generally, is that this will not really happen. In the absence of the most permanent kind of expiration, death, any *rapprochement* between the lovers will be short-lived. The persona will *still* periodically abandon his beloved, his heart's wishes notwithstanding. Successful coition with her will not be enough to bind him to her 'safe bosome', and when he does stray again he will, as before, 'fall on'—both alight upon and be degraded by—some 'unbles'd' love. The situation of the first stanza will repeat itself cyclically, Rochester's protagonist finding no pleasure in his serial infidelities yet demanding toleration for them. It is the recognition of these grim truths which makes the resolution of the problem of appetite here (as in 'The Mistress') so uneasy: for these lovers it is a resolution which, in succeeding for the most part, must also periodically fail, a fact of which they are aware from the outset. This lucid refusal of self-delusion (and especially the persona's recognition that his compulsive strayings will be worthless) is, for us, 'terrifying in itself',[83] but worse still is our realization that, because the persona foresees all this, the thing he really prays for, in the end, is not the expiration of orgasm but precisely the greater expiration of death. On a sober reading of the lyric he prays, ultimately, for the whole cycle to stop: he prays for his own extinction. Thus to expire in his beloved's arms would be truly to secure himself 'everlasting' safety. This melancholy hankering after death suggests then, rather bleakly, that *this* libertine at least is too exhausted to persevere with so contorted a form of happiness. Better, perhaps, to die than to struggle on in a life where genuine pleasure finds itself interspersed with bouts of perverse pain. And yet, lest it be thought that Rochester's lyric was thus decisive, note too that this persona is only *half* in love with easeful death: his plea is, 'May I contented there Expire', but not yet, not until he has enjoyed the painful pleasure of straying just once more.[84] Here, as in the ambiguous play on prayer versus warning (l. 13), sober seriousness is thus counterbalanced by an indeterminate degree of levity and rakishness—as indeterminate, indeed, as the boundary between sincerity and flippancy in Oldham's 'Satyr'.

It is with reference to this last uncertainty that the religious connotations of Rochester's poem assume their full significance. Superficially, the spiritual associations of the language in 'Absent'—the construction of the beloved as a Virgin-figure, home to love, peace, and truth; the references, too, to heaven, the blessed, forgiveness, rest, faithlessness, and the Fall—all contribute to the song's wit. In blasphemously applying these terms to a secular relationship, and to demands for sexual fulfilment, Rochester's libertine seems to demonstrate

---

[83] Righter, in Vieth 1988: 24.

[84] As Thormählen notes, his attitude is that of Augustine in his *Confessions*: 'Give me chastity and continence, but not just now' (N. Fisher 2000*b*: 25).

the manipulative intent of his voice.[85] To assert this, though, is to take for granted Vieth's claim that the religious imagery here provides only a vocabulary of analogies, being used 'to interpret' (or glorify) 'a secular mental state'.[86] In reality, that imagery may actually have a more substantial function. If Rochester constructs his persona's sexual experiences in cyclical terms, as a repetitive process of transgression, repentance, redemption through grace, and transgression again—just as elsewhere he construes his lovers' masochistic pains as 'sacred', after the fashion of Crashaw's Teresa—this may be because in practice he could not help but transpose the structures of Christian spiritual life on to other spheres of experience. For all that this seemingly blasphemous, free-thinking poet sought to evade the discourse of piety, Christian forms seem, periodically, to have reimposed themselves upon his consciousness (as they did on Donne's), so that when, here, he came to write of the torments of libertine appetitiousness, he found himself constructing those troubles precisely in a language of guilt and sinfulness, then looking for salvation from a transcendent presence.[87] In the same poem, if we take its sentiments seriously, that tendency is realized to the utmost, the persona's wish for death in face of his own weakness presenting, in transposed form, the Pauline desire for a mortification of the flesh. Religious idioms, then, may provide here not just a set of analogies, but a veritable grammar of experience, one from which Rochester could not, finally, escape, and in terms of which he could not help but construct the drama of regret. If so, 'Absent' needs must compare with Rochester's *Troas*, the imagery and moral and religious connotations of which again pull against the Epicurean intent of the original.[88]

The penitential, Christian impulse and the *thanatos* of 'Absent from thee' anticipate a telling observation apparently made by Rochester during his final months of life. According to Burnet, Rochester affirmed that, although he deemed religious devotion only an 'effect of Fancy', nevertheless he still felt 'they were very happy whose Fancies were under the power of such Impressions; since they had somewhat on which their thoughts rested and centred'.[89] The

---

[85] For further examples of this theologically inflected wit in Rochester's work, see Rochester 1980: 14.

[86] Vieth 1988: 183.

[87] Treglown notes that the language of a letter which Rochester wrote to Burnet in 1680 (Rochester 1980: 15, 244) betrays a continued awareness of the liturgy of the 1552 Prayer Book. The Earl probably last used the latter when he was 15, but evidently it continued to shape his consciousness even on his deathbed.

[88] Rochester's 'To the Post Boy' (1999: 42 ff.)—half boastful and blasphemous, half penitent and ashamed in tone—invites similar observations.

[89] Burnet 1680: 51.

choice of verbs here—'rest' and 'centre'—points to the authenticity of these sentiments, since it is precisely a restful centre which the persona in both 'The Mistress' and the 'Absent' lyric craves. Clearly then, viewed in such lights, the balancing of rakish levity and sober seriousness in 'Absent from thee' emerges as a poignant illustration of a tension at the heart of the poet's attitude to hedonism. In its programmatic ambiguity, 'Absent' exemplifies an oscillation recurrent in Rochester's verse, an oscillation between (1) the cynical pursuit of worldly satisfactions (which combines with a flippant misappropriation of spiritual terms) and (2) an anxious sense of the self-enslavement to which Cyrenaicism can lead (an awareness which precipitates a craving for release from all such motion, this couched in *authentic* spiritual terms). In so far as it exposes these tensions, a poem which initially seemed to paint a solution (albeit a fraught one) to the dilemma of fruition, ends up demonstrating just how extensive—how intractable—the problems of libertinism are.

Such, then, is the tangled course run by Rochester's meditations on sexual desire, that form of appetite which libertinism took to be representative. Some of the poems discussed here ('Against Constancy', 'To Love', 'Upon his leaving his Mistresse', to some extent 'Love and Life') are straightforwardly positive celebrations of a Hobbist disposition which equates felicity with the constant forward momentum of appetite. Others ('Love and Life' on a sceptical reading, for example, or 'The Fall') challenge the adequacy of such a philosophy. They question, in particular, the possibility of ever actually deriving fulfilment from a model of appetite which depends, for its pleasure, upon ignorance and a sense of anticipation—the very things that fruition would shatter. Life lived on such an assumption can never realize its goal. A third set of poems ('The Platonick Lady', 'The Mistress', 'Absent from thee') offer compromises, the latter pair in particular depicting seemingly impossible combinations of motion and stasis, pleasure and pain, in a vain attempt to escape libertinism's shortcomings. Having said this, though, it is important to emphasize that this organization of the love lyrics does not amount to a teleological development within Rochester's thought. In the first place, the lyrics are notoriously difficult to date. Secondly, by voicing them through such sensationalist personas, Rochester (like Oldham) obscures the boundary between his own and his characters' views. Hence, the poems are better viewed in the abstract, as dramatizations of different positions, different attitudes for and against the Hobbist-libertine outlook. They map out, in all their ambiguities, a pattern of oscillating attitudes towards the libertine lifestyle (albeit a pattern which, so I began by saying, is observable in the life of Rochester himself).

## SATIRES AGAINST A HOBBIST WORLD

The lyric voices of disillusionment which seem to challenge the assumptions of libertinism find a natural counterpart in Rochester's 'A Satyre against Reason and Mankind' (written during or before June 1674). The 'Satyre' develops a broadly Epicurean ideal of governance in opposition to latitudinarian theologians' concepts of right reason, but in its emphasis on self-discipline and moderated hedonism this ideal is also *implicitly* opposed to contemporary notions of libertinism. Rochester's choice of vocabulary in this poem betrays a desire to reject not only psychomachic rationalism but also the 'boundless' nature of Cyrenaic motion, a model of governance which cultivates unquenchable, overpowering desires of a kind capable of obliterating man's very self. Alongside this first concern, though, the 'Satyre' also presents a critique of other aspects of libertinism's egotistic view of man. By sketching a critical account of the wit's role in court society (a role in which Rochester was himself complicit), and then compounding that with a raft of observations about the perversity of human nature, Rochester develops an attack on the aggressive, isolating social structure which had become prevalent within Charles's court. In this Hobbist context the 'Satyre' laments, especially, the tawdry fact that man's 'best' acts are now driven only by fear of others (by the very passion which the Hobbesian contract was supposed to suppress). Rochester evokes, too, the suffocating, mutually deceitful atmosphere of a society which is probably worse than—certainly no better than—the Hobbesian state of nature. He writes, in this sense, from outside the drum, for (as Rochester told Savile) 'you att Court thinke … as if you were shutt up in a Drumme, you can thinke of nothing but the noise is made about you'.[90] The 'Satyre' thus lends itself to the more particular criticisms of the Carolean polity with which Rochester was increasingly concerned in the second half of the 1670s; but in fact the poem is wider in scope than even this emphasis might suggest. Its attack on pride and metaphysical ideas of the grandeur of reason is a theme developed in its own right, initially independently of any contrast with Rochester's own, somewhat Epicurean right reason. Since that metaphysical discussion provides the foundation for the work, it is appropriate to begin with it, before examining more Hobbist themes.

Rochester's 'Satyre' opens with five declamatory lines of pentameter which quickly degenerate into a bitter couplet:

> Were I …
> … A spírit frée to chóose for mý own sháre,

---

[90] Rochester 1980: 93.

> What cáse of flésh and blóod I pléas'd to wéar;
> I'de bé a Dóg, a Mónky, ór a Béar.
> Or ány thing bút that váin *Ánimal*
> Who is só próud of béing Rátional.

(ll. 1, 3–7)[91]

The unstressed syllables of 'any thing', '*Animal*', and 'Rational' disappear here under the weight of stressed ones and the dactyl, 'Rational', withers away (as is appropriate to the passage's sense) in the shadow of the trenchant monosyllables which begin line 7. The 'Reason' (l. 11) hereby debunked (which opposes the persona's favoured vehicles of knowledge, the five senses and 'certain Instinct' (l. 10)) is implicitly that of both contemporary Anglican rationalists and Cambridge Platonists, on the one hand, and scholastic metaphysicians, on the other.[92] These groups all conceived of reason as a transcendent faculty capable of discerning its own truths, principally because it could verify propositions on principles independent of, and superior to, the senses. According to this outlook (continuous with some of the rationalist philosophies of the sixteenth century), right reason intuited its own moral values in opposition to the corrupting influence of the passions. Like Hobbes, Théophile, and Des Barreaux, Rochester's persona is opposed to such a faith.[93] In his view the best cognitive instruments available to man are the testimonies of the senses, the intuitions of the passions, and the judgements of a purely instrumental capacity of reasoning (one which shapes the flow of passions by judging the consequences of pursuing particular appetites). This persona thus has no sympathy for the traditional rationalist whose 'wisdom' typically destroys happiness precisely in 'Ayming to *know* that World [we] should *enjoy*' (l. 34).[94] On the contrary, it is folly to pretend that man has access to some special power of right reason. The latter is a chimera,

> an Ignis fatuus of the Mind,
> Which leaving Light of Nature, sense, behind;
> Pathless and dangerous wandring wayes it takes,
> Through Errours fenny boggs and thorny brakes:
> Whilst the misguided follower climbs with pain
> Mountains of whimseys heapt in his own brain;
> Stumbling from thought to thought, falls headlong down

---

[91] Rochester 1999: 57 ff.    [92] On this idea of reason, see Beiser 1996: *passim*.

[93] On Théophile and Des Barreaux, see, as previously cited, Griffin 1973: 176–9; Farley-Hills 1978: 163–4; Thormählen 1993: 198–201.

[94] Griffin (1973: 179) suggests that, in playing on the two words I have italicized here, Rochester may be recalling Des Barreaux's precept in 'Mortels qui vous croyez': 'Estudions-nous plus à *joüir* qu'à *connoistre*'. As previously noted, these same terms are also juxtaposed in Des Barreaux's response to Vauquelin's celebrated sonnet, 'N'estre ny magistrat, ny marié', where Vallée writes, 'bien plus à jouir qu'à connoistre'.

> Into doubts boundless Sea, where like to drown,
> Books bear him up a while, and make him try
> To swim with bladders of Philosophy.
>
>                                                    (ll. 12–21)

'Pathless' is a key word here. 'Sense'—the senses—provides a safe because tried and tested route through the world. Abstract 'Reason', by contrast, leads its adherents into disaster. The imagery which encapsulates that disaster evokes various associations. The 'Ignis fatuus' idea, whilst connected to both *Leviathan*[95] and *Paradise Lost*, 9. 634–42 (where it leads straight to 'bogs and mires' and a swallowing pool), is common enough in the period to require no specific attribution. However, lines 12–21 may allude in more general terms to the Miltonic Satan's journey through Chaos. The movement through a dramatically undulating landscape replete with 'boggs' and strait 'brakes', the pilgrim's efforts too to bear himself up on parodic water-wings, certainly recall 'the Fiend' who 'O'er bog or steep, through straight, rough, dense, or rare, / With head, hands, wings, or feet pursues his way, / And swims or sinks, or wades, or creeps, or flies' (*PL* 2. 947–50). If this association holds, it would seem to underline the diabolical folly of this whole rationalist venture. Just as significant, though, is the suggestion that Rochester's passage parodies Patrick's *Parable of the Pilgrim* (which is scoffed at later in the 'Satyre' (l. 74) ): 'many steep hills he climbed, and many dangerous praecipices he narrowly escaped; he committed himself not once or twice to the anger of the Sea.'[96] The important point here is that although Rochester begins by matching Patrick's allegorical style, his shimmering Reason moving through what seems to be a 'real', physical and external landscape (ll. 14–15), 'misguided follower' in tow, the Earl quickly reverses that fancy. In lines 16 and 17 the follower's body appears, by way of a witty paradox, as internalized within his own imagination: the man climbs within his own brain. The pains he experiences (like the torments which Des Barreaux attributes to reason's activities) are thus self-generated.

This fact is reminiscent of the doctrine given early expression by Browne, and popularized by Milton and the Cambridge Platonists, which represents the landscape of Hell as a thing existent within one's own mind.[97] But besides hinting at that intellectual connection, Rochester also, I think, makes a more consequential point with his mountaineering paradox. With the image of lines 16 and 17 the allegorical mode itself is suddenly deconstructed *from within*, thereby undermining the very form which had traditionally

---

[95] Hobbes 1996: 36.        [96] Quoted in Treglown 1973: 47.
[97] See Browne 1977: 122; Patrides 1969: 45–6, 113, 123, 329–30.

facilitated and expressed psychomachic constructions of the mind. As will be evident from Chapter 2's discussion of *The Faerie Queene*, allegory thrives on the assumption that reason and the virtues, on the one hand, and the supposedly vicious extremes of sensuality and the passions, on the other, are polar opposites, discrete entities within the psyche which fight for possession of the soul and can therefore be represented as distinct objects—whether as Spenserian knight and assailants, pilgrim and tempters, or traveller and hostile landscapes. A moral psychology which reduces reason to Hobbes's instrumental role, making it a capacity which serves the passions but which does not intuit its own values (or therefore stand out as a productive faculty in its own right), does not respond so readily to allegory's polarizing tendencies. Here, Rochester emphasizes the physical diversity of the landscape he has conjured: 'wandring wayes', 'fenny boggs', 'thorny brakes', 'Mountains'; but having pushed this pictorial impression to its limit, having capitalized upon allegory's expressive power, its heroic and affective force, he then turns that allegory in on itself. What appears to be the equally concrete image of 'heaping' suddenly reveals its purely illusory status: 'heapt *in his own brain*'. The detail of this last, self-inwoven image betrays the allegory. It betrays the pretended reality of the physical externalities, the hostile landscape, exposing the whole as a self-dramatizing fantasy by means of which Spenser, Patrick, and their like torment themselves and would also torment others. What appears initially as a heroic form, ideally suited to representing struggles 'necessary' to the human condition, is suddenly reconstrued as a form which actually gives outward projection to needless, fundamentally delusional inner turmoils; to struggles which the moralizing author casts as universal in an attempt to legitimize them, but which are really particular to his mind or the mind-set of the interest group which he serves. With an uncompromising honesty typical of the Restoration libertine, Rochester strips allegory of that guise of necessity and heroism. He exposes it as no more than a fiction or 'whimsey'; an idiosyncratic fantasy in need of projection back into the mind (rather than of sympathetic identification) if it is to be understood for what it truly is, a symptom of the rationalist's folly. Allegory, thus demystified, can no longer purport to speak for Everyman—to dictate, for example, that we must all emulate Guyon's ascetic quest. Hence with this step Rochester completes, in a literary context, the same process which Hobbes had begun, that of overturning psychomachic constructions of the mind and reimagining the self on other, less delusory terms. The fact, though, that the Earl first exploits the power of this form before exposing it, and that he therefore turns its energy against itself, is typical of a poet who is ever the ventriloquist, ever the great debunker.

In light of the foregoing, lines 20 and 21 of the 'Satyre' ('Books bear him up a while, and make him try / To swim with bladders of Philosophy') assume a mildly comic dimension, but the intervening and subsequent lines are more sombre. Line 18 derives from Boileau:

> Mais l'Homme sans arrest, dans sa course insensée,
> Voltige incessamment de pensée en pensée,
> Son coeur toûjours flottant entre mille embarrass.[98]

However, crucially, Rochester's 'Stumbling' is an altogether more troubling word than 'Voltige', and this soul, so far from 'flottant', is 'like to drown' in doubt's sea. Falling 'headlong' is a not uncommon fate in seventeenth-century poetry. Quite apart from the Miltonic examples discussed at the beginning of this chapter, Quarles's *Divine Fancies*, 2. 17 also uses the adjective,[99] as does Cartwright's 'No Platonique Love', in which the lover, having 'climb'd from Sex to Soul, from Soul to Thought', suddenly finds himself rushing 'Headlong' back to 'Sex agen'.[100] These and other examples match Rochester's own interest in plummeting, dissolution, and obliteration: both his sense (in *Troas*) that the body's atoms are 'hurl'd' outwards to 'become the Lumber of the World', falling endlessly through space, and his images in 'To Love' of a persona who finds himself 'Hurl'd ... Headlong' back into a sexual appetite which inundates his mind. In the case of the 'Satyre' the fall 'headlong' into the sea wherein the would-be rationalist then drowns is a fall *into* his own mind, an internalized movement something like an implosion. The receptacle, though, 'doubts *boundless* Sea', is terrifying all the same: it compares, in its limitlessness, with Nothing's 'boundless selfe' ('Upon Nothinge') or the Epicurean 'vast *All*',[101] and in so far as it envelops the man, it robs him of his sense of self, his autonomy. It is the word 'Boundless', then—a partly Miltonic adjective which grows in significance as the poem develops—which gives this fate its most threatening aspect; and though Rochester's satyr may not pity the metaphysician who drives himself into such a plight, he does perhaps fear the fate itself. The very word which for Crashaw was, in a spiritual context, exhilarating—God offers a 'roseall spring of ... sweets, ... Boundlesse and infinite'; Christ's name is gloriously 'vnbounded'—is for Rochester, in more secular mood, disturbing.

Such is Rochester's condemnation of a wrong-headed right reason, but he is not quite finished with this theme. At line 46 he introduces a 'formal band and beard', another conventionally minded cleric who extols the virtue of 'Blest glorious' humanity (l. 60) in rationalist terms 'laden ... with laudatory epithets ... too good to be true'.[102] What Erskine-Hill dubs the 'bland facility' of this paean to man 'in shining reason drest' (l. 64) inevitably subverts

---

[98] Boileau 1966: 42. Cf. Farley-Hills 1978: 151.    [99] See Rochester 1984: 283.
[100] Quoted in Farley-Hills 1978: 22.    [101] Lucretius 1682: 66.
[102] Erskine-Hill 1966: 53–4.

the preacher's actual message. That subversion continues in the next lines where the persona, now ventriloquizing his cleric-interlocutor's part, puts the following words into his mouth:

> ... Reason, by whose aspiring Influence
> We take a flight beyond Material sense;
> Dive into Mysteries, then soaring pierce
> The flaming limits of the Universe
>
> (ll. 66–9)

The celebration of 'Div[ing] into Mysteries' is the other perspective on 'falling headlong ... / ... Into doubts boundless Sea', but the clergyman views such speculation as a flight *beyond* the 'limits' of the material 'Universe'. In saying this, he quotes verbatim (in l. 69) from Evelyn's rather loose translation of *De Rerum* 1. 73–4.[103] Evelyn loses a key nuance of Lucretius's text by conflating the flaming walls of man's planetary sphere ('flammantia moenia mundi') with the immense, *boundless* universe beyond ('omne immensum'), producing instead his own single phrase, 'flaming limits of the Universe'.[104] In Lucretius's actual view man's little world may indeed have flaming limits to be pierced, but the larger material 'Universe' does not. Line 69 is therefore oxymoronic. Rochester's persona clearly understands this point, grasping the inadequacy of Evelyn's translation. Hence, having first adopted the erroneous Lucretian perspective evoked by this confused divine, he then mocks the contradiction into which that forces his opponent:

> ... I despise ...
> This busy puzzling stirrer up of doubt ...
> Born on whose wings each heavy Sott can *pierce*
> *The limits of the boundless Universe* ... .
> ... Non-sense and Impossibilities.
>
> (ll. 75, 80, 84–5, 89)

The point exposed here is that the 'boundless', by definition, has no 'limits' which one might reach or 'pierce'. Rather, the Epicurean universe (being infinite) is centreless and disorientating, an inhospitable void through which matter drifts endlessly without ever getting anywhere. The fact that Rochester chooses the word 'boundless' in line 85 confirms the imaginative link between this Epicurean infinitude and the equally terrifying, all-absorbing sea of 'boundless' doubt into which speculative philosophy leads mankind. Here, as before, the threatened loss of autonomy is all too evident: this 'stirrer up of doubt' fosters amongst his flock an unhealthy intellectual dependency. They

---

[103] Rochester 1984: 283.
[104] Contrast Lucretius 1656: 16–17, with Lucretius 1937: 6–7.

look to, and come to depend upon, him to provide the 'wings' that will bear them up towards false revelation, in which respect the would-be sages are lost to themselves.

The fear of boundlessness and absorption which underpins the satirist's critique of metaphysical pretensions informs, too, his own model of governance established in response to the divine's contemplative right reason. Rochester's more Epicurean governance, what Griffin calls his 'instruction in how to live',[105] is founded on the axioms that 'Thoughts are given for Actions government' (l. 94) and that 'Our sphere of Action is Lifes happiness' (l. 96).[106] His better kind of Reason is therefore one that

> ... distinguishes by Sense,
> And gives us Rules of Good and Ill from thence:
> That bounds Desires with a reforming Will,
> To keep them more in vigour, not to kill.
> Your Reason [the divine's] hinders, mine helps to enjoy,
> Renewing appetites yours would destroy.
>
> (ll. 100–5)[107]

References to 'Sense' as a determinant 'of Good and Ill' in this period are inevitably ambiguous, the judgements issuing from such a standard varying according to whether or not sense is taken to include prudential assessments of an action's long-term effects. Oldham's Court-Hector uses this very criterion, 'Rule of Sence', to justify his frenetically self-indulgent lifestyle. So, likewise, does Shadwell's Don John, who insists, 'What ways soe'er conduce to my delight, / My sense instructs me, I must think 'em right' (*The Libertine*, I. i. 162–3). Don John becomes, in this context, a spokesman for Hobbes's notion of the will, proclaiming in opposition to the Hermit (with whom he argues in a parody of the Hobbes–Bramhall debate) that the will is swayed by 'the last dictate' of the judgement (III. ii. 96–7),[108] which 'judgement' in turn is only ever the register of 'present opinions' about immediate pleasure (ll. 102–4). He, like Oldham's hector then, discounts any prudential foresight in his 'Rule of Sence'.

---

[105] Griffin 1973: 222.

[106] For further comment on this Epicurean dimension in the 'Satyre's' ethics, see Wilcoxon 1974/5: 196–8.

[107] Rochester makes a legitimate shift from metaphysics to ethics at this point in the 'Satyre' on the basis that the transcendental idea of reason which informs the divine's epistemology informs, too, the latter's ethics. Typically, as Ch. 1 of this book suggests, the same Christian right reason which plumbed the mysteries of the universe in this period was also one which, in the moral sphere, tightly circumscribed man's worldly passions.

[108] *Pace* Hammond and Kewes (in N. Fisher 2000*b*: 146–7), this is clearly an allusion to Hobbes in particular, for whom the will was the last appetite of deliberation.

In marked contrast to Shadwell's caricature, Rochester's persona makes the setting of limits crucial at this point: his reason must 'bound' (l. 102) man's otherwise boundless desires in order to ensure that, in the long-term, they prove themselves truly satisfying.[109] In the lines already quoted (ll. 100–5) the *declared* contrast is between an ethic which indulges appetites and one—ultimately of the psychomachic kind—which represses them. However, in the references to 'reforming', the maintenance of 'vigour', and 'Renewing', there is clearly also an *implied* contrast with those libertine attitudes—Des Barreaux's, Oldham's, the Hobbists', Cyrenaicism—which associate felicity with constant motion and unchecked self-indulgence. In Rochester's view (as it is developed here), desires should be bounded, mixed with the self-imposed *pain* of restraint, this, first, so as to avert the disappointments of unbridled fruition dramatized in the lyric tradition, and secondly, because otherwise desire's infinitude threatens to overwhelm the self. Moderation guarantees the 'vigour', the actual power to please, of those appetites which are, in some form, indulged. Pleasure thus remains the goal, but on the understanding that an instrumental capacity of reasoning must measure out what will truly succeed in achieving that goal.[110] The resultant ethic, though lacking the freedom and *joie de vivre* of Théophile's naturalism,[111] does, more positively, invite comparison with Montaigne's 'De l'Experience'. The latter, to reiterate, makes temperance integral to the Epicurean ideal, 'limiting and cutting ... off' pleasures precisely in order to 'keep them in vse and breath', to keep them in vigour. Just as Montaigne, and indeed Cotton (in 'Clepsydra') aim to improve the quality of life by husbanding pleasures—by savouring and tasting them afresh—so too Rochester would renew and relish them. He cannot, any more than Cotton can, arrest the process of kinesis; but he can, after a fashion, make it circular, rejuvenating appetites over and again so that they continue to delight with each iteration (this rather than submitting those appetites to a linear process of exploitation, exhaustion, and abandonment).

There is a resemblance, in all this, to true Epicureanism (I noted in Ch. 7 Stanley's preoccupation with setting the 'just bounds of our Desires'); but there is also a limited resemblance to Hobbesianism. Fujimara is undoubtedly correct that Rochester's poem constitutes neither 'an attack on ... reason in its totality' nor, straightforwardly, 'an attempt to base life on an ... instinctual basis'; correct, also, that the Earl, in 'diminishing the scope of reason', strips

[109] In a striking parallel to this, *Sodom and Gomorah's* Bolloxinian suggests, in Sc. B5, ll. 7–14, that 'Cunts' no longer 'hug' nor therefore 'tickle' the 'Pintle', because through overuse they have grown 'voyd of ... bounds'. (References to this play, the authorship of which is disputed, are to Rochester 1999.)

[110] Cf. Combe 1998: 76–8.    [111] Thormählen 1993: 217.

it of the moral potency traditionally accorded it in psychomachic theories.[112] In these respects Rochester's pattern of thought mirrors Hobbes's. They both reconstruct right reason as something instrumental, a utilitarian assistant to appetite. But none of this necessarily indicates a detailed echoing of Hobbes, and, crucially, Hobbes himself never grasped the kind of critique of unchecked hedonistic motion which is implicit in Rochester's lyrics. In the *Elements of Law* he does emphasize that deliberation should identify any long-term pains which may be associated with short-term pleasures; in *Leviathan* he acknowledges that deliberation can only be based on judgements about what *appears* to be pleasant or painful; and in *De Homine* he makes a great deal of that last point. But nowhere does Hobbes recant his assertion that felicity depends upon constant forward motion, and therefore, implicitly, on Spragens's feverish pursuit of appetites. Nowhere does he acknowledge that indulged desires, even when they do not yield opportunity costs, do not provoke the sovereign's wrath, do not incur bodily suffering, may *still* be more painful than pleasant—this because fruition itself, if crudely conceived, fails to satisfy even on its own, sensual terms. Rochester recognizes exactly this, and incorporates that recognition into his notion of the deliberative process. The result is an idea of governance which 'bounds Desires' to a greater degree than Hobbesian deliberation would seem to do.

This ethic is by no means unique to the 'Satyre'. A comparable attitude underpins Rochester's 'Ramble'. Here the persona at the very least *claims* to celebrate the generosity—the openness and freedom—inherent in straightforward 'Lust' (l. 98).[113] He would never object, he argues, to his mistress, Corinna, satisfying a real sexual appetite within herself by turning to other men (ll. 91–6): 'Such nat'rall freedoms are but just' (l. 97). Granted, his acknowledgement of this ideal is not always as stable as it might be. Whereas at one moment he allows Corinna the 'wholsome Juice' (l. 94) of others, at the next, in dubbing this same dish 'a vast *Meal* of Nasty Slime' (l. 118), his equanimity gives way to jealousy.[114] Nevertheless, for the most part the 'Ramble's' spokesman professes to permit his mistress all those indulgences for which pleasure really is the 'excuse' (l. 124). What Corinna in fact does, though, so he claims, is engage in sexual liaisons indiscriminately, as a matter of unthinking, automatic habit. She turns jade 'When neither *Head* nor *Tail* perswade' (l. 100)—that is, when she accepts lovers at the behest neither of reason nor of instinctive appetite. To that extent she renders herself 'a

---

[112] Vieth 1988: 204–5.     [113] Rochester 1999: 76 ff.
[114] For other comments on such moments of slippage in this poem, see Burns 1995: 27–30; Turner 2003: 267–8, 273.

*Whore*, in understanding, / A Passive *Pot* for *Fools* to spend in' (ll. 101–2).[115] An ungoverned impulse which is thus slavish, reducing the self to something 'passive', is precisely one which no longer benefits from the rejuvenation which a bounding will would otherwise bring to it. When the persona concludes, then, that Corinna has '*prophaned* [her] Cunt' (l. 166), a serious point is made that she has violated her body's economy, an economy which (if properly governed) would yield a stream of genuine pleasures. Corinna, though, is not alone in this sin. Lady Betty Felton found herself attacked for the same reason in the Pindaric 'Let Ancients boast no more'.[116] There too the subject of the lampoon is said to have 'Cloy'd' and jaded an 'allmost boundless Appetite' (ll. 17–18); and yet still she drudges on 'in Tastless vice' (l. 19). The self-enslavement here, in rendering 'pleasure' 'Tastless', directly contradicts that Montaignian ideal the emulation of which Rochester and Cotton elsewhere implicitly recommend. To this satire one can add another, Rochester's 'Artemiza',[117] a work premised on the same values as was the 'Ramble'. Artemiza likewise venerates sexual love as 'the most gen'rous Passion of the mynde' (l. 40), but she also appreciates the value of what she calls 'Natures rule' (l. 60) and thus argues for 'restraint' (l. 58). The ladies of the town think differently. Like Corinna, they desire 'e'ne without approving', repressing private inclinations in favour of 'the publicke Voyce' of fashion (ll. 65–6). Bovey becomes a beauty in every such woman's eyes 'if some few agree, / To call him soe' (ll. 70–1). These Corinna-figures, then, 'know, what they would have, not what they like', and so far abandon the normal psychic economy of the self that 'with their Eares they see' (ll. 69, 72). Crucially, in pursuing appetite on this again slavish, automatic basis, they 'Forsake the Pleasure' which might otherwise attend it (l. 61). They perfect the 'Action' of love, but at the expense of losing its 'Passion' (l. 63), the very thing which gives it its Carewian relish.[118] It is this betrayal of 'Natures rule' which the 'Satyre's' reforming, self-restraining will would prevent.

Such, then, is the moderated ethic of pleasure which is clearly integral to one aspect of the 'Satyre's' critique of libertinism. However, in the midst of that attack a second anxiety is voiced, this time concerning the social position of the wit in the court world. That shift of satirical focus occurs at line 31, when the poem's original benighted rationalist mutates into a self-styled Wit addicted to 'pleasing others at his own expence' (l. 36). This gives Rochester the excuse to deliver a homily on the fate of the latter which perhaps reflects his own experience of playing such roles:[119]

---

[115] For a recent, comparable account of this poem, see Kramnick 2002: 286–7.
[116] Rochester 1999: 276 ff.      [117] Ibid. 63 ff.
[118] Cf. Kramnick 2002: 282–4.      [119] Cf. Thormählen 1993: 208

> ... Witts are treated just like common Whores,
> First they're enjoy'd and then kickt out of doors.
> The Pleasure past, a threatning doubt remains,
> That frights th'enjoyer with succeeding pains:
> Women and men of Witt are dangerous tools,
> And ever fatal to admiring Fools.
>
> .   .   .   .   .   .   .   .   .   .   .   .
>
> And therefore what they [the Fools] fear, at heart they hate.
>
> (ll. 37–45)

The dynamic of this passage opposes the wits to the witless (those fops whom they delight). The lines are written from the wits' viewpoint, and accuse the enjoyers because, although the latter take pleasure in seeing the wits humiliate some of their own number and are in that sense complicitous in the attack, they nevertheless conclude by turning on the wits themselves. Said wits are dismissed with the same hypocritical disgust which men reserve for the whores who please them, this because the fops who once escape a mauling recognize that they are likely to be exposed on some 'succeeding' occasion. Fearing the backbiting inconstancy of their entertainers, they turn their jesters out. Lest we be sentimental about this, though, the poem clearly implies that the wits themselves are as much to blame for this fate, because they support the divisive structure which rounds on them. The picture that emerges is thus of a society built on hostility, on a mode of humour obsessed with weakness, thereby testifying, on the one hand, to the importance of Hobbesian power and reputation in this world, and on the other, to the isolation and mistrust which accompanies that. Such is the other face of Dorimant, the fate to which he may be destined, and it perhaps also reflects Rochester's view of his own and Buckingham's position after the latter's fall.

The world of mistrust here exposed is scrutinized again immediately after the discussion of reformed right reason, the satirist now widening his scope to embrace all aspects of man's inhumanity to man. Whilst other animals hunt one another for food, 'Prest by necessity' (l. 131), 'Man undoes Man' for no good reason (l. 132), thereby 'betraying' his own nature (l. 130). This perversity is powerfully emphasized:

> ... Man with smiles, embraces, friendship, praise,
> Inhumanly his fellows life betrayes;
> With vóluntáry páins wórks his distréss,
> Nót through Necéssitý, but Wántonnéss.
>
> (ll. 135–8)

A sense of paradox is pervasive here. An initial reading of lines 137–8 might suggest that the phrase 'With voluntary pains' qualifies the object, 'distress', indicating what sort of affliction man's *victim* will suffer. This reading, though, makes little sense of 'voluntary', and the reversal of the penultimate foot in line 137 emphasizes that the man who would mistreat 'his fellows' must 'wórk' to do so. This unexpected metrical shift jars against the previous word, 'pains', and encourages the reader who might otherwise pass over this line to return to it and attend to the extraordinary implications of 'voluntary'. Far from qualifying the *object*, 'voluntary pains' actually applies to the subject, the inflictor of torment. The meaning here is that man will go out of his way—voluntarily impose pain upon himself—in order to bring distress to others. Such is the distortion to his psychic economy. He will 'wórk' hard to achieve that end, but 'Nót'—again the foot is reversed to emphasize the paradox—on grounds of necessity (hunger, for example); rather, because of his 'Wantonness', a perverse contortion of his mind's principles of action, itself reflective of a distorted view of *others'* natures.

The root of this, man's obsessive aggression towards his fellows, is an equally obsessive fear, a fear (antecedent to the aggression) of those same people whom he wantonly attacks:

> For hunger or for Love [beasts] fight and teare,
> Whilst wretched man is still in arms for Feare:
> For feare he Arms, and is of arms afraid,
> By fear to fear successively betray'd.
>
> (ll. 139–42)

Again, the rhetorical intensity of these first few lines is remarkable, a measure of the sense of absurdity which Rochester wishes to communicate. Building, perhaps, on the hint of ploche in Seneca's description of the tyrant who 'cum arma metuat, ad arma confugiens' (*De Clementia* 1. 13. 3),[120] the Earl develops here a subtle combination of anadiplosis (' … for Feare: / For feare … ') and antanaclasis ('arms … / … Arms, … arms') which lends lines 140 and 141 an enhanced severity. The sixfold repetition[121] of 'feare' likewise mimics the insistent influence of that passion upon one's life, an influence which returns us again to the verb 'betray'd', now describing man's betrayal not of others but of his own self. Man's bellicose response to his first fear—since it is matched by others around him—does nothing but exacerbate that passion: the more arms he acquires to assuage his fear, the more anxious he becomes that others are doing likewise, and the more frightening they then seem to be.

---

[120] Seneca 1928–35: i. 396.    [121] i.e., including l. 143 and 'afraid' in l. 141.

Here, as in *Sejanus*'s Rome, fear's dominion is infinite and plays a stronger role in man's nature than ambition. It underscores all human actions, whether directly or indirectly, and is the driving principle behind man's quest for 'Wisedome, Power and Glory' (l. 154):

> Base Feare! The source whence his best passion came,
> His boasted Honour, and his dear bought Fame:
> That lust of Power, to which hee's such a slave,
> And for the which alone he dares be brave,
> To which his various projects are design'd,
> Which makes him generous, affable and kind;
> For which he takes such pains to be thought wise
> And scrues his Actions in a forc'd disguise.
>
> (ll. 143–50)

There is bitter sarcasm here in the reference to man's 'lust [for] Power' as his 'best passion', and (as with fear) the anaphoric use of 'which' in various constructions from line 145 onwards stresses the pervasive influence of that hunger for supremacy. When what might seem man's real best passions emerge (line 148), they do so only as means to that other, egotistical end. What seem like 'generous' deeds—the 'generous' principles looked for by the satirist in line 125—are really only forced actions which man *makes* himself do. In the end, though, all of this, even the lust for power, is but a function of 'Base Feare', a quest 'to make [oneself] secure' (l. 156). Rochester begins this verse-paragraph by emphasizing that point, and he ends it in like fashion (ll. 156–8). Fear brackets, and is the point of origin for, all other qualities, power included. What power gathers for itself (for pride), it gathers, too, to appease a larger, underlying paranoia.

In insisting upon this point, Rochester's satirist stands apart from Hobbes and his *Elements*, otherwise a potential source here.[122] Whereas the *Elements* figures man as a being naturally rapacious and confrontational, prone to pursue power as an end in itself, Rochester makes that same quest for status a nervous, defensive response to a *prior fear*, the fear of an always diffident man. If anything, the 'Satyre', compares more nearly in this regard with *Leviathan*, which, though it still portrays man as self-seeking, nevertheless makes him less concerned with power for its own sake. *Leviathan*'s man gives more weight to Hobbes's other concern, fear. He fears for his ability to get and keep what he wants, and therefore fears for his power *qua* means rather than end. In this respect, then, *Leviathan* clearly does compare with the 'Satyre', but that said, there is no reason to assume that Rochester's poem must have been

---

[122] Cf. Vieth 1988: 212–13.

indebted to Hobbes for its content. If there is a debt, the language in question is nonetheless generic enough to suggest that Rochester owed more to popular chatter about Hobbism than to a study of actual texts, more to gossip retail than readerly detail. He could, for example, have picked up the language of fear and power from the discussion of those ten or so leaves of the Apostle of Malmesbury on which anonymous pamphleteers claimed coffee-house philosophizing was based.[123] Still more inviting is the possibility that his text (like Halifax's) simply reflects his own observations on the society around him. One should perhaps think of the poem as empiricist, in the sense that it looks directly to Charles's court—both to the headline-grabbing, libertine coterie therein, and to its imitators—for its material. It is plausible to assume that Rochester found *there* (and not just in Hobbes) the evidence both that all virtuous poses are really driven by a desire for power and that that hunger is in turn the product of a paranoid fear of others running the Hobbist race. On this hypothesis, if Rochester mirrors something of Hobbes's philosophy, he does so more because the world he moved in did, more because that society fashioned itself according to a Hobbist image, than because he studied the Malmesbury Apostle as a source. He does so, above all, because he shares with Hobbes the same root image of human nature, the same assumptions about what man, morally and psychologically speaking, must be like. The 'Satyre', though, steps well beyond simply reporting the ethos of the court (or of a dominant part thereof). It is a poem which directly attacks the debilitating, impoverished mentality nurtured *by* that ethos—in which respect Rochester repudiates something of his own courtier identity as well as other people's.

The judgement that only for power's sake will man '*dare* be brave' (l. 146 above) highlights the psychological contortions into which humans cast themselves under the pressure of a Hobbist ethic. Forced by the need for security into pursuing power, and by the need for power into asserting himself, the courtier presents both an extrovert, resplendent face and a courageous one (these, the two senses of 'brave'). He transforms his identity into a public performance. And yet doing so is stressful, demanding an effort which he would not force himself to 'dare' were it not for larger ambient pressures. Line 146 presupposes a prior indifference to such anxieties which amounts, perhaps, to man's 'natural' disposition, but which is eventually suppressed when terror of others' treachery overtakes the psyche. Man is driven to 'bravery', then, solely by the perception (overwhelming in a community where libertines set the fashion) that it is a matter of self-preservation to commit to Spragens's race: 'Meerly for safety after fame we thirst; / *For all men would be Cowards if they durst*' (ll. 157–8). Only in his cups does man recover the relaxed

---

[123] Cf. Treglown 1976: 555; Rochester 1980: 13–14; F. Russell 1986: 246.

candour of his former condition, witness Rochester's remark to Savile: 'oh that second bottle Harry ... banishes flattery from our tongues and distrust from our Hearts, [setting] us above the meane Pollicy of Court prudence, w$^{ch}$ makes us lye to one another all day, for feare of being betray'd ... att night.'[124] Alcohol alone releases the self from the oppressive game of manners.[125] That the feverish competition of the latter actually goes against the grain is evident in Rochester's dramatic choice of verb for his 'Satyre':

> [Man] scrúes his Áctions ín a fórc'd disguíse;
> Léading a tédious lífe in Mísery
> Únder labórious méan Hypócrisy.

(ll. 150–2)

There is a powerful feeling of exhaustion here. Both 'scrues' and 'forc'd' capture the sense of painful effort required by a life of pretence, a life in which man (like Halifax's Charles) cannot trust others enough to divulge his doubts and weaknesses. That same effort is mirrored stylistically in the metrical shift enacted by these lines. Rising iambic pentameter in line 150 gives way to falling dactylic tetrameter (with a trochee in the third foot) in the next couplet, each foot withering away after an initial exertion. The weight of an eleventh syllable is felt in the belaboured words, 'tédious' and 'labórious'. The impression of misery is thus all too apparent.

This preponderance of fear and misery is not, though, for Rochester an *inevitable* feature of some supposedly *given* state of nature. Rather, the prior articulation of an alternative, self-moderating vision of governance (ll. 100–5, discussed above) encourages a sense that the court and its trend-setting libertine coterie need not be this way. In sketching a more positive manner of approaching the world, the alternative ethic particularizes what might otherwise seem to be a universal critique of human nature. It encourages the perception that fear has *evolved* to become the accidental foundational passion of this uncivil society, and that misery is only the incidental condition of this peculiar court at one particular moment in history. This intuition that the *status quo* is contingent, not necessary, is further endorsed by two details at the beginning of the 'Addition' appended to the 'Satyre' in 1675.[126] There Rochester glosses his foregoing attack as directed specifically against 'the pretending part of the proud World' (l. 175), not against all human nature as it always must be. Equally, the 'Addition' is framed, superficially at least, as an appeal to any truly virtuous figure there may be 'in Court' (l. 179)—that is, within *this* court, this particular (otherwise all too Hobbist) community.

---

[124] Rochester 1980: 67.  [125] Cf. N. Fisher 2000*b*: 11.
[126] Rochester 1999: 62 ff.

The situation which prevails now is the product of a collective distortion of the psyche like that reported by Artemiza. As I suggested in my previous chapter, the *beau monde*—both its leaders and its followers—committed themselves in the 1660s to the libertine *fashion* of thinking of mankind in Hobbist terms (that is, as selfish, competitive, and unendingly rapacious). Such a perception, though, such a faith, once accepted and acted upon, needs must become a self-fulfilling prophecy. Man's basic concern may be simply a desire for security, but that desire only acquires a pathological urgency when each individual proceeds on the assumption that everyone around him wants power, and that, consequently, there really is reason to fear. Each man responds to that supposed threat by cultivating his own power; yet the very effect of that is to *substantiate* others' anxieties. It is important to recognize this fact, because it underlines all the more that, contrary to much criticism of Rochester's 'Satyre',[127] there need be no necessary contradiction between the satirist's exposition of his ideal right reason and the portrait of depraved human nature which follows it. If the latter is not—at least not in theory—an inescapable predicament, but only a contingent outlook upon man, then it cannot negate the value of the former, the hypothesis of an alternative ethic to right humanity's wrongs. On the contrary, the sketch of the *status quo* underlines all the more the value of that alternative, the possibility that man might organize court society according to other, still hedonistic but less aggressively egotistical aspirations. At the very least, therefore, the poem's vision of a reforming will compounds what was evidently a larger concern of the work, Rochester's sometime craving to break out from under the influence of so cynical a view of man.[128]

Assuming that conformity to that all too entrapping view persists, the outcome can only be a world in which individuals from the King downwards find themselves divided, neurotically suspicious, and hence unfulfilled. Contrary to any Hobbesian intention, a civil society thus grounded will perpetuate within itself a state of fear and war (albeit beneath mannerly smiles), and this to the greatest degree possible short of actually destroying the polity. Indeed, given all its 'laborious mean Hypocrisy', this world will surely be less bearable than the real Hobbesian state of nature—or so, at least, we are invited to infer. This, then, is what becomes of life lived on libertine assumptions, and Rochester's satirist, having begun by challenging the model of governance on which his libertine society depends, ends by attacking the entire ethos which that model and the associated struggle for power fosters.

[127] See R. W. Johnson 1975; J. W. Johnson 2004: 202; Knight's and Vieth's essays in Vieth 1988; Turner 2003: 266; and Gill's summary (1981: 555–7). Contrast Thormählen 1993: 224, 237.
[128] See further Cousins 1984: 433; Thormählen 1993: 237.

## ROCHESTER'S MORAL POLITICS

Although I have emphasized the *implicit* contemporary application of the 'Satyre' (its relevance to the society in which Rochester moved), the 1674 text remains, nonetheless, an essentially abstract work. It was the appending of the 'Addition' in 1675 which, in incorporating new, explicit attacks on 'Statesman' (l. 185) and 'Churchman (l. 191), drew out the political piquancy of the whole. What happened in the intervening months does much to explain that development. In October 1674 Danby requested that the bishops should draw up a series of proposals to 'pacify the minds of people against the next session of parliament'.[129] (Danby's larger aim in doing this was to court the support of the Anglican hierarchy.) The bishops' response was to advocate the enforcement of laws against Nonconformists and Papists, but also to demand 'the discountenancing of libertines, who make such mock at all religions'.[130] This was the wider setting within which Edward Stillingfleet preached his notorious sermon before the King in February 1675 in which he attacked the immorality of the Court in general and Rochester's 'Satyre' in particular.[131] Rochester's 'Addition' was written in reply to these events, and duly makes a point of attacking 'vain Prelatick pride' (l. 193). The Earl, who elsewhere satirized the 'formal bands and beards' of the priesthood in both 'Tunbridge Wells' (ll. 51–81)[132] and 'Upon Nothinge' (ll. 43–5), was far from inclined to accept lectures in ethics from either Anglican bishops or minor clergy like Stillingfleet. For him, as for Buckingham and the anti-Church party which took shape in 1675, 'prelacy' signified not moral authority but 'imperious lordliness, political ambition and a spirit of persecution against "tender consciences" '.[133] It signified, too, an impertinent intrusion on the part of clerics into the independence and privileges of the aristocracy. And it underlined, lastly—beneath all rhetoric to the contrary—the clergy's own guilty immersion in the very world of Hobbism opposed in the 'Satyre'.

The 'Addition', though, mounts its politically pointed defence of Rochester's original poem in paradoxical fashion, the persona offering to 'Recant' his text before any statesman or prelate who does *not* conform to the 'Satyre's' sketch of human depravity or who can make good his faith in what is presented as an otherwise wrong-headed right reason (l. 221). In practice, the list of transgressions which these figures would have to avoid to be deemed virtuous is so long

---

[129] Quoted in Spurr 2000: 61.     [130] Ibid. 61, 69.
[131] Paulson 1971; Rochester 1999: 385, 393–4; Thormählen 1993: 229–31.
[132] Rochester 1999: 49 ff.
[133] Goldie 1990: 80. Samuel Parker is attacked in 'Tunbridge Wells' specifically for 'trampling on Religion's liberty' (l. 71).

that it does more to elaborate on man's 'mean Hypocrisy' than to raise hopes that such paragons might exist. The grammar of the period—the 'Addition' is for the most part one sentence—may lean towards the main clause with which the recantation closes ('If upon Earth there dwell such ... men ... , / I'le here Recant' (ll. 220–1)), but the sense as a whole, the sheer number of prior conditional clauses, pulls against that possibility. The upright statesman, for instance, would have to work 'To raise his Country, not his Family' (l. 188), decline 'close Bribes' (l. 190), flatter 'Not to ... Ruine, but protect' (l. 182), and so on. The fact that this first sequence collapses in aposiopesis—a Juvenalian touch testifying to the ubiquity of evil—confirms the impression that hopes of finding such a man are forlorn. The second sequence demands, amongst other things, a divine who does not with 'sawcy Eloquence, / ... chide at Kings, and rail at men of sense' (ll. 196–7), or crave adoration 'For domineering at the [Privy] Council Board' (l. 211). These comments constitute specific attacks on Stillingfleet and Archbishop Sheldon, the latter, architect of the downfall of Charles's Declaration of Indulgence.[134] As such, they again give the 'Addition' precise political applications. The overall effect, then, of this appendage is really to reiterate, under the guise of a concession, the unwavering critique of the Hobbist court world voiced in the main poem; yet to do this in a way which maps that critique on to exact contemporary co-ordinates, co-ordinates of bitter relevance for the anti-Church (and increasingly anti-Danby) faction.

The pattern of concerns mapped out in the 'Satyre' is replicated in *Lucina's Rape* (*c.*1675). In a play which repeatedly laments a monarch's lack of moderation in the pursuit of pleasures (i. i. 105–6), it is inevitable that a debate about conflicting ideals of governance should be integral to the action. Marcellina, for example, Lucina's worldly but honest lady-in-waiting, articulates what within the framework of this drama constitutes a *healthily* lusty opinion:

> ... what Nature prompts us to
> And Reason seconds why should wee avoyd?
> This Honour is the veriest Mountebanke—
> It fills our fancies with affected Tricks
> And makes us freakish, what a cheate must that bee
> Which robbs our lives of all their softer howres?
>
> (iii. iii. 54–9)[135]

This is the outlook of one who recognizes 'something gen'rous in meer Lust' ('Ramble', l. 98) and opposes the psychological contortions of 'freakish'

---

[134] For the latter identification see Thormählen 1993: 231–3.

[135] Although much of the text of *Lucina's Rape* draws verbatim on Fletcher, this passage, like most of those cited hereafter, is unique to Rochester's text. On the Earl's adaptation of his source, see Sprague 1926: 165–78.

restraint; of one whose 'Reason' (working, perhaps, according to the 'Satyre's' model) co-operates with her 'Nature' in cultivating those delights which make up our 'softer howres'. Any similarity, though, between this attitude and that of, say, a villain like Lycias (for whom compliance with one's blood is also an imperative (iii. iii. 221–3) ) is superficial. Marcellina draws finer distinctions than he, Lycias, is capable of. Stood amidst the galleries of Whitehall Palace,[136] she dismisses its statesmen (who we have already learned include 'ill favour'd faces fill'd with Scarres' (l. 125): perhaps a nod at Lord Arlington) as corrupt. Marcellina differentiates sharply between 'The soft sins of the flesh' and all other kinds of egotistical sinning (especially those, by implication, of the politic world) which she abhors (iv. ii. 53–63). In contrast to her, the Emperor (being, like *Sodom*'s Bolloxinian, a slave to 'boundless pleasure' (Sc. 1, l. 16; Sc. A2, l. 85) ) is addicted to exactly the sorts of irrational libertinism which kill delight with their very extremism. Worse still, he is fully conscious of his folly, yet cannot help but abandon himself to his lust's boundless sea:

> I'le plunge into a Sea of my desires
> And quench my Fever though I drowne my Fame
> And tear up pleasure by the roots—no matter
> Though it never grow againe.
>
> (iv. ii. 206–9)

Even in the last moments of the play, as his assassination approaches, and at a time when it is clear to everyone else that his race is run, Vallentinian still clings to the only principle of identity left in his understanding, a familiar kind of appetitiousness. For want of any other way of responding to his predicament he persists, obsessively, in imagining himself on Hobbes's racecourse:

> Let [the dead] Æcius too …
> … run the flying Race of Life againe,
> I'll bee the foremost still and snatch fresh Glory
> To my last grasp, from the contending World.
>
> (v. v. 245–8)

There is a palpable sense here that, rather than actively governing himself, the Emperor's soul is ruled from without, by appetites with a life of their own, and by a model of conduct imposed on him by a wider ethos. These, his final words, emphasize the isolation of a figure at odds with the world, one who, in his lack of self-discipline, destroys himself and almost, too, his entire polity.

The contemporary force of the play hinges on the fact that this last point, the fate of the polity under a lascivious monarch, is treated very directly by

---

[136] On the topography of the play, see N. Fisher 2000*b*: 179–90.

Rochester. This is surely why the tragedy was not performed in the Earl's lifetime. Like his 'Satyr', 'In the Isle of Brittain', and his 'Dialogue' between the royal mistresses, *Lucina's Rape* squarely berates a monarch for thinking more about his pintle than his policies. The play opens with an exchange between Maximus and Æcius in which the latter decries a moribund Empire where 'Whole Provinces fall off', unheeded, 'and scorne to have / Him for their Prince who is his Pleasures Slave' (i. i. 26–7). Rome finds its 'worths with Forreign Nations' badly shaken (l. 108), and this Emperor gives no thought to 'how hee may by force of ... virtue / Maintaine the right of his imperiall Crowne' (ll. 22–3). Opposed to this are hints of a republican mind-set. Maximus wonders whether, in submitting to such a man's authority, he and his like can still call themselves 'sonnes of Fathers / Famous and fast to Rome?' (ll. 80–1), and at the end of the play he invokes the inspiration of that 'Roman Spirit', Lucius Junius Brutus, as he shames Vallentinian into penitence (v. v. 164–9). So too, Rochester toys at the margins with Tacitean themes. Æcius, in his plain dealing with the Emperor, likens him to his late predecessor, Nero, whose 'wantonness' and 'forgetfullness of Glory' the current ruler shares (i. i. 431, 379–80). In the same vein Æcius invokes Tiberius and Caligula and sets against them the chastening example of Germanicus (ll. 432, 424–5). The inadequacy of the monarch is further emphasized in Rochester's play on what was for him a totemic word, 'generousness'. Generosity is one of Maximus's qualities (l. 207); it is one of the properties of those soldiers who die nobly for the republic (v. v. 50); and Lucina hopes to find it in Vallentinian's heart too (iii. iii. 212). By contrast, the Emperor's understanding of the term is a corrupt, inverted one: to his degenerate mind, only the rapist's 'Force' is 'the most Generous / For what that gives it freely does bestow' (iv. ii. 202–4). Given the piquancy of these comments at a time when, to judge by Freke's *History of Insipids*, England was at its lowest ebb, it is tempting to put aside Love's cautious judgement that Rochester hints here at *York*'s depravities (because he would never attack Charles 'frontally'),[137] and to suggest instead that *Lucina's Rape*, like *Sodom*, is precisely a deliberate affront to the King. Rash that may be, but hardly implausible in a figure as impetuous as Rochester—indeed, the very directness of the play again begs the question, was it *really* an accident when the Earl likewise handed 'In the Isle of Brittain' to Charles himself? So too, was his destruction of the royal sundial simply a mishap of drunken revelry?

The sharpest criticism of Vallentinian—and, by extension, of Charles—surrounds his treatment of Æcius, who, in Act V, Scene iv, is fulsomely styled as a Stoic hero committed to Rome's best interests. Rochester ennobles the general thus, emphasizing his virtue, in order to maximize the impression of

---

[137] N. Fisher 2000*b*: 188–9.

criminality when he finally dies at the Emperor's hand. The monarch's crime, though, is not just against the republic: it is also exposed as a personal betrayal and an act of folly contrary to his own self-interest. Æcius constitutes the 'onely stay' for Vallentinian's 'sinking greatness' (v. v. 122–5), one whom it is madness to 'Lopp' off (v. iii. 27–8); yet the Emperor does for him nonetheless. The political allegory in this may (as Love suggests) point, in idealizing fashion, to Buckingham—if, that is, one pictures Villiers as one who was betrayed by Charles in 1674 yet was still loyal to his sovereign even now, in opposition, a year later.[138] Buckingham did, after all, fancy himself as a military leader (which Æcius is);[139] was, like Æcius, subjected to a trumped-up treason charge; and could claim as intimate a bond with Charles as that which Æcius claims he has with Caesar (I. i. 454–60). The Buckingham association, if valid, makes the Emperor's actual response to Æcius's death all the more poignant. Having slain the man on whom he relied for 'safety', Vallentinian now considers himself free of a dependence which 'kept'st mee still in certaine feare':

> Ah what a Lamentable Wretch is hee
> Who urg'd by feare or sloth yields up his pow'r
> To hope protection from his favourite,
> Wallowing in Ease, and Vice, feels noe contempt
> But weares the empty name of Prince with scorne
> And lives a poore Led Pageant to his Slave?
> Such have I been to thee honest Æcius!
> Thy Power kept mee in aw, thy Pride in Paine:
> Till now I liv'd, but since thou'rt dead I'le Reigne.
>
> (v. v. 80–90)

Love sees in these lines a comment on Charles's dependence upon Danby, presumably as if Rochester were imagining a moment of revelation in the King's mind just after his Lord Treasurer's fall;[140] but that fall and any revelation consequent upon it were still four years off in 1675 (the tragedy's conjectural date), besides which this argument relies on identifying prelate-friendly Danby with the emphatically admirable Æcius—a doubtful correlation, surely, since Rochester's once positive relations with the Treasurer were beginning to cloud by 1675. Perhaps the point of this speech is, rather, to expose the ingratitude of monarchs, to show how they treat their virtuous props in retrospect. Vallentinian vilifies Æcius (perhaps his Buckingham) precisely because the

---

[138] Buckingham, who had, in his own words (1985: 328), been 'bred up with [His] Maiesty from a childe', certainly presented himself as ever loyal: witness his letter to Rochester (already quoted) in which he announced his hope of making the King recognize that the latter's own interest lay with his Duke of Buckingham, not with others 'about him' (Rochester 1980: 149).

[139] See, e.g., J. H. Wilson 1954: 21, 34–5, 87–8, 157–8, 161–2, 169, 179–81.

[140] N. Fisher 2000*b*: 189.

goodness of the latter puts him in mind of his own pusillanimity—a quality which, to judge from his lampoons, Rochester evidently felt was present in his own king. The further satire here is that, having rid himself of someone whom 'we' know was actually loyal, the Emperor imagines he will now be free; whereas in fact the condition from which he thinks he will now escape is the very one which he will actually embrace—the same one, perhaps, which Charles embraced in turning from the cabal to Danby. This speech, then, may have been Rochester's sharpest blow of all against his own monarch.

There are, though, two caveats which ameliorate the otherwise critical thrust of *Lucina's Rape*. First, when Maximus addresses Vallentinian in the final scene, he reveals what may have been the benevolent, instructive intention of Rochester's play as a whole: 'I will awake thee, / I'le rouze thee, Cesar, if strong Reason can' (ll. 144–5). Secondly, Rochester also offers Charles-as-Vallentinian the consolation that he alone is not responsible for his own conduct. On the contrary, both the Emperor himself and, more tellingly, Æcius insist that this poor prince has too often been led astray by others (v. ii. 36–7; v. i. 47–50). In part this comment perhaps alludes again to Charles's dependence upon Danby, but it surely also implicates Rochester himself in the follies played out on-stage. There is other evidence to support that conclusion. Lucina's actual rape, as Love has shown, is located very precisely within the Earl's own rooms at Whitehall, his 'Appartment … / That lies upon the Garden' (III. ii. 52–3).[141] Furthermore, disparaging reference is made to those 'Rascalls' who 'with vile laughter take [the Emperor] in their Armes / And beare the drunken Cesar to his Bed' (v. v. 135–7); but this is something which Rochester himself must have done on occasion in his capacity as a Gentleman of the Bedchamber. So too, this Caesar reminds his villainous servants that he has protected them in their '*boundless* infamy', raising them 'Above the reach of Law' (I. i. 300–5): again, Charles could say as much about Rochester. Most dramatically of all, this impression of mutual complicity is confirmed towards the end of the final scene when Maximus, otherwise the spokesman for republican values, admits that his criticism of Vallentinian actually stems from a repressed sense of affinity with him:

> EMP: How … dar'st thou …
> … assault thy Emperour ?
> MAX: Because I have more Witt than honesty,
> *More of thy selfe*, more Villany than Vertue,
> More Passion, more revenge, and more Ambition
> Than foolish honour and Fantastick Glory.
>
> (v. v. 186–91)

---

141 N. Fisher 2000*b*: 186–7.

How far either Maximus or Rochester could really lay claim to 'ambition' is questionable. However, the intuition that behind the composition of this play sits a shared self, passion, and villainy, yoking together Emperor and servant; the intuition, too, that the vigour of the attack upon Vallentinian reflects a protégé's *Oedipal* turn against his monarch-father, and a turn against his own likeness, surely does point to Rochester's relationship with Charles. Just as the Earl seemed to implicate himself in his 'Satyre's' critique of the role played by wits in court society; just as he, too, was sometimes guilty of nurturing the oppressive culture of Hobbism attacked in that poem; so, here, he acknowledges his own shameful part in what he presents as Charles's tragedy. Inevitably, that concession does something to extenuate the potency of his attack.[142]

The third and last phase in the narrative which politicizes Rochester's moral critique of the polity comes with the preparation, in 1679, of a fictional preface for a projected new edition of the 'Satyre against Reason'.[143] The preface is fictional, in that Rochester casts this supportive document in the voice of a Devonshire parson, one 'William Lovesey', as if to suggest how far the Church's rank and file (who voted in Parliamentary elections for the first time this year[144]) were at odds with their high-minded masters, so dismissive of Rochester's sort. The context of this work does much to explain its contents. In December 1678, amidst a growing furore over his alleged inaction in face of the Popish Plot, Danby was impeached. His efforts of the previous March to obtain a subsidy from France (so that Charles need not depend on Parliament to pay the Army) had been exposed, and he was therefore accused of harbouring Popish sympathies, usurping royal authority in the conduct of foreign policy, and seeking to 'deprive' the King of the 'safe and wholesome councils' of his Parliament.[145] Crucially, these crimes justified the Shaftesburian opposition in reinvoking their Whiggish cry of liberty and berating the supposed threat to English freedom. In March 1679, in an attempt to shield Danby, Charles granted him a royal pardon, but that too was seen as an assault on liberty, on Parliament's right to scrutinize iniquitous ministers. MPs agreed in May that any counsel who sought to defend Danby's pardon was, *de facto*, a traitor.[146] Reflecting on Danby's previous ability to manage the two Houses, members also brought forward a bill to counteract such practices by setting a maximum

---

[142] Cf. Burns 1995: 35–6, where Clark points to further 'displaced self-loathing' in 'In the Isle of Brittain'. For this same reason one of Love's reasons for questioning Rochester's authorship of *Sodom* must be doubtful. Love claims (Rochester 1999: 498) that Rochester cannot be the author because that play, in satirizing the venality of Charles's courtiers, thereby implicates the Earl himself in that critique. Rochester seems not to be as averse to such self-laceration as Love supposes.

[143] Rochester 1999: 54 ff.     [144] See Goldie 1990: 97–9.

[145] Quoted in Spurr 2000: 269.     [146] Ibid. 276. Cf. Goldie 1990: 91.

duration of two years on any given Parliament. At the same time, the Commons edged ever closer to getting an Exclusion Bill placed on the statute book. When the latter passed its second reading on 21 May, Charles prorogued Parliament. As the wealthy departed town for the summer and judges pressed on with the prosecution of the Popish plotters, London was left bubbling with rumours about further Catholic outrages. Rochester, it should be said, took his seat in the Lords throughout this period, sat on a Commission tasked with preventing officials from 'taking undue Advantages of their Places', and (despite Danby's hopes that he might prove friendly) actively supported steps to advance the latter's impeachment.[147] Mindful, no doubt, of the prevailing rhetoric of liberty, he had began to study Livy (which did 'a little incline me to policy') some time between 1675 and 1677,[148] and he spent the last years of this decade—so Robert Wolseley later claimed—framing himself 'to publick Business': 'he begun to inform himself of the Wisdom of our Laws and the excellent Constitution of the *English* Government ...; he was inquisitive after all kinds of Histories that concern'd *England*, both ancient and modern, and set himself to read the Journals of Parliament Proceedings.'[149]

The evidence for this increasingly 'serious'-minded[150] Rochester is apparent in the Lovesey preface and the poem which he incorporated within that on 'The Freeborne English', both of which exude a preoccupation with liberty and history. On the one hand, Danby is attacked there, for ''Tis a Vile Fav'rittes Insolent pretence / To *Tyranize* att a good Kings expence' (ll. 45–6).[151] On the other, though, Lovesey berates the extremism of the sentiments aroused by the Shaftesburian faction (just as Rochester himself scorned Shaftesbury *et al.* for their cynical promotion of Oates in 'honour of the Protestant cause'[152]). Lovesey describes a London swamped with scurrilous libels and pamphlets, all glibly invoking 'that guilded Idoll Lyberty' (l. 6), and he condemns *that* understanding of liberty—lawlessness—as 'true Vassalage' (l. 17), the liberty not of Brutus but of brutes enslaved to their own self-interest (l. 18). Rochester may sketch the precious Lovesey with a touch of wry irony, but for the most part their views, actual and fictional, seem to be comparable, especially when Lovesey advocates a careful blending of liberty with authoritarian control—Brutus, after all, stood for *aristocratic* republicanism—and when

[147] Greer 2000: 23–4; J. W. Johnson 2004: 303.　　　[148] Rochester 1980: 116–17.
[149] Spingarn 1908: iii. 6.　　　[150] The adjective is Wolseley's.
[151] For other such Buckingham-circle attacks on Danby, see Buckingham 1985: 150–1, 158–61; Love 2004: 119–22.
[152] Rochester 1980: 232. Buckingham also began to distance himself from Shaftesbury's Whig extremism in 1679 (Buckingham 1985: 29–34, 331). So did both Dorset (1979: 56), whose 'My Opinion' (1682) cites the Whigs as almost as bad as the Tories ('all fools and knaves'), and Sedley, who concluded that 'Whigg and Tory' were 'much ... the same stuff at bottom ..., [all] self-interest' (quoted in Pinto 1927: 152).

(sounding like Buckingham) he condemns 'envious Inferiours' for assuming the 'prerogative of defameing' their betters (ll. 13–14). The stance which the vicar assumes is of moderated Whiggery, one wherein '*Obedience*' guarantees 'our freedome' (l. 69), and it is with reference to that ideal that Rochester (in a manœuvre which brings the story of Hobbism full circle) invokes Tacitus. I suggested earlier in this book that some of the defining attitudes of Hobbism and libertinism took their origins from the view of man propounded in the *Annals*, and it is perhaps not surprising that, at a moment when he wanted to circumscribe those boundless, individualist energies, Rochester should turn to the *Agricola* (Tacitus's more positive vision) for support. Lovesey cites from that work a description of the English people according to which they enthusiastically obey authority but only so long as the subjection required of them by their overlords does not extend to outright slavery ('*jam domiti utt pareant nondum ut serviant*' (ll. 28–9) ).[153] He adds, too, a similar precept from the *Histories* which he would place over the doors of Parliament: '*jmperaturus es Hominibus qui nec Tot[a]m Servitutem pati possunt nec tot[a]m Libertatem*' (ll. 66–7). Revealingly, the blend here of liberty and deferential allegiance anticipates that voiced by another opponent of Danby who nonetheless distanced himself from the Popish Plot madness: namely, Halifax ('the Man in the World [Rochester] valu'd most').[154] A good 'Trimmer', Halifax wrote in his 'Character' of the same, should applaud 'our blessed constitution, in which dominion and Liberty are so happily reconciled', because it 'giveth to the Prince the glorious power of commanding freemen, and to the subjects the satisfaction of seeing the power so Lodged, as that their Liberties are secure'.[155] It was the merit of England's laws, Halifax thought, to maintain 'a true distinction betweene Vassalage and Obedience', to steer a course between 'devouring prerogative, and a Licentious ungovernable freedom'.

Lovesey, then, offers an idealized image of the English as a nation hostile to 'Loath'd extreames' (ll. 21–2) and hateful of 'chaines' (l. 31), but supportive of any government which allows them their right to 'marke out Limitts of Obedience' (l. 57). Crucially, in his mind, this abstract political model approximates to the moral conclusions of the 'Satyre', to its ideal of pleasant self-indulgence tempered by a reforming, self-regulating will. In keeping with that larger poem (and not least its attack on the oppressive climate of fear fostered by Hobbism), Lovesey's version of 'The Freeborne English' describes the people of England as being, at their best, 'More govern'd by … Iudgement then … feare' (l. 35). As if recollecting *Lucina's Rape*, the inset verse in his

---

[153] The same text is also used as the epigraph in the separate manuscript of the poem 'The freeborn English' (Rochester 1999: 257 ff.).

[154] Burnet, reporting Rochester's words (quoted in Treglown 1982: 99).

[155] Halifax 1989: i. 194.

preface advises that 'Kings are Least safe with a Loose Lawless will' (l. 39), a sentiment still more poignantly evoked in the other, separate version of this same poem: 'Kings are least safe *in their unbounded will*' (l. 12). The phrasing in the latter directly recalls the project at the heart of the 'Satyre' to '*bound* Desires with a reforming *Will*'. It is perhaps not surprising, therefore, or implausible, that Lovesey concludes his preface by introducing that 'Satyre' as 'a Satyr, against Reason and Yet a Very reasonable satyr; ... against Man yett most full of humanitie ... True Witt and Morrall Philosophy' (ll. 73–5, 86).

For Rochester's parson, the moral ideal of the 'Satyre' constitutes, implicitly, a means for 'The Freeborne English' to preserve two of the defining qualities attributed to them in the opening line of that poem: namely, their wisdom and (more tellingly) their generosity. That latter word, a flickering presence across this chapter, has an extensive history within Rochester's works.[156] Indeed, its significance for him bears comparison with the significance of magnanimity for Milton. In the 'Ramble' and 'Artemiza', but also in 'A Dialogue between Strephon and Daphne' (l. 26), in 'Of Marriage' (l. 10), in 'Womans Honour' (l. 11), and in *Sodom* (Sc. 2, l. 28),[157] 'generosity' signifies an openness towards one's own bodily desires (a relaxed willingness to indulge them); a freeness, too, with one's body, sharing it with other people; and a lack of possessiveness towards others, a readiness to let them observe these same values. Here, therefore, generosity entails both giving to others and giving to oneself (allowing oneself proper pleasures). It is as such the very opposite of the ascetic disposition so furiously maintained by Guyon or Hamlet. Meanwhile, in both *Lucina's Rape*, *Sodom* (Sc. A3, l. 144), a 1676 letter which commends the 'generous philosophy' of 'Lord L——',[158] and his 'Second Prologue at Court' (l. 38),[159] Rochester casts generosity as a wider ethical ideal. There it retains its etymological associations with nobility of birth and character; it constitutes, too, the very spirit of self-sacrifice which Milton captures in 'magnanimity'; and it informs acts of kindness and pity. As such, it continues to signify a freeness with one's self towards others, a willingness to hold the self open before other people and even (in the case of pitying) to let them benefit from that openness. This is the very moral quality for which the narrator searches in the 'Satyre' but which, when he finds it, turns out to have been debased by the lust for power

---

[156] I develop here a point first broached by Griffin (1973: 234). 'Générosité' was a frequent term of approval in mid-seventeenth-century French literature. Senault, e.g., uses it obsessively in his *L'Usage des Passions* (1641). The same word became increasingly common in English plays of the 1660s and 1670s. Whereas the word is invoked two or three times in *The Mulberry Garden* or *She Would if She Could* (both 1668), it is used half a dozen times or more (often in a cluster of iterations) in *The Country Wife* (1674), *The Rover* (1677), or such heroic plays as *The Conquest of Granada, Part I* (1672) and *Aureng-Zebe* (1676).

[157] Rochester 1999: 6 ff., 40 ff., 21.          [158] Rochester 1980: 119.

[159] Rochester 1999: 118 ff.

lying behind it. The point, though, in all these cases is that, precisely in holding the self open to others, generosity (as much as Miltonic magnanimity) stands flatly opposed to Hobbism and the aggression of libertinism, since those things are premissed on a model of the self as something closed, unattached, aloof, defensive. When the Lovesey preface invokes 'generosity', it therefore invokes an ideal intrinsically opposed (like the 'Satyre' as a whole) to the Hobbist world; but the preface also politicizes that term, subsuming it within an emergent language of Whiggery (just as Milton positions 'magnanimity' in relation to republicanism).[160] Six years later, writing after Rochester's death (when the mythologizing of his identity was already under way), Wolseley could play upon this same politicizing nuance in his 'Preface to *Valentinian*'. There he emphasizes the putative 'generousness' of Rochester's temper and contrasts that with the 'ungenerous' spirit of the Yorkist, Mulgrave.[161] Rochester's pen, we are now told, was *always* 'as generous in the Aim' as Theseus's sword.[162] It was drawn in anger precisely against the likes of Danby, being used 'to stop the progress of arbitrary Oppression, and beat down the Bruitishness of headstrong Will; to do his King and Countrey justice upon such publick State-Thieves as wou'd beggar a Kingdom to enrich themselves'. This, then, is the generous, heroic Rochester: ethically the very antithesis of Oldham's libertine and of a narrow Hobbism; politically a proto-Whig ripe for appropriation by Burnet; in both senses the symbolic embodiment of one alternative, at least, to the libertine court culture which had prevailed since 1660.

---

[160] Defoe would later make 'generosity' a defining virtue of his 'True-Born Englishman' (Defoe 1997: 26 ff., ll. 594–7, 875, 1088).

[161] Spingarn 1908: iii. 7, 10. On the wider phenomenon of refashioning Restoration libertines posthumously, as serious-minded, politically engaged Whigs, see Williams 2005: 84–5, 91–2.

[162] Spingarn 1908: iii. 6.

# Coda

## PLEASURE AFTER ROCHESTER

The structure of the previous chapter, and especially its political conclusion, could be seen as imposing an implicit teleology on Rochester's life, one which matches Burnet's shaping of his biography as a progression from sin to repentant reformation. According to Burnet's *Life*, the dying Rochester admitted that in the past he had done much to consolidate the hegemony of that miserable condition of hypocrisy so censured in the 'Satyre'. By his own account, he and the wits 'cared not for [Morality], further then the reputation of it was necessary for their credit', a fact 'of which he gave … many Instances, as their … swearing Friendship, where they hated mortally; their Oaths … in their Addresses to Women, which they intended never to make good; the pleasure they took in defaming innocent Persons … because they could not engage them to comply with their ill Designs'.[1] By contrast, in his final months Rochester reportedly became 'much ashamed of his former Practices … because he had made himself a Beast, and … brought pain … on his Body'.[2] On his deathbed he told Burnet that he now (rather belatedly) lived by other maxims, the resolutions that 'he should do nothing to the hurt of any other, or that might prejudice his own health', and that 'all pleasure, when it did not interfere, with these [aforementioned considerations], was to be indulged as the gratification of our natural Appetites [for] It seemed unreasonable to imagine these were put into a man only to be restrained, or curbed to … a narrowness'.[3] The second of these points, especially, is strikingly commensurate with the reformed ethic posited in the 'Satyre', a work which presents an earlier moment of critical lucidity comparable to this later one.

As I have previously indicated, there are two problems, though, in trying to impose too linear a structure upon the story of Rochester's intellectual life. The first is that, with Rochester as with Oldham, the screen of powerful personas erected in poem after poem deliberately frustrates efforts to identify where the poet's own views lie. The libertine is not to be controlled. Secondly, most of the

---

[1] Burnet 1680: 23–4.    [2] Ibid. 35.    [3] Ibid. 38.

Earl's work is, anyway, as yet undatable, or can only be located within broad parameters. To take matters chronologically: 'The Imperfect Enjoyment', first, falls somewhere between 1672 and 1680,[4] and the 'Ramble' was certainly written before March 1673.[5] Fisher follows Hammond in dating *Troas* to 1674 or before, but Love questions this.[6] The 'Satyre', as already established, must also have been written before 1674, its 'Addition' following in 1675 (and the Lovesey preface in 1679). Love's date of 1675 for *Lucina's Rape* is a good conjecture, though within fairly wide possible boundaries.[7] 'Against Constancy' obviously predates its licensing in 1676, 'Love and Life' its publication in 1677, but by how long in each case is unclear. Love marks 'Upon Nothinge' as a mature poem, and Fisher also places it late in his chronology (albeit before May 1678); others, though, have made a case for its predating 1673.[8] (Conversely, whereas Hammond had located 'Artemiza' between 1673 and 1675, Fisher now contends that it was written early on, before May 1669.[9]) 'The Fall' must predate its publication in 1680, 'My dear Mistris' its in 1685, 'The Mistress' and 'Absent from thee' theirs in 1691; but the date of 'The Platonick Lady' remains a mystery. These marker-posts, clearly, do little to support any sense of a progressive narrative in Rochester's career, and he himself certainly performed some of his greatest 'sins'—the vandalizing of the priceless sundial, his involvement in the Downs affair—in between circulating his moralizing 'Satyre' in 1674 and reasserting its ethic (with a political slant) five years later, in the Lovesey document. Hence, despite the best efforts of Pinto, who, with boundless confidence, declared that with the 'Satyre' Rochester 'had reached the end of the cul-de-sac into which he had been led by materialism',[10] moral chronologies appear doomed to failure. It seems best to view the poems simply as dramatizations of a persistent oscillation in attitudes, an oscillation akin to that which marked Rochester's wider life, his constant shifting between fits of debauchery and study. Some poems revel in, some seek to qualify or moderate, some criticize and reject, Hobbist and libertine values. They offer no obvious linear progression—the early dating of the satires confirms that fact—but instead slip back and forth between celebratory and satirical stances.

However, if the pattern of Rochester's writing reveals no one conclusive judgement about the particular libertine ethic which animated it, time itself does—a judgement which emphasizes the inadequacies, the emotional poverty, of the Hobbist approach to society. History proved Rochester's sober side, his disillusionment with the court wit ethic, to be the harbinger of the

---

[4] N. Fisher 2000*a*: 305.    [5] Rochester 1999: 410.
[6] N. Fisher 2000*a*: 306; Rochester 1999: 370–1.    [7] Rochester 1999: 448–50.
[8] Ibid. 371; N. Fisher 2000*a*: 308; Rochester 1984: 260.
[9] N. Fisher 2000*a*: *passim*; Rochester 1999: 396.    [10] Pinto 1935: 182–3.

future: hence the structure and conclusion of my previous chapter. That disillusionment is first intimated in Dryden's *The Kind Keeper* (1678), a play which signals the decline of comedies celebrating Hobbist libertinism with Gervase's remark, 'Debauchery is upon its last Legs in *England*: witty men began the Fashion; and, now ... Fops are got into't, 'tis time to leave it.'[11] The same trend is still more apparent in Lee's *Princess of Cleve* (*c.*1680–2).[12] On the face of it, this drama, in so memorably testifying to the genius and charisma of the late Lord Rochester (the very 'Spirit of Wit' (I. ii. 101–8) ), would seem to applaud the values of libertinism. Lee's lead character, Nemours, aligns himself with a rakish view of the Earl as he quotes from the latter's lost work 'The Urn', professing that 'the Fury of Wine and ... Women possess [him]', and that true wit lies in his 'Extravagance of Pleasure' (III. i. 125–33). A serial philanderer throughout the play, Nemours displays, too, many of Dorimant's qualities, never more so than when, having successfully lured Celia into an assignation, he turns to scheduling additional conquests with the line 'So there's one in the Fernbrake' (IV. i. 28). Yet in the end Lee's hero is *not* another Dorimant, and *The Princess of Cleve* does not share Etherege's indulgent tone towards its libertine. Whereas Dorimant could hold the amused attention—even sympathy—of his audience, Lee shapes his play so as to deny his protagonist that privilege. The primary focus of Nemours's seductive attentions, Princess Cleve herself, suffers agonies of torment as she finds herself drawn by adulterous passion to this rake—torment because she recognizes her husband's virtue (albeit that she does not love him) and is therefore loath to betray him. The Prince, for his part, confronts his wife's *akrasic* condition with a comparable dignity, with the result that the couple impress upon the audience a sense of their nobility and pathos. Nowhere is this truer than in Act II, Scene iii, where Cleve confesses her transgressive passion to her consort:

PRINCE. Weep not my Chartres, for howe'er my Tongue
Upbraid thy Fame, my Heart still worships thee,
And by the Blood that chills me round—I swear
From this sad Moment, I'll ne'er urge thee more [i.e., to love me, thy husband];
All that I beg of thee, is not to hate me.
PRINCESS. The study of my Life shall be to love you.
PRINCE. Never, Oh never! I were mad to hope it,
Yet thou shalt give me leave to fold thy hand,
To press it with my Lips, to sigh upon it,
And wash it with my Tears.

(II. iii. 190–9)

---

[11] Dryden 1956–2002: xiv. 25.
[12] The play's dating is discussed in R. D. Hume 1976: 118–22.

Nemours, an unseen onlooker throughout this scene, responds to it with a triumphalism wholly insensitive to the pathos of what he has witnessed: ''tis glorious ... / To bring to such Extreams so chast a mind' (ll. 218–19). He continues in that egotistical vein even as Lee works up in his audience's mind the sense of tragedy surrounding his heroine—witness the desperation with which she confronts her ungovernable desire: 'My Heart rebels, I feel a gorgeing pain / That choaks me ... trembling from Head to Foot; / A shog of Blood and Spirits' (iv. iii. 68–70). In a sentimental touch to the plotting, the Prince, her husband, dies of grief, whereupon she abandons herself to a life of confinement. Nemours, though, remains deaf to the force of Cleve's agony, seeing her grief only as an opportunity to complete his seduction whilst she is 'in the undress of her Soul'—at which time, he avers, 'Let a man stand but right before [women], and like hunted Hares they run into his lap' (v. ii. 17–18, 21–2). In fact, Cleve does not thus capitulate, but Nemours, nonplussed, ends the play glibly, betting that he will bed her in eighteen months and three weeks' time (v. iii. 255), before rushing off to appease his other infuriated mistress. Lee, then, deliberately solicits from us a hostile, moralizing response to the callousness of this Hobbist, what in the epilogue he calls this 'Bulling Gallant' of his 'wanton Play' (l. 22). By emphasizing in his audience's minds the vulnerability, and yet also nobility, of Nemours's victims, he forces upon us a sense of the emotional cost of aggressive libertinism—this, something Etherege holds at bay in *The Man of Mode* by making Harriet as strong as Dorimant and casting Dorimant's other conquests as fools or peripheral characters. As if to complete his case, Lee also adds, in his closing line, a quick jab at Rochester's reputation, for 'Death-bed Sorrow rarely shews the Man' (v. iii. 303). Burnet's account, the playwright implies, misses much of the damage done by the libertine and conveys nothing of the tawdriness of character inherent in such figures.

Lee's play anticipates, in the sharpest of terms, the critical attitude towards Hobbism and libertinism which emerged in the next two decades. These years witnessed a rejection of the court wit ethos, a reaction which began amongst those concerned to follow Stanley in developing a more discerning model of Epicureanism, but which was then pursued by Whig essayists of the early 1700s, professional writers keen to fashion for themselves a moral identity commensurate with the godly revolution initiated by William's court. The latter group, for whom the word 'generosity' served as a totemic value, demand more attention than can be given here. Dryden, though, a representative voice in the later history of neo-Epicureanism, tellingly illustrates the story of pleasure and appetite as it developed after Rochester, and it is therefore with him that this book concludes.[13]

---

[13] Hammond 1983 and 1999 have much influenced my discussion of Dryden here.

The beginning of Book 2 of *De Rerum* succinctly articulates the 'precepts of morality'[14] for which Dryden valued Lucretius. Here, as in Rochester, the language of limits is apparent. According to Dryden's translation, he who bends his efforts to outshine others in wit and power (as the court wits, at their best/worst, did) is likely also to

> ... overfeed
> His crammed desires with more than nature needs:
> For nature wisely stints our appetite,
> And craves no more than undisturbed delight,
> Which minds unmixed with cares and fears obtain,
> A soul serene, a body void of pain.
> So little this corporeal frame requires,
> So bounded are our natural desires,
> That wanting all, and setting pain aside,
> With bare privation sense is satisfied.
>
> (2. 18–27)[15]

Lines 18–20 here, together with 'sense' in line 27, are Dryden's own additions, but they evoke familiar associations: overfeeding matches the surfeiting images of the poems 'Against Fruition'; 'crammed' recalls the feverish intensity with which appetite is pursued in Hobbes's world (particularly as characterized by Spragens); 'stints', an image of limiting, anticipates the subsequent use of 'bounded' in line 25; and 'sense' reappropriates the libertine 'rule of sense' for the true Epicurean cause. Dryden's Lucretian theme, clearly, is that moderation, not continuous indulgence, best serves the 'corporeal frame's' interests. Once pains are annulled, the body requires little else for its satisfaction. In this there are obvious parallels with Rochester's sometime ethic of bounded desires, his rules of good and ill distinguished by sense, the dissatisfactions of fruition and over-intense appetites recorded in his and others' lyrics, and his sentiment that too often man's actions 'do himself no good'. Above all, though, the message here, as in Montaigne and Théophile, is that the body and its appetites (when correctly understood, not corrupted by fashionable philosophies) dictate their own best limits. The Epicurean who heeds but this one principle may, in Jean François Sarasin's timely idiom, '*manage the fruition* of Pleasure with [such] discretion' that he suffers no 'After-Claps'.[16]

Dryden embellishes and slants his source again in selecting from Book 3:

> Yet thus the fools, that would be thought the wits,
> Disturb their mirth with melancholy fits ...

---

[14] Dryden 1995–2005: ii. 246.         [15] Ibid. ii. 312 ff.

[16] Saint-Évremond 1694: 267. (Originally composed in 1645–6, Sarasin's treatise on Epicurus first appeared in English translation in 1686, wrongly attributed to Saint-Évremond.)

> They whine, and cry, 'Let us make haste to live,
> Short are the joys that human life can give'.

(3. 97–8, 101–2)[17]

Where Lucretius has simply 'homines' (l. 913),[18] Dryden applies that text to would-be 'wits', particularly to Rochester's circle from which he had, by now, been ostracized and was therefore keen to vilify here.[19] Their unquenchable thirst for more pleasures is admonished in familiar terms, hinting at the image of the Danaïdes' leaking vessel so often invoked by Epicureans to attack Cyrenaicism:

> ... if my blessings thou hast thrown away,
> *If undigested joys passed through and would not stay,*
> Why dost thou wish for more to squander still?

(ll. 132–4)

Shortly thereafter Dryden adds significantly to Lucretius, this time tilting at the Hobbesian notion of felicity. Two lines of Latin (*De Rerum* 3. 957–8) become five in translation:

> But this is still th' effect of wishing more!
> Unsatisfied with all that Nature brings,
> Loathing the present, liking absent things;
> From hence it comes thy vain desires at strife
> Within themselves, have tantalized thy life.

(ll. 154–8)

Line 156 is something of a formula for notions of felicity which concentrate on future prosperity and lose interest in pleasures the moment they have been attained. The result is a dysfunctional psychic economy, constantly perplexed by worries as to which of its vain desires to pursue next, beset by anxieties about the opportunity cost which every such choice entails. The Hobbist libertine is tantalized by thoughts not of what he has attained but of those pleasures which he has not had world enough and time to gorge upon. This, Dryden implies, is no way to live.

What Dryden advocated in the abstract, Saint-Évremond, the *arbiter elegantiarum* of his day, then refined into an intuition. Hence, writing to the Comte d'Olonne on the subject of diet, for example, we find him advising the latter to eat when and only when he 'lightly perceives' Nature inciting him to do so.[20] As that telling phrase 'lightly perceive' ('légèrement sentir'[21]) implies, understanding how much self-indulgence is appropriate became,

---

[17] Dryden 1995–2005: ii. 317 ff.     [18] Lucretius 1937: 230.     [19] Hammond 1983: 13.
[20] Saint-Évremond 1694: 126.     [21] Saint-Évremond 1998: 119.

for Saint-Évremond, a matter not of dogmatism but simply of instinct and taste—the latter, an idiom now replacing Aristotelian talk of habituation. (We are thus a long way, here, from Stanley's laboriously codified 'Canons of Affections'.) Such tasteful intuitiveness promoted, in turn, a whole sensibility which could cope with pleasure and its vagaries much more satisfactorily than earlier ideals of libertinism had done—witness the following from a Saint-Évremond letter to Bussy-Rabutin:

> For he that still improves his present State,
> · · · · · · · · · · ·
> With Ease and Freedom tastes the present Joy,
> And distant Ills do ne'er his Thoughts employ.
> His Mind unbent, in innocent Repose,
> No real Grief, no gloomy Moments knows.
> He keeps a sweet Remembrance of the past,
> And hugs the present while the Transports last:
> He steals from the Chagrin the Future gives,
> And, as the happy Minutes come, he lives.[22]

The mind of this Epicurean hero is poised easefully in the delights of the present instead of always grasping at future pleasures. The 'happy minute'—the English translator's idiomatic rendering—is relished here (as in Montaigne) for what it is, instead of being seen only as a signal of imminent disillusionment (as it is in the lexicon of poems 'Against Fruition'). Equally, though, whilst in the fractious vision of 'Love and Life' 'The flyeing houres' are 'always gone', the past here is its own haven of 'sweet Remembrance', a pleasure cherished alongside present-moment 'Transports'. Rochester might have craved, but could never capture, such a balanced mind-set. The 'Satyre' and various of his more critical lyrics seem (even through the masks of their personas) to isolate moments of confrontation with his own, more evasive, kinetic self; but for the most part the Earl (drawn by the pull of company and the ever-beckoning promise of greater felicity) seems never to have stuck to those austere revelations.[23] He preferred at one moment to plunge into appetite's boundless sea, at the next to retreat to Woodstock: this, rather than embracing Dryden's and Saint-Évremond's challenge of learning to bound his desires even whilst remaining in town.[24]

---

[22] Saint-Évremond 1714: i. 49.

[23] On his recurring gravitation towards town and court, see N. Fisher 2000*b*: 14–16.

[24] Cf. Aubrey: 'in the country he was generally civill enough. He was wont to say that when he came to Brentford the devill entered … him and never left till he came into the country again' (Farley-Hills 1972: 178).

## CONCLUSION

Standing at the end of a narrative thread which begins with Spenserian psychomachia and ends with its antithesis, Hobbism, Rochester's works demonstrate that the libertinism with which his name is associated (and which he sometimes attacked) in fact contained, and gradually realized, the seeds of its own destruction. For some court wits that self-destruction was literal, Fanshaw, Savile, and Rochester too, all finding themselves the victims of venereal and other diseases of indulgence (and of the equally fatal methods of treatment for these).[25] For most, though, it took more intellectual, imaginative, or emotional forms. The sense of disappointment and isolation emerging from such realizations prompted the conclusion that Hobbist and libertine attitudes to governance were inadequate, and this discovery, intimated in Rochester's works, does much to explain the decline in *Hobbes's* literary fortunes especially, after 1680. Hobbes and his philosophy seem to have been associated to a significant if unreasonable extent with the moral outlook of that Hobbist libertinism propounded by the first generation of Restoration courtiers. With the collapse of this ethos, Hobbes's imaginative imprint on literary texts therefore dwindled, lingering only to enjoy a brief revival under Mandeville.[26] However, the same developments which account for this decline also help to explain that uptake on neo-Epicureanism (initially so coldly received) to which Dryden and Saint-Évremond bear witness. Furthermore, the decline of Hobbism made way, too, for an increasing engagement with an alternative and, in the end, more lasting ideal of governance, one which would ultimately exert a definitive influence over eighteenth-century moralists.

That more lasting creed took its origins from a variety of mutually resonant sources: from the traditions of Aristotelianism and Augustinianism discussed in Chapter 5 which insisted upon the value of moderated and spiritually informed passions; from the Anglican and Cambridge Platonist traditions which rooted man's ethical sensibility in an instinctive concern for sociability; and from the tradition of Cartesian ethics, grounded in Descartes's *Les Passions de l'Âme*, which again emphasized the affections' moral and practical worth, but which also made 'generosity' the guiding light of man's project to govern his

---

[25] These several parties' venereal torments are referred to in Rochester 1980: 67, 182, 184, 195, 197 ff.
[26] This notwithstanding, Skinner has noted (1966: 301–3) that various of Hobbes's *political* principles continued to attract sympathetic consideration, particularly amongst proponents of *de facto* rule, during the constitutional crisis of the late 1680s.

passions.[27] All these forces grew up in the shadow of mid-century libertinism, but in the late 1690s, when that libertinism had run its course, they emerged to supersede it, exerting their influence via a series of essays and conduct-books produced by Whig-minded authors of the time. William Ayloffe's *Government of the Passions* (1700), John Dennis's *Advancement and Reformation of Modern Poetry* (1701), and Richard Steele's *Christian Hero* (1701) all highlighted the moral value of the passions and, with Vanbrugh's and Congreve's plays, invoked the totemic values of generosity and magnanimity.[28] In so doing, these works laid the foundations for a new vocabulary of moral sentiments (an idiom then developed by the 3rd Earl of Shaftesbury, Hutcheson, *et al.*), but this always with one eye on Hobbism and the need—so much a concern of Bishop Butler—to reconcile benevolence with the realities of self-interest. All this, of course, constitutes a separate story, a story of generous sentiments which lies beyond the remit of the present book; but that subsequent narrative owes a good deal, certainly, both to Milton's language of magnanimity and to the parallel language of generosity which became associated with Rochester at his most 'Whiggish' as early as the mid-1670s. The narrative, then, of passion's sometimes libertine triumph over reason intersects in a surprising way, and at an unexpected juncture, with that of eighteenth-century moral theory. Rochester in particular—in one mood the Restoration apogee—is, in another (and like Saint-Évremond), the *arbiter elegantiarum* of a new age: the provider both of 'a Very reasonable', very Augustan measure of 'True Witt and Morrall Philosophy', and of a sober, Epicurean answer to Spenser's terror of 'passions bace'; these, two streams of thought which, in tandem with Milton's emphasis on moralized affections, foreshadow the sensibility of a new age.

[27] See Tilmouth 2007.

[28] Congreve deploys 'generosity' and its cognates precisely to signal that his libertines are of a more refined order than their Carolean forebears. In *Love for Love*, for example, Valentine is accused of having 'not a Dram of Generous Love about him: all Interest, all Interest' (Congreve 1982: III. i. 256–7); yet by the end of that play Angelica declares herself overwhelmed by his 'so generous and faithful a Passion' (v. i. 598, 609–10). *The Way of the World*'s Mirabell, a polite antithesis to the same comedy's Hobbist libertine, Fainall, is affirmed at the outset as one who has 'too much Generosity not to be tender of [a Lady's] Honour' (ibid. I. i. 98–101), and is likewise pronounced towards the end of Act v as 'generous at [the] last' (v. i. 509). Such generosity ties Mirabell to a community of like-minded figures—foremost among them being Mrs Fainall, the very 'Pattern of Generosity' (III. i. 252–3, 262–3)—who together work to exclude the more egotistical varieties of libertinism from Congreve's Whiggish world of sociability.

# References

## List of Abbreviations

| | |
|---|---|
| *17C* | *The Seventeenth Century* |
| *ELR* | *English Literary Renaissance* |
| *HJ* | *The Historical Journal* |
| *HLQ* | *Huntington Library Quarterly* |
| *HPT* | *History of Political Thought* |
| *JEGP* | *Journal of English and Germanic Philology* |
| *JHI* | *Journal of the History of Ideas* |
| *MLR* | *The Modern Language Review* |
| *MP* | *Modern Philology* |
| *MStud* | *Milton Studies* |
| *NQ* | *Notes and Queries* |
| *PQ* | *Philological Quarterly* |
| *RES* | *The Review of English Studies* |
| *RQ* | *Renaissance Quarterly* |
| *SEL* | *Studies in English Literature 1500–1900* |
| *SP* | *Studies in Philology* |
| *SQ* | *Shakespeare Quarterly* |
| *SStud* | *Shakespeare Studies* |

With the exception of journals, London is the place of publication unless otherwise stated.

## Primary Sources

Adam, Antoine (ed.) (1964). *Les Libertins au XVII^e Siècle*. Paris.

Anon. (1502). *The Ordynarye of Crystyanyte or of Crysten Men*.

_____ (1603). *The Genealogie of Vertue* and *The Anathomie of Sinne*.

_____ (1624). *The Tragedy of Nero, Newly Written*.

_____ (1630). *Pathomachia: Or, The Battel of Affections. Shadowed by a Faigned Siedge of the Citie Pathopolis*.

_____ (1641). *The Sucklington Faction: Or (Sucklings) Roaring Boyes*.

_____ (1661). *An Humble Representation of the Sad Condition of many of the Kings Party who since His Majesties Happy Restauration have No Relief and but Languishing Hopes*.

Anon. (1673). *The Character of a Coffee-House, with the Symptomes of a Town-Wit.*

———— (1675). *The Character of a Town-Gallant.*

Aquinas, St Thomas (1952–4). *The Disputed Questions on Truth,* tr. Robert William Mulligan, James V. McGlynn, and Robert W. Schmidt, 3 vols. Chicago.

———— (1964–81). *Summa Theologiæ: Latin Text and English Translation,* 61 vols.

Arias, Francis (1602). *The Litle Memorial, Concerning the Good and Fruitfull Vse of the Sacraments.*

Aristotle (1547). *The Ethiques of Aristotle, that is to saye preceptes of good behauoure and perfighte honestie,* tr. J. Wilkinson.

———— (1995). *The Complete Works of Aristotle: The Revised Oxford Translation,* ed. Jonathan Barnes, corrected edn., 2 vols. Princeton.

Aubrey, John (1960). *Aubrey's Brief Lives,* ed. Oliver Lawson Dick.

Augustine, St (1610). *Of the Citie of God,* tr. John Healey.

———— (1620). *The Confessions of the Incomparable Doctour St Augustine,* tr. Sir Tobie Matthew.

———— (1953). *Augustine: Earlier Writings,* tr. John H. S. Burleigh.

———— (1968). *Saint Augustine:* The Teacher, The Free Choice of the Will, Grace and Free Will, tr. Robert P. Russell. Washington.

Bacon, Francis (1973). *The Advancement of Learning,* ed. G. W. Kitchin, intro. Arthur Johnston.

———— (1985). *The Essayes or Counsels, Civill and Morall,* ed. Michael Kiernan. Oxford.

Boileau, Nicolas (1966). *Œuvres Complètes de Boileau,* ed. Françoise Escal, intro. Antoine Adam. Paris.

Boyle, Robert (1991). *The Early Essays and Ethics of Robert Boyle,* ed. John T. Harwood. Carbondale, Ill.

Bright, Timothy (1586). *A Treatise of Melancholie.*

Browne, Sir Thomas (1977). *The Major Works,* ed. C. A. Patrides. Harmondsworth.

Bryskett, Lodowick (1606). *A Discourse of Civill Life: Containing the Ethike part of Morall Philosophie.*

Buckingham, George Villiers, 2nd Duke of (1981). 'A Defense of His Private Life by the Second Duke of Buckingham', ed. Allan Pritchard. *HLQ* 44: 157–71.

———— (1985). *Buckingham: Public and Private Man. The Prose, Poems and Commonplace Book of George Villiers, Second Duke of Buckingham (1628–1687),* ed. Christine Phipps. New York.

Buecheler, Francis, and Riese, Alexander (eds.) (1895–1926). *Anthologia Latina,* 3 vols. Lipsiae.

Bullough, Geoffrey (ed.) (1957–75). *Narrative and Dramatic Sources of Shakespeare,* 8 vols.

Burnet, Gilbert (1680). *Some Passages of the Life and Death of the Right Honourable John Earl of Rochester.*

Burton, Robert (1989–2000). *The Anatomy of Melancholy,* ed. Thomas C. Faulkner, Nicholas K. Kiessling, and Rhonda L. Blair, commentary by J. B. Bamborough and Martin Dodsworth, 6 vols. Oxford.

Calvin, Jean (1561). *The Institution of Christian Religion,* tr. Thomas Norton.

Carew, Thomas (1949). *The Poems of Thomas Carew with his Masque,* Coelum Britannicum, ed. Rhodes Dunlap. Oxford.

Castiglione, Baldassare (1928). *The Book of the Courtier,* tr. Sir Thomas Hoby, ed. W. H. D. Rouse and Drayton Henderson.

Chapman, George (1964). *Bussy D'Ambois,* ed. Nicholas Brooke.

—— (1965). *Bussy D'Ambois,* ed. Maurice Evans.

—— (1987). *The Plays of George Chapman: The Tragedies with* Sir Gyles Goosecappe. *A Critical Edition,* ed. Allan Holaday, G. Blakemore Evans, and Thomas L. Berger. Cambridge.

Cicero, Marcus Tullius (1561). *Those Fyue Questions, which Marke Tullye Cicero, disputed in his Manor of Tusculanum,* tr. John Dolman.

Clarendon, Edward Hyde, 1st Earl of (1978). *Selections from* The History of the Rebellion *and* The Life by Himself, ed. G. Huehns, intro. Hugh Trevor-Roper. Oxford.

Coëffeteau, Nicolas (1621). *A Table of Humane Passions. With their Cause and Effects,* tr. Edward Grimestone.

Congreve, William (1982). *The Comedies of William Congreve,* ed. Anthony G. Henderson. Cambridge.

Cornwallis, Sir William (1946). *Essayes by Sir William Cornwallis the Younger,* ed. Don Cameron Allen. Baltimore.

Cowley, Abraham (1993). *The Collected Works of Abraham Cowley,* ii: *Poems (1656), Part 1: The Mistress,* ed. Thomas O. Calhoun, Laurence Heyworth, and J. Robert King. Newark, NJ.

Crashaw, Richard (1957). *The Poems English Latin and Greek of Richard Crashaw,* ed. L. C. Martin. Oxford.

Defoe, Daniel (1997). The True-Born Englishman *and Other Writings,* ed. P. N. Furbank and W. R. Owens. Harmondsworth.

De Sales, St François (1613). *An Introduction to a Deuoute Life,* tr. John Yakesley.

Digby, Sir Kenelm (1645). *Two Treatises: In the one of which, The Nature of Bodies; In the other, The Nature of Mans Soule, is Looked Into.*

Donne, John (1953–62). *The Sermons of John Donne,* ed. George R. Potter and Evelyn M. Simpson, 10 vols. Berkeley.

—— (1985). *The Complete English Poems of John Donne,* ed. C. A. Patrides.

Dorset, Charles Sackville, Lord Buckhurst, 6th Earl of (1979). *The Poems of Charles Sackville Sixth Earl of Dorset,* ed. Brice Harris. New York.

Dryden, John (1956–2002). *The Works of John Dryden,* ed. Vinton A. Dearing *et al.,* 20 vols. Berkeley.

—— (1962). *Of Dramatic Poesy and other Critical Essays,* ed. George Watson, 2 vols.

—— (1995–2005). *The Poems of John Dryden,* ed. Paul Hammond and David Hopkins, 5 vols.

'Du Plessis-Mornay', Philippe de Mornay, Sieur Du Plessis-Marly (1602). *The true knowledge of a mans owne selfe,* tr. Anthony Munday.

Du Vair, Guillaume (1598). *The Moral Philosophie of the Stoicks,* tr. Thomas James.

Dyke, Daniel (1615). *The Mystery of Selfe-Deceiving.*

Elyot, Sir Thomas (1907). *The Boke Named The Gouernour,* ed. Foster Watson.

Erasmus, Desiderius (1535). *A Lytle Treatise of the Maner and Forme of Confession.*

—— (1965). *The Praise of Folie*, tr. Sir Thomas Chaloner, ed. Clarence H. Miller. Oxford.

—— (1981). *Enchiridion Militis Christiani: An English Version*, ed. Anne M. O'Donnell. Oxford.

Etherege, Sir George (1982). *The Plays of Sir George Etherege*, ed. Michael Cordner. Cambridge.

Evelyn, John (1906). *The Diary of John Evelyn*, ed. Austin Dobson, 3 vols.

—— (1995). *The Writings of John Evelyn*, ed. Guy de la Bédoyère. Woodbridge.

Fenner, William (1651). *A Treatise of the Affections*, in *The Works of the Learned and Faithful Minister of Gods Word, Mr William Fenner.*

Ficino, Marsilio (1981). *Marsilio Ficino and the Phaedran Charioteer*, ed. Michael J. B. Allen. Berkeley.

Fludd, Robert (1992). *Robert Fludd: Essential Readings*, ed. William H. Huffman.

Ford, John (1995). *'Tis Pity She's a Whore and Other Plays*, ed. Marion Lomax. Oxford.

Gosson, Stephen (1582). *Playes Confuted in Fiue Actions.*

Greenham, Richard (1599). *The Works of the Reverend and Faithfvll Servant of Iesus Christ M. Richard Greenham*, ed. Henry Holland.

Halifax, George Savile, Marquis of (1989). *The Works of George Savile, Marquis of Halifax*, ed. Mark N. Brown, 3 vols. Oxford.

Hamilton, Anthony (1905). *The Memoirs of Count Grammont*, ed. Sir Walter Scott.

Herbert, George, and Vaughan, Henry (1986). *George Herbert and Henry Vaughan*, The Oxford Authors, ed. Louis L. Martz. Oxford.

Heywood, Thomas (1612). *An Apology for Actors.*

Hobbes, Thomas (1969). *The Elements of Law Natural and Politic*, ed. Ferdinand Tönnies, intro. M. M. Goldsmith, 2nd edn.

—— (1978). *Man and Citizen: Thomas Hobbes's De Homine, translated by Charles T. Wood, T. S. K. Scott-Craig, and Bernard Gert, and De Cive, translated by Thomas Hobbes*, ed. Bernard Gert. Hassocks.

—— (1983). *De Cive: The English Version entitled in the first edition Philosophicall Rudiments Concerning Government and Society: A Critical Edition*, ed. Howard Warrender. Oxford.

—— (1986). *The Rhetorics of Thomas Hobbes and Bernard Lamy*, ed. John T. Harwood. Carbondale, Ill.

—— (1995). *Three Discourses: A Critical Modern Edition of Newly Identified Work of the Young Hobbes*, ed. Noel B. Reynolds and Arlene W. Saxonhouse. Chicago.

—— (1996). *Leviathan*, ed. Richard Tuck, rev. edn. Cambridge.

Howard, Sir Robert (1695). 'The Duel of the Stags', in *The Temple of Death, A Poem ... With several other Excellent Poems.*

James VI and I, King (1619). *The Peace-Maker: Or, Great Brittaines Blessing.*

Jonson, Ben (1985). *Ben Jonson*, The Oxford Authors, ed. Ian Donaldson. Oxford.

—— (1990). *Sejanus His Fall*, ed. Philip J. Ayres. Manchester.

King, Henry (1657). *Poems, Elegies, Paradoxes, and Sonnets.*

Lachèvre, Frédéric (ed.) (1911). *Disciples et Successeurs de Théophile de Viau: La Vie et Les Poésies Libertines Inédites de Des Barreaux et Saint-Pavin*. Paris.

Lactantius (1964). *The Divine Institutes Books I–VII*, tr. Sister Mary Francis McDonald. Washington.

La Primaudaye, Pierre de (1618). *The French Academie. Fully Discoursed and finished in foure Bookes*, tr. T. B. C.

La Rochefoucauld, François, Duc de (1965). *Réflexions ou Sentences et Maximes Morales suivi de Réflexions Diverses*, ed. S. De Sacy, intro. Paul Morand. Paris.

Lee, Nathaniel (1955). *The Works of Nathaniel Lee*, ed. Thomas B. Stroup and Arthur L. Cooke, 2 vols. New Brunswick, NJ.

Lipsius, Justus (1939). *Two Bookes of Constancie*, tr. John Stradling, ed. Rudolf Kirk and Clayton Morris Hall. New Brunswick, NJ.

Long, A. A., and Sedley, D. N. (1987). *The Hellenistic Philosophers*, 2 vols. Cambridge.

Lord, George de F., *et al.* (eds.) (1963–75). *Poems on Affairs of State: Augustan Satirical Verse, 1660–1714*, 7 vols. New Haven.

Love, Harold (ed.) (1968). *The Penguin Book of Restoration Verse*. Harmondsworth.

Lucretius (1656). *An Essay on the First Book of T. Lucretius Carus De Rerum Natura. Interpreted and Made English verse by J. Evelyn*.

——— (1682). *T. Lucretius Carus The Epicurean Philosopher, His Six Books De Natura Rerum*, tr. Thomas Creech.

——— (1683). *T. Lucretius Carus, The Epicurean Philosopher, His Six Books De Natura Rerum*, tr. Thomas Creech, 2nd edn.

——— (1937). *De Rerum Natura With an English Translation*, tr. W. H. D. Rouse, 3rd edn.

Lucy, William, Bishop of St David's (1663). *Observations, Censures and Confutations of Notorious Errours in Mr. Hobbes His Leviathan, and other his Bookes*.

Luther, Martin (1961). *Martin Luther: Selections from his Writings*, ed. John Dillenberger. New York.

Mackay, Charles (ed.) (1863). *The Cavalier Songs and Ballads of England from 1642 to 1684*.

Manning, Gillian (ed.) (2001). *Libertine Plays of the Restoration*.

Marston, John (1978). *Antonio's Revenge*, ed. W. Reavley Gair. Manchester.

Marvell, Andrew (1971). *The Poems and Letters of Andrew Marvell*, ed. H. M. Margoliouth, rev. Pierre Legouis and E. E. Duncan-Jones, 3rd edn., 2 vols. Oxford.

——— (2003). *The Poems of Andrew Marvell*, ed. Nigel Smith.

Maus, Katharine Eisaman (ed.) (1995). *Four Revenge Tragedies:* The Spanish Tragedy, The Revenger's Tragedy, The Revenge of Bussy D'Ambois *and* The Atheist's Tragedy. Oxford.

Middleton, Thomas (1966). *A Game at Chess*, ed. J. W. Harper.

Milton, John (1953–82). *Complete Prose Works of John Milton*, ed. Don M. Wolfe *et al.*, 8 vols. New Haven.

——— (1998). *Paradise Lost*, ed. Alastair Fowler, 2nd edn.

Montaigne, Michel de (1603). *The Essayes Or Morall, Politike and Millitarie Discourses*, tr. John Florio.

Montaigne, Michel de (1952). *Essais*, ed. Maurice Rat, 3 vols. Paris.

––––– (1991). *The Complete Essays*, tr. M. A. Screech. Harmondsworth.

Myrc, John (1902). *Instructions for Parish Priests*, ed. Edward Peacock, rev. F. J. Furnivall.

Oldham, John (1987). *The Poems of John Oldham*, ed. H. F. Brooks and R. Selden. Oxford.

Ovid (1914). *Heroides and Amores*, tr. Grant Showerman.

Parsons, Robert (1680). *A Sermon Preached At the Funeral of the Rt. Honourable John Earl of Rochester*.

Patrides, C. A. (ed.) (1969). *The Cambridge Platonists*.

Pepys, Samuel (1987). *The Shorter Pepys*, ed. Robert Latham. Harmondsworth.

Perkins, William (1603). *The Works of ... M. W. Perkins*.

––––– (1604). *A Commentarie or Exposition, vpon the fiue first Chapters of the Epistle to the Galatians*.

Philips, Katherine (1990–3). *The Collected Works of Katherine Philips, 'The Matchless Orinda'*, ed. Patrick Thomas, G. Greer, and R. Little, 3 vols. Stump Cross.

Plato (1675). *Plato his Apology of Socrates, And Phaedo or Dialogue concerning the Immortality of Mans Soul, And Manner of Socrates his Death*.

Plutarch (1603). *The Philosophie, commonlie called, The Morals*, tr. Philemon Holland.

Reynolds, Edward (1640). *A Treatise of the Passions and Faculties of the Soule of Man*.

Rochester, John Wilmot, 2nd Earl of (1980). *The Letters of John Wilmot, Earl of Rochester*, ed. Jeremy Treglown. Oxford.

––––– (1984). *The Poems of John Wilmot, Earl of Rochester*, ed. Keith Walker. Oxford.

––––– (1994). *The Complete Works*, ed. Frank H. Ellis. Harmondsworth.

––––– (1999). *The Works of John Wilmot Earl of Rochester*, ed. Harold Love. Oxford.

Rogers, G. A. J. (ed.) (1995). *Leviathan: Contemporary Responses to the Political Theory of Thomas Hobbes*. Bristol.

Rogers, Richard (1603). *Seven Treatises*.

Rogers, Thomas (1576). *A philosophicall discourse, Entituled, The Anatomie of the Minde*.

Saint-Évremond, Charles Marguetel de Saint Denis, Sieur de (1694). *Miscellany Essays: By Monsieur de St Evremont*, tr. Tom Brown.

––––– (1714). *The Works of Monsieur De S$^t$ Evremond, Made English from the French Original. With the Author's Life, by Mr. Des Maizeaux*, 3 vols.

––––– (1998). *Entretiens sur Toutes Choses*, ed. David Bensoussan. Paris.

Sedley, Sir Charles (1928). *The Poetical and Dramatic Works of Sir Charles Sedley*, ed. V. De Sola Pinto.

Seneca, Lucius Annaeus (1581). *Seneca His Tenne Tragedies*, tr. Jasper Heywood *et al.*

––––– (1620). *The Workes of Lucius Annaeus Seneca Newly Inlarged and Corrected*, tr. Thomas Lodge.

––––– (1917). *Tragedies*, tr. Frank Justus Miller, 2 vols.

––––– (1928–35). *Moral Essays*, tr. John W. Basore, 3 vols.

Shaftesbury, Anthony Ashley Cooper, 1st Earl of (1675). *A Letter from a Person of Quality to his Friend in the Country*.

Shakespeare, William (1985). *Hamlet, Prince of Denmark*, ed. Philip Edwards. Cambridge.

—— (1998). *Troilus and Cressida*, ed. David Bevington.

—— (2003). *Troilus and Cressida*, ed. Anthony B. Dawson. Cambridge.

—— (2005). *The Complete Works*, ed. Stanley Wells *et al.*, 2nd edn. Oxford.

Spenser, Edmund (1977). *The Faerie Queene*, ed. A. C. Hamilton.

Spingarn, J. E. (ed.) (1908). *Critical Essays of the Seventeenth Century*, 3 vols. Oxford.

Sprat, Thomas (1959). *History of the Royal Society*, ed. Jackson I. Cope and Harold Whitmore Jones. St Louis, Mo.

Stanley, Thomas (1701). *The History of Philosophy: Containing the Lives, Opinions, Actions and Discourses of the Philosophers of every Sect*, 3rd edn.

Strode, William (1655). *The Floating Island: A Tragi-Comedy*.

Suckling, Sir John (1971). *The Works of Sir John Suckling*, ed. Thomas Clayton and L. A. Beaurline, 2 vols. Oxford.

Tacitus (1598). *The Annales of Cornelius Tacitus*, tr. Richard Greneway.

Tasso, Torquato (1981). *Godfrey of Bulloigne: A Critical Edition of Edward Fairfax's Translation of Tasso's* Gerusalemme Liberata *together with Fairfax's Original Poems*, ed. Kathleen M. Lea and T. M. Gang. Oxford.

Tawney, R. H., and Power, Eileen (eds.) (1924). *Tudor Economic Documents*, 3 vols.

Valerius, Cornelius (1571). *The Casket of Iewels: Contaynynge a Playne Description of Morall Philosophie*, tr. I. C.

Viau, Théophile de (1981). *The Cabaret Poetry of Théophile de Viau: Texts and Traditions*, ed. Claire Lynn Gaudiani.Tübingen.

—— (1984). *Œuvres Complètes*, ed. Guido Saba, 4 vols. Rome.

Wheeler, John (1601). *A Treatise of Commerce*.

Wood, Anthony à (1813–20). *Athenae Oxonienses*, 5 vols.

Wright, Thomas (1971). *The Passions of the Minde in Generall: A Reprint Based on the 1604 Edition*, intro. Thomas O. Sloan. Urbana, Ill.

Wycherley, William (1981). *The Plays of William Wycherley*, ed. Peter Holland. Cambridge.

## Secondary Sources

Adelman, Janet (1992). *Suffocating Mothers: Fantasies of Maternal Origin in Shakespeare's Plays*, Hamlet *to* The Tempest. New York.

Allison, A. F. (1948). 'Crashaw and St François de Sales'. *RES* 48: 295–302.

Anselment, Raymond A. (1988). *Loyalist Resolve: Patient Fortitude in the English Civil War*. Newark, NJ.

Anson, John (1966). '*Julius Caesar*: The Politics of the Hardened Heart'. *SStud* 2: 11–33.

Axtell, James L. (1965). 'The Mechanics of Opposition: Restoration Cambridge v. Daniel Scargill'. *Bulletin of the Institute of Historical Research*, 38: 102–11.

Babb, Lawrence (1951). *The Elizabethan Malady: A Study of Melancholia in English Literature from 1580 to 1642*. East Lansing, Mich.

Bamborough, J. B. (1952). *The Little World of Man.*

Barbour, Reid (1998). *English Epicures and Stoics: Ancient Legacies in Early Stuart Culture.* Amherst, Mass.

Beiser, Frederick C. (1996). *The Sovereignty of Reason: The Defense of Rationality in the Early English Enlightenment.* Princeton.

Bentley, Gerald Eades (1941–68). *The Jacobean and Caroline Stage,* 7 vols. Oxford.

Berger, Jun., Harry (1957). *The Allegorical Temper: Vision and Reality in Book II of Spenser's* Faerie Queene. New Haven.

Bertonasco, Marc F. (1971). *Crashaw and the Baroque.* Birmingham, Ala.

Blackburn, Thomas H. (1971). ' "Uncloister'd Virtue": Adam and Eve in Milton's Paradise'. *MStud* 3: 119–37.

Bouwsma, William J. (1975). 'Two Faces of Humanism: Stoicism and Augustinianism in Renaissance Thought', in Heiko A. Oberman and Thomas A. Brady (eds.), *Itinerarium Italicum: The Profile of the Italian Renaissance in the Mirror of its European Transformations,* 3–60. Leiden.

Bowen, Barbara E. (1993). *Gender in the Theater of War: Shakespeare's* Troilus and Cressida. New York.

Bowle, John (1951). *Hobbes and his Critics: A Study in Seventeenth-Century Constitutionalism.*

Braden, Gordon (1985). *Renaissance Tragedy and the Senecan Tradition: Anger's Privilege.* New Haven.

Bradford, Alan T. (1983). 'Stuart Absolutism and the "Utility" of Tacitus'. *HLQ* 46: 127–55.

Bradshaw, Graham (1987). *Shakespeare's Scepticism.* Brighton.

Brown, John Russell, and Harris, Bernard (eds.) (1965). *Stratford-Upon-Avon Studies, 6: Restoration Theatre.*

Brown, K. C. (ed.) (1965). *Hobbes Studies.* Oxford.

Bruster, Douglas (1992). *Drama and the Market in the Age of Shakespeare.* Cambridge.

Bryson, Anna (1998). *From Courtesy to Civility: Changing Codes of Conduct in Early Modern England.* Oxford.

Burns, Edward (ed.) (1995). *Reading Rochester.* Liverpool.

Burrow, Colin (1993). *Epic Romance: Homer to Milton.* Oxford.

Butler, Martin (1984). *Theatre and Crisis, 1632–42.* Cambridge.

—— (1985). 'Romans in Britain: *The Roman Actor* and the Early Stuart Classical Play', in Douglas Howard (ed.), *Philip Massinger: A Critical Reassessment,* 139–70. Cambridge.

Campbell, Lily B. (1930). *Shakespeare's Tragic Heroes: Slaves of Passion.* Cambridge.

Cefalu, Paul (2004*a*). *Moral Identity in Early Modern English Literature.* Cambridge.

—— (2004*b*). *Revisionist Shakespeare: Transitional Ideologies in Texts and Contexts.* New York.

Chernaik, Warren (1995). *Sexual Freedom in Restoration Literature.* Cambridge.

Clarke, Elizabeth (1997). *Theory and Theology in George Herbert's Poetry: 'Divinitie, and Poesie, Met'.* Oxford.

Collins, Jeffrey R. (2005). *The Allegiance of Thomas Hobbes.* Oxford.

Collinson, Patrick (1994). 'William Shakespeare's Religious Inheritance and Environment', in his *Elizabethan Essays*, 218–52.

Combe, Kirk (1998). *A Martyr for Sin: Rochester's Critique of Polity, Sexuality, and Society*. Newark, NJ.

Cooper, John M. (1999). *Reason and Emotion: Essays on Ancient Moral Psychology and Ethical Theory*. Princeton.

Corns, Thomas N. (ed.) (1993). *The Cambridge Companion to English Poetry, Donne to Marvell*. Cambridge.

Cottingham, John (1998). *Philosophy and the Good Life: Reason and the Passions in Greek, Cartesian and Psychoanalytic Ethics*. Cambridge.

Cousins, A. D. (1984). 'The Context, Design, and Argument of Rochester's *A Satyr against Reason and Mankind*'. *SEL* 24: 429–39.

Crocker, S. F. (1937). 'Rochester's *Satire Against Mankind*: A Study of Certain Aspects of the Background'. *West Virginia University Studies, iii: Philological Papers (Volume 2)*, 57–73.

Danielson, Dennis Richard (1982). *Milton's Good God: A Study in Literary Theodicy*. Cambridge.

Davidson, James (1997). *Courtesans and Fishcakes: The Consuming Passions of Classical Athens*.

Davies, Stevie (1991). *Milton*. Hemel Hempstead.

Devereux, E. J. (1983). *Renaissance English Translations of Erasmus: A Bibliography to 1700*. Toronto.

Devlin, Christopher (1963). *Hamlet's Divinity and Other Essays*.

Dihle, Albrecht (1982). *The Theory of Will in Classical Antiquity*. Berkeley.

Dillon, John M., and Long, A. A. (eds.) (1988). *The Question of "Eclecticism": Studies in Later Greek Philosophy*. Berkeley.

Dobrée, Bonamy (1924). *Restoration Comedy, 1660–1720*. Oxford.

Drakakis, John (2004). ' "Fashion it thus": *Julius Caesar* and the Politics of Theatrical Representation', in M. S. Alexander (ed.), *Shakespeare and Politics*, 206–18. Cambridge.

Duffy, Eamon (1992). *The Stripping of the Altars: Traditional Religion in England, 1400–1580*. New Haven.

Dutton, Richard, Findlay, Alison, and Wilson, Richard (eds.) (2003a). *Region, Religion and Patronage: Lancastrian Shakespeare*. Manchester.

—— (2003b). *Theatre and Religion: Lancastrian Shakespeare*. Manchester.

Empson, William (1986). *Essays on Shakespeare*, ed. David B. Pirie. Cambridge.

Engle, Lars (1993). *Shakespearean Pragmatism: Market of his Time*. Chicago.

Enterline, Lynn (2000). *The Rhetoric of the Body from Ovid to Shakespeare*. Cambridge.

Erskine-Hill, Howard (1966). 'Rochester: Augustan or Explorer?', in G. R. Hibbard (ed.), *Renaissance and Modern Essays Presented to Vivian de Sola Pinto in Celebration of his Seventieth Birthday*, 51–64.

Evans, Maurice (1970). *Spenser's Anatomy of Heroism: A Commentary on* The Faerie Queene. Cambridge.

Farley-Hills, David (1978). *Rochester's Poetry*. Totowa, NJ.

Farley-Hills, David (ed.) (1972). *Rochester: The Critical Heritage.*

Feiling, Keith (1924). *A History of the Tory Party, 1640–1714.* Oxford.

Fiering, Norman (1981). *Moral Philosophy at Seventeenth-Century Harvard: A Discipline in Transition.* Chapel Hill, NC.

Fish, Stanley E. (1972). *Self-Consuming Artifacts: The Experience of Seventeenth-Century Literature.* Berkeley.

——— (1997). *Surprised by Sin: The Reader in* Paradise Lost, 2nd edn. Basingstoke.

Fisher, Nicholas (2000a). 'A New Dating of Rochester's *Artemiza to Chlöe*'. *English Manuscript Studies 1100–1700*, 8: 300–19.

——— (ed.) (2000b). *'That Second Bottle': Essays on John Wilmot, Earl of Rochester.* Manchester.

Fisher, R. J. (1948). 'The Development of London as a Centre of Conspicuous Consumption in the Sixteenth and Seventeenth Centuries'. *Transactions of the Royal Historical Society*, 4th ser., 30: 37–50.

Fleischmann, Wolfgang Bernard (1964). *Lucretius and English Literature, 1680–1740.* Paris.

Florby, Gunilla (1982). *The Painful Passage to Virtue: A Study of George Chapman's* The Tragedy of Bussy D'Ambois *and* The Revenge of Bussy D'Ambois. Kävlinge.

Fowler, Alastair (2003). *Renaissance Realism: Narrative Images in Literature and Art.* Oxford.

Frye, Roland Mushat (1963). *Shakespeare and Christian Doctrine.* Princeton.

——— (1984). *The Renaissance* Hamlet: *Issues and Responses in 1600.* Princeton.

Gabbey, Alan (1982). 'Philosophia Cartesiana Triumphata: Henry More (1646–1671)', in Thomas M. Lennon, John M. Nicholas, and John W. Davis (eds.), *Problems of Cartesianism*, 171–250. Kingston, Ont.

Gallagher, Catherine, and Greenblatt, Stephen (2000). *Practicing New Historicism.* Chicago.

Gardiner, H. M., Metcalf, Ruth Clark, and Beebe-Center, John G. (1970). *Feeling and Emotion: A History of Theories.* Westport, Conn.

Gaukroger, Stephen (ed.) (1998). *The Soft Underbelly of Reason: The Passions in the Seventeenth Century.*

Gill, James E. (1981). 'Mind Against Itself: Theme and Structure in Rochester's *Satyr Against Reason and Mankind*'. *Texas Studies in Literature and Language*, 23: 555–76.

Gless, Darryl J. (1994). *Interpretation and Theology in Spenser.* Cambridge.

Goldie, Mark (1990). 'Danby, the Bishops and the Whigs', in Tim Harris, Paul Seaward, and Mark Goldie (eds.), *The Politics of Religion in Restoration England*, 75–105. Oxford.

Graves, Thornton Shirley (1923). 'Some Pre-MoHock Clansmen'. *SP* 20: 395–421.

Greenblatt, Stephen (1980). *Renaissance Self-Fashioning: From More to Shakespeare.* Chicago.

——— (2001). *Hamlet in Purgatory.* Princeton.

Greer, Germaine (2000). *John Wilmot, Earl of Rochester.* Horndon.

Griffin, Dustin H. (1973). *Satires Against Man: The Poems of Rochester.* Berkeley.

Hadfield, Andrew (2004). *Shakespeare and Renaissance Politics.*

——— (ed.) (1996). *Edmund Spenser.* Harlow.

Hamilton, A. C. (1961). *The Structure of Allegory in* The Faerie Queene. Oxford.

Hammond, Paul (1983). 'The Integrity of Dryden's Lucretius'. *MLR* 78: 1–23.

——— (1999). *Dryden and the Traces of Classical Rome.* Oxford.

Hankins, John Erskine (1941). *The Character of Hamlet and Other Essays.* Chapel Hill, NC.

——— (1971). *Source and Meaning in Spenser's Allegory: A Study of* The Faerie Queene. Oxford.

Harris, Brice (1940). *Charles Sackville, Sixth Earl of Dorset: Patron and Poet of the Restoration.* Urbana, Ill.

Hartle, Paul (2002). ' "Fruition was the Question in Debate": *Pro* and *Contra* the Renaissance Orgasm'. *17C* 17: 78–96.

Havran, Martin J. (1962). *The Catholics in Caroline England.* Stanford, Calif.

Healy, Thomas F. (1986). *Richard Crashaw.* Leiden.

Heninger, S. K. (1960). *A Handbook of Renaissance Meteorology.* Durham, NC.

Herbert, Gary B. (1989). *Thomas Hobbes: The Unity of Scientific and Moral Wisdom.* Vancouver.

Hill, Christopher (1956). *Economic Problems of the Church: From Archbishop Whitgift to the Long Parliament.* Oxford.

——— (1977). *Milton and the English Revolution.*

Hillman, David, and Mazzio, Carla (eds.) (1997). *The Body in Parts: Fantasies of Corporeality in Early Modern Europe.* New York.

Hirschman, Albert O. (1977). *The Passions and the Interests: Political Arguments for Capitalism before its Triumph.* Princeton.

Hirst, Derek (1986). *Authority and Conflict: England, 1603–1658.*

Honigmann, E. A. J. (1998a). *Myriad-Minded Shakespeare: Essays on the Tragedies, Problem Comedies and Shakespeare the Man,* 2nd edn. Basingstoke.

——— (1998b). *Shakespeare: The 'Lost Years',* 2nd edn. Manchester.

——— (2002). *Shakespeare: Seven Tragedies Revisited. The Dramatist's Manipulation of Response,* 2nd edn. Basingstoke.

Hoopes, Robert (1962). *Right Reason in the English Renaissance.* Cambridge, Mass.

Hulbert, Viola Blackburn (1931). 'A Possible Christian Source for Spenser's Temperance'. *SP* 28: 184–210.

Hume, Anthea (1984). *Edmund Spenser: Protestant Poet.* Cambridge.

Hume, Robert D. (1976). 'The Satiric Design of Nat. Lee's *The Princess of Cleve*'. *JEGP* 75: 117–38.

——— (1983). 'The Myth of the Rake in "Restoration Comedy" ', in his *The Rakish Stage: Studies in English Drama, 1660–1800,* 138–75. Carbondale, Ill.

Hunt, John (1992). ' "A Thing of Nothing": The Catastrophic Body in *Hamlet*', in Martin Coyle (ed.), *New Casebooks:* Hamlet, William Shakespeare, 168–92. Basingstoke.

Hunter, George K. (1996). 'Shakespeare and the Church', in John M. Mucciolo, Steven J. Doloff, and Edward A. Rauchut (eds.), *Shakespeare's Universe: Renaissance Ideas and Conventions. Essays in Honour of W. R. Elton,* 21–8. Aldershot.

Hunter, William B. (1994). '*Paradise Lost*: Passionate Epic'. *MStud* 31: 73–90.

Hutton, Ronald (1985). *The Restoration: A Political and Religious History of England and Wales, 1658–1667.* Oxford.

Ide, Richard S. (1980). *Possessed with Greatness: The Heroic Tragedies of Chapman and Shakespeare.*

James, Heather (1997). *Shakespeare's Troy: Drama, Politics, and the Translation of Empire.* Cambridge.

James, Susan (1997). *Passion and Action: The Emotions in Seventeenth-Century Philosophy.* Oxford.

Johnson, James William (2004). *A Profane Wit: The Life of John Wilmot, Earl of Rochester.* Rochester, NY.

Johnson, Ronald W. (1975). 'Rhetoric and Drama in Rochester's "Satyr against Reason and Mankind"'. *SEL* 15: 365–73.

Jones, Howard (1989). *The Epicurean Tradition.*

Jones, J. R. (1978). *Country and Court: England 1658–1714.*

Jones, John (1995). *Shakespeare at Work.* Oxford.

Jones, Norman (1989). *God and the Moneylenders: Usury and Law in Early Modern England.* Oxford.

Joy, Lynn S. (1992). 'Epicureanism in Renaissance Moral and Natural Philosophy'. *JHI* 53: 573–83.

Kahn, Coppélia (1997). *Roman Shakespeare: Warriors, Wounds, and Women.*

Kargon, Robert (1964). 'Walter Charleton, Robert Boyle, and the Acceptance of Epicurean Atomism in England'. *Isis,* 55: 184–92.

—— (1966). *Atomism in England from Hariot to Newton.* Oxford.

Keeble, N. H. (2002). *The Restoration: England in the 1660s.* Oxford.

Kerrigan, John (1996). *Revenge Tragedy: Aeschylus to Armageddon.* Oxford.

—— (2001). *On Shakespeare and Early Modern Literature: Essays.* Oxford.

Knowles, Ronald (1999). '*Hamlet* and Counter-Humanism'. *RQ* 52: 1046–69.

Kramnick, Jonathan Brody (2002). 'Rochester and the History of Sexuality'. *ELH* 69: 277–301.

Kretzmann, Norman (1993). 'Philosophy of Mind', in Norman Kretzmann and Eleonora Stump (eds.), *The Cambridge Companion to Aquinas,* 128–59. Cambridge.

Kroll, Richard (1991). *The Material World: Literate Culture in the Restoration and Early Eighteenth Century.* Baltimore.

Leavis, F. R. (1986). *Valuation in Criticism and Other Essays,* ed. G. S. Singh. Cambridge.

Leggatt, Alexander (1988). *Shakespeare's Political Drama: The History Plays and the Roman Plays.*

Leites, Edmund (ed.) (1988). *Conscience and Casuistry in Early Modern Europe.* Cambridge.

Lever, J. W. (1987). *The Tragedy of State: A Study of Jacobean Drama,* intro. Jonathan Dollimore, 2nd edn.

Levi, Anthony (1964). *French Moralists: The Theory of the Passions, 1585 to 1649.* Oxford.

Levitsky, Ruth M. (1973). ' "The Elements were so Mix'd … " '. *Publications of the Modern Language Association of America,* 88: 240–5.

Lewalski, Barbara Kiefer (1979). *Protestant Poetics and the Seventeenth-Century Religious Lyric.* Princeton.

Lewis, C. S. (1958). *The Allegory of Love: A Study in Medieval Tradition*. Oxford.

Loewenstein, David (2001). *Representing Revolution in Milton and his Contemporaries: Religion, Politics, and Polemics in Radical Puritanism*. Cambridge.

Love, Harold (1993). *Scribal Publication in Seventeenth-Century England*. Oxford.

—— (1995). 'Hamilton's *Mémoires de la Vie du Comte de Grammont* and the Reading of Rochester'. *Restoration: Studies in English Literary Culture, 1660–1700*, 19: 95–102.

—— (2004). *English Clandestine Satire, 1660–1702*. Oxford.

McConica, James (ed.) (1986). *The History of the University of Oxford*, iii: *The Collegiate University*. Oxford.

McDonald, Charles O. (1962). '"Decorum," "Ethos," and "Pathos" in the Heroes of Elizabethan Tragedy, with Particular Reference to *Hamlet*'. *JEGP* 61: 330–48.

McEachern, Claire, and Shuger, Debora (eds.) (1997). *Religion and Culture in Renaissance England*. Cambridge.

Malcolm, Noel (1981). 'Hobbes, Sandys, and the Virginia Company'. *HJ* 24: 297–321.

Mallin, Eric S. (1995). *Inscribing the Time: Shakespeare and the End of Elizabethan England*. Berkeley.

Marshall, Cynthia (2000). 'Shakespeare, Crossing the Rubicon'. *Shakespeare Survey*, 53: 73–88.

Marshall, William H. (1959). 'Calvin, Spenser, and the Major Sacraments'. *Modern Language Notes*, 74: 97–101.

Martinich, A. P. (1992). *The Two Gods of* Leviathan: *Thomas Hobbes on Religion and Politics*. Cambridge.

Martz, Louis L. (1962). *The Poetry of Meditation: A Study in English Religious Literature*, rev. edn. New Haven.

Matheson, Mark (1995). '*Hamlet* and "A Matter Tender and Dangerous"'. *SQ* 46: 383–97.

Mayo, Thomas Franklin (1934). *Epicurus in England (1650–1725)*. Dallas.

Mercer, Peter (1987). Hamlet *and the Acting of Revenge*. Basingstoke.

Miles, Geoffrey (1996). *Shakespeare and the Constant Romans*. Oxford.

Milward, Peter (1973). *Shakespeare's Religious Background*.

Mintz, Samuel I. (1962). *The Hunting of Leviathan: Seventeenth-Century Reactions to the Materialism and Moral Philosophy of Thomas Hobbes*. Cambridge.

Miola, Robert S. (1992). *Shakespeare and Classical Tragedy: The Influence of Seneca*. Oxford.

Monsarrat, Gilles D. (1984). *Light from the Porch: Stoicism and English Renaissance Literature*. Paris.

Montuori, Deborah (1988). 'The Confusion of Self and Role in Chapman's *Bussy D'Ambois*'. *SEL* 28: 287–99.

Moore Smith, G. C. (1908). 'Notes on Some English University Plays'. *MLR* 3: 141–56.

Morford, Mark (1993). 'Tacitean *Prudentia* and the Doctrines of Justus Lipsius', in T. J. Luce and A. J. Woodman (eds.), *Tacitus and the Tacitean Tradition*, 129–51. Princeton.

Morgan, Gerald (1986). 'The Idea of Temperance in the Second Book of *The Faerie Queene*'. *RES* 37 n.s.: 11–39.

Morrill, John (1992). *Revolution and Restoration: England in the 1650s.*

Murray, Peter B. (1996). *Shakespeare's Imagined Persons: The Psychology of Role-Playing and Acting.* Basingstoke.

Mutschmann, H., and Wentersdorf, K. (1952). *Shakespeare and Catholicism.* New York.

Norbrook, David (1999). *Writing the English Republic: Poetry, Rhetoric and Politics, 1627–1660.* Cambridge.

Nussbaum, Martha C. (1986). *The Fragility of Goodness: Luck and Ethics in Greek Tragedy and Philosophy.* Cambridge.

——— (1994). *The Therapy of Desire: Theory and Practice in Hellenistic Ethics.* Princeton.

Orgel, Stephen, and Strong, Roy (1973). *Inigo Jones: The Theatre of the Stuart Court,* 2 vols. Berkeley.

Ornstein, Robert (1960). *The Moral Vision of Jacobean Tragedy.* Madison.

Osler, Margaret J. (ed.) (1991). *Atoms, Pneuma, and Tranquillity: Epicurean and Stoic Themes in European Thought.* Cambridge.

Padelford, Frederick Morgan (1914). 'Spenser and the Theology of Calvin'. *MP* 12: 1–18.

Palmer, D. J. (1970). 'Tragic Error in *Julius Caesar*'. *SQ* 21: 399–409.

Parker, Michael P. (1982). ' "All are not born (Sir) to the Bay": "Jack" Suckling, "Tom" Carew, and the Making of a Poet'. *ELR* 12: 341–68.

Paster, Gail Kern (1993). *The Body Embarrassed: Drama and the Disciplines of Shame in Early Modern England.* Ithaca, NY.

——— (2004). *Humoring the Body: Emotions and the Shakespearean Stage.* Chicago.

——— Rowe, Katherine, and Floyd-Wilson, Mary (eds.) (2004). *Reading the Early Modern Passions: Essays in the Cultural History of Emotion.* Philadelphia.

Paulson, Kristoffer F. (1971). 'The Reverend Edward Stillingfleet and the "Epilogue" to Rochester's *A Satyr against Reason and Mankind*'. *PQ* 50: 657–63.

Peck, Linda Levy (2005). *Consuming Splendor: Society and Culture in Seventeenth-Century England.* Cambridge.

Peltonen, Markku (1995). *Classical Humanism and Republicanism in English Political Thought, 1570–1640.* Cambridge.

Pintard, René (1943). *Le Libertinage Érudit dans la Première Moitié du XVIIᵉ Siècle.* Paris.

Pinto, Vivian de Sola (1927). *Sir Charles Sedley, 1639–1701: A Study in the Life and Literature of the Restoration.*

——— (1935). *Rochester: Portrait of a Restoration Poet.*

Poole, William (2005). *Milton and the Idea of the Fall.* Cambridge.

Popkin, Richard H. (1979). *The History of Scepticism from Erasmus to Spinoza.* Berkeley.

Quaintance, Richard E. (1963). 'French Sources of the Restoration "Imperfect Enjoyment" Poem'. *PQ* 42: 190–9.

Raylor, Timothy (1994). *Cavaliers, Clubs and Literary Culture: Sir John Mennes, James Smith, and the Order of the Fancy.* Newark, NJ.

Rebhorn, Wayne A. (1990). 'The Crisis of Aristocracy in *Julius Caesar*'. *RQ* 43: 75–111.

Reid, Robert L. (1982). 'Spenserian Psychology and the Structure of Allegory in Books 1 and 2 of *The Faerie Queene*'. *MP* 79: 359–75.

Reynolds, Noel B., and Hilton, John L. (1993). 'Thomas Hobbes and Authorship of the *Horae Subsecivae*'. *HPT* 14: 361–80.

Riddell, James A., and Stewart, Stanley (1995). *Jonson's Spenser: Evidence and Historical Criticism*. Pittsburgh.

Roberts, John R. (ed.) (1990). *New Perspectives on the Life and Art of Richard Crashaw*. Columbia, Mo.

Rogers, G. A. J., and Ryan, Alan (eds.) (1988). *Perspectives on Thomas Hobbes*. Oxford.

Rogers, G. A. J., and Sorell, Tom (eds.) (2000). *Hobbes and History*.

Rorty, Amélie Oksenberg (ed.) (1980). *Essays on Aristotle's Ethics*. Berkeley.

Røstvig, Maren-Sofie (1954). *The Happy Man: Studies in the Metamorphoses of a Classical Ideal, 1600–1700*. Oslo.

Rudolph, Ross (1986). 'Conflict, Egoism and Power in Hobbes'. *HPT* 7: 73–88.

Russell, Conrad (1971). *The Crisis of Parliaments. English History 1509–1660*. Oxford.

Russell, Ford (1986). 'Satiric Perspective in Rochester's *A Satyr against Reason and Mankind*'. *Papers on Language and Literature*, 22: 245–53.

Salmon, J. H. M. (1989). 'Stoicism and Roman Example: Seneca and Tacitus in Jacobean England'. *JHI* 50: 199–225.

Sawday, Jonathan (1995). *The Body Emblazoned: Dissection and the Human Body in Renaissance Culture*.

Schmitt, Charles B. (1972). *Cicero Scepticus: A Study of the Influence of the* Academica *in the Renaissance*. The Hague.

_____ (1983). *John Case and Aristotelianism in Renaissance England*. Kingston, Ont.

Schoell, Frank L. (1926). *Études sur l'Humanisme Continental en Angleterre à la Fin de la Renaissance*. Geneva.

Schoenbaum, S. (1987). *William Shakespeare: A Compact Documentary Life*, rev. edn. Oxford.

Schoenfeldt, Michael C. (1991). *Prayer and Power: George Herbert and Renaissance Courtship*. Chicago.

_____ (1999). *Bodies and Selves in Early Modern England: Physiology and Inwardness in Spenser, Shakespeare, Herbert, and Milton*. Cambridge.

Scodel, Joshua (2002). *Excess and the Mean in Early Modern English Literature*. Princeton.

Scott, Jonathan (2000). *England's Troubles: Seventeenth-Century English Political Instability in European Context*. Cambridge.

Seaward, Paul (1989). *The Cavalier Parliament and the Reconstruction of the Old Regime, 1661–1667*. Cambridge.

Shapiro, James (2005). *1599: A Year in the Life of William Shakespeare*.

Sharp, Lindsay (1973). 'Walter Charleton's Early Life 1620–1659, and Relationship to Natural Philosophy in Mid-Seventeenth-Century England'. *Annals of Science*, 30: 311–40.

Sharpe, Kevin (1981). 'Archbishop Laud and the University of Oxford', in Hugh Lloyd-Jones, Valerie Pearl, and Blair Worden (eds.), *History and Imagination: Essays in Honour of H. R. Trevor-Roper*, 146–64.

_____ (1987*a*). *Criticism and Compliment: The Politics of Literature in the England of Charles I*. Cambridge.

_____ (1987*b*). 'The Image of Virtue: The Court and Household of Charles I, 1625–1642', in David Starkey (ed.), *The English Court: From the War of the Roses to the Civil War*, 226–60.

_____ and Lake, Peter (eds.) (1994). *Culture and Politics in Early Stuart England*.

_____ and Zwicker, Steven N. (eds.) (1987). *Politics of Discourse: The Literature and History of Seventeenth-Century England*. Berkeley.

Shifflett, Andrew (1998). *Stoicism, Politics, and Literature in the Age of Milton: War and Peace Reconciled*. Cambridge.

Sinfield, Alan (1983). *Literature in Protestant England, 1560–1660*. Totowa, NJ.

_____ (1992). *Faultlines: Cultural Materialism and the Politics of Dissident Reading*. Oxford.

Sirluck, Ernest (1951). 'The *Faerie Queene*, Book II, and the *Nicomachean Ethics*'. MP 49: 73–100.

Skinner, Quentin (1964). 'Hobbes's *Leviathan*'. HJ 7: 321–33.

_____ (1965–6). 'Thomas Hobbes and his Disciples in France and England'. *Comparative Studies in Society and History: An International Quarterly*, 8: 153–68.

_____ (1966). 'The Ideological Context of Hobbes's Political Thought'. HJ 9: 286–317.

_____ (1972). 'Conquest and Consent: Thomas Hobbes and the Engagement Controversy', in G. E. Aylmer (ed.), *The Interregnum: The Quest for Settlement, 1646–1660*, 79–98.

_____ (1978). *The Foundations of Modern Political Thought*, 2 vols. Cambridge.

_____ (1996). *Reason and Rhetoric in the Philosophy of Hobbes*. Cambridge.

Smith, Geoffrey (2003). *The Cavaliers in Exile*. Basingstoke.

Smuts, R. Malcolm (ed.) (1996). *The Stuart Court and Europe: Essays in Politics and Political Culture*. Cambridge.

Soellner, Rolf (1958). 'The Four Primary Passions: A Renaissance Theory Reflected in the Works of Shakespeare'. *SP* 55: 549–67.

Sorabji, Richard (2000). *Emotion and Peace of Mind: From Stoic Agitation to Christian Temptation*, The Gifford Lectures. Oxford.

Sorell, Tom (1996). *The Cambridge Companion to Hobbes*. Cambridge.

_____ (ed.) (1995). *The Rise of Modern Philosophy: The Tension between the New and Traditional Philosophies from Machiavelli to Leibniz*. Oxford.

Spink, J. S. (1960). *French Free-Thought from Gassendi to Voltaire*.

Spragens, Thomas A. (1973). *The Politics of Motion: The World of Thomas Hobbes*. Lexington, Ky.

Sprague, Arthur Colby (1926). *Beaumont and Fletcher on the Restoration Stage*. New York.

Spurr, John (2000). *England in the 1670s: 'This Masquerading Age'*. Oxford.

Stachniewski, John (1991). *The Persecutory Imagination: English Puritanism and the Literature of Religious Despair*. Oxford.

Strauss, Leo (1952). *The Political Philosophy of Hobbes: Its Basis and Its Genesis*, tr. Elsa M. Sinclair. Chicago.

Strier, Richard (1983). *Love Known: Theology and Experience in George Herbert's Poetry*. Chicago.

Taylor, Gary (1994). 'Forms of Opposition: Shakespeare and Middleton'. *ELR* 24: 283–314.

Thirsk, Joan (1978). *Economic Policy and Projects: The Development of a Consumer Society in Early Modern England*. Oxford.

Thormählen, Marianne (1988). 'Rochester and Jealousy: Consistent Inconsistencies'. *Durham University Journal*, 80: 213–23.

——— (1993). *Rochester: The Poems in Context*. Cambridge.

Tilmouth, Christopher (2000). 'Burton's St Bernard'. *NQ* 245: 176–9.

——— (2005). 'Burton's "Turning Picture": Argument and Anxiety in *The Anatomy of Melancholy*'. *RES* 56: 524–49.

——— (2007). 'Generosity and the Utility of the Passions: Cartesian Ethics in Restoration England'. *17C*, 22.

Treglown, Jeremy (1973). 'The Satirical Inversion of Some English Sources in Rochester's Poetry'. *RES* 24, n.s.: 42–8.

——— (1976). 'Rochester and Davenant'. *NQ* 221: 554–9.

——— (ed.) (1982). *Spirit of Wit: Reconsiderations of Rochester*. Oxford.

Trevor-Roper, Hugh (1988). *Archbishop Laud, 1573–1645*, 3rd edn. Basingstoke.

Tricomi, Albert H. (1973). 'The Revised Version of Chapman's *Bussy D'Ambois*: A Shift in Point of View'. *SP* 70: 288–305.

Tuck, Richard (1989). *Hobbes*. Oxford.

——— (1992). 'The "Christian Atheism" of Thomas Hobbes', in Michael Hunter and David Wootton (eds.), *Atheism from the Reformation to the Enlightenment*, 111–30. Oxford.

——— (1993). *Philosophy and Government, 1572–1651*. Cambridge.

Turner, James G. (1987a). *'One Flesh': Paradisal Marriage and Sexual Relations in the Age of Milton*. Oxford.

——— (1987b). 'The Properties of Libertinism', in Robert Purks Maccubbin (ed.), *'Tis Nature's Fault: Unauthorized Sexuality during the Enlightenment*, 75–87. Cambridge.

——— (2002). *Libertines and Radicals in Early Modern London: Sexuality, Politics, and Literary Culture, 1630–1685*. Cambridge.

——— (2003). *Schooling Sex: Libertine Literature and Erotic Education in Italy, France, and England, 1534–1685*. Oxford.

Tuve, Rosemond (1966). *Allegorical Imagery: Some Mediaeval Books and Their Posterity*. Princeton.

——— (1970). *Essays by Rosemond Tuve: Spenser, Herbert, Milton*, ed. Thomas P. Roche. Princeton.

Tyacke, Nicholas (ed.) (1997). *The History of the University of Oxford*, iv: *Seventeenth-Century Oxford*. Oxford.

Underwood, Dale (1957). *Etherege and the Seventeenth-Century Comedy of Manners.* New Haven.

Ure, Peter (1974). *Elizabethan and Jacobean Drama: Critical Essays by Peter Ure*, ed. J. C. Maxwell. Liverpool.

van Es, Bart (2002). *Spenser's Forms of History.* Oxford.

Vawter, Marvin L. (1974). ' "Division 'tween Our Souls": Shakespeare's Stoic Brutus'. *SStud* 7: 173–95.

——(1976). ' "After Their Fashion": Cicero and Brutus in *Julius Caesar*'. *SStud* 9: 205–19.

Vieth, David M. (ed.) (1963). *Attribution in Restoration Poetry: A Study of Rochester's Poems of 1680.* New Haven.

——(1988). *John Wilmot, Earl of Rochester: Critical Essays.* New York.

Vlastos, Gregory (1991). *Socrates: Ironist and Moral Philosopher.* Cambridge.

Warrender, Howard (1957). *The Political Philosophy of Hobbes: His Theory of Obligation.* Oxford.

Watkins, John (1973). *Hobbes's System of Ideas*, 2nd edn.

Webster, Jeremy W. (2005). *Performing Libertinism in Charles II's Court: Politics, Drama, Sexuality.* Houndmills.

Weil, Rachel (1993). 'Sometimes a Scepter is only a Scepter: Pornography and Politics in Restoration England', in Lynn Hunt (ed.), *The Invention of Pornography: Obscenity and the Origins of Modernity, 1500–1800*, 125–53. New York.

Whigham, Frank (1984). *Ambition and Privilege: The Social Tropes of Elizabethan Courtesy Theory.* Berkeley.

Wilcher, Robert (2001). *The Writing of Royalism, 1628–1660.* Cambridge.

Wilcoxon, Reba (1974/5). 'Rochester's Philosophical Premises: A Case for Consistency'. *Eighteenth-Century Studies*, 8: 183–201.

Williams, Abigail (2005). *Poetry and the Creation of a Whig Literary Culture, 1681–1714.* Oxford.

Wilson, John Harold (1954). *A Rake and his Times: George Villiers, 2nd Duke of Buckingham.*

——(1967). *The Court Wits of the Restoration: An Introduction.* New York.

Wilson, Richard (2004). *Secret Shakespeare: Studies in Theatre, Religion and Resistance.* Manchester.

Wolf, Friedrich O. (1969). *Die Neue Wissenschaft des Thomas Hobbes.* Stuttgart.

Womersley, David (1991). 'Sir Henry Savile's Translation of Tacitus and the Political Interpretation of Elizabethan Texts'. *RES* 42: 313–42.

Woodhouse, A. S. P. (1967). 'Nature and Grace in *The Faerie Queene*', in Paul J. Alpers (ed.), *Elizabethan Poetry: Modern Essays in Criticism*, 345–79. Oxford.

Wootton, David (1997). 'Thomas Hobbes's Machiavellian Moments', in Donald R. Kelley and David Harris Sacks (eds.), *The Historical Imagination in Early Modern Britain: History, Rhetoric, and Fiction, 1500–1800*, 210–42. Cambridge.

Yardley, Bruce (1992). 'George Villiers, Second Duke of Buckingham, and the Politics of Toleration'. *HLQ* 55: 317–37.

Young, R. V. (1982). *Richard Crashaw and the Spanish Golden Age.* New Haven.

# Index